Network Fact Sheet

Write down important stuff about your own network in the following spaces.

Network Servers

Hostname	IP Address	Description

Account Information

My user ID: _____

My password: <u>DON'T WRITE IT HERE!</u>

Domain Name: _____

Internet Connection Information

Your router's IP address (WAN): _____

Your IP range: _____ to _____

Subnet mask: _____

Default Gateway: _____

Nameserver 1: _____

Nameserver 2: _____

Nameserver 3: _____

Favorite snack food: _____

LAN Subnet

Subnet IP address: _____

Subnet mask: _____

For Dummies: Bestselling Book Series for Beginners

Networking All-in-One Desk Reference For Dummies, 3rd Edition

Cheat Sheet

Private IP Address Ranges

10.0.0.0	to	10.255.255.255
172.16.0.0	to	172.31.255.255
192.168.0.0	to	192.168.255.255

Coax Cabling Rules

- Segment limited to 185 meters (600 feet)
- Uses BNC connectors
- T-connectors used to connect cable to computers
- Terminators required at both ends of segment

Twisted-Pair Cabling Rules

- Maximum cable length: 100 meters (330 feet).
- All computers cabled to central wiring hub.
- Terminators not required.
- RJ-45 connector wired as follows:
  - Pin 1   orange
  - Pin 2   orange/white
  - Pin 3   green
  - Pin 6   green/white
- Up to three hubs may be daisy-chained together.
- Some hubs may also be linked using thin or thick coax.
- To create a crossover cable, reverse the connections on one end of the cable so that pin 1 is green, pin 2 is green/white, pin 3 is orange, and pin 6 is orange/white.

Secrets to Network Happiness

- Back up religiously.
- Document your network layout and keep your documentation up to date.
- Keep an adequate supply of spare parts and tools on hand.
- Never turn off or restart the server while users are logged in.
- Don't be afraid, Luke.

Best Internet Sites

General search engines

Google	Yahoo!	AltaVista	MSN Search
www.google.com	www.yahoo.com	www.altavista.com	www.msnsearch.com

Standards organizations

Institute of Electrical and Electronics Engineers	International Organization for Standards	Internet Engineering Task Force	Internet Society	American National Standards Institute
www.ieee.org	www.iso.org	www.ietf.org	www.isoc.org	www.ansi.org

Vendors

Microsoft	Novell	Red Hat	Cisco	IBM
www.microsoft.com	www.novell.com	www.redhat.com	www.cisco.com	www.ibm.com

For Dummies: Bestselling Book Series for Beginners

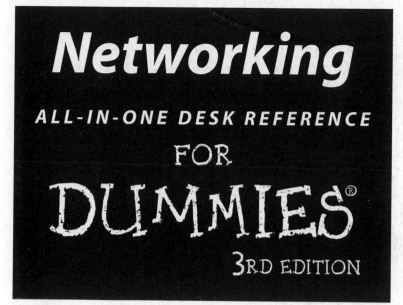

Networking

ALL-IN-ONE DESK REFERENCE

FOR

DUMMIES®

3RD EDITION

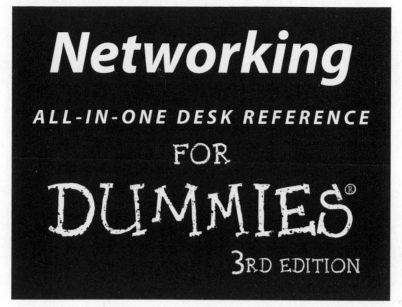

Networking

ALL-IN-ONE DESK REFERENCE

FOR

DUMMIES®

3RD EDITION

by Doug Lowe

WILEY

Wiley Publishing, Inc.

Networking All-in-One Desk Reference For Dummies,® 3rd Edition

Published by
Wiley Publishing, Inc.
111 River Street
Hoboken, NJ 07030-5774

www.wiley.com

Copyright © 2008 by Wiley Publishing, Inc., Indianapolis, Indiana

Published by Wiley Publishing, Inc., Indianapolis, Indiana

Published simultaneously in Canada

For general information on our other products and services, please contact our Customer Care Department within the U.S. at 800-762-2974, outside the U.S. at 317-572-3993, or fax 317-572-4002.

For technical support, please visit www.wiley.com/techsupport.

Wiley also publishes its books in a variety of electronic formats. Some content that appears in print may not be available in electronic books.

Library of Congress Control Number: 2008921682

ISBN: 978-0-470-17915-4

Manufactured in the United States of America

10 9 8 7 6 5 4 3 2 1

WILEY

About the Author

Doug Lowe has written a whole bunch of computer books, including more than 35 *For Dummies* books, among them *Networking For Dummies, 8th Edition, Java All-in-One Desk Reference For Dummies, PowerPoint 2007 For Dummies,* and *Word 2007 All-in-One Desk Reference For Dummies*. He lives in sunny Fresno, California, where the motto is "Fres-YES!," (unfortunately, I'm not making that up) with his wife, the youngest of his three daughters, and a couple of dogs (a goofy-looking six-month-old Shar-Pei/black Lab mix named Lucy and a yellow Lab named Odie). He's one of those obsessive-compulsive decorating nuts who creates computer-controlled Halloween decorations that rival Disney's Haunted Mansion.

Dedication

To Debbie.

Author's Acknowledgments

I'd like to thank everyone who was involved with the third edition of this book, especially project editor Christopher Morris, who put up with late submissions (it was Halloween, after all) and who did a great job following through on all the little editorial details needed to put a book of this scope together on time. Thanks also to Dan DiNicolo, who gave the manuscript a thorough review and offered many excellent suggestions for improvements, and to copy editor Heidi Unger, who whipped my prose into shape, crossing all the i's and dotting all the t's, or something like that. And, as always, thanks to all the behind-the-scenes people who chipped in with help I'm not even aware of.

Publisher's Acknowledgments

We're proud of this book; please send us your comments through our online registration form located at www.dummies.com/register/.

Some of the people who helped bring this book to market include the following:

Acquisitions, Editorial

Sr. Project Editor: Christopher Morris

Acquisitions Editor: Tiffany Ma

Copy Editors: Heidi Unger and Teresa Artman

Technical Editor: Dan DiNicolo

Editorial Manager: Kevin Kirschner

Editorial Assistant: Amanda Foxworth

Sr. Editorial Assistant: Cherie Case

Cartoons: Rich Tennant
(www.the5thwave.com)

Composition Services

Project Coordinator: Kristie Rees

Layout and Graphics: Claudia Bell, Stacie Brooks, Reuben W. Davis, Melissa K. Jester, Christine Williams

Proofreaders: David Faust, Caitie Kelly, Toni Settle

Indexer: Julie Kawabata

Publishing and Editorial for Technology Dummies

> **Richard Swadley,** Vice President and Executive Group Publisher

> **Andy Cummings,** Vice President and Publisher

> **Mary Bednarek,** Executive Acquisitions Director

> **Mary C. Corder,** Editorial Director

Publishing for Consumer Dummies

> **Diane Graves Steele,** Vice President and Publisher

> **Joyce Pepple,** Acquisitions Director

Composition Services

> **Gerry Fahey,** Vice President of Production Services

> **Debbie Stailey,** Director of Composition Services

Contents at a Glance

Table of Contents

Introduction

Welcome to the third edition of *Networking All-in-One Desk Reference For Dummies,* the one networking book that's designed to replace an entire shelf full of the dull and tedious networking books you'd otherwise have to buy. This book contains all the basic and not-so-basic information you need to know to get a network up and running and stay on top of the network as it grows, develops problems, and encounters trouble.

If you're just getting started as a network administrator, this book is ideal. As a network administrator, you have to know about a lot of different topics: installing and configuring network hardware, installing and configuring network operating systems, planning a network, working with TCP/IP, securing your network, working with wireless devices, backing up your data, and many others.

You can, and probably eventually will, buy separate books on each of these topics. It won't take long before your bookshelf is bulging with 10,000 or more pages of detailed information about every imaginable nuance of networking. But before you're ready to tackle each of those topics in depth, you need to get a birds-eye picture. This book is the ideal way to do that.

And if you already own 10,000 pages or more of network information, you may be overwhelmed by the amount of detail and wonder, "Do I really need to read 1,000 pages about Bind to set up a simple DNS server?" or "Do I really need a six-pound book to show me how to install Linux?" Truth is, most 1,000-page networking books have about 100 or so pages of really useful information — the kind you use every day — and about 900 pages of excruciating details that apply mostly to networks at places like NASA and the CIA.

The basic idea of this book is that I've tried to wring out the 100 or so most useful pages of information on nine different networking topics: network basics, building a network, network administration and security, troubleshooting and disaster planning, working with TCP/IP, home networking, wireless networking, Windows server operating systems, and Linux.

So whether you've just been put in charge of your first network or you're a seasoned pro, you've found the right book.

About This Book

Networking All-in-One Desk Reference For Dummies, 3rd edition, is intended to be a reference for all the great things (and maybe a few not-so-great things) that you may need to know when you're setting up and managing a network. You can, of course, buy a huge 1,000-page book on each of the networking topics covered in this book. But then, who would you get to carry them home from the bookstore for you? And where would you find the shelf space to store them? In this book, you get the information you need all conveniently packaged for you in between one set of covers.

This book doesn't pretend to be a comprehensive reference for every detail of these topics. Instead, this book shows you how to get up and running fast so that you have more time to do the things you really want to do. Designed using the easy-to-follow For Dummies format, this book helps you get the information you need without laboring to find it.

Networking All-in-One Desk Reference For Dummies, 3rd edition, is a big book made up of several smaller books — minibooks, if you will. Each of these minibooks covers the basics of one key element of network management, such as setting up network hardware, installing a network operating system, or troubleshooting network problems. Whenever one big thing is made up of several smaller things, confusion is always a possibility. That's why *Networking All-in-One Desk Reference For Dummies*, 3rd edition, is designed to have multiple access points (I hear an acronym coming on — MAP!) to help you find what you want. At the beginning of the book is a detailed table of contents that covers the entire book. Then, each minibook begins with a minitable of contents that shows you at a glance what chapters are included in that minibook. Useful running heads appear at the top of each page to point out the topic discussed on that page. And handy thumb tabs run down the side of the pages to help you quickly find each minibook. Finally, a comprehensive index lets you find information anywhere in the entire book.

This isn't the kind of book you pick up and read from start to finish, as if it were a cheap novel. If I ever see you reading it at the beach, I'll kick sand in your face. This book is more like a reference, the kind of book you can pick up, turn to just about any page, and start reading. You don't have to memorize anything in this book. It's a "need-to-know" book: You pick it up when you need to know something. Need to know how to set up a DHCP server in Windows? Pick up the book. Need to know how to create a user account in Linux? Pick up the book. Otherwise, put it down and get on with your life.

How to Use This Book

This book works like a reference. Start with the topic you want to find out about. Look for it in the table of contents or in the index to get going. The table of contents is detailed enough that you should be able to find most of the topics you're looking for. If not, turn to the index, where you can find even more detail.

Of course, the book is loaded with information, so if you want to take a brief excursion into your topic, you're more than welcome. If you want to know the big security picture, read the whole chapter on security. If you just want to know how to make a decent password, read just the section on passwords. You get the idea.

Whenever I describe a message or information that you see on the screen, I present it as follows:

```
A message from your friendly network
```

If you need to type something, you'll see the text you need to type like this: **Type this stuff**. In this example, you type **Type this stuff** at the keyboard and press Enter. An explanation usually follows, just in case you're scratching your head and grunting, "Huh?"

How This Book Is Organized

Each of the nine minibooks contained in *Networking All-in-One Desk Reference For Dummies*, 3rd edition, can stand by themselves. The first minibook covers the networking basics that you should know to help you understand the rest of the stuff in this book. Of course, if you've been managing a network for awhile already, you probably know all this stuff, so you can probably skip Book I or just skim it over quickly for laughs. The remaining minibooks cover a variety of networking topics that you would normally find covered in separate books. Here is a brief description of what you find in each minibook.

Book I: Networking Basics

This minibook covers the networking basics that you need to understand to get going. You find out what a network is, how networking standards work, what hardware components are required to make up a network, and what network operating systems do. You discover the difference between peer-to-peer networking and client-server networking. And you also get a comparison of the most popular network operating systems, including the current incarnations of Windows Server and Linux.

Book II: Building a Network

In this minibook, you find the ins and outs of building a network. First, you see how to create a plan for your network. After all, planning is the first step of any great endeavor. Then, you discover how to install network hardware such as network interface cards and how to work with various types of networking cable. You receive some general pointers about installing a network server operating system. And finally, you gain insight into how to configure various versions of Windows to access a network.

Book III: Network Administration and Security

In this minibook, you discover what it means to be a network administrator, with an emphasis on how to secure your network so that it's safe from intruders but at the same time allows your network's users access to everything they need. In the real world, this responsibility isn't as easy as it sounds. This minibook begins with an overview of what network administrators do. Then, it describes some of the basic practices of good network security, such as using strong passwords and providing physical security for your servers. It includes detailed information about setting up and managing network user accounts, using virus scanners, setting up firewalls, backing up network data, keeping network software up to date, and troubleshooting common network problems.

Book IV: TCP/IP and the Internet

This minibook is devoted to the most popular network technology on the planet: TCP/IP. (Actually, it may be the most popular protocol in the universe. The aliens in *Independence Day* had a TCP/IP network on their spaceship, enabling Will Smith and Jeff Goldblum to hack their way in. The aliens should have read the section on firewalls in Book III.)

Book V: Wireless Networking

In this minibook, you discover the ins and outs of setting up and securing a wireless network.

Book VI: Telecom, Convergence, and Mobile Devices

This minibook is devoted to phone systems, which are similar to computer networks in many ways but vastly different in others. You'll learn what a PBX is and how to manage one. You'll also learn how to integrate voice mail with e-mail and how to manage mobile devices.

Book VII: Windows Server 2008 Reference

This minibook describes the basics of setting up and administering a server using the latest version of Windows Server 2008. You also find helpful information about its predecessor, Windows Server 2003. You find chapters on installing a Windows server, managing user accounts, setting up a file server, and securing a Windows server. Plus, you'll find a handy reference to the many Windows networking commands that you can use from a command prompt.

Book VIII: Using Other Windows Servers

This minibook shows how the basics of setting up other popular Windows server products, including the IIS Web server, Exchange Server for managing e-mail, SQL Server for databases, and SharePoint for creating intranet sites.

Book IX: Linux Networking Reference

Linux has fast become an inexpensive alternative to Windows or NetWare. In this minibook, you discover the basics of installing and managing Fedora Core 3 Linux, the current version of the most popular Linux distribution. You find out how to install Fedora, work with Linux commands and *GNOME* (a popular graphical interface for Linux), configure Linux for networking, set up a Windows-compatible file server using Samba, and run popular Internet servers such as DHCP, Bind, and Sendmail. Plus, you get a concise Linux command reference that will turn you into a Linux command line junkie in no time.

Icons Used in This Book

Like any *For Dummies* book, this book is chock-full of helpful icons that draw your attention to items of particular importance. You find the following icons throughout this book:

Hold it — technical stuff is just around the corner. Read on only if you have your pocket protector.

Pay special attention to this icon; it lets you know that some particularly useful tidbit is at hand.

Did I tell you about the memory course I took?

Danger, Will Robinson! This icon highlights information that may help you avert disaster.

Where to Go from Here

Yes, you can get there from here. With this book in hand, you're ready to plow right through the rugged networking terrain. Browse through the table of contents and decide where you want to start. Be bold! Be courageous! Be adventurous! And above all, have fun!

Book I
Networking Basics

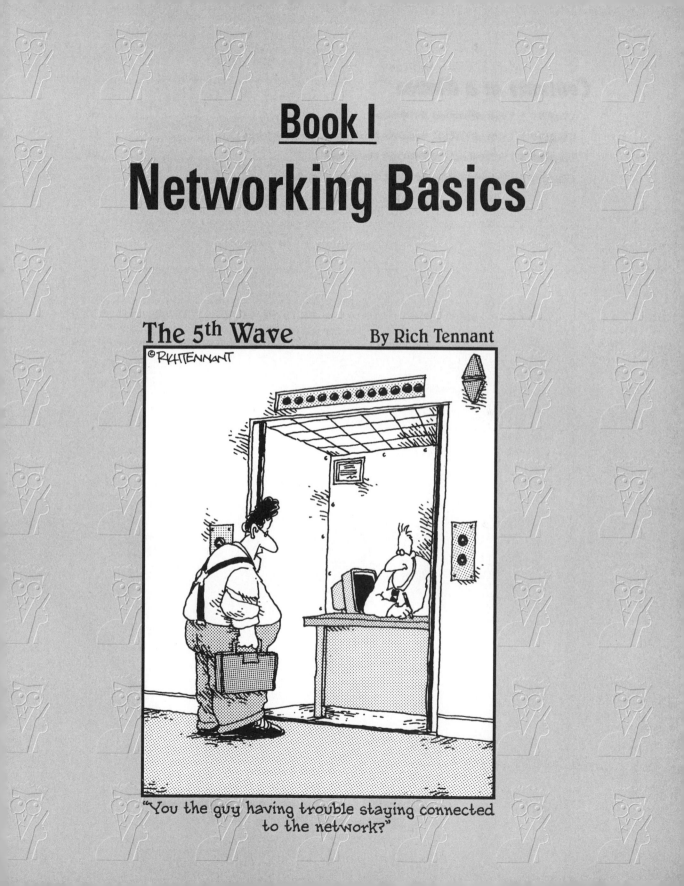

The 5th Wave

By Rich Tennant

©RICHTENNANT

"You the guy having trouble staying connected to the network?"

Contents at a Glance

Chapter 1: Understanding Networks

In This Chapter

✔ Introducing computer networks

✔ Finding out all about clients, servers, and peers

✔ Understanding the various types of networks

✔ Figuring out the disadvantages of networking

The first computer network was invented when ancient mathematicians connected their abacuses (or is it *abaci*?) together with kite string so they could instantly share their abacus answers with each other. Over the years, computer networks became more and more sophisticated. Now, instead of string, networks use electrical cables, fiber-optic cables, or wireless radio signals to connect computers to each other. The purpose, however, has remained the same: sharing information and getting work done faster.

This chapter describes the basics of what computer networking is and how it works.

What Is a Network?

A *network* is nothing more than two or more computers connected to each other so that they can exchange information, such as e-mail messages or documents, or share resources, such as disk storage or printers. In most cases, this connection is made via electrical cables that carry the information in the form of electrical signals. But in some cases, other types of connections are used. For example, fiber-optic cables let computers communicate at extremely high speeds by using impulses of light. Wireless networks let computers communicate by using radio signals, so the computers aren't restricted by physical cables.

In addition to the hardware that comprises the network, a network also requires special software to enable communications. In the early days of networking, you had to add this software to each computer on the network. Nowadays, network support is built in to all major operating systems, including all current versions of Windows, Macintosh operating systems, and Linux.

Network building blocks

All networks, large or small, require specialized network hardware to make them work. For small networks, the hardware may consist of nothing more than a network interface card in each computer, a cable for each computer, and a network switch that all the computers plug in to. Larger networks probably have additional components, such as routers or repeaters.

Small or large, all networks are built from the following basic building blocks:

+ **Client computers:** The computers that end users use to access the resources of the network. Client computers are typically located on users' desks. They usually run a desktop version of Windows such as Windows Vista or Windows XP Professional, along with application software such as Microsoft Office. Client computers are sometimes referred to as *workstations*.

+ **Server computers:** Computers that provide shared resources, such as disk storage and printers, as well as network services, such as e-mail and Internet access. Server computers typically run a specialized network operating system such as Windows Server 2008 or 2003, NetWare, or Linux, along with special software to provide network services. For example, a server may run Microsoft Exchange to provide e-mail services for the network, or it may run Apache Web Server so that the computer can serve Web pages.

+ **Network interface card (NIC):** An interface that's installed in a computer that enables the computer to communicate over a network. Almost all NICs implement a networking standard called *Ethernet*. Note that even though the "C" in "NIC" stands for "card," the NIC in most computers isn't actually a separate card. Instead, the NIC is an integral part of the computer's motherboard. Every client and every server computer must have a NIC in order to be a part of a network.

+ **Cable:** Computers in a network are usually physically connected to each other using cable. Although several types of cable have been popular over the years, the most commonly used cable today is called *twisted pair,* also known by its official designation 10BaseT. Another type of cable commonly used is *coaxial,* also called 10Base2. For high-speed network connections, *fiber-optic cable* is sometimes used.

In many cases, the cables run through the walls and converge on a central room called a *wiring closet.* But for smaller networks, the cables are often just strung along the floor.

✦ **Switches:** Network cable usually doesn't connect computers directly to each other. Instead, each computer is connected by cable to a device known as a *switch.* The switch, in turn, connects to the rest of the network. Each switch contains a certain number of *ports,* typically 8 or 16. Thus, you can use an eight-port switch to connect up to eight computers. Switches can be connected to each other to build larger networks. For more information about switches, see the section, "Network Topology," later in this chapter. (Older networks may use a more primitive type of device called a *hub* instead of a switch. A hub provides the same function as a switch, but it isn't as efficient. The term *hub* is sometimes used to mean *switch,* even though hubs and switches are not technically the same thing.)

✦ **Wireless networks:** In many networks, cables and switches are making way for wireless network connections, which enable computers to communicate via radio signals. In a wireless network, radio transmitters and receivers take the place of cables. The main advantage of wireless networking is its flexibility. With a wireless network, you don't have to run cables through walls or ceilings, and your client computers can be located anywhere within range of the network broadcast. The main disadvantage of wireless networking is that it is inherently less secure than a cabled network.

✦ **Network software:** Although network hardware is essential, what really makes a network work is software. A whole bunch of software has to be set up just right in order to get a network working. Server computers typically use a special *network operating system* (also known as a *NOS)* in order to function efficiently, and client computers need to have their network settings configured properly in order to access the network.

One of the most important networking choices to make is which network operating system you'll use on the network's servers. That's because much of the task of building a new network and managing an existing one is setting up and maintaining the network operating system on the servers.

Why bother?

If the truth be told, computer networks are a pain to set up. So, why bother? Because the benefits of having a network make the difficulty of setting one up worthwhile. You don't have to be a Ph.D. to understand the benefits of networking. In fact, you learned everything you need to know about the benefits of networking in kindergarten. Networks are all about sharing.

Specifically, networks are about sharing three things: information, resources, and applications.

✦ **Sharing information:** Networks allow users to share information in several different ways. The most common way of sharing information is to share individual files. For example, two or more people can work together on a single spreadsheet file or word-processing document. In most networks, a large hard drive on a central server computer is set up as a common storage area where users can store files to be shared with other users.

In addition to sharing files, networks allow users to communicate with each other in various ways. For example, messaging applications let network users exchange messages with each other using an e-mail application such as Microsoft Outlook. Users can also hold online meetings over the network. In fact, with inexpensive video cameras and the right software, users can hold videoconferences over the network.

✦ **Sharing resources:** Certain computer resources, such as printers or hard drives, can be set up so that network users can share them. Sharing these resources can result in significant cost savings. For example, it is cheaper to buy a single high-speed printer with advanced features such as collating, stapling, and duplex printing that can be shared by an entire workgroup than it is to buy separate printers for each user in the group.

Hard drives can also be shared resources. In fact, providing users with access to a shared hard drive is the most common method of sharing files on a network. A computer whose main purpose in life is to host shared hard drives is called a *file server*.

In actual practice, entire hard drives aren't usually shared. Instead, individual folders on a networked hard drive are shared. This way, the network administrator can allow different network users to have access to different shared folders. For example, a company may set up shared folders for its sales department and accounting department. Then, sales personnel can access the sales department's folder, and accounting personnel can access the accounting department's folder.

You can share other resources on a network. For example, a network can be used to share an Internet connection. In the early days of the Internet, it was common for each user who required access to the Internet to have his or her own modem connection. Nowadays, it's more common for the network to provide a shared, high-speed Internet connection that everyone on the network can access.

✦ **Sharing applications:** One of the most common reasons for networking in many businesses is so that several users can work together on a single business application. For example, an accounting department may have accounting software that can be used from several computers at the same time. Or a sales-processing department may have an order-entry application that runs on several computers to handle a large volume of orders.

Of Clients and Servers

The network computer that contains the hard drives, printers, and other resources that are shared with other network computers is called a *server*. This term comes up repeatedly, so you have to remember it. Write it on the back of your left hand.

Any computer that's not a server is called a *client*. You have to remember this term, too. Write it on the back of your right hand.

Only two kinds of computers are on a network: servers and clients. Look at your left hand and then look at your right hand. Don't wash your hands until you have these terms memorized.

The distinction between servers and clients in a network would be some-what fun to study in a sociology class because it's similar to the distinction between the haves and the have-nots in society:

✦ Usually, the most powerful and expensive computers in a network are the servers. This fact makes sense because every user on the network shares the server's resources.

✦ The cheaper and less powerful computers in a network are the clients. Clients are the computers used by individual users for everyday work. Because clients' resources don't have to be shared, they don't have to be as fancy.

✦ Most networks have more clients than servers. For example, a network with ten clients can probably get by with one server.

✦ In some networks, a clean line of segregation exists between servers and clients. In other words, a computer is either a server or a client, and not both. A server can't become a client, nor can a client become a server.

✦ Other networks are more progressive, allowing any computer in the net-work to be a server and allowing any computer to be both server and client at the same time. The network illustrated in Figure 1-1, later in this chapter, is this type of network.

Dedicated Servers and Peers

In some networks, a server computer is a server computer and nothing else. This server computer is dedicated solely to the task of providing shared resources, such as hard drives and printers, to be accessed by the network client computers. Such a server is referred to as a *dedicated server* because it can perform no other tasks besides network services. A network that relies on dedicated servers is sometimes called a *client/server network*.

Other networks take an alternative approach, enabling any computer on the network to function as both a client and a server. Thus, any computer can share its printers and hard drives with other computers on the network. And while a computer is working as a server, you can still use that same computer for other functions such as word processing. This type of network is called a *peer-to-peer network* because all the computers are thought of as peers, or equals.

While you're walking the dog tomorrow morning, ponder these points concerning the difference between dedicated server networks and peer-to-peer networks:

✦ Peer-to-peer networking has been built in to all versions of Windows since Windows 95. Thus, you don't have to buy any additional software to turn your computer into a server. All you have to do is enable the Windows server features.

✦ The network server features that are built into desktop versions of Windows (such as Windows XP) aren't very efficient because these versions of Windows were not designed primarily to be network servers. If you're going to dedicate a computer to the task of being a full-time server, you should use a full-fledged network operating system, such as Windows Server 2003, instead.

Networks Big and Small

Networks come in all sizes and shapes. In fact, it's common to categorize networks based on the geographical size they cover, as described in the following paragraphs:

✦ **Local area networks:** A *local area network,* or *LAN,* is a network in which computers are relatively close together, such as within the same office or building.

Note that the term *LAN* doesn't imply that the network is small. A LAN can, in fact, contain hundreds of computers. What makes a network a

LAN is that all those computers are located within close proximity to each other. Usually a LAN is contained within a single building, but a LAN can extend to several buildings on a campus — provided the buildings are close to each other.

✦ **Wide area networks:** A *wide area network,* or *WAN,* is a network that spans a large geographic territory, such as an entire city, region, or even an entire country. WANs are typically used to connect two or more LANs that are relatively far apart. For example, a WAN may connect an office in San Francisco with an office in New York.

Again, it is the geographic distance that makes a network a WAN, not the number of computers involved. If the office in San Francisco and the office in New York both have only one computer, the WAN will have a total of two computers but will span more than 3,000 miles.

✦ **Metropolitan area networks:** A *metropolitan area network,* or *MAN,* is a network that's smaller than a typical WAN but larger than a LAN. Typically, a MAN connects two or more LANs within a same city but are far enough apart that the networks can't be connected using a simple cable or wireless connection.

Network Topology

The term *network topology* refers to the shape of how the computers and other network components are connected to each other. There are several different types of network topologies, each with advantages and disadvantages.

In the following discussion of network topologies, I use two important terms:

✦ **Node:** A *node* is a device that is connected to the network. For our purposes here, a node is the same as a computer. Network topology deals with how the nodes of a network are connected to each other.

✦ **Packet:** A *packet* is a message that is sent over the network from one node to another node. The packet includes the address of the node that sent the packet, the address of the node the packet is being sent to, and data.

Bus topology

The first type of network topology is called a *bus,* in which nodes are strung together in a line, as shown in Figure 1-1. Bus topology is commonly used for LANs.

Figure 1-1:
Bus
topology.

The key to understanding how a bus topology works is to think of the entire network as a single cable, with each node "tapping" into the cable so that it can listen in on the packets being sent over that cable. If you're old enough to remember party lines, you get the idea.

In a bus topology, every node on the network can see every packet that's sent on the cable. Each node looks at each packet to determine whether the packet is intended for it. If so, the node claims the packet. If not, the node ignores the packet. This way, each computer can respond to data sent to it and ignore data sent to other computers on the network.

If the cable in a bus network breaks, the network is effectively divided into two networks. Nodes on either side of the break can continue to communicate with each other, but data can't span the gap between the networks, so nodes on opposite sides of the break can't communicate with each other.

Star topology

In a star topology, each network node is connected to a central device called a *hub* or a *switch,* as shown in Figure 1-2. Star topologies are also commonly used with LANs.

Hub

Figure 1-2:
Star
topology.

If a cable in a star network breaks, only the node connected to that cable is isolated from the network. The other nodes can continue to operate without interruption — unless, of course, the node that's isolated because of the break happens to be the file server.

You should be aware of the somewhat technical distinction between a hub and a switch. Simply put, a *hub* doesn't know anything about the computers that are connected to each of its ports. So when a computer connected to the hub sends a packet to a computer that's connected to another port, the hub sends a duplicate copy of the packet to all its ports. In contrast, a switch knows which computer is connected to each of its ports. As a result, when a switch receives a packet intended for a particular computer, it sends the packet only to the port that the recipient is connected to.

Strictly speaking, only networks that use switches have a true star topology. If the network uses a hub, the network topology has the physical appearance of a star, but is actually a bus. That's because when a hub is used, each computer on the network sees all the packets sent over the network, just like in a bus topology. In a true star topology, as when a switch is used, each computer sees only those packets that were sent specifically to it, as well as broadcast packets that were specifically sent to all computers on the network.

Expanding stars

Physicists tell us that the universe is expanding, and network administrators know they're right. A simple bus or star topology is suitable only for small networks, with a dozen or so computers, but small networks inevitably become large networks as more computers are added. For larger networks, it's common to create more complicated topologies that combine stars and buses.

For example, a bus can be used to connect several stars. In this case, two or more hubs or switches are connected to each other using a bus. Each of these hubs or switches is then the center of a star that connects two or more computers to the network. This type of arrangement is commonly used in buildings that have two or more distinct workgroups. The bus that connects the switches is sometimes called a *backbone*.

Another way to expand a star topology is to use a technique called *daisy-chaining*. When you use daisy-chaining, a hub or switch is connected to another hub or switch as if it were one of the nodes on the star. Then, this second hub or switch serves as the center of a second star.

Ring topology

A third type of network topology is called a *ring,* shown in Figure 1-3. In a ring topology, packets are sent around the circle from computer to computer. Each computer looks at each packet to decide whether the packet was intended for it. If not, the packet is passed on to the next computer in the ring.

Figure 1-3:
Ring
topology.

Years ago, ring topologies were common in LANs, as two popular networking technologies used rings: ARCNET and Token Ring. ARCNET is still used for certain applications such as factory automation, but is rarely used in business networks. Token Ring is a popular network technology for IBM midrange computers. Although plenty of Token Ring networks are still in existence, not many new networks use Token Ring any more.

Ring topology was also used by FDDI, one of the first types of fiber-optic network connections. FDDI has given way to more efficient fiber-optic techniques, however. So ring networks have all but vanished from business networks.

Mesh topology

A fourth type of network topology, known as *mesh,* has multiple connections between each of the nodes on the network, as shown in Figure 1-4. The advantage of a mesh topology is that if one cable breaks, the network can use an alternative route to deliver its packets.

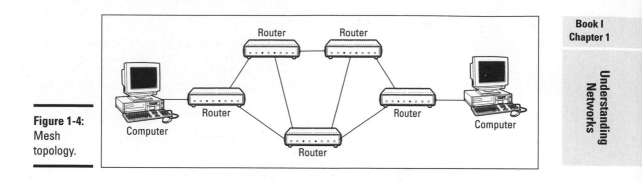

Figure 1-4:
Mesh
topology.

Mesh networks are not very practical in a LAN setting. For example, to net-work eight computers in a mesh topology, each computer would have to have seven network interface cards, and 28 cables would be required to connect each computer to the seven other computers in the network. Obviously, this scheme isn't very scalable.

However, mesh networks are common for metropolitan or wide area networks. These networks use devices called *routers* to route packets from network to network. For reliability and performance reasons, routers are usually arranged in a way that provides multiple paths between any two nodes on the network in a mesh-like arrangement.

Chapter 2: Understanding Network Protocols and Standards

In This Chapter

✔ Deciphering the layers of the OSI reference model

✔ Understanding an Ethernet

✔ Getting the inside scoop on TCP/IP and IPX/SPX

✔ Finding out about other important protocols

Protocols and standards are what make networks work together. Protocols make it possible for the various components of a network to communicate with each other. Standards also make it possible for network components manufactured by different companies to work together. This chapter introduces you to the protocols and standards that you're most likely to encounter when building and maintaining a network.

Understanding Protocols

A *protocol* is a set of rules that enables effective communications to occur. We encounter protocols every day. For example, when you pay for groceries with a check, the clerk first tells you how much the groceries cost. You then write a check, providing information such as the date, the name of the grocery store, the amount written with numerals and spelled out, and your signature, and you give the check to the clerk. The clerk accepts the check and asks to see your driver's license. You show the clerk your driver's license, and the clerk looks at it, looks at you, looks at your driver's license again, writes the driver's license number on the check, asks whether you've gained some weight since the picture was taken, and then accepts the check.

Here's another example of an everyday protocol: making a phone call. You probably take most of the details of the phone calling protocol for granted, but it's pretty complicated if you think about it:

✦ When you pick up a phone, you have to listen for a dial tone before dialing the number (unless you're using a cell phone). If you don't hear a dial tone, you know that either (1) someone else in your family is talking on the phone, or (2) something is wrong with your phone.

✦ When you hear the dial tone, you initiate the call by dialing the number of the party you want to reach. If the person you want to call is in the same area code as you, most of the time you simply dial that person's seven-digit phone number. If the person is in a different area code, you dial a one, the three-digit area code, and the person's seven-digit phone number.

✦ If you hear a series of long ringing tones, you wait until the other person answers the phone. If the phone rings a certain number of times with no answer, you hang up and try again later. If you hear a voice say, "Hello," you can begin a conversation with the other party. If the person on the other end of the phone has never heard of you, you say, "Sorry, wrong number," hang up, and try again.

✦ If you hear a voice that rambles on about how they're not home but they want to return your call, you wait for a beep and leave a message.

✦ If you hear a series of short tones, you know the other person is talking to someone else on the phone. So you hang up and try again later.

✦ If you hear a sequence of three tones that increase in pitch, then a recorded voice that begins, "We're sorry . . ." you know that the number you dialed is invalid. Either you dialed the number incorrectly, or the number has been disconnected.

I can go on and on, but I think you probably get the point. Exchanges such as writing checks or making phone calls follow the same rules every time they happen.

Computer networks depend upon many different types of protocols in order to work. These protocols are very rigidly defined, and for good reason. Network cards must know how to talk to other network cards in order to exchange information, operating systems must know how to talk to network cards in order to send and receive data on the network, and application programs must know how to talk to operating systems in order to know how to retrieve a file from a network server.

Protocols come in many different types. At the lowest level, protocols define exactly what type of electrical signal represents a one and what type of signal represents a zero. At the highest level, protocols allow a computer user in the United States to send an e-mail message to another computer user in New Zealand. And in between are many other levels of protocols. You find out more about these levels of protocols (which are often called *layers*) in the section, "The Seven Layers of the OSI Reference Model," later in this chapter.

Various protocols tend to be used together in matched sets called *protocol suites*. The two most popular protocol suites for networking are *TCP/IP* and *IPX/SPX*. TCP/IP was originally developed for Unix networks and is the protocol of the Internet. IPX/SPX was originally developed for NetWare networks and is still widely used for Windows networks. A third important protocol is *Ethernet,* a low-level protocol that's used with both TCP/IP and IPX/SPX.

Understanding Standards

A *standard* is an agreed-upon definition of a protocol. In the early days of computer networking, each computer manufacturer developed its own networking protocols. As a result, you weren't able to easily mix equipment from different manufacturers on a single network.

Then along came standards to save the day. Standards are industry-wide protocol definitions that are not tied to a particular manufacturer. With standard protocols, you can mix and match equipment from different vendors. As long as the equipment implements the standard protocols, it should be able to coexist on the same network.

Many organizations are involved in setting standards for networking. The five most important organizations are

+ **American National Standards Institute (ANSI):** The official standards organization in the United States. ANSI is pronounced *AN-see*.

+ **Institute of Electrical and Electronics Engineers (IEEE):** An international organization that publishes several key networking standards — in particular, the official standard for the Ethernet networking system (known officially as IEEE 802.3). IEEE is pronounced *eye-triple-E*.

+ **International Organization for Standardization (ISO):** A federation of more than 100 standards organizations from throughout the world. If I had studied French in high school, I'd probably understand why the acronym for International Organization for Standardization is ISO, and not IOS.

+ **Internet Engineering Task Force (IETF):** The organization responsible for the protocols that drive the Internet.

+ **World Wide Web Consortium (W3C):** An international organization that handles the development of standards for the World Wide Web.

Table 2-1 lists the Web sites for each of these standards organizations.

Table 2-1	Web Sites for Major Standards Organizations
Organization	*Web Site*
ANSI (American National Standards Institute)	`www.ansi.org`
IEEE (Institute of Electrical and Electronic Engineers)	`www.ieee.org`
ISO (International Organization for Standardization)	`www.iso.org`
IETF (Internet Engineering Task Force)	`www.ietf.org`
W3C (World Wide Web Consortium)	`www.w3c.org`

The Seven Layers of the OSI Reference Model

OSI sounds like the name of a top-secret government agency you hear about only in Tom Clancy novels. What it really stands for in the networking world is Open Systems Interconnection, as in the Open Systems Interconnection Reference Model, affectionately known as the *OSI model*.

The OSI model breaks the various aspects of a computer network into seven distinct layers. These layers are kind of like the layers of an onion: Each successive layer envelops the layer beneath it, hiding its details from the levels above. The OSI model is also like an onion in that if you start to peel it apart to have a look inside, you're bound to shed a few tears.

The OSI model is not a networking standard in the same sense that Ethernet and Token Ring are networking standards. Rather, the OSI model is a framework into which the various networking standards can fit. The OSI model specifies what aspects of a network's operation can be addressed by various network standards. So, in a sense, the OSI model is sort of a standard of standards.

Table 2-2 summarizes the seven layers of the OSI model.

Table 2-2		The Seven Layers of the OSI Model
Layer	*Name*	*Description*
1	Physical	Governs the layout of cables and devices such as repeaters and hubs.
2	Data Link	Provides MAC addresses to uniquely identify network nodes and a means for data to be sent over the Physical layer in the form of packets. Bridges and switches are layer 2 devices.
3	Network	Handles routing of data across network segments.
4	Transport	Provides for reliable delivery of packets.

Layer	Name	Description
5	Session	Establishes sessions between network applications.
6	Presentation	Converts data so that systems that use different data formats can exchange information.
7	Application	Allows applications to request network services.

The first three layers are sometimes called the *lower layers.* They deal with the mechanics of how information is sent from one computer to another over a network. Layers 4 through 7 are sometimes called the *upper layers.* They deal with how applications relate to the network through application programming interfaces.

The following sections describe each of these layers in greater detail.

The seven layers of the OSI model are a somewhat idealized view of how networking protocols should work. In the real world, actual networking protocols don't follow the OSI model to the letter. The real world is always messier than we'd like. Still, the OSI model provides a convenient — if not completely accurate — conceptual picture of how networking works.

The Physical Layer

The bottom layer of the OSI model is the *Physical layer.* It addresses the physical characteristics of the network, such as the types of cables used to connect devices, the types of connectors used, how long the cables can be, and so on. For example, the Ethernet standard for 10BaseT cable specifies the electrical characteristics of the twisted-pair cables, the size and shape of the connectors, the maximum length of the cables, and so on. The star, bus, ring, and mesh network topologies described in Book I, Chapter 1 apply to the Physical layer.

Another aspect of the Physical layer is the electrical characteristics of the signals used to transmit data over the cables from one network node to another. The Physical layer doesn't define any meaning to those signals other than the basic binary values of zero and one. The higher levels of the OSI model must assign meanings to the bits that are transmitted at the Physical layer.

One type of Physical layer device commonly used in networks is a *repeater.* A repeater is used to regenerate the signal whenever you need to exceed the cable length allowed by the Physical layer standard. 10BaseT hubs are also Physical layer devices. Technically, they're known as *multiport repeaters* because the purpose of a hub is to regenerate every packet received on any port on all of the hub's other ports. Repeaters and hubs don't examine the contents of the packets that they regenerate. If they did, they would be working at the Data Link layer, and not at the Physical layer.

The *network adapter* (also called a *network interface card* or *NIC)* that's installed in each computer on the network is a Physical layer device. You can display information about the network adapter (or adapters) installed in a Windows computer by displaying the adapter's Properties dialog box, as shown in Figure 2-1. To access this dialog box in Windows 2000 or XP, open the Control Panel and double-click the System icon, click the Hardware tab, and then click the Device Manager button. A list of all the devices on the computer appears. Double-click the network adapter to see its Properties dialog box. In Windows Vista, open the System icon in the Control Panel, click the Device Manager link, and then double-click the network adapter.

Figure 2-1:
The
Properties
dialog box
for a
network
adapter.

The Data Link Layer

The *Data Link layer* is the lowest layer at which meaning is assigned to the bits that are transmitted over the network. Data link protocols address things such as the size of each packet of data to be sent, a means of addressing each packet so that it's delivered to the intended recipient, and a way to ensure that two or more nodes don't try to transmit data on the network at the same time.

The Data Link layer also provides basic error detection and correction to ensure that the data sent is the same as the data received. If an uncorrectable error occurs, the data link standard must specify how the node is to be informed of the error so that it can retransmit the data.

At the Data Link layer, each device on the network has an address known as the *Media Access Control address,* or *MAC address.* This address is actually hard-wired into every network device by the manufacturer. MAC addresses are unique; no two network devices made by any manufacturer anywhere in the world can have the same MAC address.

You can see the MAC address for a computer's network adapter by opening a command window and running the `ipconfig /all` command, as shown in Figure 2-2. In this example, the MAC address of the network card is 00-12-3F-A7-17-BA. (The `ipconfig` command refers to the MAC address as the *physical address.*)

Figure 2-2:
Using the
`ipconfig`
command
to display
the MAC
address of
a network
adapter.

One of the most import functions of the Data Link layer is to provide a way for packets to be sent safely over the physical media without interference from other nodes attempting to send packets at the same time. The two most popular ways to do this are CSMA/CD and token passing. Ethernet networks use CSMA/CD, and Token Ring networks use token passing.

Two types of Data Link layer devices are commonly used on networks: bridges and switches. A *bridge* is an intelligent repeater that is aware of the MAC addresses of the nodes on either side of the bridge and can forward packets accordingly. A *switch* is an intelligent hub that examines the MAC address of arriving packets in order to determine which port to forward the packet to.

An important function of the Data Link layer is to make sure that two computers don't try to send packets over the network at the same time. If they do, the signals will collide with each other, and the transmission will be garbled. Ethernet accomplishes this feat by using a technique called *CSMA/CD*, which stands for carrier sense multiple access with collision detection. This phrase is a mouthful, but if you take it apart piece by piece, you'll get an idea of how it works.

Carrier sense means that whenever a device wants to send a packet over the network media, it first listens to the network media to see whether anyone else is already sending a packet. If it doesn't hear any other signals on the media, the computer assumes that the network is free, so it sends the packet.

Multiple access means that nothing prevents two or more devices from trying to send a message at the same time. Sure, each device listens before sending. However, suppose that two devices listen, hear nothing, and then proceed to send their packets at the same time? Picture what happens when you and someone else arrive at a four-way stop sign at the same time. You wave the other driver on, he or she waves you on, you wave, he or she waves, you both wave, and then you both go at the same time.

Collision detection means that after a device sends a packet, it listens carefully to see whether the packet crashes into another packet. This is kind of like listening for the screeching of brakes at the four-way stop. If the device hears the screeching of brakes, it waits a random period of time and then tries to send the packet again. Because the delay is random, two packets that collide are sent again after different delay periods, so a second collision is unlikely.

CSMA/CD works pretty well for smaller networks. After a network hits about 30 computers, however, packets start to collide like crazy, and the network slows to a crawl. When that happens, the network should be divided into two or more separate sections that are sometimes called *collision domains*.

The Network Layer

The *Network layer* handles the task of routing network messages from one computer to another. The two most popular layer 3 protocols are IP (which is usually paired with TCP) and IPX (normally paired with SPX for use with Novell and Windows networks).

Network layer protocols provide two important functions: logical addressing and routing. The following sections describe these functions.

Logical addressing

As you know, every network device has a physical address called a *MAC address,* which is assigned to the device at the factory. When you buy a network interface card to install into a computer, the MAC address of that card is fixed and can't be changed. But what if you want to use some other addressing scheme to refer to the computers and other devices on your network? This is where the concept of *logical addressing* comes in; a logical address lets you access a network device by using an address that you assign.

Logical addresses are created and used by Network layer protocols such as IP or IPX. The Network layer protocol translates logical addresses to MAC addresses. For example, if you use IP as the Network layer protocol, devices on the network are assigned IP addresses such as 207.120.67.30. Because the IP protocol must use a Data Link layer protocol to actually send packets to devices, IP must know how to translate the IP address of a device to the device's MAC address.

You can use the `ipconfig` command shown earlier in Figure 2-2 to see the IP address of your computer. The IP address shown in the figure is 192.168.1.110. Another way to display this information is to use the System Information command, found on the Start menu under Start⇨All Programs⇨ Accessories⇨System Tools⇨System Information. The IP address is highlighted in Figure 2-3. Notice that the System Information program displays a lot of other useful information about the network besides the IP address. For example, you can also see the MAC address, what protocols are being used, and other information.

Although the exact format of logical addresses varies depending on the protocol being used, most protocols divide the logical address into two parts: a network address and a device address. The network address identifies which network the device resides on, and the device address then identifies the device on that network. For example, in a typical IP address, such as 192.168.1.102, the network address is 192.168.1, and the device address (called a *host address* in IP) is 102.

Figure 2-3:
Displaying
network
information
using the
System
Information
program.

Similarly, IPX addresses consist of two parts: a network address and a node address. In an IPX address, the node address is the same as the MAC address. As a result, IPX doesn't have to translate between layer 3 and layer 2 addresses.

Routing

Routing comes into play when a computer on one network needs to send a packet to a computer on another network. In this case, a device called a *router* is used to forward the packet to the destination network. In some cases, a packet may actually have to travel through several intermediate networks in order to reach its final destination network. You can find out more about routers in Book I, Chapter 3.

An important feature of routers is that you can use them to connect networks that use different layer 2 protocols. For example, a router can be used to send a packet from an Ethernet to a Token Ring network. As long as both networks support the same layer 3 protocol, it doesn't matter if their layer 1 and layer 2 protocols are different.

TIP

A protocol is considered *routable* if it uses addresses that include a network part and a host part. Any protocol that uses physical addresses isn't routable because physical addresses don't indicate to which network a device belongs.

The Transport Layer

The *Transport layer* is the layer where you'll find two of the most well-known networking protocols: TCP (normally paired with IP) and SPX (normally paired with IPX). As its name implies, the Transport layer is concerned with the transportation of information from one computer to another.

The main purpose of the Transport layer is to ensure that packets are transported reliably and without errors. The Transport layer does this task by establishing connections between network devices, acknowledging the receipt of packets, and resending packets that aren't received or are corrupted when they arrive.

In many cases, the Transport layer protocol divides large messages into smaller packets that can be sent over the network efficiently. The Transport layer protocol reassembles the message on the receiving end, making sure that all of the packets that comprise a single transmission are received so that no data is lost.

For some applications, speed and efficiency are more important than reliability. In such cases, a *connectionless protocol* can be used. A connectionless protocol doesn't go to the trouble of establishing a connection before sending a packet. Instead, it simply sends the packet. TCP is a connection-oriented Transport layer protocol. The connectionless protocol that works alongside TCP is called *UDP.*

In Windows XP or Vista, you can view information about the status of TCP and UDP connections by running the Netstat command from a command window, as Figure 2-4 shows. In the figure, you can see that three TCP connections are established.

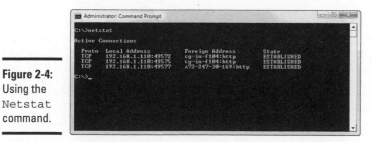

Figure 2-4:
Using the
Netstat
command.

In fact, you can use the command `Netstat /N` to see the numeric network addresses instead of the names. With the `/N` switch, the output in Figure 2-4 would look like this:

```
Active Connections
    Proto  Local Address         Foreign Address      State
    TCP    192.168.1.110:49572   209.68.34.15:21      ESTABLISHED
    TCP    192.168.1.110:49575   192.168.1.1:1079     CLOSE_WAIT
    TCP    192.168.1.110:49577   192.168.1.1:1080     CLOSE_WAIT
```

TCP is a connection-oriented Transport layer protocol. *UDP* is a connection-less Transport layer protocol.

The Session Layer

The *Session layer* establishes conversations known as *sessions* between networked devices. A *session* is an exchange of connection-oriented transmissions between two network devices. Each of these transmissions is handled by the Transport layer protocol. The session itself is managed by the Session layer protocol.

A single session can include many exchanges of data between the two computers involved in the session. After a session between two computers has been established, it is maintained until the computers agree to terminate the session.

The session layer allows three types of transmission modes:

✦ **Simplex:** In this mode, data flows in only one direction.

✦ **Half-duplex:** In this mode, data flows in both directions, but only in one direction at a time.

✦ **Full-duplex:** In this mode, data flows in both directions at the same time.

In actual practice, the distinctions in the Session, Presentation, and Application layers are often blurred, and some commonly used protocols actually span all three layers. For example, SMB — the Server Message Block protocol that is the basis of file sharing in Windows networks — functions at all three layers.

The Presentation Layer

The *Presentation layer* is responsible for how data is represented to applications. Most computers — including Windows, Unix, and Macintosh computers — use the American Standard Code for Information Interchange

(ASCII) to represent data. However, some computers (such as IBM main-frame computers) use a different code, known as Extended Binary Coded Decimal Interchange Code (EBCDIC). ASCII and EBCDIC aren't compatible with each other. To exchange information between a mainframe computer and a Windows computer, the Presentation layer must convert the data from ASCII to EBCDIC and vice versa.

Besides simply converting data from one code to another, the Presentation layer can also apply sophisticated compression techniques so that fewer bytes of data are required to represent the information when it's sent over the network. At the other end of the transmission, the Presentation layer then uncompresses the data.

The Presentation layer can also scramble the data before it is transmitted and unscramble it at the other end by using a sophisticated encryption technique that even Sherlock Holmes would have trouble breaking.

The Application Layer

The highest layer of the OSI model, the *Application layer,* deals with the techniques that application programs use to communicate with the network. The name of this layer is a little confusing. Application programs such as Microsoft Office or QuickBooks aren't a part of the Application layer. Rather, the Application layer represents the programming interfaces that application programs such as Microsoft Office or QuickBooks use to request network services.

Some of the better-known Application layer protocols are

✦ DNS (Domain Name System) for resolving Internet domain names.

✦ FTP (File Transfer Protocol) for file transfers.

✦ SMTP (Simple Mail Transfer Protocol) for e-mail.

✦ SMB (Server Message Block) for file sharing in Windows networks.

✦ NFS (Network File System) for file sharing in Unix networks.

✦ Telnet for terminal emulation.

Following a Packet through the Layers

Figure 2-5 shows how a packet of information flows through the seven layers as it travels from one computer to another on the network. The data begins its journey when an end-user application sends data to another network computer. The data enters the network through an Application layer interface, such as SMB. The data then works its way down through the proto-col stack. Along the way, the protocol at each layer manipulates the data by adding header information, converting the data into different formats, com-bining packets to form larger packets, and so on. When the data reaches the Physical layer protocol, it is actually placed on the network media (in other words, the cable) and sent to the receiving computer.

When the receiving computer receives the data, the data works its way up through the protocol stack. Then, the protocol at each layer reverses the processing that was done by the corresponding layer on the sending com-puter. Headers are removed, data is converted back to its original format, packets that were split into smaller packets are recombined into larger mes-sages, and so on. When the packet reaches the Application layer protocol, it is delivered to an application that can process the data.

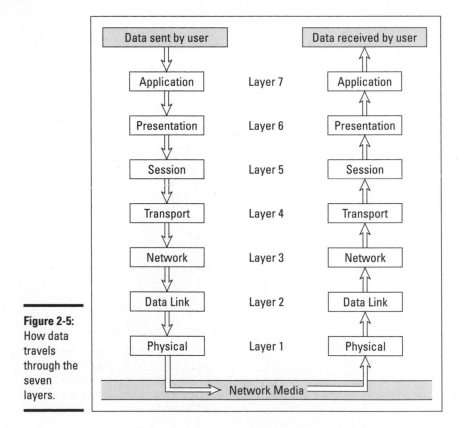

Figure 2-5:
How data travels through the seven layers.

The Ethernet Protocol

As you know, the first two layers of the OSI model deal with the physical structure of the network and the means by which network devices can send information from one device on a network to another. By far, the most popular set of protocols for the Physical and Data Link layers is *Ethernet*.

Ethernet has been around in various forms since the early 1970s. (For a brief history of Ethernet, see the sidebar, "Ethernet folklore and mythology," later in this chapter.) The current incarnation of Ethernet is defined by the IEEE standard known as 802.3. Various flavors of Ethernet operate at different speeds and use different types of media. However, all the versions of Ethernet are compatible with each other, so you can mix and match them on the same network by using devices such as bridges, hubs, and switches to link network segments that use different types of media.

The actual transmission speed of Ethernet is measured in millions of bits per second, or Mbps. Ethernet comes in three different speed versions: 10 Mbps, known as *Standard Ethernet;* 100 Mbps, known as *Fast Ethernet;* and 1,000 Mbps, known as *Gigabit Ethernet.* Keep in mind, however, that network transmission speed refers to the maximum speed that can be achieved over the network under ideal conditions. In reality, the actual throughput of an Ethernet network rarely reaches this maximum speed.

Ethernet operates at the first two layers of the OSI model — the Physical and the Data Link layers. However, Ethernet divides the Data Link layer into two separate layers known as the *Logical Link Control (LLC) layer* and the *Medium Access Control (MAC)* layer. Figure 2-6 shows how the various elements of Ethernet match up to the OSI model.

Figure 2-6: Ethernet and the OSI model.

Ethernet folklore and mythology

If you're a history buff, you may be interested in the story of how Ethernet came to be so popular. Here's how it happened: The original idea for the Ethernet was hatched in the mind of a graduate computer science student at Harvard University named Robert Metcalfe. Looking for a thesis idea in 1970, he refined a networking technique that was used in Hawaii called the AlohaNet (it was actually a wireless network) and developed a technique that would enable a network to efficiently use as much as 90 percent of its capacity. By 1973, he had his first Ethernet network up and running at the famous Xerox Palo Alto Research Center (PARC). Bob dubbed his network "Ethernet" in honor of the thick network cable, which he called "the ether." (Xerox PARC was busy in 1973. In addition to Ethernet, PARC developed the first personal computer that used a graphical user interface complete with icons, windows, and menus, and the world's first laser printer.)

In 1979, Xerox began working with Intel and DEC (a once popular computer company) to make Ethernet an industry standard networking product. Along the way, they enlisted the help of the IEEE, which formed committee number 802.3 and began the process of standardizing Ethernet in 1981. The 802.3 committee released the first official Ethernet standard in 1983.

Meanwhile, Bob Metcalfe left Xerox, turned down a job offer from Steve Jobs to work at Apple computers, and started a company called the Computer, Communication, and Compatibility Corporation — now known as 3Com. 3Com has since become one of the largest manufacturers of Ethernet equipment in the world.

The following sections describe Standard Ethernet, Fast Ethernet, and Gigabit Ethernet in more detail.

Standard Ethernet

Standard Ethernet is the original Ethernet. It runs at 10 Mbps, which was considered fast in the 1970s but is pretty slow by today's standards. Because the cost of Fast Ethernet has dropped dramatically in the past few years, Fast Ethernet has pretty much replaced Standard Ethernet for most new networks. However, plenty of existing Standard Ethernet networks are still in use.

Standard Ethernet comes in four incarnations, depending on the type of cable used to string the network together:

✦ **10Base5:** The original Ethernet cable was thick (about as thick as your thumb), heavy, and difficult to work with. It's seen today only in museums.

✦ **10Base2:** This thinner type of coaxial cable (it resembles television cable) became popular in the 1980s and lingered into the early 1990s.

Plenty of 10Base2 cable is still in use, but it's rarely installed in new networks. 10Base2 (like 10Base5) uses a bus topology, so wiring a 10Base2 network involves running cable from one computer to the next until all the computers are connected in a segment.

✦ **10BaseT:** *Unshielded twisted-pair* cable (also known as *UTP*) became popular in the 1990s because it's easier to install, lighter, more reliable, and offers more flexibility in how networks are designed. 10BaseT networks use a star topology with hubs at the center of each star. Although the maximum length of 10BaseT cable is only 100 meters, hubs can be chained together to extend networks well beyond the 100-meter limit.

10BaseT cable has four pairs of wires that are twisted together throughout the entire span of the cable. However, 10BaseT uses only two of these wire pairs, so the unused pairs are spares.

✦ **10BaseFL:** Fiber-optic cables were originally supported at 10 Mbps by the 10BaseFL standard. However, because faster fiber-optic versions of Ethernet now exist, 10BaseFL is rarely used.

Fast Ethernet

Fast Ethernet refers to Ethernet that runs at 100 Mbps, which is ten times the speed of standard Ethernet. The following are the three varieties of fast Ethernet:

✦ **100BaseT4:** The 100BaseT4 protocol allows transmission speeds of 100 Mbps over the same UTP cable as 10BaseT networks. To do this, it uses all four pairs of wire in the cable. 100BaseT4 simplifies the task of upgrading an existing 10BaseT network to 100 Mbps.

✦ **100BaseTX:** The most commonly used standard for office networks today is 100BaseTX, which transmits at 100 Mbps over just two pairs of a higher grade of UTP cable than the cable used by 10BaseT. The higher-grade cable is referred to as *Category 5*. Most new networks are wired with Category 5 or better cable.

✦ **100BaseFX:** The fiber-optic version of Ethernet running at 100 Mbps is called 10BaseFX. Because fiber-optic cable is expensive and tricky to install, it isn't used much for individual computers in a network. However, it's commonly used as a network *backbone*. For example, a fiber backbone is often used to connect individual workgroup hubs to routers and servers.

Gigabit Ethernet

Gigabit Ethernet is Ethernet running at a whopping 1,000 Mbps, which is 100 times faster than the original 10 Mbps Ethernet. Gigabit Ethernet is considerably more expensive than Fast Ethernet, so it's typically used only when the improved performance justifies the extra cost. For example, you may find Gigabit Ethernet used as the backbone for very large networks or to connect server computers to the network. And in some cases, Gigabit Ethernet is even used for desktop computers that require high-speed network connections.

Gigabit Ethernet comes in two flavors:

✦ **1000BaseT:** Gigabit Ethernet can run on Category 5 UTP cable, but higher grades such as Category 5e or Category 6 are preferred because they're more reliable.

✦ **1000BaseLX:** Several varieties of fiber cable are used with Gigabit Ethernet, but the most popular is called 1000BaseLX.

The TCP/IP Protocol Suite

TCP/IP, the protocol on which the Internet is built, is actually not a single protocol but rather an entire suite of related protocols. TCP is even older than Ethernet. It was first conceived in 1969 by the Department of Defense. For more on the history of TCP/IP, see the sidebar, "The fascinating story of TCP/IP," later in this chapter. Currently, the Internet Engineering Task Force, or IETF, manages the TCP/IP protocol suite.

The TCP/IP suite is based on a four-layer model of networking that is similar to the seven-layer OSI model. Figure 2-7 shows how the TCP/IP model matches up with the OSI model and where some of the key TCP/IP protocols fit into the model. As you can see, the lowest layer of the model, the Network Interface layer, corresponds to the OSI model's Physical and Data Link layers. TCP/IP can run over a wide variety of Network Interface layer protocols, including Ethernet, as well as other protocols, such as Token Ring and FDDI (an older standard for fiber-optic networks).

Figure 2-7:
TCP/IP and the OSI model.

OSI Layers	TCP/IP Layers	TCP/IP Protocols				
Application Layer	Application Layer	HTTP	FTP	Telnet	SMTP	DNS
Presentation Layer						
Session Layer						
Transport Layer	Transport Layer	TCP			UDP	
Network Layer	Network Layer	IP				
Data Link Layer	Network Interface Layer	Ethernet		Token Ring		Other Link-Layer Protocols
Physical Layer						

10Base what?

The names of Ethernet cable standards resemble the audible signals a quarterback might shout at the line of scrimmage. In reality, the cable designations consist of three parts:

✔ The first number is the speed of the network in Mbps. So 10BaseT is for 10 Mbps networks (Standard Ethernet), 100BaseTX is for 100 Mbps networks (Fast Ethernet), and 1000BaseT is for 1,000 Mbps networks (Gigabit Ethernet).

✔ The word *Base* indicates the type of network transmission that the cable uses. *Base* is short for *baseband.* Baseband transmissions carry one signal at a time and are relatively simple to implement. The alternative to baseband is *broadband,* which can carry more than one signal at a time but is more difficult to implement. At one time, broadband incarnations of the 802.x networking standards existed, but they have all but fizzled due to lack of use.

✔ The tail end of the designation indicates the cable type. For coaxial cables, a number is used that roughly indicates the maximum length of the cable in hundreds of meters. 10Base5 cables can run up to 500 meters. 10Base2 cables can run up to 185 meters. (The IEEE rounded 185 up to 200 to come up with the name 10Base2.) If the designation ends with a *T,* twisted-pair cable is used. Other letters are used for other types of cables.

The Application layer of the TCP/IP model corresponds to the upper three layers of the OSI model — that is, the Session, Presentation, and Application layers. Many protocols can be used at this level. A few of the most popular are HTTP, FTP, Telnet, SMTP, DNS, and SNMP.

You can find out about many of the details of these and other TCP/IP protocols in Book IV. In the rest of this section, I just want to point out a few more details of the three most important protocols in the TCP/IP suite: IP, TCP, and UDP.

IP

IP, which stands for Internet Protocol, is a Network layer protocol that is responsible for delivering packets to network devices. The IP protocol uses logical IP addresses to refer to individual devices rather than physical (MAC) addresses. A protocol called ARP (for Address Resolution Protocol) handles the task of converting IP addresses to MAC addresses.

Because IP addresses consist of a network part and a host part, IP is a *routable protocol.* As a result, IP can forward a packet to another network if the host is not on the current network. (The ability to route packets across networks is where IP gets its name. An *internet* is a series of two or more connected TCP/IP networks that can be reached by routing.)

TCP

TCP, which stands for Transmission Control Protocol, is a connection-oriented Transport layer protocol. TCP lets a device reliably send a packet to another device on the same network or on a different network. TCP ensures that each packet is delivered if at all possible. It does so by establishing a connection with the receiving device and then sending the packets. If a packet doesn't arrive, TCP resends the packet. The connection is closed only after the packet has been successfully delivered or an unrecoverable error condition has occurred.

One key aspect of TCP is that it's always used for one-to-one communications. In other words, TCP allows a single network device to exchange data with another single network device. TCP is not used to broadcast messages to multiple network recipients. Instead, the User Datagram Protocol (UDP) is used for that purpose.

Many well-known Application layer protocols rely on TCP. For example, when a user running a Web browser requests a page, the browser uses HTTP to send a request via TCP to the Web server. When the Web server receives the request, it uses HTTP to send the requested Web page back to the browser, again via TCP. Other Application layer protocols that use TCP include Telnet (for terminal emulation), FTP (for file exchange), and SMTP (for e-mail).

UDP

The *User Datagram Protocol* (or *UDP)* is a connectionless Transport layer protocol that is used when the overhead of a connection isn't required. After UDP has placed a packet on the network (via the IP protocol), it forgets about it. UDP doesn't guarantee that the packet actually arrives at its destination. Most applications that use UDP simply wait for any replies expected as a result of packets sent via UDP. If a reply doesn't arrive within a certain period of time, the application either sends the packet again or gives up.

Probably the best-known Application layer protocol that uses UDP is DNS, the Domain Name System. When an application needs to access a domain name such as `www.wiley.com`, DNS sends a UDP packet to a DNS server to look up the domain. When the server finds the domain, it returns the domain's IP address in another UDP packet. (Actually, the process is much more complicated than that. For a more detailed explanation, see Book IV, Chapter 4.)

The fascinating story of TCP/IP

Some people are fascinated by history. They subscribe to cable TV just to get the History Channel. If you're one of those history buffs, you may be interested in the following chronicle of TCP/IP's humble origins. (For maximum effect, play some melancholy violin music in the background as you read the rest of this sidebar.)

In the summer of 1969, the four mop-topped singers from Liverpool were breaking up. The war in Vietnam was escalating. Astronauts Neil Armstrong and Buzz Aldrin walked on the moon. And the Department of Defense built a computer network called ARPANET to link its defense installations with several major universities throughout the United States.

By the early 1970s, ARPANET was becoming difficult to manage. So it was split into two networks: one for military use, called MILNET, and the other for nonmilitary use. The nonmilitary network retained the name ARPANET. To link MILNET with ARPANET, a new method of connecting networks, called *Internet Protocol* or just *IP* for short, was invented.

The whole purpose of IP was to enable these two networks to communicate with each other.

Fortunately, the designers of IP realized that it wouldn't be too long before other networks wanted to join in the fun, so they designed IP to allow for more than two networks. In fact, their ingenious design allowed for tens of thousands of networks to communicate via IP.

The decision was a fortuitous one, as the Internet quickly began to grow. By the mid-1980s, the original ARPANET reached its limits. Just in time, the National Science Foundation (NSF) decided to get into the game. NSF had built a network called NSFNET to link its huge supercomputers. NSFNET replaced ARPANET as the new background for the Internet. Around that time, such magazines as *Time* and *Newsweek* began writing articles about this new phenomenon called the Internet, and the *Net* (as it became nicknamed) began to grow like wildfire. Soon NSFNET couldn't keep up with the growth, so several private commercial networks took over management of the Internet backbone. The Internet has grown at a dizzying rate ever since, and nobody knows how long this frenetic growth rate will continue. One thing is sure: TCP/IP is now the most popular networking protocol in the world.

The IPX/SPX Protocol Suite

Although TCP/IP has quickly become the protocol of choice for most networks, plenty of networks still use an alternative protocol suite called *IPX/SPX*. Novell originally developed the IPX/SPX suite in the 1980s for use with their NetWare servers. IPX/SPX also works with all Microsoft operating systems, with OS/2, and even with Unix and Linux.

Microsoft's version of the IPX/SPX protocol goes by different names, depending on which version of Windows you're using. You may see it called NWLink, IPX/SPX Compatible Protocol, or NWLINK IPX/SPX/NetBIOS Compatible Transport Protocol.

NetWare versions 5.0 and later fully support TCP/IP, so you don't have to use IPX/SPX with Novell networks unless the network has a server that runs NetWare 4.*x* or (heaven forbid) 3.*x.* If your network doesn't have one of the older NetWare servers, you're better off using TCP/IP instead of IPX/SPX.

Here are a few other points to know about IPX/SPX:

✦ IPX stands for Internetwork Package Exchange. It's a Network layer protocol that's analogous to IP.

✦ SPX stands for Sequenced Package Exchange. It's a Transport layer protocol that's analogous to TCP.

✦ Unlike TCP/IP, IPX/SPX isn't a standard protocol established by a standards group, such as IEEE. Instead, IPX/SPX is a proprietary standard developed and owned by Novell. Both IPX and IPX/SPX are registered trademarks of Novell, which is why Microsoft's versions of IPX/SPX aren't called simply "IPX/SPX."

Other Protocols Worth Knowing About

Other networks besides Ethernet, TCP/IP, and IPX/SPX are worth knowing about:

✦ **NetBIOS:** Short for Network Basic Input/Output System, this is the basic application-programming interface for network services on Windows computers. It's installed automatically when you install TCP/IP, but doesn't show up as a separate protocol when you view the network connection properties. (Refer to Figure 2-1.) NetBIOS is a Session layer protocol that can work with Transport layer protocols such as TCP, SPX, or NetBEUI.

✦ **NetBEUI:** Short for Network BIOS Extended User Interface, this is a Transport layer protocol that was designed for early IBM and Microsoft networks. NetBEUI is now considered obsolete.

✦ **AppleTalk:** Apple computers have their own suite of network protocols known as *AppleTalk.* The AppleTalk suite includes a Physical and Data Link layer protocol called *LocalTalk,* but can also work with standard lower-level protocols, including Ethernet and Token Ring.

✦ **SNA:** *Systems Network Architecture* is an IBM networking architecture that dates back to the 1970s, when mainframe computers roamed the earth and PCs had barely emerged from the primordial computer soup. SNA was designed primarily to support huge terminals such as airline reservation and banking systems, with tens of thousands of terminals attached to central host computers. Now that IBM mainframes support TCP/IP and terminal systems have all but vanished, SNA is beginning to fade away. Still, many networks that incorporate mainframe computers have to contend with SNA.

Chapter 3: Understanding Network Hardware

In This Chapter

✔ Introducing servers

✔ Working with network interface cards

✔ Becoming familiar with network cable, network hubs, and switches

✔ Exploring repeaters, bridges, and routers

✔ Figuring out network storage

The building blocks of networks are network hardware devices such as servers, adapter cards, cables, hubs, switches, routers, and so on. This chapter provides an overview of these building blocks.

Servers

Server computers are the lifeblood of any network. Servers provide the shared resources that network users crave, such as file storage, databases, e-mail, Web services, and so on. Choosing the equipment you use for your network's servers is one of the key decisions you'll make when you set up a network. In this section, I describe some of the various ways you can equip your network's servers.

Right off the bat, I want to get one thing straight: Only the smallest networks can do without at least one dedicated server computer. For a home network or a small office network with only a few computers, you can get away with true peer-to-peer networking. That's where each client computer shares its resources such as file storage or printers, and a dedicated server computer isn't needed. For a more-detailed explanation of why this isn't a good idea for larger networks, see Book II, Chapter 1.

What's important in a server

Here are some general things to keep in mind when picking a server computer for your network:

✦ **Scalability:** *Scalability* refers to the ability to increase the size and capacity of the server computer without unreasonable hassle. It's a major mistake to purchase a server computer that just meets your current needs because, you can rest assured, your needs will double within a year. If at all possible, equip your servers with far more disk space, RAM, and processor power than you currently need.

✦ **Reliability:** The old adage "you get what you pay for" applies especially well to server computers. Why spend $3,000 on a server computer when you can buy one with similar specifications at a discount electronics store for $1,000? One reason is reliability. When a client computer fails, only the person who uses that computer is affected. When a server fails, however, everyone on the network is affected. The less-expensive computer is probably made of inferior components that are more likely to fail.

✦ **Availability:** This concept of availability is closely related to reliability. When a server computer fails, how long does it take to correct the problem and get the server up and running again? Server computers are designed so that their components can be easily diagnosed and replaced, thus minimizing the downtime that results when a component fails. In some servers, components are *hot swappable,* which means that certain components can be replaced without shutting down the server. Some servers are designed to be *fault-tolerant* so that they can continue to operate even if a major component fails.

✦ **Service and support:** Service and support are factors often overlooked when picking computers. If a component in a server computer fails, do you have someone on site qualified to repair the broken computer? If not, you should get an on-site maintenance contract for the computer. Don't settle for a maintenance contract that requires you to take the computer in to a repair shop or, worse, mail it to a repair facility. You can't afford to be without your server that long.

Components of a server computer

The hardware components that comprise a typical server computer are similar to the components used in less expensive client computers. However, server computers are usually built from higher-grade components than client computers for the reasons given in the preceding section. The following paragraphs describe the typical components of a server computer:

✦ **Motherboard:** The motherboard is the computer's main electronic circuit board to which all the other components of your computer are connected. More than any other component, the motherboard *is* the computer. All other components attach to the motherboard.

The major components on the motherboard include the processor (or CPU), supporting circuitry called the *chipset,* memory, expansion slots, a standard IDE hard drive controller, and I/O ports for devices such as keyboards, mice, and printers. Some motherboards also include additional built-in features such as a graphic adapter, SCSI disk controller, or a network interface.

✦ **Processor:** The processor, or CPU, is the brain of the computer. Although the processor isn't the only component that affects overall system performance, it is the one that most people think of first when deciding what type of server to purchase. At the time of this writing, Intel had four processor models, summarized in Table 3-1, designed for use in server computers.

Each motherboard is designed to support a particular type of processor. CPUs come in two basic mounting styles: slot or socket. However, you can choose from several types of slots and sockets, so you have to make sure that the motherboard supports the specific slot or socket style used by the CPU. Some server motherboards have two or more slots or sockets to hold two or more CPUs.

The term *clock speed* refers to how fast the basic clock that drives the processor's operation ticks. In theory, the faster the clock speed, the faster the processor. However, clock speed alone is reliable only for comparing processors within the same family. In fact, the Itanium processors are faster than Xeon processors at the same clock speed. The same holds true for Xeon processors compared with Pentium D processors, as well as Pentium D processors compared with Pentium 4 processors. That's because the newer processor models contain more advanced circuitry than the older model, so they can accomplish more work with each tick of the clock.

The number of *processor cores* also has a dramatic effect on performance. Each processor core acts as if it's a separate processor. Most server computers use dual-core (two processor cores) or quad-core (four cores) chips.

Table 3-1	Intel Processors	
Processor	*Clock Speed*	*Processor Cores*
Itanium 2	1.60GHz	1–2
Xeon	1.83–2.33GHz	1–4
Pentium D	2.66–3.6GHz	2
Pentium 4	2.4–3.6GHz	1

✦ **Memory:** Don't scrimp on memory. People rarely complain about servers having too much memory. Many different types of memory are available, so you have to pick the right type of memory to match the memory supported by your motherboard. The total memory capacity of the server depends on the motherboard. Most new servers can support at least 12GB of memory, and some can handle up to 32GB.

✦ **Hard drives:** Most desktop computers use inexpensive hard drives called *IDE* drives (sometimes also called *ATA*). These drives are adequate for individual users, but because performance is more important for servers, another type of drive known as *SCSI* is usually used instead. For the best performance, use the SCSI drives along with a high-performance SCSI controller card.

Recently, a new type of inexpensive drive called *SATA* has been appearing in desktop computers. SATA drives are also being used more and more in server computers as well due to their reliability and performance.

✦ **Network connection:** The network connection is one of the most important parts of any server. Many servers have network adapters built into the motherboard. If your server isn't equipped as such, you'll need to add a separate network adapter card. See the section, "Network Interface Cards," later in this chapter, for more information.

✦ **Video:** Fancy graphics aren't that important for a server computer. You can equip your servers with inexpensive generic video cards and monitors without affecting network performance. (This is one of the few areas where it's acceptable to cut costs on a server.)

✦ **Power supply:** Because a server usually has more devices than a typical desktop computer, it requires a larger power supply (300 watts is typical). If the server houses a large number of hard drives, it may require an even larger power supply.

Server form factors

The term *form factor* refers to the size, shape, and packaging of a hardware device. Server computers typically come in one of three form factors:

✦ **Tower case:** Most servers are housed in a traditional tower case, similar to the tower cases used for desktop computers. A typical server tower case is 18-inches high, 20-inches deep, and 9-inches wide and has room inside for a motherboard, five or more hard drives, and other components. Tower cases also come with built-in power supplies.

Some server cases include advanced features specially designed for servers, such as redundant power supplies (so both servers can continue operating if one of the power supplies fails), hot-swappable fans, and hot-swappable disk drive bays. *(Hot-swappable* components can be replaced without powering down the server.)

Saving space with a KVM switch

If you have more than two or three servers in one location, you should consider getting a device called a *KVM switch* to save space. A KVM switch lets you connect several server computers to a single keyboard, monitor, and mouse. (KVM stands for keyboard, video, and mouse.) Then, you can control any of the servers from a single keyboard, monitor, and mouse by turning a dial or by pressing a button on the KVM switch.

Simple KVM switches are mechanical affairs that let you choose from among 2 to 16 or more

computers. More elaborate KVM switches can control more computers, using a pop-up menu or a special keyboard combination to switch among computers. Some advanced KVMs can even control a mix of PCs and Macintosh computers from a single keyboard, monitor, and mouse.

To find more information about KVM switches, go to a Web search engine such as Google and search for "KVM."

✦ **Rack mount:** If you need only a few servers, tower cases are fine. You can just place the servers next to each other on a table or in a cabinet that's specially designed to hold servers. If you need more than a few servers, though, space can quickly become an issue. For example, what if your departmental network requires a bank of ten file servers? You'd need a pretty long table.

Rack-mount servers are designed to save space when you need more than a few servers in a confined area. A rack-mount server is housed in a small chassis that's designed to fit into a standard 19-inch equipment rack. The rack allows you to vertically stack servers in order to save space.

✦ **Blade servers:** Blade servers are designed to save even more space than rack-mount servers. A *blade server* is a server on a single card that can be mounted alongside other blade servers in a blade chassis, which itself fits into a standard 19-inch equipment rack. A typical blade chassis holds six or more servers, depending on the manufacturer.

One of the key benefits of blade servers is that you don't need a separate power supply for each server. Instead, the blade enclosure provides power for all its blade servers. Some blade server systems provide rack-mounted power supplies that can serve several blade enclosures mounted in a single rack.

In addition, the blade enclosure provides KVM switching so that you don't have to use a separate KVM switch. You can control any of the servers in a blade server network from a single keyboard, monitor, and mouse. (For more information, see the sidebar, "Saving space with a KVM switch.")

One of the biggest benefits of blade servers is that they drastically cut down the amount of cable clutter. With rack-mount servers, each server requires its own power cable, keyboard cable, video cable, mouse cable, and network cables. With blade servers, a single set of cables can service all the servers in a blade enclosure.

Network Interface Cards

Every computer on a network, both clients and servers, requires a network interface card (or NIC) in order to access the network. A NIC is usually a separate adapter card that slides into one of the server's motherboard expansion slots. However, most newer computers have the NIC built into the motherboard, so a separate card isn't needed.

For client computers, you can usually get away with using the inexpensive built-in NIC because client computers are used to connect only one user to the network. However, the NIC in a server computer connects many network users to the server. As a result, it makes sense to spend more money on a higher-quality NIC for a heavily used server. Most network administrators prefer to use name-brand cards from manufacturers such as Intel, SMC, or 3Com.

Most NICs made today support 1 Gbps networking, and will also support slower 100 Mbps and even ancient 10 Mbps networks. These cards automatically adjust their speed to match the speed of the network. So you can use a gigabit card on a network that has older 100 Mbps cards without trouble. You can find inexpensive gigabit cards for as little as $5 each, but a typical name-brand card (such as Linksys or Intel) will cost around $25 or $30.

Here are a few other points to ponder concerning network interface cards:

✦ A NIC is a Physical layer and Data Link layer device. Because a NIC establishes a network node, it must have a physical network address, also known as a MAC address. The MAC address is burned into the NIC at the factory, so you can't change it. Every NIC ever manufactured has a unique MAC address.

✦ For server computers, it makes sense to use more than one NIC. That way, the server can handle more network traffic. Some server NICs have two or more network interfaces built into a single card.

✦ Fiber-optic networks also require NICs. Fiber-optic NICs are still too expensive for desktop use in most networks. Instead, they're used for high-speed backbones. If a server connects to a high-speed fiber backbone, it will need a fiber-optic NIC that matches the fiber-optic cable being used.

Network Cable

Nearly all modern networks are constructed using a type of cable called *twisted-pair* cable, which looks a little like phone cable but is subtly different.

You may encounter other types of cable in an existing network: coax cable that resembles TV cable, thick yellow cable that used to be the only type of cable used for Ethernet, fiber-optic cables that span long distances at high speeds, or thick twisted-pair bundles that carry multiple sets of twisted-pair cable between wiring closets in a large building. But as I mentioned, it's twisted-pair cable for nearly all new networks.

A choice that's becoming more popular every day is to forego network cable and instead build your network using wireless network components. Because Book V is devoted exclusively to wireless networking, I don't describe wireless network components in this chapter.

Coaxial cable

A type of cable that was once popular for Ethernet networks is coaxial cable, sometimes called *thinnet* or *BNC cable* because of the type of connectors used on each end of the cable. Thinnet cable operates only at 10 Mbps and is rarely used for new networks. However, you'll find plenty of existing thinnet networks still being used. Figure 3-1 shows a typical coaxial cable.

Figure 3-1:
Coax cable.

Here are some salient points about coaxial cable:

✦ You attach thinnet to the network interface card by using a goofy twist-on connector called a *BNC connector.* You can purchase preassembled cables with BNC connectors already attached in lengths of 25 or 50 feet, or you can buy bulk cable on a big spool and attach the connectors yourself by using a special tool. (I suggest buying preassembled cables. Attaching connectors to bulk cable can be tricky.)

✦ With coaxial cables, you connect your computers point-to-point in a bus topology. At each computer, a T connector is used to connect two cables to the network interface card.

✦ A special plug called a *terminator* is required at each end of a series of thinnet cables. The terminator prevents data from spilling out the end of the cable and staining the carpet.

✦ The cables strung end-to-end from one terminator to the other are collectively called a *segment.* The maximum length of a thinnet segment is about 200 meters (actually, 185 meters). You can connect as many as 30 computers on one segment. To span a distance greater than 185 meters or to connect more than 30 computers, you must use two or more segments with a device called a *repeater* to connect each segment.

✦ Although Ethernet coaxial cable resembles TV coaxial cable, the two types of cable aren't interchangeable. Don't try to cut costs by wiring your network with cheap TV cable.

Twisted-pair cable

The most popular type of cable today is *twisted-pair cable,* or *UTP.* (The U stands for unshielded, but no one says *unshielded twisted pair.* Just *twisted pair* will do.) UTP cable is even cheaper than thin coaxial cable, and best of all, many modern buildings are already wired with twisted-pair cable because this type of wiring is often used with modern phone systems. Figure 3-2 shows a twisted-pair cable.

Figure 3-2:
Twisted-pair
cable.

When you use UTP cable to construct an Ethernet network, you connect the computers in a star arrangement. In the center of the star is a device called a *hub.* Depending on the model, Ethernet hubs enable you to connect from 4 to 24 computers using twisted-pair cable.

An advantage of UTP's star arrangement is that if one cable goes bad, only the computer attached to that cable is affected; the rest of the network continues to chug along. With coaxial cable, a bad cable affects the entire network, and not just the computer to which the bad cable is connected.

Here are a few other details that you should know about twisted-pair cabling:

✦ UTP cable consists of pairs of thin wire twisted around each other; several such pairs are gathered up inside an outer insulating jacket. Ethernet uses two pairs of wires, or four wires altogether. The number of pairs in a UTP cable varies, but it's often more than two.

✦ UTP cable comes in various grades called *Categories.* Don't use anything less than Category 5 cable for your network. Although cheaper, it may not be able to support faster networks.

Although higher-Category cables are more expensive than lower-Category cables, the real cost of installing Ethernet cabling is the labor required to actually pull the cables through the walls. As a result, I recommend that you always spend the extra money to buy Category 5 cable.

✦ If you want to sound like you know what you're talking about, say "Cat 5" instead of "Category 5."

✦ Although Category 5 cable is fine for 100 Mbps networks, gigabit networks require an even better cable. Category 5e cable (the e stands for enhanced), and Category 6 cable will support 1,000 Mbps networks.

✦ UTP cable connectors look like modular phone connectors but are a bit larger. UTP connectors are officially called *RJ-45 connectors.*

✦ Like thinnet cable, UTP cable is also sold in prefabricated lengths. However, RJ-45 connectors are much easier to attach to bulk UTP cable than BNC cables are to attach to bulk coaxial cable. As a result, I suggest that you buy bulk cable and connectors unless your network consists of just two or three computers. A basic crimp tool to attach the RJ-45 connectors costs about $50.

✦ The maximum allowable cable length between the hub and the computer is 100 meters (about 328 feet).

Hubs and Switches

The biggest difference between using coaxial cable and twisted-pair cable is that when you use twisted-pair cable, you also must use a separate device called a *hub.* Years ago, hubs were expensive devices — expensive enough that most do-it-yourself networkers who were building small networks opted for thinnet cable in order to avoid the expense and hassle of using hubs.

Nowadays, the cost of hubs has dropped so much that the advantages of twisted-pair cabling outweigh the hassle and cost of using hubs. With twisted-pair cabling, you can more easily add new computers to the network, move computers, find and correct cable problems, and service the computers that you need to remove from the network temporarily.

A *switch* is simply a more-sophisticated type of hub. Because the cost of switches has come down dramatically in the past few years, most new networks are built with switches rather than hubs. If you have an older network that uses hubs and seems to run slowly, you may be able to improve the network's speed by replacing the older hubs with newer switches. For more information, see the sidebar, "Hubs and switches demystified," later in this chapter.

If you use twisted-pair cabling, you need to know some of the ins and outs of using hubs:

✦ Because you must run a cable from each computer to the hub or switch, find a central location for the hub or switch to which you can easily route the cables.

✦ The hub or switch requires electrical power, so make sure that an electrical outlet is handy.

✦ When you purchase a hub or switch, purchase one with at least twice as many connections as you need. Don't buy a four-port hub or switch if you want to network four computers because when (not *if*) you add the fifth computer, you have to buy another hub or switch.

✦ You can connect hubs or switches to one another, as shown in Figure 3-3; this is called *daisy chaining*. When you daisy chain hubs or switches, you connect a cable to a standard port on one of the hubs or switches and the daisy chain port on the other hub or switch. Be sure to read the instructions that come with the hub or switch to make sure that you daisy chain them properly.

✦ You can daisy chain no more than three hubs or switches together. If you have more computers than three hubs can accommodate, don't panic. For a small additional cost, you can purchase hubs that have a BNC connection on the back. Then you can string the hubs together using thinnet cable. The three-hub limit doesn't apply when you use thinnet cable to connect the hubs. You can also get stackable hubs or switches that have high-speed direct connections that enable two or more hubs or switches to be counted as a single hub or switch.

✦ When you shop for network hubs, you may notice that the expensive ones have network-management features that support something called *SNMP*. These hubs are called *managed hubs*. Unless your network is very large and you know what SNMP is, don't bother with the more expensive managed hubs. You'd be paying for a feature that you may never use.

Figure 3-3:
Daisy
chaining
switches
together.

✦ For large networks, you may want to consider using a *managed switch*. A managed switch allows you to monitor and control various aspects of the switch's operation from a remote computer. The switch can alert you when something goes wrong with the network, and it can keep perform-ance statistics so that you can determine which parts of the network are heavily used and which aren't. A managed switch costs two or three times as much as an unmanaged switch, but for larger networks, the benefits of managed switches are well worth the additional cost.

Hubs and switches demystified

Both hubs and switches let you connect multiple computers to a twisted-pair network. Switches are more efficient than hubs, but not just because they're faster. If you really want to know, here's the actual difference between a hub and a switch:

✔ In a hub, every packet that arrives at the hub on any of its ports is automatically sent out on every other port. The hub has to do this because it is a Physical layer device, so it has no way to keep track of which computer is connected to each port. For example, suppose that John's computer is connected to port 1 on an 8-port hub, and Andrea's computer is connected to port 5. If John's computer sends a packet of information to Andrea's computer, the hub receives the packet on port 1 and then sends it out on ports 2–8. All the computers connected to the hub get to see the packet so that they can determine whether the packet was intended for them.

✔ A switch is a Data Link layer device, which means it's able to look into the packets that pass through it to examine a critical piece of Data Link layer information: the MAC address. With this information in hand, a switch can keep track of which computer is connected to each of its ports. So if John's computer on port 1 sends a packet to Andrea's computer on port 5, the switch receives the packet on port 1 and then sends the packet out on port 5 only. This process is not only faster, but also improves the security of the system because other computers don't see packets that aren't meant for them.

Repeaters

A *repeater* is a gizmo that gives your network signals a boost so that the signals can travel farther. It's kind of like a Gatorade station in a marathon. As the signals travel past the repeater, they pick up a cup of Gatorade, take a sip, splash the rest of it on their heads, toss the cup, and hop in a cab when they're sure that no one is looking.

You need a repeater when the total length of a single span of network cable exceeds 100 meters (328 feet). The 100-meter length limit applies to the cable that connects a computer to the switch or the cable that connects switches to each other when switches are daisy chained together. In other words, you can connect each computer to the switch with no more than 100 meters of cable, and you can connect switches to each other with no more than 100 meters of cable.

Figure 3-4 shows how you can use a repeater to connect two groups of computers that are too far apart to be strung on a single segment. When you use a repeater like this, the repeater divides the cable into two segments. The cable length limit still applies to the cable on each side of the repeater.

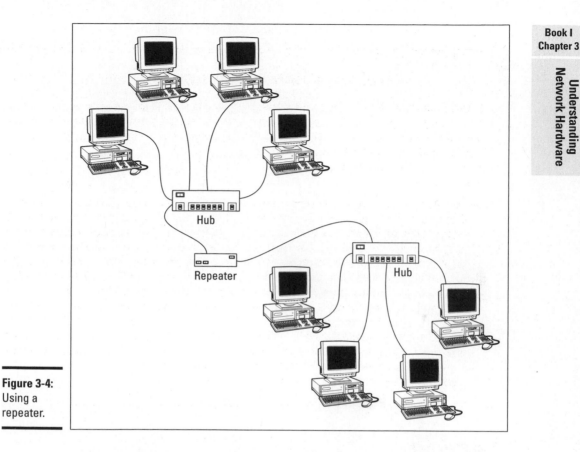

Figure 3-4:
Using a
repeater.

Here are some points to ponder when you lie awake tonight wondering
about repeaters:

✦ Repeaters are used only with Ethernet networks wired with coaxial
cable; 10/100BaseT networks don't use repeaters.

✦ Actually, that's not quite true: 10/100BaseT does use repeaters. It's just
that the repeater isn't a separate device. In a 10/100BaseT network, the
hub is actually a multiport repeater. That's why the cable used to attach
each computer to the hub is considered a separate segment.

✦ Some 10/100BaseT hubs have a BNC connector on the back. This BNC
connector is a thinnet repeater that enables you to attach a full 185-
meter thinnet segment. The segment can attach other computers,
10BaseT hubs, or a combination of both.

✦ A basic rule of Ethernet life is that a signal can't pass through more than
three repeaters on its way from one node to another. That doesn't mean

you can't have more than three repeaters or hubs, but if you do, you have to carefully plan the network cabling so that the three-repeater rule isn't violated.

✦ Repeaters are legitimate components of a by-the-book Ethernet network. They don't extend the maximum length of a single segment; they just enable you to tie two segments together. Beware of the little black boxes that claim to extend the segment limit beyond the standard 185-meter limit for thinnet or the 100-meter limit for 10/100BaseT cable. These products usually work, but playing by the rules is better.

Bridges

A *bridge* is a device that connects two networks so that they act as if they're one network. Bridges are used to partition one large network into two smaller networks for performance reasons. You can think of a bridge as a kind of smart repeater. Repeaters listen to signals coming down one network cable, amplify them, and send them down the other cable. They do this blindly, paying no attention to the content of the messages that they repeat.

In contrast, a bridge is a little smarter about the messages that come down the pike. For starters, most bridges have the capability to listen to the network and automatically figure out the address of each computer on both sides of the bridge. Then the bridge can inspect each message that comes from one side of the bridge and broadcast it on the other side of the bridge, but only if the message is intended for a computer that's on the other side.

This key feature enables bridges to partition a large network into two smaller, more efficient networks. Bridges work best in networks that are highly segregated. For example (humor me here — I'm a Dr. Seuss fan), suppose that the Sneetches networked all their computers and discovered that, although the Star-Bellied Sneetches' computers talked to each other frequently and the Plain-Bellied Sneetches' computers also talked to each other frequently, rarely did a Star-Bellied Sneetch computer talk to a Plain-Bellied Sneetch computer.

A bridge can partition the Sneetchnet into two networks: the Star-Bellied network and the Plain-Bellied network. The bridge automatically learns which computers are on the Star-Bellied network and which are on the Plain-Bellied network. The bridge forwards messages from the Star-Bellied side to the Plain-Bellied side (and vice versa) only when necessary. The overall performance of both networks improves, although the performance of any network operation that has to travel over the bridge slows down a bit.

Here are a few additional things to consider about bridges:

✦ Some bridges also have the capability to translate the messages from one format to another. For example, if the Star-Bellied Sneetches build their network with Ethernet and the Plain-Bellied Sneetches use Token Ring, a bridge can tie the two together.

✦ You can get a basic bridge to partition two Ethernet networks for about $500 from mail order suppliers. More sophisticated bridges can cost as much as $5,000 or more.

✦ If you've never read Dr. Seuss's classic story of the Sneetches, you should.

Routers

A *router* is like a bridge, but with a key difference. Bridges are Data Link layer devices, so they can tell the MAC address of the network node to which each message is sent, and can forward the message to the appropriate segment. However, they can't peek into the message itself to see what type of information is being sent. In contrast, a router is a Network layer device, so it can work with the network packets at a higher level. In particular, a router can examine the IP address of the packets that pass through it. And because IP addresses have both a network and a host address, a router can determine what network a message is coming from and going to. Bridges are ignorant of this information.

One key difference between a bridge and a router is that a bridge is essentially transparent to the network. In contrast, a router is itself a node on the network, with its own MAC and IP addresses. This means that messages can be directed to a router, which can then examine the contents of the message to determine how it should handle the message.

You can configure a network with several routers that can work cooperatively together. For example, some routers are able to monitor the network to determine the most efficient path for sending a message to its ultimate destination. If a part of the network is extremely busy, a router can automatically route messages along a less-busy route. In this respect, the router is kind of like a traffic reporter up in a helicopter. The router knows that the 101 is bumper-to-bumper all the way through Sunnyvale, so it sends the message on 280 instead.

Here's some additional information about routers:

✦ The functional distinctions between bridges and routers — and switches and hubs, for that matter — get blurrier all the time. As bridges, hubs, and switches become more sophisticated, they're able to take on some of the chores that used to require a router, thus putting many routers out of work.

✦ Some routers are nothing more than computers with several network interface cards and special software to perform the router functions.

✦ Routers can also connect networks that are geographically distant from each other via a phone line (using modems) or ISDN.

✦ You can also use a router to join your LAN to the Internet. Figure 3-5 shows a router used for this purpose.

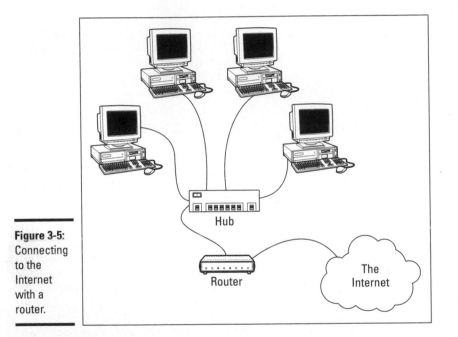

Figure 3-5:
Connecting
to the
Internet
with a
router.

Network Attached Storage

Many network servers exist solely for the purpose of making disk space available to network users. As networks grow to support more users, and users require more disk space, network administrators are constantly finding ways to add more storage to their networks. One way to do that is to add additional file servers. However, a simpler and less expensive way is to use *network attached storage,* also known as NAS.

SAN is NAS spelled backwards

It's easy to confuse the terms *storage area network* (SAN) and *network attached storage* (NAS). Both refer to relatively new network technologies that let you manage the disk storage on your network. However, NAS is a much simpler and less expensive technology. A NAS device is nothing more than an inexpensive self-contained file server. Using NAS devices actually simplifies the task of adding storage to a network because the NAS eliminates the chore of configuring a network operating system for routine file-sharing tasks.

A storage area network is designed for managing very large amounts of network storage — sometimes downright huge amounts. A SAN consists of three components: storage devices (perhaps hundreds of them), a separate high-speed network (usually fiber-optic) that directly connects the storage devices to each other, and one or more SAN servers that connect the SAN to the local area network. The SAN server manages the storage devices attached to the SAN and allows users of the LAN to access the storage.

Setting up and managing a storage area network is a job for a SAN expert. For more information about storage area networks, see the home page of the Storage Networking Industry Association at www.snia.org.

A *NAS device* is a self-contained file server that's preconfigured and ready to run. All you have to do to set it up is take it out of the box, plug it in, and turn it on. NAS devices are easy to set up and configure, easy to maintain, and less expensive than traditional file servers.

NAS should not be confused with a related technology called *storage area networks,* or *SAN.* SAN is a much more complicated and expensive technology that provides huge quantities of data storage for large networks. For more information on SAN, see the sidebar, "SAN is NAS spelled backwards."

A typical entry-level NAS device is the Dell 725N. This device is a self-contained file server built into a small rack-mount chassis. It supports up to four hard drives with a total capacity up to one terabyte (or 1,000GB). The 475N has a dual-processor motherboard that can hold up to 3GB of memory, and two built-in gigabit network ports. An LCD display on the front panel displays the device's IP address.

The Dell 725N runs a special version of Windows Server 2003 called the Windows Storage Server 2003. This version of Windows is designed specifically for NAS devices. It allows you to configure the network storage from any computer on the network by using a Web browser.

Note that some NAS devices use customized versions of Linux rather than Windows Storage Server. Also, in some systems, the operating system resides on a separate hard drive that's isolated from the shared disks. This prevents the user from inadvertently damaging the operating system.

Network Printers

Although you can share a printer on a network by attaching the printer to a server computer, many printers have network interfaces built in. This lets you connect the printer directly to the network. Then network users can connect to the printer and use it without going through a server.

Even if you connect a printer directly to the network, it's still a good idea to have the printer managed by a server computer running a network operating system such as Windows Server 2003 or 2007. That way, the server can store print jobs sent to the printer by multiple users and print the jobs in the order in which they were received.

Chapter 4: Understanding Network Operating Systems

In This Chapter

✓ Understanding what network operating systems do

✓ Figuring out the advantages of Windows Server 2003

✓ Analyzing Windows 2000 Server

✓ Taking a look at Windows NT Server

✓ Navigating NetWare

✓ Exploring other network operating systems

✓ Delving into peer-to-peer networking

*O*ne of the basic choices that you must make before you proceed any further is to decide which network operating system (NOS) to use as the foundation for your network. This chapter begins with a description of several important features found in all network operating systems. Next, it provides an overview of the advantages and disadvantages of the most popular network operating systems.

Network Operating System Features

All network operating systems, from the simplest to the most complex, must provide certain core functions. These include the ability to connect to other computers on the network, share files and other resources, provide for security, and so on. In the following sections, I describe some of these core NOS features in general terms.

Network support

It goes without saying that a network operating system should support networks. (I can picture Mike Myers in his classic Saturday Night Live role as Linda Richman, host of *Coffee Talk,* saying "I'm getting a little verklempt. . . . Talk amongst yourselves. . . . I'll give you a topic — network operating systems do not network, nor do they operate. Discuss.")

A network operating system must support a wide variety of networking protocols in order to meet the needs of its users. That's because a large network typically consists of a mixture of various versions of Windows, as well as a few scattered Macintosh (mostly in the art department) and possibly some Linux computers. The computers often have distinct protocols.

Many servers have more than one network interface card installed. In that case, the NOS must be able to support multiple network connections. Ideally, the NOS should have the ability to balance the network load among its network interfaces. In addition, in the event that one of the connections fails, the NOS should be able to seamlessly switch to another connection.

Finally, most network operating systems include a built-in ability to function as a router that connects two networks. The NOS router functions should also include firewall features in order to keep unauthorized packets from entering the local network.

File-sharing services

One of the most important functions of a network operating system is its ability to share resources with other network users. The most common resource that's shared is the server's file system. A network server must be able to share some or all of its disk space with other users so that those users can treat the server's disk space as an extension of their own computers' disk spaces.

The NOS allows the system administrator to determine which portions of the server's file system to share. Although an entire hard drive can be shared, it isn't commonly done. Instead, individual directories or folders are shared. The administrator can control which users are allowed to access each shared folder.

Because file sharing is the reason many network servers exist, network operating systems have more sophisticated disk management features than are found in desktop operating systems. For example, most network operating systems have the ability to manage two or more hard drives as if they were a single drive. In addition, most can create *mirrors,* which automatically keep backup copies of drives on a second drive.

Multitasking

Only one user at a time uses a desktop computer; however, multiple users simultaneously use server computers. As a result, a network operating system must provide support for multiple users who access the server remotely via the network.

At the heart of multiuser support is *multitasking,* which is the ability of an operating system to execute more than one program — called a *task* or a *process* — at a time. Multitasking operating systems are like the guy who used to spin plates balanced on sticks on the old *Ed Sullivan Show.* He'd run from plate to plate, trying to keep them all spinning so they wouldn't fall off the sticks. To make it challenging, he'd do it blindfolded or riding on a unicycle.

Although multitasking creates the appearance that two or more programs are executing on the computer at one time, in reality, a computer with a single processor can execute only one program at a time. The operating system switches the CPU from one program to another to create the appearance that several programs are executing simultaneously, but at any given moment, only one of the programs is actually executing. The others are patiently waiting for their turns. (However, if the computer has more than one CPU, the CPUs *can* execute programs simultaneously, which is called *multiprocessing.*)

To see multitasking in operation on a Windows computer, press Ctrl+Alt+ Delete to bring up the Windows Task Manager and then click the Processes tab. All the tasks currently active on the computer appear.

In order for multitasking to work reliably, the network operating system must completely isolate the executing programs from each other. Otherwise, one program may perform an operation that adversely affects another program. Multitasking operating systems do this by providing each task with its own unique *address space* that makes it almost impossible for one task to affect memory that belongs to another task.

In most cases, each program executes as a single task or process within the memory address space allocated to the task. However, a single program can also be split into several tasks. This technique is usually called *multithreading,* and the program's tasks are called *threads.*

The two approaches to multitasking are preemptive and non-preemptive. In *preemptive multitasking,* the operating system decides how long each task gets to execute before it should step aside so that another task can execute. When a task's time is up, the operating system's task manager interrupts the task and switches to the next task in line. All the network operating systems in widespread use today use preemptive multitasking.

The alternative to preemptive multitasking is non-preemptive multitasking. In *non-preemptive multitasking,* each task that gets control of the CPU is allowed to run until it voluntarily gives up control so that another task can run. Non-preemptive multitasking requires less operating system overhead because the operating system doesn't have to keep track of how long each task has run. However, programs have to be carefully written so that they don't hog the computer all to themselves.

Directory services

Directories are everywhere. When you need to make a phone call, you look up the number in a phone directory. When you need to find the address of a client, you look up him or her in your Rolodex. And when you need to find the Sam Goody store at a shopping mall, you look for the mall directory.

Networks have directories, too. Network directories provide information about the resources that are available on the network, such as users, computers, printers, shared folders, and files. Directories are an essential part of any network operating system.

In early network operating systems, such as Windows NT 3.1 and NetWare 3.*x*, each server computer maintained its own directory database of resources that were available on just that server. The problem with that approach was that network administrators had to maintain each directory database separately. That wasn't too bad for networks with just a few servers, but maintaining the directory on a network with dozens or even hundreds of servers was next to impossible.

In addition, early directory services were application specific. For example, a server would have one directory database for user logins, another for file sharing, and yet another for e-mail addresses. Each directory had its own tools for adding, updating, and deleting directory entries.

Most modern networks — particularly those based on Windows servers — use a directory service called *Active Directory*. Active Directory is essentially a database that organizes information about a network and allows users and computers to gain permission to access network resources. Active Directory is simple enough to use for small networks with just a few dozen computers and users, but powerful enough to work with large networks containing tens of thousands of computers.

Security services

All network operating systems must provide some measure of security to protect the network from unauthorized access. Hacking seems to be the national pastime these days. With most computer networks connected to the Internet, anyone anywhere in the world can and probably will try to break into your network.

The most basic type of security is handled through *user accounts,* which grant individual users the right to access the network resources — and govern what resources each user can access. User accounts are secured by passwords; therefore, good password policy is a cornerstone of any security system. Most network operating systems let you establish password policies, such as requiring that passwords have a minimum length and include a mix of letters and numerals. In addition, passwords can be set to expire after a certain number of days, so users can be forced to frequently change their passwords.

Most network operating systems also provide for *data encryption,* which scrambles data before it is sent over the network or saved on disk, and *digital certificates,* which are used to ensure that users are who they say they are and files are what they claim to be.

Microsoft's Server Operating Systems

Over the years, Microsoft has released several versions of its Windows-based server operating system: Windows NT Server 4, Windows 2000 Server, Windows Server 2003, and Windows Server 2008. Windows Server 2008 is the newest version, but because it's so new, most organizations are still using Windows Server 2003 — and some are still using Windows 2000 Server. (In fact, at the time I wrote this, Windows Server 2008 hadn't yet been officially released, but was scheduled for release in early 2008.) Because Microsoft discontinued support for Windows NT Server 4, it's only rarely seen these days.

It's useful to discuss these operating systems in the order they were released, because each new version builds on the previous version by introducing new and improved features. However, keep in mind as you read the following sections that Windows NT Server 4 and Windows 2000 Server are considered obsolete.

Windows NT Server 4

Windows NT Server was the last in a long series of Windows servers dubbed *NT,* which stood for New Technology. The "new technology" that got everyone so excited about Windows NT in the first place was 32-bit processing, a huge step up from the 16-bit processing of earlier versions of Windows. Windows NT was the first Microsoft operating system that was reliable enough to work as a network server on large networks. Version 4.0 shipped in July 1996, so it's now more than nine years old. That's a lifetime in operating system years (which are kind of like dog years).

Probably the most important feature of Windows NT is its directory model, which is based on the concept of *domains.* A domain is a group of computers that are managed by a single directory database. To access shared resources within a domain, you must have a valid user account within the domain and be granted rights to access the resources in which you're interested. The domain system uses 15-character NetBIOS names to access individual computers within a domain and to name the domain itself.

NTFS drives

Windows NT Server introduced a new type of formatting for hard drives, different from the standard FAT system used by MS-DOS since the early 1980s. (FAT stands for File Allocation Table, in case you're interested.) The new system, called *NTFS* (for NT File System) offers many advantages over FAT drives:

✔ NTFS is much more efficient at using the space on your hard drive. As a result, NTFS can cram more data onto a given hard drive than FAT.

✔ NTFS drives provide better security features than FAT drives. NTFS stores security information on disk for each file and directory. In contrast, FAT has only rudimentary security features.

✔ NTFS drives are more reliable because NTFS keeps duplicate copies of important information, such as the location of each file on the hard drive. If a problem develops on an NTFS drive, Windows NT Server can probably correct the problem without losing any data. In contrast, FAT drives are prone to losing information.

Here's a summary of the other features of NT:

✦ Officially, Microsoft claims that NT Server will run on any 486 processor with at least 16MB of memory. But I wouldn't try it on anything less than a 200 MHz Pentium with 64MB of RAM. Of course, these days, 200 MHz Pentiums with 64MB of RAM are given away as prizes in Cracker Jack boxes.

✦ Windows NT 4 uses the same user interface that was designed for Windows 95. In fact, the main difference between NT 4 and its predecessor, Windows NT 3.51, was this new user interface.

✦ Some of the file system limits include the following:

• Max number of users: Unlimited

• Number of disk volumes: 25

• Max size of a volume: 17,000GB

• Max hard drive space for server: 408,000GB

• Largest file: 17 billion GB (Wow! That's more than the maximum hard drive space for a server, which is impossible!)

• Max amount of RAM in server: 4GB

• Max number of open files: Unlimited

✦ Microsoft ceased support for Windows NT 4 in 2005.

Windows 2000 Server

Windows 2000 Server built on the strengths of Windows NT Server 4 by adding new features that made Windows 2000 Server faster, easier to manage, more reliable, and easier to use for large and small networks alike.

The most significant new feature offered by Windows 2000 Server is called Active Directory, which provides a single directory of all network resources and enables program developers to incorporate the directory into their programs. Active Directory drops the 15-character domain and computer names in favor of Internet-style DNS names, such as Marketing.MyCompany.com or Sales.YourCompany.com. (However, it still supports the old-style names for older clients that don't deal well with DNS names.)

Windows 2000 Server came in three versions:

✦ **Windows 2000 Server** was the basic server, designed for small- to medium-sized networks. It included all the basic server features, including file and printer sharing, and acted as a Web and e-mail server.

✦ **Windows 2000 Advanced Server** was the next step up, designed for larger networks. Advanced Server could support server computers that have up to 8GB of memory (not hard drive — RAM!) and four integrated processors instead of the single processor that desktop computers and most server computers had.

✦ **Windows 2000 Datacenter Server** supported servers that have as many as 32 processors with up to 64GB of RAM and was specially designed for large database applications.

For small networks with 50 or fewer computers, Microsoft offered a special bundle called the Small Business Server, which included the following components for one low, low price:

✦ **Windows Server 2003:** The operating system for your network server.

✦ **Exchange Server 2003:** For e-mail and instant messaging.

✦ **SQL Server 2000:** A database server.

✦ **FrontPage 2000:** For building Web sites.

✦ **Outlook 2000:** For reading e-mail.

Windows Server 2003

The most widely used Windows Server operating system today is Windows Server 2003. Windows Server 2003 builds on Windows 2000 Server, with the following added features:

✦ A new-and-improved version of Active Directory with tighter security, an easier-to-use interface, and better performance.

✦ A better and easier-to-use system management interface, called the Manage My Server window. On the flip side, for those who prefer brute-force commands, Windows Server 2003 includes a more comprehensive set of command line management tools than is offered by Windows 2000 Server. Of course, the familiar Microsoft Management Console tools from Windows 2000 Server are still there.

✦ A major change in the application-programming interface for Windows programs, known as the .NET Framework.

✦ Support for ever-larger clusters of computers. A *cluster* is a set of computers that work together as if they were a single server. Windows 2000 Server Datacenter Edition and previous versions supported clusters of four servers; Windows Server 2003 Enterprise and Datacenter Editions support clusters of eight servers. (Obviously, this is a benefit only for very large networks. The rest of us should just grin and say, "Cool!")

✦ An enhanced distributed file system that lets you combine drives on several servers to create one shared volume.

✦ Support for storage area networks.

✦ A built-in Internet firewall to secure your Internet connection.

✦ A new version of Microsoft's Web server, Internet Information Services (IIS) 6.0.

Like its predecessor, Windows Server 2003 comes in several versions. Four, to be specific:

✦ **Windows Server 2003, Standard Edition:** This is the basic version of Windows 2003. If you're using Windows Server 2003 as a file server or to provide other basic network services, this is the version you'll use. Standard Edition can support servers with up to four processors and 4GB of RAM.

✦ **Windows Server 2003, Web Edition:** A version of Windows 2003 optimized for use as a Web server.

✦ **Windows Server 2003, Enterprise Edition:** Designed for larger networks, this version can support servers with up to eight processors, 32GB of RAM, server clusters, and advanced features designed for high performance and reliability.

✦ **Windows Server 2003, Datacenter Edition:** The most powerful version of Windows 2003, with support for servers with 64 processors, 64GB of RAM, and server clusters, as well as advanced fault-tolerance features designed to keep the server running for mission-critical applications.

Windows Server 2008

At the time I wrote this, Microsoft was on the verge of releasing its latest and greatest server operating system, known as Windows Server 2008. Windows Server 2008 adds many new features to Windows Server 2003, including the following:

✦ Even more enhancements to Active Directory, including the ability to manage digital certificates, a new type of domain controller called a *read-only domain controller,* and the ability to stop and restart Active Directory services without shutting down the entire server.

✦ A new graphical user interface based on Windows Vista, including a new all-in-one management tool called the Server Manager.

✦ A new version of the operating system called *Server Core,* which has no graphical user interface. Server Core is run entirely from the command line or by a remote computer that connects to the server via Microsoft Management Console. Server Core is designed to provide efficient file servers, domain controllers, or DNS and DHCP servers.

✦ Remote connection enhancements that enable computers to establish web-based connections to the server using the HTTPS protocol without having to establish a Virtual Private Network (VPN) connection.

✦ Yet another new version of the Internet Information Services (IIS) Web server (7.0).

Other Server Operating Systems

Although Windows Server is the most popular choice for network operating systems, it isn't the only game in town. The following sections briefly describe three other server choices: Linux, Macintosh OS/X Server, and Novell's NetWare.

Linux

Perhaps the most interesting operating system available today is Linux. Linux is a free operating system that is based on Unix, a powerful network operating system often used on large networks. Linux was started by Linus Torvalds, who thought it would be fun to write a version of Unix in his free time — as a hobby. He enlisted help from hundreds of programmers throughout the world, who volunteered their time and efforts via the Internet. Today, Linux is a full-featured version of Unix; its users consider it to be as good or better than Windows.

Linux offers the same networking benefits of Unix and can be an excellent choice as a server operating system.

Apple Mac OS/X Server

All the other server operating systems I describe in this chapter run on Intel-based PCs with Pentium or Pentium-compatible processors. But what about Macintosh computers? After all, Macintosh users need networks, too. For Macintosh networks, Apple offers a special network server operating system known as Mac OS/X Server. Mac OS/X Server has all the features you'd expect in a server operating system: file and printer sharing, Internet features, e-mail, and so on.

Novell NetWare

NetWare was once the king of network operating systems. Today, NetWare networks are rare, but you can still find them if you look hard enough. NetWare has always had an excellent reputation for reliability. In fact, some network administrators swear that they have NetWare servers on their networks that have been running continuously, without a single reboot, since Ronald Reagan was president. (Unfortunately, there hasn't been a major upgrade to NetWare since George W. Bush's first term.)

Novell released the first version of NetWare in 1983, two years before the first version of Windows and four years before Microsoft's first network operating system, the now defunct LAN Manager. Over the years, NetWare has gone through many versions. The most important versions were:

+ NetWare version 3.*x,* the version that made NetWare famous. NetWare 3.*x* used a now outdated directory scheme called the *bindery.* Each NetWare 3.*x* server has a bindery file that contains information about the resources on that particular server. With the bindery, you had to log on separately to each server that contained resources you wanted to use.

+ NetWare 4.*x,* in which NetWare Directory Service, or NDS, replaced the bindery. NDS is similar to Active Directory. It provides a single directory for the entire network rather than separate directories for each server.

+ NetWare 5.*x* was the next step. It introduced a new user interface based on Java for easier administration, improved support for Internet protocols, multiprocessing with up to 32 processors, and many other features.

+ NetWare 6.0 introduced a variety of new features, including a new disk management system called Novell Storage Services, Web-based access to network folders and printers, and built-in support for Windows, Linux, Unix, and Macintosh file systems.

+ Novell released its last major version of NetWare (6.5), in summer 2003. It included improvements to its browser-based management tools and was bundled with open-source servers such as Apache and MySQL.

Beginning in 2005, NetWare has transformed itself into a Linux-based system called Open Enterprise System (OES). In OES, the core of the operating system is actually Linux, with added applications that run the traditional NetWare services such as directory services. (For more information, see "Linux" earlier in this chapter.)

Peer-to-Peer Networking with Windows

If you're not up to the complexity of dedicated network operating systems, you may want to opt for a simple peer-to-peer network based on a desktop version of Windows.

Advantages of peer-to-peer networks

The main advantage of a peer-to-peer network is that it's easier to set up and use than a network with a dedicated server. Peer-to-peer networks rely on the limited network server features that are built into Windows, such as the ability to share files and printers. Recent versions of Windows, including Vista and Windows XP, come with a Networking Wizard that automatically configures a basic network for you so that you don't have to manually configure any network settings.

Another advantage of peer-to-peer networks is that they can be less expensive than server-based networks. Here are some of the reasons that peer-to-peer networks are inexpensive:

✦ Peer-to-peer networks don't require you to use a dedicated server computer. Any computer on the network can function as both a network server and a user's workstation. (However, you can configure a computer as a dedicated server if you want to. Doing so results in better performance but negates the cost benefit of not having a dedicated server computer.)

✦ Peer-to-peer networks are easier to set up and use, which means that you can spend less time figuring out how to make the network work and keep it working. And, as Einstein proved, time is money (hence his famous equation, $E = M\$^2$).

✦ You must consider the cost of the server operating system itself. Windows Server can cost as much as $200 per user. And the total cost increases as your network grows, although the cost per user drops. For a peer-to-peer Windows server, you pay for Windows once. You don't pay any additional charges based on the number of users on your network.

Workgroups versus domains

In a Windows network, a *domain* is a group of server computers that share a common user account database. A user at a client computer can log in to a domain to access shared resources for any server in the domain. Each domain must have at least one server computer designated as the *domain controller,* which is ultimately in charge of the domain. Most domain networks share this work among at least two domain controllers, so that if one of the controllers stops working, the network can still function.

A peer-to-peer network can't have a domain because it doesn't have a dedicated server computer to act as a domain controller. Instead, computers in a peer-to-peer network are grouped in *workgroups,* which are simply groups of computers that can share resources with each other. Each computer in a workgroup keeps track of its own user accounts and security settings, so no single computer is in charge of the workgroup.

To create a domain, you have to designate a server computer as the domain controller and configure user accounts. Workgroups are much easier to administer. In fact, you don't have to do anything to create a workgroup except decide on the name you want to use. Although you can have as many workgroups as you want on a peer-to-peer network, most networks have just one workgroup. That way, any computers on the network can share resources with any other computer on the network.

One of the most common mistakes when setting up a peer-to-peer network is misspelling the workgroup name on one of the computers. For example, suppose you decide that all the computers should belong to a workgroup named MYGROUP. If you accidentally spell the workgroup name MYGRUOP for one of the computers, that computer will be isolated in its own workgroup. If you can't locate a computer on your network, the workgroup name is one of the first things to check.

Drawbacks of peer-to-peer networks

Yes, peer-to-peer networks are easier to install and manage than domain-based networks, but they do have their drawbacks:

✦ Because peer-to-peer networks are based on computers running client versions of Windows, they're subject to the inherent limitations of those Windows versions. Client versions of Windows are designed primarily to be an operating system for a single-user desktop computer rather than function as part of a network. These versions can't manage a file or printer server as efficiently as a real network operating system.

✦ If you don't set up a dedicated network server, someone (hopefully, not you) may have to live with the inconvenience of sharing his or her computer with the network. With Windows Server, the server computers are dedicated to network use so that no one has to put up with this inconvenience.

✦ Although a peer-to-peer network may have a lower cost per computer for smaller networks, the cost difference between peer-to-peer networks and Windows Server is less significant in larger networks (say, ten or more clients).

✦ Peer-to-peer networks don't work well when your network starts to grow. Peer-to-peer servers just don't have the security or performance features required for a growing network.

Windows Vista

The current version of Windows is known as Windows Vista. It has powerful peer-to-peer networking features built in, so it's easy to create a small peer-to-peer network based on Windows Vista.

Vista comes in several editions. The most popular are the following:

✦ **Home Basic:** For the simplest home users.

✦ **Home Premium:** Has more advanced features but is still designed for home users. Both of the Home versions can be used to create peer-to-peer networks but can't be used with domain-based networks.

✦ **Business:** Designed for business users with domain networks.

✦ **Ultimate:** Includes all of the available Windows features.

Windows Vista provides the following networking features:

✦ Built-in file and printer sharing allows you to share files and printers with other network users.

✦ A Network Setup Wizard automatically sets the most common configuration options. The wizard eliminates the need to work through multiple Properties dialog boxes to configure network settings.

✦ An Internet Connection Sharing feature (ICS) allows a Windows computer to share an Internet connection with other users. The ICS feature includes firewall features that protect your network from unauthorized access via the Internet connection.

✦ A built-in firewall protects the computer when it's connected to the Internet.

✦ Simple user account management lets you create multiple users and assign passwords.

✦ Built-in support for wireless networking makes connecting to a wireless network a breeze.

✦ Advanced network diagnostics and troubleshooting tools help you find and correct networking problems.

Older Windows versions

Previous versions of Windows also offer peer-to-peer networking features. The following list summarizes the networking features of the major Windows releases prior to Windows Vista:

✦ **Windows XP:** This is still the most popular version of Windows, as Windows Vista hasn't been around for long.

✦ **Windows Me:** The release of Me (short for **Millennium Edition)** was aimed at home users. It provided a Home Networking Wizard to simplify the task of configuring a network. It was the last version of Windows that was based on the old 16-bit MS-DOS code.

✦ **Windows 2000 Professional:** This is a desktop version of Windows 2000 Server. It has powerful peer-to-peer networking features similar to those found in Windows XP, although they are a bit more difficult to set up. It was the first desktop version of Windows that integrated well with Active Directory.

✦ **Windows 98 and Windows 98 Second Edition:** These were popular upgrades to Windows 95 that enhanced its basic networking features.

✦ **Windows 95:** This was the first 32-bit version of Windows. However, it still relied internally on 16-bit MS-DOS code, so it wasn't a true 32-bit operating system. It provided basic peer-to-peer network features, with built-in drivers for common network adapters and basic file- and printer-sharing features.

✦ **Windows for Workgroups:** This was the first version of Windows to support networking without requiring an add-on product. It simplified the task of creating NetBIOS-based networks for file and printer sharing. However, it had only weak support for TCP/IP.

Book II
Building a Network

The 5th Wave
By Rich Tennant

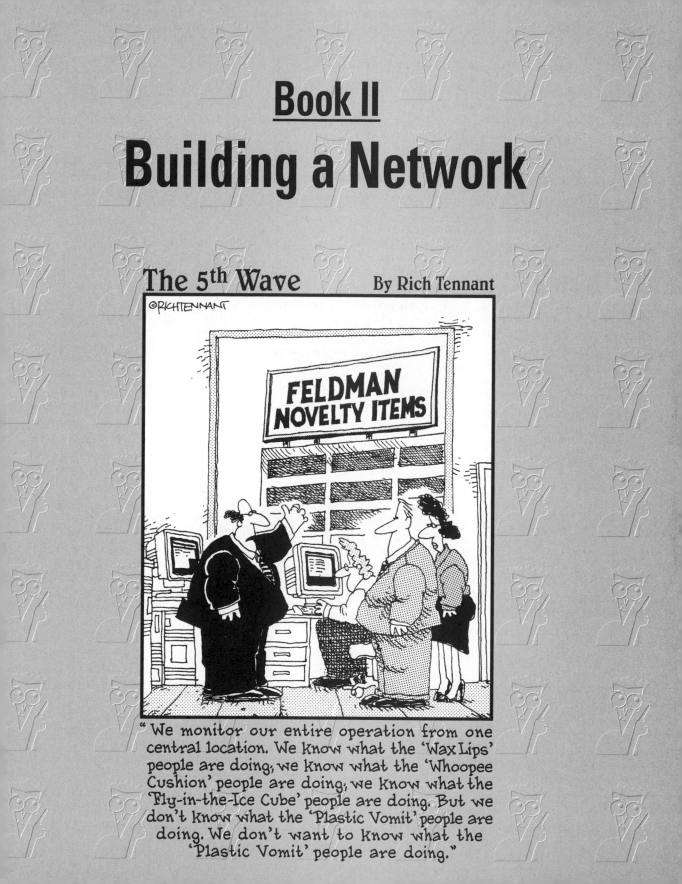

FELDMAN NOVELTY ITEMS

"We monitor our entire operation from one central location. We know what the 'Wax Lips' people are doing, we know what the 'Whoopee Cushion' people are doing, we know what the 'Fly-in-the-Ice Cube' people are doing. But we don't know what the 'Plastic Vomit' people are doing. We don't want to know what the 'Plastic Vomit' people are doing."

Contents at a Glance

Chapter 1: Planning a Network

In This Chapter

✔ Making a network plan

✔ Taking stock of your computer stock

✔ Making sure that you know why you need a network

✔ Making the three basic network decisions that you can't avoid

✔ Using a starter kit

✔ Looking at a sample network

O kay, so you're convinced that you need to network your computers. What now? Do you stop by Computers-R-Us on the way to work, install the network before morning coffee, and expect the network to be fully operational by noon?

I don't think so.

Networking your computers is just like any other worthwhile endeavor: To do it right requires a bit of planning. This chapter helps you to think through your network before you start spending money. It shows you how to come up with a networking plan that's every bit as good as the plan that a network consultant would charge thousands of dollars for. See? This book is already saving you money!

Making a Network Plan

Before you begin any networking project, whether it's a new network installation or an upgrade of an existing network, you should first make a detailed plan. If you make technical decisions too quickly, before studying all the issues that affect the project, you'll regret it. You'll discover too late that a key application won't run over the network, that the network has unacceptably slow performance, or that key components of the network don't work together.

Here are some general thoughts to keep in mind while you create your network plan:

✦ **Don't rush the plan.** The most costly networking mistakes are the ones that you make before you install the network. Think things through and consider alternatives.

✦ **Write down the network plan.** The plan doesn't have to be a fancy, 500-page document. If you want to make it look good, pick up a ½-inch three-ring binder. This binder will be big enough to hold your network plan with room to spare.

✦ **Ask someone else to read your network plan before you buy anything.** Preferably, ask someone who knows more about computers than you do.

✦ **Keep the plan up to date.** If you add to the network, dig up the plan, dust it off, and update it.

"The best laid schemes of mice and men gang oft agley, and leave us naught but grief and pain for promised joy." Robert Burns lived a few hundred years before computer networks, but his famous words ring true. A network plan isn't chiseled in stone. If you discover that something doesn't work the way you thought it would, that's okay. Just change your plan.

Being Purposeful

One of the first steps in planning your network is making sure that you understand why you want the network in the first place. Here are some of the more common reasons for needing a network, all of them quite valid:

✦ My coworker and I exchange files using CDs or flash drives just about every day. With a network, it would be easier to trade files.

✦ I don't want to buy everyone a laser printer when I know the one we have now just sits there taking up space most of the day. So wouldn't buying a network be better than buying a laser printer for every computer?

✦ I want to provide an Internet connection for all my computers. (Many networks, especially smaller ones, exist solely for the purpose of sharing an Internet connection.)

✦ Someone figured out that we're destroying seven trees a day by printing interoffice memos on paper, so we want to save the rainforest by setting up an e-mail system.

✦ Business is so good that one person typing in orders eight hours each day can't keep up. With a network, I can have two people entering orders, and I won't have to pay overtime to either person.

✦ My brother-in-law just put in a network at his office, and I don't want him to think that I'm behind the times.

✦ I already have a network, but it's so old it may as well be made of kite string and tin cans. An improved network will speed up access to shared files, provide better security, and be easier to manage.

Make sure that you identify all the reasons why you think you need a network and then write them down. Don't worry about winning the Pulitzer Prize for your stunning prose. Just make sure that you write down what you expect a network to do for you.

If you were making a 500-page networking proposal, you'd place the description of why a network is needed in a tabbed section labeled "Justification." In your ½-inch network binder, file the description under "Purpose."

As you consider the reasons why you need a network, you may conclude that you don't need a network after all. That's okay. You can always use the binder for your stamp collection.

Taking Stock

One of the most challenging parts of planning a network is figuring out how to work with the computers that you already have. In other words, how do you get from here to there? Before you can plan how to get "there," you have to know where "here" is. In other words, you have to take a thorough inventory of your current computers.

What you need to know

You need to know the following information about each of your computers:

✦ **The processor type and, if possible, its clock speed.** It would be nice if each of your computers had a shiny new 3 GHz Pentium 4 processor. In most cases, though, you find a mixture of computers: some new, some old, some borrowed, some blue. You may even find a few archaic pre-Pentium computers.

✦ **You can't usually tell what kind of processor that a computer has just by looking at the computer's case.** Most computers, however, display the processor type when you turn them on or reboot them. If the information on the startup screen scrolls too quickly for you to read it, try pressing the Pause key to freeze the information. After you finish reading it, press the Pause key again so that your computer can continue booting.

✦ **The size of the hard drive and the arrangement of its partitions.** To find out the size of your computer's hard drive in Windows Vista, open the Computer window, right-click the drive icon, and choose the Properties command from the shortcut menu that appears. Figure 1-1 shows the Properties dialog box for a 160GB hard drive that has about 145GB of free space.

Figure 1-1: The Properties dialog box for a disk drive (Windows Vista).

If your computer has more than one hard drive, Windows lists an icon for each drive in the Computer window. Jot down the size and amount of free space available on each drive.

✦ **The amount of memory.** To find this information in Windows, right-click Computer on the Start menu and choose the Properties command. The amount of memory on your computer is shown in the dialog box that appears. For example, Figure 1-2 shows the System Properties dialog box for a computer running Windows Vista with 2GB of RAM.

✦ **The operating system version.** This you can also deduce from the System Properties dialog box. For example, the Properties page shown in Figure 1-2 indicates that the computer is running Windows Vista Business Edition.

✦ **What type of network card, if any, is installed in the computer.** The easiest way to get this information is to open the Control Panel, double-click the Device Manager icon, right-click the network adapter, and choose Properties. For example, Figure 1-3 shows the Properties dialog box for an Intel Pro/100 VE network adapter, which is built into the motherboard on my computer.

Figure 1-2:
The Properties page for a Windows Vista system.

Figure 1-3:
The Properties page for a network adapter.

✦ The Device Manager is also useful for tracking down other hardware devices attached to the computer.

✦ **What network protocols are in use.** To determine this in Windows XP, open the Control Panel, double-click the Network Connections icon to open the Network Connections dialog box, and then right-click the network connection and choose the Properties command. In Windows Vista, you have to take a more circuitous route: In Control Panel, open

Network and Sharing Center, click Manage Network Connections, and then right-click the Local Area connection and choose Properties. The dialog box shown in Figure 1-4 appears.

Figure 1-4:
The Properties page for a Local Area Network connection.

✦ **What kind of printer, if any, is attached to the computer.** Usually, you can tell just by looking at the printer. You can also tell by double-clicking the Printers icon in Control Panel.

✦ **Any other devices connected to the computer.** A CD, DVD, or CD-RW drive? Scanner? Zip or Jazz drive? Tape drive? Video camera? Battle droid? Hot tub?

✦ **Which driver and installation disks are available.** Hopefully, you'll be able to locate the disks or CDs required by hardware devices such as the network card, printers, scanners, and so on. If not, you may be able to locate the drivers on the Internet.

✦ **What software is used on the computer.** Microsoft Office? AutoCAD? QuickBooks? Make a complete list and include version numbers.

Programs that gather information for you

Gathering information about your computers is a lot of work if you have more than a few computers to network. Fortunately, several software programs are available that can automatically gather the information for you. These programs inspect various aspects of a computer, such as the CPU type and speed, amount of RAM, and the size of the computer's hard drives. Then they show the information on the screen and give you the option of saving the information to a hard drive file or printing it.

Windows comes with just such a program, called Microsoft System Information. Microsoft System Information gathers and prints information about your computer. You can start Microsoft System Information by choosing Start⇨All Programs⇨Accessories⇨System Tools⇨System Information.

When you fire up Microsoft System Information, you see a window similar to the one shown in Figure 1-5. Initially, Microsoft System Information displays basic information about your computer, such as your version of Microsoft Windows, the processor type, the amount of memory on the computer, and so on. You can obtain information that is more detailed by clicking Hardware Resources, Components, or other categories in the left side of the window.

Figure 1-5: Let the System Information program gather the data you need.

To Dedicate or Not to Dedicate: That Is the Question

One of the most basic questions that a network plan must answer is whether the network will have one or more dedicated servers or rely completely on peer-to-peer networking. If the only reason for purchasing your network is to share a printer and exchange an occasional file, you may not need a dedicated server computer. In that case, you can create a peer-to-peer network by using the computers that you already have. However, all but the smallest networks will benefit from having a separate, dedicated server computer.

✦ Using a dedicated server computer makes the network faster, easier to work with, and more reliable. Consider what happens when the user of a server computer, which doubles as a workstation, decides to turn off the computer, not realizing that someone else is accessing files on his or her hard drive.

✦ You don't necessarily have to use your biggest and fastest computer as your server computer. I've seen networks where the slowest computer on the network is the server. This advice is especially true when the server is mostly used to share a printer or to store a small number of shared files. So if you need to buy a computer for your network, consider promoting one of your older computers to be the server and using the new computer as a client.

Types of Servers

Assuming that your network will require one or more dedicated servers, you should next consider what types of servers the network will need. In some cases, a single server computer can fill one or more of these roles. Whenever possible, it's best to limit each server computer to a single server function.

File servers

File servers provide centralized disk storage that can be conveniently shared by client computers on the network. The most common task of a file server is to store shared files and programs. For example, the members of a small workgroup can use disk space on a file server to store their Microsoft Office documents.

File servers must ensure that two users don't try to update the same file at the same time. The file servers do this by *locking* a file while a user updates the file so that other users can't access the file until the first user finishes. For document files (for example, word processing or spreadsheet files), the whole file is locked. For database files, the lock can be applied just to the portion of the file that contains the record or records being updated.

Print servers

Sharing printers is one of the main reasons that many small networks exist. Although it isn't necessary, a server computer can be dedicated for use as a *print server,* whose sole purpose is to collect information being sent to a shared printer by client computers and print it in an orderly fashion.

✦ A single computer may double as both a file server and a print server, but performance is better if you use separate print and file server computers.

✦ With inexpensive inkjet printers running about $100 each, just giving each user his or her own printer is tempting. However, you get what you pay for. Instead of buying $100 printers for 15 users, you may be better off buying one $1,500 laser printer and sharing it. The $1,500 laser printer will be much faster, will probably produce better-looking output, and will be cheaper to operate.

Web servers

A *Web server* is a server computer that runs software that enables the computer to host an Internet Web site. The two most popular Web server programs are Microsoft's IIS (Internet Information Services) and Apache, an open-source Web server managed by the Apache Software Foundation.

Mail servers

A *mail server* is a server that handles the network's e-mail needs. It is configured with e-mail server software, such as Microsoft Exchange Server. Exchange Server is designed to work with Microsoft Outlook, the e-mail client software that comes with Microsoft Office.

Most mail servers actually do much more than just send and receive electronic mail. For example, here are some of the features that Exchange Server offers beyond simple e-mail:

✦ Collaboration features that simplify the management of collaborative projects.

✦ Audio and video conferencing.

✦ Chat rooms and instant messaging (IM) services.

✦ Microsoft Exchange Forms Designer, which lets you develop customized forms for applications, such as vacation requests or purchase orders.

Database servers

A *database server* is a server computer that runs database software, such as Microsoft's SQL Server 2000. Database servers are usually used along with customized business applications, such as accounting or marketing systems.

Choosing a Server Operating System

If you determine that your network will require one or more dedicated servers, the next step is to determine what network operating system those servers should use. If possible, all the servers should use the same NOS so that you don't find yourself supporting different operating systems.

Although you can choose from many network operating systems, from a practical point of view, your choices are limited to the following:

✦ Windows Server 2003 or 2008

✦ Linux or another version of Unix

For more information, refer to Book I, Chapter 4.

Planning the Infrastructure

You also need to plan the details of how you will connect the computers in the network. This includes determining which network topology that the network will use, what type of cable will be used, where the cable will be routed, and what other devices, such as repeaters, bridges, hubs, switches, and routers, will be needed.

Although you have many cabling options to choose from, you'll probably use Cat 5e or better UTP for most — if not all — of the desktop client computers on the network. However, you have many decisions to make beyond this basic choice:

✦ Will you use hubs, which are cheaper, or switches, which are faster but more expensive?

✦ Where will you place workgroup hubs or switches — on a desktop somewhere within the group or in a central wiring closet?

✦ How many client computers will you place on each hub or switch, and how many hubs or switches will you need?

✦ If you need more than one hub or switch, what type of cabling will you use to connect the hubs and switches to one another?

For more information about network cabling, see Book II, Chapter 2, and Book I, Chapter 3.

If you're installing new network cable, don't scrimp on the cable itself. Because installing network cable is a labor-intensive task, the cost of the cable itself is a small part of the total cable installation cost. And if you spend a little extra to install higher-grade cable now, you won't have to replace the cable in a few years when it's time to upgrade the network.

Drawing Diagrams

One of the most helpful techniques for creating a network plan is to draw a picture of it. The diagram can be a detailed floor plan, showing the actual location of each network component. This type of diagram is sometimes called a *physical map.* If you prefer, the diagram can be a *logical map,* which is more abstract and Picasso-like. Any time you change the network layout, update the diagram. Also include a detailed description of the change, the date that the change was made, and the reason for the change.

You can diagram very small networks on the back of a napkin, but if the network has more than a few computers, you'll want to use a drawing program to help you create the diagram. One of the best programs for this purpose is Microsoft Visio, shown in Figure 1-6. Here is a rundown of some of the features that make Visio so useful:

✦ Smart shapes and connectors maintain the connections you've drawn between network components, even if you rearrange the layout of the components on the page.

✦ Stencils provide dozens of useful shapes for common network components — not just client and server computers, but routers, hubs, switches, and just about anything else you can imagine. If you're really picky about the diagrams, you can even purchase stencil sets that have accurate drawings of specific devices, such as Cisco routers or IBM mainframe computers.

**Book II
Chapter 1**

Planning a Network

Figure 1-6:
Using Visio to draw a network diagram.

✦ You can add information to each computer or device in the diagram, such as the serial number or physical location. Then, you can quickly print an inventory that lists this information for each device in the diagram.

✦ You can easily create large diagrams that span multiple pages.

Sample Network Plans

In what's left of this chapter, I present some network plans that are drawn from real-life situations. These examples illustrate many of the network design issues I've covered so far in this chapter. The stories you're about to read are true. The names have been changed to protect the innocent.

Building a small network: California Sport Surface, Inc.

California Sport Surface, Inc. (CSS) is a small company specializing in the installation of outdoor sports surfaces, such as tennis courts, running tracks, and football fields. CSS has an administrative staff of just four employees who work out of a home office. The company currently has three computers:

✦ A brand-new Dell desktop computer running Windows XP Home Edition, shared by the president (Mark) and vice president (Julie) to prepare proposals and marketing brochures, to handle correspondence, and to do other miscellaneous chores. This computer has a built-in 10/100 Mbps Ethernet network port.

✦ An older Gateway computer running Windows 98 Second Edition, used by the bookkeeper (Erin), who uses QuickBooks to handle the company's accounting needs. This computer doesn't have a network port.

✦ A notebook that runs Windows XP, used by the company's chief engineer (Daniel), who often takes it to job sites to help with engineering needs. This computer has a built-in 10 Mbps Ethernet port.

The company owns just one printer, a moderately priced inkjet printer that's connected to Erin's computer. The computers aren't networked, so whenever Mark, Julie, or Daniel need to print something, they must copy the file to a diskette and give it to Erin, who then prints the document. The computer shared by Mark and Julie is connected to the Internet via a residential DSL connection.

The company wants to install a network to support these three computers. Here are the primary goals of the network:

✦ Provide shared access to the printer so that users don't have to exchange diskettes to print their documents.

✦ Provide shared access to the Internet connection so that users can access the Internet from any of the computers.

✦ Allow for the addition of another desktop computer, which the company expects to purchase within the next six months, and potentially another notebook computer. (If business is good, the company hopes to hire another engineer.)

✦ The network should be intuitive to the users and shouldn't require extensive upkeep.

CSS's networking needs can be met with the simple peer-to-peer network diagrammed in Figure 1-7. Here's what the network requires:

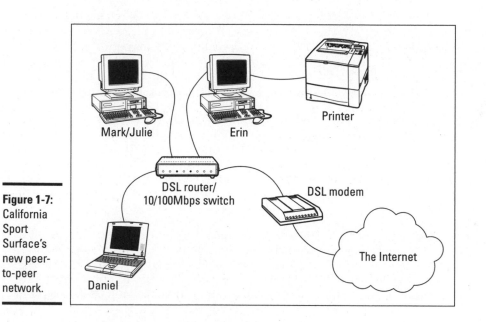

Figure 1-7: California Sport Surface's new peer-to-peer network.

✦ A 10/100 Mbps Ethernet adapter card for the Gateway computer, which is the only computer that doesn't currently have a network port.

✦ A combination DSL router and four-port 10/100 Mbps switch, such as the Linksys BEFSR41W or the Belkin F5D5231-4. The company may outgrow this device when it adds an additional laptop, but if and when that happens, another 4- or 8-port 10/100 Mbps switch can be added then.

✦ The firewall features of the DSL router will need to be enabled to protect the network from Internet hackers.

✦ File and printer sharing will need to be activated on Erin's computer, and the printer will need to be shared.

Connecting two networks: Creative Course Development, Inc.

Creative Course Development, Inc. (CCD) is a small educational publisher located in central California that specializes in integrated math and science curriculum for primary and secondary grades. It publishes a variety of course materials, including textbooks, puzzle books, and CD-ROM software.

CCD leases two office buildings that are adjacent to each other, separated only by a small courtyard. The creative staff, which consists of a dozen writers and educators, works in Building A. The sales, marketing, and administrative staff, which consists of six employees, works in Building B.

The product development and marketing staff has 14 relatively new personal computers, all running Windows XP Professional, and a server computer running Windows 2000 Server. These computers are networked by a 100 Mbps UTP network, which utilizes a single 24-port 100 Mbps switch. A fractional T1 line that's connected to the network through a small Cisco router provides Internet access.

The administrative staff has a hodgepodge of computers, some running Windows 98 Second Edition, some running Windows XP, and one still running Windows 95. They have a small Windows NT server that meets their needs. The older computers have 10BaseT network cards; the newer ones have 10/100 Mbps cards. However, the computers are all connected to a fairly old 10 Mbps Ethernet hub with 12 ports. Internet access is provided by an ISDN connection.

Both groups are happy with their computers and networks. The problem is that the networks can't communicate with each other. For example, the marketing team in Building A relies on daily printed reports from the sales system in Building B to keep track of sales, and they frequently go to the other building to follow up on important sales or to look into sales trends.

Although several solutions to this problem exist, the easiest is to bridge the networks with a pair of wireless switches. To do this, CCD will purchase two wireless access points. One will be plugged into the 100 Mbps switch in Building A, and the other will be plugged into the hub in Building B. After the access points are configured, the two networks will function as a single network. Figure 1-8 shows a logical diagram for the completed network.

Although the wireless solution to this problem sounds simple, a number of complications still need to be dealt with. Specifically:

✦ Depending on the environment, the wireless access points may have trouble establishing a link between the buildings. It may be necessary to locate the devices on the roof. In that case, CCD will have to spend a little extra money for weatherproof enclosures.

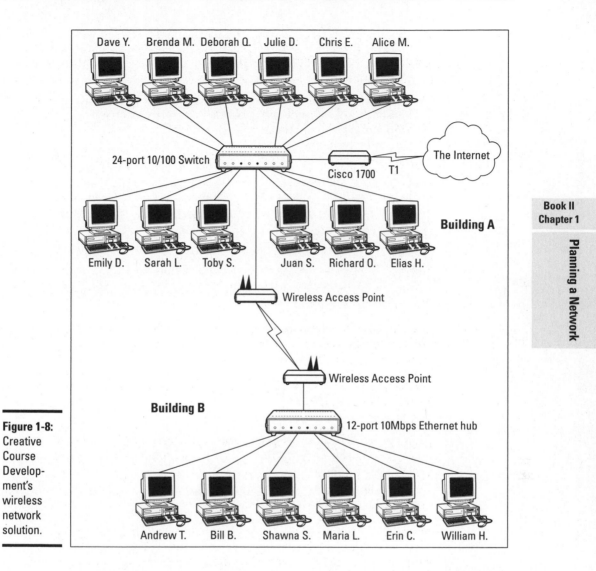

Dave Y.   Brenda M.   Deborah Q.   Julie D.   Chris E.   Alice M.

24-port 10/100 Switch

The Internet

Cisco 1700   T1

Building A

Emily D.   Sarah L.   Toby S.   Juan S.   Richard O.   Elias H.

Wireless Access Point

Wireless Access Point

Building B

12-port 10Mbps Ethernet hub

Figure 1-8:
Creative
Course
Develop-
ment's
wireless
network
solution.

Andrew T.   Bill B.   Shawna S.   Maria L.   Erin C.   William H.

✦ Because the wireless access point in Building A will be connected to a switch rather than a hub, the switch will provide some degree of isolation between the networks. As a result, overall network performance shouldn't be affected.

✦ Before the networks were connected, each network had its own DHCP server to assign IP addresses to users as needed. Unfortunately, both DHCP servers have the same local IP address (192.168.0.1). When the networks are combined, one of these DHCP servers will have to be disabled.

✦ In addition, both networks had their own Internet connections. With the networks bridged, CCD can eliminate the ISDN connection altogether. Users in both buildings can get their Internet access via the shared T1 connection.

✦ The network administrator will also have to determine how to handle directory services for the network. Previously, each network had its own domain. With the networks bridged, CCD may opt to keep these domains separate, or it may decide to merge them into a single domain. (Doing so will require considerable work, so it'll probably leave the domains separate.)

Improving network performance: DCH Accounting

DCH Accounting is an accounting firm that has grown in two years from 15 employees to 35, all located in one building. Here's the lowdown on the existing network:

✦ The network consists of 35 client computers and three servers running Windows 2003 Server.

✦ The 35 client computers run a variety of Windows operating systems. About a third (a total of 11) run Windows Vista Professional. The rest run Windows XP Professional.

✦ The Windows Vista computers all have gigabit Ethernet cards. The older computers have 10/100 Mbps cards.

✦ The servers have 10/100 Mbps cards.

✦ All the offices in the building are wired with Category 5e wiring to a central wiring closet, where a small equipment rack holds two 24-port 10/100 switches.

✦ Internet access is provided through a T1 connection with a Cisco 1700 router.

Lately, network performance has been noticeably slow, particularly Internet access and large file transfers between client computers and the servers. Users have started to complain that sometimes the network seems to crawl.

The problem is most likely that the network has outgrown the old 10/100BaseT switches. All network traffic must flow through them, and they're limited to the speed of 100 Mbps. As a result, the new computers with the gigabit Ethernet cards are connecting to the network at 100 Mbps.

The performance of this network can be dramatically improved in two steps. The first step is to replace the 10/100 Mbps network interface cards in the three servers with gigabit cards (or, better yet, replace the servers with newer models). Second, add a 24-port gigabit switch to the equipment rack. The equipment rack can be rewired, as shown in Figure 1-9.

Figure 1-9:
DCH
Account-
ing's
switched
network.

✦ Connect the servers, the Cisco router, and the gigabit clients to the new gigabit switch. This will use 15 of the 24 ports.

✦ Connect the two 10/100 switches to the new gigabit switch. This will use two more ports, leaving 7 ports for future growth.

✦ Divide the remaining clients between the two 10/100 switches. Each switch will have 12 computers connected.

This arrangement connects all the gigabit clients to gigabit switch ports and 100 Mbps clients to 100 Mbps switch ports.

For even better performance, DCH can simply replace both switches with 24-port gigabit switches.

Chapter 2: Installing Network Hardware

In This Chapter

- ✓ **Installing network interface cards**
- ✓ **Installing network cable**
- ✓ **Attaching cable connectors**
- ✓ **Figuring out pinouts for twisted-pair cabling**
- ✓ **Building a crossover cable**
- ✓ **Installing switches**

After you have your network planned out, then comes the fun of actually putting everything together. In this chapter, I describe some of the important details for installing network hardware, including cables, switches, network interface cards, and professional touches, such as patch panels.

Installing a Network Interface Card

You have to install a network interface card into each computer before you can connect the computers to the network cables. Installing a network interface card is a manageable task, but you have to be willing to roll up your sleeves.

If you've installed one adapter card, you've installed them all. In other words, installing a network interface card is just like installing a modem, a new video controller card, a sound card, or any other type of card. If you've ever installed one of these cards, you can probably install a network interface card blindfolded.

Here's a step-by-step procedure for installing a network interface card:

1. **Gather up the network card and the driver disks. While you're at it, get your Windows installation CD just in case.**

2. **Shut down Windows and then turn off the computer and unplug it.**

Never work in your computer's insides with the power on or the power cord plugged in!

3. Remove the cover from your computer.

Figure 2-1 shows the screws that you must typically remove in order to open the cover. Put the screws someplace where they won't wander off.

Remove these screws

Figure 2-1: Removing your computer's cover.

Note that if you have a name-brand computer such as a Dell or a Compaq, opening the cover may be trickier than just removing a few screws. You may need to consult the owner's manual that came with the computer to find out how to open the case.

4. Find an unused expansion slot inside the computer.

The expansion slots are lined up in a neat row near the back of the computer; you can't miss 'em. Any computer less than five years old should have at least two or three slots known as *PCI slots*.

5. When you find a slot that doesn't have a card in it, remove the metal slot protector from the back of the computer's chassis.

If a small retaining screw holds the slot protector in place, remove the screw and keep it in a safe place. Then pull the slot protector out and put the slot protector in a box with all your other old slot protectors. (After a while, you collect a whole bunch of slot protectors. Keep them as souvenirs or Christmas tree ornaments.)

6. Insert the network interface card into the slot.

Line up the connectors on the bottom of the card with the connectors in the expansion slot and then press the card straight down. Sometimes you have to press uncomfortably hard to get the card to slide into the slot.

7. **Secure the network interface card with the screw that you removed in Step 4.**

8. **Put the computer's case back together.**

   Watch out for the loose cables inside the computer; you don't want to pinch them with the case as you slide it back on. Secure the case with the screws that you removed in Step 2.

9. **Plug in the computer and turn it back on.**

If you're using a Plug and Play card with Windows, the card is automatically configured after you start the computer again. If you're working with an older computer or an older network interface card, you may need to run an additional software installation program. See the installation instructions that come with the network interface card for details.

Installing Twisted-Pair Cable

Most Ethernet networks are built using twisted-pair cable, which resembles phone cable but isn't the same. Twisted-pair cable is sometimes called *UTP.* For more information about the general characteristics of twisted-pair cable, refer to Book I, Chapter 3.

In the following sections, you find out what you need to know in order to select and install twisted-pair cable.

Cable categories

Twisted-pair cable comes in various grades called *Categories.* These Categories are specified by the ANSI/EIA standard 568. (ANSI stands for American National Standards Institute; EIA stands for Electronic Industries Association.) The standards indicate the data capacity, also known as the *bandwidth,* of the cable. Table 2-1 lists the various Categories of twisted-pair cable.

Although higher-Category cables are more expensive than lower-Category cables, the real cost of installing Ethernet cabling is the labor required to actually pull the cables through the walls. You should never install anything less than Category 5 cable. And if at all possible, you should invest in Category 5e (the e stands for enhanced) or even Category 6 cable to allow for future upgrades to your network.

If you want to sound like you know what you're talking about, say "Cat 5" instead of saying "Category 5."

Table 2-1	Twisted-Pair Cable Categories	
Category	Maximum Data Rate	Intended Use
1	1 Mbps	Voice only
2	4 Mbps	4 Mbps Token Ring
3	16 Mbps	10BaseT Ethernet
4	20 Mbps	16 Mbps Token Ring
5	100 Mbps (2 pair)	100BaseT Ethernet
	1,000 Mbps (4 pair)	Gigabit Ethernet
5e	1,000 Mbps (2 pair)	Gigabit Ethernet
6	1,000 Mbps (2 pair)	Gigabit Ethernet
6a	10,000 Mbps	10 gigabit (experimental)
7	10,000 Mbps	10 gigabit (experimental)

What's with the pairs?

Most twisted-pair cable has four pairs of wires, for a total of eight wires. Standard Ethernet actually uses only two of the pairs, so the other two pairs are unused. You may be tempted to save money by purchasing cable with just two pairs of wires, but that's a bad idea. If a network cable develops a problem, you can sometimes fix it by switching over to one of the extra pairs. But if you try to carry a separate connection over the extra pairs, electrical interference will prevent the signals from getting through.

You may also be tempted to use the extra pairs for some other purpose, such as for a voice line. Don't. The electrical noise generated by voice signals in the extra wires can interfere with your network.

To shield or not to shield

Unshielded twisted-pair cable, or *UTP,* is designed for normal office environments. When you use UTP cable, you must be careful not to route cable close to fluorescent light fixtures, air conditioners, or electric motors (such as automatic door motors or elevator motors). UTP is the least expensive type of cable.

In environments that have a lot of electrical interference, such as factories, you may want to use *shielded twisted-pair* cable, also known as *STP.* Because STP can be as much as three times more expensive than regular UTP, you won't want to use STP unless you have to. With a little care, UTP can withstand the amount of electrical interference found in a normal office environment.

Most STP cable is shielded by a layer of aluminum foil. For buildings with unusually high amounts of electrical interference, you can use more expensive, braided copper shielding for even more protection.

When to use plenum cable

The outer sheath of both shielded and unshielded twisted-pair cable comes in two varieties: PVC and Plenum. *PVC* cable is the most common and least expensive type. *Plenum cable* is a special type of fire-retardant cable that is designed for use in the plenum space of a building. Plenum cable has a special Teflon coating that not only resists heat, but also gives off fewer toxic fumes if it does burn. Unfortunately, plenum cable costs more than twice as much as ordinary PVC cable.

Most local building codes require that you use plenum cable whenever the wiring is installed within the plenum space of the building. The *plenum space* is a compartment that is part of the building's air distribution system, and is usually the space above a suspended ceiling or under a raised floor.

Note that the area above a suspended ceiling is *not* a plenum space if both the delivery and return lines of the air-conditioning and heating system are ducted. Plenum cable is required only if the air-conditioning and heating system are not ducted. When in doubt, it's best to have the local inspector look at your facility before you install cable.

Sometimes solid, sometimes stranded

The actual copper wire that composes the cable comes in two varieties: solid and stranded. Your network will have some of each.

✦ In *stranded cable,* each conductor is made from a bunch of very small wires that are twisted together. Stranded cable is more flexible than solid cable, so it doesn't break as easily. However, stranded cable is more expensive than solid cable and isn't very good at transmitting signals over long distances. Stranded cable is best used for patch cables, such as the cable used to connect a computer to a wall jack or the cable used to connect patch panels to hubs and switches.

   Strictly speaking, the cable that connects your computer to the wall jack is called a *station cable* — not a patch cable. Patch cables are used in the wiring closet, usually to connect patch panels to hubs or switches.

✦ In *solid cable,* each conductor is a single solid strand of wire. Solid cable is less expensive than stranded cable and carries signals farther, but it isn't very flexible. If you bend it too many times, it will break. Solid cable is usually used for permanent wiring within the walls and ceilings of a building.

Installation guidelines

The hardest part about installing network cable is the physical task of pulling the cable through ceilings, walls, and floors. This job is just tricky enough that I recommend that you don't attempt it yourself except for small offices. For large jobs, hire a professional cable installer. You may even want to hire a professional for small jobs if the ceiling and wall spaces are difficult to access.

Here are some general pointers to keep in mind if you decide to install cable yourself:

✦ You can purchase twisted-pair cable in prefabricated lengths, such as 50 feet, 75 feet, or 100 feet. You can also special-order prefabricated cables in any length you need. However, attaching connectors to bulk cable isn't that difficult. I recommend that you use prefabricated cables only for very small networks and only when you don't need to route the cable through walls or ceilings.

✦ Always use a bit more cable than you need, especially if you're running cable through walls. For example, when you run a cable up a wall, leave a few feet of slack in the ceiling above the wall. That way, you'll have plenty of cable if you need to make a repair later on.

✦ When running cable, avoid sources of interference, such as fluorescent lights, big motors, X-ray machines, and so on. The most common source of interference for cables that are run behind fake ceiling panels are fluorescent lights; be sure to give light fixtures a wide berth as you run your cable. Three feet should do it.

✦ The maximum allowable cable length between the hub and the computer is 100 meters (about 328 feet).

✦ If you must run cable across the floor where people walk, cover the cable so that no one trips over it. Inexpensive cable protectors are available at most hardware stores.

✦ When running cables through walls, label each cable at both ends. Most electrical supply stores carry pads of cable labels that are perfect for the job. These pads contain 50 sheets or so of precut labels with letters and numbers. They look much more professional than wrapping a loop of masking tape around the cable and writing on the tape with a marker.

   Or, if you want to scrimp, you can just buy a permanent marker and write directly on the cable.

✦ When several cables come together, tie them with plastic cable ties. Avoid masking tape if you can; the tape doesn't last, but the sticky glue stuff does. It's a mess a year later. Cable ties are available at electrical supply stores.

✦ Cable ties have all sorts of useful purposes. Once on a backpacking trip, I used a pair of cable ties to attach an unsuspecting buddy's hat to a high tree limb. He wasn't impressed with my innovative use of the cable ties, but my other hiking companions were.

✦ When you run cable above suspended ceiling panels, use cable ties, hooks, or clamps to secure the cable to the actual ceiling or to the metal frame that supports the ceiling tiles. Don't just lay the cable on top of the tiles.

Getting the tools that you need

Of course, to do a job right, you must have the right tools.

Start with a basic set of computer tools, which you can get for about $15 from any computer store or large office-supply store. These kits include the right screwdrivers and socket wrenches to open up your computers and insert adapter cards. (If you don't have a computer toolkit, make sure that you have several flat-head and Phillips screwdrivers of various sizes.)

If all your computers are in the same room and you're going to run the cables along the floor and you're using prefabricated cables, the computer tool kit should contain everything that you need.

If you're using bulk cable and plan on attaching your own connectors, you need the following tools in addition to the tools that come with the basic computer tool kit:

✦ **Wire cutters:** You need big ones for thinnet cable; smaller ones are okay for 10BaseT cable. If you're using yellow cable, you need the Jaws of Life.

✦ **Crimp tool:** You need the crimp tool to attach the connectors to the cable. Don't use a cheap $10 crimp tool. A good one will cost $100 and will save you many headaches in the long run. Remember this adage: When you crimp, you mustn't scrimp.

✦ **Wire stripper:** You need this only if the crimp tool doesn't include a wire stripper.

If you plan on running cables through walls, you need these additional tools:

✦ **A hammer.**

✦ **A bell.**

✦ **A song to sing.** Just kidding about these last two.

✦ **A keyhole saw.** This is useful if you plan on cutting holes through walls to route your cable.

- ✦ **A flashlight.**

- ✦ **A ladder.**

- ✦ **Someone to hold the ladder.**

- ✦ **Possibly a fish tape.** A *fish tape* is a coiled-up length of stiff metal tape. To use it, you feed the tape into one wall opening and fish it toward the other opening, where a partner is ready to grab it when the tape arrives. Next, your partner attaches the cable to the fish tape and yells something like "Let 'er rip!" or "Bombs away!" Then you reel in the fish tape and the cable along with it. (You can find fish tape in the electrical section of most well-stocked hardware stores.)

If you plan on routing cable through a concrete subfloor, you need to rent a jackhammer and a backhoe and hire someone to hold a yellow flag while you work.

Pinouts for twisted-pair cables

Each pair of wires in a twisted-pair cable is one of four colors: orange, green, blue, or brown. The two wires that make up each pair are complementary: One is white with a colored stripe; the other is colored with a white stripe. For example, the orange pair has a white wire with an orange stripe (called white/orange) and an orange wire with a white stripe (called orange/white). Likewise, the blue pair has a white wire with a blue stripe (white/blue) and a blue wire with a white stripe (blue/white).

When you attach a twisted-pair cable to a modular connector or jack, you must match up the right wires to the right pins. You can use several different standards to wire the connectors. To confuse matters, you can use one of the two popular standard ways of hooking up the wires. One is known as EIA/TIA 568A; the other is EIA/TIA 568B, also known as AT&T 258A. Table 2-2 shows both wiring schemes.

It doesn't matter which of these wiring schemes you use, but pick one and stick with it. If you use one wiring standard on one end of a cable and the other standard on the other end, the cable won't work.

Table 2-2	Pin Connections for Twisted-Pair Cable		
Pin Number	*Function*	*EIA/TIA 568A*	*EIA/TIA 568B AT&T 258A*
Pin 1	Transmit +	White/green	White/orange
Pin 2	Transmit -	Green	Orange
Pin 3	Receive +	White/orange	White/green
Pin 4	Unused	Blue	Blue

Pin Number	Function	EIA/TIA 568A	EIA/TIA 568B AT&T 258A
Pin 5	Unused	White/blue	White/blue
Pin 6	Receive -	Orange	Green
Pin 7	Unused	White/brown	White/brown
Pin 8	Unused	Brown	Brown

10BaseT and 100BaseT actually use only two of the four pairs, connected to pins 1, 2, 3, and 6. One pair is used to transmit data, and the other is used to receive data. The only difference between the two wiring standards is which pair is used for transmit and receive. In the EIA/TIA 568A standard, the green pair is used for transmit and the orange pair is used for receive. In the EIA/TIA 568B and AT&T 258A standards, the orange pair is used for transmit and the green pair for receive.

If you want, you can get away with connecting only pins 1, 2, 3, and 6. However, I suggest that you connect all four pairs as indicated in Table 2-2.

Attaching RJ-45 connectors

RJ-45 connectors for twisted-pair cables aren't too difficult to attach if you have the right crimping tool. The trick is in both making sure that you attach each wire to the correct pin and pressing the tool hard enough to ensure a good connection.

Here's the procedure for attaching an RJ-45 connector:

1. **Cut the end of the cable to the desired length.**

Make sure that you make a square cut — not a diagonal cut.

2. **Insert the cable into the stripper portion of the crimp tool so that the end of the cable is against the stop.**

Squeeze the handles and slowly pull the cable out, keeping it square. This strips off the correct length of outer insulation without puncturing the insulation on the inner wires.

3. **Arrange the wires so that they lay flat and line up according to Table 2-2.**

You'll have to play with the wires a little bit to get them to lay out in the right sequence.

4. **Slide the wires into the pinholes on the connector.**

Double-check to make sure that all the wires slipped into the correct pinholes.

5. **Insert the plug and wire into the crimping portion of the tool and then squeeze the handles to crimp the plug.**

Squeeze it tight!

6. **Remove the plug from the tool and double-check the connection.**

You're done!

Here are a few other points to remember when dealing with RJ-45 connectors and twisted-pair cable:

✦ The pins on the RJ-45 connectors aren't numbered, but you can tell which is pin 1 by holding the connector so that the metal conductors are facing up, as shown in Figure 2-2. Pin 1 is on the left.

Figure 2-2:
Attaching
an RJ-45
connector
to twisted-
pair cable.

Pin connections:
Pin 1 - White/Orange
Pin 2 - Orange/White
Pin 3 - White/Green
Pin 6 - Green/White

✦ Some people wire 10baseT cable differently — using the green and white pair for pins 1 and 2 and the orange and white pair for pins 3 and 6. This doesn't affect the operation of the network (the network is color-blind), *as long as the connectors on both ends of the cable are wired the same!*

✦ If you're installing cable for a Fast Ethernet system, you should be extra careful to follow the rules of Category-5 cabling. That means, among other things, making sure that you use Category-5 components through-out. The cable and all the connectors must be up to Category-5 specs. When you attach the connectors, don't untwist more than ½ inch of cable. And don't try to stretch the cable runs beyond the 100-meter max-imum. When in doubt, have cable for a 100 Mbps Ethernet system pro-fessionally installed.

Crossover cables

A *crossover cable* is a cable that you can use to directly connect two devices without a hub or switch. You can use a crossover cable to connect two computers directly to each other, but crossover cables are more often used to daisy-chain hubs and switches to each other.

If you want to create your own crossover cable, you have to reverse the wires on one end of the cable, as shown in Table 2-3. This table shows how you should wire both ends of the cable to create a crossover cable. Connect one of the ends according to the Connector A column and the other according to the Connector B column.

Note that you don't need to use a crossover cable if one of the switches or hubs that you want to connect has a crossover port, usually labeled *Uplink*. If the hub or switch has an Uplink port, you can daisy-chain it by using a normal network cable. For more information about daisy-chaining hubs and switches, see the section, "Installing Hubs and Switches," later in this chapter.

Table 2-3	Creating a Crossover Cable	
Pin	*Connector A*	*Connector B*
Pin 1	White/green	White/orange
Pin 2	Green	Orange
Pin 3	White/orange	White/green
Pin 4	Blue/white	Blue
Pin 5	White/blue	White/blue
Pin 6	Orange	Green
Pin 7	White/brown	White/brown
Pin 8	Brown	Brown

Wall jacks and patch panels

If you want, you can run a single length of cable from a network hub or switch in a wiring closet through a hole in the wall, up the wall to the space above the ceiling, through the ceiling space to the wall in an office, down the wall, through a hole, and all the way to a desktop computer. That's not a good idea, however, for a variety of reasons. For one, every time someone moves the computer or even cleans behind it, the cable will get moved a little bit. Eventually, the connection will fail, and the RJ-45 plug will have to be replaced. Then the cables in the wiring closet will quickly become a tangled mess.

The alternative is to put a *wall jack* in the wall at the user's end of the cable and connect the other end of the cable to a *patch* panel. Then, the cable itself is completely contained within the walls and ceiling spaces. To connect a computer to the network, you plug one end of a patch cable (properly called a *station cable*) into the wall jack and plug the other end into the computer's network interface. In the wiring closet, you use a patch cable to connect the wall jack to the network switch. Figure 2-3 shows how this arrangement works.

Figure 2-3:
Using wall jacks and patch panels.

Connecting a twisted-pair cable to a wall jack or a patch panel is similar to connecting it to an RJ-45 plug. However, you don't usually need any special tools. Instead, the back of the jack has a set of slots that you lay each wire across. You then snap a removable cap over the top of the slots and press it down. This forces the wires into the slots, where little metal blades pierce the insulation and establish the electrical contact.

When you connect the wire to a jack or patch panel, be sure to untwist as little of the wire as possible. If you untwist too much of the wire, the signals that pass through the wire may become unreliable.

Installing Coaxial Cable

Although twisted-pair cable is by far the most commonly used type of networking cable, some networks still rely on old-fashioned coaxial cable, usually called *thinnet* or sometimes *BNC cable* because of the type of connectors used on each end of the cable.

Here are some salient points about working with coaxial cable:

✦ You attach thinnet to the network interface card by using a goofy twist-on connector called a *BNC connector*. You can purchase preassembled cables with BNC connectors already attached in lengths of 25 or 50 feet, or you can buy bulk cable on a big spool and attach the connectors yourself by using a special tool. (I suggest buying preassembled cables. Attaching connectors to bulk coaxial cable can be tricky.)

✦ With coaxial cables, you run cable from computer to computer until all the computers are chained together. At each computer, use a T connector to connect two cables to the network interface card.

✦ A special plug called a *terminator* is required at each end of a series of thinnet cables. The terminator prevents data from spilling out the end of the cable and staining the carpet.

✦ The cables strung end-to-end from one terminator to the other are collectively called a *segment*. The maximum length of a thinnet segment is about 200 meters (actually, 185 meters). You can connect as many as 30 computers on one segment. To span a distance greater than 185 meters or to connect more than 30 computers, you must use two or more segments with a funky device called a *repeater* to connect each segment.

✦ Although Ethernet coaxial cable resembles TV coaxial cable, the two types of cable aren't interchangeable. Don't try to cut costs by wiring your network with cheap TV cable.

Attaching a BNC Connector to Coaxial Cable

Properly connecting a BNC connector to coaxial cable is an acquired skill. You need two tools — a wire stripper that can cut through the various layers of the coaxial cable at just the right location and a crimping tool that crimps the connector tightly to the cable after you get the connector into position. BNC connectors have three separate pieces, as shown in Figure 2-4.

Connector body

Center pin

Ferrule

Properly stripped cable

Figure 2-4:
Attaching a BNC connector to coaxial cable.

Here's the procedure, in case you ignore my advice and try to attach the connectors yourself:

1. **Slide the hollow tube portion of the connector (lovingly called the *ferrule*) over the cable.**

   Let it slide back a few feet to get it out of the way.

2. **Cut the end of the cable off cleanly.**

3. **Use the stripping tool to strip the cable.**

   Strip the outer jacket back ½ inch from the end of the cable; strip the braided shield back ¼ inch from the end; and then strip the inner insulation back ³⁄₁₆ inch from the end.

4. **Insert the solid center conductor into the center pin.**

   Slide the center pin down until it seats against the inner insulation.

5. **Use the crimping tool to crimp the center pin.**

6. **Slide the connector body over the center pin and inner insulation but under the braided shield.**

   After you push the body back far enough, the center pin clicks into place.

7. **Now slide the ferrule forward until it touches the connector body.**

   Crimp it with the crimping tool.

TIP

Don't get sucked into the trap of trying to use easy "screw-on" connectors. They aren't very reliable.

Installing Hubs and Switches

The biggest difference between using coaxial cable and twisted-pair cable is that when you use twisted-pair cable, you also must use a separate device called a *hub* or a *switch.* For our purposes here, you can assume a hub and a switch are the same thing. For an explanation of the difference, refer to Book I, Chapter 3.

**Book II
Chapter 2**

**Installing Network
Hardware**

You need to know only a few details when working with hubs and switches. Here they are, in no particular order:

✦ Installing a hub or switch is usually very simple. Just plug in the power cord and then plug in patch cables to connect the network.

✦ Each port on the hub or switch has an RJ-45 jack and a single LED indicator labeled *Link* that lights up when a connection has been established on the port. If you plug one end of a cable into the port and the other end into a computer or other network device, the Link light should come on. If it doesn't, something is wrong with the cable, the hub (or switch port), or the device on the other end of the cable.

✦ Each port may also have an LED indicator that flashes to indicate network activity. If you stare at a hub or switch for awhile, you can find out who uses the network most by noting which activity indicators flash the most.

✦ The ports may also have a Collision indicator that flashes whenever a packet collision occurs on the port. It's perfectly acceptable for this light to flash now and then, but if it flashes a lot, you may have a problem with the network. Usually this just means that the network is overloaded and should be segmented with a switch to improve performance. But in some cases, a flashing Collision indicator may be caused by a faulty network node that clogs up the network with bad packets.

Daisy-Chaining Hubs or Switches

If a single hub or switch doesn't have enough ports for your entire network, you can connect hubs or switches together by *daisy-chaining* them. If one of the hubs or switches has an uplink port, you can use a normal patch cable to connect the uplink port to one of the regular ports on the other hub or switch. If neither device has an uplink port, use a crossover cable to connect them. (For instructions on making a crossover cable, see the section, "Crossover cables," earlier in this chapter.)

On some hubs and switches, a button is used to switch one of the ports between a normal port and an uplink port. This button is often labeled MDI/MDIX. To use the port as a normal port, switch the button to the MDI position. To use the port as an uplink port, switch the button to MDIX.

Some hubs and switches have a separate jack for the uplink port, but it turns out that the uplink port shares one of the normal ports internally. If that's the case, plugging a cable into the uplink port disables one of the normal ports. You shouldn't plug cables into both of these jacks. If you do, the hub or switch won't work properly.

Note that the number of switches that you can chain together is limited. For 10BaseT networks, you shouldn't connect more than three switches to each other. For 100 Mbps or gigabit segments, you can chain only two switches together.

You can get around this rule by using *stackable switches*. Stackable switches have a special type of cable connector that connects two or more switches in a way that lets them function as if they were a single switch. Stackable switches are a must for large networks.

Chapter 3: Setting Up a Network Server

In This Chapter

✔ Thinking about the different ways to install a network operating system

✔ Getting ready for the installation

✔ Installing a network operating system

✔ Figuring out what to do after you install the network operating system

After you've installed the network cables and other devices, such as hubs and switches, the next step in building a network is usually setting up a server. After you've physically connected the server computer to the network, you can install the network operating system (NOS) on the server. Then, you can configure it to provide the network services that you expect and need from the server.

The Many Ways to Install a Network Operating System

Regardless of which network operating system you choose to use for your network servers, you can use any of several common ways to actually install the NOS software on the server computer. The following sections describe these alternatives.

Full install versus upgrade

One of the basic NOS installation choices is whether you want to perform a full installation or an upgrade installation. In some cases, you may be better off performing a full installation even if you're installing the NOS on a computer that already has an earlier version of the NOS installed.

✦ If you're installing the NOS on a brand-new server, you'll be performing a *full installation* that installs the operating system and configures it with default settings.

✦ If you're installing the NOS on a server computer that already has a server operating system installed, you can perform an *upgrade installation* that replaces the existing operating system with the new one but retains as many of the settings from the existing operating system as possible.

✦ You can also perform a full installation on a computer that already has an operating system installed. In that case, you have the option of deleting the existing operating system or performing a *multiboot installation* that installs the new server operating system alongside the existing operating system. Then, when you restart the computer, you can choose which operating system you want to run.

✦ Although multiboot installation may sound like a good idea, it's fraught with peril. I suggest that you avoid multiboot unless you have a specific reason to use it. For more information about multiboot setups, see the sidebar, "Giving multiboot the boot."

✦ You can't upgrade a client version of Windows to a server version. Instead, you must perform a full installation, which deletes the existing Windows operating system, or a multiboot installation, which leaves the existing client Windows intact. Either way, however, you can preserve existing data on the Windows computer when you install the server version.

Giving multiboot the boot

Multiboot installations enable you to have more than one operating system on a single computer. Of course, only one of these operating systems can be running at any time. When you boot the computer, a menu appears with each of the installed operating systems listed. You can choose which operating system to boot from this menu.

Multiboot is most useful for software developers or network managers who want to make sure that software is compatible with a wide variety of operating systems. Rather than set up a bunch of separate computers with different operating system versions, you can install several operating systems on a single PC and use that one PC to test the software. For production network servers, however, you probably don't need to have more than one operating system installed.

If you still insist on loading two or more operating systems on a network server, be sure to install each operating system into its own disk partition. Although most network operating systems let you install two (or more) operating systems into a single partition, doing so is not a very good idea. To support two operating systems in a single partition, the operating systems have to play a risky shell game with key system files — moving or renaming them each time you restart the computer. Unfortunately, things can go wrong. For example, if lightning strikes and the power goes out just as the NOS is switching the startup files around, you may find yourself with a server that can't boot to any of its installed operating systems.

The best way to set up a multiboot system is to install each operating system into its own partition. Then, you can use a boot manager program to choose the partition you want to boot from when you start the computer.

Installing over the network

Normally, you install the NOS directly from the CD-ROM distribution discs on the server's CD-ROM drive. However, you can also install the operating system from a shared drive located on another computer, provided that the server computer already has access to the network. You can either use a shared CD-ROM drive or you can copy the entire contents of the distribution CD-ROM disc onto a shared hard drive.

Obviously, the server computer must have network access in order for this technique to work. If the server already has an operating system installed, it probably already has access to the network. If not, you can boot the computer from a floppy that has basic network support.

If you're going to install the NOS onto more than one server, you can save time by first copying the distribution CD onto a shared hard drive. That's because even the fastest CD-ROM drives are slower than the network. Even with a basic 10 Mbps network, access to hard drive data over the network is much faster than access to a local CD-ROM drive.

Automated and remote installations

In case you find yourself in the unenviable position of installing a NOS onto several servers, you can use a few tricks to streamline the process:

✦ *Automated setup* lets you create a setup script that provides answers to all the questions asked by the installation program. After you've created the script, you can start the automated setup, leave, and come back when the installation is finished. Creating the setup script is a bit of work, so automated setup makes sense only if you have more than a few servers to install.

✦ Microsoft has a feature called *Remote Installation Services* (RIS) that lets you install Windows server versions from a remote network location without even going to the server computer. This is tricky to set up, however, so it's really worth it only if you have a lot of servers on which to install operating systems. (You can also use RIS to install client operating systems.)

Gathering Your Stuff

Before you install a network operating system, you should gather everything you'll need so you don't have to look for something in the middle of the setup. The following sections describe the items you're most likely to need.

A capable server computer

Obviously, you have to have a server computer on which to install the NOS. Each NOS has a list of the minimum hardware requirements supported by the operating system. For example, Table 3-1 summarizes the minimum requirements for Windows Server 2003 Standard Edition and Windows Server 2008 Standard Edition.

My suggestion is that you take these minimums with a grain of salt. Windows Server 2003 will crawl like a snail on a 133 MHz Pentium; you should consider 1 GHz the minimum clock speed for a server. And 2GB is a more realistic minimum for the memory requirement.

Table 3-1	Minimum Hardware Requirements for Microsoft Server Operating Systems	
Item	*Windows Server 2003*	*Windows Server 2008*
CPU	133 MHz Pentium	1 GHz Pentium
RAM	128MB	512MB
Free disk space	1.5GB	10GB

You should also check your server hardware against the list of compatible hardware published by the maker of your NOS. For example, Microsoft publishes a list of hardware that it has tested and certified as compatible with Windows servers. This list is called the *Hardware Compatibility List*, or *HCL* for short. You can check the HCL for your specific server by going to Microsoft's Web site at `www.microsoft.com/whdc/hcl/default.mspx`. You can also test your computer's compatibility by running the Check System Compatibility option from the Windows distribution CD-ROM.

You can find more specific details on server computer recommendations in Book I, Chapter 3.

The server operating system

You also need a server operating system to install. You'll need either the distribution CD or DVD discs or access to a copy of them over the network. In addition to the discs, you should have the following:

✦ **The product key:** The installation program asks you to enter the product key during the installation to prove that you have a legal copy of the software. If you have the actual CD or DVD discs, the product key should be on a sticker attached to the case.

✦ **Manuals:** If the operating system came with printed manuals, you should keep them handy.

✦ **Your license type:** You can purchase Microsoft operating systems on a per-server or a per-user/per device basis. You need to know which plan you have when you install the NOS.

Check the CD or DVD distribution disc for product documentation and additional last-minute information. For example, Windows servers have a \docs folder that contains several files that have useful setup information.

Other software

In most cases, the installation program should be able to automatically configure your server's hardware devices and install appropriate drivers. Just in case, though, you should dig out the driver disks that came with your devices, such as network interface cards, SCSI devices, DVD drives, printers, scanners, and so on.

A working Internet connection

This isn't an absolute requirement, but the installation will go much smoother if you have a working Internet connection before you start. The installation process may use this Internet connection for several things:

✦ **Downloading late-breaking updates or fixes to the operating system.** This can eliminate the need to install a service pack after you finish installing the NOS.

✦ **Locating drivers for nonstandard devices.** This can be a big plus if you can't find the driver disk for your obscure SCSI card.

✦ **Activating the product after you complete the installation (for Microsoft operating systems).**

A good book

You'll spend lots of time watching progress bars during installation, so you may as well have something to do while you wait. May I recommend *The Hitchhiker's Guide to the Galaxy?*

Making Informed Decisions

When you install a NOS, you have to make some decisions about how you want the operating system and its servers configured. Most of these decisions aren't cast in stone, so don't worry if you're not 100 percent sure how you want everything configured. You can always go back and reconfigure things. However, you'll save yourself time if you make the right decisions up front rather than just guess when the setup program starts asking you questions.

The following list details most of the decisions that you'll need to make. (This list is for Windows Server 2003 and 2008 installations. For other network operating systems, the decisions may vary slightly.)

+ **The existing operating system:** If you want to retain the existing operating system, the installation program can perform a multiboot setup, which allows you to choose which operating system to boot to each time you start the computer. This is rarely a good idea for server computers, so I recommend that you elect to delete the existing operating system.

+ **Partition structure:** Most of the time, you'll want to treat the entire server disk as a single partition. However, if you want to divide the disk into two or more partitions, you should do so during setup. (Unlike most of the other setup decisions, this one is hard to change later.)

+ **File system:** Windows servers provide two choices for the file system to format the server's disk: FAT32 and NTFS. In every case, you should elect to use NTFS. FAT32 should never be used for a server operating system.

+ **Computer name:** During the operating system setup, you're asked to provide the computer name used to identify the server on the network. If your network has only a few servers, you can just pick a name such as Server01 or MyServer. If your network has more than a few servers, you'll want to follow an established guideline for creating server names.

+ **Administrator password:** Okay, this one is tough. You don't want to pick something obvious, like Password, Administrator, or your last name. On the other hand, you don't want to type in something random that you'll later forget, because you'll find yourself in a big pickle if you forget the administrator password. I suggest that you make up a complex password consisting of a mix of uppercase and lowercase letters, some numerals, and a special symbol or two; then write it down and keep it in a secure location where you know it won't get lost.

+ **Networking protocols:** You'll almost always need to install the TCP/IP protocol, the Microsoft network client protocol, and file and printer sharing. Depending on how the server will be used, you may want to install other protocols as well.

+ **TCP/IP configuration:** You'll need to know what IP address to use for the server. Even if your network has a DHCP server to dynamically assign IP addresses to clients, most servers use static IP addresses.

+ **Workgroup or domain:** You'll need to decide whether the server will join a domain or just be a member of a workgroup. In either case, you'll need to know the domain name or the workgroup name.

Final Preparations

Before you begin the actual installation, you should take a few more steps:

+ Clean up the server's disk by uninstalling any software that you don't need and removing any old data that is no longer needed. This is especially important if you're converting a computer that's been in use as a client computer to a server. You probably don't need Microsoft Office or a bunch of games on the computer after it becomes a server.

+ Do a complete backup of the computer. Operating system setup programs are almost flawless, so the chances of losing data during installation are minimal. But you still face the chance that something may go wrong.

+ If the computer is connected to an uninterruptible power supply (UPS) that has a serial or USB connection to the computer, unplug the serial or USB connection. In some cases, this control connection can confuse the operating system's setup program when it tries to determine which devices are attached to the computer.

+ If the computer has hard drives compressed with DriveSpace or DoubleSpace, uncompress the drives before you begin.

+ Light some votive candles, take two Tylenol, and put on a pot of coffee.

Installing a Network Operating System

The following sections present an overview of a typical installation of Windows Server 2008. Although the details vary, the overall installation process for other network operating systems is similar.

In most cases, the best way to install Windows Server 2008 is to perform a new install directly from the DVD installation media. Although upgrade installs are possible, your server will be more stable if you perform a new install. (For this reason, most network administrators avoid upgrading to Windows Server 2008 until it's time to replace the server hardware.)

To begin the installation, insert the DVD distribution media in the server's DVD drive, then restart the server. This causes the server to boot directly from the distribution media, which initiates the setup program.

As the setup program proceeds, it leads you through two distinct installation phases: Collecting Information and Installing Windows. The following sections describe each of these installation phases in greater detail.

Phase 1: Collecting information

In the first installation phase, the setup program asks for the preliminary information that it needs to begin the installation. A setup wizard prompts you for the following information:

✦ **Language:** Select your language, time-zone, and keyboard type.

✦ **Product Key:** Enter the 25-character product key that came with the installation media. If setup says you entered an invalid product key, double-check it carefully. You probably just typed the key incorrectly.

✦ **Operating System Type:** The setup program lets you select Windows Server 2008 Standard Edition or Core. Choose Standard Edition to install the full server operating system; choose Core if you want to install the new text-only version.

✦ **License Agreement:** The official license agreement is displayed. You have to agree to its terms in order to proceed.

✦ **Install Type:** Choose an Upgrade or Clean Install type.

✦ **Disk Location:** Choose the partition in which you want to install Windows.

✦ **Upgrade to NTFS:** If you want to upgrade a FAT32 system to NTFS, you'll need to say so now.

Phase 2: Installing Windows

In this phase, Windows setup begins the actual process of installing Windows. The following steps are performed in sequence:

1. **Copying Files:** Compressed versions of the installation files are copied to the server computer.

2. **Expanding Files:** The compressed installation files are expanded.

3. **Installing Features:** Windows server features are installed.

4. **Installing Updates:** The setup program checks Microsoft's Web site and downloads any critical updates to the operating system.

5. **Completing Installation:** When the updates are installed, the setup program reboots so it can complete the installation.

Configuring Your Server

After you've installed Windows Server 2008, the computer automatically reboots, and you're presented with the Initial Configuration Tasks Wizard, as shown in Figure 3-1. This wizard guides you through the most important initial tasks for configuring your new server.

Figure 3-1:
Initial
Configu-
ration Tasks.

The following list describes the server configuration settings available from this wizard:

✦ **Set the Administrator Password:** The very first thing you should do after installing Windows is set a secure administrator password.

✦ **Set the Time Zone:** This is necessary only if the indicated time zone is incorrect.

✦ **Configure Networking:** The default network settings are usually appropriate, but you can use this option to change the defaults if you wish.

✦ **Provide Computer Name and Domain:** This option lets you change the server's computer name and join a domain.

✦ **Enable Automatic Updating:** Use this option if you want to let the server automatically check for operating system updates.

✦ **Download and Install Updates:** Use this option to check for critical operating system updates.

✦ **Add Roles:** This option launches the Add Roles Wizard, which lets you configure important roles for your server.

✦ **Add Features:** This option lets you add additional operating system features.

✦ **Enable Remote Desktop:** Use this option to enable the Remote Desktop feature, which lets you administer this server from another computer.

✦ **Configure Windows Firewall:** If you want to use the built-in Windows firewall, this option lets you configure it.

Chapter 4: Configuring Windows XP and Vista Clients

In This Chapter

✔ Configuring network connections for Windows clients

✔ Setting the computer name, description, and workgroup

✔ Joining a domain

✔ Setting logon options

*B*efore your network setup is complete, you must configure the network's client computers. In particular, you have to configure each client's network interface card so that it works properly, and you have to install the right protocols so that the clients can communicate with other computers on the network.

Fortunately, the task of configuring client computers for the network is child's play in Windows. For starters, Windows automatically recognizes your network interface card when you start up your computer. All that remains is to make sure that Windows properly installed the network protocols and client software.

With each version of Windows, Microsoft has simplified the process of configuring client network support. In this chapter, I describe the steps for configuring networking for Windows XP and Vista.

Configuring Network Connections

Windows automatically detects the presence of a network adapter; normally, you don't have to install device drivers manually for the adapter. When Windows detects a network adapter, it automatically creates a network connection and configures it to support basic networking protocols. However, you may need to change the configuration of a network connection manually. The procedures for Windows XP and Vista are described in the following sections.

Configuring Windows XP network connections

The following steps show how to configure your network connection on a Windows XP system:

1. **Choose Start➪Control Panel to open the Control Panel.**

   The Control Panel appears.

2. **Double-click the Network Connections icon.**

   The Network Connections folder appears, as shown in Figure 4-1.

3. **Right-click the connection that you want to configure, and then choose Properties from the menu that appears.**

   Or you can select the network connection and click Change Settings of This Connection in the task pane.

   Either way, the Properties dialog box for the network connection appears, as shown in Figure 4-2.

Figure 4-1:
The
Network
Connections
folder.

Figure 4-2:
The
Properties
dialog box
for a
network
connection.

4. **To configure the network adapter card settings, click Configure.**

   This action summons the Properties dialog box for the network adapter, as shown in Figure 4-3. This dialog box has five tabs that let you configure the NIC:

   - General: This tab shows basic information about the NIC, such as the device type and status. For example, the device shown in Figure 4-3 is an Intel Pro 100 adapter. (It's installed in slot 3 of the computer's PCI bus.)

Figure 4-3:
The
Properties
dialog box
for a
network
adapter.

   If you're having trouble with the adapter, you can click the Trouble shoot button to open the Windows XP Hardware Troubleshooter. You can also disable the device if it's preventing other components of the computer from working properly.

   - Advanced: This tab lets you set a variety of device-specific parameters that affect the operation of the NIC. For example, some cards allow you to set the speed parameter (typically at 10 Mbps or 100 Mbps) or the number of buffers the card should use.

   Consult the manual that came with the card before you play around with any of those settings.

   - *Driver:* This tab displays information about the device driver that's bound to the NIC and lets you update the driver to a newer version, roll back the driver to a previously working version, or uninstall the driver.

   - *Resources*: With this tab, you can use manual settings to limit the system resources used by the card — including the memory range, I/O range, IRQ, and DMA channels.

In the old days, before Plug and Play cards, you had to configure these settings whenever you installed a card, and it was easy to create resource conflicts. Windows configures these settings automatically so that you should rarely need to fiddle with them.

- *Power Management:* This tab lets you set power-management options. You can specify that the network card be shut down whenever the computer goes into sleep mode — and that the computer wake up periodically to refresh its network state.

When you click OK to dismiss the network adapter's Properties dialog box, the network connection's Properties dialog box closes. Select the Change Settings for This Connection option again to continue the procedure.

5. **Make sure that the network items your client requires are listed in the network connection Properties dialog box.**

The following list describes the items you commonly see listed here. Note that not all networks need all these items:

- *Client for Microsoft Networks:* This item is required if you want to access a Microsoft Windows network. It should always be present.

- *File and Printer Sharing for Microsoft Networks:* This item allows your computer to share its files or printers with other computers on the network.

This option is usually used with peer-to-peer networks, but you can use it even if your network has dedicated servers. However, if you don't plan to share files or printers on the client computer, you should disable this item.

- *Internet Protocol (TCP/IP):* This item enables the client computer to communicate by using the TCP/IP protocol.

If all servers on the network support TCP/IP, this protocol should be the only one installed on the client.

- *NWLink IPX/SPX/NetBIOS Compatible Transport Protocol:* This protocol is required only if your network needs to connect to an older NetWare network that uses the IPX/SPX protocol.

In most modern networks, you should enable TCP/IP only and leave this item disabled.

6. **If a protocol that you need isn't listed, click the Install button to add the needed protocol.**

A dialog box appears, asking whether you want to add a network client, protocol, or service. Click Protocol and then click Add. A list of available protocols appears. Select the one you want to add; then click OK. (You may be asked to insert a disc or the Windows CD.)

7. Make sure that the network client that you want to use appears in the list of network resources.

For a Windows-based network, make sure that Client for Microsoft Networks is listed. For a NetWare network, make sure that Client Service for NetWare appears. If your network uses both types of servers, you can choose both clients.

If you have NetWare servers, use the NetWare client software that comes with NetWare rather than the client supplied by Microsoft with Windows.

8. If the client that you need isn't listed, click the Install button to add the client that you need, click Client, and then click Add. Then choose the client that you want to add and click OK.

The client you select is added to the network connection's Properties dialog box.

9. To remove a network item that you don't need (such as File and Printer Sharing for Microsoft Networks), select the item and click the Uninstall button.

For security reasons, you should make it a point to remove any clients, protocols, or services that you don't need.

10. To configure TCP/IP settings, click Internet Protocol (TCP/IP) and click Properties to display the TCP/IP Properties dialog box. Adjust the settings, and then click OK.

The TCP/IP Properties dialog box, shown in Figure 4-4, lets you choose from these options:

- *Obtain an IP Address Automatically:* Choose this option if your network has a DHCP server that assigns IP addresses automatically. Choosing this option drastically simplifies the administering of TCP/IP on your network. (See Book IV, Chapter 3, for more information about DHCP.)

- *Use the Following IP Address:* If your computer must have a specific IP address, choose this option and then type the computer's IP address, subnet mask, and default gateway address. (For more information about these settings, see Book IV, Chapter 2.)

- *Obtain DNS Server Address Automatically:* The DHCP server can also provide the address of the Domain Name System (DNS) server that the computer should use. Choose this option if your network has a DHCP server. (See Book IV, Chapter 4, for more information about DNS.)

**Book II
Chapter 4**

**Configuring
Windows XP and
Vista Clients**

- *Use the Following DNS Server Addresses:* Choose this option if a DNS server isn't available. Then type the IP address of the primary and secondary DNS servers.

Figure 4-4:
Configuring
TCP/IP.

Configuring Windows Vista network connections

The procedure for configuring a network connection on Windows Vista is similar to the procedure for Windows XP, except that Microsoft decided to bury the configuration dialog boxes a little deeper in the bowels of Windows.

To find the settings you need, follow these steps:

1. Choose Start⇨Control Panel to open the Control Panel.

The Control Panel appears.

2. Choose View Network Status and Tasks under the Network and Internet heading.

This step opens the Network and Sharing Center, shown in Figure 4-5.

3. Click Manage Network Connections.

The Network Connections folder appears, as shown in Figure 4-6.

Figure 4-5:
The
Network
and Sharing
Center
(Windows
Vista).

Figure 4-6:
The
Network
Connections
folder.

4. **Right-click the connection that you want to configure, and then choose Properties from the menu that appears.**

The Properties dialog box for the network connection appears, as shown in Figure 4-7. If you compare this dialog box with the dialog box that was shown earlier, in Figure 4-2, you see that they're the same.

Figure 4-7:
The
Properties
dialog box
for a
network
connection
(Windows
Vista).

5. **Click Configure to configure the network connection.**

From this point, the steps for configuring the network connection are the same as they are for Windows XP. As a result, you can continue, beginning with Step 4 in the previous section, "Configuring Windows XP network connections."

Configuring Client Computer Identification

Every client computer must identify itself to participate in the network. The computer identification consists of the computer's name, an optional description, and the name of either the workgroup or the domain to which the computer belongs.

The computer name must follow the rules for NetBIOS names; it may be 1 to 15 characters long and may contain letters, numbers, or hyphens but no spaces or periods. For small networks, it's common to make the computer name the same as the username. For larger networks, you may want to develop a naming scheme that identifies the computer's location. For example, a name such as C-305-1 may be assigned to the first computer in Room 305 of Building C. Or MKTG010 may be a computer in the Marketing department.

If the computer will join a domain, you need to have access to an Administrator account on the domain, unless the administrator has already created a computer account on the domain. Note that only Windows 2000, Windows XP, and Windows Server (NT, 2000, and 2003) computers can join a domain.

(Windows 98 or 95 users can access the domain's resources by logging on to the domain as users, but domain computer accounts for Windows 9*x* clients aren't required.)

When you install Windows on the client system, the Setup program asks for the computer name and workstation or domain information. You can change this information later, if you want. The procedure varies depending on whether you're using Windows XP or Windows Vista.

Configuring Windows XP computer identification

To change the computer identification in Windows XP, follow these steps:

1. Open the Control Panel and double-click the System icon to open the System Properties dialog box.

2. Click the Computer Name tab.

The computer identification information is displayed.

3. Click the Change button.

This step displays the Computer Name Changes dialog box, as shown in Figure 4-8.

**Book II
Chapter 4**

Configuring
Windows XP and
Vista Clients

Figure 4-8:
The
Computer
Name
Changes
dialog box
(Windows
XP).

4. Type the new computer name, and then specify the workgroup or domain information.

To join a domain, select the Domain radio button and type the domain name into the appropriate text box. To join a workgroup, select the Work group radio button and type the workgroup name in the corresponding text box.

5. Click OK.

6. **If you're prompted, enter the username and password for an Administrator account.**

   You're asked to provide this information only if a computer account has not already been created for the client computer.

7. **When a dialog box appears, informing you that you need to restart the computer, click OK. Then restart the computer.**

   You're done!

Configuring Windows Vista computer identification

To change the computer identification in Windows Vista, follow these steps:

1. **Click the Start button, and then right-click Computer and choose Properties.**

   This step displays the System information window, as shown in Figure 4-9. Notice the section that lists computer name, domain, and workgroup settings.

2. **Click the Change Settings link.**

   If a dialog box appears and asks for your permission to continue, click Continue. The System Properties dialog box then appears, as shown in Figure 4-10.

Figure 4-9:
The System Information window (Windows Vista).

Figure 4-10:
The System
Properties
dialog box
(Windows
Vista).

3. Click the Change button.

This step displays the Computer Name Changes dialog box, as shown in Figure 4-11.

Figure 4-11:
The
Computer
Name/Doma
in Changes
dialog box
(Windows
Vista).

4. Enter the computer name and the workgroup or domain name.

If you want to join a domain, choose the Domain option button and type the domain name. To join a workgroup, choose the Workgroup option and type the workgroup name.

5. **Click OK.**

6. **Enter the username and password for an Administrator account when prompted.**

   You're asked to provide this information only if a computer account hasn't already been created for the client computer.

7. **When a dialog box appears, informing you that you need to restart the computer, click OK. Then restart the computer.**

   The computer is then added to the domain or workgroup.

Configuring Network Logon

Every user who wants to access a domain-based network must log on to the domain by using a valid user account. The user account is created on the domain controller — not on the client computer.

Network logon isn't required to access workgroup resources. Instead, workgroup resources can be password-protected to restrict access.

When you start a Windows computer that's been configured to join a domain, as described in the section "Configuring Client Computer Identification," earlier in this chapter, the Log On to Windows dialog box is displayed. The user can use this dialog box to log on to a domain by entering a domain username and password and then selecting the domain that she wants to log on to (from the Log On To drop-down list).

You can create local user accounts in Windows that allow users to access resources on the local computer. To log on to the local computer, the user selects This Computer from the Log On To drop-down list and enters the username and password for a local user account. When a user logs on by using a local account, he isn't connected to a network domain. To log on to a domain, the user must select the domain from the Log On To drop-down list.

If the computer isn't part of a domain, Windows can display a friendly logon screen that displays an icon for each of the computer's local users. The user can log on simply by clicking the appropriate icon and entering a password. (This feature isn't available for computers that have joined a domain.)

Note that if the user logs on by using a local computer account rather than a domain account, she can still access domain resources. A Connect To dialog box appears whenever the user attempts to access a domain resource. Then the user can enter a domain username and password to connect to the domain.

Chapter 5: Configuring Macintosh Computers for Networking

In This Chapter

✔ Hooking up a Macintosh network

✔ Using a Macintosh network

✔ Mixing Macs and PCs

This book dwells on networking Windows-based computers, as if Microsoft were the only game in town. (Hah! They wish.) To be politically correct, I should at least acknowledge the existence of an altogether different breed of computer: the Apple Macintosh.

This chapter presents what you need to know to hook up a Macintosh network, use a Macintosh network, and mix Macintoshes and Windows PCs on the same network. This chapter isn't a comprehensive tome on networking Macintoshes, but it's enough to get you started.

What You Need to Know to Hook Up a Macintosh Network

The following sections present some key things you should know about networking Macintosh computers before you start plugging in cables.

Finding out about the AppleTalk and Open Transport protocols

Every Macintosh ever built, even an original 1984 model, includes networking support. Of course, newer Macintosh computers have better built-in networking features than older Macintosh computers. The newest Macs include built-in 10/100 Mbps Ethernet adapters and sophisticated networking support built in to the operating system — similar to the networking features that come with Windows XP. The beauty of Macintosh networking is that the network card is built in, so you don't have to worry about installing and configuring the network.

Macintosh computers use a set of networking protocols collectively known as *AppleTalk*. Because AppleTalk is built in to every Mac, it's become an inarguable networking standard among Macintosh users. You don't have to worry about the differences between different network operating systems because all Macintosh networking is based on AppleTalk.

AppleTalk has gone through several major revisions since it was first introduced back in 1984. Originally, AppleTalk supported only small networks that operated only over low-speed connections. In 1989, Apple enhanced AppleTalk to support larger networks and faster connections.

In 1996, with the release of Mac OS System 7.5.3, Apple folded AppleTalk into its current networking scheme: *Open Transport*. The idea behind Open Transport is to bring all the different types of communications software used on Macintoshes under a common umbrella — and make them easy to configure and use. Currently, two types of networking are handled by Open Transport:

✦ **Open Transport/AppleTalk:** Handles local-area networks (LANs) according to the AppleTalk protocols. Open Transport/AppleTalk is a beefed-up version of AppleTalk that's more efficient and flexible.

✦ **OpenTransport/TCP:** Handles TCP/IP communications, such as Internet connections.

Open Transport is standard fare on all new Macintosh computers; old Macintosh computers can be upgraded to Open Transport, provided they're powerful enough. (The minimum system requirements for Open Transport are a 68030 processor, 5MB of RAM, and MacOS System 7.5.3.)

AppleTalk enables you to subdivide a network into *zones.* Each zone consists of the network users who regularly share information.

Who's winning in the AFP West?

AFP isn't a division of the NFL, but an acronym for AppleTalk Filing Protocol. It's the part of AppleTalk that governs how files are stored and accessed on the network. AFP allows files to be shared with non-Macintosh computers. You can integrate Macintoshes into any network operating system that recognizes AFP. NetWare and all versions of Windows since Windows 95 use AFP to support Macintoshes in their networks.

AppleTalk zones are similar to *workgroups* in Windows for Workgroups.

Although basic support for networking is built in to every Macintosh, you still have to purchase cables to connect the computers to one another. You have several types of cables to choose from. You can use AppleTalk with two different cabling schemes that connect to the Macintosh printer port, or you can use AppleTalk with faster Ethernet interface cards.

Looking at the Mac OS X Server network operating system

Apple offers a dedicated network operating system known as Mac OS X Server (the *X* is pronounced *ten,* not *ex),* which is designed for PowerMac G3 or later computers. Mac OS X Server is based on a Unix operating-system kernel known as Mach. As a result, Mac OS X Server can handle many network-server tasks as efficiently as any other network operating system, including Windows 2000, NetWare, and Unix.

(Mac OS X Server is the server version of the Mac OS X operating system, which is the current operating system version for client Macintosh computers.)

The Mac OS X Server includes the following features:

✦ **Apache Web server,** which also runs on Windows and Linux systems

✦ **NetBoot,** a feature that simplifies the task of managing network client computers

✦ **File services using AFP**

✦ **WebObjects,** a high-end tool for creating Web sites

✦ **QuickTime Streaming Server,** which lets the server broadcast multimedia programs over the network

What You Need to Know to Use a Macintosh Network

Here are some of the most common issues that come up after you install the network cable. Note that the following sections assume that you're working with AppleTalk networking using Mac OS X. The procedures may vary somewhat if you're using Open Transport networking or an earlier version of the Macintosh operating system.

Book II
Chapter 5

Configuring
Macintosh
Computers for
Networking

Configuring a Mac for networking

Before you can access the network from your Mac, you must configure your Mac for networking by activating AppleTalk and assigning your network name and password.

Activating AppleTalk

After all the cables are in place, you have to activate AppleTalk. Here's how:

1. **Choose the Chooser desk accessory from the Apple menu.**

2. **Click the Active button.**

3. **Close the Chooser.**

That's all there is to it.

Assigning your name and password

After you activate AppleTalk, you're ready to assign an owner name, a password, and a name for your computer. This process allows other network users to access your Mac. Here's how:

1. **Choose the File Sharing control panel from the Apple menu. (Choose Apple⇨Control Panels⇨File Sharing.)**

2. **Type your name in the Owner Name field.**

3. **Type a password in the Owner Password field.**

   Don't forget what the password is.

4. **Type a descriptive name for your computer in the Computer Name field.**

   Other network users will know your computer by this name.

5. **Click the Close button.**

Piece of cake, eh?

Accessing a network printer

Accessing a network printer with AppleTalk is no different than accessing a printer when you don't have a network. If more than one printer is available on the network, you use the Chooser to select the printer you want to use. The Chooser displays all the available network printers — just pick the one you want to use. And keep the following points in mind:

✦ **Be sure to enable Background Printing for the network printer.** If you don't, your Mac is tied up until the printer finishes your job — that can be a long time if someone else sends a 500-page report to the printer just before you. When you enable Background Printing, your printer output is captured to a disk file and then sent to the printer later while you continue with other work.

To enable Background Printing, follow these steps:

1. **Choose Apple⇨Chooser desk accessory.**

2. **Select the printer you want to use from the Chooser.**

3. **Click the Background Printing On button.**

✦ **Don't enable Background Printing if a dedicated print server has been set up.** In that case, print data is spooled automatically to the print server's disk so your Mac doesn't have to wait for the printer to become available.

Sharing files with other users

To share files on your Mac with other network users, you must set up a shared resource. You can share an entire disk or just individual folders and restrict access to certain users, if you want.

Before you can share files with other users, you must activate the AppleTalk file-sharing feature. Here's how:

1. **Choose the File Sharing control panel from the Apple menu.**

2. **Click the Start button in the File Sharing section of the control panel.**

3. **Click the Close button.**

To share a file or folder, click the file or folder once. Then open the File menu, choose Get Info, and choose Sharing from the submenu that appears. You can also use the Sharing section of the Info window to set access privileges to restrict access to the file or folder.

Accessing shared files

To access files on another Macintosh, follow this procedure:

1. **Choose the Chooser from the Apple menu.**

2. **Click the AppleShare icon from the Chooser window.**

3. **Click the name of the computer you want to access. (If your network has zones, you must first click the zone you want to access.)**

4. **Click OK.**

A login screen appears.

**Book II
Chapter 5**

Configuring
Macintosh
Computers for
Networking

5. **If you have a user account on the computer, click the Registered User button and enter your username and password. Otherwise, click the Guest button and then click OK.**

   A list of shared folders and disks appears.

6. **Click the folders and disks you want to access.**

   A check box appears next to each item on the list. If you select a box, you connect to the corresponding folder or disk automatically each time you start your computer.

7. **Click OK.**

With Mac OS 8.5 and later, you can also use the Network Browser, found in the Apple menu, to access network drives or folders. Just open the Network Browser from the Apple menu, double-click the server that contains the shared disk or folder, and then double-click the drive or folder you want to use.

What You Need to Know to Network Macintoshes with PCs

Life would be too boring if Macs *really* lived on one side of the tracks and PCs lived on the other. If your organization has a mix of both Macs and PCs, odds are you eventually want to network them together. Fortunately, you have several ways to do so:

✦ If your network has an OS X Server, you can use the Windows client software that comes with OS X Server to connect any version of Windows to the server. Doing so enables Windows users to access the files and printers on the Macintosh server.

✦ The server versions of Windows include a feature called Services for Macintosh that allows Macintosh computers to access files and printers managed by the Windows servers without installing special client software on the Macintosh computers.

✦ If you use NetWare, you must purchase separate NetWare client software for your Macintosh computers. After you install this client software, the Macs can access files and printers managed by your NetWare servers.

The biggest complication that occurs when you mix Macintosh and Windows computers on the same network is that the Mac OS and Windows have slightly different rules for naming files. For example:

✦ Macintosh filenames are limited to 31 characters, but Windows file-names can be up to 255 characters.

✦ Although a Macintosh filename can include any characters *other than a colon,* Windows filenames can't include backslashes, greater-than or less-than signs, and a few other oddball characters.

The best way to avoid filename problems is to stick with *short names* (under 31 characters) and limit your filenames to *letters, numbers,* and *common symbols* (such as the hyphen or pound sign). Although you can translate any filenames that violate the rules of the system being used into a form that is acceptable to both Windows and Macintosh, doing so sometimes leads to cryptic or ambiguous filenames. But hey, network administration is as much an art as a science.

**Book II
Chapter 5**

Configuring
Macintosh
Computers for
Networking

Chapter 6: Configuring Other Network Features

*A*fter you have your network servers and clients up and running, you still have many details to attend to before you can pronounce your network "finished." In this chapter, you discover a few more configuration chores that have to be done: configuring Internet access, setting up network printers, configuring e-mail, and configuring mapped network drives.

Configuring Network Printers

Before network users can print on the network, the network's printers must be properly configured. For the most part, this is a simple task. All you have to do is configure each client that needs access to the printer.

Before you configure a network printer to work with network clients, read the client configuration section of the manual that came with the printer. Many printers come with special software that provides more advanced printing and networking features than the standard features provided by Windows. If so, you may want to install the printer manufacturer's software on your client computers rather than use the standard Windows network printer support.

Adding a network printer

The exact procedure for adding a network printer varies a bit, depending on the Windows version that the client runs. The following steps describe the procedure for Windows Vista:

1. **Choose Start⇨Control Panel, and then double-click the Printers icon.**

2. **Click the Add a Printer button on the toolbar.**

   This step starts the Add Printer Wizard, as shown in Figure 6-1.

3. **Select the Add a Network, Wireless or Bluetooth Printer option.**

The wizard searches the network for available printers and displays a list of the printers it finds, as shown in Figure 6-2.

4. **Click the printer you want to use.**

If you can't find the printer you want to use, click The Printer That I Want Isn't Listed and enter the UNC or IP address for the printer when prompted.

Figure 6-1:
The Add
Printer
Wizard
comes to
life.

Figure 6-2:
The Add
Printer
Wizard asks
you to pick a
printer.

5. **Click Next to add the printer.**

The wizard copies to your computer the correct printer driver for the network printer. (You may be prompted to confirm that you want to add the driver. If so, click Install Driver to proceed.)

The Add Printer Wizard displays a screen that shows the printer's name and asks whether you want to designate the printer as your default printer.

6. **If you want, designate the printer as your default printer.**

7. **Click Next to continue.**

A final confirmation dialog box is displayed.

8. **Click Finish.**

You're done!

Accessing a network printer using a Web interface

Printers that have a direct network connection often include a built-in Web server that lets you manage the printer from any browser on the network. For example, Figure 6-3 shows the home page for a Hewlett-Packard LaserJet 4100 Series printer. This Web interface lets you view status information about the printer and check the printer's configuration. You can even view error logs to find out how often the printer jams.

Figure 6-3:
Using a printer's Web interface.

To call up a printer's Web interface, enter its IP address or host name in the address bar of any Web browser.

In addition to simply displaying information about the printer, you can also adjust the printer's configuration from a Web browser. For example, Figure 6-4 shows the Network Settings page for an HP 4100 printer. Here, you can change the network configuration details, such as the TCP/IP host name, IP address, subnet mask, domain name, and so on. Other configuration pages allow you to tell the printer to send an e-mail notification to an address that you specify whenever you encounter a problem with the printer.

As the network administrator, you may need to visit the printer's Web page frequently. I suggest that you add it to your browser's Favorites menu so that you can get to it easily. If you have several printers, add them under a folder named Network Printers.

Figure 6-4:
Changing network settings via a printer's Web interface.

Configuring Internet Access

To enable the network users to access the Internet, you need to make sure that the TCP/IP configuration settings on each client computer are set correctly. If you have a high-speed Internet connection, such as T1, DSL, cable, or ISDN, connected to the Internet via a router and your network uses DHCP for automatic TCP/IP configuration, you may not need to do anything special to get your clients connected to the Internet.

Configuring clients for DHCP

The easiest way to configure client computers to access the Internet via a shared high-speed connection is to use DHCP. DHCP automatically distributes the detailed TCP/IP configuration information to each client. Then, if your configuration changes, all you have to do is change the DHCP server's configuration. You don't have to manually change each client. Plus, the DHCP server avoids common manual configuration errors, such as assigning the same IP address to two computers.

Before you configure the clients to use DHCP, you should first set up the DHCP server. The DHCP server's configuration should include:

✦ A scope that specifies the range of IP addresses and the subnet mask to be distributed to client computers.

✦ The IP address of the router that should be used as the default gateway for client computers to reach the Internet.

✦ The IP addresses of the DNS servers that clients should use.

Note that DHCP can be provided either by a server computer or by an intelligent router that has built-in DHCP. For more information about configuring DHCP, see Book IV, Chapter 3.

After the DHCP server is configured, setting up Windows clients to use it is a snap. Just follow these steps for Windows Vista:

1. **Open the Control Panel and double-click the Network and Sharing Center icon.**

2. **Click the Manage Network Connections link.**

3. **Right-click the LAN connection icon and choose Properties.**

This brings up the connection's Properties dialog box, as shown in Figure 6-5.

**Book II
Chapter 6**

**Configuring Other
Network Features**

4. Select Internet Protocol Version 4(TCP/IPv4) from the list of items used by the connection and then click the Properties button.

This displays the Internet Protocol (TCP/IP) Properties dialog box, as shown in Figure 6-6.

Figure 6-5:
The Local
Area
Connection
Properties
dialog box.

Figure 6-6:
The IP
Properties
dialog box.

5. **Make sure that both the Obtain An IP Address Automatically and Obtain DNS Server Address Automatically options are selected.**

   These options enable DHCP for the client.

6. **Click OK to return to the Local Area Connection Properties dialog box and then click OK again.**

That's all there is to it. The computer is now configured to use DHCP. You should check to make sure that every computer on your network is configured for DHCP.

If your network doesn't have a DHCP server, you'll have to configure the TCP/IP configuration manually for each computer. Start by deciding the IP address that you want to assign to each computer. Then, follow the preceding procedure on every computer. When you get to Step 4, enter the computer's IP address as well as the IP address of the default gateway (your Internet router) and the IP addresses of your DNS servers.

Frankly, setting up a DHCP server is a lot easier than manually configuring each computer's TCP/IP information, unless your network has only two or three computers. So unless your network is tiny, get a DHCP server.

Using Internet Connection Sharing

Actually, the title of this section is misleading. It should be "*Not* Using Internet Connection Sharing." Windows XP and Vista come with a built-in feature called *Internet Connection Sharing (ICS),* designed to let you share an Internet connection with several computers on a small network. However, this feature is designed to be used only on very small networks that don't have a separate router to enable the connection to be shared.

Windows XP with Service Pack 2 as well as Windows Vista include a feature called the Windows Firewall that provides basic firewall support for home networks. This feature keeps hackers from invading your home network.

I recommend that you use ICS and the Windows Firewall only for home networks with no more than three computers. Even then, you're better off purchasing an inexpensive connection-sharing device.

If the Windows Firewall have been enabled and you don't need it, you should disable it. Otherwise, it will disrupt your network. For information about how to enable or disable this feature, refer to Book III, Chapter 4.

Mapping Network Drives

One of the main reasons that users want to use a network is to access shared disk storage located on network file servers. Although you can do this in several ways, the most common method is called *mapping*. Mapping assigns a drive letter to a shared folder on a network server. Then, the user can use the drive letter to access the shared folder as if it were a local drive.

Before you map network drives for your network's client computers, you should devise a strategy for how you'll share folders and map them to drives. Here are just two possibilities:

✦ For private storage, you can create a separate shared folder for each user on the file server and then map a drive letter on each user's computer to that user's shared folder. For example, you can create shares named jBrannan, dHodgson, and mCaldwell. Then, you can map drive N: to jBrannan on jBrannan's computer, dHodgson on dHodgson's computer, and mCaldwell on mCaldwell's computer.

✦ For shared storage for an entire department, you can create a share for the entire department and then map a drive to that share on each computer in the department. For example, you may map drive M: to a share named Marketing for the entire Marketing department to use.

After you've decided how to map the file server's shared folder, the next step is to create and share the folders on the server. For information about how to do that, refer to the appropriate chapters on specific network operating systems later in this book.

When you're ready to map drives on the client computers, follow these steps:

1. **Choose Start⇨Computer.**

2. **Click the Map Network Drive button.**

The Map Network Drive dialog box appears, as shown in Figure 6-7.

3. **Select the drive letter that you want to map in the Drive drop-down list.**

4. **Type a valid path to the server and share that you want to map in the Folder text box.**

For example, to map a folder named mCaldwell on a server named MKT-SERVER, type **MKTSERVER\mCaldwell**.

If you don't know the server or share name, click the Browse button and browse your way to the folder that you want to map.

5. **To cause the network drive to be automatically mapped each time the user logs on, select the Reconnect at Logon option.**

   If you leave this option deselected, the drive is mapped only until the next time you shut Windows down or log off.

6. **Click OK.**

   That's it! You're done.

Figure 6-7:
Mapping a
Network
Drive.

If you're the type who prefers to do things through the command line, you can quickly map network drives by using the NET USE command at a command prompt. For example, here's a NET USE command that maps drive Z: to \\MKTSERVER\mCaldwell:

```
net use z: \\MKTSERVER\mCaldwell /persistent:yes
```

Specifying /persistent:yes causes the drive to be remapped each time the user logs on. To remove a drive mapping via the command line, use a command like this:

```
net use z: /delete
```

Here, the mapping for drive Z: is removed.

Manually setting up drive mappings as described here works well enough for small networks but not so well for large networks. If a server or share name changes, would you want to go to 200 computers in order to update drive mappings? How about 2,000 computers? For larger networks, you're more likely to use either login scripts or group policies to configure network storage for end users. You can find more information about login scripts and group policies in Book VII, Chapters 4 and 6.

Chapter 7: Verifying Your Network Installation

You've installed all the network cards, plugged in all the cables, and configured all the software. However, one task remains before you can declare your network finished: You must verify that the network works as expected.

Verifying a network isn't difficult. All you have to do is make sure that users can log on and access the network resources they need. If everything works the way it should, you can declare victory, give yourself a high five, and take the afternoon off. If not, you have to do some troubleshooting to determine the source of the problem.

In this short chapter, I describe some of the tests that you should perform to make sure that your network is functioning. Along the way, I suggest a few of the most common problems that may interrupt the network. However, the focus of this chapter is on verifying that your network is functioning — not on troubleshooting it if it isn't. For information about network troubleshooting, refer to Book III, Chapters 6 and 7, as well as Book VII, Chapter 7.

Incidentally, most of the techniques described in this chapter work from an MS-DOS command prompt. You can open a command prompt by choosing Start⇨Run, typing cmd as the name of the program to run, and then clicking OK.

Is the Computer Connected to the Network?

This one is easy to check. Just check the Link light on the computer's network interface card and the light on the network hub or switch port that the computer is connected to. If both are lit, the computer is connected to the network. If one or both aren't lit, you have a connection problem. Several things may be wrong:

✦ The patch cable that connects the computer to the wall outlet or that connects to the hub or switch may be bad. Replace it with one that you know is good in order to verify this problem.

✦ The cable run between the wall outlet and the patch panel may be bad. The cable may be physically broken, or it may be routed right next to a 20,000-watt generator or an elevator motor.

✦ The computer's NIC may be bad or configured incorrectly. Check the configuration settings. If necessary, replace the card.

✦ The hub or switch may be bad.

Is the Network Configuration Working?

You can run three commands from a command window to verify the basic configuration of each computer. These commands are net config work station, net config server, and ipconfig.

The net config workstation command displays basic information about the computer's network configuration. Here's a sample of the output it displays:

```
C:>net config workstation
Computer name                           \\DOUG
Full Computer name                      doug
User name                               Doug Lowe
Workstation active on
        NetbiosSmb (000000000000)
        NetBT_Tcpip_{FC6D2F39-FDDD-448E-9B3C-0C12847F2B61}
    (0050BA843911)
Software version                        Windows 2002
Workstation domain                      WORKGROUP
Workstation Domain DNS Name             (null)
Logon domain                            DOUG
COM Open Timeout (sec)                  0
COM Send Count (byte)                   16
COM Send Timeout (msec)                 250
The command completed successfully.
```

The most important information to check in the net config workstation command's output is the computer name and domain information.

If the computer is configured to enable file and print sharing, you can also run `net config server` to display basic information about the server configuration. Here's a sample of its output:

```
C:>net config server
Server Name                          \\DOUG
Server Comment
Software version                     Windows 2002
Server is active on
        NetbiosSmb (000000000000)
        NetBT_Tcpip_{FB6D2F79-FDDF-418E-9B7C-0C82887F2A61}
   (0050ba843911)
Server hidden                        No
Maximum Logged On Users              5
Maximum open files per session       16384
Idle session time (min)              15
The command completed successfully.
```

Book II
Chapter 7

The `ipconfig` command displays information about the computer's TCP/IP configuration. If you type **ipconfig** by itself, the computer's IP address, subnet mask, and default gateway are displayed. If you type **ipconfig /all**, you see more detailed information. Here's typical output from the `ipconfig /all` command:

Verifying Your Network Installation

```
C:>ipconfig /all
Windows IP Configuration
        Host Name . . . . . . . . . . . . : doug
        Primary Dns Suffix . . . . . . . :
        Node Type . . . . . . . . . . . . : Unknown
        IP Routing Enabled. . . . . . . . : No
        WINS Proxy Enabled. . . . . . . . : No
Ethernet adapter Local Area Connection:
        Connection-specific DNS Suffix  . :
   we1.client2.attbi.com
        Description . . . . . . . . . . . : D-Link DFE-530TX+
   PCI Adapter
        Physical Address. . . . . . . . . : 00-50-BA-84-39-11
        Dhcp Enabled. . . . . . . . . . . : Yes
        Autoconfiguration Enabled . . . . : Yes
        IP Address. . . . . . . . . . . . : 192.168.1.100
        Subnet Mask . . . . . . . . . . . : 255.255.255.0
        Default Gateway . . . . . . . . . : 192.168.1.1
        DHCP Server . . . . . . . . . . . : 192.168.1.1
        DNS Servers . . . . . . . . . . . : 204.127.198.19
                                            63.240.76.19
        Lease Obtained. . . . . . . . . . : Saturday, May 24,
   2003 6:28:49 PM
        Lease Expires . . . . . . . . . . : Sunday, May 25,
   2003 6:28:49 PM
```

The most important information to glean from this output is the computer's IP address. You should also verify that the default gateway matches the IP address of your Internet router and that the IP addresses for the DHCP and DNS servers are correct.

Can the Computers Ping Each Other?

A basic test that you can perform to ensure that your network is functioning is to use the `ping` command from a command prompt to make sure that the computers on the network can contact each other. The `ping` command simply sends a packet to another computer and requests that the second computer send a packet back in reply. If the reply packet is received, `ping` displays a message indicating how long it took to hear from the other computer. If the reply packet isn't received, `ping` displays an error message indicating that the computer couldn't be reached.

You should try several `ping` tests. First, you can make sure that TCP/IP is up and running by having the computer try to ping itself. Open a command prompt and type **ping 127.0.0.1**. (127.0.0.1 is the standard loop-back address that a computer can use to refer to itself.) If you prefer, you can use the command **ping localhost** instead.

Next, have the computer ping itself by using the IP address displayed by the \ `ipconfig` command. For example, if Ipconfig says the computer's IP address is 192.168.0.100, type **ping 192.168.0.100** at the command prompt.

Now try to ping your servers. You'll have to run `ipconfig` at each of the servers to determine their IP addresses. Or, you can just ping the computer's name.

A final test is to make sure that you can ping the workstation from other computers on the network. You don't have to try to ping every computer from every other computer on the network unless you've determined that you have a connectivity problem that you need to pinpoint. However, you should try to ping each workstation from each of the servers, just to make sure the servers can see the workstations. Make a list of the IP addresses of the workstations as you test them and then take that list to the servers and ping each IP address on the list.

Can You Log On?

After you've established that the basic network connections are working, the next step is to verify that network logon works. This is as simple as attempting to log on from each computer by using the correct user account for the computer. If you can't log on, several things may be causing the problem. Here are the most common:

✦ You may not have the right user account information. Double-check the username, password, and domain.

✦ Make sure that the domain name is correct.

✦ Passwords are case-sensitive. Make sure that you type the password correctly and that the Caps Lock key isn't on.

✦ You may not have a computer account for the computer. Double-check the computer name and make sure that you have a valid computer account on the server.

✦ Double-check the user account policies to make sure that there isn't something that would prevent the user from logging on, such as a time of day restriction.

**Book II
Chapter 7**

Verifying
Your Network
Installation

Are Network Drives Mapped Correctly?

After you know the user can log on, you should make sure that mapped network drives are available. To do so, type **net use** at a command prompt. You'll see a list of all the network mappings. For example:

```
C:>net use
New connections will be remembered.
Status  Local  Remote            Network
-------------------------------------------------------------
OK      M:     \\Doug\Prod       Microsoft Windows Network
OK      X:     \\Doug\admin      Microsoft Windows Network
OK      Z:     \\Doug\Marketing  Microsoft Windows Network
The command completed successfully.
```

Here, you can see that three drives are mapped, and you can tell the server and share name for each mapped drive.

Next, try to display a directory list of each drive to make sure that you can actually reach it. For example, type **dir m:**. If everything is working, you see a directory of the shared folder you've mapped to drive M:.

Do Network Printers Work?

The final test I describe in this chapter is making sure that your network printers work. The easiest way to do this is to print a short document to the network printer and make sure that the document prints. I suggest that you open Notepad (choose Start⇨Accessories⇨Notepad), type a few words (like "Yo, Adrianne!"), and then choose File⇨Print to bring up the Print dialog box. Select the network printer and click OK.

If the network printer doesn't appear in the list of available printers, go to the Printers and Faxes window and recheck the network printer. You may have incorrectly configured the printer. If the configuration looks okay, go to the printer itself and make sure that it's turned on and ready to print.

Book III

Networking Administration and Security

The 5th Wave   By Rich Tennant

"It appears a server in Atlanta is about to go down, there's printer backup in Baltimore and an accountant in Chicago is about to make level 3 of the game 'Tomb Pirate.'"

Contents at a Glance

Chapter 1: Help Wanted: Job Description for a Network Administrator

In This Chapter

✔ Deciphering the many jobs of the network administrator

✔ Dusting, vacuuming, and mopping

✔ Managing the network users

✔ Choosing the right tools

✔ Getting certified

*H*elp wanted. Network administrator to help small business get control of a network run amok. Must have sound organizational and management skills. Only moderate computer experience required. Part time only.

Does this ad sound like one that your company should run? Every network needs a network administrator, whether the network has two computers or 200. Of course, managing a 200-computer network is a full-time job, whereas managing a two-computer network isn't. At least, it shouldn't be.

This chapter introduces you to the boring job of network administration. Oops . . . you're probably reading this chapter because you've been elected to be the network manager, so I'd better rephrase that: This chapter introduces you to the wonderful, exciting world of network management! Oh, boy! This is going to be fun!

Knowing What Network Administrators Do

Simply put, network administrators administer networks, which means that they take care of the tasks of installing, configuring, expanding, protecting, upgrading, tuning, and repairing the network. Network administrators take care of the network hardware, such as cables, hubs, switches, routers, servers, and clients, as well as network software, such as network operating systems, e-mail servers, backup software, database servers, and application software. Most importantly, network administrators take care of network users by answering their questions, listening to their troubles, and solving their problems.

On a big network, these responsibilities constitute a full-time job. Large networks tend to be volatile: Users come and go, equipment fails, cables break, and life in general seems to be one crisis after another.

Smaller networks are much more stable. After you get your network up and running, you probably won't have to spend much time managing its hardware and software. An occasional problem may pop up, but with only a few computers on the network, problems should be few and far between.

Regardless of the network's size, all network administrators must attend to several common chores:

✦ The network administrator should be involved in every decision to purchase new computers, printers, or other equipment. In particular, the network administrator should be prepared to lobby for the most network-friendly equipment possible, such as new computers that already have network cards installed and configured and printers that are network ready.

✦ The network administrator must put on the pocket protector whenever a new computer is added to the network. The network administrator's job includes considering what changes to make to the cabling configuration, what computer name to assign to the new computer, how to integrate the new user into the security system, what rights to grant the user, and so on.

✦ Every once in a while, your trusty operating system vendor (in other words, Microsoft) releases a new version of your network operating system. The network administrator must read about the new version and decide whether its new features are beneficial enough to warrant an upgrade. In most cases, the hardest part of upgrading to a new version of your network operating system is determining the *migration path* — that is, how to upgrade your entire network to the new version while disrupting the network or its users as little as possible. Upgrading to a new network operating system version is a major chore, so you need to carefully consider the advantages that the new version can bring.

✦ Between upgrades, Microsoft releases patches and service packs that fix minor problems with their server operating systems. For more information, see the section "Patching Up Your Operating System and Software" later in this chapter.

✦ One of the easiest traps that you can get sucked into is the quest for network speed. The network is never fast enough, and users always blame the hapless network manager. So the administrator spends hours and hours tuning and tweaking the network to squeeze out that last two percent of performance. You don't want to get caught in this trap, but in case you do, Chapter 7 of this book can help. It clues you in to the basics of tuning your network for best performance.

✦ Network administrators perform routine chores, such as backing up the servers, archiving old data, freeing up server hard drive space, and so on. Much of network administration is making sure that things keep working and finding and correcting problems before any users notice that something is wrong. In this sense, network administration can be a thankless job.

✦ Network administrators are also responsible for gathering, organizing, and tracking the entire network's software inventory. You never know when something is going to go haywire on Joe in Marketing's ancient Windows 95 computer and you're going to have to reinstall that old copy of Lotus Approach. Do you have any idea where the installation discs are?

Choosing the Part-Time Administrator

The larger the network, the more technical support it needs. Most small networks — with just a dozen or two computers — can get by with a part-time network administrator. Ideally, this person should be a closet computer geek: someone who has a secret interest in computers but doesn't like to admit it. Someone who will take books home with him or her and read them over the weekend. Someone who enjoys solving computer problems just for the sake of solving them.

The job of managing a network requires some computer skills, but it isn't entirely a technical job. Much of the work that the network administrator does is routine housework. Basically, the network administrator dusts, vacuums, and mops the network periodically to keep it from becoming a mess.

Here are some additional ideas on picking a part-time network administrator:

✦ The network administrator needs to be an organized person. Conduct a surprise office inspection and place the person with the neatest desk in charge of the network. (Don't warn them in advance, or everyone may mess up their desks intentionally the night before the inspection.)

✦ Allow enough time for network administration. For a small network (say, no more than 20 or so computers), an hour or two each week is enough. More time is needed upfront as the network administrator settles into the job and discovers the ins and outs of the network. After an initial settling-in period, though, network administration for a small office network doesn't take more than an hour or two per week. (Of course, larger networks take more time to manage.)

✦ Make sure that everyone knows who the network administrator is and that the network administrator has the authority to make decisions about the network, such as what access rights each user has, what files can and can't be stored on the server, how often backups are done, and so on.

**Book III
Chapter 1**

**Help Wanted:
Job Description
for a Network
Administrator**

✦ Pick someone who is assertive and willing to irritate people. A good network administrator should make sure that backups are working *before* a hard drive fails and make sure that antivirus protection is in place *before* a virus wipes out the entire network. This policing will irritate people, but it's for their own good.

✦ In most cases, the person who installs the network is also the network administrator. This is appropriate because no one understands the network better than the person who designs and installs it.

✦ The network administrator needs an understudy — someone who knows almost as much about the network, is eager to make a mark, and smiles when the worst network jobs are delegated.

✦ The network manager has some sort of official title, such as Network Boss, Network Czar, Vice President in Charge of Network Operations, or Dr. Network. A badge, a personalized pocket protector, or a set of Spock ears helps, too.

Establishing Routine Chores

Much of the network manager's job is routine stuff — the equivalent of vacuuming, dusting, and mopping. Or if you prefer, changing the oil and rotating the tires every 3,000 miles. Yes, it's boring, but it has to be done.

✦ The network manager needs to make sure that the network is properly backed up. If something goes wrong and the network isn't backed up, guess who gets the blame? On the other hand, if disaster strikes, yet you're able to recover everything from yesterday's backup with only a small amount of work lost, guess who gets the pat on the back, the fat bonus, and the vacation in the Bahamas? Chapter 8 of this book describes the options for network backups. You'd better read it soon.

✦ Another major task for network administrators is sheltering your network from the evils of the outside world. These evils come in many forms, including hackers trying to break into your network and virus programs arriving through e-mail. Chapter 8 of this book describes this task in more detail.

✦ Users think that the network server is like the attic: They want to throw files up there and leave them forever. No matter how much storage your network has, your users will fill it up sooner than you think. So the network manager gets the fun job of cleaning up the attic once in a while. Oh, joy. The best advice I can offer is to constantly complain about how messy it is up there and warn your users that spring cleaning is coming up.

Managing Network Users

Managing network technology is the easiest part of network management. Computer technology can be confusing at first, but computers aren't nearly as confusing as people. The real challenge of managing a network is managing the network's users.

The difference between managing technology and managing users is obvious: You can figure out computers, but you can never really figure out people. The people who use the network are much less predictable than the network itself. Here are some tips for dealing with users:

✦ Training is a key part of the network manager's job. Make sure that everyone who uses the network understands it and knows how to use it. If the network users don't understand the network, they may unintentionally do all kinds of weird things to it.

✦ Never treat your network users like they're idiots. If they don't understand the network, it isn't their fault. Explain it to them. Offer a class. Buy them each a copy of *Networking All-in-One Desk Reference For Dummies* and tell them to read it during their lunch hour. Hold their hands. But don't treat them like idiots.

✦ Make up a network cheat sheet that contains everything that the users need to know about using the network on one page. Make sure that everyone gets a copy.

✦ Be as responsive as possible when a network user complains of a network problem. If you don't fix the problem soon, the user may try to fix it. You probably don't want that.

✦ The better you understand the psychology of network users, the more prepared you'll be for the strangeness they often serve up. Toward that end, I recommend that you read the *Diagnostic and Statistical Manual of Mental Disorders* (also known as *DSM-IV*) cover to cover.

Book III
Chapter 1

Help Wanted:
Job Description
for a Network
Administrator

Patching Up Your Operating System and Software

One of the annoyances that every network manager faces is applying software patches to keep your operating system and other software up to date. A software *patch* is a minor update that fixes small glitches that crop up from time to time, such as minor security or performance issues. These glitches aren't significant enough to merit a new version of the software, but they're important enough to require fixing. Most of the patches correct security flaws that computer hackers have uncovered in their relentless attempts to prove that they're smarter than the security programmers at Microsoft.

Periodically, all the recently released patches are combined into a *service pack*. Although the most diligent network administrators apply all patches as they're released, many administrators just wait for the service packs.

For all versions of Windows, you can use the Microsoft Update Web site to apply patches to keep your operating system and other Microsoft software up to date. You can find Microsoft Update in the Start menu. If all else fails, just fire up Internet Explorer and go to `http://update.microsoft.com`. Microsoft Update automatically scans your computer's software and creates a list of software patches and other components that you can download and install. You can also configure Microsoft Update to automatically notify you of updates so that you don't have to remember to check for new patches.

For larger networks, you can set up a server that runs Microsoft's Software Update Services (SUS) to automate software updates. SUS essentially lets you set up your own Windows Update site on your own network. Then, you have complete control over how software updates are delivered to the computers on your network. For more information, see `www.microsoft.com/windowsserversystem/updateservices`.

Discovering Software Tools for Network Administrators

Network managers need certain tools to get their jobs done. Managers of big, complicated, and expensive networks need big, complicated, and expensive tools. Managers of small networks need small tools.

Some of the tools that the manager needs are hardware tools, such as screwdrivers, cable crimpers, and hammers. The tools that I'm talking about here, however, are software tools. Here's a sampling of the tools you'll need:

✦ A diagramming tool that lets you draw pictures of your network. Microsoft sells a program called *Visio* that's specially designed for the types of diagrams you'll want to make as a network administrator.

✦ For larger networks, you may want to invest in a *network discovery* program such as NetworkView (`www.networkview.com`) that can automatically document your network's structure for you. These programs scan the network carefully, looking for computers, printers, routers, and other devices. They then create a database of the network components, draw diagrams for you, and chug out helpful reports.

✦ Many of the software tools that you need to manage a network come with the network itself. As the network manager, you should read through the manuals that come with your network software to see what management tools are available. For example, Windows includes a `net diag` command that you can use to make sure that all the computers on a network can communicate with each other. (You can run `net diag` from an MS-DOS prompt.) For TCP/IP networks, you can use the TCP/IP diagnostic commands summarized in Table 1-1. For more information about these commands, refer to Book IV, Chapter 6.

Table 1-1	TCP/IP Diagnostic Commands
Command	*What It Does*
arp	Displays address resolution information used by the Address Resolution Protocol (ARP).
hostname	Displays your computer's host name.
ipconfig	Displays current TCP/IP settings.
nbtstat	Displays the status of NetBIOS over TCP/IP connections.
netstat	Displays statistics for TCP/IP.
nslookup	Displays DNS information.
ping	Verifies that a specified computer can be reached.
route	Displays the PC's routing tables.
tracert	Displays the route from your computer to a specified host.

✦ The System Information program that comes with Windows is a useful utility for network managers.

✦ Another handy tool available from Microsoft is the Hotfix Checker, which scans your computers to see what patches need to be applied. You can download the Hotfix Checker free of charge from Microsoft's Web site. Just go to www.microsoft.com and search for *hfnetchk.exe*.

✦ If you prefer GUI-based tools, check out Microsoft Baseline Security Analyzer. You can download it from Microsoft's Web site free of charge. To find it, go to www.microsoft.com and search for *Microsoft Baseline Security Analyzer*.

✦ I suggest that you get one of those 100-in-1 utility programs, such as Symantec's Norton Utilities. Norton Utilities includes invaluable utilities for repairing damaged hard drives, rearranging the directory structure of your hard drive, gathering information about your computer and its equipment, and so on.

Never use a hard drive repair program that wasn't designed to work with the operating system or version that your computer uses or the file system you've installed. Any time that you upgrade to a newer version of your operating system, you should also upgrade your hard drive repair programs to a version that supports the new operating system version.

**Book III
Chapter 1**

**Help Wanted:
Job Description
for a Network
Administrator**

✦ A *protocol analyzer* is a program that's designed to monitor and log the individual packets that travel along your network. (Protocol analyzers are also called *packet sniffers*.) You can configure the protocol analyzer to filter specific types of packets, watch for specific types of problems, and provide statistical analysis of the captured packets. Most network administrators agree that Sniffer, by Network General (`www.network general.com`) is the best protocol analyzer available. However, it's also one of the most expensive. If you prefer a free alternative, check out Ethereal, which you can download free from `www.ethereal.com`.

✦ All current versions of Windows include a program called Network Monitor that provides basic protocol analysis and can often help solve pesky network problems.

Building a Library

One of Scotty's best lines in the original *Star Trek* series was when he refused to take shore leave so he could get caught up on his technical journals. "Don't you ever relax?" asked Kirk. "I am relaxing!" Scotty replied.

To be a good network administrator, you need to read computer books. Lots of them. And you need to enjoy doing it. If you're the type who takes computer books with you to the beach, you'll make a great network administrator.

You need books on a variety of topics. I'm not going to recommend specific titles, but I do recommend that you get a good, comprehensive book on each of the following topics:

✦ Network security and hacking

✦ Wireless networking

✦ Network cabling and hardware

✦ Ethernet

✦ Windows Server 2003 or 2007

✦ Windows XP or Vista

✦ Linux

✦ TCP/IP

✦ DNS and BIND

✦ Sendmail

✦ Exchange Server

In addition to books, you may also want to subscribe to some magazines to keep up with what's happening in the networking industry. Here are a few you should probably consider, along with their Web addresses:

✦ *InformationWeek:* `www.informationweek.com`

✦ *InfoWorld:* `www.infoworld.com`

✦ *Network Computing:* `www.networkcomputing.com`

✦ *Network World:* `www.networkworld.com`

✦ *2600* (a great magazine on computer hacking and security): `www.2600.com`

The Internet is one of the best sources of technical information for network administrators. You'll want to stock your browser's Favorites menu with plenty of Web sites that contain useful networking information. In addition, you may want to subscribe to one of the many online newsletters that deliver fresh information on a regular basis via e-mail.

Getting Certified

Remember the scene near the end of *The Wizard of Oz* when the Wizard grants the Scarecrow a diploma, the Cowardly Lion a medal, and the Tin Man a testimonial?

Network certifications are kind of like that. I can picture the scene now:

> *The Wizard:* "And as for you, my network-burdened friend, any geek with thick glasses can administer a network. Back where I come from, there are people who do nothing but configure Cisco routers all day long. And they don't have any more brains than you do. But they do have one thing you don't have: certification. And so, by the authority vested in me by the Universita Committeeatum E Pluribus Unum, I hereby confer upon you the coveted certification of CND."
>
> *You:* "CND?"
>
> *The Wizard:* "Yes, that's, uh, *Certified Network Dummy.*"
>
> *You:* "The Seven Layers of the OSI Reference Model are equal to the Sum of the Layers on the Opposite Side. Oh, rapture! I feel like a network administrator already!"

My point is that certification in and of itself doesn't guarantee that you really know how to administer a network. That ability comes from real-world experience — not exam crams.

**Book III
Chapter 1**

Help Wanted:
Job Description
for a Network
Administrator

Nevertheless, certification is becoming increasingly important in today's competitive job market. So you may want to pursue certification — not just to improve your skills, but also to improve your resume. Certification is an expensive proposition. Each test can cost several hundred dollars, and depending on your technical skills, you may need to buy books to study or enroll in training courses before you take the tests.

You can pursue two basic types of certification: vendor-specific certification and vendor-neutral certification. The major software vendors such as Microsoft and Cisco provide certification programs for their own equipment and software. CompTIA, a nonprofit industry trade association, provides the best-known vendor-neutral certification.

The following sections describe some of the certifications offered by CompTIA, Microsoft, Novell, and Cisco.

CompTIA

www.comptia.org

+ **A+** is a basic certification for an entry-level computer technician. To attain A+ certification, you have to pass two exams: one on computer hardware, the other on operating systems.

+ **Linux+** covers basic Linux skills such as installation, operations, and troubleshooting. This certification is vendor neutral, so it doesn't depend on any particular version of Linux.

+ **Network+** is a popular vendor-neutral networking certification. It covers four major topic areas: Media and Topologies, Protocols and Standards, Network Implementation, and Network Support.

+ **Server+** covers network server hardware. It includes details such as installing and upgrading server hardware, installing and configuring a NOS, and so on.

+ **Security+** is for security specialists. The exam topics include general security concepts, communication security, infrastructure security, basics of cryptography, and operational/organizational security.

Microsoft

www.microsoft.com/learning/mcp/

+ **MCTS,** or Microsoft Certified Technology Specialist, is a certification in a specific Microsoft technology or product.

+ **MCITP,** or Microsoft Certified IT Professional, is a certification in deploying and maintaining IT infrastructure.

✦ **MCSE,** or Microsoft Certified Systems Engineer, is a prestigious certification for networking professionals who design and implement networks. To gain this certification, you have to pass a total of seven exams. Microsoft offers separate Windows 2000 Server and Windows Server 2003 certification tracks.

✦ **MCSA,** or Microsoft Certified System Administrator, is for networking professionals who administer existing networks.

Cisco

www.cisco.com/certification

✦ **CCNA,** or Cisco Certified Network Associate, is an entry-level apprentice certification. A CCNA should be able to install, configure, and operate Cisco equipment for small networks (under 100 nodes).

✦ **CCNP,** or Cisco Certified Network Professional, is a professional-level certification for Cisco equipment. A CCNP should be able to install, configure, and troubleshoot Cisco networks of virtually any size.

✦ **CCDA,** or Cisco Certified Design Associate, is an entry-level certification for network design.

✦ **CCDP,** or Cisco Certified Design Professional, is for network design professionals. Both the CCDA and CCNA certifications are prerequisites for the CCDP.

✦ **CCIP,** or Cisco Certified Internetwork Professional, is a professional-level certification that emphasizes advanced use of IP and related protocols to create intranetworks.

✦ **CCIE,** or Cisco Certified Internetwork Expert, is the top dog of Cisco certifications.

✦ **And much more!** There are many more Cisco certifications to choose from, including certification for security, voice technology, wireless networking, and more.

**Book III
Chapter 1**

**Help Wanted:
Job Description
for a Network
Administrator**

Gurus Need Gurus, Too

No matter how much you know about computers, plenty of people know more than you do. This rule seems to apply at every rung of the ladder of computer experience. I'm sure that a top rung exists somewhere, occupied by the world's best computer guru. However, I'm not sitting on that rung, and neither are you. (Not even Bill Gates is sitting on that rung. In fact, Bill Gates got to where he is today by hiring people on higher rungs.)

As the local computer guru, one of your most valuable assets can be a knowledgeable friend who's a notch or two above you on the geek scale. That way, when you run into a real stumper, you have a friend to call for advice. Here are some tips for handling your own guru:

✦ In dealing with your own guru, don't forget the Computer Geek's Golden Rule: "Do unto your guru as you would have your own users do unto you." Don't pester your guru with simple stuff that you just haven't spent the time to think through. If you have thought it through and can't come up with a solution, however, give your guru a call. Most computer experts welcome the opportunity to tackle an unusual computer problem. It's a genetic defect.

✦ If you don't already know someone who knows more about computers than you do, consider joining your local PC users' group. The group may even have a subgroup that specializes in your networking software or may be devoted entirely to local folks who use the same networking software that you use. Odds are good that you're sure to make a friend or two at a users' group meeting. Also, you can probably convince your boss to pay any fees required to join the group.

✦ If you can't find a real-life guru, try to find an online guru. Check out the various computing newsgroups on the Internet. Subscribe to online newsletters that are automatically delivered to you via e-mail.

Helpful Bluffs and Excuses

As network administrator, you just won't be able to solve a problem sometimes, at least not immediately. You can do two things in this situation. The first is to explain that the problem is particularly difficult and that you'll have a solution as soon as possible. The second solution is to look the user in the eyes and, with a straight face, try one of these phony explanations:

✦ Blame it on the version of whatever software you're using. "Oh, they fixed that with version 39."

✦ Blame it on cheap, imported memory chips.

✦ Blame it on Democrats. Or Republicans. Or hanging chads. Whatever.

✦ Blame it on oil company executives.

✦ Blame it on global warming.

✦ Hope that the problem wasn't caused by stray static electricity. Those types of problems are very difficult to track down. Tell your users that not properly discharging themselves before using their computers can cause all kinds of problems.

✦ You need more memory.

✦ You need a bigger hard drive.

✦ You need a faster processor.

✦ Blame it on Jar-Jar Binks.

✦ You can't do that in Windows Vista.

✦ You can only do that in Windows Vista.

✦ Could be a virus.

✦ Or sunspots.

✦ No beer and no TV make Homer something something something. . . .

Book III
Chapter 1

Help Wanted:
Job Description
for a Network
Administrator

Chapter 2: Security 101

In This Chapter

- ✓ **Assessing the risk for security**
- ✓ **Determining your basic security philosophy**
- ✓ **Physically securing your network equipment**
- ✓ **Figuring out user account security**
- ✓ **Using other network security techniques**

*B*efore you had a network, computer security was easy. You simply locked your door when you left work for the day. You could rest easy, secure in the knowledge that the bad guys would have to break down the door to get to your computer.

The network changes all that. Now, anyone with access to any computer on the network can break into the network and steal *your* files. Not only do you have to lock your door, but you also have to make sure that other people lock their doors, too.

Fortunately, network operating systems have built-in provisions for network security. This situation makes it difficult for someone to steal your files, even if they do break down the door. All modern network operating systems have security features that are more than adequate for all but the most paranoid users.

When I say *more* than adequate, I mean it. Most networks have security features that would make even Maxwell Smart happy. Using all these security features is kind of like Smart insisting that the Chief lower the "Cone of Silence." The Cone of Silence worked so well that Max and the Chief couldn't hear each other! Don't make your system so secure that even the good guys can't get their work done.

If any of the computers on your network are connected to the Internet, you have to contend with a whole new world of security issues. For more information about Internet security, refer to Chapter 4 of this book. Also, if your network supports wireless devices, you have to contend with wireless security issues. For more information about security for wireless networks, see Book V, Chapter 2.

Do You Need Security?

Most small networks are in small businesses or departments where everyone knows and trusts everyone else. Folks don't lock up their desks when they take a coffee break, and although everyone knows where the petty cash box is, money never disappears.

Network security isn't necessary in an idyllic setting like this one, is it? You bet it is. Here's why any network should be set up with at least some minimal concern for security:

✦ Even in the friendliest office environment, some information is and should be confidential. If this information is stored on the network, you want to store it in a directory that's available only to authorized users.

✦ Not all security breaches are malicious. A network user may be routinely scanning through his or her files and come across a filename that isn't familiar. The user may then call up the file, only to discover that it contains confidential personnel information, juicy office gossip, or your résumé. Curiosity, rather than malice, is often the source of security breaches.

✦ Sure, everyone at the office is trustworthy now. However, what if someone becomes disgruntled, a screw pops loose, and he or she decides to trash the network files before jumping out the window? What if someone decides to print a few $1,000 checks before packing off to Tahiti?

✦ Sometimes the mere opportunity for fraud or theft can be too much for some people to resist. Give people free access to the payroll files, and they may decide to vote themselves a raise when no one is looking.

✦ If you think that your network doesn't contain any data that would be worth stealing, think again. For example, your personnel records probably contain more than enough information for an identity thief: names, addresses, phone numbers, social security numbers, and so on. Also, your customer files may contain your customers' credit card numbers.

✦ Hackers who break into your network may not be interested in stealing your data. Instead, they may be looking to plant a *Trojan horse* program on your server, which enables them to use your server for their own purposes. For example, someone may use your server to send thousands of unsolicited spam e-mail messages. The spam won't be traced back to the hackers; it will be traced back to you.

✦ Finally, remember that not everyone on the network knows enough about how Windows and the network work to be trusted with full access to your network's data and systems. One careless mouse click can wipe out an entire directory of network files. One of the best reasons for activating your network's security features is to protect the network from mistakes made by users who don't know what they're doing.

Considering Two Approaches to Security

When you're planning how to implement security on your network, you should first consider which of two basic approaches to security you will take:

✦ **An open-door type of security,** in which you grant everyone access to everything by default and then place restrictions just on those resources to which you want to limit access.

✦ **A closed-door type of security,** in which you begin by denying access to everything and then grant specific users access to the specific resources that they need.

In most cases, the open-door policy is easier to implement. Typically, only a small portion of the data on a network really needs security, such as confidential employee records or secrets such as the Coke recipe. The rest of the information on a network can be safely made available to everyone who can access the network.

If you choose the closed-door approach, you set up each user so that he or she has access to nothing. Then, you grant each user access only to those specific files or folders that he or she needs.

The closed-door approach results in tighter security, but can lead to the Cone of Silence Syndrome: Like Max and the Chief who can't hear each other talk while they're under the Cone of Silence, your network users will constantly complain that they can't access the information that they need. As a result, you'll find yourself frequently adjusting users' access rights. Choose the closed-door approach only if your network contains a lot of information that is very sensitive, and only if you're willing to invest time administrating your network's security policy.

You can think of the open-door approach as an *entitlement model,* in which the basic assumption is that users are entitled to network access. In contrast, the closed-door policy is a *permissions model,* in which the basic assumption is that users aren't entitled to anything but must get permission for every network resource that they access.

Physical Security: Locking Your Doors

The first level of security in any computer network is physical security. I'm amazed when I walk into the reception area of an accounting firm and see an unattended computer sitting on the receptionist's desk. As often as not, the receptionist has logged on to the system and then walked away from the desk, leaving the computer unattended.

Physical security is important for workstations but vital for servers. Any hacker worth his or her salt can quickly defeat all but the most paranoid security measures if he or she can gain physical access to a server. To protect the server, follow these guidelines:

✦ Lock the computer room.

✦ Give the keys only to people you trust.

✦ Keep track of who has the keys.

✦ Mount the servers on cases or racks that have locks.

✦ Disable the floppy drive on the server. (A common hacking technique is to boot the server from a floppy, thus bypassing the carefully crafted security features of the network operating system.)

✦ Keep a trained guard dog in the computer room and feed it only enough to keep it hungry and mad. (Just kidding.)

There's a big difference between a locked door and a door with a lock. Locks are worthless if you don't use them.

Client computers should be physically secure as well. You should instruct users to not leave their computers unattended while they're logged on. In high-traffic areas (such as the receptionist's desk), users should secure their computers with the keylock. Additionally, users should lock their office doors when they leave.

Here are some other potential threats to physical security that you may not have considered:

✦ The nightly cleaning crew probably has complete access to your facility. How do you know that the person who vacuums your office every night doesn't really work for your chief competitor or doesn't consider computer hacking to be a sideline hobby? You don't, so you'd better consider the cleaning crew a threat.

✦ What about your trash? Paper shredders aren't just for Enron accountants. Your trash can contain all sorts of useful information: sales reports, security logs, printed copies of the company's security policy, even handwritten passwords. For the best security, every piece of paper that leaves your building via the trash bin should first go through a shredder.

✦ Where do you store your backup tapes? Don't just stack them up next to the server. Not only does that make them easy to steal, it also defeats one of the main purposes of backing up your data in the first place: securing your server from physical threats, such as fires. If a fire burns down your computer room and the backup tapes are sitting unprotected next to the server, your company may go out of business — and you'll certainly be out of a job. Store the backup tapes securely in a fireproof safe and keep a copy off-site, too.

✦ I've seen some networks in which the servers are in a locked computer room, but the hubs or switches are in an unsecured closet. Remember that every unused port on a hub or a switch represents an open door to your network. The hubs and switches should be secured just like the servers.

Securing User Accounts

Next to physical security, the careful use of user accounts is the most important type of security for your network. Properly configured user accounts can prevent unauthorized users from accessing the network, even if they gain physical access to the network. The following sections describe some of the steps that you can take to strengthen your network's use of user accounts.

Obfuscating your usernames

Huh? When it comes to security, *obfuscation* simply means picking obscure usernames. For example, most network administrators assign usernames based on some combination of the user's first and last name, such as BarnyM or baMiller. However, a hacker can easily guess such a user ID if he or she knows the name of at least one employee. After the hacker knows a username, he or she can focus on breaking the password.

You can slow down a hacker by using names that are more obscure. Here are some suggestions on how to do that:

✦ Add a random three-digit number to the end of the name. For example: BarnyM320 or baMiller977.

✦ Throw a number or two into the middle of the name. For example: Bar6nyM or ba9Miller2.

✦ Make sure that usernames are different from e-mail addresses. For example, if a user's e-mail address is baMiller@Mydomain.com, do *not* use baMiller as the user's account name. Use a more obscure name.

Do *not* rely on obfuscation to keep people out of your network! Security by obfuscation doesn't work. A resourceful hacker can discover even the most obscure names. The purpose of obfuscation is to slow intruders down — not to stop them. If you slow an intruder down, you're more likely to discover that he or she is trying to crack your network before he or she successfully gets in.

Using passwords wisely

One of the most important aspects of network security is the use of passwords. Usernames aren't usually considered secret. Even if you use obscure names, casual hackers will eventually figure them out.

Passwords, on the other hand, are top secret. Your network password is the one thing that keeps an impostor from logging on to the network by using your username and therefore receiving the same access rights that you ordinarily have. *Guard your password with your life.*

Here are some tips for creating good passwords:

✦ Don't use obvious passwords, such as your last name, your kid's name, or your dog's name.

✦ Don't pick passwords based on your hobbies, either. A friend of mine is into boating, and his password is the name of his boat. Anyone who knows him can guess his password after a few tries. Five lashes for naming your password after your boat.

✦ Store your password in your head — not on paper. Especially bad: Writing down your password on a sticky note and sticking it on your computer's monitor. Ten lashes for that. (If you must write down your password, write it on digestible paper that you can swallow after you've memorized the password.)

✦ Most network operating systems enable you to set an expiration time for passwords. For example, you can specify that passwords expire after 30 days. When a user's password expires, the user must change it. Your users may consider this process a hassle, but it helps to limit the risk of someone swiping a password and then trying to break into your computer system later.

✦ You can also configure user accounts so that when they change passwords, they can't specify a password that they've used recently. For example, you can specify that the new password can't be identical to any of the user's past three passwords.

✦ You can also configure security policies so that passwords must include a mixture of uppercase letters, lowercase letters, numerals, and special symbols. Thus, passwords like DIMWIT or DUFUS are out. Passwords like 87dIM@wit or duF39&US are in.

✦ One of the newest trends is the use of devices that read fingerprints as a way to keep passwords. These devices store your passwords in a secret encoded file, then supply them automatically to whatever programs or Web sites require them — but only after the device has read your fingerprint. Fingerprint readers used to be exotic and expensive, but you can now add a fingerprint reader to a computer for as little as $50.

A Password Generator For Dummies

How do you come up with passwords that no one can guess but that you can remember? Most security experts say that the best passwords don't correspond to any words in the English language, but they consist of a random sequence of letters, numbers, and special characters. Yet, how in the heck are you supposed to memorize a password like Dks4%DJ2? Especially when you have to change it three weeks later to something like 3pQ&X(d8.

Here's a compromise solution that enables you to create passwords that consist of two four-letter words back to back. Take your favorite book (if it's this one, you need to get a life) and turn to any page at random. Find the first four- or five-letter word on the page. Suppose that word is When. Then repeat the process to find another four- or five-letter word; say you pick the word Most the second time. Now combine the words to make your password: WhenMost. I think you agree that WhenMost is easier to remember than 3PQ&X(D8 and is probably just about as hard to guess. I probably wouldn't want the folks at the Los Alamos Nuclear Laboratory using this scheme, but it's good enough for most of us.

Here are some additional thoughts on concocting passwords from your favorite book:

- ✦ If the words end up being the same, pick another word. And pick different words if the combination seems too commonplace, such as WestWind or FootBall.

- ✦ For an interesting variation, insert a couple of numerals or special characters between the words. You end up with passwords like into#cat, ball3%and, or tree47wing.

- ✦ To further confuse your friends and enemies, use medieval passwords by picking words from Chaucer's *Canterbury Tales*. Chaucer is a great source for passwords because he lived before the days of word processors with spell-checkers. He wrote *seyd* instead of *said, gret* instead of *great, welk* instead of *walked, litel* instead of *little.* And he used lots of seven-letter and eight-letter words suitable for passwords, such as *glotenye* (gluttony), *benygne* (benign), and *opynyoun* (opinion). And he got As in English.

- ✦ If you use any of these password schemes and someone breaks into your network, don't blame me. You're the one who's too lazy to memorize D#Sc$h4@bb3xaz5.

✦ If you do decide to go with passwords such as KdI22UR3xdkL, you can find random password generators on the Internet. Just go to a search engine, such as Google (www.google.com), and search for *password generator*. You can find Web pages that generate random passwords based on criteria that you specify, such as how long the password should be, whether it should include letters, numbers, punctuation, uppercase and lowercase letters, and so on.

Securing the Administrator account

It stands to reason that at least one network user must have the authority to use the network without any of the restrictions imposed on other users. This user is called the *administrator*. The administrator is responsible for setting up the network's security system. To do that, the administrator must be exempt from all security restrictions.

Many networks automatically create an administrator user account when you install the network software. The username and password for this initial administrator are published in the network's documentation and are the same for all networks that use the same network operating system. One of the first things that you must do after getting your network up and running is to change the password for this standard administrator account. Otherwise, your elaborate security precautions will be a complete waste of time. Anyone who knows the default administrator username and password can access your system with full administrator rights and privileges, thus bypassing the security restrictions that you so carefully set up.

Don't forget the password for the administrator account! If a network user forgets his or her password, you can log in as the supervisor and change that user's password. If you forget the administrator's password, though, you're stuck.

Hardening Your Network

In addition to taking care of physical security and user account security, you should also take steps to protect your network from intruders by configuring the other security features of the network's servers and routers. The following sections describe the basics of hardening your network.

Using a firewall

A *firewall* is a security-conscious router that sits between your network and the outside world and prevents Internet users from wandering into your LAN and messing around. Firewalls are the first line of defense for any network that's connected to the Internet. You should *never* connect a network to the Internet without installing a carefully configured firewall. For more information about firewalls, refer to Chapter 4 of this book.

Disabling unnecessary services

A typical network operating system can support dozens of different types of network services: file and printer sharing, Web server, mail server, and many others. In many cases, these features are installed on servers that don't need or use them. When a server runs a network service that it doesn't really need, the service not only robs CPU cycles from other services that are needed, but also poses an unnecessary security threat.

When you first install a network operating system on a server, you should enable only those network services that you know the server will require. You can always enable services later if the needs of the server change.

Patching your servers

Hackers regularly find security holes in network operating systems. After those holes are discovered, the operating system vendors figure out how to plug the hole and release a software patch for the security fix. The trouble is that most network administrators don't stay up to date with these software patches. As a result, many networks are vulnerable because they have well-known holes in their security armor that should have been fixed but weren't.

Even though patches are a bit of a nuisance, they're well worth the effort for the protection that they afford. Fortunately, newer versions of the popular network operating systems have features that automatically check for updates and let you know when a patch should be applied.

Securing Your Users

Security techniques, such as physical security, user account security, server security, and locking down your servers, are child's play compared to the most difficult job of network security: securing your network's users. All the best-laid security plans will go for naught if your users write down their passwords on sticky notes and post them on their computers.

The key to securing your network users is to create a written network security policy and stick to it. Have a meeting with everyone to go over the security policy to make sure that everyone understands the rules. Also, make sure to have consequences when violations occur.

**Book III
Chapter 2**

Security 101

Here are some suggestions for some basic security rules you can incorporate into your security policy:

✦ Never write down your password or give it to someone else.

✦ Accounts should not be shared. Never use someone else's account to access a resource that you can't access under your own account. If you need access to some network resource that isn't available to you, you should formally request access under your own account.

✦ Likewise, never give your account information to a coworker so that he or she can access a needed resource. Your coworker should instead formally request access under his or her own account.

✦ Don't install any software or hardware on your computer — especially wireless access devices or modems — without first obtaining permission.

✦ Don't enable file and printer sharing on workstations without first getting permission.

✦ Never attempt to disable or bypass the network's security features.

Chapter 3: Managing User Accounts

In This Chapter

✔ Understanding user accounts

✔ Looking at the built-in accounts

✔ Using rights and permissions

✔ Working with groups and policies

✔ Running login scripts

*U*ser accounts are the backbone of network security administration. Through the use of user accounts, you can determine who can access your network, as well as what network resources each user can and can't access. You can restrict access to the network to just specific computers or to certain hours of the day. In addition, you can lock out users who no longer need to access your network.

The specific details for managing user accounts are unique to each network operating system and are covered in separate chapters later in this book. The purpose of this chapter is simply to introduce you to the concepts of user account management, so you know what you can and can't do, regardless of which network operating system you use.

Exploring What User Accounts Consist Of

Every user who accesses a network must have a *user account*. User accounts allow the network administrator to determine who can access the network and what network resources each user can access. In addition, the user account can be customized to provide many convenience features for users, such as a personalized Start menu or a display of recently used documents.

Every user account is associated with a *username* (sometimes called a *user ID*), which the user must enter when logging on to the network. Each account also has other information associated with it. In particular:

✦ **The user's password:** This also includes the password policy, such as how often the user has to change his or her password, how complicated the password must be, and so on.

✦ **The user's contact information:** This includes full name, phone number, e-mail address, mailing address, and other related information.

✦ **Account restrictions:** This includes restrictions that allow the user to log on only during certain times of the day. This feature enables you to restrict your users to normal working hours so that they can't sneak in at 2 a.m. to do unauthorized work. This feature also discourages your users from working overtime because they can't access the network after hours, so use it judiciously. You can also specify that the user can log on only at certain computers.

✦ **Account status:** You can temporarily disable a user account so that the user can't log on.

✦ **Home directory:** This specifies a shared network folder where the user can store documents.

✦ **Dial-in permissions:** These authorize the user to access the network remotely via a dialup connection.

✦ **Group memberships:** These grant the user certain rights based on groups to which they belong. For more information, see the section, "Assigning Permissions to Groups," later in this chapter.

Looking at Built-In Accounts

Most network operating systems come preconfigured with two built-in accounts, named *Administrator* and *Guest.* In addition, some server services, such as Web or database servers, create their own user accounts under which to run. The following sections describe the characteristics of these accounts.

The Administrator account

The Administrator account is the King of the Network. This user account isn't subject to any of the account restrictions to which other, mere mortal accounts must succumb. If you log on as the administrator, you can do anything.

Because the Administrator account has unlimited access to your network, it's imperative that you secure it immediately after you install the server. When the NOS Setup program asks for a password for the Administrator account, start off with a good random mix of uppercase and lowercase letters, numbers, and symbols. Don't pick some easy-to-remember password to get started, thinking you'll change it to something more cryptic later. You'll forget, and in the meantime, someone will break in and reformat the server's C: drive or steal your customers' credit card numbers.

Here are a few additional things worth knowing about the Administrator account:

✦ You can't delete it. The system must always have an administrator.

✦ You can grant administrator status to other user accounts. However, you should do so only for users who really need to be administrators.

✦ You should use it only when you really need to do tasks that require administrative authority. Many network administrators grant administrative authority to their own user accounts. That isn't a very good idea. If you're killing some time surfing the Web or reading your e-mail while logged on as an administrator, you're just inviting viruses or malicious scripts to take advantage of your administrator access. Instead, you should set yourself up with two accounts: a normal account that you use for day-to-day work, and an Administrator account that you use only when you need it.

✦ The default name for the Administrator account is usually simply Administrator. You may want to consider changing this name. Better yet, change the name of the Administrator account to something more obscure and then create an ordinary user account that has few — if any — rights and give that account the name Administrator. That way, hackers who spend weeks trying to crack your Administrator account password will discover that they've been duped, once they finally break the password. In the meantime, you'll have a chance to discover their attempts to breach your security and take appropriate action.

✦ Above all, don't forget the Administrator account password. Write it down in permanent ink and store it in Fort Knox, a safe deposit box, or some other secure location.

The Guest account

Another commonly created default account is called the *Guest account*. This account is set up with a blank password and few — if any — access rights. The Guest account is designed to allow anyone to step up to a computer and log on, but after they do, it then prevents them from doing anything. Sounds like a waste of time to me. I suggest you disable the Guest account.

Service accounts

Some network users aren't actual people. I don't mean that some of your users are subhuman. Rather, some users are actually software processors that require access to secure resources and therefore require user accounts. These user accounts are usually created automatically for you when you install or configure server software.

For example, when you install Microsoft's Web server (IIS), an Internet user account called IUSR is created. The complete name for this account is IUSR_ <*servername*>. So if the server is named WEB1, the account is named IUSR_WEB1. IIS uses this account to allow anonymous Internet users to access the files of your Web site.

As a general rule, you shouldn't mess with these accounts unless you know what you're doing. For example, if you delete or rename the IUSR account, you must reconfigure IIS to use the changed account. If you don't, IIS will deny access to anyone trying to reach your site. (Assuming that you *do* know what you're doing, renaming these accounts can increase your network's security. However, don't start playing with these accounts until you've researched the ramifications.)

Assigning User Rights

User accounts and passwords are only the front line of defense in the game of network security. After a user gains access to the network by typing a valid user ID and password, the second line of security defense — rights — comes into play.

In the harsh realities of network life, all users are created equal, but some users are more equal than others. The Preamble to the Declaration of Network Independence contains the statement, "We hold these truths to be self-evident, that *some* users are endowed by the network administrator with certain inalienable rights. . . ."

The specific rights that you can assign to network users depend on which network operating system you use. Here is a partial list of the user rights that are possible with Windows servers:

✦ **Log on locally:** The user can log on to the server computer directly from the server's keyboard.

✦ **Change system time:** The user can change the time and date registered by the server.

✦ **Shut down the system:** The user can perform an orderly shutdown of the server.

✦ **Back up files and directories:** The user can perform a backup of files and directories on the server.

✦ **Restore files and directories:** The user can restore backed-up files.

✦ **Take ownership of files and other objects:** The user can take over files and other network resources that belong to other users.

Controlling User Access with Permissions (Who Gets What)

User rights control what a user can do on a network-wide basis. *Permissions* enable you to fine-tune your network security by controlling access to specific network resources, such as files or printers, for individual users or groups. For example, you can set up permissions to allow users in the accounting department to access files in the server's \ACCTG directory. Permissions can also enable some users to read certain files but not modify or delete them.

Each network operating system manages permissions in a different way. Whatever the details, the effect is that you can give permission to each user to access certain files, folders, or drives in certain ways.

Any permissions that you specify for a folder apply automatically to any of that folder's subfolders, unless you explicitly specify a different set of permissions for the subfolder.

Windows refers to file system rights as *permissions.* Windows servers have six basic permissions, listed in Table 3-1. As with NetWare trustee rights, you can assign any combination of Windows permissions to a user or group for a given file or folder.

Table 3-1	Windows Basic Permissions	
Permission	*Abbreviation*	*What the User Can Do*
Read	R	The user can open and read the file.
Write	W	The user can open and write to the file.
Execute	X	The user can run the file.
Delete	D	The user can delete the file.
Change	P	The user can change the permissions for the file.
Take Ownership	0	The user can take ownership of the file.

Note the last permission listed in Table 3-1. In Windows, the concept of file or folder ownership is important. Every file or folder on a Windows server system has an owner. The *owner* is usually the user who creates the file or folder. However, ownership can be transferred from one user to another. So why the Take Ownership permission? This permission prevents someone from creating a bogus file and giving ownership of it to you without your permission. Windows doesn't allow you to give ownership of a file to another user. Instead, you can give another user the right to take ownership of the file. That user must then explicitly take ownership of the file.

You can use Windows permissions only for files or folders that are created on drives formatted as NTFS volumes. If you insist on using FAT or FAT32 for your Windows shared drives, you can't protect individual files or folders on the drives. This is one of the main reasons for using NTFS for your Windows servers.

Assigning Permissions to Groups

A *group account* is an account that doesn't represent an individual user. Instead, it represents a group of users who use the network in a similar way. Instead of granting access rights to each of these users individually, you can grant the rights to the group and then assign individual users to the group. When you assign a user to a group, that user inherits the rights specified for the group.

For example, suppose that you create a group named Accounting for the accounting staff and then allow members of the Accounting group access to the network's accounting files and applications. Then, instead of granting each accounting user access to those files and applications, you simply make each accounting user a member of the Accounting group.

Here are a few additional details about groups:

✦ Groups a key to network-management nirvana. As much as possible, you should avoid managing network users individually. Instead, clump them into groups and manage the groups. When all 50 users in the accounting department need access to a new file share, would you rather update 50 user accounts or just one group account?

✦ A user can belong to more than one group. Then, the user inherits the rights of each group. For example, suppose that you have groups set up for Accounting, Sales, Marketing, and Finance. A user who needs to access both Accounting and Finance information can be made a member of both the Accounting and Finance groups. Likewise, a user who needs access to both Sales and Marketing information can be made a member of both the Sales and Marketing groups.

✦ You can grant or revoke specific rights to individual users to override the group settings. For example, you may grant a few extra permissions for the manager of the Accounting department. You may also impose a few extra restrictions on certain users.

Understanding User Profiles

A *user profile* is a Windows feature that keeps track of an individual user's preferences for his or her Windows configuration. For a non-networked computer, profiles enable two or more users to use the same computer, each with his or her own desktop settings, such as wallpaper, colors, Start menu options, and so on.

The real benefit of user profiles becomes apparent when profiles are used on a network. A user's profile can be stored on a server computer and accessed whenever that user logs on to the network from any Windows computer on the network.

The following are some of the elements of Windows that are governed by settings in the user profile:

✦ Desktop settings from the Display Properties dialog box, including wallpaper, screen savers, and color schemes.

✦ Start menu programs and Windows toolbar options.

✦ Favorites, which provide easy access to the files and folders that the user accesses frequently.

✦ Network settings, including drive mappings, network printers, and recently visited network locations.

✦ Application settings, such as option settings for Microsoft Word.

✦ The My Documents folder.

Automating Tasks with Logon Scripts

A *logon script* is a batch file that runs automatically whenever a user logs on. Logon scripts can perform several important logon tasks for you, such as mapping network drives, starting applications, synchronizing the client computer's time-of-day clock, and so on. Logon scripts reside on the server. Each user account can specify whether to use a logon script and which script to use.

Here's a sample logon script that maps a few network drives and synchronizes the time:

```
net use m: \\MYSERVER\Acct
net use n: \\MYSERVER\Admin
net use o: \\MYSERVER\Dev
net time \\MYSERVER /set /yes
```

Logon scripts are a little out of vogue because most of what a logon script does can be done via user profiles. Still, many administrators prefer the simplicity of logon scripts, so they're still used even on Windows Server 2003 and 2008 systems.

Chapter 4: Firewalls and Virus Protection

In This Chapter

✔ **Understanding what firewalls do**

✔ **Examining the different types of firewalls**

✔ **Looking at virus protection**

✔ **Discovering Windows XP and Vista security**

I f your network is connected to the Internet, a whole host of security issues bubble to the surface. You probably connected your network to the Internet so that your network's users could access the Internet. Unfortunately, however, your Internet connection is a two-way street. Not only does it enable your network's users to step outside the bounds of your network to access the Internet, but it also enables others to step in and access your network.

And step in they will. The world is filled with hackers looking for networks like yours to break into. They may do it just for fun, or they may do it to steal your customer's credit card numbers or to coerce your mail server into sending thousands of spam messages on their behalf. Whatever their motive, rest assured that your network will be broken into if you leave it unprotected.

This chapter presents an overview of two basic techniques for securing your network's Internet connection: firewalls and virus protection.

Firewalls

A *firewall* is a security-conscious router that sits between the Internet and your network with a single-minded task: preventing *them* from getting to *us*. The firewall acts as a security guard between the Internet and your local area network (LAN). All network traffic into and out of the LAN must pass through the firewall, which prevents unauthorized access to the network.

Some type of firewall is a must-have if your network has a connection to the Internet, whether that connection is broadband (cable modem or digital subscriber line; DSL), T1, or some other high-speed connection. Without it, sooner or later a hacker will discover your unprotected network and tell his friends about it. Within a few hours, your network will be toast.

You can set up a firewall two basic ways. The easiest way is to purchase a *firewall appliance,* which is basically a self-contained router with built-in firewall features. Most firewall appliances include a Web-based interface that enables you to connect to the firewall from any computer on your network using a browser. You can then customize the firewall settings to suit your needs.

Alternatively, you can set up a server computer to function as a firewall computer. The server can run just about any network operating system, but most dedicated firewall systems run Linux.

Whether you use a firewall appliance or a firewall computer, the firewall must be located between your network and the Internet, as shown in Figure 4-1. Here, one end of the firewall is connected to a network hub, which is in turn connected to the other computers on the network. The other end of the firewall is connected to the Internet. As a result, all traffic from the LAN to the Internet and vice versa must travel through the firewall.

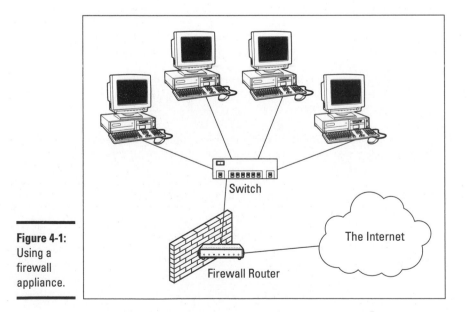

Figure 4-1:
Using a
firewall
appliance.

Switch

The Internet

Firewall Router

The term *perimeter* is sometimes used to describe the location of a firewall on your network. In short, a firewall is like a perimeter fence that completely surrounds your property and forces all visitors to enter through the front gate.

The Many Types of Firewalls

Firewalls employ four basic techniques to keep unwelcome visitors out of your network. The following sections describe these basic firewall techniques.

Packet filtering

A *packet-filtering* firewall examines each packet that crosses the firewall and tests the packet according to a set of rules that you set up. If the packet passes the test, it's allowed to pass. If the packet doesn't pass, it's rejected.

Packet filters are the least expensive type of firewall. As a result, packet-filtering firewalls are very common. However, packet filtering has a number of flaws that knowledgeable hackers can exploit. As a result, packet filtering by itself doesn't make for a fully effective firewall.

Packet filters work by inspecting the source and destination IP and port addresses contained in each Transmission Control Protocol/Internet Protocol (TCP/IP) packet. TCP/IP *ports* are numbers that are assigned to specific services that help to identify for which service each packet is intended. For example, the port number for the HTTP protocol is 80. As a result, any incoming packets headed for an HTTP server will specify port 80 as the destination port.

Port numbers are often specified with a colon following an IP address. For example, the HTTP service on a server whose IP address is 192.168.10.133 would be 192.168.10.133:80.

Literally thousands of established ports are in use. Table 4-1 lists a few of the most popular ports.

Table 4-1	Some Well-Known TCP/IP Ports
Port	**Description**
20	File Transfer Protocol (FTP)
21	File Transfer Protocol (FTP)
22	Secure Shell Protocol (SSH)
23	Telnet
25	Simple Mail Transfer Protocol (SMTP)
53	Domain Name Server (DNS)

(continued)

**Book III
Chapter 4**

Firewalls and Virus
Protection

Table 4-1 *(continued)*

Port	Description
80	World Wide Web (HyperText Transport Protocol; HTTP)
110	Post Office Protocol (POP3)
119	Network News Transfer Protocol (NNTP)
137	NetBIOS Name Service
138	NetBIOS Datagram Service
139	NetBIOS Session Service
143	Internet Message Access Protocol (IMAP)
161	Simple Network Management Protocol (SNMP)
194	Internet Relay Chat (IRC)
389	Lightweight Directory Access Protocol (LDAP)
396	NetWare over IP
443	HTTP over TLS/SSL (HTTPS)

The rules that you set up for the packet filter either permit or deny packets that specify certain IP addresses or ports. For example, you may permit packets that are intended for your mail server or your Web server and deny all other packets. Or, you may set up a rule that specifically denies packets that are heading for the ports used by NetBIOS. This rule keeps Internet hackers from trying to access NetBIOS server resources, such as files or printers.

One of the biggest weaknesses of packet filtering is that it pretty much trusts that the packets themselves are telling the truth when they say who they're from and who they're going to. Hackers exploit this weakness by using a hacking technique called *IP spoofing,* in which they insert fake IP addresses in packets that they send to your network.

Another weakness of packet filtering is that it examines each packet in isolation without considering what packets have gone through the firewall before and what packets may follow. In other words, packet filtering is *stateless.* Rest assured that hackers have figured out how to exploit the stateless nature of packet filtering to get through firewalls.

In spite of these weaknesses, packet filter firewalls have several advantages that explain why they are commonly used:

✦ **Packet filters are very efficient.** They hold up each inbound and out-bound packet for only a few milliseconds while they look inside the packet to determine the destination and source ports and addresses. After these addresses and ports are determined, the packet filter quickly applies its rules and either sends the packet along or rejects it. In contrast, other firewall techniques have a more noticeable performance overhead.

✦ **Packet filters are almost completely transparent to users.** The only time a user will be aware that a packet filter firewall is being used is when the firewall rejects packets. Other firewall techniques require that clients and/or servers be specially configured to work with the firewall.

✦ **Packet filters are inexpensive.** Most routers include built-in packet filtering.

Stateful packet inspection (SPI)

Stateful packet inspection, also known as *SPI,* is a step up in intelligence from simple packet filtering. A firewall with stateful packet inspection looks at packets in groups rather than individually. It keeps track of which packets have passed through the firewall and can detect patterns that indicate unauthorized access. In some cases, the firewall may hold on to packets as they arrive until the firewall gathers enough information to make a decision about whether the packets should be authorized or rejected.

Stateful packet inspection was once found only on expensive, enterprise-level routers. Now, however, SPI firewalls are affordable enough for small- or medium-sized networks to use.

Circuit-level gateway

A *circuit-level gateway* manages connections between clients and servers based on TCP/IP addresses and port numbers. After the connection is established, the gateway doesn't interfere with packets flowing between the systems.

For example, you could use a Telnet circuit-level gateway to allow Telnet connections (port 23) to a particular server and prohibit other types of connections to that server. After the connection is established, the circuit-level gateway allows packets to flow freely over the connection. As a result, the circuit-level gateway can't prevent a Telnet user from running specific programs or using specific commands.

Application gateway

An *application gateway* is a firewall system that is more intelligent than a packet-filtering, stateful packet inspection, or circuit-level gateway firewall. Packet filters treat all TCP/IP packets the same. In contrast, application gateways know the details about the applications that generate the packets that pass through the firewall. For example, a Web application gateway is aware of the details of HTTP packets. As a result, it can examine more than just the source and destination addresses and ports to determine whether the packets should be allowed to pass through the firewall.

In addition, application gateways work as proxy servers. Simply put, a *proxy server* is a server that sits between a client computer and a real server. The proxy server intercepts packets that are intended for the real server and processes them. The proxy server can examine the packet and decide to pass it on to the real server, or it can reject the packet. Or, the proxy server may be able to respond to the packet itself without involving the real server at all.

For example, Web proxies often store copies of commonly used Web pages in a local cache. When a user requests a Web page from a remote Web server, the proxy server intercepts the request and checks whether it already has a copy of the page in its cache. If so, the Web proxy returns the page directly to the user. If not, the proxy passes the request on to the real server.

Application gateways are aware of the details of how various types of TCP/IP servers handle sequences of TCP/IP packets to can make more intelligent decisions about whether an incoming packet is legitimate or is part of an attack. As a result, application gateways are more secure than simple packet-filtering firewalls, which can deal with only one packet at a time.

The improved security of application gateways, however, comes at a price. Application gateways are more expensive than packet filters, both in terms of their purchase price and in the cost of configuring and maintaining them. In addition, application gateways slow network performance because they do more detailed checking of packets before allowing them to pass.

The Built-In Windows Firewall

Windows comes with a built-in packet-filtering firewall. If you don't have a separate firewall router, you can use this built-in firewall to provide a basic level of protection. Here are the steps to activate this feature in Windows Vista:

1. **Choose Start⇨Control Panel.**

Control Panel appears.

Windows Firewall

2. **Double-click the Windows Firewall icon (shown in the margin).**

The dialog box shown in Figure 4-2 appears. This dialog box indicates the current status of the Windows Firewall. If Firewall is already turned on, you can skip the rest of this procedure.

3. **Click the Change Settings link.**

The dialog box shown in Figure 4-3 appears.

4. **Select the On (Recommended) option.**

This option enables Firewall.

5. **Click OK.**

That's all there is to it.

Figure 4-2:
Checking
the status of
Windows
Firewall.

Figure 4-3:
Activating
the
Windows
Firewall.

Do *not* enable Windows Firewall if you're using a separate firewall router to protect your network. Because the other computers on the network are connected directly to the router and not to your computer, Firewall won't protect the rest of the network. Additionally, as an unwanted side effect, the rest of the network will lose the ability to access your computer.

With Windows Vista as well as Windows XP Service Pack 2, Windows Firewall is turned on by default. If your computer is already behind a firewall, you need to disable Windows Firewall. (In some cases, the network's group policy settings may prevent you from disabling Firewall. In that case, you must change the group policy so that Firewall can be disabled. For more information about group policy, see Book VII, Chapter 6.)

Virus Protection

Viruses are one of the most misunderstood computer phenomena around these days. What is a virus? How does it work? How does it spread from computer to computer? I'm glad you asked.

What is a virus?

Make no mistake — viruses are real. Now that most people are connected to the Internet, viruses have really taken off. Every computer user is susceptible to attacks by computer viruses, and using a network increases your vulnerability because it exposes all network users to the risk of being infected by a virus that lands on any one network user's computer.

Viruses don't just spontaneously appear out of nowhere. Viruses are computer programs that are created by malicious programmers who've lost a few screws and should be locked up.

What makes a virus a virus is its capability to make copies of itself that can be spread to other computers. These copies, in turn, make still more copies that spread to still more computers, and so on, ad nauseam.

Then, the virus patiently waits until something triggers it — perhaps when you type a particular command or press a certain key, when a certain date arrives, or when the virus creator sends the virus a message. What the virus does when it strikes also depends on what the virus creator wants the virus to do. Some viruses harmlessly display a "gotcha" message. Some send e-mail to everyone it finds in your address book. Some wipe out all the data on your hard drive. Ouch.

A few years back, viruses moved from one computer to another by latching themselves onto floppy disks. Whenever you borrowed a floppy disk from a buddy, you ran the risk of infecting your own computer with a virus that may have stowed away on the disk.

Virus programmers have discovered that e-mail is a very efficient method to spread their viruses. Typically, a virus masquerades as a useful or interesting e-mail attachment, such as instructions on how to make $1,000,000 in your spare time, pictures of naked celebrities, or a Valentine's Day greeting from your long-lost sweetheart. When a curious but unsuspecting user double-clicks the attachment, the virus springs to life, copying itself onto the user's computer — and, in some cases, sending copies of itself to all the names in the user's address book.

After the virus works its way onto a networked computer, the virus can then figure out how to spread itself to other computers on the network.

Here are some more tidbits about protecting your network from virus attacks:

✦ The term *virus* is often used to refer not only to true virus programs (which are able to replicate themselves) but also to any other type of program that's designed to harm your computer. These programs include so-called *Trojan horse* programs that usually look like games but are, in reality, hard drive formatters.

✦ A *worm* is similar to a virus, but it doesn't actually infect other files. Instead, it just copies itself onto other computers on a network. After a worm has copied itself onto your computer, there's no telling what it may do there. For example, a worm may scan your hard drive for interesting information, such as passwords or credit card numbers, and then e-mail them to the worm's author.

✦ Computer virus experts have identified several thousand "strains" of viruses. Many of them have colorful names, such as the I Love You virus, the Stoned virus, and the Michelangelo virus.

✦ Antivirus programs can recognize known viruses and remove them from your system, and they can spot the telltale signs of unknown viruses. Unfortunately, the idiots who write viruses aren't idiots (in the intellectual sense), so they're constantly developing new techniques to evade detection by antivirus programs. New viruses are frequently discovered, and antivirus programs are periodically updated to detect and remove them.

Antivirus programs

The best way to protect your network from virus infection is to use an antivirus program. These programs have a catalog of several thousand known viruses that they can detect and remove. In addition, they can spot

**Book III
Chapter 4**

Firewalls and Virus Protection

the types of changes that viruses typically make to your computer's files, thus decreasing the likelihood that some previously unknown virus will go undetected.

It would be nice if Windows came with built-in antivirus software, but alas — it does not. You have to purchase a program on your own. The two best-known antivirus programs for Windows are Norton AntiVirus by Symantec and VirusScan by McAfee.

The people who make antivirus programs have their fingers on the pulse of the virus world and frequently release updates to their software to combat the latest viruses. Because virus writers are constantly developing new viruses, your antivirus software is next to worthless unless you keep it up to date by downloading the latest updates.

Here several approaches to deploying antivirus protection on your network:

✦ **Install antivirus software on each network user's computer.** This technique would be the most effective if you could count on all your users to keep their antivirus software up to date. Because that's an unlikely proposition, you may want to adopt a more reliable approach to virus protection.

✦ **Managed antivirus services place antivirus client software on each client computer in your network.** Then, an antivirus server automatically updates the clients on a regular basis to make sure that they're kept up to date.

✦ **Server-based antivirus software protects your network servers from viruses.** For example, you can install antivirus software on your mail server to scan all incoming mail for viruses and remove them before your network users ever see them.

✦ **Some firewall appliances include antivirus enforcement checks that don't allow your users to access the Internet unless their antivirus software is up to date.** This type of firewall provides the best antivirus protection available.

Safe computing

Besides using an antivirus program, you can take a few additional precautions to ensure virus-free computing. If you haven't talked to your kids about these safe-computing practices, you had better do so soon.

✦ **Regularly back up your data.** If a virus hits you and your antivirus software can't repair the damage, you may need the backup to recover your data. Make sure that you restore from a backup that was created before you were infected by the virus!

✦ **If you buy software from a store and discover that the seal has been broken on the disk package, take the software back.** Don't try to install it on your computer. You don't hear about tainted software as often as you hear about tainted beef, but if you buy software that's been opened, it may well be laced with a virus infection.

✦ **Use your antivirus software to scan your disk for virus infection after your computer has been to a repair shop or worked on by a consultant.** These guys don't intend harm, but they occasionally spread viruses accidentally, simply because they work on so many strange computers.

✦ **Don't open e-mail attachments from people you don't know or attachments you weren't expecting.**

✦ **Use your antivirus software to scan any floppy disk or CD that doesn't belong to you before you access any of its files.**

Using Windows Security Center

Both Windows Vista and Windows XP (beginning with Security Pack 2) include the new Security Center feature. As shown in Figure 4-4, Security Center monitors the status of your computer's security features. You can view Security Center by clicking its icon in the notification area of the Windows task bar, as shown in the margin. Or, you can summon it by clicking the Security Center icon in Control Panel.

Figure 4-4:
The Windows Vista Security Center.

Security Center monitors several aspects of your computer's security configuration:

✦ **Firewall:** Determines whether Windows Firewall or some other firewall has been enabled. Security Center can detect popular third-party firewall software. However, it can't determine whether your computer is behind a separate firewall router. If Security Center keeps warning you that you're not using a firewall when you know you are, click the Change the Way Security Center Alerts Me link in the Security Center window, and then clear the Firewall check box from the dialog box that appears.

✦ **Automatic Updating:** Ensures that the Windows Automatic Updates feature is activated so the latest security patches will be automatically downloaded.

✦ **Malware Protection:** Indicates whether you have an antivirus program installed and/or antispyware program installed and running.

Chapter 5: Managing Network Software

In This Chapter

✔ **Understanding the types of software licenses**

✔ **Using license servers**

✔ **Exploring the deployment options**

✔ **Keeping up to date with patches and service packs**

*A*n important task of any network administrator is managing all the various bits and pieces of software that are used by your users throughout the network. Most, if not all, of your network users will have a version of Microsoft Office installed on their computers. Depending on the type of business, other software may be widely used. For example, accounting firms require accounting software; engineering firms require engineering software; and the list goes on.

Long gone are the days when you could purchase one copy of a computer program and freely install it on every computer on your network. Most software has built-in features — commonly called copy protection — designed to prevent such abuse. But even in the absence of copy protection, nearly all software is sold with a license agreement that dictates how many computers you can install and use the software on. As a result, managing software licenses is an important part of network management.

Some software programs have a license feature that uses a server computer to regulate the number of users who can run the software at the same time. As the network administrator, your job is to set up the license server and keep it running.

Another important aspect of managing software on the network is figuring out the most expedient way to install the software on multiple computers. The last thing you want to do is manually run the software's Setup program individually on each computer in your network. Instead, you'll want to use the network itself to aid in the deployment of the software.

Finally, you'll want to ensure that all of the software programs installed throughout your network are kept up to date with the latest patches and updates from the software vendors.

This chapter elaborates on these aspects of network software management.

Understanding Software Licenses

Contrary to popular belief, you don't really buy software. Instead, you buy the right to use the software. When you purchase a computer program at a store, all you really own after you complete the purchase is the box the software comes in, the disks/discs the software is recorded on, and a *license* that grants you the right to use the software according to the terms offered by the software vendor. The software itself is still owned by the vendor.

That means that you are obligated to follow the terms of the *license agreement* that accompanies the software. Very few people actually read the complete text of a software agreement before they purchase and use software. If you do, you'll find that a typical agreement contains restrictions, such as the following:

✦ **You are allowed to install the software on one and only one computer.** Some license agreements have specific exceptions to this, allowing you to install the software on a single computer at work and a single computer at home, or on a single desktop computer and a single notebook computer, provided that both computers are used by the same person. However, most software licenses stick to the one-computer rule.

✦ **The license agreement probably allows you to make a backup copy of the disks/discs.** The number of backup copies you can make, though, is probably limited to one or two.

✦ **You are not allowed to reverse-engineer the software.** In other words, you can't use programming tools to dissect the software in an effort to learn the secrets of how it works.

✦ **Some software restricts the kinds of applications it can be used for.** For example, you might purchase a student or home version of a program that prohibits commercial use. And some software — for example, Sun Microsystem's Java — prohibits its use for military applications.

✦ **Some software has export restrictions that prevent you from taking it out of the country.**

✦ **Nearly all software licenses limit the liability of the software vendor to replacing defective installation disks/discs.** In other words, the software vendor isn't responsible for any damage that might be caused by bugs in the software. In a few cases, these license restrictions have been set aside in court, and companies have been held liable for damage caused by defective software. For the most part, though, you use software at your own risk.

In many cases, software vendors give you a choice of several different types of licenses to choose from. When you purchase software for use on a network, you need to be aware of the differences between these license types so you can decide which type of license to get. The most common types are

✦ **Retail:** A *retail license* is the software you buy directly from the software vendor, a local store, or an online store. A retail software license usually grants you the right for a single user to install and use the software. Depending on the agreement, the license may allow that user to install the software on two computers — one at work and one at home. The key point is that only one user may use the software. (However, it is usually acceptable to install the software on a computer that's shared by several users. In that case, more than one user can use the software, provided they use it one at a time.)

The main benefit of a retail license is that it stays with the user when the user upgrades his or her computer. In other words, if you get a new computer, you can remove the software from your old computer and install it on your new computer.

✦ **OEM:** An *OEM license* is for software that's installed by a computer manufacturer on a new computer (*OEM* stands for *original equipment manufacturer*). For example, if you purchase a computer from Dell and order Microsoft Office Professional along with the computer, you're getting an OEM license. The most important thing to know about an OEM license is that it applies only to the specific computer for which you purchased the software. You are never allowed to install the software on any computer other than the one for which you purchased the software.

Thus, if one day in a fit of rage you throw your computer out the fifth floor window of your office and the computer smashes into little pieces in the parking lot below, your OEM version of Office is essentially lost forever. When you buy a replacement computer, you'll have to buy a new OEM license of Office for the new computer. You can't install the old software on the new computer.

If this sounds like a severe limitation, it is. However, OEM licenses are usually substantially less expensive than retail licenses. For example, a retail license of Microsoft Office 2007 Professional sells for about $500. The OEM version is less than $400.

✦ **Volume:** A *volume license* allows you to install and use the software on more than one computer. The simplest type of volume license simply specifies how many computers on which you can install the software. For example, you might purchase a 20-user version of a program that allows you to install the software on 20 computers. Usually, you're on the honor system to make sure that you don't exceed the quantity. You want to set up some type of system to keep track of this type of software license. For example, you could create an Excel spreadsheet in which you record the name of each person for whom you install the software.

Volume licenses can become considerably more complicated. For example, Microsoft offers several different types of volume license programs, each with different pricing and different features and benefits. Table 5-1 summarizes the features of these license programs. For more information, refer to `www.microsoft.com/licensing`.

Table 5-1	Microsoft Volume License Plans
Plan	*Features*
Open License	Purchase as few as five end-user licenses.
Open Value	Purchase as few as five end-user licenses and receive free upgrades during the subscription term (three years)
Select License	This is a licensing program designed for companies with 250 or more employees.
Enterprise	This is an alternative to the Select License program that's designed to cost-effectively provide Windows Vista, Office, and certain other programs throughout an organization of at least 250 employees.

✦ **Subscription:** A *subscription* isn't really a separate type of license but rather an optional add-on to a volume license. The added subscription fee entitles you to technical support and free product upgrades during the term of the subscription, which is usually annual. For some types of products, the subscription also includes periodic downloads of new data. For example, anti-virus software usually includes a subscription that regularly updates your virus signature data. Without the subscription, the anti-virus software would quickly become ineffective.

Using a License Server

Some programs let you purchase network licenses that enable you to install the software on as many computers as you want, but regulate the number of people who can use the software at any given time. To control how many people use the software, a special *license server* is set up. Whenever a user starts the program, the program checks with the license server to see whether a license is available. If so, the program is allowed to start, and the number of available licenses on the licenses server is reduced by one. Later, when the user quits the program, the license is returned to the server.

One of the most commonly used license server software is FlexLM, by Macrovision. It is used by AutoCAD as well as by many other network software applications. FlexLM uses special license files that are issued by a software vendor to indicate how many licenses of a given product you have purchased. Although the license file is a simple text file, its contents are cryptic and generated by a program that only the software vendor has access to. Here's an example of a typical license file for AutoCAD:

```
SERVER server1 000ecd0fe359
    USE_SERVER
    VENDOR adskflex port=2080
    INCREMENT 57000ARDES_2008_0F adskflex 1.000 permanent 6 \
        VENDOR_STRING=commercial:permanent BORROW=4320 SUPERSEDE \
        DUP_GROUP=UH ISSUED=07-May-2007 SN=339-71570316 SIGN="102D \
        85EC 1DFE D083 B85A 46BB AFB1 33AE 00BD 975C 8F5C 5ABC 4C2F \
        F88C 9120 0FB1 E122 BA97 BCAE CC90 899F 99BB 23C9 CAB5 613F \
        E7BB CA28 7DBF 8F51 3B21" SIGN2="033A 6451 5EEB 3CA4 98B8 F92C \
        184A D2BC BA97 BCAE CC90 899F 2EF6 0B45 A707 B897 11E3 096E 0288 \
        787C 997B 0E2E F88C 9120 0FB1 782C 00BD 975C 8F5C 74B9 8BC1"
```

(Don't get any crazy ideas here. I changed the numbers in this license file so that it won't actually work. I'm not crazy enough to publish an actual valid AutoCAD license file!)

One drawback to software that uses a license server is that you have to take special steps to run the software when the server isn't available. For example, what if you have AutoCAD installed on a notebook computer and you want to use it while you're away from the office? In that case, you have two options:

✦ **Use virtual private network (VPN) software to connect to the network.** After you're connected with the VPN, the license server will be available so you can use the software.

✦ **Borrow a license.** When you borrow a license, you can use the software for a limited period of time while you're disconnected from the network. Of course, the borrowed license is subtracted from the number of available licenses on the server.

In most cases, the license server is a mission-critical application — as important as any other function on your network. If the license server goes down, all users who depend on it will be unable to work. Don't worry; they'll let you know. They'll be lining up outside your door demanding to know when you can get the license server up and running so they can get back to work.

Because the license server provides such an important function, treat it with special care. Make sure that the license server software runs on a stable, well-maintained server computer. Don't load up the license server computer with a bunch of other server functions.

And make sure that it's backed up. If possible, install the license server software on a second server computer as a backup. That way, if the main license server computer goes down and you can't get it back up and running, you can quickly switch over to the backup license server.

Book III
Chapter 5

Managing Network Software

Options for Deploying Network Software

After you acquire the correct license for your software, the next task of the network administrator is *deploying* the software — that is, installing the software on your users' computers and configuring the software so that it runs efficiently on your network. The following sections describe several approaches to deploying software to your network.

Deploying software manually

Most software is shipped on CD or DVD media along with a Setup program that you run to install the software. The Setup program usually asks you a series of questions, such as where you want the program installed, whether you want to install all of the program's features installed or just the most commonly used features, and so on. You may also be required to enter a serial number, registration number, license key, or other code that proves you purchased the software. When all these questions are answered, the Setup program then installs the program.

If only a few of your network users will be using a particular program, the Setup program may be the most convenient way to deploy the program. Just take the installation media with you to the computer you want to install the program on, insert the disc into the CD/DVD drive, and run the Setup program.

 When you finish manually installing software from a CD or DVD, don't forget to remove the disc from the drive! It's easy to leave the disc in the drive, and if the user rarely or never uses the drive, it might be weeks or months before anyone discovers that the disc is missing. By that time, you'll be hard pressed to remember where it is.

Running Setup from a network share

If you plan on installing a program on more than two or three computers on your network, you'll find it much easier to run the Setup program from a network share rather than from the original CDs or DVDs. To do so, follow these steps:

1. **Create a network share and a folder within the share where you can store the Setup program and other files required to install the program.**

I usually set up a share named Software, and then create a separate folder in this share for each program I want to make available from the network. You should enable Read access for all network users, but allow full access only for yourself and your fellow administrators.

2. **Copy the entire contents of the program's CD or DVD to the folder you create in Step 1.**

   To do so, insert the CD or DVD in your computer's CD/DVD drive. Then, use Windows Explorer to select the entire contents of the disc and drag it to the folder you create in Step 1.

   Alternatively, you can choose Start⇨Run and enter cmd to open a command prompt. Then, enter a command, such as this:

   ```
   xcopy d:\*.* \\server1\software\someprogram\*.* /s
   ```

   In this example, d: is the drive letter of your CD/DVD drive, server1 is the name of your file server, and software and someprogram are the names of the share and folder you created in Step 1.

3. **To install the program on a client computer, open a Windows Explorer window, navigate to the share and folder you create in Step 1, and double-click the Setup.exe file.**

   This launches the Setup program.

4. **Follow the instructions displayed by the Setup program.**

   When the Setup program is finished, the software is ready to use.

Copying the Setup program to a network share spares you the annoyance of carrying the installation discs to each computer you want to install the software on. It doesn't spare you the annoyance of purchasing a valid license for each computer! It's illegal to install the software on more computers than the license you acquired from the vendor allows.

Installing silently

Copying the contents of a program's installation media to a network share spares you the annoyance of carrying the installation discs from computer to computer, but you still have to run the Setup program and answer all its annoying questions on every computer. Wouldn't it be great if there were a way to automate the Setup program so that after you run it, it runs without any further interaction from you? With many programs, you can.

In some cases, the Setup program itself has a command line switch that causes it to run silently. You can usually find out what command line switches are available by entering the following at a command prompt:

```
setup /?
```

With luck, you'll find that the Setup program itself has a switch, such as /quiet or /silent, that installs the program with no interaction, using the program's default settings.

If the Setup program doesn't offer any command line switches, don't despair! The following procedure describes a technique that often lets silently install the software:

1. **Open an Explorer window and navigate to**

   - *Windows Vista:* `C:\Users\`*name*`\AppData\Local\Temp`
   - *Windows XP:* `C:\Documents and Settings\`*name*`\Local Settings\Temp`

   Then, delete the entire contents of this folder.

   This is the Temporary folder where various programs deposit temporary files. Windows may not allow you to delete every file in this folder, but it's a good idea to begin this procedure by emptying the Temp folder as much as possible.

2. **Run the Setup program and follow the installation steps right up to the final step.**

   When you get to the confirmation screen that says the program is about ready to install the software, stop! Don't click the OK or Finish button.

3. **Return to the Temp folder you open in Step 1, and then poke around until you find the `.msi` file created by the Setup program you run in Step 2.**

   The `.msi` file is the actual Windows Installer program that Setup runs to install the program. It may have a cryptic name, such as `84993882.msi`.

4. **Copy the `.msi` file to the network share from which you want to install the program on your client computers.**

   For example, `\\server1\software\someprogram`.

5. **Rename the `.msi` file to `setup.msi`.**

   This step is optional, but I prefer to run `setup.msi` rather than `84993882.msi`.

6. **Use Notepad to create a batch file to run the `.msi` file with the `/quiet` switch.**

   To create the batch file

   a. *Right-click in the folder where the `.msi` file is stored.*

   b. *Choose New⇨Text Document.*

   c. *Change the name of the text document to `Setup.bat`.*

   d. *Right-click the `Setup.bat` file and choose Edit.*

   e. *Add the following line to the file:*

   ```
   setup.msi /quiet
   ```

7. **Save the file.**

    You can now install the software by navigating to the folder you created the `setup.bat` file in and double-clicking the `setup.bat` file.

Creating an administrative installation image

Some software, such as Microsoft Office and AutoCAD, comes with tools that let you create a fully configured silent setup program that you can then use to silently install the software. For Microsoft software, this silent setup program is called an *administrative installation image.* (Note that the OEM versions of Microsoft Office don't include this feature. You need to purchase a volume license to create an administrative installation.)

To create an administrative image, you simply run the configuration tool supplied by the vendor. The configuration tool lets you choose the installation options you want to have applied when the software is installed. Then, it creates a network setup program on a network share that you specify. You can then install the software on a client computer by opening an Explorer window, navigating to the network share where you saved the network setup program, and running the network setup program.

Pushing out software with group policy

One final option you should consider for network software deployment is using Windows Group Policy to automatically install software to network users. Group Policy is a feature of Windows Server 2003 and 2007 that lets you create policies that are assigned to users. You use the Windows Group Policy feature to specify that certain users should have certain software programs available to them.

Note that group policies aren't actually assigned to individual users, but to Organizational Units (OUs), which are used to categorize users in Active Directory. Thus, you might create a Group Policy to specify that everyone in the Accounting Department OU should have Microsoft Excel.

Then, whenever anyone in the Accounting Department logs in to Windows, Windows checks to make sure that Excel is installed on the user's computer. If Excel is *not* installed, Windows advertises Excel on the computer. *Advertising* software on a computer means that a small portion of the software is downloaded to the computer — just enough to display an icon for the program on the Start menu and to associate Excel with the Excel file extensions (such as `.xls`).

If the user clicks the Start menu icon for the advertised application or attempts to open a document that's associated with the advertised application, the application is automatically installed on the user's computer. The user will have to wait a few minutes while the application is installed, but the installation is automatic.

For more information about setting up group policy software installation, search Google or any other search engine for "Group Policy Software."

Keeping Software Up to Date

One of the annoyances that every network manager faces is applying software patches to keep the operating system and other software up to date. A software *patch* is a minor update that fixes the small glitches that crop up from time to time, such as minor security or performance issues. These glitches aren't significant enough to merit a new version of the software, but they're important enough to require fixing. Most of the patches correct security flaws that computer hackers have uncovered in their relentless attempts to wreak havoc on the computer world.

Periodically, all the recently released patches are combined into a *service pack*. Although the most diligent network administrators apply all patches when they're released, many administrators just wait for the service packs.

Windows includes a feature called *Windows Update* that automatically installs patches and service packs when they become available. These patches apply not just to Windows but to other Microsoft software as well. To activate Windows Update, choose Windows Update from Control Panel. A window appears, such as the one shown in Figure 5-1.

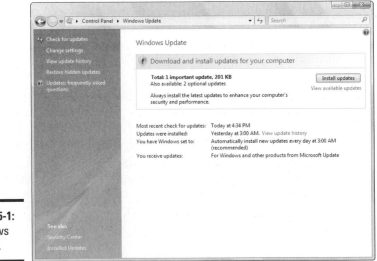

Figure 5-1:
Windows
Update.

From the Windows Update window, you can click the Install Updates button to download any updates that apply to your computer. You can also configure Windows Update so that it automatically checks for updates and installs them without asking. To set this option, click the Change Settings link. This displays the Windows Update Settings page, as shown in Figure 5-2.

Figure 5-2:
Changing the Windows Update settings.

**Book III
Chapter 5**

Managing Network Software

As you can see, Windows Update has several options for automatic operation:

✦ **Install Updates Automatically:** This option checks for updates on a regular basis and installs them without asking. You can specify how often to check for updates and at what time.

✦ **Download Updates But Let Me Choose Whether to Install Them:** If you're a picky computer user, you should choose this option. It automatically downloads the updates but then gives you the option of whether or not to install them. This lets you opt out of updates you may not want.

✦ **Check for Updates But Let Me Choose Whether to Download and Install Them:** This option lets you determine which updates should be downloaded.

✦ **Never Check for Updates:** This option disables automatic updates altogether.

Microsoft doesn't recommend selecting the Never Check for Updates option, and neither do I — unless you use some other method to keep your software up to date. For a network with more than a few dozen computers, you should consider server-based software to handle your software patches. For example, PatchLink (www.patchlink.com) is a server-based program that collects software patches from a variety of manufacturers and lets you create distributions that are automatically pushed out to client computers. With software like PatchLink, you don't have to rely on Windows Update to download patches to every computer on your network. And, you can use PatchLink to install patches from vendors other than just Microsoft.

Chapter 6: Solving Network Problems

In This Chapter

- ✔ Checking the obvious things
- ✔ Fixing computers that have expired
- ✔ Pinpointing the cause of trouble
- ✔ Restarting client and server computers
- ✔ Reviewing network event logs
- ✔ Keeping a record of network woes

*F*ace it: Networks are prone to breaking.

They have too many parts. Cables. Connectors. Cards. Switches. Routers. All these parts must be held together in a delicate balance, and the network equilibrium is all too easy to disturb. Even the best-designed computer networks sometimes act as if they're held together with baling wire, chewing gum, and duct tape.

To make matters worse, networks breed suspicion. After your computer is attached to a network, users begin to blame the network every time something goes wrong, regardless of whether the problem has anything to do with the network. You can't get columns to line up in a Word document? Must be the network. Your spreadsheet doesn't add up? The #$% network's acting up again. The stock market's down? Arghhh!!!!!!

The worst thing about network failures is that sometimes they can shut down an entire company. It's not so bad if just one user can't access a particular shared folder on a file server. If a critical server goes down, however, your network users may be locked out of their files, applications, e-mail, and everything else they need to conduct business as usual. When that happens, they'll be beating down your doors and won't stop until you get the network back up and running.

In this chapter, I review some of the most likely causes of network trouble and suggest some basic troubleshooting techniques that you can employ when your network goes on the fritz.

When Bad Things Happen to Good Computers

The following are some basic troubleshooting steps about what you should examine at the first sign of network trouble. In many (if not most) of the cases, one of the following steps can get your network back up and running:

1. **Make sure that your computer and everything attached to it is plugged in.**

   Computer geeks love it when a user calls for help and they get to tell the user that the computer isn't plugged in or that its power strip is turned off. They write it down in their geek logs so that they can tell their geek friends about it later. They may even want to take your picture so that they can show it to their geek friends. (Most "accidents" involving computer geeks are a direct result of this kind of behavior. So try to be tactful when you ask a user whether he or she is sure the computer is actually turned on.)

2. **Make sure that your computer is properly connected to the network.**

3. **Note any error messages that appear on the screen.**

4. **Try the built-in Windows network troubleshooter.**

   For more information, see the section, "Using the Windows Networking Troubleshooter," later in this chapter.

5. **Check the free disk space on your computer and on the server.**

   When a computer runs out of disk space or comes close to it, strange things can happen. Sometimes you get a clear error message indicating such a situation, but not always. Sometimes the computer just grinds to a halt; operations that used to take a few seconds now take a few minutes.

6. **Do a little experimenting to find out whether the problem is indeed a network problem or just a problem with the computer itself.**

   See the section, "Time to Experiment," later in this chapter, for some simple things that you can do to isolate a network problem.

7. **Try restarting the computer.**

   An amazing number of computer problems are cleared up by a simple restart of the computer. Of course, in many cases, the problem recurs, so you'll have to eventually isolate the cause and fix the problem. Some problems are only intermittent, and a simple reboot is all that's needed.

8. **Try restarting the network server.**

   See the section, "How to Restart a Network Server," later in this chapter.

How to Fix Dead Computers

If a computer seems totally dead, here are some things to check:

✦ **Make sure that the computer is plugged in.**

✦ **If the computer is plugged into a surge protector or a power strip, make sure that the surge protector or power strip is plugged in and turned on.** If the surge protector or power strip has a light, it should be glowing.

✦ **Make sure that the computer's On/Off switch is turned on.** This advice sounds too basic to even include here, but many computers have two power switches: an on/off switch on the back of the computer, and a push-button on the front that actually starts the computer. If you push the front button and nothing happens, check the switch on the back to make sure it's in the ON position.

To complicate matters, newer computers have a Sleep feature, in which they appear to be turned off but really they're just sleeping. All you have to do to wake such a computer is jiggle the mouse a little. (I used to have an uncle like that.) It's easy to assume that the computer is turned off, press the power button, wonder why nothing happened, and then press the power button and hold it down, hoping it will take. If you hold down the power button long enough, the computer will actually turn itself off. Then, when you turn the computer back on, you get a message saying the computer wasn't shut down properly. Arghhh! The moral of the story is to jiggle the mouse if the computer seems to have nodded off.

✦ **If you think the computer isn't plugged in but it looks like it is, listen for the fan.** If the fan is running, the computer is getting power, and the problem is more serious than an unplugged power cord. (If the fan isn't running but the computer is plugged in and the power is on, the fan may be out to lunch.)

✦ **If the computer is plugged in, turned on, and still not running, plug a lamp into the outlet to make sure that power is getting to the outlet.** You may need to reset a tripped circuit breaker or replace a bad surge protector. Or you may need to call the power company. (If you live in California, don't bother calling the power company. It probably won't do any good.)

✦ **Check the surge protector.** Surge protectors have a limited life span. After a few years of use, many surge protectors continue to provide electrical power for your computer, but the components that protect your computer from power surges no longer work. If you're using a surge protector that is more than two or three years old, replace the old surge protector with a new one.

✦ **Make sure that the monitor is plugged in and turned on.** The monitor has a separate power cord and switch. (The monitor actually has two cables that must be plugged in. One runs from the back of the monitor to the back of the computer; the other is a power cord that comes from the back of the monitor and must be plugged into an electrical outlet.)

✦ **Make sure that all cables are plugged in securely.** Your keyboard, monitor, mouse, and printer are all connected to the back of your computer by cables.

Make sure that the other ends of the monitor and printer cables are plugged in properly, too.

✦ **If the computer is running but the display is dark, try adjusting the monitor's contrast and brightness.** Some monitors have knobs that you can use to adjust the contrast and brightness of the monitor's display. They may have been turned down all the way.

Ways to Check a Network Connection

The cables that connect client computers to the rest of the network are finicky beasts. They can break at a moment's notice, and by "break," I don't necessarily mean "to physically break in two." Although some broken cables look like someone got to the cable with pruning shears, most cable problems aren't visible to the naked eye.

✦ **Twisted-pair cable:** If your network uses twisted-pair cable, you can quickly tell whether the cable connection to the network is good by looking at the back of your computer. Look for a small light located near where the cable plugs in; if this light is glowing steadily, the cable is good. If the light is dark or it's flashing intermittently, you have a cable problem (or a problem with the network card or the hub or switch that the other end of the cable is plugged in to).

If the light isn't glowing steadily, try removing the cable from your computer and reinserting it. This action may cure the weak connection.

✦ **Coaxial cable:** Detecting a cable problem in a network that's wired with *coaxial cable,* the kind that looks like cable-TV cable, is more difficult. The connector on the back of the computer forms a T. The base end of the T plugs into your computer. One or two coaxial cables plug into the outer ends of the T. If you use only one coaxial cable, you must use a special plug — a *terminator* — instead of a cable at the other end of the T. If you can't find a terminator, try conjuring one up from the future. ***Warning:*** Do not do this if your name happens to be Sarah Connor.

Don't unplug a coaxial cable from the network while the network is running. Data travels around a coaxial network the same way that a baton travels around the track in a relay race. If one person drops it, the race is over. The baton never gets to the next person. Likewise, if you unplug the network cable from your computer, the network data never gets to the computers that are "down the line" from your computer.

If you must disconnect the cable from your computer, make sure that you disconnect the T connector itself from the network card: Don't disconnect the cable from the T connector itself.

✦ **Patch cable:** Hopefully, your network is wired so that each computer is connected to the network with a short (six feet or so) patch cable. One end of the patch cable plugs into the computer, and the other end plugs into a cable connector mounted on the wall. Try quickly disconnecting and reconnecting the patch cable. If that doesn't do the trick, try to find a spare patch cable that you can use.

✦ **Hubs and switches:** Hubs and switches are prone to having cable problems, too — especially those hubs that are wired in a "professional manner," involving a rat's nest of patch cables. Be careful whenever you enter the lair of the rat's nest. If you need to replace a patch cable, be very careful when you disconnect the suspected bad cable and reconnect the good cable in its place.

A Bunch of Error Messages Just Flew By!

Error messages that display when your computer boots can provide invaluable clues to determine the source of the problem.

If you see error messages when you start up the computer, keep the following points in mind:

✦ **Don't panic if you see a lot of error messages.** Sometimes, a simple problem that's easy to correct can cause a plethora of error messages when you start your computer. The messages may look as if your computer is falling to pieces, but the fix may be very simple.

✦ **If the messages fly by so fast that you can't see them, press your computer's Pause key.** Your computer comes to a screeching halt, giving you a chance to catch up on your error-message reading. After you've read enough, press the Pause key again to get things moving. (On keyboards that don't have a Pause key, pressing Ctrl+Num Lock or Ctrl+S does the same thing.)

✦ **If you miss the error messages the first time, restart the computer and watch them again.**

✦ **Better yet, press F8 when you see the message Starting Windows.** This displays a menu that allows you to select from several startup options, including one that processes each line of your CONFIG.SYS file separately so that you can see the messages displayed by each command before proceeding to the next command.

Double-Checking Your Network Settings

I swear that there are little green men who sneak into offices at night, turn on computers, and mess up TCP/IP configuration settings just for kicks. These little green men are affectionately known as *networchons*.

Remarkably, network configuration settings sometimes get inadvertently changed so that a computer, which enjoyed the network for months or even years, one day finds itself unable to access the network. So one of the first things you do, after making sure that the computers are actually on and that the cables aren't broken, is a basic review of the computer's network settings. Check the following:

✦ **At a command prompt, run `ipconfig` to make sure that TCP/IP is up and running on the computer and that the IP addresses, subnet masks, and default gateway settings look right.**

✦ **Call up the network connection's Properties dialog box and make sure that the necessary protocols are installed correctly.**

✦ **Open the System Properties dialog box (double-click System in Control Panel) and check the Computer Name tab.**

Make sure that the computer name is unique and that the domain or workgroup name is spelled properly.

✦ **Double-check the user account to make sure that the user really has permission to access the resources he or she needs.**

For more information about network configuration settings, see Book II, Chapters 3 and 6.

Using the Windows Networking Troubleshooter

Windows comes with a built-in troubleshooter that can often help you to pin down the cause of a network problem. Figure 6-1 shows the Windows Vista version. Answer the questions asked by the troubleshooter and click Next to move from screen to screen. The Networking Troubleshooter can't solve all networking problems, but it does point out the causes of the most common problems.

Figure 6-1:
The
Windows
Vista
Network
Connection
Trouble-
shooter.

The procedure for starting Networking Troubleshooter depends on which version of Windows you're using:

✦ **Windows Vista:** Choose Start➪Help and Support, click Troubleshooting, and then click the link for the network troubleshooter that seems most directly related to the problem you're experiencing. You'll find trouble-shooters for wireless network problems, home networks, and local area network (LAN) and Internet connections.

✦ **Windows XP:** Choose Start➪Help and Support➪Networking and the Web➪Fixing Network or Web Problems. Then click Home and Small Office Networking Troubleshooter.

Time to Experiment

If you can't find some obvious explanation for your troubles — like the computer is unplugged — you need to do some experimenting to narrow down the possibilities. Design your experiments to answer one basic question: Is it a network problem or a local computer problem?

Here are some ways you can narrow down the cause of the problem:

✦ **Try performing the same operation on someone else's computer.** If no one on the network can access a network drive or printer, something is probably wrong with the network. On the other hand, if the error occurs on only one computer, the problem is likely with that computer. The wayward computer may not be reliably communicating with the network or configured properly for the network, or the problem may have nothing to do with the network at all.

✦ **If you're able to perform the operation on another computer without problems, try logging on to the network with another computer using your own username.** Then see whether you can perform the operation without error. If you can, the problem is probably on your computer. If you can't, the problem may be with the way your user account is configured.

✦ **If you can't log on at another computer, try waiting for a bit.** Your account may be temporarily locked out. This can happen for a variety of reasons — the most common of which is trying to log on with the wrong password several times in a row. If you're still locked out an hour later, call the network administrator and offer a doughnut.

Who's on First?

When troubleshooting a networking problem, it's often useful to find out who is actually logged on to a network server. For example, if a user can't access a file on the server, you can check whether the user is logged on. If so, you know that the user's account is valid, but the user may not have permission to access the particular file or folder that he's attempting to access. On the other hand, if the user isn't logged on, the problem may lie with the account itself or how the user is attempting to connect to the server.

It's also useful to find out who's logged on in the event that you need to restart the server. For more information about restarting a server, see the section, "How to Restart a Network Server," later in this chapter.

To find out who is currently logged on to a Windows server, right-click the Computer icon on the desktop (My Computer in Windows Server 2003, Computer in Windows Server 2008) and choose Manage from the menu that appears. This brings up the Computer Management window. Open System

Tools in the tree list and then open Shared Folders and select Sessions. A list of users who are logged on appears.

You can immediately disconnect all users by right-clicking Sessions in the Computer Management window and choosing All Tasks⇨Disconnect All.

How to Restart a Client Computer

Sometimes, trouble gets a computer so tied up in knots that the only thing you can do is reboot. In some cases, the computer just starts acting weird. Strange characters appear on the screen, or Windows goes haywire and doesn't let you exit a program. Sometimes, the computer gets so confused that it can't even move. It just sits there, like a deer staring at oncoming headlights. It won't move, no matter how hard you press Esc or Enter. You can move the mouse all over your desktop, or you can even throw it across the room, but the mouse pointer on the screen stays perfectly still.

When a computer starts acting strange, you need to reboot. If you must reboot, you should do so as cleanly as possible. I know this procedure may seem elementary, but the technique for safely restarting a client computer is worth repeating, even if it is basic:

1. **Save your work if you can.**

Use the File⇨Save command to save any documents or files that you were editing when things started to go haywire. If you can't use the menus, try clicking the Save button on the toolbar. If that doesn't work, try pressing Ctrl+S (the standard keyboard shortcut for the Save command).

2. **Close any running programs if you can.**

Use the File⇨Exit command or click the Close button in the upper-right corner of the program window. Or press Alt+F4.

3. **Restart the computer.**

- *Windows XP:* Choose Start⇨Turn Off Computer to summon the Shut Down Windows dialog box. Select the Restart option, and then click OK.

- *Windows Vista:* Click the Start button, click the right arrow that appears at the bottom right corner of the Start menu, and then click Restart.

If restarting your computer doesn't seem to fix the problem, you may need to turn your computer off and then turn it on again. To do so, follow the previous procedure but choose Shut Down instead of Restart.

Here are a few things to try if you have trouble restarting your computer:

1. **If your computer refuses to respond to the Start⇨Shut Down command, try pressing Ctrl+Alt+Delete.**

   This is called the "three-finger salute." It's appropriate to say, "Queueue" while you do it.

   When you press Ctrl+Alt+Delete, Windows displays a dialog box that enables you to close any running programs or shut down your computer entirely.

2. **If pressing Ctrl+Alt+Delete doesn't do anything, you've reached the last resort. The only thing left to do is turn the computer off by pressing the power On/Off button and holding it down for a few seconds.**

Powering off your computer by pressing the power button is a drastic action that you should take only after your computer becomes completely unresponsive. Any work you haven't yet saved to disk is lost. (Sniff.) (If your computer doesn't have a Reset button, turn the computer off, wait a few moments, and then turn the computer back on again.)

If at all possible, save your work before restarting your computer. Any work you haven't saved is lost. Unfortunately, if your computer is totally tied up in knots, you probably can't save your work. In that case, you have no choice but to push your computer off the digital cliff.

Restarting Network Services

Once in awhile, the operating system service that supports the task that's causing you trouble inexplicably stops or gets stuck. If users can't access a server, it may be because one of the key network services has stopped or is stuck.

You can review the status of services by using the Services tool, as shown in Figure 6-2. To display it, choose Services from the Administrative Tools menu. Review this list to make sure that all key services are running. If a key service is paused or stopped, restart it.

Which service qualifies as a *key* service depends on what roles you define for the server. Table 6-1 lists a few key services that are common to most Windows network operating systems. However, many servers require additional services besides these.

Figure 6-2:
Looking at services (Windows Vista).

Table 6-1	**Key Windows Services**
Service	*Description*
Computer Browser	Maintains a list of computers on the network that can be accessed. If this service is disabled, the computer won't be able to use browsing services, such as My Network Places.
DHCP Client	Enables the computer to obtain its IP address from a Dynamic Host Configuration Protocol (DHCP) server. If this service is disabled, the computer's Internet Protocol (IP) address won't be configured properly.
DNS Client	Enables the computer to access a Domain Name Server (DNS) server to resolve DNS names. If this service is disabled, the computer won't be able to handle DNS names, including Internet addresses and Active Directory names.
Server	Provides basic file and printer sharing services for the server. If this service is stopped, clients won't be able to connect to the server to access files or printers.
Workstation	Enables the computer to establish client connections with other servers. If this service is disabled, the computer won't be able to connect to other servers.

**Book III
Chapter 6**

Solving Network Problems

WARNING! Key services usually stop for a reason, so simply restarting a stopped service probably won't solve your network's problem — at least, not for long. You should review the System log to look for any error messages that may explain why the service stopped in the first place.

How to Restart a Network Server

Sometimes, the only way to flush out a network problem is to restart the network server that's experiencing trouble.

Restarting a network server is something you should do only as a last resort. Network operating systems are designed to run for months or even years at a time without rebooting. Restarting a server invariably results in a temporary shutdown of the network. If you must restart a server, try to do it during off hours if possible.

Before you restart a server, check whether a specific service that is required has been paused or stopped. You may be able to just restart the individual service rather than the entire server. For more information, see the section, "Restarting Network Services," earlier in this chapter.

Here is the basic procedure for restarting a network server:

1. **Make sure that everyone is logged off the server.**

   The easiest way to do that is to restart the server after normal business hours, when everyone has gone home for the day. Then, you can just shut down the server and let the shutdown process forcibly log off any remaining users.

   To find out who's logged on, refer to the earlier section, "Who's on First?"

2. **After you're sure the users have logged off, shut down the network server.**

   You want to do this step behaving like a good citizen if possible — decently, and in order. Use the Start⇨Shut Down command to shut down the server. This summons a dialog box that requires you to indicate the reason for the shutdown. The information you supply here is entered into the server's System log, which you can review by using Event Viewer.

3. **Reboot the server computer or turn it off and then on again.**

   Watch the server start up to make sure that no error messages appear.

4. **Tell everyone to log back on and make sure that everyone can now access the network.**

Remember the following when you consider restarting the network server:

- ✦ **Restarting the network server is more drastic than restarting a client computer.** Make sure that everyone saves his or her work and logs off the network before you do it! You can cause major problems if you blindly turn off the server computer while users are logged on.

- ✦ **Obviously, restarting a network server is a major inconvenience to every network user.** Better offer treats.

Looking at Event Logs

One of the most useful troubleshooting techniques for diagnosing network problems is to review the network operating system's built-in event logs. These logs contain information about interesting and potentially troublesome events that occur during the daily operation of your network. Ordinarily, these logs run in the background, quietly gathering information about network events. When something goes wrong, you can check the logs to see whether the problem generated a noteworthy event. In many cases, the event logs contain an entry that pinpoints the exact cause of the problem and suggests a solution.

To display the event logs in a Windows server, use Event Viewer, which is available from the Administrative Tools menu. For example, Figure 6-3 shows an Event Viewer from a Windows Server 2008 system. The tree listing on the left side of Event Viewer lists five categories of events that are tracked: Application, Security, System, Directory Service, and File Replication Service events. Select one of these options to see the log that you want to view. For details about a particular event, double-click the event to displays a dialog box with detailed information about the event.

**Book III
Chapter 6**

**Solving Network
Problems**

Figure 6-3:
Event
Viewer.

Event Viewer				
File Action View Help				
Event Viewer (Local)	System 399 event(s)			
Application	Type	Date	Time	Source
Security	⚠ Warning	5/29/2005	10:33:12 ...	LsaSrv
System	⚠ Warning	5/29/2005	10:33:12 ...	LsaSrv
Directory Service	⚠ Warning	5/29/2005	10:33:12 ...	LsaSrv
File Replication Service	⚠ Warning	5/29/2003	10:33:16 ...	LsaSrv
	⚠ Warning	5/29/2005	10:33:16 ...	LsaSrv
	ⓘ Information	5/29/2005	10:33:17 ...	SMTPSVC
	ⓘ Information	5/29/2005	10:34:39 ...	Service Co
	ⓘ Information	5/29/2005	10:34:39 ...	Service Co
	⚠ Warning	5/29/2005	10:35:05 ...	Dnsapi
	ⓘ Information	5/29/2005	10:35:28 ...	Service Co
	ⓘ Information	5/29/2003	10:35:28 ...	Service Co
	⚠ Warning	5/29/2005	10:36:03 ...	LsaSrv
	ⓘ Information	5/29/2005	10:36:35 ...	Service Co
	ⓘ Information	5/29/2005	10:36:36 ...	Service Co
	❌ Error	5/29/2005	10:39:21 ...	W3SVC
	❌ Error	5/29/2005	10:39:35 ...	W3SVC

Documenting Your Trials and Tribulations

For a large network, you probably want to invest in problem-management software that tracks each problem through the entire process of trouble-shooting, from initial report to final resolution. For small- and medium-sized networks, it's probably sufficient to put together a three-ring binder with pre-printed forms. Or record your log in a Word document or an Excel spreadsheet.

Regardless of how you track your network problems, the tracking log should include the following information:

✦ **The real name and the network username of the person reporting the problem**

✦ **The date the problem was first reported**

✦ **An indication of the severity of the problem**

Is it merely an inconvenience, or is a user unable to complete his or her work because of the problem? Does a workaround exist?

✦ **The name of the person assigned to resolve the problem**

✦ **A description of the problem**

✦ **A list of the software involved, including versions**

✦ **A description of the steps taken to solve the problem**

✦ **A description of any intermediate steps that were taken to try to solve the problem, along with an indication of whether those steps were "undone" when they didn't help solve the problem**

✦ **The date the problem was finally resolved**

Chapter 7: Network Performance Anxiety

In This Chapter

- ✔ Understanding performance problems
- ✔ Looking at bottlenecks
- ✔ Developing a procedure for solving performance problems
- ✔ Monitoring performance
- ✔ Implementing other tips for speeding up your network

The term *network performance* refers to how efficiently the network responds to users' needs. It goes without saying that any access to resources that involves a network will be slower than similar access that doesn't involve a network. For example, it takes longer to open a Word document that resides on a network file server than it takes to open a similar document that resides on a user's local hard drive. However, it shouldn't take *much* longer. If it does, you have a network performance problem.

This chapter is a general introduction to the practice of tuning your network so that it performs as well as possible. Keep in mind that many specific bits of network tuning advice are scattered throughout this book. In this chapter, you can find some specific techniques for analyzing your network's performance, taking corrective action when a performance problem develops, and charting your progress.

Why Administrators Hate Performance Problems

Network performance problems are among the most difficult network problems to track down and solve. If a user simply can't access the network, it usually doesn't take long to figure out why: A cable is broken, a network card or hub is malfunctioning, a user doesn't have permission to access the resource, and so on. After a little investigation, the problem usually reveals itself. You fix it and move on to the next problem.

Unfortunately, performance problems are messier. Here are just a few of the reasons that network administrators hate performance problems:

✦ **Performance problems are difficult to quantify.** Exactly how much slower is the network now than it was a week ago, a month ago, or even a year ago? Sometimes the network just *feels* slow, but you can't quite define exactly how slow it really is.

✦ **Performance problems usually develop gradually.** Sometimes, a network slows down suddenly and drastically. More often, though, the network gradually gets slower, a little bit at a time, until one day when the users notice that the network is slooow.

✦ **Performance problems often go unreported.** Users gripe about the problem to each other around the water cooler, but they don't formally contact you to let you know that their network seems 10 percent slower than usual. As long as they can still access the network, they just assume that the problem is temporary or just in their imaginations.

✦ **Many performance problems are intermittent.** Sometimes, a user calls you and complains that a certain network operation has become slower than molasses — and by the time you get to the user's desk, the operation performs like a snap. Sometimes, you can find a pattern to the intermittent behavior, such as it's slower in the morning than in the afternoon, or it's only slow while backups are running or while the printer is working. Other times, you can't find a pattern. Sometimes the operation is slow; sometimes it isn't.

✦ **Performance tuning is not an exact science.** Improving performance sometimes involves educated guesswork. Will upgrading all the users from 10 Mbps to 100 Mbps improve performance? Probably. Will segmenting the network improve performance? Maybe. Will adding another 4GB of RAM to the server improve performance? Hopefully.

✦ **The solution to performance problems is sometimes a hard sell.** If a user can't access the network because of a malfunctioning component, there's usually not much question that the purchase of a replacement is justified. However, if the network is slow and you think you can fix it by upgrading the entire network to gigabit Ethernet, you may have trouble selling management on the upgrade.

What Exactly Is a Bottleneck?

The term *bottleneck* does not in any way refer to the physique of your typical computer geek. (Well, I guess it *could,* in some cases.) Rather, computer geeks coined the phrase when they discovered that the tapered shape of a bottle of Jolt Cola limited the rate at which they could consume the beverage. "Hey," a computer geek said one day, "the gently tapered narrowness of this bottle's neck imposes a distinct limiting effect upon the rate at which I can consume the tasty caffeine-laden beverage contained within. This draws to mind a hitherto undiscovered yet obvious analogy to the limiting effect that a single slow component of a computer system can have upon the performance of the system as a whole."

"Fascinating," replied all the other computer geeks, who were fortunate enough to be present at that historic moment.

The term stuck and is used to this day to draw attention to the simple fact that a computer system is only as fast as its slowest component. It's the computer equivalent of the old truism that a chain is only as strong as its weakest link.

For a simple demonstration of this concept, consider what happens when you print a word processing document on a slow printer. Your word processing program reads the data from disk and sends it to the printer. Then you sit and wait while the printer prints the document.

Would buying a faster CPU or adding more memory make the document print faster? No. The CPU is already much faster than the printer, and your computer already has more than enough memory to print the document. The printer itself is the bottleneck, so the only way to print the document faster is to replace the slow printer with a faster one.

Here are some other random thoughts about bottlenecks:

✦ **A computer system always has a bottleneck.** For example, suppose that you decided that the bottleneck on your file server is a slow IDE hard drive, so you replace it with the fastest SCSI drive money can buy. Now, the hard drive is no longer the bottleneck: The drive can process information faster than the controller card to which the disk is connected. You haven't really eliminated the bottleneck: You just moved it from the hard drive to the disk controller. No matter what you do, the computer will always have some component that limits the overall performance of the system.

✦ **One way to limit the effect of a bottleneck is to avoid waiting for the bottleneck.** For example, print spooling lets you avoid waiting for a slow printer. Spooling doesn't speed up the printer, but it does free you to do other work while the printer chugs along. Similarly, disk caching lets you avoid waiting for a slow hard drive.

✦ **One of the reasons computer geeks are switching from Jolt Cola to Snapple is that Snapple bottles have wider necks.**

The Five Most Common Network Bottlenecks

Direct from the home office in sunny Fresno, California, here are the ten —
oops, five — most common network bottlenecks, in no particular order.

The hardware inside your servers

Your servers should be powerful computers capable of handling all the work
your network will throw at them. Don't cut corners by using a bottom-of-the-
line computer that you bought at a discount computer store.

The following are the four most important components of your server hardware:

✦ **Processor:** Your server should have a powerful processor. As a general
rule, any processor that is available in an $800 computer from a low-
cost, general appliance store is not a processor that you want to see in
your file server. In other words, avoid processors that are designed for
consumer-grade home computers.

✦ **Memory:** You can't have too much memory. Memory is cheap, so don't
skimp. Don't even think about running a server with less than 1GB of RAM.

✦ **Disk:** Don't mess around with inexpensive IDE hard drives. To be
respectable, you should have nothing but SCSI drives.

✦ **Network card:** A $9.95 network card might be fine for your home net-
work, but don't use one in a file server that supports 50 users and then
expect to be happy with the server's performance. Remember that the
server computer uses the network a lot more than any of the clients, so
equip your servers with good network cards.

The server's configuration options

All network operating systems have options that you can configure. Some of
these options can make the difference between a pokey network and a zippy
network. Unfortunately, no hard-and-fast rules exist for setting these options.
Otherwise, you wouldn't have options.

The following are some of the more important tuning options available for
most servers:

✦ **Virtual memory options:** *Virtual memory* refers to disk paging files that
the server uses when it doesn't have enough real memory to do its work.
Few servers ever have enough real memory, so virtual memory is always
an important server feature. You can specify the size and location of the
virtual memory paging files. For best performance, you should provide
at least 1.5 times the amount of real memory. For example, if you have 4GB
of real memory, allocate at least 6GB of virtual memory. If necessary, you
can increase this size later.

✦ **Disk striping:** Use Disk Defragmenter to optimize the data storage on your server's disks. If the server has more than one hard drive, you can increase performance by creating *striped volumes,* which allow disk I/O operations to run concurrently on each of the drives in the stripe set.

✦ **Network protocols:** Make sure that your network protocols are configured correctly; remove any protocols that aren't necessary.

✦ **Free disk space on the server:** Servers like to have plenty of breathing room on their disks. If the amount of free disk space on your server drops precipitously low, the server chokes up and slows to a crawl. Make sure that your server has plenty of space: A few GBs of unused disk space provide a healthy buffer.

Servers that do too much

One common source of network performance problems is servers that are overloaded with too many duties. Just because modern network operating systems come equipped with dozens of different types of services doesn't mean that you should enable and use them all on a single server. If a single server is bogged down because of too much work, add a second server to relieve the first server of some of its chores. Remember the old saying: "Many hands make light work."

For example, if your network needs more disk space, consider adding a second file server rather than adding another drive to the server that already has four drives that are nearly full. Or better yet, purchase a file server appliance that is dedicated just to the task of serving files.

As a side benefit, your network will be easier to administer and more reliable if you place separate functions on separate servers. For example, if you have a single server that doubles as a file server and a mail server, you'll lose both services if you have to take down the down to perform an upgrade or repair a failed component. However, if you have separate file and mail server computers, only one of the services will be interrupted if you have to take down one of the servers.

The network infrastructure

A network *infrastructure* comprises the cables and any switches, hubs, routers, and other components that sit between your clients and your servers. The following network infrastructure items can slow down your network:

✦ **Hubs:** Because switches are so inexpensive now, you can affordably solve a lot of performance problems by replacing outdated hubs with switches. Using switches instead of hubs reduces the overall load on your network.

Book III
Chapter 7

**Network
Performance
Anxiety**

✦ **Segment sizes:** Keep the number of computers and other devices on each network segment to a reasonable number. About 20 devices is usually the right number. (Note that if you replace your hubs with switches, you instantly cut the size of each segment because each port on a switch constitutes a separate segment.)

✦ **The network's speed:** If you have an older network, you'll probably discover that many — if not all — of your users are still working at 10 Mbps. Upgrading to 100 Mbps will speed up the network dramatically.

✦ **The backbone speed:** If your network uses a backbone to connect segments, consider upgrading the backbone to 1 Gbps.

The hardest part about improving the performance of a network is determining what the bottlenecks are. With sophisticated test equipment and years of experience, network gurus can make pretty good educated guesses. Without the equipment and experience, you can still make pretty good uneducated guesses.

Malfunctioning components

Sometimes a malfunctioning network card or other component slows down the network. For example, a switch may malfunction intermittently, occasionally letting packets through but dropping enough of them to slow down the network. After you identify the faulty component, replacing it will restore the network to its original speed.

Tuning Your Network the Compulsive Way

You have two ways to tune your network. The first is to think about it a bit, take a guess at what may improve performance, try it, and see whether the network seems to run faster. This approach is how most people go about tuning the network.

Then you have the compulsive way, which is suitable for people who organize their sock drawers by color and their food cupboards alphabetically by food groups. The compulsive approach to tuning a network goes something like this:

1. **Establish a method for objectively testing the performance of some aspect of the network.**

This method is *benchmarking,* and the result of your benchmark is a *baseline.*

2. **Change one variable of your network configuration and rerun the test.**

For example, suppose you think that increasing the size of the disk cache can improve performance. Change the cache size, restart the server, and run the benchmark test. Note whether the performance improves, stays the same, or becomes worse.

3. **Repeat Step 2 for each variable that you want to test.**

Here are some salient points to keep in mind if you decide to tune your network the compulsive way:

✦ **If possible, test each variable separately.** In other words, reverse the changes you made to other network variables before proceeding.

✦ **Write down the results of each test.** That way, you have an accurate record of the impact that each change made on your network's performance.

✦ **Be sure to change only one aspect of the network each time you run the benchmark.** If you make several changes, you won't know which one caused the change. One change may improve performance, but the other change may worsen performance so that the changes cancel each other out — kind of like offsetting penalties in a football game.

✦ **If possible, conduct the baseline test during normal working hours.** That way, the network is undergoing its normal workload.

✦ **To establish your baseline performance, run your benchmark test two or three times to make sure that the results are repeatable.**

Monitoring Network Performance

One way to monitor network performance is to use a stopwatch to see how long it actually takes to complete common network tasks, such as opening documents or printing reports. If you choose to monitor your network by using the stopwatch technique, you'll want to get a clipboard, baseball cap, and gray sweat suit to complete the ensemble.

A more high-tech approach to monitoring network performance is to use a monitor program that automatically gathers network statistics for you. After you set up the monitor, it plugs away, silently spying on your network and recording what it sees in performance logs. You can then review the performance logs to see how your network is doing.

For large networks, you can purchase sophisticated monitoring programs that run on their own dedicated servers. For small- and medium-sized networks, you can probably get by with the built-in monitoring facilities that come with the network operating system. For example, Figure 7-1 shows the Performance Monitor tool that comes with Windows Server 2003. Other operating systems come with similar tools.

Figure 7-1:
Monitoring
performance.

Windows Performance Monitor lets you keep track of several different aspects of system performance at once. You track each performance aspect by setting up a counter. You can choose from dozens of different counters. Table 7-1 describes some of the most commonly used counters. Note that each counter refers to a server object, such as physical disk, memory, or the processor.

Table 7-1	Commonly Used Performance Counters	
Object	*Counter*	*Description*
Physical Disk	% Free Space	The percentage of free space on the server's physical disks. Should be at least 15 percent.
Physical Disk Length	Average Queue	Indicates how many disk operations are waiting while the disk is busy servicing other disk operations. Should be two or fewer.
Memory	Pages/second	The number of pages retrieved from the virtual memory page files per second. A typical threshold is about 2,500 pages per second.
Processor	% Processor Time	Indicates the percentage of the processor's time that it's busy doing work rather than sitting idle. Should be 85 percent or less.

Here are a few more things to consider about performance monitoring:

✦ **Performance Monitor enables you to view real-time data or to view data that you can save in a log file.** Real-time data gives you an idea about what's happening with the network at a particular moment, but the more useful information comes from the logs.

✦ **You can schedule logging to occur at certain times of the day and for certain intervals.** For example, you may schedule the log to gather data every 15 seconds from 9:00 to 9:30 every morning and then again from 3:00 to 3:30 every afternoon.

✦ **Even if you don't have a performance problem now, you should set up performance logging and let it run for a few weeks to gather baseline data.** If you develop a problem, this baseline data will prove invaluable while you research the problem.

✦ **Don't leave performance logging on all the time.** Gathering performance data slows down your server. Use it only occasionally to gather baseline data or when you're experiencing a performance problem.

More Performance Tips

Here are a few last-minute performance tips that barely made it in:

✦ **You can often find the source of a slow network by staring at the network hubs or switches for a few minutes.** These devices have colorful arrays of green and red lights. The green lights flash whenever data is transmitted; the red lights flash when a collision occurs. An occasional red flash is normal, but if one or more of the red lights is flashing repeatedly, the network interface card (NIC) connected to that port may be faulty.

✦ **Check for scheduled tasks, such as backups, batched database updates, or report jobs.** If at all possible, schedule these tasks to run after normal business hours, such as at night when no one is in the office. These jobs tend to slow down the network by hogging the server's hard drives.

✦ **Sometimes, faulty application programs can degrade performance.** For example, some programs develop a *memory leak:* They use memory but then forget to release the memory after they finish. Programs with memory leaks can slowly eat up all the memory on a server, until the server runs out and grinds to a halt. If you think a program has a memory leak, contact the manufacturer of the program to see whether a fix is available.

**Book III
Chapter 7**

Network
Performance
Anxiety

✦ **Spyware can slow a system to a crawl.** A common source of performance problems on client computers is *spyware,* those annoying programs that you almost can't help but pick up when you surf the Internet. Fortunately, you can remove spyware with a variety of free or inexpensive spyware removal tools. For more information, use Google or another search engine to search for spyware removal.

Chapter 8: Backing Up Your Data

In This Chapter

- ✔ Understanding the need for backups
- ✔ Working with tape drives and other backup media
- ✔ Understanding the different types of backups
- ✔ Mastering tape rotation and other details

*I*f you're the hapless network manager, the safety of the data on your network is your responsibility. In fact, it's your primary responsibility. You get paid to lie awake at night worrying about your data. Will it be there tomorrow? If it's not, can you get it back? And — most importantly — if you can't get it back, will you have a job tomorrow?

This chapter covers the ins and outs of being a good, responsible, trustworthy network manager. No one gives out merit badges for this stuff, but someone should.

Backing Up Your Data

Having data backed up is the cornerstone of any disaster recovery plan. Without backups, a simple hard drive failure can set your company back days or even weeks while it tries to reconstruct lost data. In fact, without backups, your company's very existence is in jeopardy.

The main goal of a backup is simple: Keep a spare copy of your network's critical data so that no matter what happens, you never lose more than one day's work. The stock market may crash, hanging chads may factor into another presidential election, and George Lucas may decide to make a pre-prequel. When you stay on top of your backups, though, you'll never lose more than one day's work.

The way to do this, naturally, is to make sure that data is backed up on a daily basis. For many networks, you can back up all the network hard drives every night. And even if full nightly backups aren't possible, you can still use techniques that can ensure that every file on the network has a backup copy that's no more than one day old.

All about Tapes and Tape Drives

If you plan on backing up the data on your network server's hard drives, you obviously need some type of media on which to back up the data. You could copy the data onto CDs, but a 500GB hard drive would need more than 750 CDs to do a full backup. That's a few more discs than most people want to keep in the closet. And you could use DVDs, but you'll still need about a dozen of them as well as an hour or so to fill each one. Sigh. That means devoting a Saturday to creating your backup.

Because of the limitations of CDs and DVDs, most network administrators back up network data to tape. Depending on the make and model of the tape drive, you can copy as much as 800GB of data onto a single tape.

One of the benefits of tape backup is that you can run it unattended. In fact, you can schedule a tape backup to run automatically during off hours when no one is using the network. For unattended backups to work, though, you must ensure that you have enough tape capacity to back up your entire network server's hard drive without having to manually switch tapes. If your network server has only 100GB of data, you can easily back it up onto a single tape. However, if you have 1,000GB of data, invest in a tape drive that features a magazine changer that can hold several tapes and automatically cycle them in and out of the drive. That way, you can run your backups unattended.

Here are some additional thoughts concerning tape backups:

✦ **Travan drives:** A popular style of tape backup for small servers is a Travan drive, which comes in a variety of models with tape capacities ranging from 20GB to 40GB. You can purchase a 20GB drive for less than $200.

✦ **DAT and DLT units:** For larger networks, you can get tape backup units that offer higher capacity and faster backup speed than Travan drives — for more money, of course. Digital audio tape (DAT) units can back up as much as 80GB on a single tape, and DLT (digital linear tape) drives can store up to 200GB on one tape. DAT and DLT drives can cost $1,000 or more, depending on the capacity.

✦ **Robotic units:** If you're really up the backup creek with hundreds of gigabytes to back up, you can get robotic tape backup units that automatically fetch and load tape cartridges from a library. That way, you can do complete backups without having to load tapes manually. As you can likely guess, these units aren't inexpensive: Small ones, which have a library of about eight tapes and a total backup capacity of more than 5,000GB, start at about $4,000.

Backup Software

All versions of Windows come with a built-in backup program. In addition, most tape drives come with backup programs that are often faster or more flexible than the standard Windows backup.

You can also purchase sophisticated backup programs that are specially designed for networks that have multiple servers with data that must be backed up. For a basic Windows file server, you can use the backup program that comes with Windows Server. Server versions of Windows come with a decent backup program that can run scheduled, unattended tape backups.

Backup programs do more than just copy data from your hard drive to tape. Backup programs use special compression techniques to squeeze your data so that you can cram more data onto fewer tapes. Compression factors of 2:1 are common, so you can usually squeeze 100GB of data onto a tape that would hold only 50GB of data without compression. (Tape drive manufacturers tend to state the capacity of their drives by using compressed data, assuming a 2:1 compression ratio. Thus, a 200GB tape has an uncompressed capacity of 100GB.)

Whether you achieve a compression factor of 2:1 depends on the nature of the data you're backing up:

✦ **Documents:** If your network is used primarily for Office applications and is filled with Word and Excel documents, you'll probably get better than 2:1 compression.

✦ **Graphics:** If your network data consists primarily of graphic image files, you probably won't get much compression. Most graphic image file formats are already compressed, so they can't be compressed much more by the backup software's compression methods.

Backup programs also help you keep track of which data has been backed up and which hasn't. They also offer options, such as incremental or differential backups that can streamline the backup process, as I describe in the next section.

If your network has more than one server, invest in good backup software. The most popular is Yosemite Backup, made by Yosemite Technologies (www.yosemitetech.com). Besides being able to handle multiple servers, one of the main advantages of backup software (such as Yosemite Backup) is that it can properly back up Microsoft Exchange server data.

Types of Backups

You can perform five different types of backups. Many backup schemes rely on full daily backups, but for some networks, using a scheme that relies on two or more of these backup types is more practical.

The differences among the fives types of backup involve a little technical detail known as the *archive bit*. The archive bit indicates whether a file has been modified since it was backed up. The archive bit is a little flag that's stored along with the filename, creation date, and other directory information. Any time that a program modifies a file, the archive bit is set to the On position. That way, backup programs know that the file has been modified and needs to be backed up.

The differences among the various types of backup center around whether they use the archive bit to determine which files to back up as well as whether they flip the archive bit to the Off position after they back up a file. Table 8-1 summarizes these differences, which I explain in the following sections.

Backup programs allow you to select any combination of drives and folders to back up. As a result, you can customize the file selection for a backup operation to suit your needs. For example, you can set up one backup plan that backs up all a server's shared folders and drives plus its mail server stores but then leaves out folders that rarely change, such as the operating system folders or installed program folders. You can then back up those folders on a less regular basis. The drives and folders that you select for a backup operation are collectively called the *backup selection*.

Table 8-1	How Backup Types Use the Archive Bit	
Backup Type	*Selects Files Based on Archive Bit?*	*Resets Archive Bits After Backing Up?*
Normal	No	Yes
Copy	No	No
Daily	No*	No
Incremental	Yes	Yes
Differential	Yes	No

*Selects files based on the Last Modified date.

The archive bit would have made a good Abbott and Costello routine. ("All right, I wanna know who modified the archive bit." "What." "Who?" "No, what." "Wait a minute . . . just tell me what's the name of the guy who modified the archive bit!" "Right.")

Normal backups

A *normal backup* — also called a *full backup* — is the basic type of backup. In a normal backup, all files in the backup selection are backed up regardless of whether the archive bit has been set. In other words, the files are backed up even if they haven't been modified since the last time they were backed up. When each file is backed up, its archive bit is reset, so backups that select files based on the archive bit setting won't back up the files.

When a normal backup finishes, none of the files in the backup selection have their archive bits set. As a result, if you immediately follow a normal backup with an incremental backup or a differential backup, no files will be selected for backup by the incremental or differential backup because no files will have their archive bits set.

The easiest backup scheme is to simply schedule a normal backup every night. That way, all your data is backed up on a daily basis. Then, if the need arises, you can restore files from a single tape or set of tapes. Restoring files is more complicated when other types of backups are involved.

Do normal backups nightly if you have the tape capacity to do them unattended: that is, without having to swap tapes. If you can't do an unattended normal backup because the amount of data to be backed up is greater than the capacity of your tape drive(s), you have to use other types of backups in combination with normal backups.

If you can't get a normal backup on a single tape and you can't afford a second tape drive or a tape changer, take a hard look at the data that's being included in the backup selection. I recently worked on a network that was difficult to back up onto a single tape. When I examined the data that was being backed up, I discovered a large amount of static data that was essentially an online archive of old projects. This data was necessary because network users needed it for research purposes, but the data was read-only. Even though the data never changed, it was being backed up to tape every night, and the backups required two tapes. After we removed this data from the cycle of nightly backups, the backups were able to squeeze onto a single tape again.

If you remove static data from the nightly backup, make sure that you have a secure backup of the static data on tape, CD-RW, or some other media.

Copy backups

A *copy backup* is similar to a normal backup except that the archive bit isn't reset when each file is copied. As a result, copy backups don't disrupt the cycle of normal and incremental or differential backups.

Copy backups are usually not incorporated into regular, scheduled backups. Instead, you use a copy backup when you want to do an occasional one-shot backup. For example, if you're about to perform an operating system upgrade, you should back up the server before proceeding. If you do a full backup, the archive bits are reset, and your regular backups are disrupted. However, if you do a copy backup, the archive bits of any modified files remain unchanged. As a result, your regular normal and incremental or differential backups are unaffected.

If you don't incorporate incremental or differential backups into your backup routine, the difference between a copy backup and a normal backup is moot.

Daily backups

A *daily backup* backs up just those files that have been changed the same day when the backup is performed. A daily backup examines the modification date stored with each file's directory entry to determine whether a file should be backed up. Daily backups don't reset the archive bit.

I'm not a big fan of this option because of the small possibility that some files may slip through the cracks. Someone may be working late one night and modify a file after the evening's backups have completed — but before midnight — meaning that those files won't be included in the following night's backups. Incremental or differential backups, which rely on the archive bit rather than the modification date, are more reliable.

Incremental backups

An *incremental backup* backs up only those files that were modified since the last time you did a backup. Incremental backups are a lot faster than full backups because your network users probably modify only a small portion of the files on the server in any given day. As a result, if a full backup takes three tapes, you can probably fit an entire week's worth of incremental backups on a single tape.

When an incremental backup copies each file, it resets the file's archive bit. That way, the file will be backed up again before your next normal backup only when a user modifies the file again.

Here are some thoughts about using incremental backups:

✦ **The easiest way to use incremental backups is the following:**

- A *normal* backup every Monday

  If your full backup takes more than 12 hours, you may want to do it on Friday so that it can run over the weekend.

- An *incremental* backup on each remaining normal business day (for example, Tuesday, Wednesday, Thursday, and Friday)

✦ **When you use incremental backups, the complete backup consists of the full backup tapes and all the incremental backup tapes that you've made since you did the full backup.**

If the hard drive crashes and you have to restore the data onto a new drive, you first restore Monday's normal backup and then you restore each of the subsequent incremental backups.

✦ **Incremental backups complicate restoring individual files because the most recent copy of the file may be on full backup tape or on any of the incremental backups.**

Backup programs keep track of the location of the most recent version of each file in order to simplify the process.

✦ **When you use incremental backups, you can choose whether you want to**

- Store each incremental backup on its own tape.

- Append each backup to the end of an existing tape.

Often, you can use a single tape for a week of incremental backups.

Differential backups

A *differential backup* is similar to an incremental backup except that it doesn't reset the archive bit when files are backed up. As a result, each differential backup represents the difference between the last normal backup and the current state of the hard drive.

To do a full restore from a differential backup, you first restore the last normal backup and then you restore the most recent differential backup.

For example, suppose that you do a normal backup on Monday and differential backups on Tuesday, Wednesday, and Thursday, and then your hard drive crashes Friday morning. On Friday afternoon, you install a new hard drive. To restore the data, you first restore the normal backup from Monday. Then, you restore the differential backup from Thursday. The Tuesday and Wednesday differential backups aren't needed.

The main difference between incremental and differential backups is that

✦ *Incremental* backups result in smaller and faster backups.

✦ *Differential* backups are easier to restore.

If your users often ask you to restore individual files, consider using differential backups.

Local versus Network Backups

When you back up network data, you have two basic approaches to running the backup software: You can perform a *local backup,* in which the backup software runs on the file server itself and backs up data to a tape drive that's installed in the server. Or, you can perform a *network backup,* in which you use one network computer to back up data from another network computer. In a network backup, the data has to travel over the network to get to the computer that's running the backup.

If you run the backups from the file server, you'll tie up the server while the backup is running — and users will complain that their server access has slowed to a snail's pace. On the other hand, if you run the backup over the network from a client computer or a dedicated backup server, you'll flood the network with gigabytes of data being backed up. Your users will then complain that the entire network has slowed to a snail's pace.

Network performance is one of the main reasons why you should try to run your backups during off hours, when other users aren't accessing the network. Another reason to run backups during off hours is so that you can perform a more thorough backup. If you run your backup while other users are accessing files, the backup program is likely to skip over any files that are being accessed by users at the time the backup runs. As a result, your backup won't include those files. Ironically, the files most likely to get left out of the backup are often the files that need backing up the most because they're the files that are being used and modified.

Here are some extra thoughts on client and server backups:

✦ **Backing up directly from the server isn't necessarily be more efficient than backing up from a client because data doesn't have to travel over the network.** The network may well be faster than the tape drive. The network probably won't slow down backups unless you back up during the busiest time of the day, when hordes of network users are storming the network gates.

 ✦ **To improve network backup speed and to minimize the effect that network backups have on the rest of the network, consider using a 1,000 Mbps switch instead of a normal 100 Mbps switch to connect the servers and the backup client.** That way, network traffic between the server and the backup client won't bog down the rest of the network.

✦ **Any files that are open while the backups are running won't get backed up.** That's usually not a problem because backups are run at off hours when people have gone home. However, if someone leaves his computer on with a Word document open, that Word document won't be backed up. One way to solve this problem is to set up the server so that it automatically logs everyone off the network before the backups begin.

✦ **Some backup programs have special features that enable them to back up open files.** For example, the Windows Server 2003 and 2008 backup programs do this by creating a snapshot of the volume when it begins, thus making temporary copies of any files that are modified during the backup. The backup backs up the temporary copies rather than the versions being modified. When the backup finishes, the temporary copies are deleted.

How Many Sets of Backups Should You Keep?

Don't try to cut costs by purchasing one backup tape and reusing it every day. What happens if you accidentally delete an important file on Tuesday and don't discover your mistake until Thursday? Because the file didn't exist on Wednesday, it won't be on Wednesday's backup tape. If you have only one tape that's reused every day, you're outta luck.

The safest scheme is to use a new backup tape every day and keep all your old tapes in a vault. Pretty soon, though, your tape vault can start looking like the warehouse where they stored the Ark of the Covenant at the end of *Raiders of the Lost Ark*.

As a compromise between these two extremes, most users purchase several tapes and rotate them. That way, you always have several backup tapes to fall back on, just in case the file you need isn't on the most recent backup tape. This technique is *tape rotation,* and several variations are commonly used:

✦ **The simplest approach is to purchase three tapes and label them A, B, and C.** You use the tapes on a daily basis in sequence: A the first day, B the second day, C the third day; then A the fourth day, B the fifth day, C the sixth day, and so on. On any given day, you have three generations of backups: today's, yesterday's, and the day-before-yesterday's. Computer geeks like to call these the *grandfather, father,* and *son* tapes.

✦ **Another simple approach is to purchase five tapes and use one each day of the workweek.**

✦ **A variation of the preceding bullet is to buy eight tapes.** Take four of them and write *Tuesday* on one label, *Wednesday* on the second, *Thursday* on the third, and *Friday* on the fourth label. On the other four tapes, write *Monday 1, Monday 2, Monday 3,* and *Monday 4.* Now, tack up a calendar on the wall near the computer and number all the Mondays in the year: 1, 2, 3, 4, 1, 2, 3, 4, and so on.

On Tuesday through Friday, you use the appropriate daily backup tape. When you run a full backup on Monday, consult the calendar to decide which Monday tape to use. With this scheme, you always have four weeks' worth of Monday backup tapes, plus individual backup tapes for the rest of the week.

✦ **If bookkeeping data lives on the network, make a backup copy of all your files (or at least all your accounting files) immediately before closing the books each month; then retain those backups for each month of the year.** This doesn't necessarily mean that you should purchase 12 additional tapes. If you back up just your accounting files, you can probably fit all 12 months on a single tape. Just make sure that you back up with the "append to tape" option rather than the "erase tape" option so that the previous contents of the tape aren't destroyed. Also, treat this accounting backup as completely separate from your normal daily backup routine.

Keep at least one recent full backup at another location. That way, if your office should fall victim to an errant Scud missile or a rogue asteroid, you can re-create your data from the backup copy that you stored offsite. Make sure the person entrusted with the task of taking the backups to this off-site location is trustworthy.

A Word about Tape Reliability

From experience, I've found that although tape drives are very reliable, they do run amok once in a while. The problem is that they don't always tell you when they're not working. A tape drive (especially the less-expensive Travan drives) can spin along for hours, pretending to back up your data — but in reality, your data isn't being written reliably to the tape. In other words, a tape drive can trick you into thinking that your backups are working just fine. Then, when disaster strikes and you need your backup tapes, you may just discover that the tapes are worthless.

Don't panic! Here's a simple way to assure yourself that your tape drive is working. Just activate the "compare after backup" feature of your backup software. Then, as soon as your backup program finishes backing up your data, it rewinds the tape, reads each backed-up file, and compares it with the original version on the hard drive. If all files compare, you know your backups are trustworthy.

Here are some additional thoughts about the reliability of tapes:

✦ The compare-after-backup feature doubles the time required to do a backup, but that doesn't matter if your entire backup fits on one tape. You can just run the backup after hours. Whether the backup and repair operation takes one hour or ten doesn't matter, as long as it's finished by the time the network users arrive at work the next morning.

✦ If your backups require more than one tape, you may not want to run the compare-after-backup feature every day. However, be sure to run it periodically to check that your tape drive is working.

✦ If your backup program reports errors, throw away the tape and use a new tape.

✦ Actually, you should ignore that last comment about waiting for your backup program to report errors. You should discard tapes *before* your backup program reports errors. Most experts recommend that you should use a tape only about 20 times before discarding it. If you use the same tape every day, replace it monthly. If you have tapes for each day of the week, replace them twice yearly. If you have more tapes than that, figure out a cycle that replaces tapes after about 20 uses.

About Cleaning the Heads

An important aspect of backup reliability is proper maintenance of your tape drives. Every time you back up to tape, little bits and specks of the tape rub off onto the read and write heads inside the tape drive. Eventually, the heads become too dirty to reliably read or write data.

To counteract this problem, clean the tape heads regularly. The easiest way to clean them is to use a cleaning cartridge for the tape drive. The drive automatically recognizes when you insert a cleaning cartridge and then performs a routine that wipes the cleaning tape back and forth over the heads to clean them. When the cleaning routine is done, the tape is ejected. The whole process takes only about 30 seconds.

Because the maintenance requirements of each drive differ, check the drive's user's manual to find out how and how often to clean the drive. As a general rule, clean the drives once weekly.

The most annoying aspect of tape drive cleaning is that the cleaning cartridges have a limited lifespan. And, unfortunately, if you insert a used-up cleaning cartridge, the drive accepts it and pretends to clean the drive. For this reason, keep track how many times you used the cleaning cartridge and replace it as recommended by the manufacturer.

Backup Security

Backups create an often-overlooked security exposure for your network. No matter how carefully you set up user accounts and enforce password policies, if any user (including a guest) can perform a backup of the system, that user may make an unauthorized backup. In addition, your backup tapes themselves are vulnerable to theft. As a result, make sure that your backup policies and procedures are secure by taking the following measures:

✦ **Set up a user account for the user who does backups.** Because this user account has backup permission for the entire server, guard its password carefully. Anyone who knows the username and password of the backup account can log in and bypass any security restrictions that you place on that user's normal user ID.

✦ **Counter potential security problems by restricting the backup user ID to a certain client and a certain time of the day.** If you're really clever (and paranoid), you can probably set up the backup user's account so that only the program it can run is the backup program.

✦ **Use encryption to protect the contents of your backup tapes.**

✦ **Secure the backup tapes in a safe location, such as, um, a safe.**

Chapter 9: Disaster Recovery and Business Continuity Planning

In This Chapter

✓ Realizing the need for backups

✓ Making a plan

✓ Practicing disaster recovery

✓ Remembering tape rotation and other details

On April Fools Day about 20 years ago, my colleagues and I discovered that some loser had broken into the office the night before and pounded our computer equipment to death with a crowbar. (I'm not making this up.)

Sitting on a shelf right next to the mangled piles of what used to be a Wang minicomputer system was an undisturbed disk pack that contained the only complete backup of all the information that was on the destroyed computer. The vandal didn't realize that one more swing of the crowbar would have escalated this major inconvenience into a complete catastrophe. Sure, we were up a creek until we could get the computer replaced. And in those days, you couldn't just walk into your local Computer Depot and buy a new computer off the shelf — this was a Wang minicomputer system that had to be specially ordered. After we had the new computer, though, a simple restore from the backup disk brought us right back to where we were on March 31. Without that backup, getting back on track would have taken months.

I've been paranoid about disaster planning ever since. Before then, I thought that disaster planning meant doing good backups. That's a part of it, but I can never forget the day we came within one swing of the crowbar of losing everything. Vandals are probably much smarter now: They know to smash the backup disks as well as the computers themselves. Being prepared for disasters entails much more than just doing regular backups.

Nowadays, the trendy term for disaster planning is a *business continuity plan* (BCP). I suppose the term *disaster planning* sounded too negative, like we were planning for disasters to happen. The new term refocuses attention on the more positive aspect of preparing a plan that will enable a business to carry on with as little interruption as possible in the event of a disaster.

For more in-depth information about this topic, please refer to *IT Disaster Recovery Planning For Dummies* by Peter Gregory, published by Wiley, of course.

Assessing Different Types of Disasters

Disasters come in many shapes and sizes. Some types of disasters are more likely than others. For example, your building is more likely to be struck by lightning than to be hit by a comet. In some cases, the likelihood of a particular type of disaster depends on where you're located. For example, crippling snowstorms are more likely in New York than in Florida.

In addition, the impact of each type of disaster varies from company to company. What may be a disaster for one company may only be a mere inconvenience for another. For example, a law firm may tolerate a disruption in telephone service for a day or two. Loss of communication via phone would be a major inconvenience but not a disaster. To a telemarketing firm, however, a day or two with the phones down is a more severe problem because the company's revenue depends on the phones.

One of the first steps in developing a business continuity plan is to assess the risk of the various types of disasters that may affect your organization. Weigh the likelihood of a disaster happening with the severity of the impact that the disaster would have. For example, a meteor crashing into your building would probably be pretty severe, but the odds of that happening are miniscule. On the other hand, the odds of your building being destroyed by fire are much higher, and the consequences of a devastating fire would be about the same as those from a meteor impact.

The following sections describe the most common types of risks that most companies face. Notice throughout this discussion that although many of these risks are related to computers and network technology, some are not. The scope of business continuity planning is much larger than just computer technology.

Environmental disasters

Environmental disasters are what most people think of first when they think of disaster recovery. Some types of environmental disasters are regional. Others can happen pretty much anywhere.

✦ **Fire:** Fire is probably the first disaster that most people think of when they consider disaster planning. Fires can be caused by unsafe conditions; carelessness, such as electrical wiring that isn't up to code; natural causes, such as lightning strikes; or arson.

✦ **Earthquakes:** Earthquakes can cause not only structural damage to your building, but they can also disrupt the delivery of key services and utilities, such as water and power. Serious earthquakes are rare and unpredictable, but some areas experience them with more regularity than others. If your business is located in an area known for earthquakes, your BCP should consider how your company would deal with a devastating earthquake.

✦ **Weather:** Weather disasters can cause major disruption to your business. Moderate weather may close transportation systems so that your employees can't get to work. Severe weather may damage your building or interrupt delivery of services, such as electricity and water.

✦ **Water:** Flooding can wreak havoc with electrical equipment, such as computers. If floodwaters get into your computer room, chances are good that the computer equipment will be totally destroyed. Flooding can be caused not only by bad weather but also by burst pipes or malfunctioning sprinklers.

✦ **Lightning:** Lightning storms can cause electrical damage to your computer and other electronic equipment from lightning strikes as well as surges in the local power supply.

Deliberate disasters

Some disasters are the result of deliberate actions by others. For example

✦ **Intentional damage:** Vandalism or arson may damage or destroy your facilities or your computer systems. The vandalism or arson may be targeted at you specifically by a disgruntled employee or customer, or it may be random. Either way, the effect is the same.

Don't neglect the possibility of sabotage. A disgruntled employee who gets hold of an administrator's account and password can do all sorts of nasty things to your network.

✦ **Theft:** Theft is always a possibility. You may come to work someday to find that your servers or other computer equipment have been stolen.

✦ **Terrorism:** Terrorism used to be something that most Americans weren't concerned about, but September 11, 2001, changed all that. No matter where you live in the world, the possibility of a terrorist attack is real.

Disruption of services

You may not realize just how much your business depends on the delivery of services and utilities. A BCP should take into consideration how you will deal with the loss of certain services:

✦ **No juice:** Electrical power is crucial for computers and other types of equipment. During a power failure once (I live in California, so I'm used to it), I discovered that I can't even work with pencil and paper because all my pencil sharpeners are electric. Electrical outages are not uncommon, but the technology to deal with them is readily available. UPS (uninterruptible power supply) equipment is reliable and inexpensive.

✦ **No communications:** Communication connections can be disrupted by many causes. A few years ago, a railroad overpass was constructed across the street from my office. One day, a backhoe cut through the phone lines, completely cutting off our phone service — including our Internet connection — for a day and a half.

✦ **No water:** An interruption in the water supply may not shut down your computers, but it can disrupt your business by forcing you to close your facility until the water supply is reestablished.

Equipment failure

Modern companies depend on many different types of equipment for their daily operations. The failure of any of these key systems can disrupt business until the systems are repaired:

✦ **Computer equipment failure can obviously affect business operations.**

✦ **Air-conditioning systems are crucial to regulate temperatures, especially in computer rooms.** Computer equipment can be damaged if the temperature climbs too high.

✦ **Elevators, automatic doors, and other equipment may also be necessary for your business.**

Other disasters

You should assess many other potential disasters. Here are just a few:

✦ Labor disputes

✦ Loss of key staff because of resignation, injury, sickness, or death

✦ Workplace violence

✦ Public health issues, such as epidemics, mold infestations, and so on

✦ Loss of a key supplier

✦ Nearby disaster, such as a fire or police action across the street that results in your business being temporarily blocked off

Analyzing the Impact of a Disaster

With a good understanding of the types of disasters that can affect your business, you can turn your attention to the impact that these disasters can have on your business. The first step is to identify the key business processes that can be impacted by different types of disasters. These business processes are different for each company. For example, here are a few of the key business processes for a publishing company:

+ Editorial processes, such as managing projects through the process of technical editing, copyediting, and production

+ Acquisition processes, such as determining product development strategies, recruiting authors, and signing projects

+ Human resource processes, such as payroll, hiring, employee review, and recruiting

+ Marketing processes, including sales tracking, developing marketing materials, sponsoring sales conferences, exhibiting at trade events, and so on

+ Sales and billing processes, such as filling customer orders, maintaining the company Web site, managing inventory, and handling payments

+ Executive and financial processes, such as managing cash flow, securing credit, raising capital, deciding when to go public, and deciding when to buy a smaller publisher or sell out to a bigger publisher

The impact of a disruption to each of these processes will vary. One common way to assess the impact of business process loss is to rate the impact of various degrees of loss for each process. For example, you may rate the loss of each process for the following time frames:

+ 0 to 2 hours

+ 2 to 24 hours

+ 1 to 2 days

+ 2 days to one week

+ More than one week

For some business processes, an interruption of two hours or even one day may be minor. For other processes, even the loss of a few hours may be very costly.

Developing a Business Continuity Plan

A BCP is simply a plan for how you will continue operation of your key business processes should the normal operation of the process fail. For example, if your primary office location is shut down for a week because of a major fire across the street, you won't have to suspend operations if you have a business continuity plan in place.

The key to a BCP is redundancy of each component that is essential to your business processes. These components include:

✦ **Facilities:** If your company already has multiple office locations, you may be able to temporarily squeeze into one of the other locations for the duration of the disaster. If not, you should secure arrangements in advance with a real estate broker so that you can quickly arrange an alternate location. By having an arrangement made in advance, you can move into an emergency location on a moment's notice.

✦ **Computer equipment:** It doesn't hurt to have a set of spare computers in storage somewhere so that you can dig them out to use in an emergency. Preferably, these computers would already have your critical software installed. The next best thing would be to have detailed plans available so that your IT staff can quickly install key software on new equipment to get your business up and running.

Always keep a current set of backup tapes at an alternate location.

✦ **Phones:** Discuss emergency phone services in advance with your phone company. If you're forced to move to another location on 24-hour notice, how quickly can you get your phones up and running? And can you arrange to have your incoming toll-free calls forwarded to the new location?

✦ **Staff:** Unless you work for a government agency, you probably don't have redundant employees. However, you can make arrangements in advance with a temp agency to provide clerical and administrative help on short notice.

✦ **Stationery:** This sounds like a small detail, but you should store a supply of all your key stationery products (letterhead, envelopes, invoices, statements, and so on) in a safe location. That way, if your main location is suddenly unavailable, you don't have to wait a week to get new letterhead or invoices printed.

✦ **Hard copy files:** Keep a backup copy of important printed material (customer billing files, sales records, and so on) at an alternate location.

Holding a Fire Drill

Remember in grade school when the fire alarm would go off and your teacher would tell the kids to calmly put down their work and walk out to the designated safe zone in an orderly fashion? Drills are important so that if a real fire occurs, you don't run and scream and climb all over each other in order to be the first one to get out.

Any disaster recovery plan is incomplete unless you test it to see whether it works. Testing doesn't mean that you should burn your building down one day to see how long it takes you to get back up and running. You should, though, periodically simulate a disaster in order to prove to yourself and your staff that you can recover.

The most basic type of disaster recovery drill is a simple test of your network backup procedures. You should periodically attempt to restore key files from your backup tapes just to make sure that you can. You achieve several benefits by restoring files on a regular basis:

✦ **Tapes are unreliable.** The only way to be sure that your tapes are working is to periodically restore files from them.

✦ **Backup programs are confusing to configure.** I've seen people run backup jobs for years that don't include all the data they think they're backing up. Only when disaster strikes and they need to recover a key file do they discover that the file isn't included in the backup.

✦ **Restoring files can be a little confusing, especially when you use a combination of normal and incremental or differential backups.** Add to that the pressure of having the head of the company watching over your shoulder while you try to recover a lost file. If you regularly conduct file restore drills, you'll familiarize yourself with the restore features of your backup software in a low-pressure situation. Then, you can easily restore files for real when the pressure's on.

You can also conduct walkthroughs of more serious disaster scenarios. For example, you can set aside a day to walk though moving your entire staff to an alternate location. You can double-check that all the backup equipment, documents, and data are available as planned. If something is missing, it's better to find out now rather than while the fire department is still putting water on the last remaining hot spots in what used to be your office.

Book IV

TCP/IP and the Internet

The 5th Wave   By Rich Tennant

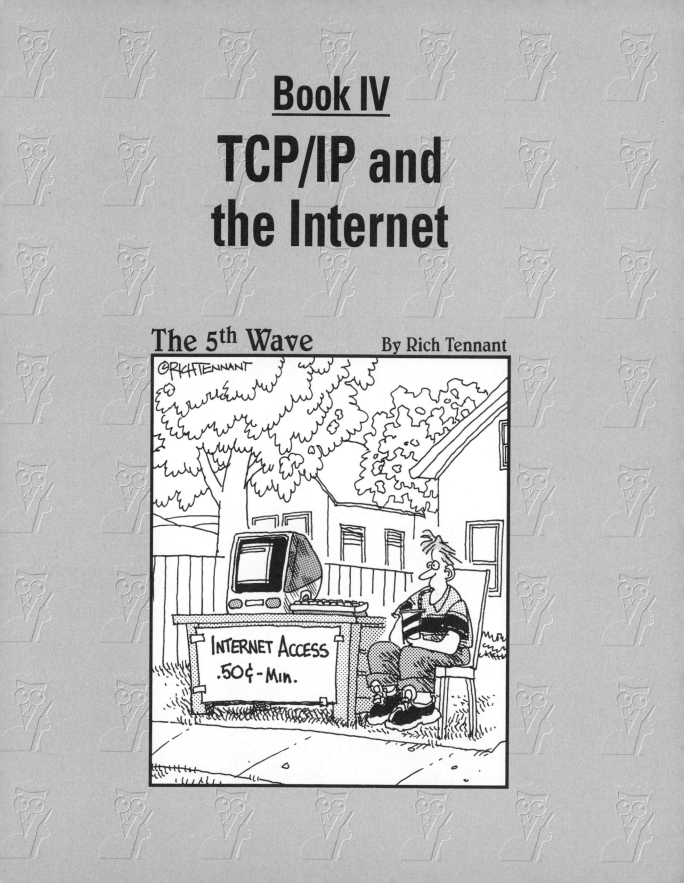

INTERNET ACCESS
.50¢ - Min.

Contents at a Glance

Chapter 1: Introduction to TCP/IP and the Internet

In This Chapter

✔ Introducing the Internet

✔ Familiarizing yourself with TCP/IP standards

✔ Figuring out how TCP/IP lines up with the OSI reference model

✔ Discovering important TCP/IP applications

*J*ust a few short years ago, Transmission Control Protocol/Internet Protocol (TCP/IP) was known primarily as the protocol of the Internet. The biggest challenge of getting a local area network (LAN) connected to the Internet was figuring out how to mesh TCP/IP with the proprietary protocols that were the basis of the LANs — most notably Internetwork Packet Exchange/Sequenced Packet Exchange (IPX/SPX) and NetBIOS Extended User Interface (NetBEUI). A few years ago, network administrators realized that they could save the trouble of combining TCP/IP with IPX/SPX and NetBEUI by eliminating IPX/SPX and NetBEUI from the equation altogether. As a result, TCP/IP is not just the protocol of the Internet now, but it's also the protocol on which most LANs are based.

This chapter is a gentle introduction to the Internet in general and the TCP/IP suite of protocols in particular. After I get the introductions out of the way, you'll be able to focus more in-depth on the detailed TCP/IP information given in the remaining chapters of Book IV.

What Is the Internet?

The Goliath of all computer networks, the Internet links hundreds of millions of computer users throughout the world. Strictly speaking, the Internet is a network of networks. It consists of tens of thousands of separate computer networks, all interlinked, so that a user on any of those networks can reach out and potentially touch a user on any of the other networks. This network of networks connects nearly 5 million computers to each other.

TECHNICAL STUFF

Just how big is the Internet?

Because the Internet is not owned or controlled by any one organization, no one knows how big the Internet really is. Several organizations do attempt to periodically determine the size of the Internet, including the Internet Systems Consortium (ISC), which completed its last survey in January 2007. ISC found that more than 433 million host computers are connected to the Internet. The same survey showed a mere 317 million hosts in January 2005, so the size of the Internet has grown considerably in just a few years. The first year the ISC did the survey (1993), it found only 1.3 million host computers.

Unfortunately, no one knows how many actual users are on the Internet. Each host can support a single user, or in the case of domains — such as `aol.com` (America Online) or `msn.com` (MSN) — hundreds of thousands or perhaps even millions of users. No one really knows. Still, the indisputable point is that the Internet is big and growing every day.

If you're already on the Net and are interested, you can check up on the latest Internet statistics from ISC by visiting its Web site at `www.isc.org/ds`.

One of the official documents (RFC 2026) of the Internet Engineering Task Force (IETF) defines the Internet as "a loosely organized international collaboration of autonomous, interconnected networks." Broken down piece by piece, this definition encompasses several key aspects of what the Internet is:

✦ **Loosely organized:** No single organization has authority over the Internet. As a result, the Internet is not highly organized. Online services, such as America Online or MSN, are owned and operated by individual companies that control exactly what content appears on the service and what software can be used with the service. No one exercises that kind of control over the Internet. As a result, you can find just about any kind of material imaginable on the Internet. No one guarantees the accuracy of information that you find on the Internet, so you have to be careful as you work your way through the labyrinth.

✦ **International:** At least 192 countries are represented on the Internet, from Afghanistan to Zimbabwe.

✦ **Collaboration:** The Internet exists only because many different organizations cooperate to provide the services and support needed to sustain it. For example, much of the software that drives the Internet is open source software that's developed collaboratively by programmers throughout the world, who constantly work to improve the code.

✦ **Autonomous:** The Internet community respects that organizations that join the Internet are free to make their own decisions about how they configure and operate their networks. Although legal issues sometimes boil up, for the most part, each player on the Internet operates independently.

✦ **Interconnected:** The whole key to the Internet is the concept of *interconnection,* which uses standard protocols that enable networks to communicate with each other. Without the interconnection provided by the TCP/IP protocol, the Internet would not exist.

✦ **Networks:** The Internet would be completely unmanageable if it consisted of 317 million individual users, all interconnected. That's why the Internet is often described as a network of networks. Most individual users on the Internet don't access the Internet directly. Instead, they access the Internet indirectly through another network, which may be a LAN in a business or academic environment, or a dialup or broadband network provided by an Internet service provider (ISP). In each case, however, the users of the local network access the Internet via a gateway IP router.

The Internet is composed of several distinct types of networks: Government agencies, such as the Library of Congress and the White House; military sites (did you ever see *War Games*?); educational institutions, such as universities and colleges (and their libraries); businesses, such as Microsoft and IBM; ISPs, which allow individuals to access the Internet; and commercial online services, such as America Online and MSN.

A Little Internet History

The Internet has a fascinating history, if such things interest you. There's no particular reason why you should be interested in such things, of course, except that a superficial understanding of how the Internet got started may help you to understand and cope with the way this massive computer network exists today. So here goes.

The Internet traces its beginnings back to a small network called ARPANET, built by the Department of Defense in 1969 to link defense installations. ARPANET soon expanded to include not only defense installations but universities as well. In the 1970s, ARPANET was split into two networks: one for military use (renamed MILNET) and the original ARPANET (for nonmilitary use). The two networks were connected by a networking link called IP — the *Internet protocol* — so called because it allowed communication between two networks.

The good folks who designed IP had the foresight to realize that soon, more than two networks would want to be connected. In fact, they left room for tens of thousands of networks to join the game, which is a good thing because it wasn't long before the Internet began to take off.

By the mid-1980s, ARPANET was beginning to reach the limits of what it could do. Enter the National Science Foundation (NSF), which set up a nationwide network designed to provide access to huge *supercomputers,* those monolithic computers used to discover new prime numbers and calculate the orbits of distant galaxies. The supercomputers were never put to much use, but the network that was put together to support the supercomputers — NSFNET — was used. In fact, NSFNET replaced ARPANET as the new backbone for the Internet.

Then, out of the blue, it seemed as if the whole world became interested in the Internet. Stories about it appeared in *Time* and *Newsweek.* Any company that had "dot com" in its name practically doubled in value every month. Al Gore claimed he invented the Internet. The Net began to grow so fast that even NSFNET couldn't keep up, so private commercial networks got into the game. The size of the Internet nearly doubled every year for most of the 1990s. Then, in the first few years of the millennium, the growth rate slowed a bit. However, the Internet still seems to be growing at the phenomenal rate of about 30 to 50 percent per year, and who knows how long this dizzying rate of growth will continue.

TCP/IP Standards and RFCs

The TCP/IP protocol standards that define how the Internet works are managed by the IETF. However, the IETF doesn't impose standards. Instead, it simply oversees the process by which ideas are developed into agreed-upon standards.

An Internet standard is published in the Request for Comments (RFC) document. When a document is accepted for publication, it is assigned an RFC number by the IETF. The RFC is then published. After it's published, an RFC is never changed. If a standard is enhanced, the enhancement is covered in a separate RFC.

At the time of this writing, more than 3,500 RFCs were available from the IETF Web site (`www.ietf.org`). The oldest RFC is RFC 0001, published in 1969. It describes how the host computers communicated with each other in the original ARPANET. The most recent RFC (as of December, 2007) is RFC 5092, a proposed standard entitled "IMAP URL Scheme."

Not all RFCs represent Internet standards. The following paragraphs summarize the various types of RFC documents:

✦ **Internet Standards Track:** This type of RCF represents an Internet standard. Standards Track RFCs have one of three maturity levels, as described in Table 1-1. An RFC enters circulation with Proposed Standard status but may be elevated to Draft Standard status — and, ultimately, to Internet Standard status.

Table 1-1	Maturity Levels for Internet Standards Track RFCs
Maturity Level	*Description*
Proposed Standard	Proposed standards are generally stable, have resolved known design choices, are believed to be well understood, have received significant community review, and appear to enjoy enough community interest to be considered valuable.
Draft Standard	Draft standards are well understood and known to be quite stable. At least two interoperable implementations must exist, developed independently from separate code bases. The specification is believed to be mature and useful.
Internet Standard	Internet Standards have been fully accepted by the Internet community as highly mature and useful standards.

✦ **Experimental specifications:** These are a result of research or development efforts. They're not intended to be standards, but the information they contain may be of use to the Internet community.

✦ **Informational specifications:** These simply provide general information for the Internet community.

✦ **Historic specifications:** These RFCs have been superceded by a more recent RFC and are thus considered obsolete.

✦ **Best Current Practice (BCP):** RFCs are documents that summarize the consensus of the Internet community's opinion on the best way to perform an operation or procedure. BCPs are guidelines, not standards.

Table 1-2 summarizes the RFCs that apply to the key Internet standards described in this book.

Table 1-2	RFCs for Key Internet Standards	
RFC	*Date*	*Description*
768	August 1980	User Datagram Protocol (UDP)
791	September 1981	Internet Protocol (IP)
792	September 1981	Internet Control Message Protocol (ICMP)
793	September 1981	Transmission Control Protocol (TCP)
826	November 1982	Ethernet Address Resolution Protocol (ARP)
950	August 1985	Internet Standard Subnetting Procedure
959	October 1985	File Transfer Protocol (FTP)
1034	November 1987	Domain Names — Concepts and Facilities (DNS)

Book IV
Chapter 1

Introduction to
TCP/IP and
the Internet

(continued)

Table 1-2 *(continued)*

RFC	Date	Description
1035	November 1987	Domain Names — Implementation and Specification (DNS)
1939	May 1996	Post Office Protocol Version 3 (POP3)
2131	March 1997	Dynamic Host Configuration Protocol (DHCP)
2236	November 1997	Internet Group Management Protocol (IGMP) (Updates RFC 1112)
2616	June 1999	Hypertext Transfer Protocol — HTTP/1.1
2821	April 2001	Simple Mail Transfer Protocol (SMTP)

My favorite RFC is 1149, an experimental specification for the "Transmission of IP datagrams on avian carriers." The specification calls for IP datagrams to be written in hexadecimal on scrolls of paper and secured to "avian carriers" with duct tape. (Not surprisingly, it's dated 1 April, 1990. Similar RFCs are submitted on April 1 almost every year.)

The TCP/IP Protocol Framework

Like the seven-layer OSI Reference Model, TCP/IP protocols are based on a layered framework. TCP/IP has four layers, as shown in Figure 1-1. These layers are described in the following sections.

Figure 1-1:
The four layers of the TCP/IP framework.

TCP/IP Layers	TCP/IP Protocols				
Application Layer	HTTP	FTP	Telnet	SMTP	DNS
Transport Layer	TCP			UDP	
Network Layer	IP		ARP	ICMP	IGMP
Network Interface Layer	Ethernet		Token Ring		Other Link-Layer Protocols

Network Interface layer

The lowest level of the TCP/IP architecture is the Network Interface layer. It corresponds to the OSI Physical and Data Link layers. You can use many different TCP/IP protocols at the Network Interface layer, including Ethernet and Token Ring for LANs and protocols such as X.25, Frame Relay, and ATM for wide area networks (WANs).

The Network Interface layer is assumed to be unreliable.

Network layer

The Network layer is where data is addressed, packaged, and routed among networks. Several important Internet protocols operate at the Network layer:

✦ **Internet Protocol (IP):** A routable protocol that uses IP addresses to deliver packets to network devices. IP is an intentionally unreliable protocol, so it doesn't guarantee delivery of information.

✦ **Address Resolution Protocol (ARP):** Resolves IP addresses to hardware MAC addresses, which uniquely identify hardware devices.

✦ **Internet Control Message Protocol (ICMP):** Sends and receives diagnostic messages. ICMP is the basis of the ubiquitous `ping` command.

✦ **Internet Group Management Protocol (IGMP):** Used to multicast messages to multiple IP addresses at once.

Transport layer

The Transport layer is where sessions are established and data packets are exchanged between hosts. Two core protocols are found at this layer:

✦ **Transmission Control Protocol (TCP):** Provides reliable connection-oriented transmission between two hosts. TCP establishes a session between hosts, and then ensures delivery of packets between the hosts.

✦ **User Datagram Protocol (UDP):** Provides connectionless, unreliable, one-to-one or one-to-many delivery.

**Book IV
Chapter 1**

**Introduction to
TCP/IP and
the Internet**

Application layer

The Application layer of the TCP/IP model corresponds to the Session, Presentation, and Application layers of the OSI Reference Model. A few of the most popular Application layer protocols are

+ **HyperText Transfer Protocol (HTTP):** The core protocol of the World Wide Web

+ **File Transfer Protocol (FTP):** A protocol that enables a client to send and receive complete files from a server

+ **Telnet:** The protocol that lets you connect to another computer on the Internet in a terminal emulation mode

+ **Simple Mail Transfer Protocol (SMTP):** One of several key protocols that are used to provide e-mail services

+ **Domain Name System (DNS):** The protocol that allows you to refer to other host computers by using names rather than numbers

Chapter 2: Understanding IP Addresses

*O*ne of the most basic components of TCP/IP is IP addressing. Every device on a TCP/IP network must have a unique IP address. In this chapter, I describe the ins and outs of these IP addresses. Enjoy!

Understanding Binary

Before you can understand the details of how IP addressing works, you need to understand how the binary numbering system works because binary is the basis of IP addressing. If you already understand binary, please skip to the section, "Introducing IP Addresses." I don't want to bore you with stuff that's too basic.

Counting by ones

Binary is a counting system that uses only two numerals: 0 and 1. In the decimal system (with which most people are accustomed), you use 10 numerals: 0–9. In an ordinary decimal number — such as 3,482 — the rightmost digit represents ones; the next digit to the left, tens; the next, hundreds; the next, thousands; and so on. These digits represent powers of ten: first 10^0 (which is 1); next, 10^1 (10); then 10^2 (100); then 10^3 (1,000); and so on.

In binary, you have only two numerals rather than ten, which is why binary numbers look somewhat monotonous, as in 110011, 101111, and 100001.

The positions in a binary number (called *bits* rather than *digits*) represent powers of two rather than powers of ten: 1, 2, 4, 8, 16, 32, and so on. To figure the decimal value of a binary number, you multiply each bit by its corresponding power of two and then add the results. The decimal value of binary 10111, for example, is calculated as follows:

```
  1 × 20 = 1 ×  1 =   1
+ 1 × 21 = 1 ×  2 =   2
+ 1 × 22 = 1 ×  4 =   4
+ 0 × 23 = 0 ×  8 =   0
+ 1 × 24 = 1 × 16 =  16
                     23
```

Fortunately, converting a number between binary and decimal is something a computer is good at — so good, in fact, that you're unlikely ever to need to do any conversions yourself. The point of learning binary is not to be able to look at a number such as 1110110110110 and say instantly, "Ah! Decimal 7,606!" (If you could do that, Barbara Walters would probably interview you, and they would even make a movie about you — starring Dustin Hoffman.)

Instead, the point is to have a basic understanding of how computers store information and — most important — to understand how the binary counting system works, which I describe in the following section.

Here are some of the more interesting characteristics of binary and how the system is similar to and differs from the decimal system:

✦ **In decimal, the number of decimal places allotted for a number determines how large the number can be.** If you allot six digits, for example, the largest number possible is 999,999. Because 0 is itself a number, however, a six-digit number can have any of 1 million different values.

   Similarly, the number of bits allotted for a binary number determines how large that number can be. If you allot eight bits, the largest value that number can store is 11111111, which happens to be 255 in decimal.

✦ **To quickly figure how many different values you can store in a binary number of a given length, use the number of bits as an exponent of two.** An eight-bit binary number, for example, can hold 2^8 values. Because 2^8 is 256, an eight-bit number can have any of 256 different values. This is why a *byte* — eight bits — can have 256 different values.

✦ **This "powers of two" thing is why computers don't use nice, even, round numbers in measuring such values as memory or disk space.** A value of 1K, for example, is not an even 1,000 bytes: It's actually 1,024 bytes because 1,024 is 2^{10}. Similarly, 1MB is not an even 1,000,000 bytes but instead 1,048,576 bytes, which happens to be 2^{20}.

One basic test of computer nerddom is knowing your powers of two because they play such an important role in binary numbers. Just for the fun of it, but not because you really need to know, Table 2-1 lists the powers of two up to 32.

Table 2-1 also shows the common shorthand notation for various powers of two. The abbreviation *K* represents 2^{10} (1,024). The *M* in *MB* stands for 2^{20}, or 1,024K, and the *G* in *GB* represents 2^{30}, which is 1,024MB. These shorthand notations don't have anything to do with TCP/IP, but they're commonly used for measuring computer disk and memory capacities, so I thought I'd throw them in at no charge because the table had extra room.

Table 2-1			Powers of Two		
Power	*Bytes*	*Kilobytes*	*Power*	*Bytes*	*K, MB, or GB*
2^1	2		2^{17}	131,072	128K
2^2	4		2^{18}	262,144	256K
2^3	8		2^{19}	524,288	512K
2^4	16		2^{20}	1,048,576	1MB
2^5	32		2^{21}	2,097,152	2MB
2^6	64		2^{22}	4,194,304	4MB
2^7	128		2^{23}	8,388,608	8MB
2^8	256		2^{24}	16,777,216	16MB
2^9	512		2^{25}	33,554,432	32MB
2^{10}	1,024	1K	2^{26}	67,108,864	64MB
2^{11}	2,048	2K	2^{27}	134,217,728	128MB
2^{12}	4,096	4K	2^{28}	268,435,456	256MB
2^{13}	8,192	8K	2^{29}	536,870,912	512MB
2^{14}	16,384	16K	2^{30}	1,073,741,824	1GB
2^{15}	32,768	32K	2^{31}	2,147,483,648	2GB
2^{16}	65,536	64K	2^{32}	4,294,967,296	4GB

Doing the logic thing

One of the great things about binary is that it's very efficient at handling special operations: namely, logical operations. Four basic logical operations exist although additional operations are derived from the basic four operations. Three of the operations — AND, OR, and XOR — compare two binary digits (bits). The fourth (NOT) works on just a single bit.

The following list summarizes the basic logical operations:

✦ **AND:** An AND operation compares two binary values. If both values are 1, the result of the AND operation is 1. If one or both of the values are 0, the result is 0.

✦ **OR:** An OR operation compares two binary values. If at least one of the values is 1, the result of the OR operation is 1. If both values are 0, the result is 0.

✦ **XOR:** An XOR operation compares two binary values. If exactly one of them is 1, the result is 1. If both values are 0 or if both values are 1, the result is 0.

✦ **NOT:** The NOT operation doesn't compare two values. Instead, it simply changes the value of a single binary value. If the original value is 1, NOT returns 0. If the original value is 0, NOT returns 1.

Table 2-2 summarizes how AND, OR, and XOR work.

Table 2-2	Logical Operations for Binary Values			
First Value	*Second Value*	*AND*	*OR*	*XOR*
0	0	0	0	0
0	1	0	1	1
1	0	0	1	1
1	1	1	1	0

Logical operations are applied to binary numbers that have more than one binary digit by applying the operation one bit at a time. The easiest way to do this manually is to line the two binary numbers on top of one another and then write the result of the operation beneath each binary digit. The following example shows how you would calculate 10010100 AND 11011101:

```
    10010100
AND 11011101
    10010100
```

As you can see, the result is 10010100.

Working with the binary Windows Calculator

The Calculator program that comes with all versions of Windows has a special Scientific mode that many users don't know about. When you flip the Calculator into this mode, you can do instant binary and decimal conversions, which can occasionally come in handy when you're working with IP addresses.

To use the Windows Calculator in Scientific mode, launch the Calculator by choosing Start➪All Programs➪Accessories➪Calculator. Then, choose the View➪Scientific command from the Calculator menu. The Calculator changes to a fancy scientific model — the kind I paid $200 for when I was in college. All kinds of buttons appear, as shown in Figure 2-1.

Figure 2-1:
The free
Windows
scientific
Calculator.

You can select the Bin and Dec radio buttons to convert values between decimal and binary. For example, to find the binary equivalent of decimal 155, enter **155** and then select the Bin radio button. The value in the display changes to 10011011.

Here are a few other things to note about the Scientific mode of the Calculator:

✦ Although you can convert decimal values to binary values with the scientific Calculator, the Calculator can't handle the dotted-decimal IP address format that's described later in this chapter. To convert a dotted-decimal address to binary, just convert each octet separately. For example, to convert 172.65.48.120 to binary, first convert 172; then convert 65; then convert 48; and finally, convert 120.

✦ The scientific Calculator has several features that are designed specifically for binary calculations, such as AND, XOR, NOT, NOR, and so on.

✦ The scientific Calculator can also handle hexadecimal conversions. Hexadecimal doesn't come into play when dealing with IP addresses, but it is used for other types of binary numbers, so this feature sometimes proves to be useful.

**Book IV
Chapter 2**

Understanding IP
Addresses

Introducing IP Addresses

An *IP address* is a number that uniquely identifies every host on an IP network. IP addresses operate at the Network layer of the TCP/IP protocol stack, so they are independent of lower-level Data Link layer MAC addresses, such as Ethernet MAC addresses.

IP addresses are 32-bit binary numbers, which means that theoretically, a maximum of something in the neighborhood of 4 billion unique host addresses can exist throughout the Internet. You'd think that would be enough, but TCP/IP places certain restrictions on how IP addresses are allocated. These restrictions severely limit the total number of usable IP addresses. Many experts predict that we will run out of IP addresses as soon as the year 2010. However, new techniques for working with IP addresses have helped to alleviate this problem, and a new standard for 128-bit IP addresses has been adopted but is not yet in widespread use.

Networks and hosts

IP stands for *Internet Protocol,* and its primary purpose is to enable communications between networks. As a result, a 32-bit IP address actually consists of two parts:

✦ The *network ID* (or *network address*): Identifies the network on which a host computer can be found

✦ The *host ID* (or *host address*): Identifies a specific device on the network indicated by the network ID

Most of the complexity of working with IP addresses has to do with figuring out which part of the complete 32-bit IP address is the network ID and which part is the host ID. The original IP specification uses a system called *address classes* to determine which part of the IP address is the network ID and which part is the host ID. A newer system — classless IP addresses — is rapidly taking over the address classes system.

As I describe the details of how host IDs are assigned, you may notice that two host addresses seem to be unaccounted for. For example, the Class C addressing scheme, which uses eight bits for the host ID, allows only 254 hosts — not the 256 hosts you'd expect. That's because host 0 (the host ID is all zeros) is always reserved to represent the network itself. The host ID can't be 255 (the host ID is all ones) because that host ID is reserved for use as a broadcast request that's intended for all hosts on the network.

The dotted-decimal dance

IP addresses are usually represented in a format known as *dotted-decimal notation.* In dotted-decimal notation, each group of eight bits — an *octet* — is represented by its decimal equivalent. For example, consider the following binary IP address:

```
11000000101010001000100000011100
```

To convert this value to dotted-decimal notation, first divide it into four octets, as follows:

```
11000000 10101000 10001000 00011100
```

Then, convert each of the octets to its decimal equivalent:

```
11000000 10101000 10001000 00011100
192      168      136      28
```

Then, use periods to separate the four decimal numbers, like this:

```
192.168.136.28
```

This is the format in which you'll usually see IP addresses represented.

Figure 2-2 shows how the 32 bits of an IP address are broken down into four octets of eight bits each. As you can see, the four octets of an IP address are often referred to as *w, x, y,* and *z.*

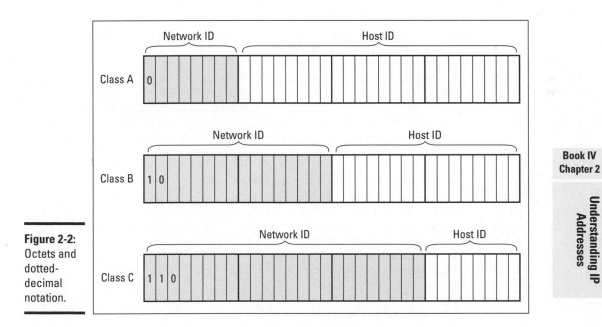

Figure 2-2:
Octets and dotted-decimal notation.

Classifying IP Addresses

When the original designers of the IP protocol created the IP addressing scheme, they could have assigned an arbitrary number of IP address bits for the network ID. The remaining bits would then be used for the host ID. For example, suppose that the designers decided that half of the address (16 bits) would be used for the network, and the remaining 16 bits would be used for the host ID. The result of that scheme would be that the Internet could have a total of 65,536 networks, and each of those networks could have 65,536 hosts.

In the early days of the Internet, this scheme probably seemed like several orders of magnitude more than would ever be needed. However, the IP designers realized from the start that few networks would actually have tens of thousands of hosts. Suppose that a network of 1,000 computers joins the Internet and is assigned one of these hypothetical network IDs. Because that network will use only 1,000 of its 65,536 host addresses, more than 64,000 IP addresses would be wasted.

What about IPv6?

Most of the current Internet is based on version 4 of the Internet Protocol, also known as IPv4. IPv4 has served the Internet well for more than 20 years. However, the growth of the Internet has put a lot of pressure on IPv4's limited 32-bit address space. This chapter describes how IPv4 has evolved to make the best possible use of 32-bit addresses. Eventually, though, all the addresses will be assigned, and the IPv4 address space will be filled to capacity. When that happens, the Internet will have to migrate to the next version of IP, known as IPv6.

IPv6 is also called *IP next generation,* or *IPng,* in honor of the favorite television show of most Internet gurus, *Star Trek: The Next Generation.*

IPv6 offers several advantages over IPv4, but the most important is that it uses 128 bits for Internet addresses instead of 32 bits. The number of host addresses possible with 128 bits is a number so large that it would have made Carl Sagan proud. It doesn't just double or triple the number of available addresses, or even a thousand-fold or even a million-fold. Just for the fun of it, here is the number of unique Internet addresses provided by IPv6:

340,282,366,920,938,463,463,374,607,431,768, 211,456

This number is so large it defies understanding. If the IANA had been around at the creation of the universe and started handing out IPv6 addresses at a rate of one per millisecond — that is, 1,000 addresses every second — it would now, 15 billion years later, have not yet allocated even 1 percent of the available addresses.

The transition from IPv4 to IPv6 has been a slow one. IPv6 is available on all new computers and has been supported on Windows since Windows XP Service Pack 1 (released in 2002). However, most Internet service providers (ISPs) still base their service on IPv4. Thus, the Internet will continue to be driven by IPv4 for at least a few more years.

As a solution to this problem, the idea of IP address classes was introduced. The IP protocol defines five different address classes: A, B, C, D, and E. The first three classes, A–C, each use a different size for the network ID and host ID portion of the address. Class D is for a special type of address called a *multicast address.* Class E is an experimental address class that isn't used.

The first four bits of the IP address are used to determine into which class a particular address fits, as follows:

- ✦ **If the first bit is a zero,** the address is a Class A address.
- ✦ **If the first bit is one and if the second bit is zero,** the address is a Class B address.
- ✦ **If the first two bits are both one and if the third bit is zero,** the address is a Class C address.
- ✦ **If the first three bits are all one and if the fourth bit is zero,** the address is a Class D address.
- ✦ **If the first four bits are all one,** the address is a Class E address.

Because Class D and E addresses are reserved for special purposes, I focus the rest of the discussion here on Class A, B, and C addresses. Table 2-3 summarizes the details of each address class.

Table 2-3		IP Address Classes			
Class	*Address Number Range*	*Starting Bits*	*Length of Network ID*	*Number of Networks*	*Hosts*
A	1–126 .x.y.z	0	8	126	16,777,214
B	128–191 .x.y.z	10	16	16,384	65,534
C	192–223 .x.y.z	110	24	2,097,152	254

Class A addresses

Class A addresses are designed for very large networks. In a Class A address, the first octet of the address is the network ID, and the remaining three octets are the host ID. Because only eight bits are allocated to the network ID and the first of these bits is used to indicate that the address is a Class A address, only 126 Class A networks can exist in the entire Internet. However, each Class A network can accommodate more than 16 million hosts.

Only about 40 Class A addresses are actually assigned to companies or organizations. The rest are either reserved for use by the Internet Assigned Numbers Authority (IANA) or are assigned to organizations that manage IP assignments for geographic regions such as Europe, Asia, and Latin America.

Just for fun, Table 2-4 lists some of the better-known Class A networks. You'll probably recognize many of them. In case you're interested, you can find a complete list of all the Class A address assignments at

`www.iana.org/assignments/ipv4-address-space`

You may have noticed in Table 2-3 that Class A addresses end with $126.x.y.z$, and Class B addresses begin with $128.x.y.z$. What happened to $127.x.y.z$? This special range of addresses is reserved for loopback testing, so these addresses aren't assigned to public networks.

Table 2-4	Some Well-Known Class A Networks		
Net	*Description*	*Net*	*Description*
3	General Electric Company	32	Norsk Informasjonsteknology
4	Bolt Beranek and Newman Inc.	33	DLA Systems Automation Center
6	Army Information Systems Center	35	MERIT Computer Network
8	Bolt Beranek and Newman Inc.	38	Performance Systems International
9	IBM	40	Eli Lilly and Company
11	DoD Intel Information Systems	43	Japan Inet
12	AT&T Bell Laboratories	44	Amateur Radio Digital Communications
13	Xerox Corporation	45	Interop Show Network
15	Hewlett-Packard Company	46	Bolt Beranek and Newman Inc.
16	Digital Equipment Corporation	47	Bell-Northern Research
17	Apple Computer Inc.	48	Prudential Securities Inc.
18	MIT	51	Department of Social Security of UK
19	Ford Motor Company	52	E.I. duPont de Nemours and Co., Inc.
20	Computer Sciences Corporation	53	Cap Debis CCS (Germany)

Net	Description	Net	Description
22	Defense Information Systems Agency	54	Merck and Co., Inc.
25	Royal Signals and Radar Establishment	55	Boeing Computer Services
26	Defense Information Systems Agency	56	U.S. Postal Service
28	Decision Sciences Institute (North)	57	SITA
29–30	Defense Information Systems Agency		

Class B addresses

In a Class B address, the first two octets of the IP address are used as the network ID, and the second two octets are used as the host ID. Thus, a Class B address comes close to my hypothetical scheme of splitting the address down the middle, using half for the network ID and half for the host ID. It isn't identical to this scheme, however, because the first two bits of the first octet are required to be 10, in order to indicate that the address is a Class B address. As a result, a total of 16,384 Class B networks can exist. All Class B addresses fall within the range $128.x.y.z$ to $191.x.y.z$. Each Class B address can accommodate more than 65,000 hosts.

The problem with Class B networks is that even though they are much smaller than Class A networks, they still allocate far too many host IDs. Very few networks have tens of thousands of hosts. Thus, careless assignment of Class B addresses can lead to a large percentage of the available host addresses being wasted on organizations that don't need them.

Class C addresses

In a Class C address, the first three octets are used for the network ID, and the fourth octet is used for the host ID. With only eight bits for the host ID, each Class C network can accommodate only 254 hosts. However, with 24 network ID bits, Class C addresses allow for more than 2 million networks.

The problem with Class C networks is that they're too small. Although few organizations need the tens of thousands of host addresses provided by a Class B address, many organizations need more than a few hundred. The large discrepancy between Class B networks and Class C networks is what led to the development of *subnetting,* which I describe in the next section.

**Book IV
Chapter 2**

Understanding IP Addresses

Subnetting

Subnetting is a technique that lets network administrators use the 32 bits available in an IP address more efficiently by creating networks that aren't limited to the scales provided by Class A, B, and C IP addresses. With subnetting, you can create networks with more realistic host limits.

Subnetting provides a more flexible way to designate which portion of an IP address represents the network ID and which portion represents the host ID. With standard IP address classes, only three possible network ID sizes exist: 8 bits for Class A, 16 bits for Class B, and 24 bits for Class C. Subnetting lets you select an arbitrary number of bits to use for the network ID.

Two reasons compel people to use subnetting. The first is to allocate the limited IP address space more efficiently. If the Internet were limited to Class A, B, or C addresses, every network would be allocated 254, 65 thousand, or 16 million IP addresses for host devices. Although many networks with more than 254 devices exist, few (if any) exist with 65 thousand, let alone 16 million. Unfortunately, any network with more than 254 devices would need a Class B allocation and probably waste tens of thousands of IP addresses.

The second reason for subnetting is that even if a single organization has thousands of network devices, operating all those devices with the same network ID would slow the network to a crawl. The way TCP/IP works dictates that all the computers with the same network ID must be on the same physical network. The physical network comprises a single *broadcast domain,* which means that a single network medium must carry all the traffic for the network. For performance reasons, networks are usually segmented into broadcast domains that are smaller than even Class C addresses provide.

Subnets

A *subnet* is a network that falls within a Class A, B, or C network. Subnets are created by using one or more of the Class A, B, or C host bits to extend the network ID. Thus, instead of the standard 8-, 16-, or 24-bit network ID, subnets can have network IDs of any length.

Figure 2-3 shows an example of a network before and after subnetting has been applied. In the unsubnetted network, the network has been assigned the Class B address `144.28.0.0`. All the devices on this network must share the same broadcast domain.

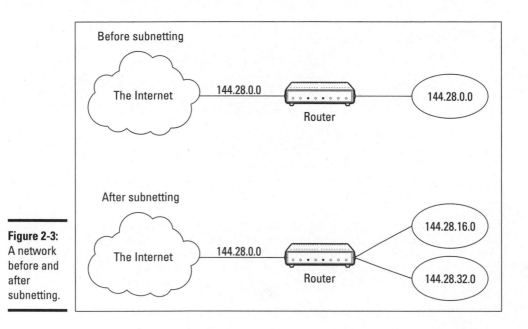

Figure 2-3:
A network
before and
after
subnetting.

In the second network, the first four bits of the host ID are used to divide the network into two small networks, identified as subnets 16 and 32. To the outside world (that is, on the other side of the router), these two networks still appear to be a single network identified as 144.28.0.0. For example, the outside world considers the device at 144.28.16.22 to belong to the 144.28.0.0 network. As a result, a packet sent to this device will be delivered to the router at 144.28.0.0. The router then considers the subnet portion of the host ID to decide whether to route the packet to subnet 16 or subnet 32.

Subnet masks

In order for subnetting to work, the router must be told which portion of the host ID should be used for the subnet network ID. This little sleight of hand is accomplished by using another 32-bit number, known as a *subnet mask*. Those IP address bits that represent the network ID are represented by a 1 in the mask, and those bits that represent the host ID appear as a 0 in the mask. As a result, a subnet mask always has a consecutive string of ones on the left, followed by a string of zeros.

For example, the subnet mask for the subnet shown in Figure 2-3, where the network ID consists of the 16-bit network ID plus an additional 4-bit subnet ID, would look like this:

```
11111111 11111111 11110000 00000000
```

**Book IV
Chapter 2**

**Understanding IP
Addresses**

In other words, the first 20 bits are ones, and the remaining 12 bits are zeros. Thus, the complete network ID is 20 bits in length, and the actual host ID portion of the subnetted address is 12 bits in length.

To determine the network ID of an IP address, the router must have both the IP address and the subnet mask. The router then performs a bitwise operation called a *logical AND* on the IP address in order to extract the network ID. To perform a logical AND, each bit in the IP address is compared with the corresponding bit in the subnet mask. If both bits are 1, the resulting bit in the network ID is set to 1. If either of the bits are 0, the resulting bit is set to 0.

For example, here's how the network address is extracted from an IP address using the 20-bit subnet mask from the previous example:

```
                144  .    28  .    16  .    17
IP address:   10010000 00011100 00010000 00010001
Subnet mask:  11111111 11111111 11110000 00000000
Network ID:   10010000 00011100 00010000 00000000
                144  .    28  .    16  .    0
```

Thus, the network ID for this subnet is `144.28.16.0`.

The subnet mask itself is usually represented in dotted-decimal notation. As a result, the 20-bit subnet mask used in the previous example would be represented as `255.255.240.0`:

```
Subnet mask:  11111111 11111111 11110000 00000000
                255  .    255  .    240  .    0
```

Don't confuse a subnet mask with an IP address. A subnet mask doesn't represent any device or network on the Internet. It's just a way of indicating which portion of an IP address should be used to determine the network ID. (You can spot a subnet mask right away because the first octet is always 255, and 255 is not a valid first octet for any class of IP address.)

Network prefix notation

Because a subnet mask always begins with a consecutive sequence of ones to indicate which bits to use for the network ID, you can use a shorthand notation — a *network prefix* — to indicate how many bits of an IP address represent the network ID. The network prefix is indicated with a slash immediately after the IP address, followed by the number of network ID bits to use. For example, the IP address `144.28.16.17` with the subnet mask `255.255.240.0` can be represented as `144.28.16.17/20` because the subnet mask `255.255.240.0` has 20 network ID bits.

Network prefix notation is also called *classless interdomain routing* notation (*CIDR,* for short) because it provides a way of indicating which portion of an address is the network ID and which is the host ID without relying on standard address classes.

Default subnets

The *default subnet masks* are three subnet masks that correspond to the standard Class A, B, and C address assignments. These default masks are summarized in Table 2-5.

Table 2-5	The Default Subnet Masks		
Class	*Binary*	*Dotted-Decimal*	*Network Prefix*
A	11111111 00000000 00000000 00000000	255.0.0.0	/8
B	11111111 11111111 00000000 00000000	255.255.0.0	/16
C	11111111 11111111 11111111 00000000	255.255.255.0	/24

Keep in mind that a subnet mask is not actually required to use one of these defaults because the IP address class can be determined by examining the first three bits of the IP address. If the first bit is 0, the address is Class A, and the subnet mask 255.0.0 is applied. If the first two bits are 10, the address is Class B, and 255.255.0.0 is used. If the first three bits are 110, the Class C default mask 255.255.255.0 is used.

The great subnet roundup

You should know about a few additional restrictions that are placed on subnets and subnet masks. In particular

✦ **The minimum number of network ID bits is eight.** As a result, the first octet of a subnet mask is always 255.

✦ **The maximum number of network ID bits is 30.** You have to leave at least two bits for the host ID portion of the address to allow for at least two hosts. If you use all 32 bits for the network ID, that leaves no bits for the host ID. Obviously, that won't work. Leaving just one bit for the host ID won't work, either, because a host ID of all ones is reserved for a broadcast address, and all zeros refers to the network itself. Thus, if you use 31 bits for the network ID and leave only 1 for the host ID, host ID 1 would be used for the broadcast address, and host ID 0 would be the network itself, leaving no room for actual hosts. That's why the maximum network ID size is 30 bits.

✦ **Because the network ID portion of a subnet mask is always composed of consecutive bits set to 1, only nine values are possible for each octet of a subnet mask:** 0, 128, 192, 224, 248, 252, 254, and 255.

✦ **A subnet address can't be all zeros or all ones.** Thus, the number of unique subnet addresses is two less than two raised to the number of subnet address bits. For example, with three subnet address bits, six unique subnet addresses are possible ($2^3 - 2 = 6$). This implies that you must have at least two subnet bits. (If a single-bit subnet mask were allowed, it would violate the "can't be all zeros or all ones" rule because the only two allowed values would be 0 or 1.)

IP block parties

A subnet can be thought of as a range or block of IP addresses that have a common network ID. For example, the CIDR 192.168.1.0/28 represents the following block of 14 IP addresses:

```
192.168.1.1    192.168.1.2    192.168.1.3    192.168.1.4
192.168.1.5    192.168.1.6    192.168.1.7    192.168.1.8
192.168.1.9    192.168.1.10   192.168.1.11   192.168.1.12
192.168.1.13   192.168.1.14
```

Given an IP address in CIDR notation, it's useful to be able to determine the range of actual IP addresses that the CIDR represents. This matter is straightforward when the octet within which the network ID mask ends happens to be 0, as in the preceding example. You just determine how many host IDs are allowed based on the size of the network ID and count them off.

However, what if the octet where the network ID mask ends is not 0? For example, what are the valid IP addresses for 192.168.1.100 when the subnet mask is 255.255.255.240? In that case, the calculation is a little harder. The first step is to determine the actual network ID. You can do that by converting both the IP address and the subnet mask to binary and then extracting the network ID as in this example:

```
                192  .   168  .    1  .   100
IP address:   11000000 10101000 00000001 01100100
Subnet mask:  11111111 11111111 11111111 11110000
Network ID:   11000000 10101000 00000001 01100000
                192  .   168  .    1  .   96
```

As a result, the network ID is 192.168.1.96.

Network Address Translation **285**

Next, determine the number of allowable hosts in the subnet based on the network prefix. You can calculate this by subtracting the last octet of the subnet mask from 254. In this case, the number of allowable hosts is 14.

To determine the first IP address in the block, add 1 to the network ID. Thus, the first IP address in my example is `192.168.1.97`. To determine the last IP address in the block, add the number of hosts to the network ID. In my example, the last IP address is `192.168.1.110`. As a result, the `192.168.1.100` with subnet mask `255.255.255.240` designates the following block of IP addresses:

```
192.168.1.97   192.168.1.98   192.168.1.99   192.168.1.100
192.168.1.101  192.168.1.102  192.168.1.103  192.168.1.104
192.168.1.105  192.168.1.106  192.168.1.107  192.168.1.108
192.168.1.109  192.168.1.110
```

Private and public addresses

Any host with a direct connection to the Internet must have a globally unique IP address. However, not all hosts are connected directly to the Internet. Some are on networks that are not connected to the Internet. Some hosts are hidden behind firewalls, so their Internet connection is indirect.

Several blocks of IP addresses are set aside just for this purpose, for use on private networks that are not connected to the Internet or to use on networks that are hidden behind a firewall. Three such ranges of addresses exist, summarized in Table 2-6. Whenever you create a private TCP/IP network, you should use IP addresses from one of these ranges.

Table 2-6	Private Address Spaces	
CIDR	*Subnet Mask*	*Address Range*
`10.0.0.0/8`	`255.0.0.0`	`10.0.0.1–10.255.255.254`
`172.16.0.0/12`	`255.255.240.0`	`172.16.1.1–172.31.255.254`
`192.168.0.0/16`	`255.255.0.0`	`192.168.0.1–192.168.255.254`

Network Address Translation

Many firewalls use a technique called *network address translation* (NAT) to hide the actual IP address of a host from the outside world. When that's the case, the NAT device must use a globally unique IP to represent the host to the Internet. Behind the firewall, though, the host can use any IP address it

Book IV
Chapter 2

Understanding IP Addresses

wants. When packets cross the firewall, the NAT device translates the private IP address to the public IP address and vice versa.

One of the benefits of NAT is that it helps to slow down the rate at which the IP address space is assigned. That's because a NAT device can use a single public IP address for more than one host. It does so by keeping track of outgoing packets so that it can match incoming packets with the correct host. To understand how this works, consider the following sequence of steps:

1. A host whose private address is 192.168.1.100 sends a request to 216.239.57.99, which happens to be www.google.com. The NAT device changes the source IP address of the packet to 208.23.110.22, the IP address of the firewall. That way, Google will send its reply back to the firewall router. The NAT records that 192.168.1.100 sent a request to 216.239.57.99.

2. Now another host, at address 192.168.1.107, sends a request to 207.46.134.190, which happens to be www.microsoft.com. The NAT device changes the source of this request to 208.23.110.22 so that Microsoft will reply to the firewall router. The NAT records that 192.168.1.107 sent a request to 207.46.134.190.

3. A few seconds later, the firewall receives a reply from 216.239.57.99. The destination address in the reply is 208.23.110.22, the address of the firewall. To determine to whom to forward the reply, the firewall checks its records to see who is waiting for a reply from 216.239.57.99. It discovers that 192.168.1.100 is waiting for that reply, so it changes the destination address to 192.168.1.100 and sends the packet on.

Actually, the process is a little more complicated than that, because it's very likely that two or more users may have pending requests from the same public IP. In that case, the NAT device uses other techniques to figure out to which user each incoming packet should be delivered.

Chapter 3: Using DHCP

In This Chapter

✔ **Discovering the basics of DHCP**

✔ **Exploring scopes**

✔ **Configuring a DHCP server**

✔ **Setting up a DHCP client**

*E*very host on a Transmission Control Protocol/Internet Protocol (TCP/IP) network must have a unique IP address. Each host must be properly configured so that it knows its IP address. When a new host comes online, it must be assigned an IP address that's both within the correct range of addresses for the subnet and but not already in use. Although you can manually assign IP addresses to each computer on your network, that task quickly becomes overwhelming if the network has more than a few computers.

That's where DHCP — Dynamic Host Configuration Protocol — comes into play. *DHCP* automatically configures the IP address for every host on a network, thus assuring that each host has a valid, unique IP address. DHCP even automatically reconfigures IP addresses as hosts come and go. As you can imagine, DHCP can save a network administrator many hours of tedious configuration work.

In this chapter, you discover the ins and outs of DHCP: what it is, how it works, and how to set it up.

Understanding DHCP

DHCP allows individual computers on a TCP/IP network to obtain their configuration information — in particular, their IP address — from a server. The DHCP server keeps track of which IP addresses are already assigned so that when a computer requests an IP address, the DHCP server offers it an IP address that's not already in use.

Configuration information provided by DHCP

Although the primary job of DHCP is to dole out IP addresses and subnet masks, DHCP actually provides more configuration information than just the

IP address to its clients. The additional configuration information are DHCP options. The following is a list of some common DHCP options that can be configured by the server:

✦ The router address, also known as the Default Gateway address

✦ The expiration time for the configuration information

✦ Domain name

✦ Domain Name Server (DNS) server address

✦ Windows Internet Name Service (WINS) server address

DHCP servers

A DHCP server can be a server computer located on the TCP/IP network. All modern server operating systems have a built-in DHCP server. To set up DHCP on a network server, all you have to do is enable the server's DHCP function and configure its settings. In the upcoming section, "Working with a DHCP Server," I show you how to configure a DHCP server for Windows Server 2008. (The procedure for Windows Server 2003 is similar.)

A server computer running DHCP doesn't have to be devoted entirely to DHCP unless the network is very large. For most networks, a file server can share duty as a DHCP server. This is especially true if you provide long leases for your IP addresses. (I explain the idea of leases later in this chapter.)

Many multifunction routers also have built-in DHCP servers. If you don't want to burden one of your network servers with the DHCP function, you can enable the router's built-in DHCP server. An advantage of allowing the router to be your network's DHCP server is that you rarely need to power-down a router. In contrast, you occasionally need to restart or power-down a file server to perform system maintenance, apply upgrades, or perform troubleshooting.

Most networks require only one DHCP server. Setting up two or more servers on the same network requires that you carefully coordinate the IP address ranges (known as *scopes*) for which each server is responsible. If you accidentally set up two DHCP servers for the same scope, you may end up with duplicate address assignments if the servers attempt to assign the same IP address to two different hosts. To prevent this from happening, just set up one DHCP server unless your network is so large that one server can't handle the workload.

How DHCP actually works

You can configure and use DHCP without knowing the details of how DHCP client configuration actually works. However, a basic understanding of the process can help you to understand what DHCP is actually doing. This

understanding is not only enlightening, but it can also help when you're trouble
shooting DHCP problems.

The following paragraphs contain a blow-by-blow account of how DHCP
configures TCP/IP hosts. This procedure happens every time you boot up a
host computer. It also happens when you release an IP lease and request
a fresh lease.

1. When a host computer starts up, the DHCP client software sends a special
   broadcast packet, known as a *DHCP Discover message*.

   This message uses the subnet's broadcast address (all host ID bits set to
   one) as the destination address and 0.0.0.0 as the source address.

   The client has to specify 0.0.0.0 as the source address because it doesn't
   yet have an IP address, and it specifies the broadcast address as the
   destination address because it doesn't know the address of any DHCP
   servers. In effect, the DHCP Discover message is saying, "Hey! I'm new
   here. Are there any DHCP servers out there?"

2. The DHCP server receives the broadcast DHCP Discover message and
   responds by sending a *DHCP Offer message*.

   The DHCP Offer message includes an IP address that the client can use.

   Like the DHCP Discover message, the DHCP Offer message is sent to the
   broadcast address. This makes sense because the client to which the
   message is being sent doesn't yet have an IP address and won't have one
   until it accepts the offer. In effect, the DHCP Offer message is saying,
   "Hello there, whoever you are. Here's an IP address you can use, if you
   want it. Let me know."

   What if the client never receives a DHCP Offer message from a DHCP
   server? In that case, the client waits for a few seconds and tries again.
   The client will try four times — at 2, 4, 8, and 16 seconds. If it still doesn't
   get an offer, it will try again after five minutes.

3. The client receives the DHCP Offer message and sends back a message
   known as a *DHCP Request message*.

   At this point, the client doesn't actually own the IP address: It's simply
   indicating that it's ready to accept the IP address that was offered by the
   server. In effect, the DHCP Request message says, "Yes, that IP address
   would be good for me. Can I have it, please?"

4. When the server receives the DHCP Request message, it marks the IP
   address as assigned to the client and broadcasts a *DHCP Ack message*.

   The DHCP Ack message says, in effect, "Okay, it's all yours. Here's the
   rest of the information you need to use it."

5. When the client receives the DHCP Ack message, it configures its TCP/IP
   stack by using the address it accepted from the server.

Book IV
Chapter 3

Using DHCP

Understanding Scopes

A *scope* is simply a range of IP addresses that a DHCP server is configured to distribute. In the simplest case, where a single DHCP server oversees IP configuration for an entire subnet, the scope corresponds to the subnet. However, if you set up two DHCP servers for a subnet, you can configure each with a scope that allocates only one part of the complete subnet range. In addition, a single DHCP server can serve more than one scope.

You must create a scope before you can enable a DHCP server. When you create a scope, you can provide it with the following properties:

✦ A **scope name,** which helps you to identify the scope and its purpose

✦ A **scope description,** which lets you provide additional details about the scope and its purpose

✦ A **starting IP address** for the scope

✦ An **ending IP address** for the scope

✦ A **subnet mask** for the scope

    You can specify the subnet mask with dotted-decimal notation or with Classless Interdomain Routing (CIDR) notation.

✦ **One or more ranges of excluded addresses**

    These addresses won't be assigned to clients. For more information, see the section, "Feeling excluded?" later in this chapter.

✦ **One or more reserved addresses**

    These are addresses that will always be assigned to particular host devices. For more information, see the section, "Reservations suggested," later in this chapter.

✦ The **lease duration,** which indicates how long the host will be allowed to use the IP address

    The client will attempt to renew the lease when half of the lease duration has elapsed. For example, if you specify a lease duration of eight days, the client will attempt to renew the lease after four days pass. This allows the host plenty of time to renew the lease before the address is reassigned to some other host.

✦ The **router address** for the subnet

    This value is also known as the Default Gateway address.

✦ The **domain name and the IP address of the network's DNS servers and WINS servers**

Feeling excluded?

Everyone feels excluded once in awhile. With a wife, three daughters, and a female dog, I know how it feels. Sometimes, however, being excluded is a good thing. In the case of DHCP scopes, exclusions can help you to prevent IP address conflicts and can enable you to divide the DHCP workload for a single subnet among two or more DHCP servers.

An *exclusion* is a range of addresses that are not included in a scope. The exclusion range falls within the range of the scope's starting and ending addresses. In effect, an exclusion range lets you punch a hole in a scope. The IP addresses that fall within the hole won't be assigned.

Here a few reasons for excluding IP addresses from a scope:

+ **The computer that runs the DHCP service itself must usually have a static IP address assignment.** As a result, the address of the DHCP server should be listed as an exclusion.

+ **Some hosts may not be able to support DHCP.** In that case, the host will require a static IP address. For example, you may have a really old MS-DOS computer that doesn't have a DHCP client. By excluding its IP address from the scope, you can prevent that address from being assigned to any other host on the network.

Reservations suggested

In some cases, you may want to assign a particular IP address to a particular host. One way to do this is to configure the host with a static IP address so that the host doesn't use DHCP to obtain its IP configuration. However, here are two major disadvantages to that approach:

+ **TCP/IP configuration supplies more than just the IP address.** If you use static configuration, you must manually specify the subnet mask, the Default Gateway address, the DNS server address, and other configuration information required by the host. If this information changes, you have to change it not only at the DHCP server, but also at each host that you configured statically.

+ **You must remember to exclude the static IP address from the DHCP server's scope.** Otherwise, the DHCP server won't know about the static address and may assign it to another host. Then, you'll have two hosts with the same address on your network.

A better way to assign a fixed IP address to a particular host is to create a DHCP reservation. A *reservation* simply indicates that whenever a particular host requests an IP address from the DHCP server, the server should provide

**Book IV
Chapter 3**

Using DHCP

it the address that you specify in the reservation. The host won't receive the IP address until the host requests it from the DHCP server, but whenever the host does request IP configuration, it will always receive the same address.

To create a reservation, you associate the IP address that you want assigned to the host with the host's MAC address. As a result, you need to get the MAC address from the host before you create the reservation. You can get the MAC address by running the command ipconfig /all from a command prompt. (If that fails because TCP/IP has not yet been configured on the computer, you can also get the MAC address [the number that uniquely identifies the hardware device] by running the System Information command, which is Start⇨All Programs⇨Accessories⇨System Tools⇨System Information.)

If you set up more than one DHCP server, each should be configured to serve a different range of IP addresses. Otherwise, the servers might assign the same address to two different hosts.

How long to lease?

One of the most important decisions that you'll make when you configure a DHCP server is the length of time to specify for the lease duration. The default value is eight days, which is appropriate in many cases. However, you may encounter situations in which a longer or shorter interval may be appropriate:

✦ **The more stable your network,** the longer the lease duration can safely exist. If you only periodically add new computers to the network or replace existing computers, you can safely increase the lease duration past eight days.

✦ **The more volatile the network,** the shorter the lease duration should be. For example, a wireless network in a university library is used by students who bring their laptop computers into the library to work for a few hours at a time. For this network, a duration such as one hour may be appropriate.

Don't configure your network to allow infinite duration leases. Some administrators feel that this cuts down the workload for the DHCP server on stable networks. However, no network is permanently stable. Whenever you find a DHCP server that's configured with infinite leases, look at the active leases. I guarantee you'll find IP leases assigned to computers that no longer exist.

What about BootP?

BootP — Bootstrap Protocol — is an Internet protocol that enables diskless workstations to boot themselves over the Internet. Like DHCP, BootP allows a computer to receive an IP address assigned from a server. However, unlike DHCP, BootP also enables the computer to download a *boot image file,* which the computer can then use to boot itself from. A significant difference between BootP and DHCP is that BootP comes into play before the computer actually loads an operating system. In contrast, DHCP is used after an operating system has been loaded, during the configuration of network devices.

Most DHCP servers can also support the BootP protocol. If your network has diskless workstations, you can use the DHCP server's BootP support to boot those computers. At one time, diskless workstations were all the rage because network administrators thought they'd be easier to manage. Users hated them, however. Most diskless workstations have now buried in landfills, and the BootP protocol isn't used much.

Working with a DHCP Server

The exact steps that you should follow when configuring and managing a DHCP server depend on the network operating system that you're using. The following procedures show you how to work with a DHCP server in Windows Server 2008. The procedures for other operating systems are similar.

Installing and configuring a DHCP server

To install the DHCP server role on Windows Server 2008, follow these steps:

1. **Choose Start➪Administrative Tools➪Server Manager.**

   The Manage Your Server application appears.

2. **Click the Roles link and then click Add a Role.**

   The Add Roles Wizard appears.

3. **Click Next to get the wizard started.**

   The wizard displays a list of available server roles.

4. **Select DHCP Server from the list of roles and then click Next.**

   The wizard displays an explanation of DHCP.

5. **Click Next.**

   The wizard displays a list of the server's network connections that have static IP addresses, as shown in Figure 3-1. (In this example, only one network connection has a static IP address assigned. Most network servers will have at least two.)

Figure 3-1:
Select the
static IP
addresses
to use for
this DHCP
server.

6. **Select the static IP addresses you want to use for the DHCP server. Then click Next.**

   The wizard asks for the DNS configuration information, as shown in Figure 3-2.

Figure 3-2:
Specify the
DNS
information.

7. **Enter the domain name and DNS servers. To enter a DNS server, type its address in the IP address text box and then click Add.**

   You typically have more than one DNS server.

8. **Click Next.**

   The wizard next asks for the WINS configuration information.

9. **(Optional) If you want to enable WINS, enter the WINS server configuration and then click Next.**

   If you don't want to use WINS, skip this step and just click Next.

   Either way, the next screen lets you configure scopes.

10. **To create a new scope, click the Add Scope button.**

    The wizard asks for a name and description for the new scope, as shown in Figure 3-3.

Figure 3-3:
Creating a
new scope.

11. **Enter the information the new scope.**

    You must enter the following information:

    • *Scope Name:* The name can be anything you want. I suggest that you use a generic name such as *Office* or your company name unless you're creating two or more scopes. Then, the names should indicate the function of each scope.

    • *Scope Starting IP Address:* This is the lowest IP address that will be issued for this scope.

    • *Scope Ending IP Address:* This is the highest IP address that will be issued for this scope.

**Book IV
Chapter 3**

Using DHCP

- *Subnet Mask:* This is the subnet mask issued for IP addresses in this scope.

- *Default Gateway:* This is the default gateway address that will be used for this scope. This is usually the address of your router.

- *Subnet type:* Choose Wired or Wireless. The difference is how long the IP address will be valid. For Wired network, the addresses will be valid for six days. For Wireless networks, the addresses will expire in eight hours.

12. **Select the Activate This Scope option and then Click Next.**

The scope is created, as shown in Figure 3-4.

Add Roles Wizard					✕

Add or Edit DHCP Scopes

Before You Begin
Select Server Roles
DHCP Server
  Bindings
  DNS settings
  WINS settings
  DHCP scopes
  IPv6 Operation Mode
  IPv6 DNS settings
  DHCP Server Authorization
Confirm Installation Selections
Installation Progress
Installation Results

A scope is the full consecutive range of possible IP addresses for a network. The DHCP server cannot fully distribute IP addresses to clients until a scope is created.

Scopes:

Name	IP address range		Add...
Office	192.168.1.20 - 192.168.1.250		Edit
			Delete

Properties
  Add a scope to view its properties.

Why are scopes required for the DHCP server?

< Previous | Next > | Install | Cancel

Figure 3-4:
The scope is
created.

13. **If you want to create additional scopes, repeat steps 10–12.**

You can create as many scopes as you want for your DHCP server.

14. **When you finish creating scopes, click Next.**

The wizard asks whether you want to enable stateless mode, which is used for IPv6. I recommend disabling this mode unless dealing with IPv6 clients is important to your network.

15. **Click Next.**

The wizard asks for the credentials to use when creating this DHCP server. The default is to use your current login credentials.

16. **Click Next.**

The wizard displays a confirmation screen that summarizes the settings you've entered for the DHCP server.

17. **Click Install.**

The DHCP server is created. This might take a few minutes. When the server is finished, a final results page is displayed to confirm that the server was properly installed.

18. **Click Close.**

You're done!

Managing a DHCP server

You can bring up the DHCP management console by choosing Start⇨ Administrative Tools⇨DHCP or by clicking Manage This DHCP Server from the Manage Your Server application. Either way, the DHCP management console appears, as shown in Figure 3-5.

Figure 3-5:
The DHCP management console.

From the DHCP console, you have complete control over the DHCP server's configuration and operation. The following list summarizes some of the things that you can do from the DHCP console:

✦ **You can** *authorize* **the DHCP server,** which allows it to begin assigning client IP addresses. To authorize a server, select the server, choose Action⇨Manage Authorized Servers, and then click Authorize.

Book IV
Chapter 3

Using DHCP

✦ **To add another scope,** right-click the server in the tree and choose the New Scope command from the menu that appears. This brings up the New Scope Wizard. You can follow Steps 5–20 in the preceding section to complete the wizard.

✦ **To activate or deactivate a scope,** right-click the scope in the tree and then choose the Activate or Deactivate command.

✦ **To change scope settings,** right-click the scope and choose the Properties command. This brings up the Scope Properties dialog box, as shown in Figure 3-6. From this dialog box, you can change the scope's start and end IP addresses, subnet mask, and DNS configuration.

✦ **To change the scope exclusions,** click Address Pool under the scope in the tree. This lists each range of addresses that's included in the scope. You can add or delete a range by right-clicking the range and choosing the Delete command from the menu that appears. You can also add a new exclusion range by right-clicking Address Pool in the tree and choosing Add New Exclusion from the contextual menu that appears.

✦ **To view or change reservations,** click Reservations in the tree.

✦ **To view a list of assigned addresses,** click Address Leases in the tree.

Figure 3-6:
The Scope
Properties
dialog box.

How to Configure a Windows DHCP Client

Configuring a Windows client for DHCP is easy. The DHCP client is automatically included when you install the TCP/IP protocol, so all you have to do is configure TCP/IP to use DHCP. To do this, bring up the Network Properties dialog box by choosing Network or Network Connections in the Control

Panel (depending on which version of Windows the client is running). Then, select the TCP/IP protocol and click the Properties button. This brings up the TCP/IP Properties dialog box, as shown in Figure 3-7. To configure the computer to use DHCP, select the Obtain an IP Address Automatically option and the Obtain DNS Server Address Automatically option.

Figure 3-7:
Configuring a Windows client to use DHCP.

Automatic Private IP Addressing

If a Windows computer is configured to use DHCP but the computer can't obtain an IP address from a DHCP server, the computer automatically assigns itself a private address by using a feature called Automatic Private IP Addressing (APIPA). APIPA assigns a private address from the $169.254.x.x$ range and uses a special algorithm to ensure that the address is unique on the network. As soon as the DHCP server becomes available, the computer requests a new address, so the APIPA address is used only while the DHCP server is unavailable.

Renewing and releasing leases

Normally, a DHCP client attempts to renew its lease when the lease is halfway to the point of being expired. For example, if a client obtains an eight-day lease, it attempts to renew the lease after four days. However, you can renew a lease sooner by issuing the `ipconfig /renew` command at a command prompt. You may want to do this if you changed the scope's configuration or if the client's IP configuration isn't working correctly.

You can also release a DHCP lease by issuing the `ipconfig /release` command at a command prompt. When you release a lease, the client computer no longer has a valid IP address. This is shown in the output from the `ipconfig /release` command:

```
C:\>ipconfig /release
Windows IP Configuration
Ethernet adapter Local Area Connection:
        Connection-specific DNS Suffix  . :
        IP Address. . . . . . . . . . . : 0.0.0.0
        Subnet Mask . . . . . . . . . . : 0.0.0.0
        Default Gateway . . . . . . . . :
```

Here, you can see that the IP address and subnet masks are set to `0.0.0.0` and that the Default Gateway address is blank. When you release an IP lease, you can't communicate with the network by using TCP/IP until you issue an `ipconfig /renew` command to renew the IP configuration or restart the computer.

Chapter 4: Using DNS

Domain Name Server — DNS — is the TCP/IP facility that lets you use names rather than numbers to refer to host computers. Without DNS, you'd buy books from `207.171.182.16` instead of from `www.amazon.com`, you'd sell your used furniture at `66.135.192.87` instead of on `www.ebay.com`, and you'd search the Web at `216.239.51.100` instead of at `www.google.com`.

Understanding how DNS works and how to set up a DNS server is crucial to setting up and administering a Transmission Control Protocol/Internet Protocol (TCP/IP) network. This chapter introduces you to the basics of DNS, including how the DNS naming system works and how to set up a DNS server.

If you want to review the complete official specifications for DNS, look up RFC 1034 and 1035 at `www.ietf.org/rfc/rfc1034.txt` and `www.ietf.org/rfc/rfc1035.txt`, respectively.

Understanding DNS Names

DNS is a name service that provides a standardized system for providing names to identify TCP/IP hosts as well as a way to look up the IP address of a host, given the host's DNS name. For example, if you use DNS to look up the name `www.ebay.com`, you get the IP address of the eBay Web host: `66.135.192.123`. Thus, DNS allows you to access the eBay Web site by using the DNS name `www.ebay.com` instead of the site's IP address.

The following sections describe the basic concepts of DNS.

Domains and domain names

To provide a unique DNS name for every host computer on the Internet, DNS uses a time-tested technique: Divide and conquer. DNS uses a hierarchical naming system that's similar to how folders are organized hierarchically on a Windows computer. Instead of folders, however, DNS organizes its names into domains. Each domain includes all the names that appear directly beneath it in the DNS hierarchy.

For example, Figure 4-1 shows a small portion of the DNS domain tree. At the very top of the tree is the *root domain,* which is the anchor point for all domains. Directly beneath the root domain are four top-level domains, named `edu`, `com`, `org`, and `gov`.

In reality, many more top-level domains than this exist in the Internet's root domain. For more information, see the section, "Top-Level Domains," later in this chapter.

Beneath the `com` domain in Figure 4-1 is another domain called `LoweWriter`, which happens to be my own personal domain. (Pretty clever, eh?) To completely identify this domain, you have to combine it with the name of its *parent domain* (in this case, `com`) to create the complete domain name: `LoweWriter. com`. Notice that the parts of the domain name are separated from each other with periods, which are called dots. As a result, when you read this domain name, you pronounce it *LoweWriter dot com.*

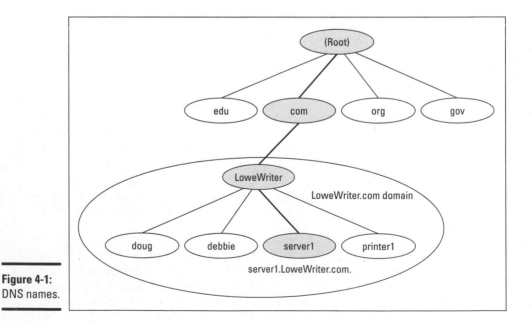

Figure 4-1:
DNS names.

Beneath the `LoweWriter` node are four host nodes, named `doug`, `debbie`, `server1`, and `printer1`. Respectively, these correspond to three computers and a printer on my home network. You can combine the host name with the domain name to get the complete DNS name for each of my network's hosts. For example, the complete DNS name for my server is `server1.LoweWriter.com`. Likewise, my printer is `printer1.LoweWriter.com`.

Here are a few additional details that you need to remember about DNS names:

✦ **DNS names are not case sensitive.** As a result, `LoweWriter` and `Lowewriter` are treated as the same name, as are `LOWEWRITER`, `LOWEwriter`, and `LoWeWrItEr`. When you use a domain name, you can use capitalization to make the name easier to read, but DNS ignores the difference between capital and lowercase letters.

✦ **The name of each DNS node can be up to 63 characters long (not including the dot) and can include letters, numbers, and hyphens.**

No other special characters are allowed.

✦ **A *subdomain* is a domain that's beneath an existing domain.** For example, the `com` domain is actually a subdomain of the root domain. Likewise, `LoweWriter` is a subdomain of the `com` domain.

✦ **DNS is a hierarchical naming system that's similar to the hierarchical folder system used by Windows.**

However, one crucial difference exists between DNS and the Windows naming convention. When you construct a complete DNS name, you start at the bottom of the tree and work your way up to the root. Thus, `doug` is the lowest node in the name `doug.LoweWriter.com`. In contrast, Windows paths are the opposite: They start at the root and work their way down. For example, in the path `\Windows\System32\dns`, `dns` is the lowest node.

✦ **The DNS tree can be up to 127 levels deep.** However, in practice, the DNS tree is pretty shallow. Most DNS names have just three levels (not counting the root). And although you'll sometimes see names with four or five levels, you'll rarely see more levels than that.

✦ **Although the DNS tree is shallow, it's very broad.** In other words, each of the top-level domains has a huge number of second-level domains immediately beneath it. For example, at the time of this writing, the `com` domain had well over a million second-level domains beneath it.

Fully qualified domain names

If a domain name ends with a trailing dot, that trailing dot represents the root domain, and the domain name is said to be a *fully qualified domain name* (also known as an *FQDN*). A fully qualified domain name is also called an *absolute name*. A fully qualified domain name is unambiguous because it identifies itself all the way back to the root domain. In contrast, if a domain name doesn't end with a trailing dot, the name may be interpreted in the context of some other domain. Thus, DNS names that don't end with a trailing dot are called *relative names*.

This is similar to how relative and absolute paths work in Windows. For example, if a path begins with a backslash, such as `\Windows\System32\dns`, the path is absolute. However, a path that doesn't begin with a backslash, such as `System32\dns`, uses the current directory as its starting point. If the current directory happens to be `\Windows`, then `\Windows\System32\dns` and `System32\dns` refer to the same location.

In many cases, relative and fully qualified domain names are interchangeable because the software that interprets them always interprets relative names in the context of the root domain. That's why, for example, you can type `www.wiley.com` (without the trailing dot) — not `www.wiley.com.` — to go to the Wiley home page in a Web browser. Some applications, such as DNS servers, may interpret relative names in the context of a domain other than the root.

Top-Level Domains

A *top-level domain* appears immediately beneath the root domain. Top-level domains come in two categories: generic domains and geographic domains. These categories are described in the following sections. (Actually, a third type of top-level domain exists, which is used for reverse lookups. I describe it later in this chapter, in the section, "Reverse Lookup Zones.")

Generic domains

Generic domains are the popular top-level domains that you see most often on the Internet. Originally, seven top-level organizational domains existed. In 2002, seven more were added to help ease the congestion of the original seven — in particular, the `com` domain.

Table 4-1 summarizes the original seven generic top-level domains. Of these, you can see that the com domain is far and away the most populated, with nearly 1.9 million second-level domains beneath it.

The Size column in this table indicates approximately how many second-level domains existed under each top-level domain as of January 2007, according to an Internet Software Consortium survey, found at `www.isc.org`.

Table 4-1	The Original Seven Top-Level Domains	
Domain	*Description*	*Size*
com	Commercial organizations	1,291,296
edu	Educational institutions	3,873
gov	U.S. government institutions	966
int	International treaty organizations	119
mil	U.S. military institutions	110
net	Network providers	253,741
org	Noncommercial organizations	140,968

Because the com domain ballooned to an almost unmanageable size in the late 1990s, the Internet authorities approved seven new top-level domains in an effort to take some of the heat off of the com domain. Most of these domains, listed in Table 4-2, became available in 2002. As you can see, they haven't really caught on yet even though they've been around for several years.

Table 4-2	The New Seven Top-Level Domains	
Domain	*Description*	*Size*
aero	Aerospace industry	147
biz	Business	11,399
coop	Cooperatives	263
info	Informational sites	16,276
museum	Museums	11
name	Individual users	710
pro	Professional organizations	30

Geographic domains

Although the top-level domains are open to anyone, U.S. companies and organizations dominate them. An additional set of top-level domains corresponds to international country designations. Organizations outside the United States often use these top-level domains to avoid the congestion of the generic domains.

Table 4-3 lists those geographic top-level domains with more than 200 registered subdomains at the time of this writing, in alphabetical order. In all, about 150 geographic top-level domains exist. The exact number varies from time to time as political circumstances change.

Table 4-3 **Geographic Top-Level Domains with More Than 200 Subdomains**

Domain	Description	Domain	Description
ac	Ascension Island	hu	Hungary
ae	United Arab Emirates	ie	Ireland
ag	Antigua And Barbuda	in	India
am	Armenia	is	Iceland
an	Netherlands Antilles	it	Italy
as	American Samoa	jp	Japan
at	Austria	kz	Kazakhstan
be	Belgium	la	Lao People's Democratic Republic
bg	Bulgaria	li	Liechtenstein
br	Brazil	lk	Sri Lanka
by	Belarus	lt	Lithuania
bz	Belize	lu	Luxembourg
ca	Canada	lv	Latvia
cc	Cocos (Keeling) Islands	ma	Morocco
ch	Switzerland	md	Moldova
cl	Chile	nl	Netherlands
cn	China	no	Norway
coop	Cooperatives	nu	Niue
cx	Christmas Island	pl	Poland
cz	Czech Republic	pt	Portugal
de	Germany	ro	Romania
dk	Denmark	ru	Russian Federation
ee	Estonia	se	Sweden
es	Spain	si	Slovenia
eu	European Union	sk	Slovakia
fi	Finland	st	Sao Tome and Principe
fm	Micronesia	su	Soviet Union
fo	Faroe Islands	to	Tonga
fr	France	tv	Tuvalu
ge	Georgia	tw	Taiwan
gov	Government	ua	Ukraine
gr	Greece	us	United States
hr	Croatia	ws	Samoa

The Hosts File

Long ago, in a network far, far away, the entire Internet was small enough that network administrators could keep track of it all in a simple text file. This file, called the *Hosts file,* simply listed the name and IP address of every host on the network. Each computer had its own copy of the Hosts file. The trick was keeping all those Hosts files up to date. Whenever a new host was added to the Internet, each network administrator would manually update his copy of the Hosts file to add the new host's name and IP address.

As the Internet grew, so did the Hosts file. In the mid-1980s, it became obvious that a better solution was needed. Imagine trying to track the entire Internet today by using a single text file to record the name and IP address of the millions of hosts on the Internet! DNS was invented to solve this problem.

Understanding the Hosts file is important for two reasons:

✦ **The Hosts file is not dead.** For small networks, a Hosts file may still be the easiest way to provide name resolution for the network's computers. In addition, a Hosts file can coexist with DNS. The Hosts file is always checked before DNS is used, so you can even use a Hosts file to override DNS if you want.

✦ **The Hosts file is the precursor to DNS.** DNS was devised to circumvent the limitations of the Hosts file. You'll be in a better position to appreciate the benefits of DNS when you understand how the Hosts file works.

The Hosts file is a simple text file that contains lines that match IP addresses with host names. You can edit the Hosts file with any text editor, including Notepad or by using the MS-DOS EDIT command. The exact location of the Hosts file depends on the client operating system, as listed in Table 4-4.

Table 4-4	Location of the Hosts File
Operating System	*Location of Hosts File*
Windows 9*x*/Me	`c:\windows\hosts`
Windows NT/2000	`c:\winnt\system32\drivers\etc\hosts`
Windows XP and Vista	`c:\windows\system32\drivers\etc\hosts`
Unix/Linux	`/etc/hosts`

All TCP/IP implementations are installed with a starter Hosts file. For example, Listing 4-1 shows the sample Windows Vista TCP/IP Hosts file. As you can see, the starter file begins with some comments that explain the purpose of the file. It also includes a host mapping for the host name localhost, mapped to the IP address 127.0.0.1. The IP address 127.0.0.1 is the standard loopback address. As a result, this entry allows a computer to refer to itself by using the name localhost.

Note that after the 127.0.0.1 localhost entry, another localhost entry defines the standard IPv6 loopback address (::2). This is required because unlike previous versions of Windows, Vista provides built-in support for IPv6.

Listing 4-1: A Sample Hosts File

```
# Copyright (c) 1993-2006 Microsoft Corp.
#
# This is a sample HOSTS file used by Microsoft TCP/IP for Windows.
#
# This file contains the mappings of IP addresses to host names. Each
# entry should be kept on an individual line. The IP address should
# be placed in the first column followed by the corresponding host name.
# The IP address and the host name should be separated by at least one
# space.
#
# Additionally, comments (such as these) may be inserted on individual
# lines or following the machine name denoted by a '#' symbol.
#
# For example:
#
#      102.54.94.97     rhino.acme.com          # source server
#       38.25.63.10     x.acme.com              # x client host

127.0.0.1       localhost
::1             localhost
```

To add an entry to the Hosts file, simply edit the file in any text editor. Then, add a line at the bottom of the file, after the localhost entry. Each line that you add should list the IP address and the host name that you want to use for the address. For example, to associate the host name server1.Lowe Writer.com with the IP address 192.168.168.201, you add this line to the Hosts file:

```
192.168.168.201 server1.LoweWriter.com
```

Then, whenever an application requests the IP address of the host name server1, the IP address 192.168.168.201 is returned.

You can also add an alias to a host mapping. This enables users to access a host by using the alias as an alternate name. For example, consider the following line:

```
192.168.168.201 server1.LoweWriter.com s1
```

Here, the device at address 192.168.168.201 can be accessed as server1.LoweWriter.com or just s1.

Listing 4-2 shows a Hosts file with several hosts defined.

Listing 4-2: A Hosts File with Several Hosts Defined

```
# Copyright (c) 1993-2006 Microsoft Corp.
#
# This is a sample HOSTS file used by Microsoft TCP/IP for Windows.
#
# This file contains the mappings of IP addresses to host names. Each
# entry should be kept on an individual line. The IP address should
# be placed in the first column followed by the corresponding host name.
# The IP address and the host name should be separated by at least one
# space.
#
# Additionally, comments (such as these) may be inserted on individual
# lines or following the machine name denoted by a '#' symbol.
#
# For example:
#
#      102.54.94.97     rhino.acme.com          # source server
#       38.25.63.10     x.acme.com              # x client host

127.0.0.1       localhost
::1             localhost
192.168.168.200 doug.LoweWriter.com            #Doug's computer
192.168.168.201 server1.LoweWriter.com s1      #Main server
192.168.168.202 debbie.LoweWriter.com          #Debbie's computer
192.168.168.203 printer1.LoweWriter.com p1     #HP Laser Printer
```

Even if your network uses DNS, every client still has a Hosts file that defines at least `localhost`.

Understanding DNS Servers and Zones

A *DNS server* is a computer that runs DNS server software, helps to maintain the DNS database, and responds to DNS name resolution requests from other computers. Although many DNS server implementations are available, the two most popular are Bind and the Windows DNS service. Bind runs on Unix-based computers (including Linux computers), and Windows DNS (naturally) runs on Windows computers. Both provide essentially the same services and can interoperate.

The key to understanding how DNS servers work is to realize that the DNS database — that is, the list of all the domains, subdomains, and host mappings — is a massively distributed database. No single DNS server contains the entire DNS database. Instead, authority over different parts of the database is delegated to different servers throughout the Internet.

For example, suppose that I set up a DNS server to handle name resolutions for my `LoweWriter.com` domain. Then, when someone requests the IP address of `doug.LoweWriter.com`, my DNS server can provide the answer.

**Book IV
Chapter 4**

Using DNS

However, my DNS server wouldn't be responsible for the rest of the Internet. Instead, if someone asks my DNS server for the IP address of some other computer, such as `coyote.acme.com`, my DNS server will have to pass the request on to another DNS server that knows the answer.

Zones

To simplify the management of the DNS database, the entire DNS namespace is divided into zones, and the responsibility for each zone is delegated to a particular DNS server. In many cases, zones correspond directly to domains. For example, if I set up a domain named `LoweWriter.com`, I can also set up a DNS zone called `LoweWriter.com` that's responsible for the entire `LoweWriter.com` domain.

However, the subdomains that make up a domain can be parceled out to separate zones, as shown in Figure 4-2. Here, a domain named `LoweWriter.com` has been divided into two zones. One zone, `us.LoweWriter.com`, is responsible for the entire `us.LoweWriter.com` subdomain. The other zone, `LoweWriter.com`, is responsible for the entire `LoweWriter.com` domain except for the `us.LoweWriter.com` subdomain.

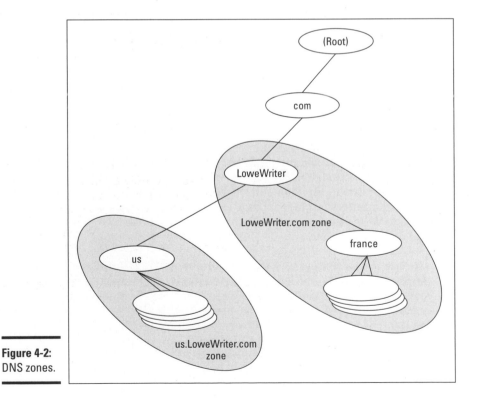

Figure 4-2:
DNS zones.

Why would you do that? The main reason is to delegate authority for the zone to separate servers. For example, Figure 4-2 suggests that part of the `LoweWriter.com` domain is administered in the United States and that part of it is administered in France. The two zones in the figure allow one server to be completely responsible for the U.S. portion of the domain, and the other server handles the rest of the domain.

The following are the two basic types of zones:

✦ A **primary zone** is the master copy of a zone. The data for a primary zone is stored in the local database of the DNS server that hosts the primary zone. Only one DNS server can host a particular primary zone. Any updates to the zone must be made to the primary zone.

✦ A **secondary zone** is a read-only copy of a zone. When a server hosts a secondary zone, the server doesn't store a local copy of the zone data. Instead, it obtains its copy of the zone from the zone's primary server by using a process called *zone transfer*. Secondary servers must periodically check primary servers to see whether their secondary zone data is still current. If not, a zone transfer is initiated to update the secondary zone.

The old phony Hosts file trick

The Hosts file can be the basis of a fun, practical joke. Of course, neither I nor my editors or publishers recommend that you actually do this. If it gets you into trouble, don't send your lawyers to me. This sidebar is here only to let you know what to do if it happens to you.

The idea is to edit your poor victim's Hosts file so that whenever the user tries to access his favorite Web site, a site of your choosing comes up instead. For example, if you're trying to get your husband to take you on a cruise, add a line to his Hosts file that replaces his favorite Web site with the Web site for a cruise line.

For example, this line should do the trick:

```
151.124.250.181 www.espn.com
```

Now, whenever your husband tries to call up the ESPN Web site, he'll get the Carnival Cruise Lines home page instead.

Of course, to actually pull a stunt like this would be completely irresponsible. Especially if you didn't first make a backup copy of the Hosts file, just in case it somehow gets messed up.

Be warned: If the wrong Web sites suddenly start coming up, check your Hosts file to see whether it's been tampered with.

Primary and secondary servers

Each DNS server is responsible for one or more zones. The following are the two different roles that a DNS server can take:

✦ **Primary server for a zone,** which means that the DNS server hosts a primary zone. The data for the zone is stored in files on the DNS server. Every zone must have one primary server.

✦ **Secondary server for a zone,** which means that the DNS server obtains the data for a secondary zone from a primary server. Every zone should have at least one secondary server. That way, if the primary server goes down, the domain defined by the zone can be accessed via the secondary server or servers.

A secondary server should be on a different subnet than the zone's primary server. If the primary and secondary servers are on the same subnet, both servers will be unavailable if the router that controls the subnet goes down.

Note that a single DNS server can be the primary server for some zones and a secondary server for other zones. A server is said to be *authoritative* for the primary and secondary zones that it hosts because it can provide definitive answers for queries against those zones.

Root servers

The core of DNS comprises the *root servers,* which are authoritative for the entire Internet. The main function of the root servers is to provide the address of the DNS servers that are responsible for each of the top-level domains. These servers, in turn, can provide the DNS server address for subdomains beneath the top-level domains.

The root servers are a major part of the glue that holds the Internet together. As you can imagine, they're swamped with requests day and night. A total of 13 root servers are located throughout the world. Table 4-5 lists the IP address and location of each of the 13 root servers.

Table 4-5		The 13 Root Servers	
Server	*IP Address*	*Operator*	*Location*
A	198.41.0.4	VeriSign Global Registry Services	Dulles, VA
B	128.9.0.107	Information Sciences Institute	Marina Del Rey, CA
C	192.33.4.12	Cogent Communications	Herndon, VA and Los Angeles, CA

Server	IP Address	Operator	Location
D	128.8.10.90	University of Maryland	College Park, MD
E	192.203.230.10	NASA Ames Research Center	Mountain View, CA
F	192.5.5.241	Internet Systems Consortium	Palo Alto, CA; San Jose, CA; New York City; San Francisco; Madrid; Hong Kong; Los Angeles
G	192.112.36.4	U.S. DOD Network Information	Vienna, VA Center
H	128.63.2.53	U.S. Army Research Lab	Aberdeen, MD
I	192.36.148.17	Autonomica	Stockholm
J	192.58.128.30	VeriSign Global Registry Services	Dulles, VA; Mountain View CA; Sterling, VA (two locations); Seattle, WA; Amsterdam, NL; Atlanta, GA; Los Angeles
K	193.0.14.129	Reseaux IP Europeens Network	London Coordination Centre
L	198.32.64.12	IANA	Los Angeles
M	202.12.27.33	WIDE Project	Tokyo

DNS servers learn how to reach the root servers by consulting a *root hints* file that's located on the server. In the Unix/Linux world, this file is known as named.root and can be found at /etc/named.root. For Windows DNS servers, the file is called cache.dns and can be found in \windows\system32\dns\ or \winnt\system32\dns\, depending on the Windows version. Listing 4-3 shows the file itself.

Listing 4-3: The Named.Root File

```
;       This file holds the information on root name servers needed to
;       initialize cache of Internet domain name servers
;       (e.g. reference this file in the "cache  .  <file>"
;       configuration file of Bind domain name servers).
;
;       This file is made available by InterNIC registration services
;       under anonymous FTP as
;           file                /domain/named.root
;           on server           FTP.RS.INTERNIC.NET
;       -OR- under Gopher at    RS.INTERNIC.NET
;           under menu          InterNIC Registration Services (NSI)
;               submenu         InterNIC Registration Archives
;           file                named.root
;
;       last update:    Aug 22, 1997
```

(continued)

Listing 4-3 *(continued)*

```
;       related version of root zone:   1997082200
;
;
; formerly NS.INTERNIC.NET
;
.                        3600000   IN  NS   A.ROOT-SERVERS.NET.
A.ROOT-SERVERS.NET.      3600000       A    198.41.0.4
;
; formerly NS1.ISI.EDU
;
.                        3600000       NS   B.ROOT-SERVERS.NET.
B.ROOT-SERVERS.NET.      3600000       A    128.9.0.107
;
; formerly C.PSI.NET
;
.                        3600000       NS   C.ROOT-SERVERS.NET.
C.ROOT-SERVERS.NET.      3600000       A    192.33.4.12
;
; formerly TERP.UMD.EDU
;
.                        3600000       NS   D.ROOT-SERVERS.NET.
D.ROOT-SERVERS.NET.      3600000       A    128.8.10.90
;
; formerly NS.NASA.GOV
;
.                        3600000       NS   E.ROOT-SERVERS.NET.
E.ROOT-SERVERS.NET.      3600000       A    192.203.230.10
;
; formerly NS.ISC.ORG
;
.                        3600000       NS   F.ROOT-SERVERS.NET.
F.ROOT-SERVERS.NET.      3600000       A    192.5.5.241
;
; formerly NS.NIC.DDN.MIL
;
.                        3600000       NS   G.ROOT-SERVERS.NET.
G.ROOT-SERVERS.NET.      3600000       A    192.112.36.4
;
; formerly AOS.ARL.ARMY.MIL
;
.                        3600000       NS   H.ROOT-SERVERS.NET.
H.ROOT-SERVERS.NET.      3600000       A    128.63.2.53
;
; formerly NIC.NORDU.NET
;
.                        3600000       NS   I.ROOT-SERVERS.NET.
I.ROOT-SERVERS.NET.      3600000       A    192.36.148.17
;
; temporarily housed at NSI (InterNIC)
;
.                        3600000       NS   J.ROOT-SERVERS.NET.
J.ROOT-SERVERS.NET.      3600000       A    198.41.0.10
;
; housed in LINX, operated by RIPE NCC
;
.                        3600000       NS   K.ROOT-SERVERS.NET.
K.ROOT-SERVERS.NET.      3600000       A    193.0.14.129
;
; temporarily housed at ISI (IANA)
;
```

```
.                        3600000     NS    L.ROOT-SERVERS.NET.
L.ROOT-SERVERS.NET.      3600000     A     198.32.64.12
;
; housed in Japan, operated by WIDE
;
.                        3600000     NS    M.ROOT-SERVERS.NET.
M.ROOT-SERVERS.NET.      3600000     A     202.12.27.33
; End of File
```

Caching

DNS servers don't really like doing all that work to resolve DNS names, but they're not stupid. They know that if a user visits www.wiley.com today, he'll probably do it again tomorrow. As a result, name servers keep a cache of query results. The next time the user visits www.wiley.com, the name server is able to resolve this name without having to query all those other name servers.

The Internet is constantly changing, however, so cached data can quickly become obsolete. For example, suppose that Wiley Publishing, Inc., switches its Web site to a different server? It can update its name servers to reflect the new IP address, but any name servers that have a cached copy of the query will be out of date.

To prevent this from being a major problem, DNS data is given a relatively short expiration time. The expiration value for DNS data is called the *TTL* (Time to Live). TTL is specified in seconds. Thus, a TTL of 60 means the data is kept for one minute.

Understanding DNS Queries

When a DNS client needs to resolve a DNS name to an IP address, it uses a library routine — a *resolver* — to handle the query. The resolver takes care of sending the query message over the network to the DNS server, receiving and interpreting the response, and informing the client of the results of the query.

A DNS client can make two basic types of queries: recursive and iterative. The following list describes the difference between these two query types. (The following discussion assumes that the client is asking the server for the IP address of a host name, which is the most common type of DNS query. You find out about other types of queries later; they, too, can be either recursive or iterative.)

✦ **Recursive queries:** When a client issues a *recursive DNS query,* the server must reply with either the IP address of the requested host name or an error message indicating that the host name doesn't exist. If the server doesn't have the information, it asks another DNS server for the

IP address. When the first server finally gets the IP address, it sends it back to the client. If the server determines that the information doesn't exist, it returns an error message.

✦ **Iterative queries:** When a server receives an iterative query, it returns the IP address of the requested host name if it knows the address. If the server doesn't know the address, it returns a *referral,* which is simply the address of a DNS server that should know. The client can then issue an iterative query to the server to which it was referred.

Normally, DNS clients issue recursive queries to DNS servers. If the server knows the answer to the query, it replies directly to the client. If not, the server issues an iterative query to a DNS server that it thinks should know the answer. If the original server gets an answer from the second server, it returns the answer to the client. If the original server gets a referral to a third server, the original server issues an iterative query to the third server. The original server keeps issuing iterative queries until it either gets the answer or an error occurs. It then returns the answer or the error to the client.

A real-life DNS example

Confused? I can understand why. An example may help to clear things up. Suppose that a user wants to view the Web page `www.wiley.com`. The following sequence of steps occurs to resolve this address:

1. The browser asks the client computer's resolver to find the IP address of `www.wiley.com`.

2. The resolver issues a recursive DNS query to its name server.

   In this case, I'll call the name server `ns1.LoweWriter.com`.

3. The name server `ns1LoweWriter.com` checks whether it knows the IP address of `www.wiley.com`.

   It doesn't, so the name server issues an iterative query to one of the root name servers to see whether it knows the IP address of `www.wiley.com`.

4. The root name server doesn't know the IP address of `www.wiley.com`, so it returns a list of the name servers that are authoritative for the com domain.

5. The `ns1.LoweWriter.com` name server picks one of the com domain name servers and sends it an iterative query for `www.wiley.com`.

6. The `com` name server doesn't know the IP address of `www.wiley.com`, so it returns a list of the name servers that are authoritative for the `wiley.com` domain.

7. The `ns1.LoweWriter.com` name server picks one of the name servers for the `wiley.com` domain and sends it an iterative query for `www.wiley.com`.

8. The `wiley.com` name server knows the IP address for `www.wiley.com`, so the name server returns it.

9. The `ns1.LoweWriter.com` name server shouts with joy for having finally found the IP address for `www.wiley.com`. It gleefully returns this address to the client. It also caches the answer so that the next time the user looks for `www.wiley.com`, the name server won't have to contact other name servers to resolve the name.

10. The client also caches the results of the query.

    The next time the client needs to look for `www.wiley.com`, the client can resolve the name without troubling the name server.

Zone Files and Resource Records

Each DNS zone is defined by a *zone file* (also known as a *DNS database* or a *master file*). For Windows DNS servers, the name of the zone file is *domain*.zone. For example, the zone file for the `LoweWriter.com` zone is named `Lowe Writer.com.zone`. For Bind DNS servers, the zone files are named `db.`*domain*. Thus, the zone file for the `LoweWriter.com` domain would be `db.LoweWriter.com`. The format of the zone file contents is the same for both systems, however.

A zone file consists of one or more resource records. Creating and updating the resource records that comprise the zone files is one of the primary tasks of a DNS administrator. The Windows DNS server provides a friendly graphical interface to the resource records. However, you should still be familiar with how to construct resource records.

Resource records are written as simple text lines, with the following fields:

```
Owner    TTL    Class    Type    RDATA
```

These fields must be separated from each other by one or more spaces. The following list describes the five resource record fields:

✦ **Owner:** The name of the DNS domain or the host that the record applies to. This is usually specified as a fully qualified domain name (with a trailing dot) or as a simple host name (without a trailing dot), which is then interpreted in the context of the current domain.

You can also specify a single @ symbol as the owner name. In that case, the current domain is used.

**Book IV
Chapter 4**

Using DNS

◆ **TTL:** Also known as *Time to Live;* the number of seconds that the record should be retained in a server's cache before it's invalidated. If you omit the TTL value for a resource record, a default TTL is obtained from the Start of Authority (SOA) record. (For your reference, Table 4-6 lists commonly used TTL values.)

◆ **Class:** Defines the protocol to which the record applies. You should always specify IN, for the Internet protocol. If you omit the class field, the last class field that you specified explicitly is used. As a result, you'll sometimes see zone files that specify IN only on the first resource record (which must be an SOA record) and then allow it to default to IN on all subsequent records.

◆ **Type:** The resource record type. The most commonly used resource types are summarized in Table 4-6 and are described separately later in this section. Like the Class field, you can also omit the Type field and allow it to default to the last specified value.

◆ **RDATA:** Resource record data that is specific to each record type.

Table 4-6	Common Resource Record Types	
Type	**Name**	**Description**
SOA	Start Of Authority	Identifies a zone
NS	Name Server	Identifies a name server that is authoritative for the zone
A	Address	Maps a fully qualified domain name to an IP address
CNAME	Canonical Name	Creates an alias for a fully qualified domain name
MX	Mail Exchange	Identifies the mail server for a domain
PTR	Pointer	Maps an IP address to a fully qualified domain name for reverse lookups

Most resource records fit on one line. If a record requires more than one line, you must enclose the data that spans multiple lines in parentheses.

You can include comments to clarify the details of a zone file. A comment begins with a semicolon and continues to the end of the line. If a line begins with a semicolon, the entire line is a comment. You can also add a comment to the end of a resource record. You see examples of both types of comments later in this chapter.

SOA records

Every zone must begin with as SOA record, which names the zone and provides default information for the zone. Table 4-7 lists the fields that appear in the RDATA section of an SOA record. Note that these fields are positional, so you should include a value for all of them and list them in the order specified. Because the SOA record has so many RDATA fields, you'll probably need to use parentheses to continue the SOA record onto multiple lines.

Table 4-7	RDATA Fields for an SOA Record
Name	*Description*
MNAME	The domain name of the name server that is authoritative for the zone.
RNAME	An e-mail address (specified in domain name format; not regular e-mail format) of the person responsible for this zone.
SERIAL	The serial number of the zone. Secondary zones use this value to determine whether they need to initiate a zone transfer to update their copy of the zone.
REFRESH	A time interval that specifies how often a secondary server should check whether the zone needs to be refreshed. A typical value is 3600 (one hour).
RETRY	A time interval that specifies how long a secondary server should wait after requesting a zone transfer before trying again. A typical value is 600 (ten minutes).
EXPIRE	A time interval that specifies how long a secondary server should keep the zone data before discarding it. A typical value is 86400 (one day).
MINIMUM	A time interval that specifies the TTL value to use for zone resource records that omit the TTL field. A typical value is 3600 (one hour).

Note two things about the SOA fields:

✦ **The e-mail address of the person responsible for the zone is given in DNS format, not in normal e-mail format.** Thus, you separate the user from the mail domain with a dot rather than an @ symbol. For example, `doug@LoweWriter.com` would be listed as `doug.lowewriter.com`.

✦ **The serial number should be incremented every time you change the zone file.** If you edit the file via the graphic interface provided by Windows DNS, the serial number is incremented automatically. However, if you edit the zone file via a simple text editor, you have to manually increment the serial number.

Book IV
Chapter 4

Using DNS

Here's a typical example of an SOA record, with judicious comments to identify each field:

```
lowewriter.com. IN  SOA (
    ns1.lowewriter.com                ; authoritative name server
    doug.lowewriter.com               ; responsible person
    148                               ; version number
    3600                              ; refresh (1 hour)
    600                               ; retry (10 minutes)
    86400                             ; expire (1 day)
    3600 )                            ; minimum TTL (1 hour)
```

NS records

Name Server (NS) records identify the name servers that are authoritative for the zone. Every zone must have at least one NS record. Using two or more NS records is better so that if the first name server is unavailable, the zone will still be accessible.

The owner field should either be the fully qualified domain name for the zone, with a trailing dot, or an @ symbol. The RDATA consists of just one field: the fully qualified domain name of the name server.

The following examples show two NS records that serve the lowewriter.com domain:

```
lowewriter.com.   IN  NS  ns1.lowewriter.com.
lowewriter.com.   IN  NS  ns2.lowewriter.com.
```

A records

Address (A) records are the meat of the zone file: They provide the IP addresses for each of the hosts that you want to make accessible via DNS. In an A record, you usually list just the host name in the owner field, thus allowing DNS to add the domain name to derive the fully qualified domain name for the host. The RDATA field for the A record is the IP address of the host.

The following lines define various hosts for the LoweWriter.com domain:

```
doug        IN  A   192.168.168.200
server1     IN  A   192.168.168.201
debbie      IN  A   192.168.168.202
printer1    IN  A   192.168.168.203
router1     IN  A   207.126.127.129
www         IN  A   64.71.129.102
```

Notice that for these lines, I didn't specify the fully qualified domain names for each host. Instead, I just provide the host name. DNS will add the name of the zone's domain to these host names in order to create the fully qualified domain names.

If I wanted to be more explicit, I could list these A records like this:

```
doug.lowewriter.com.     IN  A  192.168.168.200
server1.lowewriter.com.  IN  A  192.168.168.201
debbie.lowewriter.com.   IN  A  192.168.168.202
printer1.lowewriter.com. IN  A  192.168.168.203
router1.lowewriter.com   IN  A  207.126.127.129
www.lowewriter.com.      IN  A  64.71.129.102
```

However, all this does is increase the chance for error. Plus, it creates more work for yourself later if you decide to change your network's domain.

CNAME records

A *Canonical Name* (CNAME) record creates an alias for a fully qualified domain name. When a user attempts to access a domain name that is actually an alias, the DNS system substitutes the real domain name — known as the *canonical name* — for the alias. The owner field in the CNAME record provides the name of the alias that you want to create. Then, the RDATA field provides the canonical name — that is, the real name of the host.

For example, consider these resource records:

```
ftp.lowewriter.com.    IN  A      207.126.127.132
files.lowewriter.com.  IN  CNAME  www1.lowewriter.com.
```

Here, the host name of an FTP server at `207.126.127.132` is `ftp.lowewriter.com`. The CNAME record allows users to access this host as `files.lowewriter.com` if they prefer.

PTR records

A *Pointer* (PTR) record is the opposite of an address record: It provides the fully qualified domain name for a given address. The owner field should specify the reverse lookup domain name, and the RDATA field specifies the fully qualified domain name. For example, the following record maps the address `64.71.129.102` to `www.lowewriter.com`:

```
102.129.71.64.in-addr.arpa. IN  PTR  www.lowewriter.com.
```

**Book IV
Chapter 4**

Using DNS

PTR records don't usually appear in normal domain zones. Instead, they appear in special reverse lookup zones. For more information, see the section, "Reverse Lookup Zones," later in this chapter.

MX records

Mail Exchange (MX) records identify the mail server for a domain. The owner field provides the domain name that users address mail to. The RDATA section of the record has two fields. The first is a priority number used to determine which mail servers to use when several are available. The second is the fully qualified domain name of the mail server itself.

For example, consider the following MX records:

```
lowewriter.com.    IN  MX  0   mail1.lowewriter.com.
lowewriter.com.    IN  MX  10  mail2.lowewriter.com.
```

In this example, the `lowewriter.com` domain has two mail servers, named `mail1.lowewriter.com` and `mail2.lowewriter.com`. The priority numbers for these servers are `0` and `10`. Because it has a lower priority number, mail will be delivered to `mail1.lowewriter.com` first. The `mail2.lowewriter.com` server will be used only if `mail1.lowewriter.com` isn't available.

The server name specified in the RDATA section should be an actual host name, not an alias created by a CNAME record. Although some mail servers can handle MX records that point to CNAMEs, not all can. As a result, you shouldn't specify an alias in an MX record.

Be sure to create a reverse lookup record (PTR, described in the next section) for your mail servers. Some mail servers won't accept mail from a server that doesn't have valid reverse lookup entries.

Reverse Lookup Zones

Normal DNS queries ask a name server to provide the IP address that corresponds to a fully qualified domain name. This kind of query is a *forward lookup*. A *reverse lookup* is the opposite of a forward lookup: It returns the fully qualified domain name of a host based on its IP address.

Reverse lookups are possible because of a special domain called the `in-addr.arpa` domain, which provides a separate fully qualified domain name for every possible IP address on the Internet. To enable a reverse lookup for a particular IP address, all you have to do is create a PTR record in a reverse lookup zone (a zone that is authoritative for a portion of the in-addr.arpa domain). The PTR record maps the in-addr.arpa domain name for the address to the host's actual domain name.

The technique used to create the reverse domain name for a given IP address is pretty clever. It creates subdomains beneath the in-addr.arpa domain by using the octets of the IP address, listing them in reverse order. For example, the reverse domain name for the IP address 207.126.67.129 is 129.67.126.207.in-addr.arpa.

Why list the octets in reverse order? Because that correlates the network portions of the IP address (which work from left to right) with the subdomain structure of DNS names (which works from right to left). The following description should clear this up:

✦ The 255 possible values for the first octet of an IP address each have a subdomain beneath the in-addr.arpa domain. For example, any IP address that begins with 207 can be found in the 207.in-addr.arpa domain.

✦ Within this domain, each of the possible values for the second octet can be found as a subdomain of the first octet's domain. Thus, any address that begins with 207.126 can be found in the 126.207.in-addr.arpa domain.

✦ The same holds true for the third octet, so any address that begins with 207.126.67 can be found in the 67.126.207.in-addr.arpa domain.

✦ By the time you get to the fourth octet, you've pinpointed a specific host. The fourth octet completes the fully qualified reverse domain name. Thus, 207.126.67.129 is mapped to 129.67.126.207. in-addr.arpa.

As a result, to determine the fully qualified domain name for the computer at 207.126.67.129, the client queries its DNS server for the FQDN that corresponds to 129.67.126.207.in-addr.arpa.

Working with the Windows DNS Server

Installing and managing a DNS server depends on the network operating system that you're using. The following sections are specific to working with a DNS server in Windows 2003. Working with Bind in a Unix/Linux environment is similar but without the help of a graphical user interface (GUI).

You can install the DNS server on Windows Server 2008 from the Server Manager application. Choose Start⇨Administrative Tools⇨Server Manager. Click the Server Roles, click the Add Roles link, and then follow the wizard instructions to add the DNS role.

After you set up a DNS server, you can manage the DNS server from the DNS management console. From this management console, you can perform common administrative tasks, such as adding additional zones, changing zone settings, adding A or MX records to an existing zone, and so on. The DNS management console hides the details of the actual resource records from you, thus allowing you to work with a friendly GUI instead.

To add a new host (that is, an A record) to a zone, right-click the zone in the DNS management console and choose the Add New Host command. This brings up the New Host dialog box, as shown in Figure 4-3. From this dialog box, specify the following information.

✦ **Name:** The host name for the new host.

✦ **IP Address:** The host's IP address.

✦ **Create Associated Pointer (PTR) Record:** Automatically creates a PTR record in the reverse lookup zone file. Select this option if you want to allow reverse lookups for the host.

✦ **Allow Any Authenticated User to Update:** Select this option if you want to allow other users to update this record or other records with the same host name. You should usually leave this option unchecked.

You can add other records, such as MX or CNAME records, in the same way.

Figure 4-3: The New Host dialog box.

How to Configure a Windows DNS Client

Client computers don't need much configuration in order to work properly with DNS. The client must have the address of at least one DNS server. Usually, this address is supplied by DHCP, so if the client is configured to obtain its IP address from a DHCP server, it will also obtain the DNS server address from DHCP.

To configure a client computer to obtain the DNS server location from DHCP, bring up the Network Properties dialog box by choosing Network or Network Connections in Control Panel (depending on which version of Windows the client is running). Then, select the Internet Protocol Version 4 (TCP/IPv4) protocol and click the Properties button. This summons the dialog box shown in Figure 4-4. To configure the computer to use Dynamic Host Configuration Protocol (DHCP), select the Obtain an IP Address Automatically and the Obtain DNS Server Address Automatically options.

If the computer doesn't use DHCP, you can use this same dialog box to manually enter the IP address of your DNS server.

Figure 4-4:
Configuring
a Windows
client to
obtain its
DNS
address
from DHCP.

Chapter 5: Using FTP

In This Chapter

✔ **Figuring out the basics of FTP**

✔ **Setting up an FTP server**

✔ **Retrieving files from an FTP server**

✔ **Using FTP commands**

*F*ile Transfer Protocol (FTP) is the basic method for exchanging files over the Internet. If you need to access files from someone's FTP site, this chapter shows you how to do so by using a Web browser or a command line FTP client. If you need to set up your own FTP server to share files with other users, this chapter shows you how to do that, too.

Introducing FTP

FTP is as old as the Internet. The first versions of FTP date to the early 1970s, and even the current FTP standard (RFC 959) dates to 1985. You can use FTP with the command line FTP client (which has a decidedly 1980s feel to it), or you can access FTP sites with most modern Web browsers if you prefer a graphic interface. Old computer hounds prefer the FTP command line client, probably for nostalgic reasons.

In spite of its age, FTP is still commonly used on the Internet. For example, InterNIC (the organization that manages Internet names) maintains an FTP site at `ftp.rs.internic.net`. There, you can download important files, such as `named.root`, which provides the current location of the Internet's root name servers. Many other companies maintain FTP sites from which you can download software, device drivers, documentation, reports, and so on. FTP is also one of the most common ways to publish HTML files to a Web server. Because FTP is still so widely used, it pays to know how to use it from both the command line and from a browser.

In the Windows world, an FTP server is integrated with the Microsoft Web server, Internet Information Services (IIS). As a result, you can manage FTP from the IIS management console along with other IIS features. Note that the FTP component is an optional part of IIS, so you may need to install it separately if you opted to not include it when you first installed IIS.

On Unix and Linux systems, FTP isn't usually integrated with a Web server. Instead, the FTP server is installed as a separate program. You're usually given the option to install FTP when you install the operating system. If you choose not to, you can always install it later.

When you run an FTP server, you expose a portion of your file system to the outside world. As a result, you need to be careful about how you set up your FTP server so that you don't accidentally allow hackers access to the bowels of your file server. Fortunately, the default configuration of FTP is pretty secure. You shouldn't tinker much with the default configuration unless you know what you're doing.

Configuring an FTP Server

In this section, I show you how to configure FTP services in Microsoft IIS. The examples show IIS version 6 running on Windows Server 2008, but the procedures are essentially the same for other IIS versions.

Installing FTP

Although FTP is integrated with IIS, FTP is not installed by default when you install IIS. As a result, if you didn't specifically select FTP when you installed IIS, you'll need to install FTP before you can set up an FTP site. Here are the procedures for Windows Server 2003 and 2008:

✦ For Windows Server 2003, you install the FTP protocol by choosing Control Panel➪Add or Remove Programs➪Add/Remove Windows Components. Then, select Application Server from the list of components, click Details, and choose Internet Information Services (IIS). Click Details again and then select File Transfer Protocol (FTP) from the list of IIS subcomponents. Finally, click OK to install FTP. If asked, you'll need to insert the Windows Server 2003 setup disc.

✦ For Windows Server 2008, choose Start➪Server Manager and select the Web Server (IIS) role. Scroll down to the Role Services section, then click Add Role Services. Select the FTP Publishing Services service and click Next, then click Install.

When you first install FTP, a default FTP site is created automatically. To manage the default site, open the Internet Information Services Manager by choosing Start➪Administrative Programs➪Internet Information Services Manager. Then, select the default FTP site, as shown in Figure 5-1.

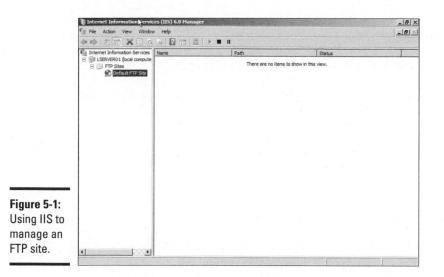

Figure 5-1:
Using IIS to
manage an
FTP site.

Changing the FTP site properties

You can change the properties for an FTP site by right-clicking the site in the Internet Information Services Manager and choosing the Properties command. This brings up the FTP Site Properties dialog box, as shown in Figure 5-2.

Figure 5-2:
The FTP Site
Properties
dialog box.

**Book IV
Chapter 5**

Using FTP

The FTP Site Properties dialog box contains the following tabs that let you configure the properties of your FTP site:

✦ **FTP Site:** The only item that you're likely to change on the main FTP Site tab is the name of the FTP site. You can also specify the IP address and port number for the site, but you'll usually leave these items set to their default values. You can also limit the number of connections allowed and disable logging.

✦ **Security Accounts:** From the Security Accounts tab, specify whether you want to allow anonymous logons for the FTP site. If the site is open to the general public to download files, you'll want to enable anonymous logons. If you want to control access to the site, use this tab to disable anonymous logons.

Also use the Security Accounts tab to specify under which Windows account anonymous users will be logged on. The default value, IUSR_computername, is usually appropriate.

✦ **Messages:** From this tab, as shown in Figure 5-3, you can create four customized messages that appear when users access the site:

- The *Banner message* appears when a user first accesses the site, before he or she has logged on. If the site allows anonymous logons, you may mention that in the Banner message.

- The *Welcome message* appears after the user has successfully logged on to your site.

- The *Exit message* appears when the user leaves the site.

- The *Maximum Connections message* appears when the connection limit has been exceeded.

Figure 5-3:
Customizing the site's messages.

✦ **Home Directory:** From this tab, specify the location of the site's home directory. This directory can be a folder on the server's hard drive, or it can be a shared folder on another server. To the user, this directory appears to be the FTP site's root directory. As a result, the user can access any child folders that appear beneath the home directory. However, the user won't be able to access any other directories on the server's hard drive.

✦ **Directory Security:** From this tab, limit access to your FTP site based on the client computer's IP address. You can either deny access to all computers except the ones you specifically list or grant access to all computers except the ones you specifically list.

Adding content to your FTP site

When you set up an FTP site, IIS creates an empty home directory for the site. Then it's up to you to add to this directory whatever files you want to make available on the site. The easiest way to do that is to simply open a My Computer window and copy the files to the site's home directory. If you're not sure where the site's home directory is located, you can find it by right-clicking the site in the IIS Manager, choosing Properties, and then choosing the Home Directory tab.

The following list offers some useful tips for setting up FTP site content:

✦ **Create a `readme.txt` file in the FTP site's home directory that describes the content and rules for your site.** Hopefully, users will view this file when they visit your site. There's no guarantee that they will, but you can always hope.

✦ **If your site has a lot of files, organize them into subdirectories beneath the home directory.**

✦ **Stick to short filenames.** Users working with command line clients appreciate brevity because they'll have to type the filenames accurately to retrieve your files.

✦ **Don't use spaces in filenames.** Some clients balk at names that include spaces.

Adding an additional FTP site

IIS can host more than an FTP site on the same computer. If you need to host multiple sites, you can add additional sites by using the FTP Site Creation Wizard. To start this wizard, right-click the FTP Sites folder in IIS Manager and choose New⇨Ftp Site.

Accessing an FTP Site with a Browser

Modern Web browsers include built-in support for FTP. Internet Explorer lets you access an FTP site almost as if it were a local disk. You can even drag and drop files to and from an FTP site.

To access an FTP site in a Web browser, just type the name of the site in the Address bar. If you want, you can explicitly specify the FTP protocol by typing **ftp://** before the FTP site name, but that's usually not necessary. The browser determines that the name you type is an FTP site and invokes the FTP protocol automatically.

Figure 5-4 shows you how a typical FTP site appears when accessed with Windows Explorer on a Windows Vista system. As you can see, the files and folders appear as if they were on a local disk. Double-click a folder to display the files contained in that folder; download files by dragging them from the browser window to the desktop or to another window. You can also upload files by dragging them from the desktop or another window into the FTP browser window.

If the contents of an FTP site don't appear in the browser window, you may need to log on to the site. Choose File⇨Login As to display the Log On As dialog box. If the site administrator has given you a name and password, you can enter it here to access the site. Otherwise, select the Log On Anonymously check box and then click the Log On button.

Figure 5-4:
Browsing
an FTP site.

Using an FTP Command Line Client

If you're a command line junkie, you'll appreciate the FTP command that comes with Windows. It isn't pretty, but it gets the job done. At the end of this chapter, you can find a command reference that details all the subcommands you can use with the FTP command. In this section, I just show you a typical session in which I sign on to an FTP server named ftp.lowewriter.com, switch to a directory named pics, download a file, and then log off.

First, open a command window: Choose Start⇨Run, type **Command** in the text box, and then click OK. Navigate to the directory to where you want to download files. This step is important because although you can change the local working directory from within the FTP command, it's much easier to just start FTP from the right directory.

To start FTP, type **ftp** with the name of the FTP server as the parameter, like this:

```
C:\>ftp ftp.lowewriter.com
```

Assuming that you typed the site name correctly, the FTP command connects to the site, displays the banner message, and prompts you to log on:

```
Connected to ftp.lowewriter.com.
220-Microsoft FTP Service
220 We have 999 spooks here, but there's always room
    for one more! To volunteer, log in as Anonymous.
User (ftp.lowewriter.com:(none)):
```

To log on anonymously, type **Anonymous** and then press Enter. The server responds by telling you that Anonymous access is allowed and asks for your e-mail address as a password:

```
331 Anonymous access allowed, send identity (e-mail name)
    as password.
Password:
```

Type your e-mail address as the password and then press Enter. The Welcome message appears, followed by the ftp> prompt:

```
230-Welcome to my FTP site! For spooky Halloween pictures,
    check out the Pics folder.
230 Anonymous user logged in.
ftp>
```

Whenever you see the `ftp>` prompt, the `FTP` command is waiting for you to enter a subcommand. Start by entering **dir** to see a directory listing:

```
200 PORT command successful.
150 Opening ASCII mode data connection for /bin/ls.
06-30-07  08:05PM        <DIR>          pics
06-30-07  07:55PM                  2365 readme.txt
06-30-07  07:55PM        <DIR>          sounds
06-30-07  07:56PM        <DIR>          videos
226 Transfer complete.
ftp: 190 bytes received in 0.00Seconds 190000.00Kbytes/sec.
ftp>
```

As you can see, the response from the `dir` command is not quite as clean as the display from an MS-DOS command. Still, you can pick out that the directory includes three subdirectories, named `pics`, `sounds`, and `videos`; and a single file, named `readme.txt`. The size of the file is 2,365 bytes.

Here's a good question: If you enter a `dir` command, why does the response read `200 PORT command successful`? The answer has to do with how the FTP protocol works. When you enter a `dir` command, the FTP client forwards a `PORT` command to the server that opens a data transfer port that is then used to return the resulting directory listing. The server replies that the `PORT` command has successfully opened a data transfer port. Then, it sends back the directory listing. Finally, it sends two more lines: one to indicate that the transfer is complete (that is, that the `dir` output has been successfully sent); and the other to summarize the number of bytes of data that were sent and the data transfer rate.

The files that I want to download are located in the `pics` subdirectory, so the next command to issue is `cd pics`. This results in the following output:

```
250 CWD command successful.
ftp>
```

Once again, the command's output isn't exactly what you'd expect. The FTP protocol doesn't actually have a `CD` command. Instead, it uses a command named `CWD`, which stands for *change working directory,* to change the directory. The Windows FTP client uses command `CD` instead of `CWD` to be more consistent with the Windows/MS-DOS user interface, which uses the command `CD` to change directories. When you type a `CD` command at the `ftp>` prompt, the FTP client sends a `CWD` command to the FTP server. The server then replies with the message CWD command successful to indicate that the directory has been changed.

Next, type **dir** again. The FTP server displays the directory listing for the pics directory:

```
200 PORT command successful.
150 Opening ASCII mode data connection for /bin/ls.
06-27-07  10:04PM              123126 door.jpg
06-27-07  10:06PM              112457 echair.jpg
06-27-07  10:06PM               81610 fence.jpg
06-27-07  10:09PM              138102 fog.jpg
06-27-07  10:09PM               83712 gallows.jpg
06-27-07  10:10PM              166741 ghost.jpg
06-27-07  09:58PM              119859 skel01.jpg
06-27-07  10:05PM               87720 wall.jpg
226 Transfer complete.
ftp: 400 bytes received in 0.00Seconds 400000.00Kbytes/sec.
ftp>
```

Here, you can see that the pics directory contains eight files. To download a file, you use the GET command, specifying the name of the file that you want to download. For example, to download the door.jpg file, type **get door.jpg**. The FTP server transfers the file to your computer and displays the following response:

```
200 PORT command successful.
150 Opening ASCII mode data connection for door.jpg(123126 bytes).
226 Transfer complete.
ftp: 123126 bytes received in 0.13Seconds 985.01Kbytes/sec.
ftp>
```

Notice again that the response indicates that the command actually processed by the server is a PORT command. The file is transferred in ASCII mode. The entire transfer takes 0.13 seconds, which works out to a transfer rate of about 985K per second.

After you download the file, you can end the session by typing **bye**. FTP responds by displaying the site's goodbye message; then it returns you to the MS-DOS command prompt:

```
221 Hurry back...
C:\>
```

Of course, FTP is a lot more involved than this simple session suggests. Still, the most common use of FTP is to download files, and most downloads are no more complicated than this example.

**Book IV
Chapter 5**

Using FTP

FTP Command and Subcommand Reference

The rest of this chapter is an FTP command reference. In the following sections, you can find complete reference information for the FTP command and all its subcommands. The first command in this section is the FTP command itself. After that, all the FTP command subcommands are listed in alphabetical order.

The FTP command

What it does: Starts the FTP client so that you can transfer files to and from an FTP server

Syntax: **ftp** [**-v**] [**-d**] [**-i**] [**-n**] [**-g**] [**-s:***filename*] [**-a**] [**-w:***windowsize*] [**-A**] [*host*]

Parameters: **-v** Turns off Verbose mode.

-d Turns on Debug mode.

-i Turns off Prompt mode.

-n Forces manual logon.

-g Turns off Glob mode.

-s Specifies a script file that contains FTP commands.

-a Specifies that any network interface can be used to bind the data connection.

-w Specifies the size of the transmission buffer. The default is 4K.

-A Automatically logs on as Anonymous.

Host: The FTP server to which you want to connect. This can be the server's DNS name or an IP address.

Examples: **ftp ftp.lowewriter.com**
ftp ftp.lowewriter.com -A

More info:	Unlike most Windows commands, the switches for this command begin with a hyphen, not a slash.
	If you want to script subcommands, use the -s switch. Input redirection doesn't work with FTP.
	When FTP is running, the prompt ftp> appears. When this prompt is displayed, you can enter any of the FTP subcommands described in the rest of this chapter.

! (Escape)

What it does:	Escape to a command shell
Syntax:	**!**
More info:	This command brings up a temporary command prompt so that you can enter commands. To return to the ftp> prompt, type **exit**.

? (Help)

What it does:	Displays Help information
Syntax:	**?** [*command*]
	help [*command*]
Example:	**help mput**
More info:	? and help are interchangeable. If you enter **?** or **help** by itself, a list of FTP commands appears. If you enter **?** or **help** followed by a command name, a summary of that command's function appears.

append

What it does:	Uploads a file and appends it to the end of an existing file on the remote system
Syntax:	**append** *localfile* [*remotefile*]
Example:	**append extra.txt start.txt**
More info:	If you omit the *remotefile* parameter, the remote file is assumed to have the same name as the local file.

**Book IV
Chapter 5**

Using FTP

ascii

What it does:	Sets the ASCII transfer mode
Syntax:	**ascii**
More info:	This command sets the transfer type of ASCII, which is best suited for text files. ASCII is the default transfer type.

bell

What it does:	Causes the FTP client to beep when each transfer is complete
Syntax:	**bell**
More info:	This command is useful when you're downloading long files and want to take a nap during the download. Unfortunately, it doesn't beep when it sees your boss approaching your office, so you'll need some other alarm system to cover that contingency.

binary

What it does:	Sets the binary transfer type
Syntax:	**binary**
More info:	The binary file type is best for executable files and other nontext files.

bye

What it does:	Ends the FTP session and exits the FTP client
Syntax:	**bye**
More info:	This is the command to use when you're done. It's the same as the `quit` command.

cd

What it does:	Changes the working directory on the remote computer
Syntax:	**cd** *remotedirectory*
Example:	**cd pics**

More info:	Use this to change to the directory that contains the files you want to download or the directory to which you want to upload files. Type **cd ** to go to the root directory.

close

What it does:	Closes the session with the remote computer but doesn't leave the FTP program
Syntax:	**close**
More info:	You can use this command if you want to switch to another FTP server without leaving and restarting the FTP program. This command is the same as the disconnect command.

debug

What it does:	Toggles Debug mode
Syntax:	**debug**
More info:	When Debug mode is on, the FTP client displays the actual FTP commands that are sent to the FTP server. This can be useful if you're an FTP guru trying to diagnose a problem with a server or a client, but it can also be fun if you just want to see how FTP client commands (like CD) get translated into FTP server commands (like CWD).

delete

What it does:	Deletes the specified file on the remote computer
Syntax:	**delete** *remotefile*
Example:	**delete fright.txt**
More info:	You can delete only one file at a time with this command. To delete more than one file in a single command, use the mdelete command.

dir

What it does:	List contents of remote directory
Syntax:	**dir** [*remotedirectory*] [*localfile*]

**Book IV
Chapter 5**

Using FTP

Examples:	**dir** **dir \pics** **dir \pics picdir.txt**
More info:	The first parameter lets you list a directory other than the current working directory. The second parameter lets you capture the output to a file on the local computer.

disconnect

What it does:	Disconnects from the remote computer but doesn't leave the FTP program
Syntax:	**disconnect**
More info:	You can use this command if you want to switch to another FTP server without leaving and restarting the FTP program. This command is the same as the close command.

get

What it does:	Downloads a file from the remote computer
Syntax:	**get** *remotefile* [*localfile*]
Examples:	**get boo.exe** **get boo.exe bar.exe**
More info:	This command downloads the specified file from the current working directory on the remote system to the current directory on the local system. The second parameter lets you save the file using a different name than the name used on the remote system.
	You can use this command to download only one file at a time. To download multiple files, use the mget command.
	This command is the same as the recv command.

glob

What it does:	Toggles the use of wildcards for local filenames
Syntax:	**glob**
More info:	If globbing is on, you can use * and ? characters in local filenames. Globbing is on by default.

hash

What it does: Toggles the display of hash marks (#) to indicate transfer progress

Syntax: **hash**

More info: Hash is off by default. If you turn it on by issuing the hash command, a hash mark (#) appears each time a 2K data block is transferred. This helps you track the progress of transfers.

help

What it does: Displays Help information

Syntax: **?** [*command*]

help [*command*]

Example: **help mput**

More info: ? and help are interchangeable. If you enter **?** or **help** by itself, a list of FTP commands appears. If you enter **?** or **help** followed by a command name, a summary of that command's function appears.

lcd

What it does: Changes the working directory on the local computer

Syntax: **lcd** *localdirectory*

Example: **lcd \docs**

More info: Use this to change to the directory you want to download files to or that contains files you want to upload.

literal

What it does: Sends a native FTP command directly to the server

Syntax: **literal** *arguments* . . .

Example: **literal cwd pics**

More info: Use this command if you're an FTP guru and you want to send a native FTP command to the server. It's the same as the quote command.

ls

What it does:	List contents of remote directory
Syntax:	**ls** [remotedirectory] [localfile]
Examples:	**ls** **ls \pics** **ls \pics picdir.txt**
More info:	The first parameter lets you list a directory other than the current working directory. The second parameter lets you capture the output to a file on the local computer.

mdelete

What it does:	Delete multiple files
Syntax:	**mdelete** remotefile . . .
Examples:	**mdelete file1.txt** **mdelete file1.txt file2.txt file3.txt**
More info:	This command deletes one or more files from the current working directory on the remote system.

mdir

What it does:	Lists the contents of multiple remote directories
Syntax:	**mdir** *remotedirectory* . . . [*localfile*]
Example:	**mdir pics videos**
More info:	Specify a hyphen as the last parameter to display the output on the screen. Otherwise, the last parameter will be interpreted as the name of the local file you want the directory listing captured to.

mget

What it does:	Downloads multiple files
Syntax:	**mget** remotefile . . .
Example:	**mget file1.txt** **mget file1.txt file2.txt file3.txt**

More info:	This command downloads one or more files from the current working directory on the remote system to the current directory on the local computer.

mkdir

What it does:	Creates a directory on the remote system
Syntax:	**mkdir** *remotedirectory*
Example:	**mdir plans**
More info:	The new subdirectory is created in the current working directory on the remote system.

mls

What it does:	Lists the contents of multiple remote directories
Syntax:	**mls** *remotedirectory . . .* [*localfile*]
Example:	**mls pics videos**
More info:	Specify a hyphen as the last parameter to display the output on the screen. Otherwise, the last parameter will be interpreted as the name of the local file you want the directory listing captured to.

mput

What it does:	Uploads multiple files
Syntax:	**mput** *localfile . . .*
Examples:	**mput file1.txt** **mput file1.txt file2.txt file3.txt**
More info:	This command uploads one or more files from the current directory on the local system to the current working directory on the remote system.

open

What it does:	Connects to an FTP server
Syntax:	**open** *remotesystem* [*port*]

Examples:	**open ftp.microsoft.com** **open ftp.weirdport.com 1499**
More info:	Specify the port number only if the remote system does not use the standard FTP ports (20 and 21).

prompt

What it does:	Toggles prompting for multiple transfers
Syntax:	**prompt**
More info:	When prompt mode is on, you're prompted for each file before the file is transferred. Prompt mode is on by default.

put

What it does:	Uploads a file to the remote computer
Syntax:	**put** *localfile* [*remotefile*]
Examples:	**put boo.exe** **put boo.exe bar.exe**
More info:	This command uploads the specified file from the current directory on the local system to the current working directory on the remote system. The second parameter lets you save the file with a different name than the name used on the local system.
	You can use this command to upload only one file at a time. To upload multiple files, use the mput command.
	This command is the same as the send command.

pwd

What it does:	Displays the current working directory on the remote computer
Syntax:	**pwd**
More info:	If you aren't sure what the current directory is on the remote system, use this command to find out.

quit

What it does: Ends the FTP session and quits the FTP program

Syntax: **quit**

More info: This is the command to use when you're done. It's the same as the `bye` command.

quote

What it does: Sends a native `FTP` command directly to the server

Syntax: **quote** *arguments* . . .

Example: **quote cwd pics**

More info: Use this command if you're an FTP guru and you want to send a native `FTP` command to the server. It's the same as the `literal` command.

recv

What it does: Downloads a file from the remote compute

Syntax: **recv** *remotefile* [*localfile*]

Examples: **recv boo.exe**
recv boo.exe bar.exe

More info: This command downloads the specified file from the current working directory on the remote system to the current directory on the local system. The second parameter lets you save the file with a different name than the name used on the remote system.

You can use this command to download only one file at a time. To download multiple files, use the `mget` command.

This command is the same as the `get` command.

Book IV
Chapter 5

Using FTP

remotehelp

What it does: Displays help for remote commands

Syntax: **remotehelp** [*command*]

Example: **remotehelp cwd**

More info: If you enter remotehelp by itself, a list of FTP commands is displayed. If you enter remotehelp followed by a command name, a summary of that command's function appears.

rename

What it does: Renames a file on the remote system

Syntax: **rename** *filename newfilename*

Example: **rename door.jpg doorway.jpg**

More info: Use this command to change the name of a file on the remote system.

rmdir

What it does: Removes a directory on the remote system

Syntax: **rmdir** *directoryname*

Example: **rmdir oldpics**

More info: This command removes a directory and all the files in it, so use it with caution!

send

What it does: Uploads a file to the remote computer

Syntax: **send** *localfile* [*remotefile*]

Examples: **send boo.exe**
send boo.exe bar.exe

More info:	This command uploads the specified file from the current directory on the local system to the current working directory on the remote system. The second parameter lets you save the file with a different name than the name used on the local system.

You can use this command to upload only one file at a time. To upload multiple files, use the `mput` command.

This command is the same as the `put` command.

status

What it does:	Displays the current status of the FTP client
Syntax:	**status**
More info:	Use this command to display the current settings of options, such as `bell`, `prompt`, and `verbose`, as well as the current connection status.

trace

What it does:	Activates Trace mode
Syntax:	**trace**
More info:	When Trace mode is on, detailed information about each packet transmission is displayed. `trace` is off by default and should be left off unless you're digging deep into the bowels of FTP or just want to show off.

type

What it does:	Sets the transfer type to ASCII or binary or displays the current mode
Syntax:	**type** [**ascii** or **binary**]
Examples:	**type ascii** **type binary** **type**

**Book IV
Chapter 5**

Using FTP

More info:	Use ASCII transfers for text files and binary transfers for nontext files.
	If you don't specify a type, the current transfer type appears.
	You can also use the `ascii` or `binary` commands to switch the transfer type.

user

What it does:	Logs you on to a remote system
Syntax:	**user** *username* [*password*]
Examples:	**user doug** **user doug notmypw**
More info:	This command logs you on to the remote system by using the username and password you provide. If you omit the password, you're prompted to enter it.

verbose

What it does:	Toggles Verbose mode
Syntax:	**verbose**
More info:	When Verbose mode is on, FTP responses appear. Verbose mode is on by default.

Chapter 6: TCP/IP Tools and Commands

In This Chapter

↳ **Recognizing tools and commands**

↳ **Making all your hosts sing with IPConfig and Ping**

Most client and server operating systems that support Transmission Control Protocol/Internet Protocol (TCP/IP) come with a suite of commands and tools that are designed to let you examine TCP/IP configuration information and diagnose and correct problems. Although the exact form of these commands varies between Windows and Unix/Linux, most are surprisingly similar. This chapter is a reference to the most commonly used TCP/IP commands.

Using the arp Command

Using the arp command allows you to display and modify the Address Resolution Protocol (ARP) cache. An *ARP cache* is a simple mapping of IP addresses to MAC addresses. Each time a computer's TCP/IP stack uses ARP to determine the Media Access Control (MAC) address for an IP address, it records the mapping in the ARP cache so that future ARP lookups go faster.

If you use the arp command without any parameters, you get a list of the command's parameters. To display the ARP cache entry for a specific IP address, use an -a switch followed by the IP address. For example:

```
C:\>arp -a 192.168.168.22
Interface: 192.168.168.21 --- 0x10004
  Internet Address      Physical Address      Type
  192.168.168.22        00-60-08-39-e5-a1     dynamic
C:\>
```

You can display the complete ARP cache by using -a without specifying an IP address, like this:

```
C:\>arp -a
Interface: 192.168.168.21 --- 0x10004
  Internet Address      Physical Address      Type
  192.168.168.9         00-02-e3-16-e4-5d     dynamic
```

```
192.168.168.10       00-50-04-17-66-90    dynamic
192.168.168.22       00-60-08-39-e5-a1    dynamic
192.168.168.254      00-40-10-18-42-49    dynamic
C:\>
```

ARP is sometimes useful when diagnosing duplicate IP assignment problems. For example, suppose you can't access a computer that has an IP address of `192.168.168.100`. You try to ping the computer, expecting the ping to fail; but lo and behold, the ping succeeds. One possible cause for this may be that two computers on the network have been assigned the address `192.168.168.100`, and your ARP cache is pointing to the wrong one. The way to find out is to go to the `192.168.168.100` computer that you want to access, run `ipconfig /all`, and make a note of the physical address. Then return to the computer that's having trouble reaching the `192.168.168.100` computer, run `arp -a`, and compare the physical address with the one you noted. If they're different, that two computers are assigned the same IP address. You can then check the Dynamic Host Configuration Protocol (DHCP) or static TCP/IP configuration of the computers involved to find out why.

Using the `hostname` Command

The `hostname` command is the simplest of all the TCP/IP commands presented in this chapter. It simply displays the computer's host name. For example:

```
C:\>hostname
doug
C:\>
```

Here, the host name for the computer is `doug`. The Windows version of the `hostname` command has no parameters. However, the Unix/Linux versions of `hostname` let you set the computer's host name as well as display it. You do that by specifying the new host name as an argument.

Using the `ipconfig` Command

Using the `ipconfig` command displays information about a computer's TCP/IP configuration. It can also be used to update DHCP and Domain Name Server (DNS) settings.

Displaying basic IP configuration

To display the basic IP configuration for a computer, use the ipconfig command without any parameters, like this:

```
C:\>ipconfig

Windows IP Configuration


Ethernet adapter Local Area Connection:

    Connection-specific DNS Suffix  . :
    Link-local IPv6 Address . . . . . :
     fe80::cca:9067:9427:a911%8
    IPv4 Address. . . . . . . . . . . : 192.168.1.110
    Subnet Mask . . . . . . . . . . . : 255.255.255.0
    Default Gateway . . . . . . . . . : 192.168.1.1

Tunnel adapter Local Area Connection* 6:

    Connection-specific DNS Suffix  . :
    IPv6 Address. . . . . . . . . . . :
     2001:0:4136:e38c:2c6c:670:3f57:fe91
    Link-local IPv6 Address . . . . . :
     fe80::2c6c:670:3f57:fe91%9
    Default Gateway . . . . . . . . . : ::

Tunnel adapter Local Area Connection* 7:

    Connection-specific DNS Suffix  . :
    Link-local IPv6 Address . . . . . :
     fe80::5efe:192.168.1.110%10
    Default Gateway . . . . . . . . . :
C:\>
```

When you use ipconfig without parameters, the command displays the name of the adapter, the domain name used for the adapter, the IP address, the subnet mask, and the default gateway configuration for the adapter. This is the easiest way to determine a computer's IP address.

If your computer indicates an IP address in the 169.254.x.x block, odds are good that the DHCP server isn't working. 169.254.x.x is the Class B address block that Windows uses when it resorts to IP Autoconfiguration. This usually happens only when the DHCP server can't be reached or isn't working.

**Book IV
Chapter 6**

**TCP/IP Tools and
Commands**

Displaying detailed configuration information

You can display detailed IP configuration information by using an `/all` switch with the `ipconfig` command, like this:

```
C:\>ipconfig /all

Windows IP Configuration

    Host Name . . . . . . . . . . . . : WK07-001
    Primary Dns Suffix  . . . . . . . :
    Node Type . . . . . . . . . . . . : Hybrid
    IP Routing Enabled. . . . . . . . : No
    WINS Proxy Enabled. . . . . . . . : No

Ethernet adapter Local Area Connection:

    Connection-specific DNS Suffix  . :
    Description . . . . . . . . . . . : Intel(R) PRO/100 VE Network Connection
    Physical Address. . . . . . . . . : 00-12-3F-A7-17-BA
    DHCP Enabled. . . . . . . . . . . : No
    Autoconfiguration Enabled . . . . : Yes
    Link-local IPv6 Address . . . . . : fe80::cca:9067:9427:a911%8(Preferred)
    IPv4 Address. . . . . . . . . . . : 192.168.1.110(Preferred)
    Subnet Mask . . . . . . . . . . . : 255.255.255.0
    Default Gateway . . . . . . . . . : 192.168.1.1
    DNS Servers . . . . . . . . . . . : 192.168.1.10
                                        68.87.76.178
    NetBIOS over Tcpip. . . . . . . . : Enabled

C:\>
```

You can determine a lot of information about the computer from the `ip config /all` command. For example:

✦ The computer's host name is `WK07-001`.

✦ The computer's IPv4 address is `192.168.1.110`, and the subnet mask is `255.255.255.0`.

✦ The default gateway is a router located at `192.168.1.1`.

✦ This router is also the network's DHCP server.

✦ The DNS servers are at `192.168.1.10` and `68.87.76.178`.

Renewing an IP lease

If you're having an IP configuration problem, you can often solve it by renewing the computer's IP lease. To do that, use a `/renew` switch, like this:

```
C:\>ipconfig /renew
Windows IP Configuration
Ethernet adapter Local Area Connection:
        Connection-specific DNS Suffix  . :
        IP Address. . . . . . . . . . . . : 192.168.1.110
```

```
        Subnet Mask . . . . . . . . . . . : 255.255.255.0
        Default Gateway . . . . . . . . . : 192.168.1.1
C:\>
```

When you renew an IP lease, the `ipconfig` command displays the new lease information.

This command won't work if you configured the computer to use a static IP address.

Releasing an IP lease

You can release an IP lease by using an `ipconfig` command with the `/release` parameter, like this:

```
C:\>ipconfig /release
Windows IP Configuration
Ethernet adapter Local Area Connection:
        Connection-specific DNS Suffix  . :
        IP Address. . . . . . . . . . . . : 0.0.0.0
        Subnet Mask . . . . . . . . . . . : 0.0.0.0
        Default Gateway . . . . . . . . . :
C:\>
```

As you can see, the DNS suffix and default gateway for the computer are blank, and the IP address and subnet mask are set to `0.0.0.0`.

After you release the DHCP lease, you can use an `ipconfig /renew` command to obtain a new DHCP lease for the computer.

Flushing the local DNS cache

You probably won't need to do this unless you're having DNS troubles. If you've been tinkering with your network's DNS configuration, you may need to flush the cache on your DNS clients so that they'll be forced to reacquire information from the DNS server. You can do that by using a `/flushdns` switch:

```
C:\>ipconfig /flushdns
Windows IP Configuration
Successfully flushed the DNS Resolver Cache.
C:\>
```

Even if you don't need to do this, it's fun just to see the computer read flushed. If I worked at Microsoft, you'd be able to revert Windows Vista computers back to XP by using a `/flushVista` switch.

Using the **nbtstat** Command

nbtstat is a Windows-only command that can help solve problems with NetBIOS name resolution. (*nbt* stands for *NetBIOS over TCP/IP.*) You can use any of the switches listed in Table 6-1 to specify what nbtstat output you want to display. For example, you can use an -a switch to display the cached name table for a specified computer, like this:

```
C:\>nbtstat -a WK07-001

Local Area Connection:
Node IpAddress: [192.168.1.110] Scope Id: []

          NetBIOS Remote Machine Name Table

       Name               Type         Status
    ---------------------------------------------
    WK07-001       <00>  UNIQUE      Registered
    WORKGROUP      <00>  GROUP       Registered
    WK07-001       <20>  UNIQUE      Registered
    WORKGROUP      <1E>  GROUP       Registered
    WORKGROUP      <1D>  UNIQUE      Registered
    ..__MSBROWSE__.<01>  GROUP       Registered

    MAC Address = 00-12-3F-A7-17-BAC:\>
C:\>
```

Table 6-1 lists the switches that you can use with nbtstat and explains the function of each switch.

Table 6-1	**nbtstat Command Switches**
Switch	*What It Does*
-a *name*	Lists the specified computer's name table given the computer's name
-A *IP-address*	Lists the specified computer's name table given the computer's IP address
-c	Lists the contents of the NetBIOS cache
-n	Lists locally registered NetBIOS names
-r	Displays a count of the names resolved by broadcast and via WINS
-R	Purges and reloads the cached name table from the LMHOSTS file
-RR	Releases and then reregisters all names
-S	Displays the sessions table using IP addresses
-s	Displays the sessions table and converts destination IP addresses to computer NetBIOS names

Using the `netdiag` *Utility*

`netdiag` is a powerful, network-testing utility that performs a variety of network diagnostic tests that can help you to pinpoint a networking problem. Listing 6-1 shows the output from a typical execution of the `Netdiag` command. (I took the liberty of editing it somewhat to make it more compact.) You can scan this listing to see the types of tests that the `netdiag` command performs.

Unfortunately, the `netdiag` command is not available for Windows 9*x* computers (including Windows Me), and it isn't installed by default in Windows XP nor Vista. However, you can install it in Windows XP or Vista by inserting your Windows installation disc in your computer's optical drive. If you're asked to reinstall Windows, say no. Instead, choose to browse the install CD. Navigate your way down to the `\Support\Tools` folder on the install CD and then double-click the Setup.exe icon in the `\Support\Tools` folder.

The `netdiag` command has several switches that let you control the output generated by the command:

✦ `/q`: Lists only those tests that fail

✦ `/v`: Generates verbose output (even more verbose than usual)

✦ `/debug`: Generates extremely verbose output — way more than when you use `/v`

✦ `/l`: Stores the output from the command in a file named `NetDiag.log`

✦ `/fix`: Attempts to fix DNS problems that are discovered

Listing 6-1: Output from the `netdiag` Command

```
. . . . . . . . . . . . . . . . . . . . . . . . . . . .
     Computer Name: DOUG
     DNS Host Name: Doug
     System info : Windows 2000 Professional (Build 2600)
     Processor : x86 Family 15 Model 2 Stepping 4,
     GenuineIntel
     List of installed hotfixes :
          Q147222
          Q308677
          Q308678
          Q310601
          Q311889
          Q315000
Netcard queries test . . . . . . . : Passed
Per interface results:
     Adapter : Local Area Connection
          Netcard queries test . . . : Passed
          Host Name. . . . . . . . . : Doug
```

(continued)

**Book IV
Chapter 6**

**TCP/IP Tools and
Commands**

Listing 6-1 *(continued)*

```
        IP Address . . . . . . . . : 192.168.168.21
        Subnet Mask. . . . . . . . : 255.255.255.0
        Default Gateway. . . . . . : 192.168.168.254
        Dns Servers. . . . . . . . : 192.168.168.10
                                     168.215.210.50
                                     192.9.9.3
        AutoConfiguration results. . . . . . : Passed
        Default gateway test . . . : Passed
        NetBT name test. . . . . . : Passed
        WINS service test. . . . . : Skipped
            There are no WINS servers configured for this
    interface.
Global results:
Domain membership test . . . . . . : Passed
    Dns domain name is not specified.
    Dns forest name is not specified.
NetBT transports test. . . . . . . : Passed
    List of NetBt transports currently configured:
        NetBT_Tcpip_{4A526104-BAEB-44F0-A2F6-A804FE31BBAA}
    1 NetBt transport currently configured.
Autonet address test . . . . . . . : Passed
IP loopback ping test. . . . . . . : Passed
Default gateway test . . . . . . . : Passed
NetBT name test. . . . . . . . . . : Passed
Winsock test . . . . . . . . . . . : Passed
DNS test . . . . . . . . . . . . . : Passed
Redir and Browser test . . . . . . : Passed
    List of NetBt transports currently bound to the Redir
        NetBT_Tcpip_{4A526104-BAEB-44F0-A2F6-A804FE31BBAA}
    The redir is bound to 1 NetBt transport.
    List of NetBt transports currently bound to the browser
        NetBT_Tcpip_{4A526104-BAEB-44F0-A2F6-A804FE31BBAA}
    The browser is bound to 1 NetBt transport.
DC discovery test. . . . . . . . . : Skipped
DC list test . . . . . . . . . . . : Skipped
Trust relationship test. . . . . . : Skipped
Kerberos test. . . . . . . . . . . : Skipped
LDAP test. . . . . . . . . . . . . : Skipped
Bindings test. . . . . . . . . . . : Passed
WAN configuration test . . . . . . : Skipped
    No active remote access connections.
Modem diagnostics test . . . . . . : Passed
IP Security test . . . . . . . . . : Passed
    Service status  is: Started
    Service startup is: Automatic
    IPSec service is available, but no policy is assigned
    or active
    Note: run "ipseccmd /?" for more detailed information
The command completed successfully
```

Using the netstat Command

Use the Netstat command displays a variety of statistics about a computer's active TCP/IP connections. It's a useful tool to use when you're having trouble with TCP/IP applications, such as File Transfer Protocol (FTP), HyperText Transport Protocol (HTTP), and so on.

Displaying connections

If you run netstat without specifying any parameters, you get a list of active connections, something like this:

```
C:\>netstat
Active Connections
   Proto  Local Address   Foreign Address                State
   TCP    Doug:1463       192.168.168.10:1053            ESTABLISHED
   TCP    Doug:1582       192.168.168.9:netbios-ssn      ESTABLISHED
   TCP    Doug:3630       192.168.168.30:9100            SYN_SENT
   TCP    Doug:3716       192.168.168.10:4678            ESTABLISHED
   TCP    Doug:3940       192.168.168.10:netbios-ssn     ESTABLISHED
C:\>
```

This list shows all the active connections on the computer and indicates the local port used by the connection, as well as the IP address and port number for the remote computer.

You can specify the -n switch to display both local and foreign addresses in numeric IP form:

```
C:\>netstat -n
Active Connections
   Proto  Local Address          Foreign Address         State
   TCP    192.168.168.21:1463    192.168.168.10:1053     ESTABLISHED
   TCP    192.168.168.21:1582    192.168.168.9:139       ESTABLISHED
   TCP    192.168.168.21:3658    192.168.168.30:9100     SYN_SENT
   TCP    192.168.168.21:3716    192.168.168.10:4678     ESTABLISHED
   TCP    192.168.168.21:3904    207.46.106.78:1863      ESTABLISHED
   TCP    192.168.168.21:3940    192.168.168.10:139      ESTABLISHED
C:\>
```

Finally, you can specify the -a switch to display all TCP/IP connections and ports that are being listened to. I won't list the output from that command here because it would run several pages, and I want to do my part for the rainforests. Suffice it to say that it looks a lot like the netstat output shown previously, but a lot longer.

**Book IV
Chapter 6**

**TCP/IP Tools and
Commands**

Displaying interface statistics

If you use an `-e` switch, `netstat` displays various protocol statistics, like this:

```
C:\>netstat -e
Interface Statistics
                              Received              Sent
Bytes                       672932849         417963911
Unicast packets               1981755           1972374
Non-unicast packets            251869             34585
Discards                            0                 0
Errors                              0                 0
Unknown protocols                1829
C:\>
```

The items to pay attention to in this output are the Discards and Errors. These numbers should be zero, or at least close to it. If they're not, the network may be carrying too much traffic or the connection may have a physical problem. If no physical problem exists with the connection, try segmenting the network to see whether the error and discard rate drops.

You can display additional statistics by using an `-s` switch, like this:

```
C:\>netstat -s

IPv4 Statistics

    Packets Received                    = 9155
    Received Header Errors              = 0
    Received Address Errors             = 0
    Datagrams Forwarded                 = 0
    Unknown Protocols Received          = 0
    Received Packets Discarded          = 0
    Received Packets Delivered          = 14944
    Output Requests                     = 12677
    Routing Discards                    = 0
    Discarded Output Packets            = 71
    Output Packet No Route              = 0
    Reassembly Required                 = 0
    Reassembly Successful               = 0
    Reassembly Failures                 = 0
    Datagrams Successfully Fragmented   = 0
    Datagrams Failing Fragmentation     = 0
    Fragments Created                   = 0

IPv6 Statistics

    Packets Received                    = 3
    Received Header Errors              = 0
    Received Address Errors             = 0
    Datagrams Forwarded                 = 0
```

```
            Unknown Protocols Received          = 0
            Received Packets Discarded          = 0
            Received Packets Delivered          = 345
            Output Requests                     = 377
            Routing Discards                    = 0
            Discarded Output Packets            = 0
            Output Packet No Route              = 0
            Reassembly Required                 = 0
            Reassembly Successful               = 0
            Reassembly Failures                 = 0
            Datagrams Successfully Fragmented   = 0
            Datagrams Failing Fragmentation     = 0
            Fragments Created                   = 0

    ICMPv4 Statistics

                                      Received      Sent
            Messages                  6             14
            Errors                    0             0
            Destination Unreachable   6             14
            Time Exceeded             0             0
            Parameter Problems        0             0
            Source Quenches           0             0
            Redirects                 0             0
            Echo Replies              0             0
            Echos                     0             0
            Timestamps                0             0
            Timestamp Replies         0             0
            Address Masks             0             0
            Address Mask Replies      0             0
            Router Solicitations      0             0
            Router Advertisements     0             0

    ICMPv6 Statistics

                                      Received      Sent
            Messages                  3             7
            Errors                    0             0
            Destination Unreachable   0             0
            Packet Too Big            0             0
            Time Exceeded             0             0
            Parameter Problems        0             0
            Echos                     0             0
            Echo Replies              0             0
            MLD Queries               0             0
            MLD Reports               0             0
            MLD Dones                 0             0
            Router Solicitations      0             6
            Router Advertisements     3             0
            Neighbor Solicitations    0             1
            Neighbor Advertisements   0             0
```

Book IV
Chapter 6

TCP/IP Tools and
Commands

```
Redirects                        0             0
Router Renumberings              0             0

TCP Statistics for IPv4

Active Opens                           = 527
Passive Opens                          = 2
Failed Connection Attempts             = 1
Reset Connections                      = 301
Current Connections                    = 1
Segments Received                      = 8101
Segments Sent                          = 6331
Segments Retransmitted                 = 301

TCP Statistics for IPv6

Active Opens                           = 1
Passive Opens                          = 1
Failed Connection Attempts             = 0
Reset Connections                      = 1
Current Connections                    = 0
Segments Received                      = 142
Segments Sent                          = 142
Segments Retransmitted                 = 0

UDP Statistics for IPv4

Datagrams Received       = 6703
No Ports                 = 0
Receive Errors           = 0
Datagrams Sent           = 6011

UDP Statistics for IPv6

Datagrams Received       = 32
No Ports                 = 0
Receive Errors           = 0
Datagrams Sent           = 200
C:\>
```

Using the `nslookup` Command

The `nslookup` command is a powerful tool for diagnosing DNS problems. You know you're experiencing a DNS problem when you can access a resource by specifying its IP address but not its DNS name. For example, if you can get to www.ebay.com by typing **66.135.192.87** in your browser's address bar but not by typing **www.ebay.com**, you have a DNS problem.

Looking up an IP address

The simplest use of `nslookup` is to look up the IP address for a given DNS name. For example, how did I know that `66.135.192.87` was the IP address for `ebay.com`? I used `nslookup` to find out:

```
C:\>nslookup ebay.com
Server:  ns1.orng.twtelecom.net
Address:  168.215.210.50
Non-authoritative answer:
Name:    ebay.com
Address:  66.135.192.87
C:\>
```

As you can see, just type **nslookup** followed by the DNS name you want to look up. Nslookup issues a DNS query to find out. This DNS query was sent to the name server named `ns1.orng.twtelecom.net` at `168.215.210.50`. It then displayed the IP address that's associated with `ebay.com`: namely, `66.135.192.87`.

In some cases, you may find that using an `nslookup` command gives you the wrong IP address for a host name. To know that for sure, of course, you have to know with certainty what the host IP address *should* be. For example, if you know that your server is `203.172.182.10` but Nslookup returns a completely different IP address for your server when you query the server's host name, something is probably wrong with one of the DNS records.

Get me out of here!

One of my pet peeves is that it seems as if every program that uses subcommands chooses a different command to quit the application. I can never remember whether the command to get out of `nslookup` is `quit`, `bye`, or `exit`. I usually end up trying them all. And no matter what program I'm using, I always seem to choose the one that works for some other program first. When I'm in `nslookup`, I use `bye` first. When I'm in FTP, I try `exit` first. Arghh! If I were King of the Computer Hill, every program that had subcommands would respond to the following commands by exiting the program and returning to a command prompt:

```
Quit   Sayonara

Exit   Ciao

Bye    Mañana

Leave  Makelikeatree
```

Of course, the final command to try would be `Andgetouttahere` (in honor of Biff from the *Back to the Future* movies).

Using `nslookup` subcommands

If you use `nslookup` without any arguments, the `nslookup` command enters a subcommand mode. It displays a prompt character (>) to let you know that you're in `nslookup` subcommand mode rather than at a normal Windows command prompt. In subcommand mode, you can enter various subcommands to set options or to perform queries. You can type a question mark (?) to get a list of these commands. Table 6-2 lists the subcommands you'll use most.

Table 6-2	The Most Commonly Used `nslookup` Subcommands
Subcommand	*What It Does*
`name`	Queries the current name server for the specified name.
`server name`	Sets the current name server to the server you specify.
`root`	Sets the root server as the current server.
`set type=x`	Specifies the type of records to be displayed, such as A, CNAME, MX, NS, PTR, or SOA. Specify ANY to display all records.
`set debug`	Turns on Debug mode, which displays detailed information about each query.
`set nodebug`	Turns off Debug mode.
`set recurse`	Enables recursive searches.
`set norecurse`	Disables recursive searches.
`exit`	qExits the `nslookup` program and returns you to a command prompt.

Displaying DNS records

One of the main uses of `nslookup` is to examine your DNS configuration to make sure that it's set up properly. To do that, follow these steps:

1. **At a command prompt, type** nslookup **without any parameters.**

   `nslookup` displays the name of the default name server and displays the > prompt.

   ```
   C:\>nslookup
   Default Server:  ns1.orng.twtelecom.net
   Address:  168.215.210.50
   >
   ```

2. **Type the subcommand** set type=any.

   `nslookup` silently obeys your command and displays another prompt:

   ```
   > set type=any
   >
   ```

3. **Type your domain name.**

`nslookup` responds by displaying the name servers for your domain:

```
> lowewriter.com
Server:  ns1.orng.twtelecom.net
Address:  168.215.210.50
Non-authoritative answer:
lowewriter.com   nameserver = NS000.NS0.com
lowewriter.com   nameserver = NS207.PAIR.com
lowewriter.com   nameserver = NS000.NS0.com
lowewriter.com   nameserver = NS207.PAIR.com
>
```

4. **Use a server command to switch to one of the domain's name servers.**

For example, to switch to the first name server listed above, type **server NS000.NS0.com**. `nslookup` replies with a message that indicates the new default server:

```
> server ns000.ns0.com
Default Server:  ns000.ns0.com
Address:  216.92.61.61
>
```

5. **Type your domain name again.**

This time, `nslookup` responds by displaying the DNS information for your domain:

```
> lowewriter.com
Server:  ns000.ns0.com
Address:  216.92.61.61
lowewriter.com
        primary name server = ns207.pair.com
        responsible mail addr = root.pair.com
        serial  = 2001121009
        refresh = 3600 (1 hour)
        retry   = 300 (5 mins)
        expire  = 604800 (7 days)
        default TTL = 3600 (1 hour)
lowewriter.com   nameserver = ns000.ns0.com
lowewriter.com   nameserver = ns207.pair.com
lowewriter.com   MX preference = 50, mail exchanger =
    sasi.pair.com
lowewriter.com   internet address = 209.68.34.15
>
```

6. **Type exit to leave the Nslookup program.**

You return to a command prompt.

```
> exit
C:\>
```

Wasn't that fun?

**Book IV
Chapter 6**

**TCP/IP Tools and
Commands**

Locating the mail server for an e-mail address

If you're having trouble delivering mail to someone, you can use `nslookup` to determine the IP address of the user's mail server. Then, you can use the `ping` command to see whether you can contact the user's mail server. If not, you can use the `tracert` command to find out where the communication breaks down.

To find a user's mail server, start `nslookup` and enter the command **set type=MX**. Then, enter the domain portion of the user's e-mail address. For example, if the user's address is Doug@LoweWriter.com, enter **Lowe Writer.com**. `nslookup` will display the MX (Mail eXchanger) information for the domain, like this:

```
C:\>nslookup
Default Server:  ns7.attbi.com
Address:  204.127.198.19
> set type=mx
> lowewriter.com
Server:  ns7.attbi.com
Address:  204.127.198.19
lowewriter.com  MX preference = 50, mail exchanger = sasi.pair.com
lowewriter.com  nameserver = ns000.ns0.com
lowewriter.com  nameserver = ns207.pair.com
ns000.ns0.com    internet address = 216.92.61.61
ns207.pair.com   internet address = 209.68.2.52
>
```

Here, you can see that the name of the mail server for the `LoweWriter.com` domain is `sasi.pair.com`.

Taking a ride through DNS-Land

Ever find yourself wondering how DNS really works? I mean, how is it that you can type a DNS name like `www.disneyland.com` into a Web browser and you're almost instantly transported to the Magic Kingdom? Is it really magic?

Nope. It isn't magic; it's DNS. In Book IV, Chapter 4, I present a somewhat dry and theoretical overview of DNS. After you have the `nslookup` command in your trusty TCP/IP toolbox, take a little trip through the Internet's maze of DNS servers to find out how DNS gets from `www.disneyland.com` to an IP address in just a matter of milliseconds.

DNS does its whole name resolution thing so fast, it's easy to take it for granted. If you follow this little procedure, you'll gain a deeper appreciation for what DNS does literally tens of thousands of times every second of every day.

1. **At a command prompt, type** nslookup **without any parameters.**

`nslookup` displays the name of the default name server and displays the > prompt.

```
C:\>nslookup
Default Server:  ns1.orng.twtelecom.net
Address:  168.215.210.50
>
```

2. **Type** root **to switch to one of the Internet's root servers.**

`nslookup` switches to one of the Internet's 13 root servers and then displays the > prompt.

```
> root
Default Server:  A.ROOT-SERVERS.NET
Address:  198.41.0.4
```

3. **Type** www.disneyland.com.

`nslookup` sends a query to the root server to ask if it knows the IP address of www.disneyland.com. The root server answers with a referral, meaning that it doesn't know about www.disneyland.com, but you should try one of these servers because they know all about the com domain.

```
> www.disneyland.com
Server:  A.ROOT-SERVERS.NET
Address:  198.41.0.4
Name:    www.disneyland.com
Served by:
- A.GTLD-SERVERS.NET
        192.5.6.30
        com
- G.GTLD-SERVERS.NET
        192.42.93.30
        com
- H.GTLD-SERVERS.NET
        192.54.112.30
        com
- C.GTLD-SERVERS.NET
        192.26.92.30
        com
- I.GTLD-SERVERS.NET
        192.43.172.30
        com
- B.GTLD-SERVERS.NET
        192.33.14.30
        com
- D.GTLD-SERVERS.NET
        192.31.80.30
        com
- L.GTLD-SERVERS.NET
```

**Book IV
Chapter 6**

**TCP/IP Tools and
Commands**

```
                192.41.162.30
                com
 - F.GTLD-SERVERS.NET
                192.35.51.30
                com
 - J.GTLD-SERVERS.NET
                192.48.79.30
                com

>
```

4. Type server **followed by the name or IP address of one of the** com **domain name servers.**

It doesn't really matter which one you pick. `nslookup` switches to that server. (The server may spit out some other information besides what I've shown here; I left it out for clarity.)

```
> server 192.48.79.30
Default Server:  [192.5.6.30]
Address:  192.5.6.30
>
```

5. Type www.disneyland.com **again.**

`nslookup` sends a query to the com server to ask whether it knows where the Magic Kingdom is. The com server's reply indicates that it doesn't know where `www.disneyland.com` is, but it does know which server is responsible for `disneyland.com`.

```
Server:  [192.5.6.30]
Address:  192.5.6.30
Name:    www.disney.com
Served by:
 - huey.disney.com
            204.128.192.10
            disney.com
 - huey11.disney.com
            208.246.35.40
            disney.com

>
```

Doesn't it figure that Disney's name server is `huey.disney.com`? There's probably also a `dewey.disney.com` and a `louie.disney.com`.

6. Type server **followed by the name or IP address of the second-level domain name server.**

`nslookup` switches to that server:

```
> server huey.disney.com
Default Server:  huey.disney.com
Address:  204.128.192.10
>
```

7. **Type** www.disneyland.com **again.**

Once again, `nslookup` sends a query to the name server to find out whether it knows where the Magic Kingdom is. Of course, `huey.disney.com` *does* know, so it tells us the answer:

```
> www.disneyland.com
Server:   huey.disney.com
Address:  204.128.192.10
Name:     disneyland.com
Address:  199.181.132.250
Aliases:  www.disneyland.com
>
```

8. **Type** Exit, **and then shout like Tigger in amazement at how DNS queries work.**

And be glad that your DNS resolver and primary name server do all this querying for you automatically.

Okay, maybe that wasn't an E Ticket ride, but it never ceases to amaze me that the DNS system can look up any DNS name hosted anywhere in the world almost instantly.

Using the `pathping` *Command*

`pathping` is an interesting command that's unique to Windows. It's sort of a cross between the `ping` command and the `tracert` command, combining the features of both into one tool. When you run `pathping`, it first traces the route to the destination address much the way `tracert` does. Then, it launches into a 25-second test of each router along the way, gathering statistics on the rate of data loss to each hop. If the route has a lot of hops, this can take a long time. However, it can help you to spot potentially unreliable hops. If you're having intermittent trouble reaching a particular destination, using `pathping` may help you pinpoint the problem.

The following command output is typical of the `pathping` command. (Using an -n switch causes the display to use numeric IP numbers only, instead of DNS host names. Although fully qualified host names are convenient, they tend to be very long for network routers, which makes the `pathping` output very difficult to decipher.)

```
C:\>pathping -n www.lowewriter.com
Tracing route to lowewriter.com [209.68.34.15]
over a maximum of 30 hops:
  0   192.168.168.21
  1   66.193.195.81
  2   66.193.200.5
  3   168.215.55.173
```

```
 4   168.215.55.101
 5   168.215.55.77
 6   66.192.250.38
 7   66.192.252.22
 8   208.51.224.141
 9   206.132.111.118
10   206.132.111.162
11   64.214.174.178
12   192.168.1.191
13   209.68.34.15
Computing statistics for 325 seconds...
              Source to Here    This Node/Link
Hop  RTT Lost/Sent = Pct    Lost/Sent = Pct   Address
 0                                             192.168.168.21
                            0/ 100 =  0%     |
 1   1ms    0/ 100 =  0%    0/ 100 =  0%   66.193.195.81]
                            0/ 100 =  0%     |
 2   14ms   0/ 100 =  0%    0/ 100 =  0%   66.193.200.5
                            0/ 100 =  0%     |
 3   10ms   0/ 100 =  0%    0/ 100 =  0%   168.215.55.173
                            0/ 100 =  0%     |
 4   10ms   0/ 100 =  0%    0/ 100 =  0%   168.215.55.101
                            0/ 100 =  0%     |
 5   12ms   0/ 100 =  0%    0/ 100 =  0%   168.215.55.77
                            0/ 100 =  0%     |
 6   14ms   0/ 100 =  0%    0/ 100 =  0%   66.192.250.38
                            0/ 100 =  0%     |
 7   14ms   0/ 100 =  0%    0/ 100 =  0%   66.192.252.22
                            0/ 100 =  0%     |
 8   14ms   0/ 100 =  0%    0/ 100 =  0%   208.51.224.141
                            0/ 100 =  0%     |
 9   81ms   0/ 100 =  0%    0/ 100 =  0%   206.132.111.118
                            0/ 100 =  0%     |
10   81ms   0/ 100 =  0%    0/ 100 =  0%   206.132.111.162]
                            0/ 100 =  0%     |
11   84ms   0/ 100 =  0%    0/ 100 =  0%   64.214.174.178]
                            0/ 100 =  0%     |
12   --- 100/ 100 =100%  100/ 100 =100%   192.168.1.191
                            0/ 100 =  0%     |
13   85ms   0/ 100 =  0%    0/ 100 =  0%   209.68.34.15
Trace complete.
```

Using the `ping` Command

`ping` is probably the most basic TCP/IP command line tool. Its main purpose is to determine whether you can reach another computer from your computer. It uses Internet Control Message Protocol (ICMP) protocol to send mandatory ECHO_REQUEST datagrams to the specified host computer. When the reply is received back from the host, the `ping` command displays how long it took to receive the response.

You can specify the host to ping by using an IP address, as in this example:

```
C:\>ping 192.168.168.10
Pinging 192.168.168.10 with 32 bytes of data:
Reply from 192.168.168.10: bytes=32 time<1ms TTL=128
Reply from 192.168.168.10: bytes=32 time<1ms TTL=128
Reply from 192.168.168.10: bytes=32 time<1ms TTL=128
Reply from 192.168.168.10: bytes=32 time<1ms TTL=128
Ping statistics for 192.168.168.10:
    Packets: Sent = 4, Received = 4, Lost = 0 (0% loss),
Approximate round trip times in milli-seconds:
    Minimum = 0ms, Maximum = 0ms, Average = 0ms
C:\>
```

By default, the ping command sends four packets to the specified host. It displays the result of each packet sent. Then it displays summary statistics: how many packets were sent, how many replies were received, the error loss rate, and the approximate round-trip time.

You can also ping by using a DNS name, as in this example:

```
C:\>ping www.lowewriter.com
Pinging lowewriter.com [209.68.34.15] with 32 bytes of data:
Reply from 209.68.34.15: bytes=32 time=84ms TTL=53
Reply from 209.68.34.15: bytes=32 time=84ms TTL=53
Reply from 209.68.34.15: bytes=32 time=84ms TTL=53
Reply from 209.68.34.15: bytes=32 time=84ms TTL=53
Ping statistics for 209.68.34.15:
    Packets: Sent = 4, Received = 4, Lost = 0 (0% loss),
Approximate round trip times in milli-seconds:
    Minimum = 84ms, Maximum = 84ms, Average = 84ms
C:\>
```

The ping command uses a DNS query to determine the IP address for the specified host, and then pings the host based on its IP address.

The ping command has a number of other switches that you'll use rarely, if ever. Some of these switches are available only for some operating systems. To find out which switches are available for your version of Ping, type **ping /?** (Windows) or **man ping** (Unix/Linux).

You can find a very interesting story about the creation of the ping command written by the command's author, Mike Muus, at his Web site at http://ftp. arl.mil/~mike/ping.html. (Sadly, Mr. Muus was killed in an automobile accident in November of 2000.)

Using the route Command

Using the route command displays or modifies the computer's routing table. For a typical computer that has a single network interface and is connected to a local area network (LAN) that has a router, the routing table is pretty simple and isn't often the source of network problems. Still, if you're having trouble accessing other computers or other networks, you can use the route command to make sure that a bad entry in the computer's routing table isn't the culprit.

For a computer with more than one interface and that's configured to work as a router, the routing table is often a major source of trouble. Setting up the routing table properly is a key part of configuring a router to work.

Displaying the routing table

To display the routing table (both IPv4 and IPv6) in Windows, use the route print command. In Unix/Linux, you can just use route without any command line switches. The output displayed by the Windows and Unix/Linux commands are similar. Here's an example from a typical Windows client computer:

```
C:\>route print
===========================================================================
Interface List
  8 ...00 12 3f a7 17 ba ...... Intel(R) PRO/100 VE Network Connection
  1 ........................... Software Loopback Interface 1
  9 ...02 00 54 55 4e 01 ...... Teredo Tunneling Pseudo-Interface
 10 ...00 00 00 00 00 00 00 e0  isatap.{D0F85930-01E2-402F-B0FC-31DFF887F06F}
===========================================================================

IPv4 Route Table
===========================================================================
Active Routes:
Network Destination        Netmask          Gateway       Interface  Metric
          0.0.0.0          0.0.0.0      192.168.1.1   192.168.1.110    276
        127.0.0.0        255.0.0.0        On-link         127.0.0.1    306
        127.0.0.1  255.255.255.255        On-link         127.0.0.1    306
  127.255.255.255  255.255.255.255        On-link         127.0.0.1    306
      192.168.1.0    255.255.255.0        On-link     192.168.1.110    276
    192.168.1.110  255.255.255.255        On-link     192.168.1.110    276
    192.168.1.255  255.255.255.255        On-link     192.168.1.110    276
        224.0.0.0        240.0.0.0        On-link         127.0.0.1    306
        224.0.0.0        240.0.0.0        On-link     192.168.1.110    276
  255.255.255.255  255.255.255.255        On-link         127.0.0.1    306
  255.255.255.255  255.255.255.255        On-link     192.168.1.110    276
===========================================================================
Persistent Routes:
  Network Address          Netmask  Gateway Address  Metric
          0.0.0.0          0.0.0.0      192.168.1.1  Default
===========================================================================

IPv6 Route Table
===========================================================================
Active Routes:
 If Metric Network Destination      Gateway
```

```
9     18 ::/0                                  On-link
1    306 ::1/128                               On-link
9     18 2001::/32                             On-link
9    266 2001:0:4136:e38c:2c6c:670:3f57:fe91/128
                                               On-link
8    276 fe80::/64                             On-link
9    266 fe80::/64                             On-link
10   281 fe80::5efe:192.168.1.110/128
                                               On-link
8    276 fe80::cca:9067:9427:a911/128
                                               On-link
9    266 fe80::2c6c:670:3f57:fe91/128
                                               On-link
1    306 ff00::/8                              On-link
9    266 ff00::/8                              On-link
8    276 ff00::/8                              On-link
===========================================================================
Persistent Routes:
  None
C:\>
```

For each entry in the routing table, five items of information are listed:

✦ **The destination IP address**

Actually, this is the address of the destination subnet, and must be interpreted in the context of the subnet mask.

✦ **The subnet mask that must be applied to the destination address to determine the destination subnet**

✦ **The IP address of the gateway to which traffic intended for the destination subnet will be sent**

✦ **The IP address of the interface through which the traffic will be sent to the destination subnet**

✦ **The *metric*, which indicates the number of hops required to reach destinations via the gateway**

Each packet that's processed by the computer is evaluated against the rules in the routing table. If the packet's destination address matches the destination subnet for the rule, the packet is sent to the specified gateway via the specified network interface. If not, the next rule is applied.

The computer on which I ran the route command in this example is on a private 192.168.1.0 subnet. The computer's IP address is 192.168.1.100, and the default gateway is a router at 192.168.1.1.

Book IV
Chapter 6

TCP/IP Tools and Commands

Here's how the rules shown in this example are used. Notice that you have to read the entries from the bottom up:

✦ **The first rule is for packets sent to 255.255.255.255, with subnet mask 255.255.255.255.** This special IP address is for broadcast packets. The rule specifies that these broadcast packets should be delivered to the local network interface (192.168.1.100).

✦ **The next rule is for packets sent to 192.168.1.255, again with subnet mask 255.255.255.255.** These are also broadcast packets and are sent to the local network interface.

✦ **The next rule is for packets sent to 192.168.1.100, again with subnet mask 255.255.255.255.** This is for packets that the computer is sending to itself via its own IP address. This rule specifies that these packets will be sent to the local loopback interface on 127.0.0.1.

✦ **The next rule is for packets sent to 192.168.1.0 with subnet mask 255.255.255.0.** These are packets intended for the local subnet. They're sent to the subnet via the local interface at 192.169.1.100.

✦ **The next rule is for packets sent to the loopback address (127.0.0.1, subnet mask 255.0.0.0).** These packets are sent straight through to the loopback interface, 127.0.0.1.

✦ **The last rule is for everything else.** All IP addresses will match the destination IP address 0.0.0.0 with subnet mask 0.0.0.0 and will be sent to the default gateway router at 192.168.1.1 via the computer's network interface at 192.168.1.100.

One major difference between the Windows version of route and the Unix/Linux version is the order in which they list the routing table. The Windows route command lists the table starting with the most general entry and works toward the most specific. The Unix/Linux version is the other way around: It starts with the most specific and works toward the more general. The Unix/Linux order makes more sense — the Windows route command displays the routing list upside down.

Modifying the routing table

Besides displaying the routing table, the route command also lets you modify it by adding, deleting, or changing entries.

You shouldn't do this unless you know what you're doing. If you mess up the routing table, your computer may not be able to communicate with anyone.

The syntax for the route command for adding, deleting, or changing a route entry is

```
route [-p] command dest [mask subnet] gateway [-if interface]
```

The following list describes each of the route command's parameters:

✦ -p: Makes the entry persistent. If you omit -p, the entry will be deleted the next time you reboot. (Use this only with add commands.)

✦ *command*: Add, delete, or change.

✦ *dest*: The IP address of the destination subnet.

✦ mask *subnet*: The subnet mask. If you omit the subnet mask, the default is 255.255.255.255, meaning that the entry will apply only to a single host rather than a subnet. You usually want to include the mask.

✦ *gateway*: The IP address of the gateway to which packets will be sent.

✦ -if *interface*: The IP address of the interface through which packets will be sent. If your computer has only one network interface, you can omit this.

Suppose that your network has a second router that serves as a link to another private subnet, 192.168.2.0 (subnet mask 255.255.255.0). The interface on the local side of this router is at 192.168.1.200. To add a static route entry that sends packets intended for the 192.168.2.0 subnet to this router, use a command like this:

```
C:\>route -p add 192.168.2.0 mask 255.255.255.0 192.168.1.200
```

Now, suppose that you later change the IP address of the router to 192.168.1.222. You can update this route with the following command:

```
C:\>route change 192.168.2.0 mask 255.255.255.0 192.168.1.222
```

Notice that I specify the mask again. If you omit the mask from a route change command, the command changes the mask to 255.255.255.255!

Finally, suppose that you realize that setting up a second router on this network wasn't such a good idea after all, so you want to just delete the entry. The following command will do the trick:

```
C:\>route delete 192.168.2.0
```

Using the tracert *Command*

The tracert command (spelled *traceroute* in Unix/Linux implementations) is one of the key diagnostic tools for TCP/IP. It displays a list of all the routers that a packet must go through to get from the computer where tracert is run to any other computer on the Internet. Each one of these routers is called a *hop,* presumably because the original designers of the IP protocol played a lot of hopscotch when they were young. If you can't connect to another computer, you can use `tracert` to find out exactly where the problem is occurring.

`tracert` makes three attempts to contact the router at each hop and displays the response time for each of these attempts. Then, it displays the DNS name of the router (if available) and the router's IP address.

To use `tracert`, type the `tracert` command followed by the host name of the computer to which you want to trace the route. For example, suppose that you're having trouble sending mail to a recipient at `wiley.com`. You've used `nslookup` to determine that the mail server for `wiley.com` is `xmail. wiley.com`, so now you can use `tracert` to trace the routers along the patch from your computer to `xmail.wiley.com`:

Understanding how `tracert` works

Understanding how `tracert` works can provide some insight that may help you to interpret the results it provides. Plus, you can use this knowledge to impress your friends, who probably don't know how it works.

The key to `tracert` is a field that's a standard part of all IP packets called TTL, which stands for *Time to Live*. In most other circumstances, a value called TTL would be a time value — not in IP packets, however. In an IP packet, the TTL value indicates how many routers a packet can travel through on its way to its destination. Every time a router forwards an IP packet, it subtracts one from the packet's TTL value. When the TTL value reaches zero, the router refuses to forward the packet.

The `tracert` command sends a series of special messages called ICMP Echo Requests to the destination computer. The first time it sends this message, it sets the TTL value of the packet to 1. When the packet arrives at the first router along the path to the destination, that router subtracts one from the TTL value, sees that the TTL value has become 0, so it sends a

Time Exceeded message back to the original host. When the `tracert` command receives this Time Exceeded message, it extracts the IP address of the router from it, calculates the time it took for the message to return, and displays the first hop.

Then the `tracert` command sends another Echo Request message: this time, with the TTL value set to 2. This message goes through the first router to the second router, which sees that the TTL value has been decremented to 0 and then sends back a Time Exceeded message. When `tracert` receives the Time Exceeded message from the second router, it displays the line for the second hop. This process continues, each time with a greater TTL value, until the Echo Request finally reaches the destination.

Pretty clever, eh?

(Note that the Unix/Linux `traceroute` command uses a slightly different set of TCP/IP messages and responses to accomplish the same result.)

```
C:\>tracert xmail.wiley.com
Tracing route to xmail.wiley.com [208.215.179.78]
over a maximum of 30 hops:
  1    27 ms    14 ms    10 ms  10.242.144.1
  2    11 ms    43 ms    10 ms  bar01-p5-0-0.frsnhe4.ca.attbb.net [24.130.64.125]
  3     9 ms    14 ms    12 ms  bar01-p4-0-0.frsnhe1.ca.attbb.net [24.130.0.5]
  4    25 ms    30 ms    29 ms  bic01-p6-0.elsgrdc1.ca.attbb.net [24.130.0.49]
  5    25 ms    29 ms    43 ms  bic02-d4-0.elsgrdc1.ca.attbb.net [24.130.0.162]
  6    21 ms    19 ms    20 ms  bar01-p2-0.1sanhe4.ca.attbb.net [24.130.0.197]
  7    37 ms    38 ms    19 ms  bic01-p2-0.1sanhe3.ca.attbb.net [24.130.0.193]
  8    20 ms    22 ms    21 ms  12.119.9.5
  9    21 ms    21 ms    22 ms  tbr2-p012702.la2ca.ip.att.net [12.123.199.241]
 10    71 ms   101 ms    62 ms  tbr2-p013801.sl9mo.ip.att.net [12.122.10.13]
 11    68 ms    77 ms    71 ms  tbr1-p012401.sl9mo.ip.att.net [12.122.9.141]
 12    79 ms    81 ms    83 ms  tbr1-cl4.wswdc.ip.att.net [12.122.10.29]
 13    83 ms   107 ms   103 ms  tbr1-p012201.n54ny.ip.att.net [12.122.10.17]
 14   106 ms    85 ms   105 ms  gbr6-p30.n54ny.ip.att.net [12.122.11.14]
 15   104 ms    96 ms    88 ms  gar3-p370.n54ny.ip.att.net [12.123.1.189]
 16    98 ms    86 ms    83 ms  12.125.50.162
 17    85 ms    90 ms    87 ms  xmail.wiley.com [208.215.179.78]
Trace complete.
```

Wow, when I send mail to my editors at Wiley, the mail travels through 17 routers along the way. No wonder I'm always missing deadlines!

The most likely problem that you'll encounter when you use tracert is a timeout during one of the hops. Timeouts are indicated by asterisks where you'd expect to see a time. For example, the following tracert output shows the fourth hop timing out on all three attempts:

```
C:\>tracert xmail.wiley.com
Tracing route to xmail.wiley.com [208.215.179.78]
over a maximum of 30 hops:
  1    27 ms    14 ms    10 ms  10.242.144.1
  2    11 ms    43 ms    10 ms  bar01-p5-0-0.frsnhe4.ca.attbb.net [24.130.64.125]
  3     9 ms    14 ms    12 ms  bar01-p4-0-0.frsnhe1.ca.attbb.net [24.130.0.5]
  4     *         *         *    Request timed out.
```

Sometimes, timeouts are caused by temporary problems, so you should try the tracert again to see if the problem persists. If you keep getting timeouts at the same router, the router could be having a genuine problem.

**Book IV
Chapter 6**

TCP/IP Tools and Commands

Book V
Wireless Networking

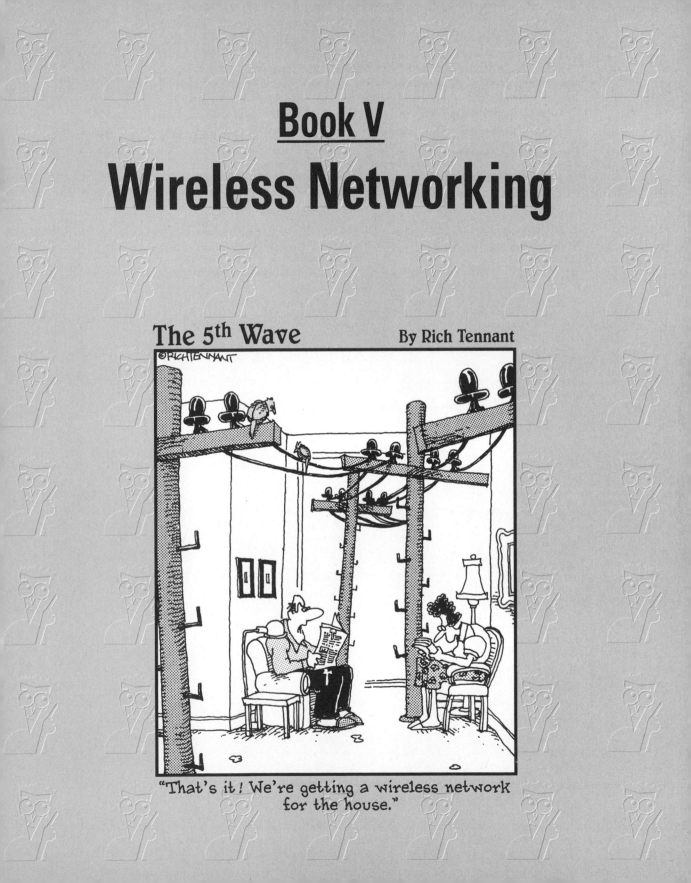

The 5th Wave   By Rich Tennant

"That's it! We're getting a wireless network for the house."

Contents at a Glance

Chapter 1: Setting Up a Wireless Network

In This Chapter

✔ Looking at wireless network standards

✔ Reviewing some basic radio terms

✔ Considering infrastructure and ad-hoc networks

✔ Working with a wireless access point

✔ Configuring Windows for wireless networking

Since the beginning of Ethernet networking, cable has been getting smaller and easier to work with. The original Ethernet cable was about as thick as your thumb, weighed a ton, and was difficult to bend around tight corners. Then came coaxial cable, which was lighter and easier to work with. Coaxial cable was supplanted by unshielded twisted-pair (UTP) cable, which is the cable used for most networks today. Coaxial and UTP cable is still *cable*, though, which means that you have to drill holes and pull cable through walls and ceilings in order to wire your entire home or office.

That's why wireless networking has become so popular. With wireless networking, you don't need cables to connect your computers. Instead, wireless networks use radio waves to send and receive network signals. As a result, a computer can connect to a wireless network at any location in your home or office.

Wireless networks are especially useful for notebook computers. After all, the main benefit of a notebook computer is that you can carry it around with you wherever you go. At work, you can use your notebook computer at your desk, in the conference room, in the break room, or even out in the parking lot. At home, you can use it in the bedroom, kitchen, den, game room, or out by the pool. With wireless networking, your notebook computer can be connected to the network, no matter where you take it.

This chapter introduces you to the ins and outs of setting up a wireless network. I tell you what you need to know about wireless networking standards, how to plan a wireless network, how to install and configure wireless network components, and how to create a network that mixes both wireless and cabled components.

Diving into Wireless Networking

A *wireless network* is a network that uses radio signals rather than direct cable connections to exchange information. A computer with a wireless network connection is like a cell phone. Just as you don't have to be connected to a phone line to use a cell phone, you don't have to be connected to a network cable to use a wireless networked computer.

The following paragraphs summarize some of the key concepts and terms that you need to understand in order to set up and use a basic wireless network:

✦ A wireless network is often referred to as a *WLAN,* for *wireless local area network.* Some people prefer to switch the acronym around to *local area wireless network,* or *LAWN.* The term *Wi-Fi* is often used to describe wireless networks, although it technically refers to just one form of wireless networks: the 802.11b standard. (See the section, "Eight-Oh-Two-Dot-Eleventy Something? (Or, Understanding Wireless Standards)" later in this chapter, for more information.)

✦ A wireless network has a name, known as a *SSID.* SSID stands for *service set identifier* — wouldn't that make a great *Jeopardy!* question? (I'll take obscure four-letter acronyms for $400, please!) Each of the computers that belong to a single wireless network must have the same SSID.

✦ Wireless networks can transmit over any of several channels. In order for computers to talk to each other, they must be configured to transmit on the same channel.

✦ The simplest type of wireless network consists of two or more computers with wireless network adapters. This type of network is called an *ad-hoc mode network.*

✦ A more complex type of network is an *infrastructure mode network.* All this really means is that a group of wireless computers can be connected not only to each other, but also to an existing cabled network via a device called a *wireless access point,* or WAP. (I tell you more about ad-hoc and infrastructure networks later in this chapter.)

A Little High School Electronics

I was a real nerd in high school: I took three years of electronics. The electronics class at my school was right next door to the auto shop. Of course, all the cool kids took auto shop, and only nerds like me took electronics. We hung in there, though, and learned all about capacitors and diodes while the cool kids were learning how to raise their cars and install 2-gigawatt stereo systems.

It turns out that a little of that high school electronics information proves useful when it comes to wireless networking. Not much, but a little. You'll understand wireless networking much better if you know the meanings of some basic radio terms.

Waves and frequencies

For starters, *radio* consists of electromagnetic waves that are sent through the atmosphere. You can't see or hear them, but radio receivers can pick them up and convert them into sounds, images, or — in the case of wireless networks — data. Radio waves are actually cyclical waves of electronic energy that repeat at a particular rate, called the *frequency*. Figure 1-1 shows two frequencies of radio waves: The first is one cycle per second; the second is two cycles per second. (Real radio doesn't operate at that low of a frequency, but I figured one and two cycles per second would be easier to draw than 680,000 cycles per second or 2.4 million cycles per second.)

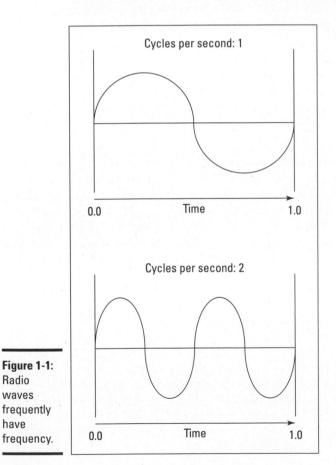

Figure 1-1: Radio waves frequently have frequency.

The measure of a frequency is *cycles per second,* which indicates how many complete cycles the wave makes in one second (duh). In honor of Heinrich Hertz, who didn't invent catsup, rather was the first person to successfully send and receive radio waves (it happened in the 1880s), *cycles per second* is usually referred to as *Hertz,* abbreviated Hz. Thus, 1 Hz is one cycle per second. Incidentally, when the prefix *K* (for *kilo,* or 1,000), *M* (for *mega,* 1 million), or *G* (for *giga,* 1 billion) is added to the front of Hz, the *H* is still capitalized. Thus, 2.4 MHz is correct (not 2.4 Mhz).

The beauty of radio frequencies is that transmitters can be tuned to broadcast radio waves at a precise frequency. Likewise, receivers can be tuned to receive radio waves at a precise frequency, ignoring waves at other frequencies. That's why you can tune the radio in your car to listen to dozens of different radio stations: Each station broadcasts at its own frequency.

Wavelength and antennas

A term related to frequency is *wavelength.* Radio waves travel at the speed of light. The term *wavelength* refers to how far the radio signal travels with each cycle. For example, because the speed of light is roughly 300,000,000 meters per second, the wavelength of a 1-Hz radio wave is about 300,000,000 meters. The wavelength of a 2-Hz signal is about 150,000,000 meters.

As you can see, the wavelength decreases as the frequency increases. The wavelength of a typical AM radio station broadcasting at 580 KHz is about 500 meters. For a TV station broadcasting at 100 MHz, it's about 3 meters. For a wireless network broadcasting at 2.4 GHz, the wavelength is about 12 centimeters.

It turns out that the shorter the wavelength, the smaller the antenna needs to be in order to adequately receive the signal. As a result, higher frequency transmissions need smaller antennas. You may have noticed that AM radio stations usually have huge antennas mounted on top of tall towers, but cell phone transmitters are much smaller and their towers aren't nearly as tall. That's because cell phones operate on a higher frequency than do AM radio stations. So who decides what type of radio gets to use specific frequencies? That's where spectrums and the FCC come in.

Spectrums and the FCC

The term *spectrum* refers to a continuous range of frequencies on which radio can operate. In the United States, the Federal Communications Commission (FCC) regulates not only how much of Janet Jackson can be shown at the Super Bowl, but also how various portions of the radio spectrum can be used. Essentially, the FCC has divided the radio spectrum into dozens of small ranges called *bands* and restricted certain uses to certain bands. For example, AM radio operates in the band from 535 KHz to 1,700 KHz.

And now a word from the irony department

I was an English literature major in college, so I like to use literary devices such as irony. Of course, irony doesn't come up much in computer books. So when it does, I like to jump on it like a hog out of the water.

So here's my juicy bit of irony for today: The very first Ethernet system was actually a wireless network. Ethernet traces its roots back to a network developed at the University of Hawaii in 1970, called the AlohaNet. This network transmitted its data by using small radios. If two computers tried to broadcast data at the same time, the computers detected the collision and tried again after a short, random delay. This technique was the inspiration for the basic technique of Ethernet, now called *carrier sense multiple access with collision detection,* or *CSMA/CD.* The wireless AlohaNet was the network that inspired Robert Metcalfe to develop his cabled network, which he called *Ethernet,* as his doctoral thesis at Harvard in 1973.

For the next 20 years or so, Ethernet was pretty much a cable-only network. It wasn't until the mid-1990s that Ethernet finally returned to its wireless roots.

Table 1-1 lists some of the most popular bands. Note that some of these bands are wide — for example, UHF television begins at 470 MHz and ends at 806 MHz, but other bands are restricted to a specific frequency. The difference between the lowest and highest frequency within a band is called the *bandwidth.*

Table 1-1	Popular Bands of the Radio Spectrum
Band	*Use*
535 KHz–1,700 KHz	AM radio
5.9 MHz–26.1 MHz	Short wave radio
26.96 MHz–27.41 MHz	Citizens Band (CB) radio
54 MHz–88 MHz	Television (VHF channels 2 through 6)
88 MHz–108 MHz	FM radio
174 MHz–220 MHz	Television (VHF channels 7 through 13)
470 MHz–806 MHz	Television (UHF channels)
806 MHz–890 MHz	Cellular networks
900 MHz	Cordless phones
1850 MHz–1990 MHz	PCS cellular
2.4 GHz–2.4835 GHz	Cordless phones and wireless networks (802.11b and 802.11g)
4 GHz–5 GHz	Large dish satellite TV
5 GHz	Wireless networks (802.11a)
11.7 GHz–12.7 GHz	Small dish satellite TV

Two of the bands in the spectrum are allocated for use by wireless networks: 2.4 GHz and 5 GHz. Note that these bands aren't devoted exclusively to wireless networks. In particular, the 2.4-GHz band shares its space with cordless phones. As a result, cordless phones can sometimes interfere with wireless networks.

Eight-Oh-Two-Dot-Eleventy Something? (Or, Understanding Wireless Standards)

The most popular standards for wireless networks are the IEEE 802.11 standards. These standards are essential wireless Ethernet standards and use many of the same networking techniques that the cabled Ethernet standards (in other words, 802.3) use. Most notably, 802.11 networks use the same CSMA/CD technique as cabled Ethernet to recover from network collisions.

The 802.11 standards address the bottom two layers of the IEEE seven-layer model: The Physical layer and the Media Access Control (MAC) layer. Note that TCP/IP protocols apply to higher layers of the model. As a result, TCP/IP runs just fine on 802.11 networks.

The original 802.11 standard was adopted in 1997. Two additions to the standard, 802.11a and 802.11b, were adopted in 1999. The latest and greatest version is 802.11g.

Table 1-2 summarizes the basic characteristics of the three variants of 802.11.

Table 1-2		802.11 Variations	
Standard	*Speeds*	*Frequency*	*Typical Range (Indoors)*
802.11a	Up to 54 Mbps	5 GHz	150 feet
802.11b	Up to 11 Mbps	2.4 GHz	300 feet
802.11g	Up to 54 Mbps	2.4 GHz	300 feet

Currently, most wireless networks are based on the 802.11g standard. In late 2008, this standard is expected to be replaced by a new standard, known as 802.11n, which will be more than three times as fast as 802.11g and have almost twice the range.

Home on the Range

The maximum range of an 802.11g wireless device indoors is about 300 feet.
This can have an interesting effect when you get a bunch of wireless computers
together — such that some of them are in range of each other, but others are
not. For example, suppose that Wally, Ward, and the Beaver all have wireless
notebooks. Wally's computer is 200 feet away from Ward's computer, and
Ward's computer is 200 feet away from Beaver's in the opposite direction. (See
Figure 1-2.) In this case, Ward is able to access both Wally's computer and
Beaver's computer. But Wally can access only Ward's computer, and Beaver
can access only Ward's computer. In other words, Wally and Beaver won't be
able to access each other's computers because they're outside of the 300-feet
range limit. (This is starting to sound suspiciously like an algebra problem.
Now suppose that Wally starts walking toward Ward at 2 miles per hour, and
Beaver starts running toward Ward at 4 miles per hour. . . .)

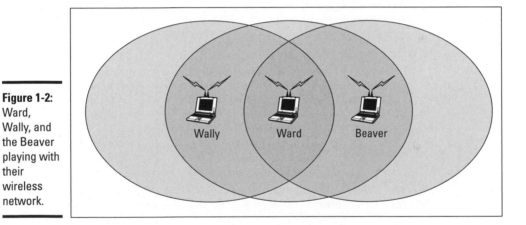

Figure 1-2:
Ward,
Wally, and
the Beaver
playing with
their
wireless
network.

Although the normal range for 802.11g is 300 feet, the range may be less in
actual practice. Obstacles such as solid walls, bad weather, cordless phones,
microwave ovens, backyard nuclear reactors, and so on can all conspire
together to reduce the effective range of a wireless adapter. If you're having
trouble connecting to the network, sometimes just adjusting the antenna helps.

Also, wireless networks tend to slow down when the distance increases.
802.11g network devices claim to operate at 54 Mbps, but they usually
achieve that speed only at ranges of 100 feet or less. At 300 feet, they often
slow down to a crawl. You should also realize that when you're at the edge of
the wireless device's range, you're more likely to suddenly lose your connection
due to bad weather.

Wireless Network Adapters

Each computer that will connect to your wireless network needs a *wireless network adapter*. The wireless network adapter is similar to the network interface card (NIC) that is used for a standard Ethernet connection. However, instead of having a cable connector on the back, a wireless network adapter has an antenna.

You can get several basic types of wireless network adapters, depending on your needs and the type of computer you will use it with:

✦ A wireless PCI card is a wireless network adapter that you install into an available slot inside a desktop computer. In order to install this type of card, you need to take your computer apart. So use this type of card only if you have the expertise and the nerves to dig into your computer's guts.

✦ A wireless USB adapter is a separate box that plugs into a USB port on your computer. Because the USB adapter is a separate device, it takes up extra desk space. However, you can install it without taking your computer apart.

✦ A wireless PC card is designed to slide into the PC card slot found in most notebook computers. This is the type of card to get if you want to network your notebook.

You can purchase a combination 802.11b/g PCI adapter for less than $50. USB versions cost about $10 more.

At first, you may think that wireless network adapters are prohibitively expensive. After all, you can buy a regular Ethernet adapter for as little as $20. However, when you consider that you don't have to purchase and install cable to use a wireless adapter, the price of wireless networking becomes more palatable. And if you shop around, you can sometimes find wireless adapters for as little as $19.95.

Figure 1-3 shows a typical wireless network adapter. This one is a Linksys WUSB11, which sells for about $50. To install this device, you simply connect it to one of your computer's USB ports with the included USB connector. You then install the driver software that comes on the CD, and you're ready to network. The device is relatively small. You'll find a little strip of Velcro on the back, which you can use to mount it on the side of your computer or desk if you want. The adapter gets its power from the USB port itself, so there's no separate power cord to plug in.

Figure 1-3:
A typical
wireless
networking
adapter.

Wireless Access Points

Unlike cabled networks, wireless networks don't need a hub or switch. If all you want to do is network a group of wireless computers, you just purchase a wireless adapter for each computer, put them all within 300 feet of each other, and *voilà!* — instant network.

But what if you already have an existing cabled network? For example, suppose that you work at an office with 15 computers all cabled up nicely, and you just want to add a couple of wireless notebook computers to the network. Or suppose that you have two computers in your den connected to each other with network cable, but you want to link up a computer in your bedroom without pulling cable through the attic.

That's where a *wireless access point,* also known as a *WAP,* comes in. A WAP actually performs two functions. First, it acts as a central connection point for all your computers that have wireless network adapters. In effect, the WAP performs essentially the same function as a hub or switch performs for a wired network.

Second, the WAP links your wireless network to your existing wired network so that your wired computer and your wireless computers get along like one big happy family. Sounds like the makings of a Dr. Seuss story. ("Now the wireless sneeches had hubs without wires. But the twisted-pair sneeches had cables to thires. . . .")

Wireless access points are sometimes just called *access points,* or *APs.* An access point is a box that has an antenna (or often a pair of antennae) and an RJ-45 Ethernet port. You just plug the access point into a network cable and then plug the other end of the cable into a hub or switch, and your wireless network should be able to connect to your cabled network.

Figure 1-4 shows how an access point acts as a central connection point for wireless computers and how it bridges your wireless network to your wired network.

Figure 1-4:
A wireless access point connects a wireless network to a cabled network.

Infrastructure mode

When you set up a wireless network with an access point, you are creating an *infrastructure mode* network. It's called *infrastructure mode* because the access point provides a permanent infrastructure for the network. The access points are installed at fixed physical locations, so the network has relatively stable boundaries. Whenever a mobile computer wanders into the range of one of the access points, it has come into the sphere of the network and can connect.

An access point and all the wireless computers that are connected to it are referred to as a *Basic Service Set,* or *BSS.* Each BSS is identified by a *Service Set Identifier,* or *SSID.* When you configure an access point, you specify the SSID that you want to use. The SSID is often a generic name such as *wireless,* or it can be a name that you create. Some access points use the MAC address of the WAP as the SSID.

Multifunction WAPs

Wireless access points often include other built-in features. For example, some access points double as Ethernet hubs or switches. In that case, the access point will have more than one RJ-45 port. In addition, some access points include broadband cable or DSL firewall routers that enable you to connect to the Internet. For example, Figure 1-5 shows a Linksys BEFW11S4 wireless access point router. I have one of these little guys in my home. This inexpensive (about $60) device includes the following features:

✦ An 802.11b wireless access point that lets me connect a notebook computer and a computer located on the other side of the house because I didn't want to run cable through the attic.

✦ A four-port 10/100 MHz switch that I can connect up to four computers to via twisted-pair cable.

✦ A DSL/cable router that I connect to my cable modem. This enables all the computers on the network (cabled and wireless) to access the Internet.

A multifunction access point that's designed to serve as an Internet gateway for home networks sometimes is called a *residential gateway.*

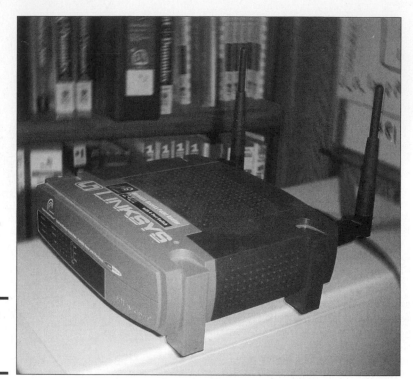

Figure 1-5:
A typical
wireless
router.

Roaming

You can use two or more wireless access points to create a large wireless network in which computer users can roam from area to area and still be connected to the wireless network. As the user moves out of the range of one access point, another access point automatically picks up the user and takes over without interrupting the user's network service.

To set up two or more access points for roaming, you must carefully place the WAPs so that all areas of the office or building that are being networked are in range of at least one of the WAPs. Then, just make sure that all the computers and access points use the same SSID and channel.

Two or more access points joined for the purposes of roaming, along with all the wireless computers connected to any of the access points, form what's called an *Extended Service Set,* or *ESS.* The access points in the ESS are usually connected to a wired network.

One of the current limitations of roaming is that each access point in an ESS must be on the same TCP/IP subnet. That way, a computer that roams from one access point to another within the ESS retains the same IP address. If the access points had a different subnet, a roaming computer would have to change IP addresses when it moved from one access point to another.

Wireless bridging

Another use for wireless access points is to bridge separate subnets that can't easily be connected by cable. For example, suppose that you have two office buildings that are only about 50 feet apart. To run cable from one building to the other, you'd have to bury conduit — a potentially expensive job. Because the buildings are so close, though, you can probably connect them with a pair of wireless access points that function as a *wireless bridge* between the two networks. Connect one of the access points to the first network and the other access point to the second network. Then, configure both access points to use the same SSID and channel.

Ad-hoc networks

A wireless access point is not necessary to set up a wireless network. Any time two or more wireless devices come within range of each other, they can link up to form an *ad-hoc network*. For example, if you and a few of your friends all have notebook computers with 802.11b/g wireless network adapters, you can meet anywhere and form an ad-hoc network.

All of the computers within range of each other in an ad-hoc network are called an *Independent Basic Service Set*, or *IBSS*.

Configuring a Wireless Access Point

The physical setup for a wireless access point is pretty simple: You take it out of the box, put it on a shelf or on top of a bookcase near a network jack and a power outlet, plug in the power cable, and plug in the network cable.

The software configuration for an access point is a little more involved, but still not very complicated. It's usually done via a Web interface. To get to the configuration page for the access point, you need to know the access point's IP address. Then, you just type that address into the address bar of a browser from any computer on the network.

Multifunction access points usually provide DHCP and NAT services for the networks and double as the network's gateway router. As a result, they typically have a private IP address that's at the beginning of one of the Internet's private IP address ranges, such as 192.168.0.1 or 10.0.0.1. Consult the documentation that came with the access point to find out more.

If you use a multifunction access point that is both your wireless access point and your Internet router and you can't remember the IP address, run the IPCONFIG command at a command prompt from any computer on the network. The Default Gateway IP address should be the IP address of the access point.

Basic configuration options

Figure 1-6 shows the main configuration screen for a Linksys BEFW11S4 wireless access point router that is pictured in Figure 1-5. I called up this configuration page by entering **192.168.1.1** in the address bar of a Web browser and then supplying the login password when prompted.

Figure 1-6:
The main configuration page for a Linksys wireless router.

This configuration page offers the following configuration options that are related to the wireless access point functions of the device. Although these options are specific to this particular device, most access points have similar configuration options.

✦ **Enable/Disable:** Enables or disables the device's wireless access point functions.

✦ **SSID:** The Service Set Identifier used to identify the network. Most access points have well-known defaults. You can talk yourself into thinking that your network is more secure by changing the SSID from the default to something more obscure, but in reality, that only protects you from first-grade hackers. By the time most hackers get into the second grade, they learn that even the most obscure SSID is easy to get around. So I recommend that you leave the SSID at the default and apply better security measures, as described in the next chapter.

✦ **Allow broadcast SSID to associate?** Disables the access point's periodic broadcast of the SSID. Normally, the access point regularly broadcasts its SSID so that wireless devices that come within range can detect the network and join in. For a more secure network, you can disable this function. Then, a wireless client must already know the network's SSID in order to join the network.

✦ **Channel:** Lets you select one of 11 channels on which to broadcast. All the access points and computers in the wireless network should use the same channel. If you find that your network is frequently losing connections, try switching to another channel. You may be experiencing interference from a cordless phone or other wireless device operating on the same channel.

Switching channels is also a friendly way for neighbors with wireless networks to stay out of each other's way. For example, if you share a building with another tenant who also has a wireless network, you can agree to use separate channels so that your wireless networks won't interfere with each other. Keep in mind that this doesn't give you any real measure of security because your neighbor could secretly switch back to your channel and listen in on your network. So you still need to secure your network as described in the next chapter.

✦ **WEP — Mandatory or Disable:** Lets you use a security protocol called *wired equivalent privacy*. I have more to say about this in the next chapter.

DHCP configuration

You can configure most multifunction access points to operate as a DHCP server. For small networks, it's common for the access point to also be the DHCP server for the entire network. In that case, you need to configure the access point's DHCP server. Figure 1-7 shows the DHCP configuration page for the Linksys WAP router. To enable DHCP, you select the Enable option and then specify the other configuration options to use for the DHCP server.

Larger networks that have more demanding DHCP requirements are likely to have a separate DHCP server running on another computer. In that case, you can defer to the existing server by disabling the DHCP server in the access point.

For more information on configuring a DHCP server, please refer to Book IV, Chapter 3.

Figure 1-7:
Configuring
DHCP for a
Linksys
wireless
router.

Configuring Windows XP for Wireless Networking

The first step in configuring Windows XP for wireless networking is to install the appropriate device driver for your wireless network adapter. To do that, you need the installation CD that came with the adapter. Follow the instructions that came with the adapter to install the drivers.

Windows XP has some nice built-in features for working with wireless networks. You can configure these features by opening the Network Connections folder. Choose Start⇨Control Panel and then double-click the Network Connections icon. Right-click the wireless network connection and then choose Properties to bring up the Properties dialog box. Then, click the Wireless Networks tab to display the wireless networking options shown in Figure 1-8.

Figure 1-8:
Configuring wireless networking in Windows XP.

Each time you connect to a wireless network, Windows XP adds that network to this dialog box. Then, you can juggle the order of the networks in the Preferred Networks section to indicate which network you'd prefer to join if you find yourself within range of two or more networks at the same time. You can use the Move Up and Move Down buttons next to the Preferred Networks list to change your preferences.

To add a network that you haven't yet actually joined, click the Add button. This brings up the dialog box shown in Figure 1-9. Here, you can type the SSID value for the network that you want to add. You can also specify other information, such as whether to use data encryption, how to authenticate yourself, and whether the network is an ad-hoc rather than an infrastructure network.

Figure 1-9:
Adding a
wireless
network in
Windows
XP.

Using a Wireless Network with Windows XP

Windows XP also has some nice built-in features that simplify the task of using a wireless network. For example, when your computer comes within range of a wireless network, a pop-up balloon appears in the taskbar, indicating that a network is available.

If one of your preferred networks is within range, clicking the balloon automatically connects you to that network. If Windows XP doesn't recognize any of the networks, clicking the balloon displays the dialog box shown in Figure 1-10. With this dialog box, you can choose the network that you want to join (if more than one network is listed) and then click Connect to join the selected network.

Figure 1-10:
Joining a
wireless
network in
Windows
XP.

After you've joined a wireless network, a network status icon appears in the notification area of the taskbar. You can quickly see the network status by hovering the mouse cursor over this icon; a balloon appears to indicate the state of the connection. For more detailed information, you can click the status icon to display the Wireless Network Connection Status dialog box, shown in Figure 1-11.

Figure 1-11:
The
Wireless
Network
Connection
Status
dialog box
(Windows
XP).

This dialog box provides the following items of information:

✦ **Status:** Indicates whether you are connected.

✦ **Duration:** Indicates how long you've been connected.

✦ **Speed:** Indicates the current network speed. Ideally, this should say 11 Mbps for an 802.11b network, or 54 Mbps for an 802.11a or 802.11g network. However, if the network connection is not of the highest quality, the speed may drop to a lower value.

✦ **Signal Strength:** Displays a graphic representation of the quality of the signal.

✦ **Packets Sent & Received:** Indicates how many packets of data you've sent and received over the network.

You can click the Properties button to bring up the Connection Properties dialog box for the wireless connection.

Connecting to a Wireless Network with Windows Vista

Wireless networking in Windows Vista is similar to Windows XP. When Windows Vista detects that a wireless network is within range, a balloon notification appears on the screen to indicate that one or more wireless networks are available. You can double-click this balloon to summon the dialog box shown in Figure 1-12. Then, you can double-click the network you want to connect to.

Figure 1-12:
Choosing a wireless network in Vista.

Chapter 2: Securing a Wireless Network

In This Chapter

✔ Reviewing the threats posed by wireless networks

✔ Examining the strange world of wardriving and warchalking

✔ Enabling the security features of your wireless access point

*B*efore you dive headfirst into the deep end of the wireless networking pool, you should first consider the inherent security risks in setting up a wireless network. With a cabled network, the best security tool that you have is the lock on the front door of your office. Unless someone can physically get to one of the computers on your network, he or she can't get into your network. (Well, I'm sort of ignoring your wide-open broadband Internet connection for the sake of argument.)

If you go wireless, an intruder doesn't have to get into your office to hack into your network. He or she can do it from the office next door. Or the lobby. Or the parking garage beneath your office. Or the sidewalk outside. In short, when you introduce wireless devices into your network, you usher in a whole new set of security issues to deal with.

This chapter explores some of the basic security issues that come with the territory when you go wireless.

Understanding Wireless Security Threats

Wireless networks have the same basic security considerations as wired networks. As a network administrator, you need to balance the need of legitimate users to access network resources against the risk of illegitimate users breaking into your network. That's the basic dilemma of network security. Whether the network uses cables, wireless devices, kite strings and tin cans, or smoke signals, the basic issues are the same.

On one extreme of the wireless network security spectrum is the totally open network, in which anyone within range of your wireless transmissions can log in as an administrator and gain full access to every detail of your network. On the other end is what I call the "cone-of-silence syndrome," in which the network is so secure that no one can gain access to the network — not even legitimate users.

The goal of securing a wireless network is to find the happy medium between these two extremes that meets the access and risk-management needs of your organization.

The following sections describe the most likely types of security threats that wireless networks encounter. You should take each of these kinds of threats into consideration when you plan your network's security.

Intruders

With a wired network, an intruder must usually gain access to your facility to physically connect to your network. Not so with a wireless network — in fact, with wireless, hackers equipped with notebooks that have wireless network capability can gain access to your network if they can place themselves physically within range of your network's radio signals. Consider these possibilities:

+ If you share a building with other tenants, the other tenants' offices may be within range.

+ If you're in a multifloor building, the floor immediately above or below you may be in range.

+ The lobby outside your office may be within range of your network.

+ The parking lot outside or the parking garage in the basement may be in range.

If a would-be intruder can't get within normal broadcast range, he or she may try one of several tricks to increase the range:

+ A would-be intruder can switch to a bigger antenna to extend the range of his or her wireless computer. Some experiments have shown that big antennas can receive signals from wireless networks that are miles away. In fact, I once read of someone who listened in on wireless networks based in San Francisco from the Berkeley hills, which is across the San Francisco Bay.

+ If a would-be intruder is serious about breaking into your network, he or she may smuggle a wireless repeater device into your facility — or near it — to extend the range of your wireless network to a location that he or she *can* get to.

Of course, a *physical* connection to your network is not the only way an intruder can gain access. You must still take steps to prevent an intruder from sneaking into your network through your Internet gateway. In most cases, this means that you need to set up a firewall to block unwanted and unauthorized traffic.

Freeloaders

Freeloaders are intruders who want to piggyback on your wireless network to get free access to the Internet. If they manage to gain access to your wireless network, they probably won't do anything malicious: They'll just fire up their Web browsers and surf the Internet. These are folks who are too cheap to spend $40 per month on their own broadband connection at home, so they'd rather drive into your parking lot and steal yours.

Even though freeloaders may be relatively benign, they can be a potential source of trouble. In particular:

✦ Freeloaders use bandwidth that you're paying for. As a result, their mere presence can slow down Internet access for your legitimate users.

✦ After freeloaders gain Internet access through your network, they can potentially cause trouble for you or your organization. For example, they may use your network to download illegal pornography. Or they may try to send spam via your mail server. Most ISPs will cut you off cold if they catch you sending spam, and they won't believe you when you tell them the spam came from a kid parked in a Pinto out in your parking lot.

✦ If you're in the business of *selling* access to your wireless network, freeloaders are obviously a problem.

✦ Freeloaders may start out innocently looking for free Internet access. But once they get in, curiosity may get the better of them, leading them to snoop around your network.

✦ If freeloaders can get in, so can more malicious intruders.

Eavesdroppers

Eavesdroppers just like to listen to your network traffic. They don't actually try to gain access via your wireless network — at least, not at first. They just listen.

Unfortunately, wireless networks give them plenty to listen to. For example:

✦ Most wireless access points regularly broadcast their SSID to anyone who's listening.

✦ When a legitimate wireless network user joins the network, an exchange of packets occurs as the network authenticates the user. An eavesdropper can capture these packets and, if security isn't set up right, determine the user's logon name and password.

✦ An eavesdropper can steal files that are opened from a network server. For example, if a wireless user opens a confidential sales report that's saved on the network, the sales report document is broken into packets that are sent over the wireless network to the user. A skilled eavesdropper can copy those packets and reconstruct the file.

✦ When a wireless user connects to the Internet, an eavesdropper can see any packets that the user sends to or receives from the Internet. If the user purchases something online, the transaction may include a credit card number and other personal information. (Hopefully, these packets will be encrypted so the eavesdropper won't be able to decipher the data.)

Spoilers

A *spoiler* is a hacker who gets kicks from jamming networks so that they become unusable. A spoiler usually accomplishes this by flooding the network with meaningless traffic so that legitimate traffic gets lost in the flow. Spoilers may also try to place viruses or worm programs on your network via an unsecured wireless connection.

Rogue access points

One of the biggest problems that network administrators have to deal with is the problem of rogue access points. A *rogue access point* is an access point that suddenly appears out of nowhere on your network. What usually happens is that an employee decides to connect a notebook computer to the network via a wireless computer. So the user stops at Computers-R-Us on the way home from work one day and buys a Fisher-Price wireless access point for $25 and plugs it into the network, without asking permission.

Now, in spite of all the elaborate security precautions you've taken to fence in your network, this well-meaning user has opened the barn door. It's *very* unlikely that the user will enable the security features of the wireless access point; in fact, he or she probably isn't even aware that wireless access devices *have* security features.

Unless you take some kind of action to find it, a rogue access point can operate undetected on your network for months or even years. You may not discover it until you report to work one day and find that your network has been trashed by an intruder who found his or her way into your network via an unprotected wireless access point that you didn't even know existed.

Here are some steps you can take to reduce the risk of rogue access points appearing on your system:

✦ Establish a policy prohibiting users from installing wireless access points on their own. Then, make sure that you inform all network users of the policy and let them know why installing an access point on their own can be such a major problem.

✦ If possible, establish a program that quickly and inexpensively grants wireless access to users who want it. The reasons rogue access points show up in the first place are (1) users need it, and (2) it's hard to get through channels. If you make it easier for users to get legitimate wireless access, you're less likely to find wireless access points hidden behind file cabinets or in flower pots.

✦ Once in awhile, take a walk through the premises looking for rogue access points. Take a look at every network outlet in the building and see what's connected to it.

✦ Turn off all your wireless access points and then walk around the premises with a wireless-equipped notebook computer that has scanning software, such as NetStumbler (www.netstumbler.com), looking for wireless access. (Of course, just because you detect a wireless network doesn't mean you have found a rogue access point — you may have stumbled onto a wireless network from a nearby office or home.)

✦ If your network is large, consider using a software tool such as AirWave (www.airwave.com) to snoop for unauthorized access points.

What About Wardrivers and Warchalkers?

The recent explosion of wireless networking has led to a few new terms, including *wardriving* and *warchalking*. Whether wardriving and warchalking actually represent security threats is a question that's subject to a lot of debate.

Wardriving

Wardriving refers to the practice of driving around town with notebook computers looking for open access to wireless networks just to see what networks are out there. Some wardrivers even make maps and put them on the Internet.

The basic intent of wardriving is to discover open wireless networks that can be accessed from public places. A side benefit is that it can help network administrators discover holes in their network security. If your network shows up on a wardriving map, be grateful for the wardrivers who discovered your vulnerability. And by publishing it, they've given you incentive to plug the hole!

The downside of wardriving is that intruders can check the wardriving maps posted on the Internet to find potential targets.

Wardrivers arm themselves with the following equipment:

✦ A car

✦ A notebook computer with a wireless adapter

✦ An external antenna isn't a must, but it helps

✦ Software that can scan for open wireless networks

✦ A GPS, or *global positioning system,* a device that can automatically track where you are

✦ Software that correlates the discovery of open networks with location data obtained from the GPS device

✦ Free time

For more information about wardriving, check out the Web site `www.war driving.com`.

Warchalking

Warchalking refers to marking the location of open access points with special chalk symbols on the sidewalk. The chalk symbols indicate that a network is nearby. So if you're wandering around in downtown San Francisco and you spot a warchalk symbol on the curb, you can sit down at the nearest park bench, fire up your notebook computer, and start surfing the Internet.

Figure 2-1 shows the common warchalking symbol for an open (unprotected) wireless network. The SSID of the open network is listed above the symbol. You may also find other information written, such as the bandwidth of the Internet connection available through the access point.

Figure 2-1:
A warchalking symbol.

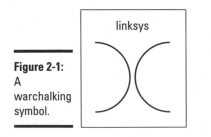

The origins of war

Where does the term *wardriving* come from? Although the term has nothing to do with actual combat, I've heard two plausible explanations for its origin:

✔ It derives from the popular hacker word *warez* (pronounced *wayrz)*, which refers to pirated software. Thus, wardriving refers to looking for pirated wireless network access.

✔ It derives from the movie *War Games,* in which a very young Matthew Broderick hacks his way into the Pentagon's top-secret nuclear defense network by setting up his computer to dial numbers sequentially until it finds a computer worth hacking into. This practice was called *wardialing.*

Warchalking Web sites like to relate that the practice of warchalking dates back to the Great Depression in the United States, when homeless people used chalk or coal to write symbols on sidewalks, fences, or railroad trestles to provide information or warnings to their fellow travelers. For example, some symbols represented food, water, or safe places to camp, while other symbols represented dangerous areas or aggressive police. I leave it up to you to decide whether college kids wandering the streets looking for free Internet access is analogous to the unemployed and homeless of the Great Depression looking for food.

Securing Your Wireless Network

Hopefully, you're convinced that wireless networks do indeed pose many security risks. In the following sections, I describe some steps that you can take to help secure your wireless network.

Changing the password

Probably the first thing you should do when you install a wireless access point is to change its administrative password. Most access points have a built-in, Web-based setup page that you can access from any Web browser to configure the access point's configuration settings. The setup page is protected by a username and password. However, the username and password are initially set to default values that are easy to guess.

For example, the default username for Linksys access points is blank, and the password is "admin." If you leave the username and password set to their default values, anyone can access the access point and change its configuration settings, thus bypassing any other security features that you enable for the access point.

So, the first step in securing your wireless access point is changing the setup password to a value that can't be guessed. I suggest that you use a random combination of numerals and both uppercase and lowercase letters. Be sure to store the password in a secure location. (If you forget the password, you can press the Reset button on the router to restore it to its factory default. Then, you can log in using the default password, which you can find with the documentation that came with the router.)

Securing the SSID

The next step is to secure the SSID that identifies the network. A client must know the access point's SSID in order to join the wireless network. If you can prevent unauthorized clients from discovering the SSID, you can prevent them from accessing your network.

Securing the SSID is not a complete security solution, so you shouldn't rely on it as your only security mechanism. SSID security can slow down casual intruders and wardrivers who are just looking for easy and free Internet access, but it isn't possible to prevent serious hackers from discovering your SSID.

You can do three things to secure your SSID:

✦ **Change the SSID from the default.** Most access points come preconfigured with well-known default SSIDs. For example, Table 2-1 lists some well-known default SSIDs. By changing your access point's SSID, you can make it more difficult for an intruder to determine your SSID and gain access.

Table 2-1	Common Default SSID Values
SSID	*Manufacturer*
3com	3Com
Compaq	Compaq
linksys	Linksys
tsunami	Cicso
Wireless	NetGear
WLAN	DLink
WLAN	SMC

✦ **Disable SSID broadcast.** Most access points frequently broadcast their SSIDs so that clients can discover the network when they come within range. Clients that receive this SSID broadcast can then use the SSID to join the network.

You can increase network security somewhat by disabling the SSID broadcast feature. That way, clients won't automatically learn the access point's SSID. To join the network, a client computer must figure out the SSID on its own. You can then tell your wireless network users the SSID to use when they configure their clients.

✦ Unfortunately, when a client computer connects to a wireless network, it sends the SSID to the access point in an unencrypted packet. So a sophisticated intruder who's using a packet sniffer to eavesdrop on your wireless network can determine your SSID as soon as any legitimate computer joins the network.

✦ **Disable guest mode.** Many access points have a guest mode feature that enables client computers to specify a blank SSID or to specify "any" as the SSID. If you want to ensure that only clients that know the SSID can join the network, you must disable this feature.

Enabling WEP

WEP stands for *wired equivalent privacy* and is designed to make wireless transmission as secure as transmission over a network cable. WEP encrypts your data by using either a 40-bit key or a 128-bit key. 40-bit encryption is faster than 128-bit encryption and is adequate for most purposes. So I suggest that you enable 40-bit encryption unless you work for the CIA.

Note that in order to use WEP, both the client and the server must know the encryption keys being used. So a client that doesn't know the access point's encryption keys won't be able to join the network.

You can specify encryption keys for WEP in two ways. The first is to create the 10-digit key manually by making up a random number. The second method, which I prefer, is to use a *passphrase,* which can be any word or combination of numerals and letters that you want. WEP automatically converts the pass phrase to the numeric key used to encrypt data. If the client knows the passphrase used to generate the keys on the access point, the client will be able to access the network.

As it turns out, security experts have identified a number of flaws with WEP that compromise its effectiveness. As a result, with the right tools, a sophisticated intruder can get past WEP. So although it's a good idea to enable WEP, you shouldn't count on it for complete security.

Besides just enabling WEP, you should take two steps to increase its effectiveness:

✦ **Make WEP mandatory.** Some access points have a configuration setting that enables WEP but makes it optional. This may prevent eavesdroppers from viewing the data transmitted on WEP connections, but it doesn't prevent clients that don't know your WEP keys from accessing your network.

✦ **Change the encryption keys.** Most access points come preconfigured with default encryption keys that make it easy for even casual hackers to defeat your WEP security. You should change the default keys either by using a passphrase or by specifying your own keys. Figure 2-2 shows the WEP key configuration page for a typical access point (in this case, a Linksys BEFW11).

Figure 2-2:
Changing the WEP settings on a Linksys wireless router.

Using WPA

WPA, which stands for *Wi-Fi Protected Access,* is a new and improved form of security for wireless networks that's designed to plug some of the holes of WEP. WPA is similar in many ways to WEP. But the big difference is that when you use WPA, the encryption key is automatically changed at regular intervals, thus thwarting all but the most sophisticated efforts to break the key. Most newer wireless devices support WPA. If your equipment supports it, I suggest you use it.

Here are a few additional things to know about WPA:

✦ A small office and home version of WPA, called WPA-PSK, bases its encryption keys on a passkey value that you supply. However, true WPA devices rely on a special authentication server to generate the keys.

✦ Windows XP with Service Pack 2 has built-in support for WPA, as does Windows Vista.

✦ The official IEEE standard for WPA is 802.11i. However, WPA devices were widely available before the 802.11i standard was finalized. As a result, not all WPA devices implement every aspect of 802.11i. In Wi-Fi circles, the 802.11i standard is sometimes called WPA2.

Using MAC address filtering

MAC address filtering allows you to specify a list of MAC addresses for the devices that are allowed to access the network. If a computer with a different MAC address tries to join the network via the access point, the access point will deny access.

MAC address filtering is a great idea for wireless networks with a fixed number of clients. For example, if you set up a wireless network at your office so that a few workers can connect their notebook computers, you can specify the MAC addresses of those computers in the MAC filtering table. Then, other computers won't be able to access the network via the access point.

Unfortunately, it isn't difficult to configure a computer to lie about its MAC address. Thus, after a potential intruder determines that MAC filtering is being used, he or she can just sniff packets to determine an authorized MAC address and then configure his or her computer to use that address. (This is called *MAC spoofing.*) So you shouldn't rely on MAC address filtering as your only means of security.

Figure 2-3 shows the screen used to edit the MAC address table for a Linksys wireless access point.

Don't neglect the basics

The security techniques described in this chapter are specific to wireless networks. They should be used alongside the basic security techniques that are presented in Book III. In other words, don't forget the basics, such as:

✔ Use strong passwords for your user accounts.

✔ Apply security patches to your servers.

✔ Change default server account information (especially the administrator password).

✔ Disable unnecessary services.

✔ Regularly check your server logs.

✔ Install virus protection.

✔ Back up!

Figure 2-3:
A MAC address table for a Linksys wireless router.

Placing your access points outside the firewall

The most effective security technique for wireless networking is to place all your wireless access points *outside* of your firewall. That way, all network traffic from wireless users will have to travel through the firewall to access the network.

As you can imagine, doing this can significantly limit network access for wireless users. To get around those limitations, you can enable a virtual private network (VPN) connection for your wireless users. The VPN will allow full network access to authorized wireless users.

Obviously, this solution requires a bit of work to set up and can be a little inconvenient for your users. However, it's the only way to completely secure your wireless access points.

Chapter 3: Hotspotting

In This Chapter

- ✓ Exploring hotspots
- ✓ Using hotspots safely
- ✓ Comparing free and fee-based hotspots
- ✓ Creating your own hotspot

*W*ireless networks aren't just for private use within your home or at your place of work. Nowadays, many public places such as airports, libraries, hotels, restaurants, and coffee houses host public-access wireless networks, called *hotspots*. If you visit one of these establishments with a wireless-equipped laptop computer in tow, you can use these hotspots to access the Internet.

In this chapter, you read about these public hotspots and find out how to use them. As you read this chapter, keep in mind that public hotspots use the same 802.11 technology as private wireless networks described in the first two chapters of this minibook. So the techniques that you use to connect to a hotspot are the same as you use to connect to any wireless network. And the security implications are the same, too.

What Is a Hotspot?

A *hotspot* is an area that has wireless networking available to the public. The first public hotspots were in airports and hotels, where business travelers could connect to the Internet with their laptop computers to pick up e-mail while on the road. Soon libraries jumped on the bandwagon, providing Internet access to anyone who brings a wireless-equipped laptop into the library.

Lately, restaurants and trendy coffee houses have been providing wireless hotspots so that you can stream music and video or play an online game while sipping a vanilla latte. Starbucks is probably the best-known trendy hotspot, but many others are joining in. For example, many Schlotzsky's Deli locations have free hotspot access. And even McDonald's is equipping many of its restaurants with hotspots. Bookstores like Borders and Barnes & Noble also provide access.

What's So Great about Hotspots?

If you're puzzled about why so many businesses are getting into the hotspotting business, the following paragraphs offer some of the most common reasons:

✦ **To increase traffic and, therefore, business.** For example, the CEO of Schlotzsky's Deli (www.schlotzskys.com) has said that free Internet access results in 15,000 additional visits to each store every year. And those people who come in simply to use the free Internet access usually buy something, even if it's just a soda and a bag of chips.

✦ **To identify the business as hip or trendy.**

✦ **To make money directly from the hotspot.** Note that just because a business charges for its wireless access doesn't mean it is making a significant amount of money from it. Some must charge fees to help cover the costs because they can't justify the expense of commercial-quality broadband access simply on the basis of good will and a little increased traffic.

Safe Hotspotting

To simplify the connection process, most hotspots — both free and fee-based — disable the security features that are available for wireless networks. As a result, you should take some basic precautions when you use a public hotspot:

✦ Make sure that you have a firewall installed and running. If you don't have a separate firewall program, enable the Windows Firewall that's built in to Windows.

✦ Disable file sharing on your laptop computer.

✦ Avoid sites that ask for confidential information but don't use the secure HTTPS protocol.

✦ Use a VPN if you plan on accessing your company's network.

✦ Disconnect from the wireless network when you're finished using it.

Free Hotspots

Many hotspots are free of charge. For example, the hotspots at Schlotzsky's Deli are free. And hotspots at libraries are typically free.

To use a free hotspot, all you have to do is turn on your wireless-equipped laptop computer in the vicinity of the hotspot access point. Then, when you see the notification bubble in the bottom-right corner indicating that a wireless network is in range, click it to connect to the network. You can then fire up your Web browser to surf the Web.

Connecting to a free hotspot is easy. The hard part is finding an available hotspot to connect to, especially a free one. If you happen to live across the street from a library or a Schlotzsky's Deli, you're in luck. Otherwise, you'll have to search to find a hotspot. Fortunately, there are several Web sites you can consult to locate hotspots in your area:

✦ `www.freenetworks.org`: An organization of free networks around the world.

✦ `www.sflan.org`: Free networks in the San Francisco area.

✦ `www.socalfreenet.org`: Free networks in Southern California.

✦ `www.seattlewireless.org`: Free networks in the Seattle, WA area.

With Google and a little perseverance, you may be able to find a Web site devoted to your city. Note, however, that you're much more likely to find free hotspot access in a big city than in Mayberry.

Fee-Based Hotspots

Although some hotspots are free, most charge a fee. Although some charge for hourly use, others offer subscriptions that give you unlimited use for a monthly fee, usually in the neighborhood of $30 per month.

When you connect to a fee-based hotspot, a login page is displayed. On this login page, you can enter your user ID and password if you are already a subscriber. If not, you can join on the spot — just have your credit card handy. After you've joined and logged in, you can access the Internet using your Web browser.

Many fee-based providers have roaming agreements with one another that effectively increase the number of locations that are available. However, you may have to pay an additional surcharge if you use roaming.

The following sections describe several well-known wireless service providers.

T-Mobile

A well-known and widely available subscription hotspot provider is T-Mobile, which provides the hotspots found in Starbucks, Barnes & Noble, FedEx/Kinkos, and many other locations. At the time I wrote this (August 2007), T-Mobile had more than 8,000 hotspot locations in the United States and more than 37,000 additional locations worldwide.

Of course, T-Mobile is also a cell phone company, and like any cell phone company, it offers a variety of plans you can choose from. If you're willing to commit to the service for a year, the monthly fee is $29.95. This gives you unlimited access to any T-Mobile hotspot within the United States. Without the one-year commitment, the plan costs $39.95 per month. You can also purchase a one-day pass for $9.95 or pay for the service hourly. The hourly rate is $6 for the first hour and $0.10 per minute for each additional minute.

For information about T-Mobile's hotspot subscriptions, visit `www.tmobile.com/hotspot`.

Boingo

With more than 100,000 locations worldwide, Boingo Wireless may be the biggest wireless network on earth. Plus it has the coolest name. Boingo is designed primarily for business travelers, so most of its hotspots are in hotels, airports, and business service centers.

Boingo has three basic service plans:

✦ $21.95 per month for unlimited access in the U.S.

✦ $39 per month for unlimited access worldwide

✦ $9.95 per day for an as-you-go plan

Unlike most other providers, Boingo uses its own software to connect you to its wireless network. This simplifies the task of connecting to the network. Boingo's Wi-Fi software is available for Windows, Macs, and Pocket PCs.

For more information, check out `www.boingo.com`.

Wayport

With more than 12,000 locations, Wayport is another large hotspot provider. Most of Wayport's locations are in hotels and airports. Wayport has also recently branched into McDonald's, so you can hook your McLaptop up to the McWeb while you eat your Big Mac.

In addition to wireless access, many hotels also offer cabled Wayport access in their rooms. In other words, you can plug your computer directly into an Ethernet port without paying additional fees or worrying about wireless connection problems.

Wayport has several pricing plans to choose from:

✦ $9.95 per day for a hotel connection

✦ $6.95 per day for an airport connection

✦ Prepaid connections at three for $25, eight for $50, and 20 for $100

✦ Monthly membership for $29.95 per month with a one-year commitment ($49.95 per month without the commitment)

For more information, visit www.wayport.com.

Setting Up Your Own Hotspot

So you own a little café and you think it would be cool to set up a hotspot for your customers to use, eh? If you want to set up a free hotspot, here's all you need:

✦ A reliable broadband Internet connection. DSL, cable, or T-1 will work nicely.

✦ A wireless access point. For a small hotspot, a simple consumer-grade access point (like a Linksys wireless router) will do fine.

✦ A sign to tell your customers about the hotspot and how to connect to it.

Of course, there's a lot more to it than this. Here are a few additional issues to consider:

✦ You need a firewall to prevent your customers from poking around inside your private network. The wireless access point should be *outside* of the firewall.

✦ No matter how good your sign is, your customers will have questions about how to connect. So in addition to how to make a mocha latte, you need to teach your employees how to help customers connect to your hotspot.

✦ Your broadband provider may not appreciate it if you let the general public access the Internet through your wireless access point. In fact, your service contract may prohibit it. As a result, you probably need to pay a bit more to share your broadband connection with the general public.

If you want to charge for hotspot access, you've got a lot more work to do. In particular, you need to devise a way to charge your customers. The easiest way to do this is to purchase a single-box solution that includes the necessary wireless devices as well as software that handles the authentication and billing.

Chapter 4: Troubleshooting a Wireless Network

In This Chapter

✔ Isolating the cause of wireless problems

✔ Changing channels

✔ Hardware that can improve wireless connections

✔ Resetting your access point/router password

*W*ireless networks are great until something goes haywire. When a regular network doesn't work, you usually know about it right away because the network simply becomes unavailable. You can't display Web pages, read e-mail, or access files on shared drives. The troubleshooting chapters in Book III address the most common problems encountered on cabled networks.

But wireless networks can cause problems of their own. And to add to the frustration, wireless networks tend to degrade rather than completely fail. Performance gets slower. Web pages that usually pop up in a second or two take 15 to 20 seconds to appear. Or sometimes they don't appear at all, but then if you try again a few minutes later, they download fine.

This chapter offers some troubleshooting tips that can help you restore normalcy to a failing wireless network.

Checking for Obvious Problems

Before you roll up your sleeves and take drastic corrective action, you should check for a few obvious things if you're having wireless network trouble. The following list highlights some basic things you should check for:

✦ Is everything turned on? Make sure you have lights on your wireless access point/router as well as on your cable or DSL modem.

✦ Many access point/routers use a power supply transformer that plugs into the wall. Make sure that the transformer is plugged into the wall outlet and that the small cable that comes out of the transformer is plugged into the power connector on the access point/router.

✦ Are the cables connected? Check the network cable that connects your access point/router to the cable or DSL modem.

✦ Try restarting everything. Turn off the computer, the access point/router, and your cable or DSL modem. Leave everything off for at least two minutes. Then turn everything back on. Sometimes this clears up a connection problem.

Pinpointing the Problem

If you can't connect to the Internet, one of the first steps (after you've made sure everything is turned on) is to find out if the problem is with your access point/router or with your broadband connection. Here is one way you can check to find out if your wireless connection is working:

1. **Open a command prompt window by choosing Start⇨Run, typing** cmd, **and pressing Enter.**

2. **At the command prompt, type** ipconfig **and press Enter.**

You should get a display similar to this:

```
Ethernet adapter Wireless Network Connection:
        Connection-specific DNS Suffix  . : hsd1.ca.comcast.net)).
        IP Address. . . . . . . . . . . : 192.168.1.101
        Subnet Mask . . . . . . . . . . : 255.255.255.0
        Default Gateway . . . . . . . . : 192.168.1.1
```

If the display resembles this but with different numbers, you're connected to the wireless network, and the problem most likely lies with your broadband modem.

But if the IP Address, Subnet Mask, and Default Gateway indicate 0.0.0.0 instead of valid IP addresses, you have a problem with your wireless network.

Changing Channels

One of the most common problems of wireless network trouble is interference from other wireless devices. The culprit might be a cordless phone, or it could be a neighbor who also has a wireless network.

The simplest solution to this type of interference is to change channels. 802.11b access points let you select one of 11 different channels to broadcast on. If you're having trouble connecting to your access point, try changing the channel. To do that, you must log in to the router with the administrator password. Then, hunt around the router's administrator pages until you find the controls that let you change the channel.

You may have to try changing the channel several times before you solve the problem. Unfortunately, 802.11b channels overlap slightly, which means that broadcasts on one channel may interfere with broadcasts on adjacent channels. Thus, if you're having trouble connecting on channel 1, don't bother switching to channel 2. Instead, try switching to channel 5 or 6. If that doesn't work, switch to channel 10 or 11.

Fiddle with the Antennas

Sometimes you can fix intermittent connection problems by fiddling with the antennas on the access point and your computer's wireless adapter. This is similar to playing with old-fashioned rabbit-ear antennas on a TV to get the best reception.

The angle of the antennas can sometimes make a difference, so try adjusting the antenna angles. In addition, you usually have better results if you place the access point at a high location, such as on top of a bookshelf.

In some cases, you may actually need to add a high-gain antenna to the access point to increase its range. These high-gain antennas simply snap or screw on to the access point to provide a bigger antenna. For example, Figure 4-1 shows high-gain antennas that are designed to work with Linksys access points. Antennas such as these cost about $70 for the pair.

A more drastic fix is to add a signal booster to your access point. A *signal booster* is a power amplifier that increases the transmission power of most wireless devices by a factor of five. A typical signal booster costs about $100.

Adding Another Access Point

If you have a computer that's out of range of your access point, one solution is to add a second access point closer to the problematic computer. Most likely, the only difficulty will be getting an Ethernet cable to the location where you want to put your second access point.

Figure 4-1:
High-gain
antennas for
a Linksys
wireless
router.

Photo courtesy of Linksys.

If possible, you can simply run a length of cable through your walls or attic to the second access point. If that isn't feasible, you can use a PowerLine or Phone (HPNA) network connection for the second access point.

An alternative to a second access point is to simply add a repeater, such as the Linksys Wireless-G Range Expander shown in Figure 4-2. All you have to do is place this device midway between your access point and the computer that's having trouble connecting.

Figure 4-2:
A wireless
repeater
such as this
one from
Linksys can
help
increase the
range of
your
wireless
network.

Photo courtesy of Linksys.

Help! I Forgot My Router's Password!

I mention many times throughout this book that you should always change default passwords that come with computer and operating systems to more secure passwords, usually consisting of a random combination of letters, digits, and special symbols.

Hopefully, you've already taken my sage advice and changed the password on your combination wireless access point/router. Good for you. But what if you later forget the password? Is there any way to get back into your access point/router then?

Fortunately, there is. Most access point/routers have a reset button. It's usually located on the back or on the bottom of the router's case. Press this button to restore the access point/router to its factory default settings. That will reset the administrator password to the factory default. It will also reset any other custom settings you've applied, so you may have to reconfigure your router to get it working again.

Chapter 5: Wireless Networking with Bluetooth

In This Chapter

✔ Discovering how Bluetooth works

✔ Digging into some of Bluetooth's technical issues

✔ Installing a USB Bluetooth adapter

✔ Using Bluetooth in Windows XP and Vista

A vast! If 'twere up to me, Bluetooth would be the name of a pirate, not a network technology. Aye, and make no mistake. Blame it on those scurvy bilge rats whats call themselves Engineers. The next blaggard Engineer whats wastes a perfectly good pirate name on some network technology will soon be feeding fish in Davey Jones' locker, says I. But the deed be done. Aye, so now Bluetooth be the topic of a chapter in a networking book instead of a chapter in the annals of piracy. Arrrrr!

Understanding Bluetooth

Bluetooth is the name of a short-range wireless network technology that's designed to let devices connect to each other without need for cables or a Wi-Fi network access point. The two main uses for Bluetooth are to connect peripheral devices such as keyboards or mice to a computer and to connect hand-held devices such as phones and PDAs (Personal Digital Assistants) to computers.

Here are just a few of the many uses of Bluetooth:

✦ Wirelessly connecting a keyboard and mouse to a computer so that you don't have to fuss with cables. This is marginally useful for desktop computers because it eliminates the need for cables. But it's even more useful for laptop computers because it lets you use a keyboard and mouse simply by placing them next to the laptop.

✦ Synchronizing the address book in your cell phone with your computer's address book, with no cables.

✦ Exchanging files between your Pocket PC or Palm PDA and your laptop or desktop computers.

✦ Using a cord-free headset with your cell phone.

✦ Connecting a Global Positioning System (GPS) device to a computer so that it can track your location. This is especially useful when used in your car with a laptop, Pocket PC, or Palm PDA.

✦ Swapping electronic business cards between handheld computers.

Bluetooth Technical Stuff

For you technical enthusiasts out there, here's a whole section that gets the Technical Stuff icon. The following paragraphs point out some of the important and obscure technical highlights of Bluetooth:

✦ Bluetooth was originally developed in 1998 by a consortium of companies, including IBM, Intel, Ericsson, Nokia, and Toshiba. Not wanting to be left out of the action, IEEE turned Bluetooth into a standard called 802.15.

✦ Bluetooth operates in the same 2.4-GHz bandwidth as 802.11 Wi-Fi networks. Although it is possible for Bluetooth and Wi-Fi networks to interfere with one another, Bluetooth includes features that usually minimize or eliminate this interference.

✦ Bluetooth is slow — about 721 Kbps, way slower than Wi-Fi networks. Blue tooth isn't designed to transport large amounts of data, such as huge video files. For that, you should use Wi-Fi.

✦ Bluetooth devices periodically "sniff" the air to see if other Bluetooth devices are nearby so that they can automatically hook up.

✦ Bluetooth has very low power requirements. As a result, it's ideal for battery-powered devices such as cell phones and PDAs.

✦ Bluetooth comes in three flavors, as described in Table 5-1. Class 1 is the most powerful form of Bluetooth and the most commonly used. Class 2 is ideal for devices such as wireless mice or keyboards and wireless cell phone headsets, which need to communicate only at close range. Class 3 is for devices that operate at even closer range, but few Bluetooth devices actually implement Class 3.

Table 5-1	Bluetooth Classes	
Class	*Power*	*Range*
Class 1	100 mW	300 feet (100 meters)
Class 2	10 mW	30 feet (10 meters)
Class 3	1 mW	< 30 feet (10 meters)

✦ Bluetooth was originally conceived by cell phone giant Ericsson as a way to connect a wireless earpiece to a cell phone. As the developers worked on the idea, they soon realized that the technology had uses far beyond wireless earpieces for cell phones.

✦ The name Bluetooth is an English translation of Harald Blatand, a Viking king who united Denmark and Norway in the 10th century.

How to Add Bluetooth to Your Computer

Many computers sold today — especially laptop computers and PDAs — come equipped with Bluetooth technology. If your computer doesn't already support Bluetooth, you can easily add Bluetooth support. Just purchase a USB Bluetooth adapter, which is a small device that plugs into any available USB port on your computer. After you plug it in, your computer is Bluetooth enabled and can connect to any other Bluetooth device that's in range.

Many companies make Bluetooth USB adapters, and most look and work similarly. Figure 5-1 shows an adapter made by Linksys that sells for about $40.

Figure 5-1:
A typical
USB
Bluetooth
adapter.

Photo courtesy of Linksys.

Using Bluetooth in Windows

Unfortunately, the original version of Windows XP didn't have any support for Bluetooth. When Microsoft released Windows XP Service Pack 1 a few years later, it included limited Bluetooth support. Windows XP Service Pack 2 included excellent built-in support for Bluetooth, as does Windows Vista.

If your computer has Bluetooth, a special Bluetooth icon will appear in the System Tray (the panel at the right side of the taskbar). You can click this icon to bring up a menu with the following choices:

✦ Add a Bluetooth Device

✦ Show Bluetooth Devices

✦ Send a File

✦ Receive a File

✦ Join a Personal Area Network

✦ Open Bluetooth Settings

✦ Remove Bluetooth Icon

Installing a USB Bluetooth Adapter

Installing a USB Bluetooth adapter is easy. All you have to do is install the software provided with the adapter and plug the adapter into a free USB port. Usually, you can start the installation process by inserting the CD that comes with the adapter into your CD drive. Then, the installation program automatically starts up. After the installation program starts, follow its steps and plug the adapter in when the installation program instructs you to.

Be sure to follow the installation instructions that come with the adapter. In most cases, you should install the software that comes with the adapter *before* you plug the adapter in.

Enabling Discovery

By default, your computer remains hidden from other Bluetooth devices. If you want other Bluetooth devices to be able to recognize your computer, you need to enable a feature called *discovery.* Here are the steps:

1. **Right-click the Bluetooth icon in the System Tray and select Open Bluetooth Settings from the shortcut menu.**

2. **In the Bluetooth Properties dialog box that appears, click the Options tab.**

3. **Select the Turn Discovery On check box.**

4. **Select the Allow Bluetooth Devices to Connect to This Computer check box.**

5. **Select the Alert Me When a New Bluetooth Device Wants to Connect check box.**

6. **Click OK.**

Installing a Bluetooth Mouse or Keyboard

Installing a Bluetooth-enabled mouse or keyboard is easy. The only trick, ironically, is that you have to have a normal mouse or keyboard installed before you can install a Bluetooth mouse or keyboard. However, after you install the Bluetooth mouse or keyboard, you can unplug the normal mouse or keyboard.

The main trick to installing a Bluetooth mouse or keyboard is that you must first enable discovery on the mouse or keyboard. Most Bluetooth mice and keyboards have a button on the bottom to do this. After Bluetooth is enabled, you can install the mouse or keyboard by right-clicking the Bluetooth icon in the system and choosing the Add a Bluetooth Device command. Then, follow the wizard's steps to install the mouse or keyboard.

Book VI

Telecom, Convergence, and Mobile Devices

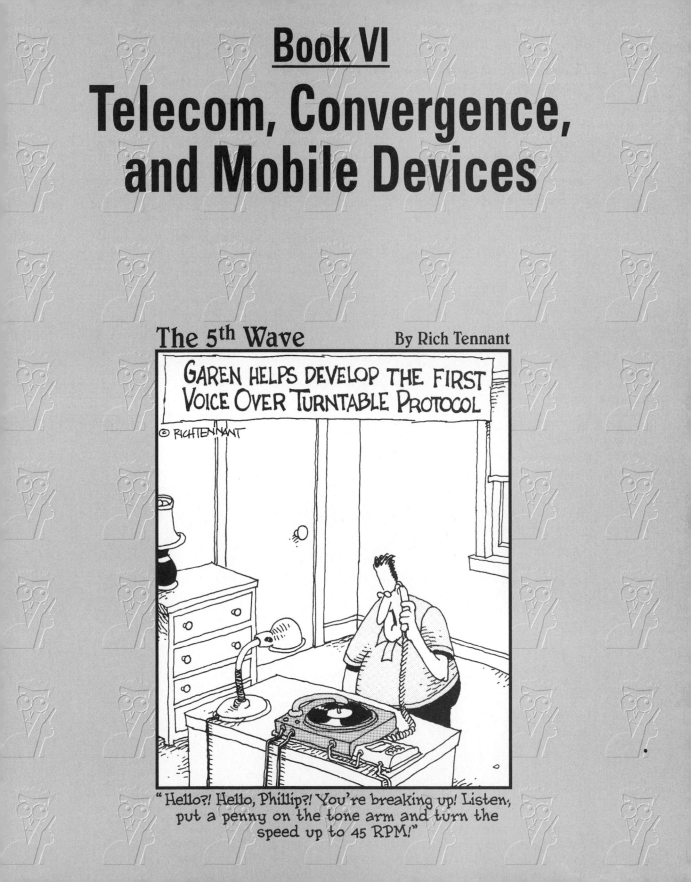

The 5th Wave   By Rich Tennant

GAREN HELPS DEVELOP THE FIRST VOICE OVER TURNTABLE PROTOCOL

"Hello?! Hello, Phillip?! You're breaking up! Listen, put a penny on the tone arm and turn the speed up to 45 RPM!"

Contents at a Glance

Chapter 1: Understanding Telecom Systems

In This Chapter

✔ Looking at telecom companies

✔ Understanding how analog phone systems work

✔ Examining PBX systems and their features

✔ Exploring phone system cabling

*U*p to this point, this book has been entirely about the world of computer networking — specifically, Ethernet, TCP/IP, Windows networking, and Linux. These are the elements that make up the computer network infrastructure for small and large businesses alike. The primary goal of such networks is to carry data to and from the computers in your organization.

However, there exists a parallel universe to computer networking: the world of telephones, commonly known as *telecom*. Rather than data, the primary role of telecom networks is to carry voice traffic to and from the telephones within your organization.

To be sure, these two worlds intersect and overlap. Telecom systems have carried data as well as voice for decades, and computer networks have recently began to carry voice traffic as well as data. But for the most part, telecom networks have evolved along separate paths from computer networks. As a result, telecom networks are built from fundamentally different building blocks than computer networks.

As an IT professional, you may find it your responsibility to support your organization's telecom systems as well as its computer systems. This chapter provides a general introduction to those systems — at least enough to help you understand the basic components and terminology of telecom networks.

Understanding Telecom Carriers

In the not-so-distant past, there was essentially only one telecom company: *AT&T*, colloquially known as *Ma Bell*. Originally descended from the company founded by Alexander Graham Bell, it had a nation-wide monopoly on long distance phone systems and was also the largest provider of local phone systems. All of that changed in the 1980s, however, when the monopoly was broken up by a number of antitrust settlements. The result is that there are now a plethora of telecom companies.

The following paragraphs describe three different types of telecom carriers that exist today:

✦ *Local carriers,* officially known as *Local Exchange Carriers* or *LECs*. These are companies that provide local service — that is, these companies connect individual phones in businesses and homes to the outside world. When Ma Bell was originally broken up, LECs such as Bell Atlantic and Bell South were given regional monopolies to provide local service. There are also *Competing LECs,* or *CLECs,* which provide local service that competes with the original LECs.

✦ *Long distance carriers* are companies that provide service between geographical areas known as *LATAs* (for *Local Access Transport Areas*). These include the big companies such as AT&T, Sprint, and MCI, which physically own nation-wide networks, as well as providers that don't physically own networks but lease space on other companies' networks.

✦ *Wireless carriers* are companies that have built mobile cell networks to support wireless phones. Wireless technology is constantly changing, and today's hottest wireless technology will seem like coffee cans and kite string within just a few years. Wireless carriers are in furious competition with one another to upgrade their networks based on the latest and greatest technology and win your service.

In all likelihood, your organization will deal at one time or another with all three types of telecom carriers.

Understanding Telecom Basics

In its most basic form, a telecommunications network consists of three basic elements:

✦ **Transmitter:** Telecommunication signals originate with a *transmitter,* which converts information into a form that can be sent to a remote destination and sends the information. For example, in a smoke signal telecom network, the transmitter consists of a fire that creates smoke and a person who waves a blanket over the fire to modulate the smoke into a series of puffs that convey the desired information. In more advanced telecom networks, the transmitters are electronic devices that convert information — typically spoken words — into modulated electrical signals.

✦ **Receiver:** The receiver is at the other end of the telecommunications network. It observes the signals sent by the transmitter and converts them from their coded or modulated form back into an understandable form. In our smoke signal network, the receiver is typically a person standing on a hilltop some distance away from the transmitter, watching the smoke signals and interpreting their meaning.

✦ **Medium:** All telecom networks also involve the use of a *medium* through which signals pass from the transmitter to the receiver. In the smoke signal network, the medium is the air through which the receiver observes the smoke signals. In this example, the air is not a particularly good medium because it is prone to wind currents that frequently distort the original signals and often make them unreadable. More modern telecom networks use electrical or fiber-optic wire as the medium, although the air is still a popular choice for wireless networks.

This is no different than with computer networks, of course. In a computer network, the transmitters and receivers are embedded into devices such as NICs, switches, and routers. The medium consists of the cables that run through the walls to connect the NICs, switches, and routers.

The following paragraphs briefly describe some additional basics of telecommunication networks:

✦ *Analog communications* refers to signals that convey information by varying the frequency or intensity of the signals. *Digital communications* refers to signals that transmit information in discrete units that represent 0s and 1s. Analog systems are still popular for basic voice communications, but digital signals are more reliable and cost-effective for more complicated systems. Even analog phone signals are typically converted to digital signals at some point along the system, then converted back to analog signals at the other end.

✦ A *circuit* refers to an end-to-end connection between a transmitter and a receiver. Originally, telephone systems were circuit based: When you placed a phone call by dialing a number, you established a circuit between your phone and the other party's phone. However, circuit-based systems are limited by the number of unique circuits that can be created at any given time. When all of the circuits are in use, no additional calls can be placed.

✦ An alternative to circuit-based networks is a *packet*-based network. In a packet-based network, circuits are not established between end points. Instead, information is divided into small packets, which are addressed to a particular destination and sent over the network. The receiver collects the packets at the other end and reassembles them. Packet-based networks are more complicated, but they aren't limited by a maximum number of concurrent circuits.

✦ *Channels* refer to the ability of a single medium to carry more than one signal at a time. For example, a single cable is able to deliver hundreds of different channels of TV to your home. In a similar way, a single telecom cable, whether electrical or fiber-optic, can carry many simultaneous channels.

Understanding Analog Phone Systems

Most residential phone service is of the analog circuit-switching type and hasn't changed fundamentally in several decades. When you pick up your phone, you hear a *dial tone,* which is a signal placed on the network to indicate that the system is ready to place a call. Specifically, the dial tone means that the network has recognized an *off-hook* condition. In the old days, that meant literally that you had picked up the phone's handset from its hook; when the phone was removed, the spring-loaded hook closed a switch that opened a connection to the phone system; hence, the phone was "off hook."

You may not have noticed before, but if you listen carefully to a dial tone (at least in the US), you'll notice that it is actually two distinct pitches that interfere with each other to produce a distinct buzzing sound. The two pitches are at 350 Hz and 440 Hz. (Musically, 440 Hz is the A above Middle C, and 350 Hz is a slightly out-of-tune F.)

When you hear a dial tone, you can dial a phone number. In the old days, of course, you literally spun a spring-loaded wheel that had ten contact switches on the back. Holes were arranged around the dial so that you could select the number of contact switches that would operate when you released the wheel so that the spring would return it to its home position. This generated electrical pulses, which the telephone exchange system counted to determine the number that was dialed. This form of dialing was referred to as *pulse dialing*.

These days, of course, phones don't use dialing wheels, but the term *dialing* is still used. *Touch-tone dialing* is now the norm. In touch-tone dialing, the digits zero through nine are represented by different combinations of pitches technically known as *DTMF* tones — *Dual Tone Multi-Frequency*. Each digit is represented by a different combination of two frequencies.

When you press the first digit of a phone number, the dial tone disappears to indicate that the dialing process has begun. If you take a phone off-hook for an extended period without initiating a call, the dial tone is replaced by an *off-hook tone,* which is a disconcerting combination of the four pitches 1400 Hz, 2600 Hz, 2450 Hz, and 2600 Hz. (If you want to amuse your friends and there's a piano nearby, tell 'em you're working on a new song called "My Baby Left the Phone Off the Hook," then bang really fast on the four keys F, C, D#, and E an octave above Middle C. It isn't exactly the off-hook tone, but it's close enough for jazz.)

DTMF frequencies decoded

Each DTMF tone used for touch-tone dialing is a combination of two frequencies. One of the frequencies is 697 Hz, 770 Hz, 852 Hz, or 941 Hz. The other is 1209 Hz, 1336 Hz, 1477 Hz, or 1633 Hz. The following table shows how these two frequencies are selected:

	1209 Hz	1336 Hz	1477 Hz	1633 Hz
697 Hz	1	2	3	A
770 Hz	4	5	6	B
852 Hz	7	8	9	C
941 Hz	*	0	#	D

For example, the digit 1 is the combination of 697 Hz and 1209 Hz. Notice that the codes that use the 1633 Hz are for the letters A through D. These were originally intended to let you choose menu options from automated systems, but that usage never caught on and few phones include A through D keys. However, the A through D codes are used internally within the telephone system for network control.

A lot of thought went into the selection of the frequencies used for the DTMF tones. The frequencies do not correspond with musical notes. Instead, they were carefully chosen so that none of the combinations produce harmonics that can confuse the system.

Each digit you dial while placing a phone call places you one step closer to completing a circuit with the receiving party. Back in the old days, the first two or three digits of the phone number actually represented the exchange office to which the phone was connected. The first two digits were usually spelled with letters that were abbreviations for the station name. For example, the Ricardo's phone number on *I Love Lucy* was Murray Hill 5-9975 (535-9975). The use of letters in phone numbers was phased out in the 1960s, and modern electronic switching equipment doesn't rely on the first several digits of the number to identify local exchange stations. Even so, we still use hyphens to separate phone numbers into groups of three and four digits.

Understanding PBX Systems

Most businesses with more than a few phones use what is referred to as a *PBX,* or *Private Branch Exchange,* system. The primary purpose of a PBX is to manage access for a large number of internal phones, called *extensions,* to a smaller number of external telephone circuits, called *lines.* For example, a business with 100 telephones might be connected to a service with 16 phone lines. Then, any of the company's 100 employees can access any of the 16 lines. If the company finds that all 16 of the lines are frequently in use at the same time, it can acquire additional lines from the carrier to ease the congestion.

Originally, PBX systems were manually operated by phone operators who sat at a *switchboard* to connect incoming calls to the correct extension. Now, of course, the switchboard operators are replaced by computerized controls. But the basic operation is the same: The PBX connects incoming calls to specific extensions and provides internal users with access to lines to make outgoing calls.

One of the most recognizable features of PBX systems is the need to dial 9 to get an outside line. With a PBX system, you can connect directly to any other extension by picking up the handset and dialing the extension's number. To distinguish between this type of internal call and an outgoing call, you first dial a 9 to access an outgoing line, and then you dial the external phone number.

There are two types of systems that are similar, but distinct from PBX systems:

✦ **Centrex:** A *Centrex* system is functionally similar to a PBX system. But instead of residing at the company's site, Centrex is a service provided by a phone company. As such, the equipment for the Centrex system is owned by the phone company and located at the phone company's facilities.

✦ **Key system:** A *key system* is similar to a PBX system but doesn't automatically connect internal users to outgoing lines. Instead, the phones in a key system have buttons that correspond to outgoing lines. For example, if the company has four outgoing lines, each phone will have four buttons, one for each line. To place a call, the user picks up the phone, presses one of the buttons to select a line, and then places the call. The key buttons light up when the lines are in use. Key systems are often used in smaller offices, typically with a dozen or fewer phones.

Common Features of PBX Systems

Besides the basic ability to make and receive external calls and to directly connect to extensions, PBX systems offer a variety of additional useful features. Unfortunately, most of these features have obscure names such as DID or Camp-On. In the following paragraphs, I decode the more commonly used features for your edification, presented in alphabetical order:

✦ **Auto-attendant:** The Auto-attendant feature enables callers to navigate through your phone system without human intervention. In its simplest form, the caller simply dials an extension to reach a particular person. But the auto-attendant feature can usually be programmed to let callers access a plethora of choices by selecting menu choices. ("For sales, press 1. For technical support, press 2 . . .")

When programmed well, with just a few simple choices, the auto-attendant feature can be a real time-saver for callers. But most auto-attendant systems are not programmed with customer service in mind. Instead, they are programmed to minimize the costs associated with letting your customers talk to actual human beings who can help them connect with the people they need to talk to. If you can't resist the urge to program your PBX's auto-attendant feature, please put yourself in your customer's shoes before you design an overly complicated phone menu.

✦ **Call-forwarding:** This feature can automatically forward calls for a particular extension to another number if no one answers the original number. Most often, the call is forwarded to a voice mailbox, where the caller can leave a voice message. However, the call can also be forwarded to another extension on the PBX or to a different external number such as a cell phone.

✦ **Call parking:** This feature lets you "park" a call so that you or someone else can resume the call from a different extension. It is similar to placing a call on hold, except that when you park a call, anyone can retrieve the call. In contrast, when you place a call on hold, only you can resume the call.

When you park a call, you are actually transferring the call to one of several designated extensions that are not associated with actual phones. Instead, these extensions are used as holding areas for parked calls. When you retrieve a parked call, you are actually transferring the call from the parked extension to your extension.

The person who programs your PBX system will determine which extensions are used for call parking.

There are two basic uses for call parking. The first is for transferring a call to someone when you aren't certain of that person's location. Rather than transferring the call directly to the person's extension, you park the call. Then, you can page the person to let them know they have a parked call.

The second common use is when you need to interrupt a call but resume it later from a different location. For example, I often make technical support phone calls from my desk, but find that I need to go into the computer server room to continue the call. So I'll park the call, go into the server room, and then retrieve the parked call from the phone in the server room.

✦ **Call transfer:** This feature lets you transfer an incoming call from your extension to another extension. This feature is most often used by a telephone receptionist who answers an incoming call, asks the caller who he or she wishes to speak with, and then transfers the call accordingly. Most PBX systems give you the option of announcing the call to the recipient of the transfer. This gives the recipient the heads-up on who is calling, so he or she can decide whether or not to answer the call.

✦ **Camp-on:** When this feature is enabled, the system keeps calling an extension until it gets an answer. If the extension is busy, the call "camps" itself on to the extension, waiting for the busy signal to end. When the signal ends, the extension immediately rings, and the extension that originally made the call also rings so the two parties can connect.

✦ **Conference calls:** The conference call feature lets you engage in phone calls with more than two parties. In some PBX systems, the conference call feature can include a scheduling component in which participants are sent e-mail that invites them to participate in the call, providing a special phone number for the call and a password that must be used to access the call. As each participant joins or leaves the call, the system automatically announces their arrival or departure to the other participants.

✦ **Direct Inward Dialing (DID):** A DID number is an external number that the PBX automatically routes to a specific extension. This creates the impression that the user of the extension has a separate external phone line. In actuality, he or she doesn't have a separate external line.

Suppose a company's main phone number is 555-1200, and the carrier has provided a block of 20 DID numbers ranging from 555-1201 to 555-1220. You might assign 555-1215 as the DID number for extension 115. When a caller dials 555-1215, the phone system actually connects the caller to 555-1200 but passes the DID number 555-1215 to the PBX. Then, the PBX automatically transfers the call to extension 115. To the caller, it appears as if that extension has its own separate outside line.

✦ **Follow-me:** This feature lets you associate one or more extension numbers with an individual. When the PBX system receives a call for that individual, it tries each of the numbers in the list until one of them answers. Usually, the last number in the list is the person's voice mailbox.

✦ **Hotel/motel features:** Many PBX systems offer features designed for hotels and motels — most notably wake-up calls. Even though I don't work for a hotel, I still like to program my company PBX system's wake-up call feature to give me a wake-up call at about 3:00 p.m., when that mid-afternoon drowsiness starts to kick in.

✦ **Hunt groups:** A *hunt group* is a group of lines that are available for receiving incoming calls. The PBX can be programmed to use one of several methods for determining which of the available lines in the hunt group will receive a particular call. The most common methods are as follows:

  • *Linear:* The first available line always gets the call. For example, suppose there are four lines numbered 1 through 4. When the first call comes in, it is assigned to line 1. When the second call comes in, it is assigned to line 2 if line 1 is still busy. If the call on line 1 has ended, the new call will be assigned to line 1.

  • *Circular:* Incoming calls are assigned sequentially to lines. For example, suppose there are four lines numbered 1 through 4. When the first call comes in, it is assigned to line 1. When the second call comes in, it is assigned to line 2, even if the call on line 1 has already ended.

  • *Most idle:* Incoming calls are assigned to the line that has been idle the longest.

✦ **Music On Hold (MOH):** The Music On Hold feature lets you play cheesy music for your customers while they wait on hold. The feature usually consists of an audio jack located on the side of the PBX cabinet, often labeled "MOH." You can use a standard audio cable to connect a music source such as a CD or MP3 player.

Copyright laws apply strictly to Music On Hold systems. Technically, playing music through an MOH system is a form of broadcasting. Thus, it is illegal to purchase CDs from a normal retail outlet and use a CD player to play them through your MOH system. The same applies to MP3 players or even to radio broadcasts. To legally play music on hold, you must obtain permission from the copyright holder to use the music. The easiest way to do that is to purchase music specifically recorded for this purpose. You can purchase inexpensive generic music in a variety of formats (jazz, soft rock, and so on), or you can have custom recordings made that include annoying sales messages.

✦ **Night service:** This feature lets you schedule the PBX to respond differently to calls made after hours than it does to calls made during business hours. For example, you might route incoming calls automatically to a generic voice mailbox, with a greeting that states your business hours and invites the caller to leave a message.

✦ **Voice mail:** *Voice mail* is an essential feature of any PBX system. Its primary purpose is to let callers leave messages when you aren't available to take calls. However, it is also widely used to screen calls. If you aren't sure whether you want to accept a particular call, you can have the call directed to your voice mail. Then, you can listen to the message (if the caller leaves one) and determine whether to return the call.

For more information about voice mail, refer to Chapter 3 of this minibook.

**Book VI
Chapter 1**

**Understanding
Telecom Systems**

Working with Phone System Cabling

The last topic for this chapter is phone system cabling. Fortunately, phone system cabling is simpler than network cabling — at least, the part of the cabling that resides within your building and that connects extensions to your central PBX system. The cabling that connects the PBX system to the outside world is another matter, but you probably don't want to have anything to do with those cables. They are the responsibility of your carrier.

While network connections typically use 8-pin RJ-45 connectors, phone connections usually use 6-pin RJ-11 connections. Standard analog phones use only one pair of wires — usually the blue pair — connected on pins 3 and 4. Digital phones used as extensions with PBX systems usually use two pairs — the blue pair and the orange pair — connected on pins 2 through 5 as shown in the following table:

Pin	Color	Type
2	orange/white stripe	tip
3	solid blue	ring
4	blue/white stripe	tip
5	solid orange	ring

The electrical requirements for these cables are much less stringent than for Ethernet network cables because much less data is carried on them. Connectors, cables, jacks, and crimping tools are readily available at suppliers such as Home Depot and Lowe's.

The two wires in each pair of phone cable are called *tip* and *ring*. The tip wire is ground, and the ring wire carries the negative voltage. The terms *tip* and *ring* originated with the plugs that were used in manual switchboards: The tip wire was connected to the tip of the plug, while the ring wire was connected to the ring around the shaft of the plug. Within a given pair, the striped wire is used for tip, while the solid wire is used for ring.

Chapter 2: Managing a PBX System

In This Chapter

✔ **Accessing browser-based PBX administration pages**

✔ **Setting up extension data**

✔ **Programming function keys**

✔ **Swapping extensions**

Managing a large PBX system with hundreds or even thousands of extensions is a job for specialists with extensive telecom training. However, the job of managing a smaller PBX system — say, with 100 or fewer extensions — is often left to the lowly network administrator. You will probably have a telecom provider that does the initial setup for you, and you'll call them out periodically whenever hardware changes need to be made. But you may find yourself tasked with the day-to-day operation of the system.

Fortunately, modern PBX systems have Web-based interfaces you can use for basic management tasks such as adding new users, changing basic extension data such as the user's name, and relocating extensions. This chapter shows you how to use a Web-based PBX interface for such tasks.

PBX systems from different manufacturers use different management programs, but the concepts are similar. The illustrations in this chapter are from one specific system manufactured by NEC, called the *NEC Electra Elite IPK,* which I refer to as simply *IPK.* If you are working with a different PBX system, you'll need to learn its idiosyncrasies. (And believe me, PBX systems have plenty of idiosyncrasies.)

The word *idiosyncrasy* comes from two Latin words, *syncrasis,* which means "the ability to make you feel like something," and *idios,* which means "an idiot."

Accessing the Web-Based PBX Interface

Most PBX systems include a TCP/IP port that lets you connect the system to your network. In addition, the PBX system runs a small Web server that supports a management application. In the case of the NEC IPK system, the

Web-based interface is called *WebPro,* and it can be accessed simply by opening a browser window and entering the IP address of the PBX system into the address bar. This displays a login screen, as shown in Figure 2-1.

Figure 2-1:
Logging in
to a PBX
system.

To log in, simply enter your username and password. Your telecom provider will have to give you the initial administrator credentials to access the system. When you're in, you can use the Accounts setup page to create additional accounts. I recommend you create your own account rather than use the main administrator account.

When you have logged in, the Home page shown in Figure 2-2 appears. This page displays the main links you'll use to access the various administrative pages provided by the Web interface.

Figure 2-2:
The Home
page for the
IPK system.

In the case of the NEC IPK system, almost all of the basic administrative tasks are performed from the System Data page, shown in Figure 2-3. This page consists of a large menu on the left side of the page. When you select a menu item, the corresponding page is displayed in the central portion of the page.

The menu items are numbered for easy reference. Each top-level menu choice has a number that's a multiple of 10, beginning with 10. Then, the pages within each top-level choice are numbered sequentially. For example, the page shown in Figure 2-3 is page 10-01, which is titled "Time and Date Setup." This page, as its title suggests, lets you change the PBX system's time and date.

Each field on each page also has a number. For example, the Year field is 01, the Month is 02, and the Day of the Month is 03. You can combine these numbers with the page numbers to uniquely identify every configurable field on the IPK system. For example, the complete number for the Year field is 10-01-01. Here, 10-01 is the page (Time and Date Setup), and the final 01 is the field number (Year).

**Book VI
Chapter 2**

**Managing a PBX
System**

Figure 2-3:
The System
Data page.

Playing with IP Addresses

You might find that the PBX system has been configured to run on a different subnet than the rest of your network. In that case, you'll have to devise a way to access the PBX from your subnet. Here are three suggested approaches:

✦ **Use a router to connect the PBX system's subnet to your network's subnet.** Then, you'll be able to browse directly to the PBX system from any computer on your network.

✦ **Add a second network card to your computer and configure it with an IP address on the PBX system's subnet.** Then, you'll be able to access the PBX system from your computer. The PBX system still won't be accessible to other computers on the network, but that's probably for the best anyway. You don't want your users stumbling into the PBX system and guessing at passwords.

✦ **Change the PBX system's IP address to match your subnet.** You can do that by accessing page 10-12, as shown in Figure 2-4.

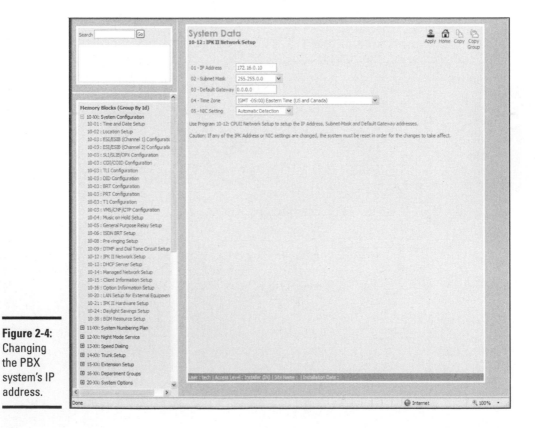

Figure 2-4:
Changing the PBX system's IP address.

Before the IP address change takes effect, you will have to reboot the PBX system. This is not something to be done lightly, as phone service will be interrupted. You'll probably want to do it on a weekend or late at night. If you have a service contract with a telecom provider to maintain the PBX system, you should first get its advice and consent. In fact, you should probably just have the company make the IP address change for you as part of its service.

Changing a User's Name

One of the most common administrative tasks you'll need to perform is changing the basic configuration of an extension. For example, many PBX systems display the user's name on a small LCD screen on the user's phone. If the extension is reassigned to a different user, you'll need to change the name associated with the extension.

Here are the steps you can follow to do that on a NEC IPK system:

1. **Open the WebPro interface and log in.**

2. **Click the System Data icon.**

3. **Select menu item 15-XX, Extension Setup.**

   This opens a list of the Extension Setup pages.

4. **Select menu item 15-01, Basic Extension Setup.**

   This displays the Basic Extension Setup page, as shown in Figure 2-5.

5. **Select the extension you want to change from the Extension drop-down list.**

   The data for the extension you selected is displayed.

6. **Change the user's name.**

   The user's name is displayed in field 01.

7. **Click Apply.**

   You're done! You can log out if this is the only configuration change you need to make. Otherwise, you can browse to other extensions or other administration pages to make additional changes.

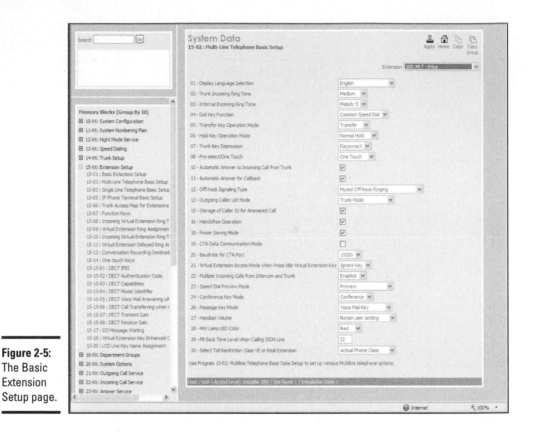

Figure 2-5:
The Basic
Extension
Setup page.

Changing Other Extension Settings

Besides the user's name, there are many other settings you can change for an extension. In the IPK system, you can access these additional settings via page 15-02, which is shown in Figure 2-6.

You can use this page to change many different settings. Here are the most popular:

✦ **Display Language Selection:** This is the user's preferred language.

✦ **Trunk Incoming Ring Tone:** This option lets you select the ring tone used for incoming calls that originate from an outside line.

✦ **Internal Incoming Ring Tone:** Lets you change the ring tone used for internal calls — that is, calls originating from another extension.

Figure 2-6:
The Multi-
Line
Telephone
Basic Setup
page.

Programming Function Keys

Most phones used in PBX systems have one or more programmable buttons called *function keys*. A typical desk phone has 16 function keys arranged in two rows of eight. Usually, the top row of keys is assigned to predefined phone functions such as Park or Retrieve, while the bottom row is reserved for the user to assign speed-dial numbers for his or her eight favorite people.

You can program these keys by using page 15-07, as described in the following procedure:

1. **Open the WebPro interface and log in.**
2. **Click the System Data icon.**
3. **Select menu item 15-XX, Extension Setup.**

   This opens a list of the Extension Setup pages.

4. **Select menu item 15-07, Function Keys.**

   This displays the Function Keys page, as shown in Figure 2-7.

5. **Select the extension you want to change from the Extension drop-down list.**

   The data for the extension you selected is displayed.

6. **Set the function and additional data value for each of the eight function keys.**

   For each button, select the function you want to assign to the button by using the button's function drop-down list. Then, enter any additional data that's required for the function in the Additional Data text box.

   In Figure 2-7, I've programmed the first eight function keys as follows:

   - *Key 1 — CAP Key 2:* This key allows the user to access an outside line.

   - *Key 2 — CAP Key 3:* This key provides a second outside line so the user can have two simultaneous external calls.

   - *Key 3 — DSS/One Touch #6:* This is a code that lets the user park calls. To park a call, the user presses Transfer, this key, then a park number.

   - *Key 4 — DSS/One Touch *6:* This code lets the user retrieve parked calls. To retrieve a call, the user presses this key followed by the park number.

   - *Key 5 — External All Call Paging:* This key lets the user access the paging system.

   - *Key 6 — Call Forward Immediate:* This key lets the user forward a call to another extension.

   - *Key 7 — Trunk Key 1:* This key answers the door phone, which rings at night when someone outside the building presses the Phone button. Hopefully you aren't working late at night, so you don't get bugged by skateboarding kids who think it's funny to press the door phone button repeatedly.

   - *Key 8 — Virtual Extension 191:* This key lets the user answer the phone when the system is in night mode. (In night mode, incoming calls can be answered by phones other than the operator's console.)

7. **Click Apply.**

   The changes are applied.

8. **Click the Right Arrow next to the Function Key text box.**

   This displays the next set of eight function keys for the phone.

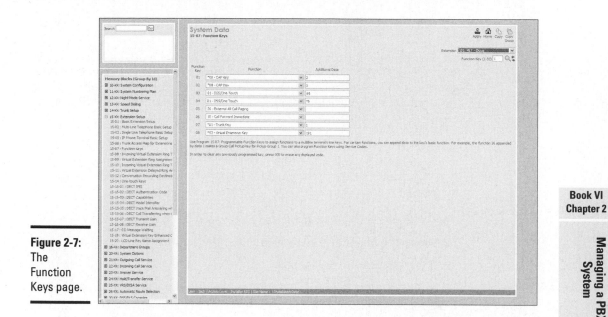

Book VI
Chapter 2

Managing a PBX
System

Figure 2-7:
The
Function
Keys page.

9. **Set the function and additional value for the next set of function keys.**

10. **Click Apply.**

The changes are applied.

11. **If the phone has more than 16 buttons, repeat Steps 8 through 10 for each additional set of buttons.**

12. **You're done!**

Well, not quite. You really should go to the phone you just modified and make sure the buttons work correctly.

Here are just a few tips regarding the function keys:

✦ I strongly recommend you program the first eight buttons on all of the desk phones consistently. Otherwise, your users will be hopelessly confused.

✦ Be sure to physically label the keys on each of your phones. Your phone vendor should be able to supply faceplate labels you can write on and may be able to provide software that will let you create the faceplates and print them on a laser printer.

✦ If you have users who are complaining that sometimes they can't get a dial tone when they press 9, check the virtual extension numbers. Odds are you've assigned two or more users the same numbers.

Swapping Extensions

If a user physically moves from one office to another, you don't have to actually move the user's phone, provided there's an unused phone in the user's new office. Instead, you can use the PBX system to swap the extensions, so the user's new phone will assume the identity of his or her old extension. This feature is called *extension swap* and can be a real time-saver.

The easiest way to accomplish an extension swap is from one of the phones involved in the swap, rather than from the PBX system's browser interface. The procedure is similar for most PBX systems. For the NEC IPK system, follow these steps:

1. **Go to one of the extensions to be swapped.**

2. **Press the Speaker button or pick up the handset.**

3. **Type the Station Swap code.**

On my system, it is 777, but it might be different on yours. I show you how to find out at the end of this section.

4. **Type the password.**

A password is required to access this feature. This prevents users from accidentally swapping their extensions by randomly pressing keys.

5. **Type the extension of the other phone.**

6. **Hang up.**

The extensions are now swapped.

To find out the access code assigned to the Station Swap function on a NEC IPK system, open the Web browser and go to page 11-10, which lists the service codes for system functions. Other PBX systems should have similar pages that list the codes that have been assigned to various service functions.

Chapter 3: Unified Messaging: Voice Mail, E-Mail, and Fax Together

In This Chapter

✔ **Looking at unified messaging**

✔ **Integrating Outlook with your voice mail**

✔ **Listening to voice mail in Outlook**

✔ **Configuring ViewMail options**

*E*very day when I get to work, I run Outlook on my computer to see if I have any new e-mail. Then I glance at my phone to see if the message light is flashing. If so, I use the phone to listen to my voice mail. Then I pull my cell phone out of my pocket, too, and check to see if I have any voice mail there. Then I walk down the hall to the fax machine to see if I have any faxes. Then I . . .

Does this sound familiar? If so, you need *unified messaging*. The idea of unified messaging is to combine all of these different repositories of messages into one convenient location, so you can check for messages in just one place.

When the unified messaging idea was first hatched about ten years ago, the idea was that this one single repository of messages could also be accessed from all your different devices. So, you could use your e-mail program to check your voice mail, and you could use your cell phone to listen to your e-mail.

This idea never really caught on, for the simple reason that people don't really want to listen to their e-mail over a cell phone. However, mobile devices such as BlackBerrys have given the idea new life, as these devices work like hand-held versions of your desktop computer, and allow you to read your e-mail just as you would at your desk.

This chapter focuses on the most basic form of unified messaging, in which Microsoft Outlook is extended so that it handles not only e-mail, but also voice mail for your phone system and faxing. This all but eliminates the need for a message light on your phone and a fax machine down the hall.

Integrating Voice Mail with Outlook

The most basic form of unified messaging is integrating your voice mail with Outlook. That way, any voice mail messages you receive will appear in your Outlook inbox.

The exact method used to integrate voice mail with Outlook depends on the PBX vendor. The simplest approach lets you associate an e-mail address with each voice mailbox. Then, whenever the mailbox receives a message, the message is converted to an audio file (typically in .WAV format) and sent as an attachment to the specified address.

This approach works well enough, but Outlook doesn't give you much help when it comes to listening to the message. Typically, when you double-click the attachment, it opens with your preferred media player, which plays the message over your computer's speakers. The entire audio file must be downloaded to the computer before the message begins to play, so you'll experience a brief delay before you can hear the message.

A better approach is to use software provided by your PBX vendor to integrate Outlook with the voice mail system. Typically, you must install this software on each client computer. The software works as an Outlook add-in and adds the ability to listen to voice mail from within Outlook.

Different PBX vendors use different software. One common program is called *ViewMail,* originally Active Voice, and also offered by Cisco as part of its Unity package. ViewMail installs as an add-on to Microsoft Outlook and displays a special applet when you open a message that contains voice mail. This applet then plays the voice mail over your computer system's speakers.

Configuring ViewMail

When you install ViewMail, you must configure it to retrieve your voice mail. This configuration happens in two steps. First, you must tell ViewMail where and how to locate your voice mail server. The Setup program displays a screen similar to the one in Figure 3-1 to obtain this information.

This screen asks for the name or IP address of your voice mail server, as well as the protocol used to connect to it.

Figure 3-1:
Configuring
your voice
mail server's
IP address.

Second, you must identify the specific voice mailbox that will be accessed. The Setup program displays a screen similar to the one in Figure 3-2 to solicit this information. Here, you must enter the extension number of the voice mailbox, along with the password, if the mailbox has one.

After the Setup program has completed this configuration, Outlook should begin receiving messages with voice mail and fax attachments.

Figure 3-2:
Configuring
the mailbox
number.

Listening to Voice Mail in Outlook

Without an add-in program such as ViewMail, voice mail messages appear as regular e-mail items with sound file attachments. You can open the message and then open the attachment to hear the voice mail played with Microsoft Media Player or some other media player.

With an add-in program such as ViewMail, however, the process is much slicker. Here is the procedure:

1. **Double-click the message to open it.**

You must actually open the message to listen to it; voice mail messages cannot be played from the Preview pane.

When you open a message that has a voice mail attachment, the standard Outlook e-mail form is not used. Instead, you'll see a form like the one in Figure 3-3.

2. **Click the Play button.**

The message begins playing over your computer's speakers.

Figure 3-3:
Playing a voice mail with ViewMail.

Additional buttons let you pause the message, start over, or skip to any part of the message.

Here are a few additional thoughts regarding voice mail messages:

✦ If you get a voice mail message that you think was intended for someone else, or if you think someone else should hear it (maybe it contains a juicy bit of gossip!), you can forward the message to another recipient. Just click the Forward button, type the address of the person you want to forward the message to, and click Send.

✦ You can delete a voice mail message by selecting it in your Inbox and pressing the Delete key, or by clicking the Delete button when viewing the message. Either way, the message is removed not only from your Inbox but also from the voice mail system. (By default, Outlook copies the message to your Deleted Items folder rather than actually deleting it. So if you decide you want the message back, open the Deleted Items folder and restore the message.)

✦ If your computer is equipped with a microphone, you can reply to voice mail messages via Outlook. Open the voice mail message and click the Reply button. Then click the Record button and record your reply. Note that this feature works only for internal voice mails — that is, voice mails from recipients who also have a voice mailbox on the same system.

✦ If you prefer, you can listen to your voice mail on your telephone's headset rather than on your computer's speakers. More information on how to do that is found in the next section.

Changing ViewMail Settings

ViewMail has several options you can set to change how it handles your voice mail. To change these options, open Outlook and choose Tools➪ ViewMail Options. This displays an options dialog box that has several tabs. The following sections describe the options found in each of these tabs.

The General tab

Figure 3-4 shows the General tab. It offers the following options:

✦ **Workstation Extension:** The extension number for your phone.

✦ **Play Voice Automatically:** If you select this option, you won't have to click the Play button when you open a voice mail message. Instead, the voice mail will automatically play when you open the message.

✦ **View Fax Automatically:** If you select this option, ViewMail will automatically load the fax viewer if the message contains a fax attachment.

✦ **Keep Only Message Header in the Sent Items Folder:** If you deselect this item, ViewMail stores a copy of the original voice mail in the Sent Items folder when you reply to a message.

Figure 3-4:
The General
tab of the
ViewMail
options
dialog box.

The Notification tab

Figure 3-5 shows the Notification tab. The options in this tab let you control the sound played when voice messages arrive. You can set the sound that is played when a normal-priority voice mail is received, when an urgent voice mail is received, and when a fax is received. You can also indicate whether you want the computer to play the sender's name if it is available.

Figure 3-5:
The
Notification
tab of the
ViewMail
options
dialog box.

The Record tab

The Record tab, shown in Figure 3-6, lets you control options for how messages are recorded. The most important option is the Device: You can use this drop-down list to indicate whether you want to record messages using your computer's sound card (if it has a microphone plugged in) or your telephone. You can also set the audio format used to record messages and specify how the size of the audio buffers, which affects the quality of the recorded audio.

Figure 3-6:
The Record
tab of the
ViewMail
options
dialog box.

The Playback tab

Figure 3-7 shows the Playback tab, which lets you control options that govern how messages are played. You can choose whether to play messages using your computer's sound card or using your telephone. If you choose the telephone, your phone will ring when you click the Play button to play a message. Then, the message will be played when you answer the phone.

Figure 3-7:
The
Playback
tab of the
ViewMail
options
dialog box.

The Advanced tab

Figure 3-8 shows the Advanced tab. This tab contains several useful options:

+ **When a message is delivered, automatically download it.** This option tells ViewMail to download voice mail messages from the voice mail server as soon as they arrive. If you deselect this option, messages are not downloaded until you listen to them. You can select this option for better performance; however, it may cause your inbox to fill up with large attachments if you receive a lot of voice mail.

+ **When downloading a message, remove the original from the voice mail server.** If you select this option, messages are automatically deleted from the voice mail server when they are downloaded to your mailbox. If you leave this option deselected, messages are not deleted from the voice mail server until you delete them from your inbox.

Figure 3-8:
The
Advanced
tab of the
ViewMail
options
dialog box.

Figure 3-8: The Advanced tab of the ViewMail options dialog box.

✦ **When deleting messages that have not been downloaded . . . Move it to the deleted items folder.** If you select this option, messages that you have not yet listened to (let alone downloaded) are sent to the Deleted Items folder when you delete them.

✦ **Delete it permanently from the voice mail system.** If you select this option, messages are permanently deleted from the voice mail system when you delete them in Outlook, even if you have not yet listened to or downloaded the message.

Note that the Connectivity and Diagnostics tabs are used only for trouble shooting purposes, so you probably won't ever need them.

Chapter 4: Using VoIP

In This Chapter

↙ **How VoIP works**

↙ **Advantages of VoIP**

↙ **Disadvantages of VoIP**

↙ **Some popular VoIP providers**

*O*ne of the newest trends in networking is replacing your traditional telephone service with an Internet-based service known as *VoIP*. Why? Two reasons. First, because you can. And second, because you might save money, depending on how big your long distance bills are.

This chapter gives you a brief introduction to VoIP: what it is, what it can do, and how you can get it. It isn't a complete guide to VoIP. For that, check out *VoIP For Dummies* by Timothy V. Kelly, published by Wiley, of course.

Understanding VoIP

VoIP, which stands for *Voice over IP (Internet Protocol)* works much the same as a regular telephone. However, instead of connecting to the public telephone network, your phone system connects directly to the Internet. The main benefit is reduced cost, especially if you make a lot of long distance phone calls.

When you use a normal phone to make a long distance call, your voice is transmitted (usually in digital form) over a network called the *Public Switched Telephone Network,* or *PSTN.* Along the way, you're charged by-the-minute fees by your long distance service provider.

When you use VoIP, your voice is still converted into digital form. However, instead of being sent over private networks owned by telephone companies, it is sent over the Internet. Because the Internet uses the IP protocol, the digital data that represents your voice must be converted into packets that can be sent reliably over IP. Hence the name, Voice over IP, or VoIP.

Carrying telephone conversations over the Internet isn't new. In fact, the technology has been around for many years. But only recently has the technology become inexpensive enough to catch on for residential or commercial service. That's why you may not have heard of VoIP until now.

There are three basic approaches to setting up VoIP:

✦ **Software-only VoIP systems:** These run on your computer and enable you to talk free with anyone else anywhere in the world provided they are using the same software you are. The best-known software-only VoIP system is Skype (`www.skype.com`). The advantage of Skype is that it's free. But software-only VoIP has two major drawbacks:

- You can only use it from your computer. You can't just pick up a phone, dial a number, and make a call via Skype.

- The person you're calling must also use Skype. You can't just call any number. (However, there is a fee-based system called SkypeOut that lets you call regular phone numbers from Skype. At about two cents per minute, SkypeOut is pretty cheap.)

Skype is great if you do most of your long distance calling to just a few other people and you and your friends are computer geeks who don't mind sitting at the computer while you have your phone conversations.

✦ **VoIP services such as Vonage and AT&T CallVantage:** These services don't require the use of a computer. Instead, they use a special adapter called an *Analog Telephone Adapter* (*ATA*) that connects a normal telephone to the Internet. The adapter lets you use VoIP pretty much as if it were a regular telephone. You just pick up the phone and dial a number. The fact that the call is routed over the Internet instead of the public phone network is, for the most part, transparent.

✦ **VoIP PBX systems:** These are PBX systems such as the ones described in Chapter 2, except that they carry the phone traffic over TCP/IP rather than the public telephone system. For more information, see the section "Using a VoIP PBX System" later in this chapter.

Advantages of VoIP

VoIP service has several compelling advantages over traditional telephone service. Here are but a few:

✦ **Long distance calls over VoIP are cheaper than they are over traditional phone service.** With VoIP, you typically pay a fixed monthly rate of $25–$35 for unlimited calls, long distance or not. So if your phone bill currently runs more than $35 per month, you may want to consider VoIP.

✦ **You can take your ATA device with you on the road and use it anywhere that you can plug into the Internet.** For example, you can go on vacation and take your ATA with you. Then, you can plug into the Internet and receive or make calls using your home phone number. (Of course, you don't *have* to take your ATA with you. After all, avoiding calls from your in-laws may be the reason you're going on vacation in the first place.)

✦ **Because calls are carried over the Internet and not over the public switched telephone network, your phone isn't tied to a specific area code.** In fact, VoIP lets you choose any area code you want. For example, if you're a small company located in, say, Fresno, you could get a VoIP service with a 415 area code so your customers will think you're in San Francisco.

TIP

In fact, an enterprising small business in Fresno might set up two VoIP lines, one with a 415 area code and another with a 212 area code. Then, your customers will think you have offices in San Francisco and New York, even though both numbers ring phones in sunny Fresno.

TIP

Choosing an area code other than your real area code isn't always just for looks. Suppose your office is in Fresno, but nearly all of your clients are in San Francisco. Setting up a 415 VoIP number lets your clients dial your number as a local call.

✦ **Most VoIP services have features such as Call Waiting, Call Forwarding, Caller ID, 3-way Calling, Voice Mail, and others as part of the standard package.** These features are usually an additional charge with traditional phone services.

✦ **Although early VoIP services had poor audio quality, modern VoIP is as good as traditional phone service.** In fact, sometimes it's better.

✦ **VoIP services have additional features that you can use if you connect a computer to the ATA device.** For example, some services can send your voice mail messages to an e-mail account as an attachment. Then, you can use Microsoft Outlook or another mail program to listen to your voice mail.

Disadvantages of VoIP

Although VoIP services have many advantages, there are a few disadvantages to consider before you switch your phone service over to VoIP. Here are the most important ones:

✦ **You must have a reliable broadband Internet connection.** If your Internet connection goes down, so will your VoIP phone connection.

✦ **The ATA requires electrical power to work.** As a result, you won't be able to use your VoIP phone during a power outage. In contrast, traditional telephones draw their power directly from the phone lines. That's why traditional phones continue to work even during power outages.

✦ **Although you can take your ATA with you, VoIP isn't really mobile in the same sense as a cell phone.** As a result, you'll probably need a cell phone too.

✦ **911 emergency calls are a bit problematic with VoIP services.** The basic problem with 911 calls is that the 911 system is designed to contact a local emergency dispatcher. Because VoIP services aren't tied to a particular location, you must notify your VoIP provider of your location for 911 to work. If you take your VoIP ATA with you on a trip, forget to notify your provider of your new location, and then dial 911, you'll be connected to emergency services in your hometown, not in your present location.

Popular VoIP Providers

The following list describes several of the more popular providers for VoIP services. If you're thinking of switching to VoIP, you should investigate the following services:

✦ **Vonage:** Vonage is one of the oldest and most popular VoIP providers. For residential customers, you can get an unlimited access plan for $24.95 per month. Or you can get a 500-minute plan for $14.95 per month. For more information, see www.vonage.com.

✦ **AT&T CallVantage:** Not wanting to be left out of the VoIP game, AT&T offers a service called CallVantage. The basic plan for residential customers, with unlimited long distance, costs $24.95 per month. For more information, see www.usa.att.com/callvantage.

✦ **Comcast:** Comcast offers residential VoIP service over its cable network. Typically, this service is combined with cable TV and broadband Internet for one monthly price, in the neighborhood of $135 per month for all three. For more information, see www.comcast.com.

✦ **Verizon VoiceWing:** Verizon is best known for its wireless services, but it also offers a VoIP service called VoiceWing. The basic unlimited service is $24.95 per month, and like Vonage, Verizon offers a 500-minute plan for $19.95 per month. For more information, see www.voicewing.com.

Using a VoIP PBX System

Residential VoIP services usually provide just a few VoIP phones on one or two phone numbers. Other than small mom-and-pop operations, most businesses will require something more, such as a VoIP-based PBX system.

A VoIP PBX consists of the following components:

✦ **A high-speed Internet connection, typically T1 service.**

✦ **An internal TCP/IP network complete with cables and switches.** This can be the same network that services your computers, or it can be a separate network dedicated to the phones.

✦ **IP phones that plug into the network.** You can use special IP-only phones, or you can purchase IP adapters that let you connect regular analog phones to the network.

✦ **The PBX itself, which can be a dedicated hardware device or a software-only PBX system running on a generic computer.**

High-speed Internet connections and TCP/IP networks are covered elsewhere throughout this book, so I won't elaborate on those elements here. In the rest of this section, I'll expand on the other elements: the IP phones and the PBX itself.

IP phones

An IP phone resembles a standard phone, but instead of a standard phone jack, it provides an Ethernet interface that lets you plug the phone into an Ethernet network. Then, the phone uses TCP/IP to communicate via VoIP.

Many manufacturers make IP phones. Figure 4-1 illustrates the D-Link model DPH-140S, which can be purchased for about $135. It offers the following features:

✦ Built-in 10/100 Ethernet port

✦ Speakerphone

✦ Common phone functions including hold, redial, mute, transfer, voice mail, and a 200-entry address book

**Book VI
Chapter 4**

Using VoIP

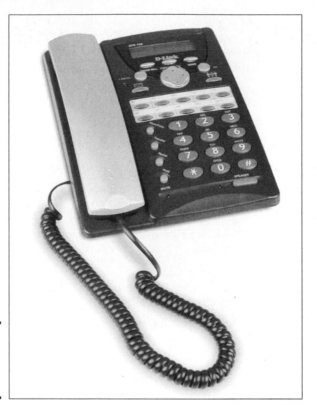

Figure 4-1:
The D-Link
DPH-140S
IP Phone.

Photo courtesy D-Link.

IP PBX

There are several choices available to create an IP-based PBX. One of the most popular is an open-source software program called Asterisk. Here are some things you should know about Asterisk:

✦ **Asterisk is open-source software, which means you don't have to buy it.** Instead, you can download it from www.asterisk.org.

✦ **Asterisk will run on just about any Pentium-based computer.** Many companies run Asterisk on older computers.

✦ **Asterisk runs on Linux, not Windows.** For more information about Linux, refer to Book IX.

For more information about Asterisk, refer to the Asterisk Web site at www.asterisk.org. And pick up a copy of *Asterisk For Dummies* by Stephen P. Olejniczak and Brady Kirby, published by Wiley, of course.

Chapter 5: Managing Mobile Devices

In This Chapter

✓ **Looking at mobile devices**

✓ **Configuring Windows Mobile devices for Exchange access**

✓ **Examining BlackBerrys and BlackBerry Enterprise Server (BES)**

✓ **Considering security implications**

*I*n August of 2003, a computer consultant purchased a used BlackBerry device on eBay for $15.50. When he put in a new battery and turned the device on, he discovered that it contained confidential e-mails and personal contact information for executives of a well known financial institution.

Oops!

It turns out that a former executive with the company sold his old BlackBerry on eBay a few months after he left the firm. He had assumed that because he had removed the battery, everything on the BlackBerry had been erased.

The point of this true story is that mobile devices such as BlackBerrys pose a new set of challenges for network administrators and that these challenges are now being faced even by administrators of small networks. For example, just a few years ago, only large companies had BlackBerrys or other mobile devices that integrated with Exchange e-mail. But now it isn't uncommon for companies with just a few employees to have mobile devices.

This chapter is a brief introduction to mobile devices and the operating systems they run, with an emphasis on Windows Mobile and BlackBerry devices. You'll learn how these devices can interact with Exchange e-mail and the steps you can take to ensure their security.

The Many Types of Mobile Devices

Once upon a time, there were mobile phones and PDAs. A mobile phone was just that — a handheld telephone you could take with you. The good ones had nice features such as a call log, an address book, and perhaps a crude game, but not much else. PDAs — *Personal Digital Assistants* — were handheld computers that were designed to replace the old-fashioned Day Timer books people used to carry around with them to keep track of their appointment calendars and address books.

All that changed a few years ago when cellular providers began adding data capabilities to their networks. Now, cell phones can have complete mobile Internet access. This has resulted in sophisticated PDA features being added to mobile phones and phone features being added to PDAs so that the distinctions are now blurred.

The term *mobile device* is used to describe a wide assortment of devices that you can hold in one hand and that are connected through a wireless network. The term *handheld* is a similar generic name for such devices. The following list describes some of the more common specifics of mobile devices:

✦ **Mobile phone:** A *mobile phone* (or *cell phone*) is a mobile device whose primary purpose is to enable phone service. Most mobile phones include features such as text messaging, address books, appointment calendars, games, and may provide Internet access.

✦ **Smartphone:** A *smartphone* is a mobile phone with advanced features that aren't typically found on mobile phones. There's no clearly drawn line between mobile phones and smartphones. One distinction is whether the phone can provide integrated access to corporate e-mail. The screen on a smartphone is typically bigger than the screen on a traditional cell phone, but the device still resembles a cell phone with a keyboard located beneath the screen.

✦ **Personal Digital Assistant (PDA):** A PDA is a handheld device whose main function is to provide Personal Information Management (PIM) applications such as contact lists, appointment calendars, and e-mail. A typically PDA has a full (albeit small) QWERTY keyboard and a relatively large display. PDAs can also have phone capabilities.

✦ **PocketPC:** A *PocketPC* is a very specific type of handheld that meets a set of specifications published by Microsoft. PocketPCs use a touch screen, so they often do not include a separate keyboard. PocketPCs run the mobile version of Windows, known as *Windows Mobile.*

✦ **BlackBerry:** BlackBerry devices are sophisticated PDAs made by Research In Motion (RIM) with cell phone capabilities. The most distinctive feature of BlackBerrys is their ability to synchronize with Exchange e-mail servers to provide instant access to your corporate e-mail. Typically, this synchronization requires a special server called *BlackBerry Enterprise Server (BES)* running on the corporate network. BlackBerry devices use a proprietary operating system developed by RIM.

Configuring Windows Mobile Devices

Many mobile devices run a special version of Windows known as Windows Mobile. Windows Mobile includes a mobile version of Outlook known as *Outlook Mobile* that has the ability to synchronize in real time with Exchange. The features that accomplish this synchronization are called *Outlook Mobile Access* and *Exchange ActiveSync,* and they are easy to configure. Just follow these steps:

1. **Log in to the Exchange server with an Exchange administrator account.**

2. **Choose Start↪Administrative Tools↪Exchange System Manager.**

3. **In the navigation pane, expand the Global Settings node.**

4. **Right-click Mobile Services, then choose Properties.**

   The dialog box shown in Figure 5-1 appears.

5. **Select all of the check boxes on the General tab.**

   This enables all of the capabilities of Outlook Mobile Access and Exchange ActiveSync.

6. **Click OK.**

7. **Close Exchange System Manager.**

8. **Choose Start↪Administrative Tools↪Active Directory Users and Computers.**

   The Active Directory Users and Computers console opens.

Figure 5-1:
Enabling
Outlook
Mobile
Access.

9. **Expand the domain and locate the user you want to enable mobile access for.**

10. **Right-click the user and choose Properties.**

11. **Click the Exchange Features tab.**

The Exchange Features options are displayed, as shown in Figure 5-2.

12. **Enable all three options listed under Mobile Services.**

If the options are not already enabled, right-click each option and choose Enable.

13. **Click OK.**

14. **Repeat Steps 12 and 13 for any other users you want to enable mobile access for.**

15. **Close Active Directory Users and Computer.**

16. **Test the configuration by opening a browser window and browsing to the address** `http:`*servername*`/oma.`

If everything is configured correctly, you should see a page similar to the one shown in Figure 5-3.

That's all there is to it. After you have enabled these features, any users running Windows Mobile will be able to synchronize their handhelds with their Exchange mailboxes.

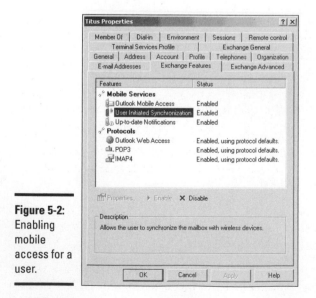

Figure 5-2:
Enabling
mobile
access for a
user.

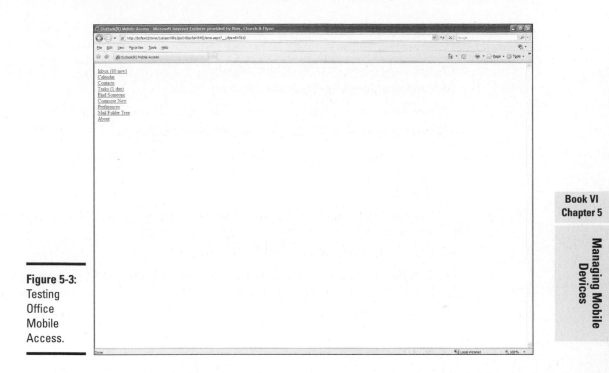

Figure 5-3:
Testing
Office
Mobile
Access.

Configuring BlackBerry Devices

Unfortunately, configuring BlackBerry devices is considerably more difficult than configuring Windows Mobile devices. That's because Microsoft includes support for Windows Mobile devices in Exchange server, but you must use additional software to support BlackBerry devices.

If you have just a few BlackBerry users, you can synchronize their handhelds with Exchange by using a service called *BlackBerry Internet Service,* or *BIS.* BIS is a Web site you log in to and to which you provide the Exchange account information for each of your BlackBerry users. BIS then handles the synchronization for you. In a nutshell, BIS masquerades as an Office Web Access (OWA) user to access the user's Exchange data. It then forwards the data it retrieves via OWA to the BlackBerry.

BIS works surprisingly well, but it isn't instantaneous. The delay between when an e-mail appears in the user's Exchange inbox and when it shows up on the BlackBerry is often 15 minutes or more.

For more timely access, you should install *BlackBerry Enterprise Server,* or *BES,* on a server computer. For small organizations, you can install BES on the same physical server as Exchange. But if you have more than a few dozen BlackBerry users, you're better off using a separate server dedicated to BES.

After you've installed BES, you can use it to manage your BlackBerry users. Figure 5-4 shows the BlackBerry Manager application, which you use to manage your BES administration. From this page, you can configure new BlackBerry users, modify or delete existing users, and perform other tasks required to manage your BlackBerry environment.

Figure 5-4:
The
BlackBerry
Manager
application.

Considering Security for Mobile Devices

As a network administrator, one of your main responsibilities regarding mobile devices is to keep them secure. Unfortunately, that's a significant challenge. Here are some of the reasons why:

✦ **Mobile devices connect to your network via other networks that are out of your control.** You can go to great lengths to set up firewalls, encryption, and a host of other security features. But mobile devices connect via public networks whose administrators may not be as conscientious as you.

✦ **Mobile devices are easy to lose.** A user might leave his or her BlackBerry at a restaurant or hotel, or it might fall out of his pocket on the subway.

✦ **Mobile devices run operating systems that aren't as security-conscious as Windows.**

✦ **Users who wouldn't dare install renegade software on their desktop computers will think nothing of downloading free games or ring tones to their handhelds.** Who knows what kinds of viruses or Trojans these downloads carry?

✦ **Inevitably, someone will buy his own handheld device and connect it to your network without your knowledge or permission.**

Here are some recommendations for beefing up security for your mobile devices:

✦ Establish clear and consistent policies for mobile devices and enforce them.

✦ Make sure employees understand that they are not allowed to bring their own devices into your network. Allow only company-owned devices to connect.

✦ Train your users in the security risks associated with using mobile devices.

✦ Implement antivirus protection for your mobile devices.

**Book VI
Chapter 5**

**Managing Mobile
Devices**

Book VII
Windows Server 2008 Reference

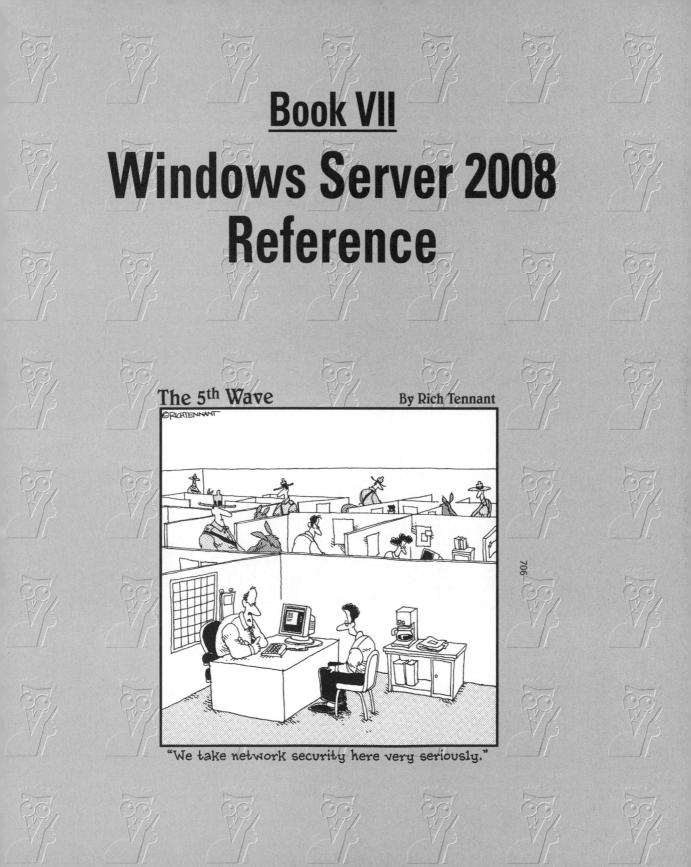

The 5th Wave   By Rich Tennant

"We take network security here very seriously."

Contents at a Glance

Chapter 1: Installing and Configuring Windows Server 2008

In This Chapter

✔ **Making sure you have everything you need**

✔ **Planning how you will install Windows Server 2008**

✔ **Installing Windows Server 2008**

*T*his chapter presents the procedures that you need to follow in order to install Windows Server — specifically, Windows Server 2008. Note that although the specific details provided are for Windows Server 2008, installing Windows Server 2003 is very similar. So you won't have any trouble adapting these procedures if you're installing Windows Server 2003.

Planning a Windows Server Installation

Before you begin the Setup program to actually install a Windows Server operating system, you need to make a number of preliminary decisions, as the following sections describe.

Checking system requirements

Before you install a Windows Server operating system, you should make sure that the computer meets the minimum requirements. Table 1-1 lists the official minimum requirements for Windows Server 2008. (The minimums for Windows Server 2003 are a bit less.) Table 1-1 also lists what I consider to be more realistic minimums if you expect satisfactory performance from the server as a moderately used file server.

Table 1-1	Minimum Hardware Requirements for Windows Server 2008 (Standard Edition)	
Item	*Official Minimum*	*A More Realistic Minimum*
CPU	1G Hz	3 GHz
RAM	512MB	2GB
Free disk space	8GB	80GB

Besides meeting the minimum requirements, you should also make sure that your specific hardware has been checked out and approved for use with Windows Server 2008. Microsoft publishes an official list of supported hardware, called the *Hardware Compatibility List,* or *HCL.* You can find the HCL at `www.microsoft.com/whdc/hcl/default.mspx`.

The Windows Server 2008 distribution DVD includes a feature called the *Check System Compatibility* option that automatically checks your hardware against the HCL.

Reading the release notes

The Windows Server 2008 distribution DVD includes a file called `readme.rtf`, located in the Sources folder. When you open this file, the page shown in Figure 1-1 is displayed. You should read this file before you start Setup, just to check whether any of the specific procedures or warnings it contains apply to your situation.

Figure 1-1:
The
Windows
Server 2008
Readme file.

Deciding whether to upgrade or install

Windows offers two installation modes to choose from: full installation or upgrade installation.

A *full installation* deletes any existing operating system(s) it finds on the computer and configures the new operating system from scratch. If you do a full installation onto a disk that already has an operating system installed, the full installation offers to keep any existing data files that it finds on the disk.

An *upgrade installation* assumes that you already have a previous Windows Server 2003 installation in place. The operating system is upgraded to Windows Server 2008, preserving as many settings from the previous installation as possible.

Here are some points to ponder before you perform an upgrade installation:

✦ You can't upgrade a client version of Windows to a server version.

✦ With an upgrade installation, you don't have to reinstall any applications that were previously installed on the disk.

✦ Always perform a full backup before doing an upgrade installation!

Considering your licensing options

You can purchase Microsoft operating systems on either a per-server or a per-user basis. You need to know which plan you have when you install the operating system.

✦ **Per-user licensing:** In this licensing mode, each client that accesses the server must have a Windows Server license. If your network has 25 users, you need a license that allows for 25 users — one for each client.

✦ **Per-server licensing:** In per-server licensing, the server itself has a license that allows a specific number of concurrent client connections. This is a good choice if you have a large number of users, but only a small number of them use the computer at any given time. For example, if you have a large number of dialup or VPN users, you may want to opt for per-server licensing.

**Book VII
Chapter 1**

Installing and
Configuring
Windows
Server 2008

Thinking about multiboot

Windows includes a *multiboot* feature that lets you set up the computer so that it has more than one operating system. Then, when you boot up the computer, you can select which operating system you want to boot up from a menu.

If you're a software developer or a network manager who needs to make sure that software is compatible with multiple operating systems, the multiboot feature can be useful. For most servers, however, you want to install just one operating system.

A much better alternative to a multiboot installation is to use virtual machine software such as VMware. This software allows you to install a development version of an operating system such as Windows Server 2008 within an already installed operating system. For more information, see www.vmware.com.

Choosing a file system

Windows servers provide three choices for the file system format: FAT, FAT32, and NTFS. In most cases, you should choose NTFS. Well, actually, you should use NTFS in almost *all* cases. Come to think of it, you should *always* use NTFS.

The name *FAT* refers to the *file allocation table,* which was used in the original version of MS-DOS back when disco was still popular. FAT was a simple but effective way to track disk space allocated to files on diskettes and on small hard drives. The original FAT system used 16-bit disk addresses to divide the total space on a disk into 65,526 units, called *clusters,* each of which could be allocated to any file on the disk. The size of each cluster could vary from as little as 2K to as much as 256K, depending on the size of the drive.

When disk drives started to get bigger than 512MB (can you remember when 512MB was a *huge* disk?), FAT was upgraded to FAT32, which used 32-bit addresses for clusters. That allowed a maximum of 524,208 clusters on the disk with the size of each cluster ranging from 4K to 32K, depending on the size of the drive.

FAT32 was a nice improvement over FAT, but both suffer from several inherent problems:

✦ Even with 32-bit addresses, FAT32 is stretched by today's 200GB+ disk drives.

✦ Neither FAT nor FAT32 has built-in security features.

✦ Frankly, FAT and FAT32 are inherently unreliable. Most users, at one time or another, lose files due to the unreliability of FAT/FAT32.

✦ FAT and FAT32 allocate space inefficiently on large volumes because the smallest unit of space that they can allocate must be large — as much as 256K in some cases.

Here are just a few of the reasons why choosing NTFS for Windows servers is a no-brainer:

✦ NTFS has built-in security features that track security information for individual files and directories.

✦ NTFS tracks clusters with 64-bit disk addresses rather than 32-bit addresses (FAT32) or 16-bit addresses (FAT). As a result, an NTFS volume can theoretically have something in the neighborhood of 18 million billion disk clusters, which should keep you going for awhile.

✦ The benefit of having so many clusters available is that the size of each cluster can be kept small. NTFS can efficiently use 4KB clusters for even the largest drives available today.

✦ NTFS drives are more reliable because NTFS keeps duplicate copies of important information, such as the location of each file on the hard drive. If a problem develops on an NTFS drive, Windows can usually correct the problem automatically without losing any data. In contrast, FAT drives are prone to losing data.

✦ The system that FAT uses to keep track of which disk clusters belong to a given file is prone to errors. In contrast, NTFS has more redundancy built into its record keeping, so it's less likely to scramble up your files.

✦ NTFS has better support for large drives and large files. Table 1-2 compares some of the upper limits of the FAT, FAT32, and NTFS file systems.

Table 1-2	File System Limits		
Limit	*FAT*	*FAT32*	*NTFS*
Maximum volume size	4GB	32GB	16TB
Maximum file size	2GB	4GB	16TB
Maximum files per folder	512	65,534	4,294,967,295
Maximum files per volume	65,526	524,208	Too many to count.

Planning your partitions

Partitioning enables you to divide a physical disk into one or more separate units called *partitions*. Each disk can have up to four partitions. All four of the partitions can be *primary partitions,* each of which can be formatted with a different file system, such as NTFS or FAT32. Or you can create up to three primary partitions and one *extended partition,* which can then be subdivided into one or more *logical drives.* Then, each logical drive can be formatted with a file system.

Although you can set up partitions for a Windows server in many ways, the following two approaches are the most common:

✦ **Allocate the entire disk as a single partition that will be formatted with NTFS.** The operating system is installed into this partition, and disk space that isn't needed by the operating system or other network applications can be shared.

✦ **Divide the disk into two partitions.** Install the operating system and any other related software (such as Exchange Server or a backup utility) on the first partition. If the first partition will contain just the operating system, 10GB is a reasonable size, although you can get by with as little as 4GB if space is at a premium. Then, use the second partition for application data or network file shares.

Book VII
Chapter 1

Installing and
Configuring
Windows
Server 2008

Note that the disk partitioning scheme is independent of any hardware-based RAID configuration your server might employ. For example, your server might actually include five physical hard drives that are combined by the hardware disk controller to form a single logical drive. Within this logical drive, you can create one or more operating system partitions.

Deciding your TCP/IP configuration

Before you install the operating system, you should have a plan for how you will implement TCP/IP on the network. Here are some of the things you need to decide or find out:

✦ What is the IP subnet address and mask for your network?

✦ What is the domain name for the network?

✦ What is the host name for the server?

✦ Will the server obtain its address from DHCP?

✦ Will the server have a static IP address? If so, what?

✦ Will the server be a DHCP server?

✦ What is the Default Gateway for the server? (That is, what is the IP address of the network's Internet router?)

✦ Will the server be a DNS server?

If the server will host TCP/IP services (such as DHCP or DNS), you should assign the server a static IP address.

For more information about planning your TCP/IP configuration, see Book IV.

Choosing workgroups or domains

A *domain* is a method of placing user accounts and various network resources under the control of a single directory database. Domains ensure that security policies are consistently applied throughout a network and greatly simplify the task of managing user accounts on large networks.

A *workgroup* is a simple association of computers on a network that makes it easy to locate shared files and printers. Workgroups don't have sophisticated directory databases, so they can't enforce strict security.

Microsoft says that workgroups should be used only for very small networks with just a few users. In fact, any network that is large enough to have a dedicated server running Windows Server 2008 is too large to use workgroups. As a result, if you're installing a Windows server, you should always opt for domains.

After you decide to use domains, you have to make two basic decisions:

✦ **What will the domain name be?** If you have a registered Internet domain name, such as `mydomain.com`, you may want to use it for your network's domain name. Otherwise, you can make up any name you want.

✦ **What computer or computers will be the domain controllers for the domain?** If this is the first server in a domain, you must designate it as a domain controller. If you already have a server acting as a domain controller, you can either add this computer as an additional domain controller or designate it as a *member server.*

You can always change the role of a server from a domain controller to a member server and vice versa if the needs of your network change. If your network has more than one server, it's always a good idea to create at least two domain controllers. That way, if one fails, the other one can take over.

Before You Install . . .

After you've made the key planning decisions for your Windows server installation, you should take a few precautionary steps before you actually start the Setup program. The following sections describe the steps that you should take before you perform an upgrade installation. Note that all these steps except the last one apply only to upgrades. If you're installing a Windows server on a new system, you can skip the first steps.

Backing up

Do a complete backup of the server before you begin. Although Windows Setup is reliable, sometimes something serious goes wrong, and data is lost.

Note that you don't have to back up the drive to external media, such as tape. If you can find a network disk share with enough free space, back up to it.

Checking the event logs

Look at the event logs of the existing server computer to check for recurring errors. You may discover that you have a problem with a SCSI device or your current TCP/IP configuration. Better to find out now rather than in the middle of setup.

**Book VII
Chapter 1**

Installing and
Configuring
Windows
Server 2008

Uncompressing data

If you've used DriveSpace or any other disk compression software to compress a drive, you have to uncompress the drive before you run Setup. Neither Windows 2000 Server nor Windows Server 2008 supports DriveSpace or other disk compression programs.

Disconnecting UPS devices

If you have installed an uninterruptible power supply (UPS) device on the server and connected it to your computer via a serial cable, you should temporarily disconnect the serial cable before you run Setup. After Setup is complete, you can reconnect the serial cable.

Running Setup

Now that you've planned your installation and prepared the computer, you're ready to run the Setup program. The following procedure describes the steps that you must follow in order to install Windows Server 2008 on a new computer that has a bootable DVD drive.

1. **Insert the distribution CD in the DVD drive and restart the computer.**

After a few moments, the Windows Setup Wizard fires up, as shown in Figure 1-2.

Figure 1-2:
Welcome to
Windows
Setup!

2. Click Install Now to start the installation.

The wizard next asks for the product key, which is printed on a sticker attached to the CD case.

3. Enter the 25-character product key and then click Next.

Because the key is so long, it's easy to make a mistake. If Setup complains that the product key is invalid, don't panic. Just try again.

After you input the correct product key, the wizard asks which edition of the operating system you want to install. The options here depend on which version you have purchased. For the Standard Edition, you can choose to install the full Standard Edition server operating system or the Core edition.

4. Select the edition you want to install, and then click Next.

The Setup Wizard displays the License Agreement information. Read it if you enjoy legalese.

5. Click I Accept the License Terms, and then click Next.

The Setup Wizard then asks whether you want to perform an upgrade installation or a full installation.

6. Click the installation option you want to use.

Setup continues by displaying the computer's current partition information. Here, you can select the partition that you want to use for the installation. If necessary, you can reconfigure your partitions from this screen by deleting existing partitions or creating new ones. I assume here that you want to create a single partition that uses all available space on the drive.

7. Select the partition on which you want to install Windows, and then click Next.

Setup now formats the drive and then copies files to the newly formatted drive. This step usually takes awhile. I suggest you bring along your favorite book. Start reading at Chapter 1.

After all the files have been copied, Setup reboots your computer. Then, Setup examines all the devices on the computer and installs any necessary device drivers. You can read Chapter 2 of your book during this time.

When Setup finishes installing drivers, it displays the Initial Configuration Tasks page, as shown in Figure 1-3. You can use this page to perform additional configuration tasks that are required to make your server usable.

**Book VII
Chapter 1**

Installing and Configuring Windows Server 2008

Figure 1-3:
The Initial
Configur-
ation
Tasks page.

In particular, the Initial Configuration Tasks page provides the following capabilities:

- Set the time zone.

- Configure networking.

- Provide the computer name and domain.

- Enable automatic updating.

- Download and install updates.

- Add additional server roles and features.

- Enable remote desktop access.

- Configure the Windows Firewall.

You'll want to work your way through each of these steps. The steps are pretty self-explanatory, and simple wizards help guide you through each task.

You'll find more information about adding additional server roles and features in the next section, "Adding Server Roles and Features."

Adding Server Roles and Features

Server roles refer to the roles that your server can play on your network — roles such as a file server, a Web server, or a DHCP or DNS server. *Features* refer to additional capabilities of the Windows operating system itself, such as the .NET Framework or Windows Backup. Truthfully, the distinctions between roles and features are a bit arbitrary. For example, the Web server is considered a role, but the telnet server is a feature. Go figure.

The Initial Configuration Tasks page that was shown in Figure 1-3 lets you add additional roles or features to your server. After you have finished with the initial configuration of your server, you can choose Start⇨Administrative Tools⇨Server Manager to bring up the Server Manager page, as shown in Figure 1-4. As you can see, this page also provides links that let you add roles or features.

Figure 1-4:
The Server
Manager
page.

Book VII
Chapter 1

Installing and
Configuring
Windows
Server 2008

The following procedure describes how to install server roles. The procedure for installing server features is similar.

1. **Click the Add Roles link either on the Server Manager page or the Initial Server Configuration Tasks page.**

Either way, the Add Roles Wizard appears, as shown in Figure 1-5.

2. **Click Next.**

The Select Server Roles page shown in Figure 1-6 appears. This page lets you select one or more roles to add to your server.

3. **Select one or more roles to install.**

You can click each role to display a brief description of the role. For example, if you click the File Services role, the following text is displayed:

```
File Services provide technologies that help you manage storage, enable
file replication, manage shared folders, ensure fast file searching, and
enable access for UNIX client computers.
```

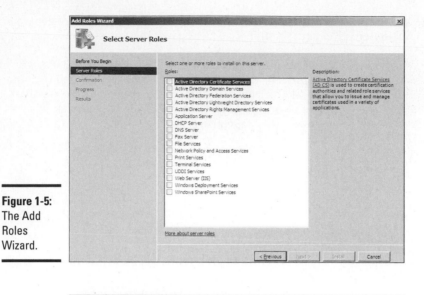

Figure 1-5:
The Add
Roles
Wizard.

Figure 1-6:
The Select
Server
Roles page.

4. Click Next.

Depending on the role or roles you select, an additional page may be displayed asking you to select the role services you want to install. For example, Figure 1-7 shows the Role Services page for the File Services role.

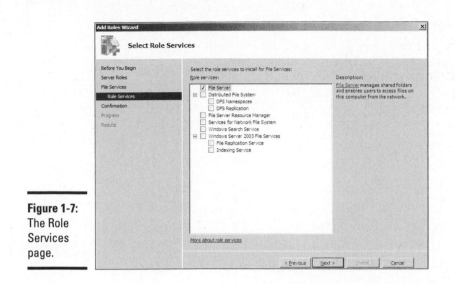

Figure 1-7:
The Role
Services
page.

5. **Select the services you want to install.**

   Again, you can select each service to see a brief text description of the
   service. For example, if you select the Windows Search Services service,
   the following text is displayed:

   ```
   Windows Search Service permits fast file searches on this server from
   clients that are compatible with Windows Search Service. Windows Search
   Service is intended for desktop search or small file server scenarios,
   and not for enterprise scenarios.
   ```

6. **Click Next.**

   A confirmation page appears, listing the roles and services you have
   selected.

7. **Click Install.**

   Windows installs the server role and its services. A progress screen is
   displayed during the installation so you can gauge the installation's
   progress. When the installation finishes, a final results page is displayed.

8. **Click OK.**

   You're done!

**Book VII
Chapter 1**

Installing and
Configuring
Windows
Server 2008

Chapter 2: Managing Windows Server 2008

In This Chapter

↳ **Working with the trusty Administrator account**

↳ **Using Remote Desktop Connection to administer a server from the comfort of your desktop**

↳ **Perusing the list of Microsoft Management Consoles**

↳ **Customizing your own management console**

This chapter provides an introduction to the most important tools that you'll use to administer Windows Server 2008.

Using the Administrator Account

Windows comes with a built-in account named *Administrator* that has complete access to all the features of the server. As a network administrator, you frequently log on using the Administrator account to perform maintenance chores.

Because the Administrator account is so powerful, you should always enforce good password practices for it. In other words, don't use your dog's name as the Administrator account password. Instead, pick a random combination of letters and numbers. Then, change the password periodically.

 Write down the Administrator account password and keep it in a secure location. Note that by "secure location," I don't mean taped to the front of the monitor. Keep it in a safe place where you can retrieve it if you forget it, but where it won't easily fall into the hands of someone looking to break into your network.

Note that you cannot delete or disable the Administrator account. If Windows allowed you to do that, you could potentially find yourself locked out of your own system.

 As much as possible, you should avoid using the Administrator account. Instead, you should create accounts for each of your system administrators and grant them administrator privileges by assigning their accounts to the Administrators group.

Although you can't delete or disable the Administrator account, you can rename it. Some network managers use this ability to hide the true Administrator account. To do this, just follow these steps:

1. **Rename the Administrator account.**

   Write down the new name you use for the Administrator account, along with the password, and store it in a top-secret secure location.

2. **Create a new account named Administrator and assign it a strong password, but don't give this account any significant privileges.**

   This will become a "decoy" Administrator account. The idea is to get hackers to waste time trying to crack this account's password. Even if a hacker does manage to compromise this account, he won't be able to do anything when he gets in.

Using Remote Desktop Connection

One of the most useful tools available to system administrators is a program called *Remote Desktop Connection,* or *RDC* for short. RDC lets you connect to a server computer from your own computer and use it as if you were actually sitting at the server. In short, RDC lets you administer your server computers from your own office.

Enabling remote access

Before you can use Remote Desktop Connection to access a server, you must first enable remote access on the server. To do that, follow these steps (on the server computer, not your desktop computer):

1. **Open the Control Panel, and then double-click System.**

   This brings up the System applet.

2. **Click the Remote tab.**

   This brings up the remote access options, as shown in Figure 2-1.

3. **Select one of the two Allow Connections check boxes.**

   Which one should you select? If you select Allow Connections Only from Computers Running Remote Desktop with Network Level Authentication, you will be able to connect to the server only from clients running Windows Vista. The other option, Allow Connections from Computers Running Any Version of Remote Desktop, will let you connect from Windows XP clients.

4. **Click OK.**

You're done! Repeat this procedure for each server computer you want to allow access to.

System Properties

Computer Name | Hardware | Advanced | Remote

Remote Assistance

☐ Allow Remote Assistance connections to this computer

Advanced...

Remote Desktop

Click an option, and then specify who can connect, if needed.

⊙ Don't allow connections to this computer

○ Allow connections from computers running any version of Remote Desktop (less secure)

○ Allow connections only from computers running Remote Desktop with Network Level Authentication (more secure)

Help me choose   Select Users...

OK   Cancel   Apply

Figure 2-1:
Configuring remote access.

Here are a few other points to ponder concerning remote access:

✦ You can click the Select Users button to create a list of users who are authorized to access the computer remotely. Note that all members of the Administrators group are automatically granted access, so you don't have to add administrators to this list.

✦ There's no question that RDC is convenient and useful. However, it's also inherently dangerous. Don't enable it unless you've also taken precautions to secure your Administrator accounts by using strong passwords; you should also already have a firewall installed to keep unwanted visitors out of your network. For more information on account security, see Book VII, Chapter 6.

Connecting remotely

After you've enabled remote access on a server, you can connect to the server by using the Remote Desktop Client that's automatically installed with Windows XP or Vista. Here is the procedure for Windows XP:

1. **Choose Start⇨All Programs⇨Accessories⇨Communications⇨Remote Desktop Connection.**

The Remote Desktop Connection client comes to life, as shown in Figure 2-2.

2. **Enter the name of the computer you want to connect to.**

Alternatively, you can use the drop-down list to select the computer from the list of available computers.

Figure 2-2:
Connecting
with Remote
Desktop
Connection.

Remote Desktop Connection

Remote Desktop
Connection

Computer: server1

Connect Cancel Help Options >>

3. **Click the Connect button.**

   You're connected to the computer you selected, and the computer's logon screen is displayed.

4. **Log on and use the computer.**

   After you log on, you can use the computer as if you were sitting right in front of it.

Here are a few other tips for working with the Remote Desktop Connection client:

✦ After you're in the Remote Desktop Connection client, you can't just Alt+Tab to another program running on the client computer. Instead, you must first minimize the RDC client's window by clicking its minimize button. Then, you can access other programs running on your computer.

✦ If you minimize the RDC client window, you have to provide your logon credentials again when you return. This is a security feature that's there in case you forget you have an RDC session open.

✦ If you use RDC a lot on a particular computer (such as your own desktop computer), I suggest you create a shortcut to RDC, either on the desktop, at the top of the Start menu, or in the Quick Launch portion of the taskbar.

✦ RDC has several useful configuration options that you can access by clicking the Options button.

Using Microsoft Management Console

Microsoft Management Console, also known as *MMC,* is a general-purpose management tool that's used to administer many different types of objects on a Windows system. Throughout this minibook, you see many examples of MMC for working with objects such as user accounts, disk drives, event logs, and so on. This section provides a general overview of how to use MMC.

By itself, MMC doesn't actually manage anything. Instead, it's a framework that accepts management *snap-ins.* It's the snap-ins that do the actual managing.

The main point of MMC is that it provides a consistent framework for building management snap-ins. That way, the snap-ins all behave in similar ways. As a result, you don't have to struggle to learn completely different tools to manage various aspects of Windows Server 2008.

Another advantage of MMC is that you can create your own custom management consoles with just the right combination of snap-ins. For example, suppose that you spend most of your time managing user accounts, disk devices, IIS (Internet Information Services, the Web server that comes with Windows Server 2008), and studying event logs. You can easily craft a management console with just these four snap-ins. For more information, see the section, "Customizing MMC," later in this chapter.

Working with MMC

There are several ways to open a Microsoft Management Console window. The easiest is to open one of the predefined consoles that comes with Windows Server 2008. These consoles are available from the Start⇨Administrative Tools menu.

You can also start MMC from a command prompt or from the Run dialog box (opened by choosing Start⇨Run). To start MMC without opening a snap-in, just type **mmc** at a command prompt or in the Run dialog box. To open a specific console, type the path to the console file after mmc. For example, the following command opens the Computer Management console:

```
mmc \Windows\System32\compmgmt.msc
```

Figure 2-3 shows a typical Microsoft Management Console window, displaying the Active Directory Users and Computers snap-in. As you can see, the MMC window consists of two panes. The pane on the left is a tree pane that displays a hierarchical tree of the objects that you can manage. The pane on the right is a details pane that shows detailed information about the object that's selected in the tree pane.

The procedures for working with the information in the Details pane vary depending on the console you're viewing. However, most of the consoles display a list of some kind, such as a list of settings or a list of user accounts. Double-clicking an item usually brings up a properties box that lets you view or set properties for the object. In most cases, you can click the column headings at the top of the list to change the order in which the list items are displayed.

MMC also includes a menu and toolbar with commands and buttons that vary depending on the item selected in the tree. In particular, the Action menu contains commands that apply to the current item. For example, the Action menu includes a New User command when you're working with the Active

Directory Users and Computers console and a Defragment command when you view the Disk Defragmenter item in the Computer Management Console. As you work with different items within the different consoles, be sure to check the Action menu frequently to find out what commands are available.

Figure 2-3: A typical MMC window.

An overview of the MMC consoles

The Start⇨Administrative Tools menu gives you direct access to many useful management consoles. You find detailed descriptions of several of these tools later in this minibook. The following paragraphs give you a brief overview of the most important of these consoles:

✦ **Active Directory Domains and Trusts:** Manages the domains and trusts relationships for the server.

✦ **Active Directory Sites and Services:** Manages Active directory services.

✦ **Active Directory Users and Computers:** This is the console where you create and modify user accounts.

✦ **Certification Authority:** If you have configured your server to act as a Certificate Authority, you can use this console to manage certificate services.

✦ **Cluster Administrator:** This console is available only on Windows Server 2008 Enterprise Server. It lets you manage clustering, which allows several servers to work together as a single unit.

✦ **Component Services:** This console lets you manage how COM+ (Component Object Model) services work on the server. You mess with this console only if you're involved in developing applications that use

COM+ services.

✦ **Computer Management:** This console provides access to several useful tools for managing a server. In particular, the Computer Management console provides the following management tools:

- *Event Viewer:* Lets you view event logs.

- *Shared Folders:* Lets you manage shared folders for a file server. In addition to finding out what shares are available, you can use this tool to find out what users are connected to the server and what files are open.

- *Local Users and Groups:* This tool is available only on servers that are not domain controllers. It lets you manage local user and group accounts. For a domain controller, you use the Active Directory Users and Computers console to manage user accounts.

- *Performance Logs and Alerts:* Use this tool to monitor system performance counters.

- *Device Manager:* This tool lets you manage the hardware devices connected to a server. You'll probably use it only if you're having a problem with the server that you suspect may be hardware related.

- *Removable Storage:* You can use this tool to manage removable storage devices such as CD-ROM drives and tape drives.

- *Disk Defragmenter:* This tool lets you defragment the server's disks.

- *Disk Management:* This console tool lets you view the physical disks and volumes that are available to the system. You can also use this tool to create and delete partitions, set up RAID volumes, format disks, and so on.

- *Services:* This tool lets you manage system services. You can use this tool to start or stop services such as Exchange e-mail services, TCP/IP services such as DNS and DHCP, and so on.

- *WMI Control:* This tool lets you configure *Windows Management Instrumentation services,* which are used to track management data about computers, users, applications, and other objects in large Enterprise networks.

- *Indexing Service:* The Indexing Service is a service that dynamically builds indexes to make searching for documents easier. Although these indexes are useful, keeping them constantly up to date can consume a lot of system resources, thus slowing down the server. As a result, many administrators disable this service to improve the server's performance.

- *Telephony:* This console lets you configure telephony services if you've enabled them on the server.

✦ **Data Sources (ODBC):** Manages database connections that use ODBC. You'll probably use this console only if you're a developer or database administrator.

✦ **DHCP:** Manages the DHCP server.

✦ **Distributed File System:** Manages Distributed File System, which lets you create the appearance of a single disk file structure from multiple shares that may be located on different drives and even different servers.

✦ **DNS:** Manages the DNS server.

✦ **Domain Controller Security Policy:** Lets you set security policy for a domain controller.

✦ **Domain Security Policy:** Lets you set security policies that apply to an entire domain.

✦ **Event Viewer:** Lets you view event logs.

✦ **Group Policy Management:** Lets you set system policies that can be applied to objects such as users and groups.

✦ **Health Monitor:** Displays a console that lets you monitor the health of the server.

✦ **Internet Information Services (IIS) Manager:** If IIS (Microsoft's Web server) is installed on the server, this console lets you manage the services it provides.

✦ **Performance:** This console lets you monitor a server's performance and twiddle with various settings that can have a positive or negative effect on performance.

✦ **Routing and Remote Access:** This console lets you manage *Routing and Remote Access Services,* also known as *RRAS.* The first *R* in *RRAS* refers to routing, which essentially lets you configure Windows Server 2008 to function as a router. The *RAS* in *RRAS* refers to setting up the server so that remote clients can access it via dialup lines or VPN connections.

✦ **Server Management:** The Server Management console is a general-purpose console that combines several of the most commonly used management consoles for specific server roles, such as file servers, Web servers, and so on.

✦ **Services:** This console lets you start and stop Windows services. (It's also available via the Computer Management console.)

Customizing MMC

One of the best things about Microsoft Management Console is that you can customize it so that the tools you use most often are grouped together in whatever combination you choose. To create a custom console, first start Microsoft Management Console without loading a console by choosing Start⇨Run, typing **mmc** in the Open text box, and clicking OK or pressing Enter. This creates an empty console, as shown in Figure 2-4.

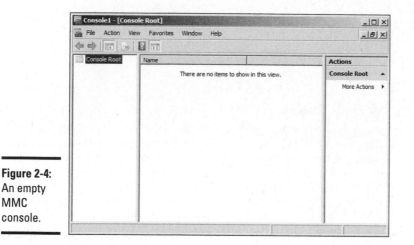

Figure 2-4:
An empty
MMC
console.

**Book VII
Chapter 2**

**Managing Windows
Server 2008**

Adding snap-ins

After you've created an empty console, you can customize it by adding whatever snap-ins you want to make use of in the console. To add a snap-in, follow these steps:

1. **Choose File⇨Add/Remove Snap-In.**

This brings up the Add/Remove Snap-In dialog box, shown in Figure 2-5.

2. **Select the snap-in you want to add, and then click the Add button.**

Depending on which snap-in you select, a dialog box will appear asking if you want to use the add-in to manage settings on your own computer or on a local computer.

3. **Repeat Step 2 if you want to add other snap-ins to the console.**

4. **Click OK.**

The console is now equipped with the snap-ins you've selected.

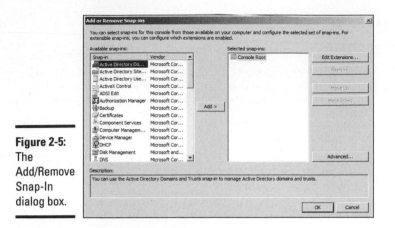

Figure 2-5:
The
Add/Remove
Snap-In
dialog box.

Adding taskpads

A *taskpad* is a customized page that's displayed within a console. Taskpads are designed to provide quick access to the most common chores for a particular snap-in. A taskpad can display shortcuts that run programs, execute menu commands, open Web pages, or open folders. For example, Figure 2-6 shows a simple taskpad that I created for managing local user accounts. As you can see, it includes icons that let you quickly add an account, delete an account, and change an account's password.

Figure 2-6:
A taskpad
for
managing
user
accounts.

To add a taskpad, follow these steps:

1. **Select the tree node where you want the taskpad to appear.**

Each taskpad you create is specific to a tree node. For example, the taskpad shown in Figure 2-6 is displayed only when you select a user account. To create this taskpad, I opened the Local Users and Groups node and selected the Users node.

2. **Choose Action⇨New Taskpad View.**

This brings up the New Taskpad View Wizard, as shown in Figure 2-7.

3. **Click Next.**

The Taskpad Display page appears, as shown in Figure 2-8.

Figure 2-7:
The New
Taskpad
View
Wizard.

Figure 2-8:
Setting the
display
options for a
new
taskpad
page.

This page provides the following options for formatting the taskpad display:

- *Vertical List:* If you want to include the list from the details page, you can select this option to place taskpad icons to the left of the list. This is the option I selected for the taskpad shown in Figure 2-6.

- *Horizontal List:* This option places the taskpad icons beneath the details page list.

- *No List:* This option creates a task pad with no list, just task icons.

- *Hide Standard Tab:* Each taskpad can have a standard view, which simply lists all of the items in the taskpad without showing custom tasks. The Hide Standard Tab checkbox, which is checked by default, hides this tab. Most of the time, you'll want to leave this checkbox checked.

- *Text:* This option displays descriptive information beneath each taskpad icon.

- *InfoTip:* This option displays descriptive information as a pop-up tip that appears when you hover the mouse over the icon.

- *List Size:* This drop-down list lets you select how much of the taskpad area should be devoted to the list. The options are Small, Medium, or Large.

It's a good thing this wizard wasn't designed by a fast food company. If it was, the options for List Size would be Large, Extra Large, and MegaSuperKing.

4. Select the taskpad options you want, and then click Next.

The next page of the wizard presents two options that let you control when the taskpad should be displayed. The choices are:

- *Selected Tree Item:* The taskpad will be displayed only for the specific tree item that you selected in Step 1.

- *All Tree Items That Are the Same Type as the Selected Item:* The taskpad will be displayed not only for the selected tree item, but also for other items of the same type. This is the more common option.

5. Select the taskpad display option, and then click Next.

The next page of the wizard asks for a name and description for the taskpad.

6. **Type a name and description for the taskpad, and then click Next.**

The final page of the New Taskpad View Wizard is displayed, as shown in Figure 2-9.

7. **Select the Add New Tasks to This Taskpad After the Wizard Closes checkbox, and then click Finish.**

This completes the New Taskpad View Wizard but automatically launches the New Task Wizard so that you can begin adding tasks to the task pad. The New Task Wizard begins by displaying a typical greeting page.

Figure 2-9: The final page of the New Taskpad View Wizard.

8. **Click Next.**

The page shown in Figure 2-10 is displayed. This page lets you select one of three types of shortcuts to create on the taskpad:

- *Menu Command:* This option lets you choose one of the console's menu commands. All three of the shortcuts shown in the taskpad in Figure 2-6 are menu commands.

- *Shell Command:* Lets you run another program, start a batch file, or open a Web page.

- *Navigation:* Lets you go to one of the views you've added to the Favorites menu. (If you want to add shortcuts that navigate to different taskpads in a console, first add each taskpad view to your Favorites menu by navigating to the taskpad and choosing Favorites⇨Add to Favorites.)

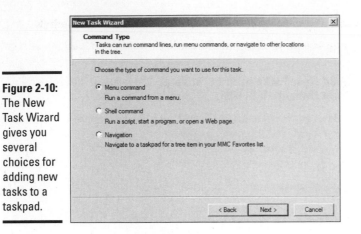

Figure 2-10:
The New Task Wizard gives you several choices for adding new tasks to a taskpad.

9. **Choose the type of shortcut command you want to create, and then click Next.**

   The page that's displayed next depends on which option you selected in Step 8. The rest of this procedure assumes you selected the Menu Command option, which displays the page shown in Figure 2-11.

10. **Choose the command you want to use, and then click Next.**

    The available commands are listed in the Available Commands list box. Note that you can bring up several different lists of available commands by choosing an option in the Command Source drop-down list.

    When you click Next, the wizard asks for a name and description for the command you've selected.

Figure 2-11:
Choosing a menu command for a taskpad shortcut.

11. **Enter a name and description for the command, and then click Next.**

This brings up the page shown in Figure 2-12.

Figure 2-12:
Selecting an
icon.

12. **Choose the icon you want to use, and then click Next.**

Note that in many cases, the New Task Wizard suggests an appropriate icon. For example, if you select a Delete command, the standard Delete icon will be selected.

When you click Next, the final page of the wizard is displayed, as shown in Figure 2-13.

13. **If you want to create additional tasks, select the When I Click Finish, Run This Wizard Again check box, and then click Finish and repeat Steps 8 through 13.**

You can run the wizard as many times as necessary to add tasks to your taskpad.

14. **When you're finished adding tasks, deselect the When I Click Finish, Run This Wizard Again check box and click Finish.**

You're done!

**Book VII
Chapter 2**

**Managing Windows
Server 2008**

Figure 2-13:
The final
page of the
New Task
Wizard.

Here are a few other pointers for working with taskpads:

✦ You can edit an existing taskpad by selecting the tree node that displays
the taskpad and choosing Action➪Edit Taskpad View. This brings up a
Properties dialog box that lets you change the taskpad layout options
and add or remove tasks.

✦ To delete a taskpad, select the tree node that displays the taskpad and
choose Action➪Delete Taskpad View.

✦ Don't forget to save (File➪Save) often while you're creating custom
taskpads.

Chapter 3: Dealing with Active Directory

In This Chapter

✔ Discovering directories

✔ Examining how Active Directory is structured

✔ Setting up a domain controller

✔ Creating organizational units

A ctive Directory is among the most important features of Windows Server 2008, and much of your time as a network administrator will be spent keeping Active Directory neat and tidy. In Chapter 4 of this minibook, I discuss the details of working with the most common and troublesome types of Active Directory objects, users and groups. But first, this chapter lays some foundation by explaining what Active Directory is and how it works.

What Directories Do

Everyone uses directory services of one type or another every day. When you look up someone's name in a phone book, you're using a directory service. But you're also using a directory service when you make a call: When you enter someone's phone number into your touch-tone phone, the phone system looks up that number in its directory to locate that person's phone.

Almost from the very beginning, computers have had directory services. I remember when I first got started in the computer business back in the 1970s, using IBM mainframe computers and a transaction-processing system called CICS that is still in widespread use today. CICS relied on many different directories to track such things as files available to the system, users that were authorized to access the system, and application programs that could be run.

But the problem with this directory system, and with most other directory systems until recently, is that it was made up of many small directory systems that didn't know how to talk to each other. I have the very same problem at home. We have our own little personal address book that has phone numbers and addresses for our friends and family. And I have a Day-Timer book with a bunch of other phone numbers and addresses. Then I have a church directory that lists everyone who goes to my church. Oh, and there's the list of players on the softball team I coach. And of course, my cell phone has a directory.

All counted, I probably have a dozen sources for phone numbers that I routinely call. So when I need to look up someone's phone number, I first have to decide which directory to look in. And, of course, some of my friends are listed in two or three of these sources, which raises the possibility that their listings might be out of synch.

That's exactly the type of problem that Active Directory is designed to address. Before I get into the specifics of Active Directory, however, I show you the directory system that Microsoft used on Windows networks before Active Directory became available.

Remembering the Good-Ol' Days of NT Domains

Active Directory was introduced with Windows 2000 Server. Before then, the directory management system in a Windows network was managed by Windows NT *domains,* which stored directory information in a database called the Security Account Manager (SAM) database.

PDCs and BDCs

The most important thing to know about NT domains is that they are *server-centric.* That is, every Windows NT domain is under the control of a Windows NT server computer that hosts the primary copy of the SAM database. This server is called the *Primary Domain Controller,* or *PDC.*

Of course, large networks couldn't work efficiently if all directory access had to be channeled through a single computer. To solve that bottleneck problem, Windows NT domains can also be serviced by one or more *Backup Domain Controllers,* or *BDCs.* Each BDC stores a read-only copy of the SAM database, and any changes made to the SAM database on the PDC must be propagated down to the BDC copies of the database.

Note that although any of the BDC servers can service access requests such as user logons, all changes to the SAM database must be made via the PDC. Then, those changes are copied to the BDC servers. Naturally, this raises the possibility that the PDC and BDC database can get out of synch.

If the PDC should fail for some reason, one of the BDCs can be *promoted* so that it becomes the PDC for the domain. This allows the domain to continue to function while the original PDC is repaired. Because the BDC is an important backup for the PDC, it's important that all NT networks have at least one BDC.

Trusts

Many organizations have directory needs that are too complicated to store on just one NT domain PDC. In that case, the organization can create two or more separate domains for its network, each with its own PDC and BDCs. Then, the organization can set up trusts among its domains.

Simply put, a *trust* is a relationship in which one domain trusts the directory information stored in another domain. The domain that does the trusting is called — you guessed it — the *trusting domain,* while the domain that contains the information being trusted is called the *trusted domain.*

Trust relationships work in one direction. For example, suppose you have two domains, named DomainA and DomainB, and a trust relationship is set up so that DomainA trusts DomainB. That means that users whose accounts are defined in DomainB can log on to DomainA and access resources. However, the trust relationship doesn't work in the other direction: Users in DomainA can't log on and access resources defined in DomainB.

Also, trust relationships are not *transitive.* (There's a word that takes you back to high school algebra.) That means that even if DomainA trusts DomainB and DomainB trusts DomainC, DomainA does not automatically trust DomainC. For DomainA to trust DomainC, you'd have to create a separate trust relationship between DomainA and DomainC.

NetBIOS names

One other important characteristic of Windows NT domains is that they use NetBIOS names. Thus, NT names such as computer names and domain names are limited to 15 characters.

Actually, NetBIOS names are 16 characters long. But NT uses the last character of the 16-character NetBIOS name for its own purposes, so that character isn't available for use. As a result, NT names can be only 15 characters long.

Active Directory to the Rescue

Active Directory solves many of the inherent limitations of Windows NT domains by creating a distributed directory database that keeps track of every conceivable type of network object.

Active Directory is a comprehensive directory management system that tracks just about everything worth tracking in a Windows network, including users, computers, files, folders, applications, and much more. Much of your job as a network administrator involves working with Active Directory. So it's vital that you have a basic understanding of how it works.

One of the most important differences between Active Directory and NT domains is that Active Directory is not server-centric. In other words, Active Directory isn't tied to a specific server computer the way a Windows NT domain is. Although Active Directory still uses domains and domain controllers, these concepts are much more flexible in Active Directory than they are in Windows NT.

Another important difference between Active Directory and NT domains is that Active Directory uses the same naming scheme that's used on the Internet: Domain Name Service (DNS). Thus, an Active Directory domain might have a name like `sales.mycompany.com`.

Understanding How Active Directory Is Structured

Like all directories, Active Directory is essentially a database management system. The Active Directory database is where the individual objects tracked by the directory are stored. Active Directory uses a *hierarchical* database model, which groups items in a tree-like structure.

The terms *object, organizational unit, domain, tree,* and *forest* are used to describe the way Active Directory organizes its data. The following sections explain the meaning of these important Active Directory terms.

Objects

The basic unit of data in Active Directory is called an *object*. Active Directory can store information about many different kinds of objects. The objects you work with most are users, groups, computers, and printers.

Figure 3-1 shows the Active Directory Manager displaying a list of built-in objects that come preconfigured with Windows Server 2008. To get to this management tool, choose Start➪Administrative Tools➪Active Directory Users and Computers. Then click the Builtin node to show the built-in objects.

Objects have descriptive characteristics called *properties* or *attributes*. You can call up the properties of an object by double-clicking the object in the management console.

Figure 3-1:
Objects
displayed by
Active
Directory
Manager
console.

Domains

A *domain* is the basic unit for grouping related objects in Active Directory. Typically, domains correspond to departments in a company. For example, a company with separate Accounting, Manufacturing, and Sales departments might have domains named (you guessed it) `Accounting`, `Manufacturing`, and `Sales`. Or the domains correspond to geographical locations. For example, a company with offices in Detroit, Dallas, and Denver might have domains named `det`, `dal`, and `den`.

Note that because Active Directory domains use DNS naming conventions, you can create subdomains that are considered to be child domains. You should always create the top-level domain for your entire network before you create any other domain. For example, if your company is named Nimbus Brooms and you've registered `NimbusBroom.com` as your domain name, you should create a top-level domain named `NimbusBroom.com` before you create any other domains. Then, you can create subdomains such as `Accounting.NimbusBroom.com`, `Manufacturing.Nimbus Broom.com`, and `Sales.NimbusBroom.com`.

If you have Microsoft Visio, you can use it to draw diagrams for your Active Directory domain structure. Visio includes several templates that provide cool icons for various types of Active Directory objects. For example, Figure 3-2 shows a diagram that shows an Active Directory with four domains created with Visio.

Book VII
Chapter 3

Dealing with
Active Directory

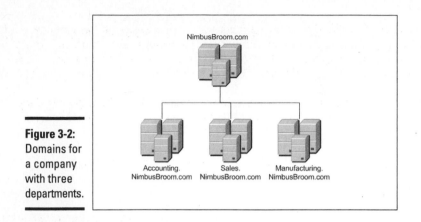

Figure 3-2:
Domains for
a company
with three
departments.

Note that these domains have little to do with the physical structure of your network. In Windows NT, domains usually are related to the network's physical structure.

Every domain must have at least one *domain controller,* which is a server that's responsible for the domain. However, unlike a Windows NT PDC, an Active Directory domain controller doesn't have unique authority over its domain. In fact, a domain can have two or more domain controllers that share administrative duties. A feature called *replication* works hard at keeping all the domain controllers in sync with each other.

Organizational units

Many domains have too many objects to manage all together in a single group. Fortunately, Active Directory lets you create one or more *organizational units,* also known as *OUs.* OUs let you organize objects within a domain, without the extra work and inefficiency of creating additional domains.

One reason to create OUs within a domain is so that you can assign administrative rights to each OU to different users. Then, these users can perform routine administrative tasks such as creating new user accounts or resetting passwords.

For example, suppose the domain for the Denver office, named den, houses the Accounting and Legal departments. Rather than create separate domains for these departments, you could create organizational units for the departments.

Trees

A *tree* is a set of Active Directory names that share a common namespace. For example, the domains `NimbusBroom.com`, `Accounting.NimbusBroom.com`, `Manufacturing.NimbusBroom.com`, and `Sales.NimbusBroom.com` make up a tree that is derived from a common root domain, `NimbusBroom.com`.

The domains that make up a tree are related to each other through *transitive trusts*. In a transitive trust, if DomainA trusts DomainB and DomainB trusts DomainC, then DomainA automatically trusts DomainC.

Note that a single domain all by itself is still considered to be a tree.

Forests

As its name suggests, a *forest* is a collection of trees. In other words, a forest is a collection of one or more domain trees that do *not* share a common parent domain.

For example, suppose Nimbus Brooms acquires Tracorum Technical Enterprises, which already has its own root domain named `Tracorum Tech.com`, with several subdomains of its own. Then, you can create a forest from these two domain trees so the domains can trust each other. Figure 3-3 shows this forest.

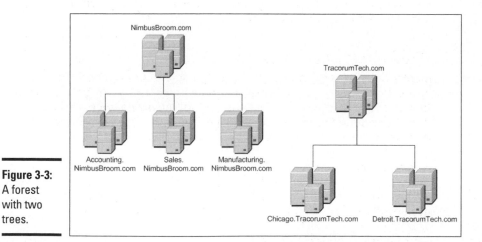

Figure 3-3: A forest with two trees.

The key to Active Directory forests is a database called the global catalog. The *global catalog* is sort of a super-directory that contains information about all of the objects in a forest, regardless of the domain. Then, if a user account can't be found in the current domain, the global catalog is searched for the account. The global catalog provides a reference to the domain in which the account is defined.

Creating a Domain

To create a domain, you start by designating a Windows Server 2008 system to be the new domain's controller. You can do that by using the Configure Your Server Wizard as described in Chapter 1 of this minibook. This wizard is automatically started when you first install Windows Server 2008. However, you can start it at any time by choosing Start⇨Administrative Tools⇨Configure Your Server.

From the Configure Your Server Wizard, select Domain Controller (Active Directory) to start the Active Directory Installation Wizard. This wizard lets you create a new domain by choosing the Domain Controller for a New Domain option. You can also create a new forest or create the new domain in an existing forest.

The Active Directory Installation Wizard asks for a name for the new domain. If you're creating the first domain for your network, use your company's domain name, such as `NimbusBroom.com`. If you're creating a subdomain, use a name such as `Sales.NimbusBroom.com`.

Creating an Organizational Unit

Organizational units can simplify the task of managing large domains by dividing users, groups, and other objects into manageable collections. By default, Active Directory domains include several useful OUs. For example, the Domain Controllers OU contains all of the domain controllers for the domain.

If you want to create additional organizational units to help manage a domain, follow these steps:

1. **Choose Start⇨Administrative Tools⇨Active Directory Users and Computers.**

The Active Directory Users and Computers console appears, as shown in Figure 3-4.

Figure 3-4:
The Active
Directory
Users and
Computers
console.

2. **Right-click the domain you want to add the OU to and choose**
   New⇨Organizational Unit.

   The New Object — Organizational Unit dialog box appears, as shown in
   Figure 3-5.

3. **Type a name for the new organization unit.**

4. **Click OK.**

   You're done!

Figure 3-5:
Creating a
new
organiza-
tional unit.

Here are just a few more thoughts about OUs to ponder as you drift off to sleep:

✦ You can delegate administrative authority for an OU to another user by right-clicking the OU and choosing Select Delegate Control. Then you can select the user or group that will have administrative authority over the OU. You can also choose which administrative tasks will be assigned to the selected user or group.

✦ Remember that OUs are not the same as groups. *Groups* are security principals, which means that you can assign them rights. Then, when you assign a user to a group, the user is given the rights of the group. In contrast, an OU is merely an administrative tool that lets you control how user and group accounts are managed.

✦ For more information about how to create user and group accounts as well as other Active Directory objects, turn to the next chapter.

Chapter 4: Managing Windows User Accounts

In This Chapter

✔ Understanding user accounts

✔ Creating user accounts

✔ Setting account options

✔ Working with groups

✔ Creating a roaming profile

*E*very user who accesses a network must have a *user account*. User accounts let you control who can access the network and who can't. In addition, user accounts let you specify what network resources each user can use. Without user accounts, all your resources would be open to anyone who casually dropped by your network.

Understanding Windows User Accounts

User accounts are one of the basic tools for managing a Windows server. As a network administrator, you'll spend a large percentage of your time dealing with user accounts — creating new ones, deleting expired ones, resetting passwords for forgetful users, granting new access rights, and so on. Before I get into the specific procedures of creating and managing user accounts, this section presents an overview of user accounts and how they work.

Local accounts versus domain accounts

A *local account* is a user account that's stored on a particular computer and applies only to that computer. Typically, each computer on your network will have a local account for each person who uses that computer.

In contrast, a *domain account* is a user account that's stored by Active Directory and can be accessed from any computer that's a part of the domain. Domain accounts are centrally managed. This chapter deals primarily with setting up and maintaining domain accounts.

User account properties

Every user account has a number of important *account properties* that specify the characteristics of the account. The three most important account properties are

✦ **Username:** A unique name that identifies the account. The user must enter the username when logging on to the network. The username is public information. In other words, other network users can (and often should) find out your username.

✦ **Password:** A secret word that must be entered in order to gain access to the account. You can set up Windows so that it enforces password policies, such as the minimum length of the password, whether the password must contain a mixture of letters and numerals, and how long the password remains current before the user must change it.

✦ **Group membership:** The group or groups to which the user account belongs. Group memberships are the key to granting access rights to users so that they can access various network resources, such as file shares or printers or to perform certain network tasks, such as creating new user accounts or backing up the server.

Many other account properties record information about the user, such as the user's contact information, whether the user is allowed to access the system only at certain times or from certain computers, and so on. I describe some of these features in later sections of this chapter, and some are described in more detail in Chapter 6 of this minibook.

Creating a New User

To create a new domain user account in Windows Server 2008, follow these steps:

1. **Choose Start⇨Administrative Tools⇨Active Directory Users and Computers.**

This fires up the Active Directory Users and Computers management console, as shown in Figure 4-1.

2. **Right-click the domain that you want to add the user to and then choose New⇨User.**

This summons the New Object — User Wizard, as shown in Figure 4-2.

3. **Type the user's first name, middle initial, and last name.**

As you type the name, the New Object Wizard automatically fills in the Full Name field.

Figure 4-1:
The Active Directory Users and Computers management console.

Figure 4-2:
Creating a new user.

4. **Change the Full Name field if you want it to appear differently than proposed.**

For example, you may want to reverse the first and last names so the last name appears first.

5. **Type the user logon name.**

This name must be unique within the domain.

Pick a naming scheme to follow when creating user logon names. For example, use the first letter of the first name followed by the complete last name, the complete first name followed by the first letter of the last name, or any other scheme that suits your fancy.

6. Click Next.

The second page of the New Object — User Wizard appears, as shown in Figure 4-3.

Figure 4-3:
Setting the
user's
password.

7. Type the password twice.

You're asked to type the password twice, so type it correctly. If you don't type it identically in both boxes, you're asked to correct your mistake.

8. Specify the password options that you want to apply.

The following password options are available:

- User must change password at next logon.
- User cannot change password.
- Password never expires.
- Account is disabled.

For more information about these options, see the section "Setting account options," later in this chapter.

9. Click Next.

You're taken to the final page of the New Object — User Wizard, as shown in Figure 4-4.

Figure 4-4:
Verifying the
user
account
information.

10. **Verify that the information is correct and then click Finish to create the account.**

    If the account information is not correct, click the Back button and correct the error.

    You're done! Now you can customize the user's account settings. At a minimum, you'll probably want to add the user to one or more groups. You may also want to add contact information for the user or set up other account options.

Setting User Properties

After you've created a user account, you can set additional properties for the user by right-clicking the new user and choosing Properties. This brings up the User Properties dialog box, which has about a million tabs that you can use to set various properties for the user. Figure 4-5 shows the General tab, which lists basic information about the user, such as the user's name, office location, phone number, and so on.

The following sections describe some of the administrative tasks that you can perform via the various tabs of the User Properties dialog box.

**Book VII
Chapter 4**

**Managing Windows
User Accounts**

Figure 4-5:
The General
tab.

Changing the user's contact information

Several tabs of the User Properties dialog box contain contact information
for the user:

+ **Address:** Lets you change the user's street address, post office box, city,
  state, zip code, and so on.

+ **Telephones:** Lets you specify the user's phone numbers.

+ **Organization:** Lets you record the user's job title and the name of his or
  her boss.

Setting account options

The Account tab of the User Properties dialog box, shown in Figure 4-6,
features a variety of interesting options that you can set for the user. From
this dialog box, you can change the user's logon name. In addition, you can
change the password options that you set when you created the account
and set an expiration date for the account.

The following account options are available in the Account Options list box:

+ **User must change password at next logon:** This option, which is selected
  by default, allows you to create a one-time-only password that can get
  the user started with the network. The first time the user logs on to the
  network, he or she is asked to change the password.

Figure 4-6:
The
Account
tab.

+ **User cannot change password:** Use this option if you don't want to allow users to change their passwords. (Obviously, you can't use this option and the previous one at the same time.)

+ **Password never expires:** Use this option if you want to bypass the password expiration policy for this user so that the user will never have to change his or her password.

+ **Store password using reversible encryption:** This option stores passwords using an encryption scheme that hackers can easily break, so you should avoid it like the plague.

+ **Account is disabled:** This option allows you to create an account that you don't yet need. As long as the account remains disabled, the user won't be able to log on. See the section "Disabling and Enabling User Accounts," later in this chapter, to find out how to enable a disabled account.

+ **Smart card is required for interactive logon:** If the user's computer has a smart card reader to automatically read security cards, check this option to require the user to use it.

+ **Account is trusted for delegation:** This option indicates that the account is trustworthy and can set up delegations. This is an advanced feature that's usually reserved for administrator accounts.

+ **Account is sensitive and cannot be delegated:** Prevents other users from impersonating this account.

✦ **Use DES encryption types for this account:** Beefs up the encryption for applications that require extra security.

✦ **Do not require Kerberos preauthentication:** Select this option if you use a different implementation of the Kerberos protocol.

Specifying logon hours

You can restrict the hours during which the user is allowed to log on to the system by clicking the Logon Hours button from the Account tab of the User Properties dialog box. This brings up the Logon Hours for [User] dialog box, shown in Figure 4-7.

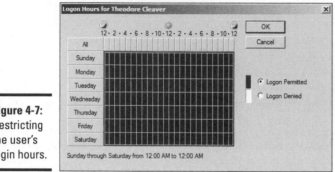

Figure 4-7: Restricting the user's login hours.

Initially, the Logon Hours dialog box is set to allow the user to log on at any time of day or night. To change the hours that you want the user to have access to, click a day and time or a range of days and times and choose either Logon Permitted or Logon Denied.

Restricting access to certain computers

Normally, a user can use his or her user account to log on to any computer that's a part of the user's domain. However, you can restrict a user to certain computers by clicking the Logon To button on the Account tab of the User Properties dialog box. This brings up the Logon Workstations dialog box, as shown in Figure 4-8.

To restrict the user to certain computers, select the radio button labeled The Following Computers. Then, for each computer you want to allow the user to log on from, type the computer's name in the text box and click Add.

If you make a mistake, you can select the incorrect computer name and either click Edit to change the name or click Remove to delete the name.

Figure 4-8:
Restricting
the user to
certain
computers.

Setting the user's profile information

The Profile tab, shown in Figure 4-9, lets you configure the user's profile information. This dialog box lets you configure three bits of information related to the user's profile:

✦ **Profile Path:** This field specifies the location of the user's roaming profile. For more information, see the section "User Profiles," later in this chapter.

Figure 4-9:
The Profile
tab.

✦ **Logon Script:** This is the name of the user's logon script. A *logon script* is a batch file that's run whenever the user logs on. The main purpose of the logon script is to map the network shares that the user requires access to. Logon scripts are a carryover from the early versions of Windows NT Server. In Windows Server 2008, profiles are the preferred way to configure the user's computer when the user logs on, including setting up network shares. However, many administrators still like the simplicity of logon scripts. For more information, see the section "Creating a Logon Script" later in this chapter.

✦ **Home Folder:** This is where you specify the default storage location for the user.

The Profile tab lets you specify the location of an existing profile for the user, but it doesn't actually let you set up the profile. For more information about setting up a profile, see the section "User Profiles," later in this chapter.

Resetting User Passwords

By some estimates, the single most time-consuming task of most network administrators is resetting user passwords. It's easy to just think users are forgetful idiots, but put yourself in their shoes. We insist that they set their passwords to something incomprehensible, such as 94kD82leL384K, that they change it a week later to something more unmemorable, such as dJUQ63DWd8331, and that they don't write it down. Then we get mad when they forget their passwords.

So when a user calls and says he or she forgot his or her password, the least we can do is be cheerful when we reset it for them. After all, they've probably already spent 15 minutes trying to remember it before they finally gave up and admitted failure.

Here's the procedure to reset the password for a user domain account:

1. **Log on as an administrator.**

   You must have administrator privileges in order to perform this procedure.

2. **Choose Start⇨Administrative Tools⇨Active Directory Users and Computers.**

   The Active Directory Users and Computers management console appears.

3. **Click Users in the console tree.**

4. **In the Details pane, right-click the user who forgot his or her password and choose Reset Password.**

5. **Type the new password in both password boxes.**

   You have to type the password twice to ensure that you type it correctly.

6. **If desired, select the User Must Change Password at Next Logon option.**

   If you select this option, the password that you assign will work for only one logon. As soon as the user logs on, he or she will be required to change the password.

7. **Click OK.**

   That's all there is to it! The user's password is now reset.

Disabling and Enabling User Accounts

If you want to temporarily prevent a user from accessing the network, you can disable his or her account. Then you can enable the account later, when you're ready to restore the user to full access. Here's the procedure:

1. **Log on as an administrator.**

   You must have administrator privileges to perform this procedure.

2. **Choose Start⇨Administrative Tools⇨Active Directory Users and Computers.**

   The Active Directory Users and Computers management console appears.

3. **Click Users in the console tree.**

4. **In the Details pane, right-click the user that you want to enable or disable. Then choose either Enable Account or Disable Account to enable or disable the user.**

Deleting a User

Deleting a user account is surprisingly easy. Just follow these steps:

1. **Log on as an administrator.**

   You must have administrator privileges in order to perform this procedure.

2. **Choose Start⇨Administrative Tools⇨Active Directory Users and Computers.**

   The Active Directory Users and Computers management console appears.

3. **Click Users in the console tree.**

4. **In the details pane, right-click the user that you want to delete and then choose Delete.**

   Windows asks whether you really want to delete the user, just in case you're kidding.

5. **Click Yes.**

   Poof! The user account is deleted.

Working with Groups

A *group* is a special type of account that represents a set of users who have common network access needs. Groups can dramatically simplify the task of assigning network access rights to users. Rather than assigning access rights to each user individually, groups let you assign rights to the group itself. Then, those rights automatically extend to any user that you add to the group.

The following sections describe some of the key concepts that you need to understand in order to use groups and some of the most common procedures you'll employ when setting up groups for your server.

Group types

Two distinct types of groups exist:

✦ **Security groups:** Most groups are security groups, which extend access rights to members of the group. For example, if you want to allow a group of users to access your high-speed color laser printer, you can create a group called ColorPrintUsers. Then, you can grant permission to use the printer to the ColorPrintUsers group. Finally, you can add individual users to the ColorPrintUsers group.

✦ **Distribution groups:** Distribution groups aren't used as much as security groups. They're designed as a way to send e-mail to a group of users by specifying the group as the recipient.

Group scope

Three distinct group scopes exist:

✦ **Domain local:** A group with *domain local scope* can have members from any domain. However, the group can be granted permissions only from the domain in which the group is defined.

✦ **Global:** A group with *global scope* can have members only from the domain in which the group is defined. However, the group can be granted permissions in any domain in the forest. (For more information about forests, refer to Chapter 3 of this minibook.)

✦ **Universal scope:** Groups with *universal scope* are available in all domains that belong to the same forest.

As you can probably guess, universal scope groups are usually found only on very large networks.

One common way you can use domain local and global groups is as follows:

1. **Use domain local groups to assign access rights for network resources.**

For example, to control access to a high-speed color printer, create a domain local group for the printer. Grant the group access to the printer, but don't add any users to the group.

2. **Use global groups to associate users with common network access needs.**

For example, create a global group for users who need to access color printers. Then, add each user who needs access to a color printer membership to the group.

3. **Finally, add the global group to the domain local group.**

That way, access to the printer will be extended to all members of the global group.

This technique gives you the most flexibility when your network grows.

Default groups

Windows Server 2008 comes with a number of predefined groups that you can use. Although you shouldn't be afraid to create your own groups when you need them, there's no reason to create your own group if you find a default group that meets your needs.

Some of these groups are listed in the Builtin container in the Active Directory Users and Computers management console. Others are found in the Users container. Table 4-1 lists the more useful default groups found in Builtin, while Table 4-2 lists the default groups found in the Users container.

Table 4-1   **Default Groups Located in the Builtin Container**

Group	Description
Account Operators	This group is for users who should be allowed to create, edit, or delete user accounts but shouldn't be granted full administrator status.
Administrators	These are the system administrators who have full control over the domain. The Administrator account is a default member of this group. You should create only a limited number of accounts that belong to this group.
Backup Operators	This group is for users who need to perform backup operations. Because this group must have access to the files that are backed up, it presents a security risk. So you should limit the number of users that you add to this group.
Guests	This group allows members to log on, but little else. The default Guest account is a member of this group.
Network Configuration	This group is allowed to twiddle with network configuration settings, including releasing and renewing DHCP leases.
Print Operators	This group grants users access to printers, including the ability to create and share new printers and manage print queues.
Remote Desktop Users	This group can remotely log on to domain controllers in the domain.
Replicator	This group is required to support directory replication. Don't add users to this group.
Server Operators	These users can log on locally to a domain controller.
Users	These users can perform common tasks, such as running applications and using local and network printers.

Table 4-2   **Default Groups Located in the Users Container**

Group	Description
Cert Publishers	These users can publish security certificates for users and computers.
DnsAdmins	This group is installed if you install DNS. It grants administrative access to the DNS Server service.
DnsUpdateProxy	This group is installed if you install DNS. It allows DNS clients to perform dynamic updates on behalf of other clients, such as DHCP servers.

Group	Description
Domain Admins	These users have complete control of the domain. By default, this group is a member of the Administrators group on all domain controllers, and the Administrator account is a member of this group.
Domain Computers	This group contains all computers that belong to the domain. Any computer account created becomes a member of this group automatically.
Domain Controllers	This group contains all domain controllers in the domain.
Domain Guests	This group contains all domain guests.
Domain Users	This group contains all domain users. Any user account created in the domain is added to this group automatically.
Group Policy	These users can modify Group Policy for the domain.
IIS_WPG	This group is created if you install IIS. It is required in order for IIS to operate properly.
RAS and IAS Servers	This group is required in order for RAS and IAS servers to work properly.

Creating a group

If none of the built-in groups meets your needs, you can create your own group by following these steps:

1. **Log on as an administrator.**

You must have administrator privileges to perform this procedure.

2. **Choose Start⇨Administrative Tools⇨Active Directory Users and Computers.**

The Active Directory Users and Computers management console appears.

3. **Right-click the domain to which you want to add the group and then choose New⇨Group.**

The New Object — Group dialog box appears, as shown in Figure 4-10.

4. **Type the name for the new group.**

Enter the name in both text boxes.

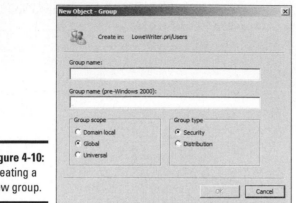

Figure 4-10:
Creating a
new group.

5. Choose the group scope.

The choices are Domain Local, Global, and Universal. For groups that will be granted access rights to network resources, choose Domain Local. Use Global for groups to which you'll add users and Domain Local groups. Use Universal groups only if you have a large network with multiple domains.

6. Choose the group type.

The choices are Security and Distribution. In most cases, choose Security.

7. Click OK.

The group is created.

Adding a member to a group

Groups are collections of objects, called *members*. The members of a group can be user accounts or other groups. When you create a group, it has no members. As a result, the group isn't useful until you add at least one member.

Follow these steps to add a member to a group:

1. Log on as an administrator.

You must have administrator privileges to perform this procedure.

2. Choose Start⇨Administrative Tools⇨Active Directory Users and Computers.

The Active Directory Users and Computers management console appears.

3. **Open the folder that contains the group to which you want to add members and then double-click the group.**

The Group Properties dialog box appears.

4. **Click the Members tab.**

The members of the group are displayed, as shown in Figure 4-11.

Figure 4-11:
Adding
members to
a group.

5. **Type the name of a user or other group that you want to add to this group and then click Add.**

The member is added to the list.

6. **Repeat Step 5 for each user or group that you want to add.**

Keep going until you've added everyone!

7. **Click OK.**

That's all there is to it.

The Group Properties dialog box also has a Member Of tab that lists each group that the current group is a member of.

Adding members to a group is only half the process of making a group useful. The other half is adding access rights to the group so that the members of the group can actually *do* something. The procedures for doing that are covered in the next chapter.

User Profiles

User profiles automatically maintain desktop settings for Windows users. By default, user profiles are stored on each user's local computer. The following items are just some of the settings that are stored as part of the user profile:

✦ Desktop settings in the Display Properties dialog box, including wallpaper, screen savers, and color schemes.

✦ Start menu programs and Windows toolbar options.

✦ Favorites, which provide easy access to the files and folders that the user accesses frequently.

✦ Application Data, such as option settings, custom dictionaries, and so on.

✦ Cookies, used for Internet browsing.

✦ My Recent Documents, which keeps shortcuts to the documents most recently accessed by the user.

✦ Templates, which stores user templates.

✦ Network Neighborhood, which keeps shortcuts to the user's network locations.

✦ Send To, which keeps shortcuts to document-handling utilities.

✦ Local Settings, such as history and temporary files.

✦ Printers, which keeps shortcuts to the user's printers.

✦ My Documents.

Types of user profiles

Four types of user profiles exist:

✦ **Local user profile:** A *local user profile* is stored on the user's local computer and is applied only when the user logs on to that computer. A local user profile is created automatically when a new user logs on.

✦ **Roaming user profile:** A *roaming user profile* is created on a network share. That way, the user can access the roaming profile when he or she logs on to any computer on the network.

✦ **Mandatory user profile:** A *mandatory user profile* is a roaming user profile that the user is not allowed to change. One benefit of mandatory user profiles is that users can't mess up their desktop settings. Another is that you can create a single mandatory profile that can be used by multiple users.

✦ **Temporary user profile:** If a roaming or mandatory profile is not available for some reason, a *temporary user profile* is automatically created for the user. The temporary profile is deleted when the user logs off, so any changes that the user makes while using a temporary profile are lost at the end of the session.

Creating a roaming profile

A *roaming user profile* is simply a user profile that has been copied to a network share so that it can be accessed from any computer on the network.

Before you can create roaming user profiles, you should create a shared folder on the server to hold the profiles. You can name the shared folder anything you like, but most administrators call it Users. For information on the procedure to create a shared folder, see Chapter 3 of this minibook.

After you've created the shared Users folder, you can copy the profile to the server by following these steps at the user's local computer:

1. **Log on to the computer by using an account other than the one you want to make a user account.**

   Windows won't let you copy the profile that you're logged on with.

2. **Open the Control Panel and then double-click the System icon.**

3. **Click the Advanced tab and then click the Settings button in the User Profile section.**

   This step brings up the User Profiles dialog box shown in Figure 4-12.

Figure 4-12: The User Profiles dialog box.

4. **Select the profile that you want to copy and then click Copy To.**

   A Copy To dialog box appears.

5. **Type the path and name for the roaming profile in the Copy Profile To box.**

   For example, to copy a profile named Doug to the User share on a server named Server01, type **\\Server01\Users\Doug**.

6. **Click OK.**

   The profile is copied.

Now, you can go back to the server, log on as an administrator, and follow these steps to designate a roaming profile for the user's domain account:

1. **Choose Start➪Administrative Tools➪Active Directory Users and Computers.**

   The Active Directory Users and Computers management console appears.

2. **Right-click the user account and choose Properties.**

   The User Properties dialog box appears.

3. **Click the Profile tab.**

   The Profile tab appears. This tab was shown in Figure 4-9, so I won't repeat it again here.

4. **Type the path and name of the profile in the Profile Path text box.**

   The path and name that you type here should be the same path and name that you used to copy the profile to the server.

5. **Click OK.**

Creating a Logon Script

A *logon script* is a batch file that's run automatically whenever a user logs on. The most common reason for using a logon script is to map the network shares that the user needs access to. For example, here's a simple logon script that maps three network shares:

```
echo off
net use m: \\server1\shares\admin
net use n: \\server1\shares\mktg
net use o: \\server2\archives
```

Here, two shares on server1 are mapped to drives M and N, and a share on server2 is mapped as drive O.

If you want, you can use the special variable %username% to get the user's username. This is useful if you've created a folder for each user and you want to map a drive to each user's folder. For example:

```
net use u: \\server1\users\%username%
```

For example, if a user logs on with the username dlowe, drive U is mapped to \\server1\users\dlowe.

Scripts should be saved in the Scripts folder, which is buried deep in the bowels of the SYSVOL folder — typically, c:\Windows\SYSVOL\Sysvol\ *domainname*\Scripts, where *domainname* is your domain name. Because you frequently need to access this folder, I suggest creating a shortcut to it on your desktop.

After you've created a logon script, you can assign it to a user by using the Profile tab of the User Properties dialog box. For more information, see the section "Setting the user's profile information" earlier in this chapter.

**Book VII
Chapter 4**

**Managing Windows
User Accounts**

Chapter 5: Managing a File Server

*I*n this chapter, you discover how to set up and manage file and print servers Windows Server 2008. Because the features for file and print servers are essentially the same for both operating systems, the techniques presented in this chapter should work for either system.

Understanding Permissions

Before I get into the details of setting up a file server, you need to have a solid understanding of the concept of permissions. *Permissions* allow users to access shared resources on a network. Simply sharing a resource such as a disk folder or a printer doesn't guarantee that a given user is able to access that resource. Windows makes this decision based on the permissions that have been assigned to various groups for the resource and group memberships of the user. If the user belongs to a group that has been granted permission to access the resource, the access is allowed. If not, access is denied.

In theory, permissions sound pretty simple. In practice, however, they can get pretty complicated. The following paragraphs explain some of the nuances of how access control and permissions work:

✦ Every object — that is, every file and folder — on an NTFS volume has a set of permissions called the *Access Control List,* or *ACL,* associated with it.

✦ The ACL identifies the users and groups who can access the object and specifies what level of access each user or group has. For example, a folder's ACL may specify that one group of users can read files in the folder, while another group can read and write files in the folder, and a third group is denied access to the folder altogether.

✦ Container objects — files and volumes — allow their ACLs to be inherited by the objects that they contain. As a result, if you specify permissions for a folder, those permissions extend to the files and child folders that appear within it.

✦ Table 5-1 lists the six permissions that can be applied to files and folders on an NTFS volume.

Table 5-1	File and Folder Permissions
Permission	*Description*
Full control	The user has unrestricted access to the file or folder.
Modify	The user can change the file or folder's contents, delete the file or folder, read the file or folder, or change the attributes of the file or folder. For a folder, this permission allows you to create new files or subfolders within the folder.
Read & Execute	For a file, this permission grants the right to read or execute the file. For a folder, this permission grants the right to list the contents of the folder or to read or execute any of the files in the folder.
List Folder Contents	This permission applies only to folders; it grants the right to list the contents of the folder.
Write	Grants the right to change the contents of a file or its attributes. For a folder, grants the right to create new files and subfolders within the folder.
Read	Grants the right to read the contents of a file or folder.

✦ Actually, the six file and folder permissions comprise various combinations of *special permissions* that grant more detailed access to files or folders. Table 5-2 lists the special permissions that apply to each of the six file and folder permissions.

✦ It's best to assign permissions to groups rather than to individual users. Then, if a particular user needs access to a particular resource, add that user to a group that has permission to use the resource.

Table 5-2	Special Permissions					
Special Permission	*Full Control*	*Modify*	*Read & Execute*	*List Folder Contents*	*Read*	*Write*
Traverse Folder/ Execute File	✔	✔	✔	✔		
List Folder/ Read Data	✔	✔	✔	✔	✔	

Special Permission	Full Control	Modify	Read & Execute	List Folder Contents	Read	Write
Read Extended Attributes	✓	✓	✓	✓	✓	
Create Files/ Write Data	✓	✓				✓
Create Folders/ Append Data	✓	✓				✓
Write Attributes	✓	✓				✓
Write Extended Attributes	✓	✓				✓
Delete Sub- folders and Files	✓					
Delete	✓	✓				
Read Permissions	✓	✓	✓	✓	✓	✓
Change Permissions	✓					
Take Ownership	✓					
Synchronize	✓	✓	✓	✓	✓	✓

Understanding Shares

A *share* is simply a folder that is made available to other users via the network. Each share has the following elements:

+ **Share name:** The name by which the share is known over the network. To be compatible with older computers, you should stick to eight-character share names whenever possible.

+ **Path:** The path to the folder on the local computer that's being shared, such as C:\Accounting.

+ **Description:** A one-line description of the share.

+ **Permissions:** A list of users or groups who have been granted access to the share.

When you install Windows and configure various server roles, special shared resources are created to support those roles. You shouldn't disturb these special shares unless you know what you're doing. Table 5-3 lists some of the more common special shares.

Table 5-3	Special Shares
Share Name	*Description*
drive$	The root directory of a drive.
ADMIN$	Used for remote administration of a computer. This share points to the operating system folder (usually, C:\Windows).
IPC$	Used by named pipes, a programming feature that lets processes communicate with one another.
NETLOGON	Required in order for domain controllers to function.
SYSVOL	Another required domain controller share.
PRINT$	Used for remote administration of printers.
FAX$	Used by fax clients.

Notice that some of the special shares end with a dollar sign ($). These shares are *hidden shares* that aren't visible to users. However, you can still access them by typing the complete share name (including the dollar sign) when the share is needed. For example, the special share C$ is created to allow you to connect to the root directory of the C: drive from a network client. You wouldn't want your users to see this share, would you? (Of course, shares such as C$ are also protected by privileges so that if an ordinary user finds out that C$ is the root directory of the server's C: drive, he or she still can't access it.)

Configuring the File Server Role

To use Windows Server 2003 or 2008 as a file server, you must first enable the file server role. In Windows Server 2003, you can do so by running Manage Your Server (choose Start⇨Administrative Tools⇨Manage Your Server). Then, choose Add or Remove a Role and select the File Server role. In Windows Server 2008, choose Start⇨Administrative Tools⇨Server Management, choose Roles, then enable the File Services role.

Managing Your File Server

Windows Server 2008 includes a useful new management console called Share and Storage Management, as shown in Figure 5-1. From this console, you can easily create new shares, set up the permissions for a share, remove a share, and so on. To summon the File Server Manager, choose Start⇨ Administrative Tools⇨Share and Storage Management.

Figure 5-1:
The Share and Storage Management console.

The following sections describe some of the more common procedures that you'll use when managing your file server.

Using the Provision a Shared Folder Wizard

To be useful, a file server should offer one or more *shares* — folders that have been designated as publicly accessible via the network. You can see a list of the current shares available from a file server by firing up the File Server Manager and clicking Shares in the console tree. The Share and Storage Management console displays the share name, description, and network path for each share that you've already created.

To create additional shares, use the Provision a Shared Folder Wizard, as described in the following procedure.

1. **In the Share and Storage Management console, choose Provision Share.**

The opening screen of the Provision a Shared Folder Wizard appears, as shown in Figure 5-2. Here, the wizard asks you what folder you want to share.

Figure 5-2:
The
Provision a
Shared
Folder asks
what folder
you want to
share.

2. **Type the path of the folder that you want to share over the network and then click Next.**

If you aren't sure of the path, you can click Browse. This action calls up a dialog box that lets you search the server's hard drive for a folder to share. You can also create a new folder from this dialog box if the folder that you want to share doesn't yet exist. After you've selected or created the folder to share, click OK to return to the wizard.

Next, the dialog box shown in Figure 5-3 appears.

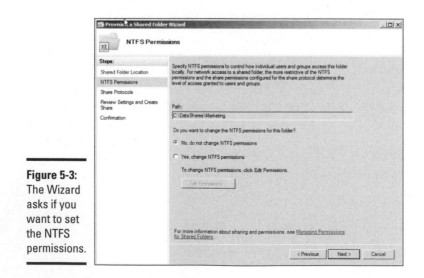

Figure 5-3:
The Wizard
asks if you
want to set
the NTFS
permissions.

3. Change the NTFS Permissions if you want, then click Next.

The NTFS permissions are the permissions that are applied to the folder that you are sharing, not to the share itself. If you want to change the underlying NTFS permissions for the folder you are sharing, click Edit Permissions and set the permissions the way you want. Otherwise, click Next to proceed to the next step. The Wizard displays the dialog box shown in Figure 5-4, which lets you set the name this share will be known by.

Figure 5-4:
Specifying
the share
name.

**Book VII
Chapter 5**

Managing a
File Server

4. Type the name that you want to use for the share in the Share Name box and type a description of the share in the Description box.

The default name is the name of the folder being shared. If the folder name is long, you can use a more succinct name here.

The description is strictly optional but can sometimes help users determine the intended contents of the folder.

Windows Server 2008 includes the ability to share files using the Unix NFS file protocol. If you have enabled NFS sharing on this computer, this dialog box also lets you set the sharing information for NFS.

5. Click Next.

The dialog box shown in Figure 5-5 appears.

Figure 5-5:
Entering a
description
for the
share.

6. **Enter a description for the share, then click Next.**

The dialog box shown in Figure 5-6 appears.

Figure 5-6:
Setting the
share
permissions.

7. Select the sharing permissions you want to impose.

You have four choices:

- **All users have read-only access.** Use this option to share information that you want everyone to have access to, but you don't want to allow anyone to change the information.

- **Administrators have full control, everyone else has read-only access.**

- **Administrators have full control, and everyone else has read/write access.**

- **Custom permissions:** When you select this option, you can then click the Permissions button to set custom permissions.

8. Click Next.

The dialog box shown in Figure 5-7 appears.

**Book VII
Chapter 5**

Figure 5-7:
Joining a
Distributed
File System
network.

Managing a
File Server

9. If you have set up a Distributed File System (DFS) namespace and want to connect this share to it, check the Public button.

DFS is a system that lets you combine two or more separate file shares under a single name. Its purpose is to simplify the management of large file server networks, so it is typically used only on networks that have a large number of file servers.

If you've never heard of DFS until now, skip this step.

10. **Click Next.**

The dialog box shown in Figure 5-8 appears.

11. **Verify that all the settings are correct, then click Next.**

The share is created, and a final confirmation dialog box is displayed, as shown in Figure 5-9.

Figure 5-8:
Joining a Distributed File System network.

Figure 5-9:
You're done!

Sharing a folder without the wizard

If you think wizards should be confined to *Harry Potter* movies, you can set up a share without bothering with the wizard. Just follow these steps:

1. **Open the My Computer window and navigate to the folder that you want to share.**

2. **Right-click the folder and choose Properties.**

   This action brings up the Properties dialog box for the folder.

3. **Click the Sharing tab.**

   The Sharing tab comes to the front, as shown in Figure 5-10.

4. **Click the Advanced Sharing button.**

   The dialog box shown in Figure 5-11 appears.

5. **Select the Share This Folder option to designate the folder as shared.**

   The rest of the controls on this dialog box will be unavailable until you check this box.

6. **Type the name that you want to use for the share in the Share Name box and type a description of the share in the Description box.**

   The default name is the name of the folder being shared. If the folder name is long, you can use a more succinct name here.

   The description is strictly optional but can sometimes help users determine the intended contents of the folder.

Figure 5-10:
Manually
sharing a
folder.

Figure 5-11:
Setting the
share name.

7. If you want to specify permissions now, click Permissions.

This brings up a dialog box that lets you create permissions for the share. For more information, see the next section, "Granting permissions."

8. Click OK.

The folder is now shared.

Granting permissions

When you first create a file share, all users are granted read-only access to the share. If you want to allow users to modify files in the share or allow them to create new files, you need to add additional permissions. Here's how to do this via the Share and Storage Management console:

1. Choose Start➪Administrative Tools➪Share and Storage Management.

The Share and Storage Management console appears.

2. Right-click the share you want to set permissions for, choose Properties, and then click the Permissions tab.

The dialog box shown in Figure 5-12 appears. This dialog box lets you set the permissions for the share itself or the NTFS permissions for the folder being shared.

3. Click Share Permissions.

The dialog box shown in Figure 5-13 appears. This dialog box lists all the users and groups to whom you've granted permission for the folder. When you select a user or group from the list, the check boxes at the bottom of the list change to indicate which specific permissions you've assigned to each user or group.

Figure 5-12:
Setting
permissions.

Figure 5-13:
Setting the
Share
Permissions.

4. **Click Add.**

The dialog box shown in Figure 5-14 appears.

5. **Type the name of the user or group to whom you want to grant permission and then click OK.**

You return to the Share Permissions tab, with the new user or group added.

Figure 5-14:
The Select
Users,
Computers,
and Groups
dialog box.

Select Users, Computers, or Groups	? X
Select this object type:	
Users, Groups, or Built-in security principals	Object Types...
From this location:	
LoweWriter.pri	Locations...
Enter the object names to select (examples):	
	Check Names
Advanced...	OK	Cancel

If you're not sure of the name, click Advanced. This action brings up the Select Users, Computers, and Groups dialog box shown. Then, you can click the Find Now button to display a list of all users and groups in the domain.

Alternatively, you can enter the first part of the name that you're looking for before you click Find Now to search more specifically. When you find the user or group that you're looking for, click OK.

6. **Check the appropriate Allow or Deny check boxes to specify which** permissions to allow for the user or group.

7. **Repeat Steps 3 through 5 for any other permissions that you want to add.**

8. **When you're done, click OK.**

Here are a few other thoughts to ponder concerning adding permissions:

✦ If you want to grant full access to everyone for this folder, don't bother adding another permission. Instead, select the Everyone group and then check the Allow box for each permission type.

✦ You can remove a permission by selecting the permission and then clicking Remove.

✦ If you'd rather not fuss with the Share and Storage Management console, you can set the permissions from My Computer. Right-click the shared folder and choose Sharing and Security and then click Permissions. You can then follow the preceding procedure, picking up at Step 4.

✦ The permissions assigned in this procedure apply only to the share itself. The underlying folder can also have permissions assigned to it. If that's the case, whichever of the restrictions is more restrictive always applies. For example, if the Share Permissions grant a user Full Control permission, but the folder permission grants the user only Read permission, the user has only Read permission for the folder.

Chapter 6: Using Group Policy

In This Chapter

✔ **Looking at group policy concepts**

✔ **Enabling group policy on a Windows Server**

✔ **Editing group policy objects**

*G*roup policy refers to a feature of Windows operating systems that lets you control how certain aspects of Windows and other Microsoft software work throughout your network. Many features that you might expect to find in a management console such as Active Directory Users and Computers are controlled instead by group policy. For example, you must use group policy to control how often users must change their passwords and how complicated their passwords must be. As a result, group policy is an important tool for any Windows network administrator.

Unfortunately, group policy can be a confusing beast. In fact, it's one of the more confusing aspects of Windows network administration. So don't be put off if you find this chapter more confusing than other chapters in this section. Group policy becomes clear after you spend some time actually working with it.

Understanding Group Policy

Here it is in a nutshell: Group policy consists of a collection of *group policy objects* (also called *GPOs*) that define individual policies. These policy objects are selectively applied to both users and computers. Each policy object specifies how some aspect of Windows or some other Microsoft software should be configured. For example, a group policy object might specify the home page that's initially displayed when any user launches Internet Explorer. Then, when a user logs in to the domain, that policy object is retrieved and applied to the user's Internet Explorer configuration.

Group policy objects can apply to either computers or users. A policy that applies to a computer will be enforced for any user of the computer. And a policy that applies to a user will be enforced for that user no matter what computer he or she logs on to. As a network administrator, you'll be mostly concerned with policies that apply to users. But computer policies are useful from time to time as well.

To use group policy, you have to know how to do two things: (1) create individual group policy objects, and (2) apply — or *link* — those objects to user and computer objects. Both tasks can be a little tricky.

The trick to creating group policy objects is finding the particular setting you want to employ. Trying to find a specific group policy among the thousands of available policies can be frustrating. For example, suppose you want to force all network users to change their passwords every 30 days. You know there is a group policy that controls the password expiration date. But where is it? You'll find help with this aspect of working with group policy in the section titled "Creating Group Policy Objects," later in this chapter.

After you've created a group policy object, you then are faced with the task of linking it to the users or computers you want it to apply to. Creating a policy that applies to all users or computers is simple enough. But things get more complicated if you want to be more selective — for example, if you want the policy to apply only to users in a particular organizational unit (OU) or to users that belong to a particular group. You'll find help for this aspect of working with group policy in the section "Filtering Group Policy Objects," later in this chapter.

Enabling Group Policy Management on Windows Server 2008

Before you can work with group policy on a Windows Server 2008, you must enable group policy on the server. The procedure is simple enough and needs to be done only once for each server. Here are the steps:

1. **Choose Start⇨Administrative Tools⇨Server Manager.**

2. **Click Features in the console tree.**

3. **Click Add Features.**

   Be patient — it takes a few minutes for the list of features to populate. Eventually, the dialog box shown in Figure 6-1 appears.

4. **Select the Group Policy Management check box and then click Next.**

5. **When the confirmation page appears, click Install.**

   Be patient again — it may take a few minutes to install.

6. **Click Close — you're done!**

After you've completed this procedure, a new command titled Group Policy Management appears on the Start⇨Administrative Tools menu. You use this command to create and link Group Policy objects.

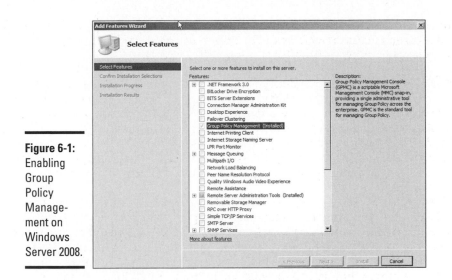

Figure 6-1:
Enabling
Group
Policy
Manage-
ment on
Windows
Server 2008.

Creating Group Policy Objects

The easiest way to create group policy objects is to use the Group Policy Management Console, which you can run by clicking Start, and then choosing Administrative Tools⇨Group Policy Management.

A single group policy object can consist of one or many individual group policy settings. The Group Policy Management Console presents the thousands of group policy settings that are available for your use in several categories. The more you work with group policy, the more these categories will begin to make sense. When you first get started, you can expect to spend a lot of time hunting through the lists of policies to find the specific one you're looking for.

The easiest way to learn how to use the Group Policy Management Console is to use it to create a simple group policy object. In the following procedure, I'll show you how to create a GPO that defines a group policy that sets the browser's home page to www.dummies.com.

1. **Choose Start⇨Administrative Tools⇨Group Policy Management.**

The Group Policy Management console appears, as shown in Figure 6-2.

2. **In the Navigation pane, drill down to the Group Policy Objects node for your domain.**

Figure 6-2:
The Group
Policy
Manage-
ment
console.

3. **Right-click the Group Policy Objects node, and then choose New from the menu that appears.**

   This brings up the dialog box shown in Figure 6-3.

Figure 6-3:
Creating a
new group
policy
object.

4. **Type a name for the group policy object, and then click OK.**

   For this example, I typed **IE Home Page** as the group policy object name.

   When you click OK, the group policy object is created.

5. **Double-click the new group policy.**

   The group policy opens, as shown in Figure 6-4. Note that at this stage, the Location section of the group policy does not list any objects. As a result, this policy is not yet linked to any Active Directory domains or groups. I'll get to that in a moment. But first, I'll create the policy settings.

6. **Click the Settings tab.**

The group policy settings are displayed, as shown in Figure 6-5.

Figure 6-4:
A new
group policy
object.

Figure 6-5:
A new
group policy
object.

7. Right-click User Configuration, and then choose Edit.

This opens the Group Policy Management Editor to edit the User Configuration policies, as shown in Figure 6-6.

Figure 6-6:
Editing
group
policy.

8. In the Navigation pane, navigate to User Configuration⇨Windows Settings⇨Internet Explorer Maintenance⇨URLs.

This brings up the Internet Explorer URL settings, as shown in Figure 6-7.

Figure 6-7:
The Internet
Explorer
Settings
URLs page.

9. **Double-click Important URLs.**

This brings up the Important URLs dialog box, as shown in Figure 6-8.

10. **Select the Customize Home Page URL check box.**

11. **Enter the URL you want to use for the home page.**

For this example, I entered `http://www.dummies.com`.

12. **Click OK.**

You are returned to the Group Policy Management Editor.

13. **Close the Group Policy Management Editor window.**

This returns you to the Group Policy Management settings window you opened in Step 5.

14. **Right-click User Configuration and choose Refresh.**

The IE home page policy is now visible, as shown in Figure 6-9.

15. **Click the Scope tab.**

The Scope tab is displayed. Refer to Figure 6-4.

Book VII
Chapter 6

Using Group Policy

Figure 6-8:
The Internet
Explorer
Settings
URLs page.

| Important URLs | ?|x |

Important URLs

You can specify a custom Home page, Search bar URL, and Online support page. The Home page is opened when the browser is started or when the user clicks the Home button.

Home page URL: ☐ Customize Home page URL

Internet Explorer 6 lets you specify a custom Search bar URL which opens in a separate frame when the user clicks on the Search button. The Search bar must be written in HTML and has some special requirements.

Search bar URL: ☐ Customize Search bar URL

When the user clicks Help in the browser menu bar, and then clicks Online support, the URL you specify below will be displayed in the browser.

Online support page URL: ☐ Customize Online support page URL

OK   Cancel   Apply   Help

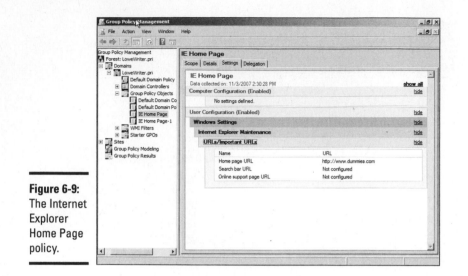

Figure 6-9:
The Internet
Explorer
Home Page
policy.

16. **In the navigation pane, drag the new IE Home Page object to the top-level domain (in this case, LoweWriter.pri).**

When you release the mouse button, the dialog box shown in Figure 6-10 appears.

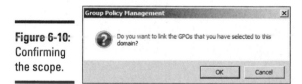

Figure 6-10:
Confirming
the scope.

17. **Click OK.**

The domain is added to the scope, as shown in Figure 6-11.

18. **Close the Group Policy Management window.**

The new group policy is now active, so the Internet Explorer home page is now set to www.dummies.com for all users in the domain.

Figure 6-11:
The policy is
finished.

Filtering Group Policy Objects

One of the more confusing aspects of group policy is that even though it applies to users and computers, you don't associate group policy objects with users or computers. Instead, you link them to sites, domains, or organizational units (OUs). At first glance, this might seem to limit the usefulness of group policy. For most simple networks, you'll work with group policy mostly at the domain level, and occasionally at the OU level. Site-level group policy objects are used only for very large or complex networks.

Group policy wouldn't be very useful if you had to assign the exact same policy to every user or computer within a domain. And although OUs can help break down group policy assignments, even that is limiting because a particular user or computer can be a member of only one OU. Fortunately, group policy objects can have *filters* that further refine which users or computers the policy applies to. Although you can filter policy objects so they apply only to individual users or computers, you're more likely to use groups to apply your group policy objects.

For example, suppose you want to use group policy to set the home page for your marketing staff to www.dummies.com, but you want the accounting staff to go to www.beancounters.com by default. You can easily accomplish this by creating a Marketing group and an Accounting group in Active Directory Users and Computers and assigning the marketing and accounting users to the appropriate groups. Then, you can create two group policy objects: one for the marketing department's home page, the other to assign the accounting department's home page. You can then link both of these policy objects to the domain, and use filters to specify which group each policy applies to.

For the following procedure, I have created two group policies, named IE Home Page Dummies and IE Home Page Beancounter, as well as two Active Directory groups, named Marketing and Accounting. Here are the steps for filtering these policies to link correctly to the groups:

1. **Choose Start⇨Administrative Tools⇨Group Policy Management.**

The Group Policy Management console appears. (Refer to Figure 6-2 for a refresher on what it looks like.)

2. **In the Navigation pane, navigate to the group policy object you want to apply the filter to.**

For this example, I navigated to the IE Home Page Dummies policy as shown in Figure 6-12.

Figure 6-12:
The IE Home Page Dummies policy.

3. **In the Security Filtering section, click Authenticated Users, and then click Remove.**

This removes Authenticated Users, so the policy will not be applied to all users.

4. **Click Add.**

This brings up the Select User, Computer, or Group dialog box as shown in Figure 6-13.

5. **Type** Marketing **in the text box, and then click OK.**

The policy is updated to indicate that it applies to members of the Marketing group, as shown in Figure 6-14.

Book VII
Chapter 6

Using Group Policy

Figure 6-13:
The Select User, Computer, or Group dialog box.

6. **Repeat Steps 2-5 for the IE Home Page Beancounter policy, applying it to the Accounting group.**

You're done!

Figure 6-14:
A policy that uses a filter.

Chapter 7: Troubleshooting

In This Chapter

✔ **Examining the Event Viewer**

✔ **Perusing the Performance console**

✔ **Checking out the Computer Management console**

✔ **Surveying the Services console**

*B*oth Windows Server 2003 and Windows Server 2008 are extremely reliable. Get them configured right in the first place, and they'll chug along without incident. That is, at least until something goes wrong. Which is inevitable.

In this chapter, I review some of the tools that Windows provides to help you diagnose trouble. Before I start, however, I want to point you to a few other chapters that also contain troubleshooting information. This chapter deals only with those tools that apply specifically to Windows servers. You can find other information in these chapters:

✦ Book II, Chapter 7 gives you some guidance on verifying that the network is functioning.

✦ Book III, Chapter 6 gives some basic network troubleshooting tips.

✦ Book III, Chapter 7 gives some basic performance management tips.

✦ Book IV, Chapter 6 explains how to use the TCP/IP troubleshooting tools, such as `ping` and `ipconfig`.

Working with the Event Viewer

Windows has a built-in event-tracking feature that automatically logs a variety of interesting system events. Usually, when something goes wrong with your server, you can find at least one and maybe dozens of events in one of the logs. All you have to do is open the Event Viewer and check the logs for suspicious-looking entries.

Using the Event Viewer

To display the event logs, choose Start⇨Administrative Tools⇨Event Viewer. This brings up the Event Viewer, as shown in Figure 7-1. The tree on the left side of the Event Viewer lists the various categories of events that are tracked:

Figure 7-1:
The Event
Viewer.

✦ **Application:** Lists events that were generated by application programs. In most cases, these are events that the application's developers purposely wrote to the event log in order to inform you of error conditions or developing trouble.

✦ **Security:** Lists security-related events, such as unsuccessful logon attempts, changes to security policy, and so on. For information about how to change the events that are written to the security log, see Chapter 5 of this minibook.

✦ **Setup:** Lists events generated during operating system setup.

✦ **System:** This is where you find events related to hardware or operating system failures. For example, if you're having trouble with a hard drive, you should check here for events related to the hard drive.

✦ **Forwarded events:** Lists other events that were forwarded to this server.

Note that you may find other categories in this list, depending on the roles you have configured for the server.

Select one of these options to see the log that you want to view. In Figure 7-1, I clicked the System Events log.

Notice the cute little icons next to each item in the log. Table 7-1 summarizes the meaning of these icons.

Table 7-1		Icons Used in the Event Log
Icon	*Name*	*Description*
(i)	Information	This message simply indicates that some noteworthy operation completed successfully.
(!)	Warning	An event developed a problem that wasn't fatal, but it may indicate a problem looming on the horizon.
(!)	Error	This message indicates that something has gone wrong.

To see the details for a particular event, double-click the event to bring up the Event Properties dialog box, shown in Figure 7-2. Here you can see the details of the event. In some cases, you may be able to diagnose a problem just by reading the error message displayed in this dialog box. In other cases, this information just points you in the right direction — it tells you *what* went wrong, but you still have to figure out *why*.

Figure 7-2:
The Event
Properties
dialog box.

Event Properties - Event 6008, EventLog

General | Details

The previous system shutdown at 10:21:53 PM on 8/15/2007 was unexpected.

Log Name:	System		
Source:	EventLog	Logged:	8/28/2007 9:52:56 PM
Event ID:	6008	Task Category:	None
Level:	Error	Keywords:	Classic
User:	N/A	Computer:	LH-36BC23815NV2
OpCode:			
More Information:	Event Log Online Help		

Copy   Close

Setting event log policies

You can set default policies that affect how application, security, and system event logs are kept by opening the Group Policy Management Editor. You'll find the event log policies under Computer Configuration, Windows Settings, Security Settings in the tree to the left. See Figure 7-3.

Figure 7-3:
Setting the event log policies.

You can use these policies to specify the following options for the Application, Security, and System logs:

✦ **Maximum Log Size:** Lets you specify the maximum size of the log in KB.

✦ **Prevent Local Guests from Accessing Log:** Prevents users who are logged on using a guest account from viewing the logs. This is a good security precaution.

✦ **Retain Log:** This policy sounds like it may let you disable the log, but it doesn't. Instead, it specifies the number of days that log data should be kept if you specify By Days as the Retention Method policy.

✦ **Retention Method for Log:** Specifies how log events should be overwritten when the log becomes full. Options are By Days, As Needed, or Do Not Overwrite.

Monitoring Performance

The Performance console is a troubleshooting tool that can help you track down nasty and elusive problems — particularly the type that don't cause the server to crash, but just cause it to run slowly. With the Performance console, you can look at many different aspects of system performance to figure out why your system is dragging.

Using the Reliability and Performance Monitor

To run the Performance console, choose Start⇨Administrative Tools⇨Reliability and Performance Monitor. The Reliability and Performance Monitor comes to life, as shown in Figure 7-4.

Figure 7-4:
The Reliability and Performance Monitor.

The display in Figure 7-4 shows essential performance data for the CPU, memory, network, and disk. Although it isn't apparent from the figure, the display constantly updates itself as it gathers new data.

You can summon more specific performance information by clicking Performance Monitor in the console tree. This brings up the Performance Monitor, as shown in Figure 7-5.

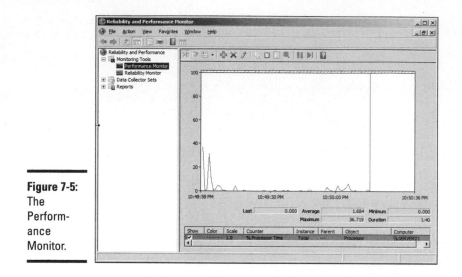

The Performance Monitor lets you keep track of several different aspects of system performance at once. You track each performance aspect by setting up a *counter.* You can choose from hundreds of different counters. Table 7-2 describes some of the most commonly used counters. Notice that each counter refers to a server object, such as physical disk, memory, or the processor.

Table 7-2	Commonly Used Performance Counters	
Object	*Counter*	*Description*
Physical Disk	% Free Space	The percentage of free space on the server's physical disks. Should be at least 15%.
Physical Disk	Average Queue Length	The number of disk operations that are waiting while the disk is busy servicing other disk operations. Should be two or less.
Memory	Pages/second	The number of pages retrieved per second from the virtual memory page files. A typical value is about 2,500.
Processor	% Processor Time	The percentage of the processor's time that it is busy doing work rather than sitting idle. Should be 85% or less.

To add a counter, click the Add button to bring up the Add Counters dialog box, as shown in Figure 7-6. Then select the object that you want to track from the drop-down list, choose the counter that you want to add from the list, and click Add. You can add more than one counter from this dialog box; when you're finished adding counters, click OK to dismiss the Add Counters dialog box.

Figure 7-6:
The Add Counters dialog box.

The act of gathering performance data slows down your server, so don't leave performance logging on all the time. Use it only occasionally to gather baseline data or when you're experiencing a performance problem.

Creating performance logs

Instead of staring at the Performance Monitor for hours on end waiting for a performance glitch to occur, you can create a performance log — which in Windows Server 2008 is called a *Data Collector Set.* (In Windows Server 2003, it was called a *Performance Log.* I guess the intellectuals at Microsoft think the term "Data Collector Set" is more meaningful than "Performance Log." I disagree, but they didn't ask for my opinion.)

When the network is running well, you can collect data to act as a baseline, so you'll know if performance has slipped. When the network is not acting well, you can collect data to help isolate the problem.

To set up a performance log, follow these steps:

1. **Open the Data Collector Sets node in the console tree, and then right-click the User Defined node and choose New⇨Data Collector Set.**

This action brings up a wizard that steps you through the process of creating a new log, as shown in Figure 7-7.

Figure 7-7:
Creating a
new Data
Collector
Set (er,
Perform-
ance Log).

2. Type a name for your log, choose whether you want to use a pre-defined template or create your own custom log, and then click Next.

For this example, I use one of the templates. The dialog box shown in Figure 7-8 lists the available templates.

Figure 7-8:
Data
Collector
Set
templates.

3. Select System Performance, and then click Finish.

Note that creating the log doesn't actually start the logging activity. To start the log, right-click it and choose Start. Alternatively, you can click the big green Start button in the toolbar. When you want to stop the log, select the log and click the Stop button or right-click the log and choose Stop.

To display the data accumulated by a performance log, right-click the log and choose Latest Report. A summary of the logged data is displayed, as shown in Figure 7-9.

Figure 7-9:
Data
collected
by a
performance
log.

Using the Computer Management Console

The Start⇨Administrative Tools⇨Computer Management command leads you to the Computer Management console, which is a tool that's often useful when tracking down problems in a Windows Server 2008 system. Poke around the console tree in Computer Management and you'll find

**Book VII
Chapter 7**

Troubleshooting

✦ **Event Viewer:** Refer to the section "Using the Event Viewer," earlier in this chapter, for more information.

✦ **Shared Folders:** Here, you can manage your shared folders, current sessions, and open files. For more information, see Chapter 4 of this minibook.

✦ **Performance Logs and Alerts:** Refer to the section "Using the Reliability and Performance Monitor," earlier in this chapter, for more information.

✦ **Device Manager:** This is a handy tool for diagnosing problems with hardware devices. Device Manager lists all the hardware devices currently installed on the computer, as shown in Figure 7-10. You can double-click a device to bring up a Properties dialog box that displays information about the status of the device and lets you change drivers or configuration settings.

Figure 7-10:
The Device
Manager.

✦ **Removable Storage:** This lets you track removable storage media, such as tapes and CDs, and manage tape and CD libraries.

✦ **Disk Defragmenter:** This tool lets you optimize the way data is stored on your disks.

✦ **Disk Management:** This tool lets you work with disk partitions, format disks, create mirror sets, and perform other disk operations.

✦ **Services and Applications:** Here, you can manage services and applications that you've installed on the computer, such as DHCP, DNS, IIS, and so on.

Working with Services

The last troubleshooting tool I want to describe in this chapter is the Services console, which you can access by choosing Start⇨Administrative Tools⇨ Services. As Figure 7-11 shows, the Services console displays a list of all the services that are currently running on your system.

If a Windows server feature isn't working properly, the problem is often that something has caused one of the services associated with the feature to stop. You can often correct the problem by calling up the Services console and restarting the service. To do that, just select the service and then click the Start the Service link.

Figure 7-11:
The
Services
console.

Of course, this action doesn't correct the underlying cause of the problem. If the service stopped because of a one-time error, simply restarting the service may be all that you need to do. In many cases, though, the problem that caused the service to start will resurface and cause the service to stop again.

So, if you fix a problem by restarting a service, you must keep an eye out for the problem's resurgence. Usually, if the problem doesn't recur within a few days, you can safely assume that you encountered a one-time glitch and fixed it by restarting the service. But if the problem happens again, you'll need to investigate more to get to the bottom of the problem.

**Book VII
Chapter 7**

Troubleshooting

Chapter 8: Windows Commands

In This Chapter

✔ Getting started with a command window

✔ Taking advantage of command tricks and techniques

✔ Looking at batch files

✔ Using the amazing Net commands

A lthough Windows sports a fancy graphical interface that makes it possible to perform most network management tasks by pointing and clicking, you can also do almost any network management task from a command prompt. Whether you choose to do so is largely a matter of personal style. Some network administrators pride themselves in being able to type Windows commands blindfolded and with two fingers from each hand tied behind their backs. Others have fully embraced the graphical user interface and think the command line is for administrators with Unix envy.

So the choice is yours. Skip this chapter if the thought of typing commands causes you to lose sleep. For those of you who are willing to venture forth, this chapter begins with an overview of working from the command prompt. Then, it describes some of the more useful Windows commands. Finally, this chapter introduces the fine (and almost lost) art of writing batch files.

Windows Server 2008 includes a brand new command environment known as *PowerShell*. PowerShell is an advanced command processor that has many sophisticated features that are designed especially for creating powerful scripts. For more information, see Microsoft's PowerShell site at www. microsoft.com/powershell.

Using a Command Window

Command prompts are even older than video monitors. The first computer I worked on used a teletype machine as its terminal, so the command prompt was printed on paper rather than displayed onscreen. Surprisingly, though, the concept of the command prompt hasn't changed much since those days. The system displays a prompt to let you know it's waiting for a command. When you type the command and press the Enter key, the system reads your command, interprets it, executes it, displays the results, and then displays the prompt again so that you can enter another command.

Opening and closing a command window

To get to a command prompt on a Windows server, follow these steps:

1. **Choose Start⇨Run.**

   The Run dialog box appears.

2. **Type** cmd.

   The name of the command processor for Windows NT and Windows Server is cmd.exe.

   If you type **Command** instead, you get Command.com, the old MS-DOS command processor, which is considerably less powerful than cmd.exe.

3. **Click OK.**

   The command prompt window appears, as shown in Figure 8-1.

Figure 8-1:
The command prompt.

You can now type any commands that you want in the window.

To exit the command prompt, type **Exit** and press Enter. This properly terminates cmd.exe and closes the command prompt window. If you try to close the command prompt window by clicking its Close button, Windows is forced to shut down cmd.exe. The process will work, but you'll have to click your way through an intervening dialog box and wait a few seconds while Windows terminates cmd.exe. Entering the Exit command is a much faster method.

Editing commands

Most of the time, you just type commands by using the keyboard. If you make a mistake, you just retype the command, being careful not to repeat the mistake. However, cmd.exe has several built-in editing features that can simplify the task of correcting a mistaken command or entering a sequence of similar commands:

✦ Press the right-arrow key to recall the text of the last command that you entered, one letter at a time. When you get to the spot where the new command should differ from the previous command, start typing.

✦ Press F3 to recall all of the previous command, from the current cursor position to the end of the line.

✦ If you want to repeat a command that you've used recently, press the up-arrow key. This recalls up to 50 of the most recently executed commands. You can press Enter to execute a command as is, or you can edit the command before you execute it.

Using the Control menu

Although the command window has no menu bar, it does have a menu that you can access via the control box at the top-left corner of the window. Besides the commands found on this menu for all windows (such as Move, Size, and Minimize), this menu includes three additional commands:

✦ **Edit:** The Edit command leads to a submenu with several choices. Several of these commands work together so that you can copy information from the command window to the Clipboard and vice versa. If you choose Edit⇨ Mark, you're placed in a special editing mode that lets you highlight text in the command window with the mouse. (Normally, the mouse doesn't do anything in the command window.) You can then choose Edit⇨Copy or just press Enter to copy the text that you selected to the Clipboard.

You can also use the Edit menu to paste text from the Clipboard, to scroll the window, and to search the window for text.

✦ **Default:** Lets you set default properties for the command window.

✦ **Properties:** Displays a Properties dialog box that you can use to change the appearance of the window. You can change the font size, choose background colors, and make other adjustments to make the command window look good on your computer.

Special Command Tricks

Before I get into the details of using specific commands, I want to describe some techniques you should familiarize yourself with. In many cases, these techniques can let you accomplish in a single command what would otherwise take dozens of separate commands.

Wildcards

Wildcards are one of the most compelling reasons to use the command prompt. With wildcards, you can process all the files that match a particular naming pattern with a single command. For example, suppose that you have a folder containing 500 files, and you want to delete all the files that contain the letters *Y2K* and end with the extension .doc, which happens to be 50 files. If you open a My Documents window, you'll spend ten minutes picking these files out from the list. From a command window, you can delete them all with the single command Del *Y2K*.doc.

You can use two wildcard characters: An asterisk stands for any number of characters, including zero, and an exclamation point stands for just one character. Thus, !Text.doc would match files with names like aText.doc, xText.doc, and 4Text.doc, but not abcText.doc or just Text.doc. However, *Text.doc would match any of the names mentioned in the previous sentence.

Wildcards work differently in Windows than they did in MS-DOS. In MS-DOS, anything you typed after an asterisk was ignored. Thus, ab*cd.doc was the same as ab*.doc. In Windows, the asterisk wildcard can come before static text, so ab*cd.doc and ab*.doc are *not* the same.

Chaining commands

You can enter two or more commands on the same line by separating the commands with an ampersand (&), like this:

```
C:\>copy *.doc a: & del *.doc
```

Here, the Copy command copies all the .doc files to the A: drive. Then, the Del command deletes the .doc files.

Although that may be convenient, it's also dangerous. What if the A: drive fills up so that all the files can't be copied? In that case, the Del command executes anyway, deleting the files that didn't get copied.

A safer alternative is to use two ampersands, which says to execute the second command only if the first command finishes successfully. Thus:

```
C:\>copy *.doc a: && del *.doc
```

Now, the Del command will be executed only if the Copy command succeeds.

You can also use two pipe characters (the *pipe* is the vertical bar character that's above the backslash on the keyboard) to execute the second command only if the first command fails. Thus,

```
C:\>copy *.doc a: || echo Oops!
```

displays the message "Oops!" if the Copy command fails.

Finally, you can use parentheses to group commands. Then, you can use the other symbols in combination. For example:

```
C:\>(opy *.doc a: && del *.doc) || echo Oops!
```

Here, the files are copied and then deleted if the copy was successful. If either command fails, the message is displayed.

Redirection and piping

Redirection and piping are related techniques. *Redirection* lets you specify an alternate destination for output that will be displayed by a command or an alternate source for input that should be fed into a command. For example, you can save the results of an ipconfig /all command to a file named myconfig.txt like this:

```
C:\>iconfig /all > myconfig.txt
```

Here, the greater-than sign (>) is used to redirect the command's console output.

If a command accepts input from the keyboard, you can use input redirection to specify a file that contains the input you want to feed to the command. For example, you can create a text file named lookup.txt with subcommands for a command such as nslookup. Then, you can feed those scripted subcommands to the nslookup command, like this:

```
C:\>nslookup < lookup.txt
```

Piping is a similar technique. It takes the console output from one command and feeds it into the next command as input. Piping is often used with special commands called *filters,* which are designed to read input from the console, modify the data in some way, and then write it to the console.

For example, suppose that you want to display the contents of a file named users.txt sorted into alphabetical order. You can use the Type command, which displays a file on the console, and then you can pipe the output into the Sort command, a filter that sorts its input and displays the sorted output on the console. The resulting command would look like this:

```
C:\>type users.txt | sort
```

The vertical bar is often called the *pipe character* because it's the symbol used to indicate piping.

Environment variables

The command shell makes several *environment variables* available to commands. Environment variables all begin and end with percent signs. You can use an environment variable anywhere in a command. For example,

```
C:\>echo %OS% running on a %PROCESSOR_IDENTIFIER%
```

displays a line such as this:

```
Windows_NT running on an x86 Family 15 Model 2 Stepping 8,
    GenuineIntel
```

Interestingly, Windows NT, Windows 2000 Server, Windows Server 2003, and Windows Server 2008 all display "Windows_NT" for the operating system name.

If the environment variable represents a path, you may need to enclose it in quotation marks, like this:

```
C:\>dir "%HOMEPATH%"
```

This command displays the contents of the user's home directory. The quotation marks are required here because the environment variable expands to a pathname that may include spaces, and the command shell requires that long filenames that include spaces must be enclosed in quotation marks.

Table 8-1 lists the environment variables that are available to you and your commands.

Table 8-1	Environment Variables
Variable	*Description*
%ALLUSERSPROFILE%	The location of the All Users profile.
%APPDATA%	The path where applications store data by default.
%CD%	The path to the current directory.
%CMDCMDLINE%	The command line that was used to start the command shell.
%CMDEXTVERSION%	The version number of the command shell.
%COMPUTERNAME%	The computer's name.
%COMSPEC%	The path to the command shell executable (cmd.exe).
%DATE%	The current date in the format generated by the date /t command.

Variable	Description
%ERRORLEVEL%	The error returned by the most recent command.
%HOMEDRIVE%	The drive letter of the user's home directory.
%HOMEPATH%	The path to the user's home directory.
%HOMESHARE%	The network path to the user's shared home directory.
%LOGONSERVER%	The name of the domain controller the user logged on to.
%NUMBER_OF_ PROCESSORS%	The number of processors on the computer
%OS%	The name of the operating system.
%PATH%	The current search path.
"%PATHEXT%"	A list of the extensions the operating system treats as executable files.
%PROCESSOR _ARCHITECTURE%	The chip architecture of the processor.
%PROCESSOR _IDENTIFIER%.	A description of the processor
%PROCESSOR_REVISION%	The revision level of the processor.
%PROMPT%	The current prompt string.
%RANDOM%	A random number between 1 and 32,767.
%SYSTEMDRIVE%	The drive containing the operating system.
%SYSTEMROOT%	The path to the operating system.
%TEMP%	The path to a temporary folder for temporary files.
%TMP%	Same as %TEMP%.
%TIME%	The time in the format produced by the time /t command.
%USERDOMAIN%	The name of the user's domain.
%USERNAME%	The user's account name.
%USERPROFILE%	The path to the user's profile.
%WINDIR%	The path to the operating system directory.

Batch files

A *batch file* is simply a text file that contains one or more commands. Batch files are given the extension .bat and can be run from a command prompt as if they were commands or programs. You can also run a batch file from the Start menu by choosing Start⇨Run, typing the name of the batch file, and clicking OK.

As a network administrator, you'll find plenty of uses for batch files. Most of them won't be very complicated. For example, here are some examples of very simple batch files I've used:

✦ I once used a one-line file to copy the entire contents of an important shared network drive to a user's computer every night at 10 p.m. The user had just purchased a new Dell computer with a 100GB drive, and the server had only a 20GB drive. The user wanted a quick-and-dirty backup solution that would complement the regular tape backups that ran every night.

✦ I've also used a pair of short batch files to stop and then restart Exchange server before and after nightly backups for backup software that didn't have an Exchange plug-in that could back up the mail store while it was open.

✦ If I frequently need to work with several related folders at once, I create a short batch file that opens Explorer windows for each of the folders. (You can open an Explorer window from a batch file simply by typing the path to the folder that you want to open as a command.) Then, I place the batch file on my desktop so I can get to it quickly.

You can also use batch files to create logon scripts that are executed whenever a user logs on. Microsoft keeps trying to get users to use profiles instead of logon scripts, but many networks still use logon scripts.

The EventCreate Command

The `EventCreate` command lets you create an event that's added to one of the Windows event logs. This can be useful if you want to make a note of something unusual that's happened. It's often used in batch files to mark the start or completion of a task such as a nightly backup.

Here's the basic syntax:

```
eventcreate [options]
eventcreate /T type /D "description" /ID eventide
    [/L logname] [/SO sourcename]        [/S system
    [/U username [/P password]]]
```

Here's a description of the options:

✦ **/T:** Specifies the type. The options are `Information`, `Warning`, or `Error`.

✦ **/D:** Provides a descriptive message that's saved in the log. Use quotes if the message contains more than one word.

✦ **/ID:** A number from 1 to 1000.

✦ **/L:** The name of the log to write the event to. The default is `Application`.

✦ **/SO:** A string that represents the source of the event. The default is `EventCreate`. If you specify this option, you must also specify the /L option.

✦ **/S:** The name of the system on which the event should be recorded.

✦ **/U:** The user account to use when logging the event. You can specify this option only if you also specify /S.

✦ **/P:** The password. You can specify this option only if you also specify /U.

Here's an example that writes an informational message to the Application log:

```
eventcreate /t information /id 100 /d "Nightly processing
    complted" /L Application /SO Nightly
```

Figure 8-2 shows an event created by the above command.

Figure 8-2: An event generated by the EventCreate command.

Book VII
Chapter 8

Windows
Commands

Net Commands

Among the more useful commands for network administrators are the Net Services commands. These commands are all two-word commands, beginning with Net — such as Net Use and Net Start. In the following sections, I present each of the Net commands, in alphabetical order for handy reference. First, though, I want to point out a few details about the Net commands:

✦ You can get a quick list of the available `Net` commands by typing **net /?** at a command prompt.

✦ You can get brief help for any `Net` command by typing **net help *command***. For example, to display help for the `Net Use` command, type **net help use**. (Yes, we all could use some help.)

✦ Many of the `Net` commands prompt you for confirmation before completing an operation. For these commands, you can specify `/Y` or `/N` to bypass the confirmation prompt. You'll want to do that if you include these commands in a batch file that runs unattended. Note that you can use `/Y` or `/N` on any `Net` command, even if it doesn't prompt you for confirmation. So I suggest that you place `/Y` on every `Net` command in a batch file that you intend on running unattended.

The Net Accounts command

This command updates user account policies for password requirements. Here's the command syntax:

```
net accounts [/forcelogoff:{minutes | no}]
    [/minwlen:length]                [/maxpwage:{days |
    unlimited}]                 [/minpwage:days]
    [/uniquepw:number]               [/domain]
```

The following paragraphs describe the parameters for the `Net Accounts` command:

✦ **Forcelogoff:** Specifies how long to wait before forcing a user off the system when the user's logon time expires. The default value, `no`, prevents users from being forced to log off. If you specify a number, the user will be warned a few minutes before being forcibly logged off.

✦ **Minpwlen:** Specifies the minimum length for the user's password. *Length* can be from 0 through 127. The default is 6.

✦ **Maxpwage:** Specifies the number of days a user's password is considered valid. `Unlimited` means the password will never expire. *Days* can be from 1 through 49,710, which is about 135 years. The default is 90.

✦ **Minpwage:** Specifies the minimum number of days after a user changes a password before the user can change it again. The default value is 0. You should usually set this value to 1 day in order to prevent users from bypassing the `Uniquepw` policy.

✦ **Uniquepw:** Indicates how many different passwords the user must use before he or she is allowed to reuse the same password again. The default setting is 5. The range is from 0 to 24.

✦ **Domain:** Specifies that the operation should be performed on the primary domain controller rather than on the local computer.

If you enter Net Accounts without any parameters, the command simply displays the current policy settings.

Here's an example that sets the minimum and maximum password ages:

```
C:\>net accounts /minpwage:7 /maxpwage:30
```

The Net Computer command

This command creates or deletes a computer account. Here's the syntax:

```
net computer \\computername {/add | /del}
```

The following paragraphs describe the parameters for the Net Computer command:

✦ **Computername:** The name of the computer to add or delete.

✦ **Add:** Create a computer account for the specified computer.

✦ **Del:** Deletes the specified computer account.

Here's an example that adds a computer named Theodore:

```
C:\>net computer \\theodore /add
```

The Net Config command

This command lets you view or configure various network services. Here's the syntax:

```
net config [{server|workstation}]
```

To configure server settings, use this syntax:

```
net cnfig server [/autodisconnect:time]
    [/srvcomment:"text"] [/hidden:{yes | no}]
```

The following paragraphs describe the parameters for the Net Config command:

✦ **Server:** Lets you display and configure the Server service while it's running.

✦ **Workstation:** Lets you display and configure the Workstation service while it's running.

**Book VII
Chapter 8**

**Windows
Commands**

✦ **Autodisconnect:** Specifies how long a user's session can be inactive before it's disconnected. Specify –1 to never disconnect. The range is –1 to 65535 minutes, which is about 45 days. The default is 15 minutes.

✦ **Srvcomment:** Specifies a description of the server. The comment can be up to 48 characters long and should be enclosed in quotation marks.

✦ **Hidden:** Specifies whether the server appears in screens that display available servers. Hiding a server doesn't make the server unavailable; it just means that the user will have to know the name of the server in order to access it. The default is No.

Here's an example that sets a server's descriptive comment:

```
C:\>net config server /srvcomment:"DHCP Server"
```

The Net Continue command

This command continues a service you've suspended with the Net Pause command. Here's the syntax:

```
net continue service
```

Here are some typical services that you can pause and continue.

✦ **Netlogon:** The Net Logon service.

✦ **Schedule:** The Task Scheduler service.

✦ **Server:** The Server service.

✦ **Workstation:** The Workstation service.

Here's an example that continues the Workstation service:

```
C:>net continue workstation
```

If the service name has embedded spaces, enclose the service name in quotation marks. For example, this command continues the NT LM Security Support Provider service:

```
C:\>net continue "nt lm security support provider"
```

The Net File command

This command lists all open shared files and the number of file locks placed on each file. You can also use this command to close files and remove locks, which is a useful procedure when a user manages to accidentally leave a file open or locked. Here's the syntax:

```
C:\>net file [id [/close]]
```

The following paragraphs describe the Net File command's parameters:

✦ *ID:* The file's identification number.

✦ **Close:** Closes an open file and releases any locks that were placed on the file.

To close a file, you must issue the command from the server where the file is shared.

Net Files works, too.

To close an open file, first run Net File without any parameters to list the open files. Here's a sample of the output that you can expect from Net File:

```
File        Path            Username    #locks
------------------------------------------------
0           C:\BUDGET.DOC   WARD        0
1           C:\RECIPE.MDF   JUNE        4
```

Next, run Net File again, specifying the file number displayed for the file that you want to close. For example, to close the RECIPE.MDF file, use this command:

```
C:\>net file 1 /close
```

The Net Group command

This command lets you add, display, or change global groups. This command has a number of different syntaxes, depending on how you intend to use it.

To display information about a group or to change a group's comment, use this syntax:

```
net group groupname [/comment:"text"] [/domain]
```

To create a new group, use this syntax:

```
net group groupname /add [/comment:"text"] [/domain]
```

To delete a group, use this syntax:

```
net group groupname /delete [/domain]
```

Book VII
Chapter 8

Windows
Commands

Finally, to add or remove users from a group, use this syntax:

```
net group groupname username[ ...] {/add | /delete} [/domain]
```

The following paragraphs describe the parameters that you can use with the `NetGroup` command:

✦ ***Groupname:*** The name of the group to add, change, or delete. If you specify this parameter and no others, a list of users in the group appears.

✦ **Comment:** Specifies a comment for the group. The comment can be up to 48 characters in length and should be enclosed in quotation marks.

✦ **Domain:** Specifies that the operation should be performed on the primary domain controller rather than on the local computer.

✦ **Add:** Creates a new group or adds users to an existing group. Before you add a user to a group, you must first create a user account for the user.

✦ **Delete:** Removes a group or removes users from the group.

✦ ***Username:*** One or more usernames to be added to or removed from the group. If you list more than one name, separate the names with spaces.

Windows isn't picky: You can specify `Net Groups` rather than `Net Group` if you want.

This example lists all the groups on a server:

```
C:\>net group
```

This example adds a group named Admin:

```
C:\>net group Admin /add
```

This example adds three users to the Admin group:

```
C:\>net group Admin Ward Wally June /add
```

This example lists the users in the Admin group:

```
C:\>net group Admin
```

The Net Help command

This command displays help for the Net command or for a specific Net sub-command. Here's the basic syntax:

```
net help [command]
```

The *command* parameter can be any of the following commands:

ACCOUNTS	HELP	SHARE
COMPUTER	HELPMSG	START
CONFIG	LOCALGROUP	STATISTICS
CONFIG SERVER	NAME	STOP
CONFIG WORKSTATION	PAUSE	TIME
CONTINUE	PRINT	USE
FILE	SEND	USER
GROUP	SESSION	VIEW

You can type **net help services** to display a list of services that you can start via the Net Start command.

The Net Helpmsg command

This command displays an explanation of network error codes. Here's the syntax:

```
net helpmsg message#
```

The *message#* parameter should be the four-digit number displayed when the error occurred. For example, if you get an error with message 2180, use this command to see an explanation of the error:

```
C:\>net helpmsg 2180
The service database is locked.
EXPLANATION
Another program is holding the service database lock.
ACTION
Wait for the lock to be released and try again later.  If it
    is possible to determine which program is holding the
    lock, then end that program.
```

The Net Localgroup command

This command lets you add, display, or change local groups. This command has a number of different syntaxes, depending on how you intend to use it.

To display information about a local group or to change a local group's comment, use this syntax:

```
net localgroup groupname [/comment:"text"] [/domain]
```

To create a new group, use this syntax:

```
net localgroup groupname /add [/comment:"text"] [/domain]
```

To delete a group, use this syntax:

```
net localgroup groupname /delete [/domain]
```

Finally, to add users to or remove users from a group, use this syntax:

```
net localgroup groupname username[ ...] {/add | /delete}
    [/domain]
```

The following paragraphs describe the parameters that you can use with the Net Localgroup command:

+ ✦ *Groupname:* The name of the group to add, change, or delete. If you specify this parameter and no others, a list of users in the group appears.

+ ✦ **Comment:** Specifies a comment for the group. The comment can be up to 48 characters in length and should be enclosed in quotation marks.

+ ✦ **Domain:** Specifies that the operation should be performed on the primary domain controller rather than on the local computer.

+ ✦ **Add:** Creates a new group or adds users to an existing group. Before you add a user to a group, you must first create a user account for the user.

+ ✦ **Delete:** Removes a group or removes users from the group.

+ ✦ *Username:* One or more usernames to be added to or removed from the group. If you list more than one name, separate the names with spaces.

This example lists all the local groups:

```
C:\>net localgroup
```

This example adds a local group named Admin:

```
C:\>net localgroup Admin /add
```

This example adds three users to the Admin local group:

```
C:\>net localgroup Admin Ward Wally June /add
```

This example lists the users in the Admin group:

```
C:\>net localgroup Admin
```

The Net Name command

This command creates or removes an alias that can be used to send messages to the computer, or it lists any existing aliases. Here's the syntax:

```
net name [name {/add|/delete}]
```

You can use the following parameters with the Net Name command:

✦ **Name:** The name of the alias to create or remove.

✦ **Add:** Creates the alias.

✦ **Delete:** Removes the alias.

Use net name to specify a name for receiving messages. You must start the Messenger service before you can use net name. Each messaging name must be unique on the network. Names created with net name are strictly for messaging — not for group names. Windows XP uses three name types.

To list the current names for a computer, use the Net Name command like this:

```
C:\>net name
Name
-------------------------------------------------------
DOUG
DOUG LOWE
The command completed successfully.
```

To add the name T1000 to your computer, use this command:

```
C:\>net name T1000 /add
```

To delete the name, use this command:

```
C:\>net name T1000 /delete
```

The Net Pause command

This command temporarily pauses a service. It's a good idea to pause a service for a while before you stop the service altogether. That gives users who are currently using the service a chance to finish up any pending tasks, while at the same time preventing other users from beginning new sessions with the service. To reactivate the service later, use the `Net Continue` command.

The syntax to pause a service is:

```
net pause service
```

Here are some typical services you can pause:

- ✦ **Netlogon:** The Net Logon service.
- ✦ **Schedule:** The Task Scheduler service.
- ✦ **Server:** The Server service.
- ✦ **Workstation:** The Workstation service.

Here's an example that pauses the Workstation service:

```
CL>net pause workstation
```

If the service name has embedded spaces, enclose the service name in quotation marks. For example, this command pauses the NT LM Security Support Provider service:

```
C:\>net pause "nt lm security support provider"
```

The Net Print command

This command displays information about print jobs and shared print queues. To display information about a print queue, use this syntax:

```
net print \\computername\sharename
```

To display information about a specific print job or to change the status of a print job, use this syntax:

```
net print [\\computername] job# [/HOLD | /RELEASE | /DELETE]
```

The following paragraphs describe the parameters of the Net Print command:

✦ **\\\computername:** The name of the computer sharing the printer.

✦ **Sharename:** The name of the shared printer.

✦ **job#:** The identification number for the print job.

✦ **Hold:** Prevents a job in a queue from printing. The job remains in the queue but is not printed until released.

✦ **Release:** Releases a job that was held.

✦ **Delete:** Removes a job from the print queue.

To display the status of the print queue for a printer named LASER1 on a computer named PSERVER, use this command:

```
C:\>net print \\PSERVER\LASER1
Printers at \\PSERVER
Name                Job #      Size      Status
-------------------------------------------------------
LASER1Queue         3 jobs               *Printer Active*
    Ward            54         43546     Printing
    Wally           55         13565     Waiting
    Beaver          56         18321     Waiting
```

Now suppose that you happen to be user Beaver and you want to crowd ahead of Wally's print job. All you have to do is issue this command:

```
C:\>net print \\PSERVER 55 /hold
```

The Net Send command

This command lets you send messages to other users on the network. The message pops up, interrupting whatever the user is doing. Use this command sparingly, or you'll lose friends quickly. Here's the syntax:

```
net send {name | * | /domain[:name] | /users} message
```

Here's what each of the parameters do:

✦ **Name:** Provides the name of the user or computer to whom you want to send the message. (This can also be an alias created by the Net Name command.) If the name includes spaces, enclose it in quotes.

✦ ***:** Sends the message to all computers in the domain or workgroup.

✦ **Domain:** Sends the message to everyone in the computer's domain or workgroup. If you specify a domain name, the message is sent to all users in the specified domain or workgroup.

✦ **Users:** Sends the message to all users who are currently connected to the server.

✦ *Message:* The message to be sent. Interestingly, you don't have to enclose the message in quotes even if it contains spaces.

To send the message "I'm shutting down the server in 10 minutes" to everyone on the network, use this command:

```
C:\>net send * I'm shutting down the server in 10 minutes
```

To send the message "How about lunch?" to a user named Pooh, use this command:

```
C:\>net send pooh How about lunch?
```

The Net Session command

This command lets you view current server connections and kick users off, if you feel inclined. Here's the syntax:

```
net session [\\ComputerName] [/delete]
```

Here's what the parameters do:

✦ *ComputerName:* Indicates which computer's session you want to view or disconnect. If you omit this parameter, all sessions are listed.

✦ **Delete:** Disconnects the computer's session. Any open files are immediately closed. If you use this parameter without specifying a computer name, all computers currently connected to the server are disconnected.

This is an obviously dangerous command. If you disconnect users while they're updating files or before they have a chance to save their work, they will be hopping mad.

To find out who is connected to a computer, use this command:

```
C:\>net session
Computer    User name      Client type   Opens Idle time
-------------------------------------------------------
\\DEN       Ward           Windows XP    1     00:00:4
\\BEDROOM   Administrator  Windows 2008  0     02:15:17
```

The Net Share command

This command lets you manage shared resources. To display information about all shares or a specific share, use this syntax:

```
net share [ShareName]
```

To create a new share, use this syntax:

```
net share ShareName=path  [{/users:number|/unlimited}]
    [/remark:"text"]    [/cache: {manual|automatic|no}]
```

To change the properties of an existing share, use this syntax:

```
net share ShareName [{/users:number|unlimited}]
    [/remark:"text"]                [/cache: {manual|automatic|no}]
```

To delete an existing share, use this syntax:

```
net share {ShareName|drive:path} /delete
```

Here's what each of the parameters do:

+ ***ShareName***: Specifies the share name. Use this parameter by itself to display information about the share.

+ ***Path***: Specifies the path to the folder to be shared. The path should include a drive letter. If the path includes spaces, enclose it in quotation marks.

+ **Users:** Specifies how many users can access the share concurrently.

+ **Unlimited:** Specifies that an unlimited number of users can access the share concurrently.

+ **Remark:** Creates a descriptive comment for the share. The comment should be enclosed in quotation marks.

+ **Cache:** Specifies the caching option for the share.

+ **Delete:** Stops sharing the folder.

If you use `Net Share` without any parameters, all the current shares are listed, as shown in this example:

```
C:\>net share
Sharename  Resource                 Remark
-------------------------------------------------
ADMIN$     C:\WINNT                 Remote Admin
C$         C:\                      Default Share
print$     C:\WINNT\SYSTEM\SPOOL
IPC$                                Remote IPC
LASER      LPT1                     Spooled Laser printer
```

The following example creates a share named Docs:

```
C:\>net share Docs=C:\SharedDocs /remark:"Shared documents"
```

The Net Start command

This command lets you start a networking service or display a list of all the services that are currently running. The syntax is

```
net start [service]
```

In most cases, you'll use this command to start a service that you've previously stopped with the `Net Stop` command. In that case, you should first run the `Net Start` command without any parameters to find the name of the service that you want to stop. Make a note of the exact spelling of the service that you want to stop. Then, use the `Net Stop` command to stop the service. When you want to restart the service, use the `Net Start` command again — this time specifying the service to start.

For example, suppose that you need to stop your DNS server. Using `Net Start`, you discover that the name of the service is "DNS Server," so you use the following command to stop it:

```
C:\>net stop "DNS Server"
```

Then, you can later use this command to restart the service:

```
C:\>net start "DNS Server"
```

The Net Statistics command

This command lists the statistics log for the local Workstation or Server service. The syntax is

```
net statistics [{workstation | server}]
```

You can specify `Workstation` or `Server` to indicate for which service you'd like to view statistics.

If you use `Net Statistics Workstation`, the following information appears:

+ The computer name.

+ The date and time the statistics were last updated.

+ The number of bytes and server message blocks (SMB) received and transmitted.

+ The number of read and write operations that succeeded or failed.

+ The number of network errors.

+ The number of sessions that failed, disconnected, or were reconnected.

+ The number of connections to shared resources that succeeded or failed.

If you use `Net Statistics Server`, the following information is listed.

+ The computer name.

+ The date and time the statistics were last updated.

+ The number of sessions that have been started, disconnected automatically, and disconnected because of errors.

+ The number of kilobytes sent and received and the average response time.

+ The number of password and permission errors and violations.

+ The number of times the shared files, printers, and communication devices were used.

+ The number of times the size of the memory buffer was exceeded.

**Book VII
Chapter 8**

**Windows
Commands**

The Net Stop command

This command lets you stop a networking service. The syntax is

```
net stop service
```

To use this command, first run the `Net Start` command to determine the exact spelling of the service that you want to stop. If the service name includes spaces, enclose it in quotation marks.

You can restart the service later using the `Net Start` command.

The following example stops the DNS Server service:

```
C:\>net stop "DNS Server"
```

The Net Time command

This command synchronizes the computer's clock with the clock on another computer. To access a clock on another computer in the same domain or workgroup, use this form:

```
net time \\ComputerName [/set]
```

To synchronize time with a domain, use this form:

```
net time /domain[:DomainName] [/set]
```

To use an RTS time server, use this syntax:

```
net time /rtsdomain[:DomainName] [/set]
```

To specify the computer to use for Network Time Protocol, use this syntax:

```
net time [\\ComputerName] [/querysntp]
    [/setsntp[:NTPServerList]]
```

For example, to set the computer's clock to match the Server01, use this command:

```
C:\>net time \\Server01 /set
```

The Net Use command

This command connects or disconnects to a shared resource on another computer and maps the resource to a drive letter. Here's the complete syntax:

```
net use [{drive | *}]
        [{\\ComputerName\ShareName]
        [{Password | *}]]
        [/user:[DomainName\]UserName]
        [/savecred]
        [/smartcard]
        [{/delete | /persistent:{yes | no}}]
```

To set up a home directory, use this syntax:

```
net use [drive [/home[{password | *}]
        [/delete:{yes | no}]]
```

And to control whether connections should be persistent, use this:

```
net use [/persistent:{yes | no}]
```

Here's what the parameters do:

✦ ***DeviceName:*** Specifies the drive letter. (Note that for a printer, you should specify a printer device such as LPT1: here instead of a drive letter.) If you specify an asterisk, Windows will determine what drive letter to use.

✦ ***\\ComputerName\ShareName:*** The server and share name to connect to.

✦ ***Password:*** The password needed to access the shared resource. If you use an asterisk, you're prompted for the password.

✦ **User:** Specifies the username to use for the connection.

✦ **Savecred:** Saves the credentials for reuse later if the user is prompted for a password.

✦ **Smartcard:** Specifies that the connection should use a smart card for authorization.

✦ **Delete:** Deletes the specified connection. If you specify an asterisk (*), all network connections are canceled.

✦ **Persistent:** Specifies whether connections should be persistent.

✦ **Home:** Connects to the home directory.

To display all current connections, type **net use** with no parameters.

The following example shows how to create a persistent connection to a drive named Acct on a server named Server01, using drive K:

```
C:\>net use k: \\Server01\Acct /persistent: yes
```

The following example drops the connection:

```
C:\>net use k: /delete
```

The Net User command

This command creates or changes user accounts. To display a user's information, use this form:

```
net user username
```

To update user information, use this form:

```
net user [username [password | *] [options]] [/domain]
```

To add a new user, use this form:

```
net user username [password | *] /add [options] [/domain]
```

To delete a user, use this form:

```
net user username /delete [/domain]
```

Most of the parameters for this command are straightforward. However, the `options` parameters can have a variety of different settings. Table 8-2 lists the descriptions of these options as presented by the `Net Help Users` command:

Table 8-2	The Options Parameters
Options	*Description*
`/ACTIVE:{YES	NO}`	Activates or deactivates the account. If the account is not active, the user can't access the server. The default is `YES`.
`/COMMENT:"text"`	Provides a descriptive comment about the user's account (maximum of 48 characters). Enclose the text in quotation marks.
`/COUNTRYCODE:nnn`	Uses the operating system country code to implement the specified language files for a user's help and error messages. A value of 0 signifies the default country code.
`/EXPIRES:{date	NEVER}`	Causes the account to expire if date is set. `NEVER` sets no time limit on the account. An expiration date is in the form *mm/dd/yy* or *dd/mm/yy*, depending on the country code. Months can be a number, spelled out, or abbreviated with three letters. The year can be two or four numbers. Use slashes(/) (no spaces) to separate parts of the date.
`/FULLNAME:"name"`	Is a user's full name (rather than a username). Enclose the name in quotation marks.
`/HOMEDIR:pathname`	Sets the path for the user's home directory. The path must exist.
`/PASSWORDCHG:{YES	NO}`	Specifies whether users can change their own passwords. The default is `YES`.
`/PASSWORDREQ:{YES	NO}`	Specifies whether a user account must have a password. The default is `YES`.

Options	Description
/PROFILEPATH[:*path*]	Sets a path for the user's logon profile.
/SCRIPTPATH:*pathname*	Is the location of the user's logon script.
/TIMES:{times | ALL}	Is the logon hours. TIMES is expressed as *day*[-*day*][,*day*[-*day*]],*time*[-*time*] [,*time*[-*time*]], limited to 1-hour increments. Days can be spelled out or abbreviated. Hours can be 12- or 24-hour notation. For 12-hour notation, use am or pm (without periods) or a.m., or p.m. ALL means a user can always log on, and a blank value means a user can never log on. Separate day and time entries with a comma, and separate multiple day and time entries with a semicolon.
/USERCOMMENT:"*text*"	Lets an administrator add or change the User Comment for the account.
/WORKSTATIONS:	Lists as many as eight computers from which a user {*ComputerName*[,...] | *} can log on to the network. If /WORKSTATIONS has no list or if the list is *, the user can log on from any computer.

To display information for a particular user, use the command like this:

```
C:\>net user Doug
```

To add a user account for Theodore Cleaver with the username Beaver, use this command:

```
C:\>net user Beaver /add /fullname:"Theodore Cleaver"
```

The Net View command

This command displays information about your network. If you use it without parameters, it displays a list of the computers in your domain. You can use parameters to display resources that are being shared by a particular computer. Here's the syntax:

```
net view [\\ComputerName] [/domain[:DomainName]]
net view /network:nw [\\ComputerName]
```

Here's what the parameters do:

✦ *ComputerName:* The computer whose shared resources you want to view.

✦ *DomainName:* The domain you want to view if other than the current domain.

Here's typical output from a Net View command:

```
C:\>net view
Server Name            Remark
-------------------------------------------------
\\Server01             Main file server
\\Print01              Main print server
```

The RunAs Command

The RunAs command lets you run a program from a command prompt using the credentials of another user account. Here's the basic syntax:

```
runas /user:username [other parameters] program
```

For example, to run the Microsoft Management Console with the dom1 domain's administrator account, you can use this command:

```
runas /user:dom1\administrator mmc
```

Assuming that the username is valid, you'll be prompted for the user's password. Then, the program will be run using the specified user's account.

Here are some of the parameters you can use with the RunAs command:

✦ **/user:** Specifies the domain and username. You can use one of two forms to specify the domain and username: *domain\username* or *username@domain*.

✦ **/profile:** Specifies that the user's profile should be loaded. (This option is on by default, so you don't have to explicitly specify it.)

✦ **/noprofile:** Doesn't load the user's profile. Although this can cause the application to load more quickly, it can also prevent some applications from functioning properly.

✦ **/env:** Uses the current environment instead of the user's.

✦ **/netonly:** Indicates that the user account isn't valid in the current domain. (If you use /netonly, the username must be specified in the form *domain\username*; the *username@domain* form won't work.)

✦ **/savecred:** Saves the password so it has to be entered only the first time the RunAs command is used.

The /savecred parameter is an extremely bad idea, as it creates a gaping security hole. In short, once you've used /savecred, any user at the computer can use the RunAs command to run any program with administrator privileges.

✦ **/smartcard:** Specifies that the user's credentials will be supplied by a smartcard device.

Book VIII
Using Other Windows Servers

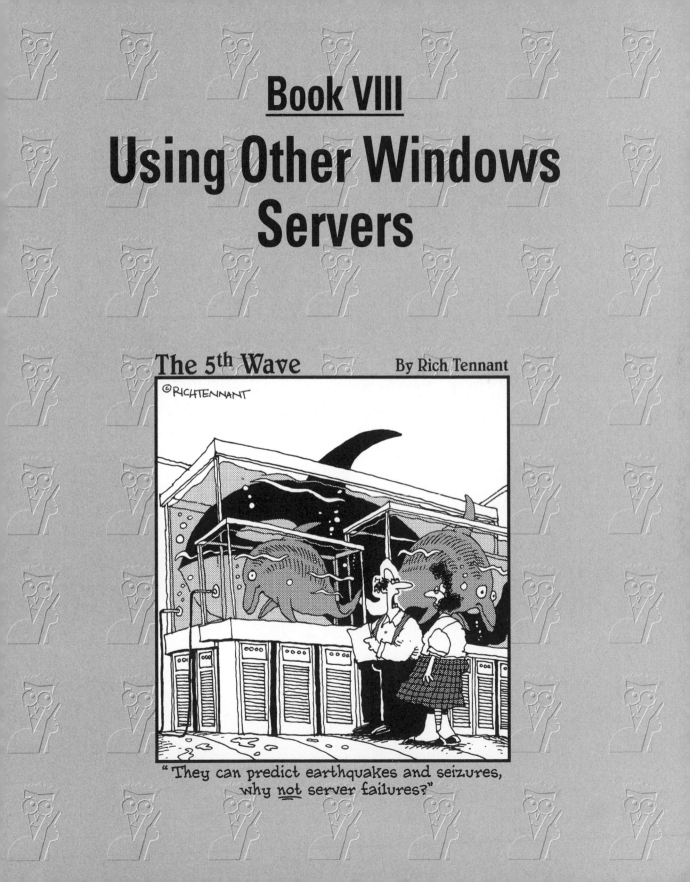

The 5th Wave   By Rich Tennant

"They can predict earthquakes and seizures, why not server failures?"

Contents at a Glance

Chapter 1: Using Internet Information System (IIS)

In This Chapter

✔ Configuring a server to use IIS

✔ Working with the default Web site

✔ Creating your own Web sites

*I*nternet Information Services, also known as *IIS,* is the Web server that comes with Windows Server 2003 and 2008. It is an essential piece of software for hosting public Web sites, and it's also a must for any network that includes an intranet with Web pages designed to be used by your network users.

In this chapter, you'll learn how to set up IIS and perform the most common types of maintenance chores, such as creating new Web sites.

Installing IIS

IIS is a free component of Windows Server 2003 and 2008, but it's not installed by default. After you have completed the installation of Windows Server, you must add the Web Server role to enable IIS. The following procedure is for Windows Server 2008, but the procedure for Windows Server 2003 is similar:

1. **Choose Start⇨Administrative Tools⇨Server Manager.**

The Server Manager comes to life.

2. **Choose Roles in the navigation pane.**

The roles configured for the server are displayed.

3. **Click Add Roles.**

This launches the Welcome page of the Add Roles Wizard.

4. **Click Next.**

The Select Server Roles page appears, as shown in Figure 1-1.

5. **Check the Web Server (IIS) role, and then click Next.**

The Web Server (IIS) page appears, as shown in Figure 1-2.

6. Click Next.

The Role Services page appears, as shown in Figure 1-3. This page lists a variety of optional services that can be configured for IIS.

7. Select the services you want to configure for IIS.

If you want, you can study this list and try to anticipate which features you think you'll need. Or you can just leave the default options selected.

You can always return to the Add Roles Wizard to add features you leave out here.

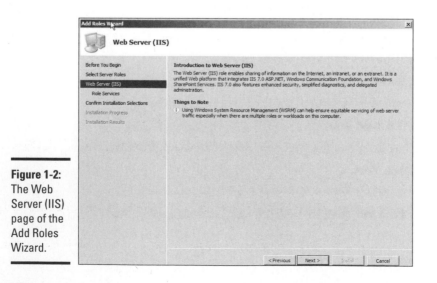

Figure 1-1:
The Select Server Roles page of the Add Roles Wizard.

Figure 1-2:
The Web Server (IIS) page of the Add Roles Wizard.

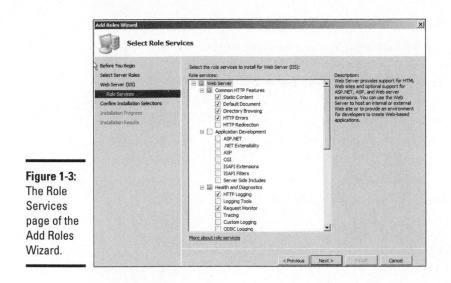

Figure 1-3:
The Role
Services
page of the
Add Roles
Wizard.

8. **Click Next.**

The Confirm Installation Selections page appears, as shown in Figure 1-4.

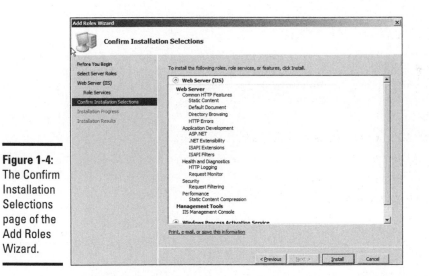

Figure 1-4:
The Confirm
Installation
Selections
page of the
Add Roles
Wizard.

9. **Click Install.**

The features you selected are installed. This may take a few minutes, so now would be a good time to take a walk.

When the installation finishes, the Installation Results page is displayed, as shown in Figure 1-5.

10. **Click Close.**

IIS is now installed and ready to use!

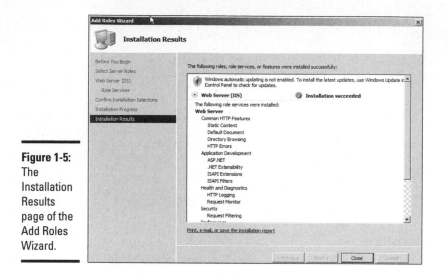

Figure 1-5:
The
Installation
Results
page of the
Add Roles
Wizard.

Understanding the Default Web Site

Initially, IIS is configured with a single Web site, called the *default Web site*. You can test that IIS is up and running by opening a browser window on the server and typing **localhost** in the address bar. You can also reach this page by entering your local domain name in the address bar. For example, **lowewriter.pri**. Figure 1-6 shows the standard welcome page that appears when you browse to the default site.

The actual files that make up the default Web site are stored on the server's C: drive in a folder named \inetpub\wwwroot. When you browse to the default Web site without requesting a specific file (for example, by entering simply **localhost** in the address bar), IIS looks for the following files, in this order:

+ default.htm
+ default.asp
+ index.htm
+ index.html
+ iisstart.htm
+ default.aspx

Figure 1-6:
The default
Web site.

Initially, `c:\inetpub\wwwroot` contains just two files: `iisstart.htm` and `welcome.png`. The `iisstart.htm` file is the file that's displayed when you browse to the Web site; it contains the HTML markup necessary to display the image contained in the `welcome.png` file, which is the image you actually see on the page.

You can preempt the standard page for the default Web site by providing your own file with one of the preceding names. For example, you can follow these steps to create a simple `default.htm` file that displays the words "Hello World!" as the start page for the default Web site:

1. **Open an Explorer window and browse to `c:\inetpub\wwwroot`.**

2. **Choose File⇨New⇨Text Document, type** default.htm **for the filename, and press Enter.**

3. **Right-click the `default.htm` file you just created and choose Open With⇨Notepad.**

4. **Enter the following text in the Notepad window:**

```
<HTML>
<BODY>
<H1>Hello World!</H1>
</BODY>
</HTML>
```

**Book VIII
Chapter 1**

**Using Internet
Information
System (IIS)**

5. **Choose File⇨Save to save the file, and then choose File⇨Exit to quit Notepad.**

6. **Open a browser window.**

7. **Type** localhost **in the address bar and press Enter.**

The page shown in Figure 1-7 appears.

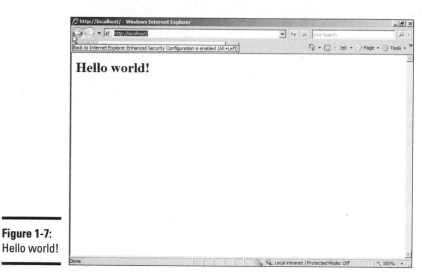

Figure 1-7:
Hello world!

Creating Web Sites

IIS has the ability to host multiple Web sites. This is an extremely useful feature not only for Web servers that host public sites, but also for Web servers that host internal (intranet) sites. For example, you might create a separate intranet Web site for Human Resources and assign it the Web site name hr. Then, assuming the domain name is lowewriter.pri, users can browse to the Web site by using the address hr.lowewriter.pri.

Here are the steps:

1. **Using Windows Explorer, create a folder in which you will save the files for the new Web site.**

For this example, I created a folder named c:\HR-Web-Site.

2. **Choose Start⇨Administrative Tools⇨Internet Information Services (IIS) Manager.**

The IIS Manager springs to life, as shown in Figure 1-8.

Figure 1-8:
The IIS Manager.

3. Right-click Sites, and then choose Add Web Site.

The Add Web Site dialog box appears, as shown in Figure 1-9.

4. Enter a name for the Web site in the Web Site Name text box.

For this example, I used HR.

Figure 1-9:
The Add Web Site dialog box.

Book VIII Chapter 1

Using Internet Information System (IIS)

5. **Click the Browse button, browse to the folder you created in Step 1, and then click OK.**

   For this example, I browsed to `C:\HR-Web-Site`.

6. **In the Host Header text box, enter the exact DNS name you want to use for the site.**

   For this example, I entered `hr.lowewriter.pri`.

7. **Click OK.**

   The newly created Web site appears beneath the Sites node in the IIS Manager, as shown in Figure 1-10.

Figure 1-10: The HR Web site appears in the IIS Manager.

8. **Close the IIS Manager.**

9. **Create a Web page to display in the folder you created in Step 1.**

   For this example, I used Notepad to create a text file named `default.htm`, with the following text:

```
<HTML>
<BODY>
<H1>Welcome to the HR Web Site!</H1>
</BODY>
</HTML>
```

10. **Choose Start⇨Administrative Tools⇨DNS.**

    This brings up the DNS Management console, as shown in Figure 1-11.

Figure 1-11:
The DNS
Management
console.

11. **In the navigation pane, navigate to the node for your domain.**

In this example, I navigated to LoweWriter.pri.

12. **Choose Action⇨New Alias (CNAME).**

The New Resource Record dialog box appears, as shown in Figure 1-12.

13. **Enter the alias name you want to use in the Alias text box.**

For this example, I entered simply hr.

Figure 1-12:
Creating a
CNAME
record.

14. Enter the computer name of your Web server in the target host text box.

For this example, I entered `lserver01`.

15. Click OK.

The DNS alias is created.

16. Close the DNS Management Console.

17. Open a browser window.

18. Browse to the alias address you just created.

For this example, I browsed to `hr.lowewriter.pri`. Figure 1-13 shows the resulting page.

Figure 1-13:
Viewing a
Web site.

Chapter 2: Managing Exchange Server 2007

In This Chapter

✔ Working with the Exchange Server consoles

✔ Managing mailboxes

✔ Granting mailbox access

Although not strictly a part of Windows Server 2008, Exchange Server 2007 is the mail server software that's used on most Windows networks. Yes, I know Microsoft doesn't call Exchange Server a *mail server*. It's a *messaging and collaboration server*. But the basic reason for Exchange Server's existence is e-mail. The other messaging and collaboration features are just icing on the cake.

In this chapter, you discover how to perform the most commonly requested maintenance chores for Exchange Server, such as how to create a new mailbox, grant a user access to an additional mailbox, and deal with mailbox size limits.

Managing Mailboxes

When you create a new user by using the Add User Wizard from the Server Management Console, an Exchange mailbox is automatically created for the new user. As a result, you don't usually have to create Exchange mailboxes separately. But on occasion, you may need to modify some aspect of a user's Exchange configuration.

Several tabs of the user account Properties dialog box let you manage basic mailbox settings. To summon this dialog box, choose Start➪Administrative Tools➪Active Directory Users and Computers. Then, drill down to the user account you need to modify and double-click it. This brings up the Properties dialog box. The following sections describe the Exchange features that are available from the various tabs of this dialog box.

The Exchange General tab

The Exchange General tab, shown in Figure 2-1, lets you set the following options:

+ **Alias:** The default is the user's name, but you can change it if you want.

+ **Delivery Restrictions:** This button brings up a dialog box that lets you set a message size limit for incoming and outgoing messages. You can also specify who the user can receive messages from.

+ **Delivery Options:** This button brings up a dialog box that lets you create a forwarding address and grant permission to other users to send on behalf of this account.

+ **Storage Limits:** This button brings up a dialog box that lets you set the storage limits for the user's mailbox. You can specify that a warning message should be sent when the mailbox reaches a specified size. Then, you can specify another size after which the user will not be allowed to send or receive mail.

Figure 2-1:
The
Exchange
General tab.

The E-mail Addresses tab

The E-mail Addresses tab of the User Properties dialog box, shown in Figure 2-2, displays the e-mail addresses that are associated with a user account. If an e-mail address has been incorrectly assigned, you can use this dialog box to change it. Just select the incorrect e-mail address, click the Edit button, and enter the correct e-mail address. You can also add or remove an e-mail address from this dialog box.

Figure 2-2:
The E-mail
Addresses
tab.

The Exchange Features tab

Figure 2-3 shows the Exchange Features tab of the user Properties dialog box, which lets you configure optional Exchange features for the user. The following paragraphs describe these features:

✦ **Outlook Mobile Access:** Lets the user access Exchange data from a mobile device such as a cell phone or PDA.

✦ **User Initiated Synchronization:** Lets the user start a synchronization operation, which updates the mobile device's data from the data on the Exchange server.

✦ **Up-to-Date Notifications:** Enables automatic synchronizations.

✦ **Outlook Web Access:** Lets the user access his or her Exchange mailbox from a Web browser rather than from an Outlook client. With this feature enabled, the user can read e-mail from any computer that has an Internet connection.

✦ **POP3:** Enables Internet e-mail using the POP3 protocol.

✦ **IMAP4:** Enables Internet e-mail using the IMAP4 protocol.

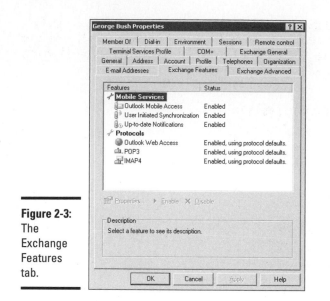

Figure 2-3:
The
Exchange
Features
tab.

The Exchange Advanced tab

The Exchange Advanced tab, shown in Figure 2-4, lets you configure various advanced features of Exchange. The following list describes these features:

✦ **Simple Display Name:** Lets you specify a display name that's used by computers that can't display the full display name. You probably won't have to mess with this unless you have computers that can't display ASCII characters.

✦ **Hide from Exchange Address Lists:** Select this option to prevent this user from appearing in address lists. This option is useful for mailboxes that you don't want to be widely known.

✦ **Downgrade High Priority Mail Bound for X.400:** This option is compatible with the original X.400 standard, which was first released in 1984. If you exchange mail with old-style X.400 systems, you may need to use this option.

✦ **Custom Attributes:** This button leads to a dialog box that lets you track up to 15 different custom attributes for a user. You can safely ignore this option.

✦ **ILS Settings:** If you have an Internet Locator Service server installed, you can click this button to configure it. ILS lets online users find each other. It's used by applications such as NetMeeting.

✦ **Mailbox Rights:** Of all the features on the Exchange Advanced tab, this is the one you'll probably use most. It lets you grant access to this user's mailbox to other users. For more information, see the section, "Viewing Another Mailbox," later in this chapter.

Figure 2-4:
The Exchange Advanced tab.

Configuring Outlook for Exchange

When you create an Active Directory user, the user is automatically set up with a mailbox. However, you must still configure that user's Outlook client software to connect to the user's account. The following procedure describes how to do that:

1. **Start Outlook on the user's computer.**

There's usually an icon for Outlook near the top of the Start menu.

2. **Choose Tools⇨Account Settings.**

The E-mail Accounts dialog box appears, as shown in Figure 2-5.

3. **Click the New button.**

An Add E-mail Account dialog box appears. Do not enter your e-mail address as prompted in this dialog box. Instead, proceed to Step 4.

**Book VIII
Chapter 2**

Managing
Exchange
Server 2007

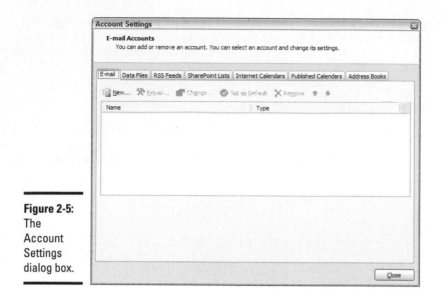

Figure 2-5:
The
Account
Settings
dialog box.

4. **Click the Manually Configure Server Settings Or Additional Server Types option, and then click Next.**

   This brings up a dialog box that asks you what type of e-mail account you want to create. The choices are Internet E-mail, Microsoft Exchange, and Other.

5. **Select the Microsoft Exchange option, and then click Next.**

   The dialog box shown in Figure 2-6 appears.

Figure 2-6:
You must
identify the
Exchange
server and
provide a
username.

6. **Enter the name of the Exchange server and the username in the appropriate text boxes, and then click Next.**

The dialog box with the following message appears:

```
The E-Mail account you have just added will not
start until you choose Exit from the File menu,
and then restart Microsoft Outlook.
```

7. **Click OK.**

The message dialog box disappears, and the last page of the E-Mail Accounts Wizard appears.

8. **Click the Finish button.**

The wizard is dismissed.

9. **Choose File⇨Exit to close Outlook, and then restart Outlook.**

The mailbox should now be configured.

Viewing Another Mailbox

Sometimes, you want to set up Outlook so that in addition to the user's main mailbox, he or she has access to another user's mailbox. For example, suppose you create a user named Support so that your customers can send e-mail to Support@YourCompany.com to ask technical support questions. If you don't set up at least one of your users so that he or she can read the Support mailbox, any mail sent to Support@YourCompany.com will languish unanswered. Assuming that's not what you want, you can set up one or more of your users to access the Support mailbox so that they can read and respond to the mail.

First, you must configure the Support user account's mailbox so that it grants access rights to the user that you want to have access to the account. To do that, follow these steps:

1. **On the server, choose Start⇨Active Directory Users and Computers, and then find and double-click the e-mail account you want to access from another user's Outlook.**

The Properties dialog box appears.

2. **Click the Exchange Advanced tab, and then click the Mailbox Rights button.**

The Permissions for Support dialog box appears, as shown in Figure 2-7.

Figure 2-7:
The Mailbox
Rights tab.

3. **Click the Add button.**

   This brings up a dialog box titled Select Users, Computers, or Groups.

4. **Type the name of the user you want to grant access to, and then click OK.**

   You're returned to the Permissions for Support dialog box. The user you added will be selected in the list of users with access to the mailbox.

5. **Select the Allow check box for the Full Mailbox Access option to grant the user full access to the mailbox, and then click OK.**

   The Mailbox Rights dialog box is dismissed.

6. **Click OK.**

   The user Properties dialog box is dismissed.

After you've granted access to the account, you can configure the user's Outlook to read the Support account. Follow these steps:

1. **On the user's computer, start Outlook and choose Tools⇨Account.**

   The Account Settings dialog box is displayed.

2. **Select your main e-mail account, and then click Change.**

   The Microsoft Exchange Settings dialog box appears, as shown in Figure 2-8.

Figure 2-8:
The
Exchange
Server
Settings
dialog box.

3. **Click the More Settings button, and then click the Advanced tab.**

The Advanced tab of the Microsoft Exchange Server dialog box appears, as shown in Figure 2-9.

Figure 2-9:
The
Advanced
tab.

4. **Click the Add button.**

   A dialog box appears to prompt you for the name of the mailbox you want to add.

5. **Type the name of the mailbox you want to add, and then click OK.**

   The mailbox is added to the list box in the Microsoft Exchange Server dialog box.

6. **Click OK.**

   You're returned to the Exchange Settings dialog box.

7. **Click Next, and then click Finish.**

   You're done! You can now view the Support mailbox.

To actually view the mailbox, you need to open the Folder List window in Outlook (by choosing View⇨Folder List). Then, you can double-click the Support mailbox in the list to open it.

Chapter 3: Using SQL Server 2008

*S*QL Server is the most common database server used on Microsoft networks. At the time of this writing, the most widely used version of SQL Server was SQL Server 2005, but a new version known as SQL Server 2008 was close to being released.

This chapter introduces you to the basics of installing and running SQL Server 2008. It begins with a basic introduction to relational databases and SQL. Then, it shows you how to install SQL Server 2008. Finally, it shows you how to use SQL Management Suite to create and manipulate databases. Note that the information in this chapter applies to SQL Server 2005 as well.

What Is a Database?

A *database* is simply an organized collection of information. Here are some examples of databases from everyday life:

✦ Your personal address book

✦ The shoebox that contains your tax records for the year

✦ Your baseball card collection

✦ All those parking tickets conveniently stuffed into your car's glove compartment

✦ The phone book

✦ That pile of score cards that has been accumulating in the bottom of your golf bag for 15 years

You can think of each of these databases as a collection of records. In database lingo, a *record* consists of all the useful information that you can gather about a particular thing. In your address book, each record represents one of your friends (or enemies). For your tax records database, each receipt in the shoebox is a record.

Each little snippet of information that makes up a record is called a *field*. Using the address book as an example once again, each person's record — that is, each entry in your address book — consists of several fields: name, street address, city, state, zip code, phone number, e-mail address, as well as other information that may be optional, such as the person's birthday, whether you sent a Christmas card to the person last year, or how much money the person owes you.

SQL Server is designed to create and manage computerized databases that are similar to these noncomputerized databases. Like your address book or shoebox full of tax records, a SQL Server database is a collection of records, and each record is a collection of fields. The biggest difference is that in a SQL Server database, the information is stored on a server computer's hard disk rather than in a shoe box.

What Is a Relational Database?

"Say Al, do you think they call it a *relational database* because it's good at dealing with relationships?"

"I don't think so, Tim."

SQL Server is a database management server that creates and maintains relational databases. Unfortunately, the term *relational database* is one of the most used and abused buzzwords in the computer business. The term has at least three meanings. A *relational database* can be:

✦ *A database in which data is stored in tables.* In a relational database, groups of similar records are called *tables.* A database usually consists of more than one table — in fact, it isn't uncommon for a single database to have dozens of different tables. You can establish relationships between and among these tables based on common information. For example, a sales database might contain a table of customer information and a table of invoices, with both tables containing a customer number column that establishes a relationship between the tables.

✦ *A database model based on a Conehead branch of mathematics called Set Theory.* This is actually the most technically precise definition of a relational database, but only computer geeks know or care. Contrary to popular belief, the term *relational database* is not derived from the ability to create relationships among tables, but from the term *relation,* a mathematical term that refers to the way data is arranged into tables of rows and columns.

(It is a little known fact that relational database theory was developed at around the same time that the Coneheads from the planet Remulak first visited the Earth, back in the 1970s. I have always suspected that these two developments are — dare I say it? — related.)

✦ *A database that is accessed via SQL.* SQL, which stands for *Structured Query Language*, provides a practical way to access data stored in relational tables. A database that is based on SQL is inherently relational because SQL stores its data in tables and is based on Set Theory. SQL Server, as its name implies, is based on SQL.

From a practical point of view, the third definition is the most important: A relational database is a database that you can access via SQL. Thus, SQL Server is used for relational databases. The next section dives a little more deeply into what SQL is.

What Is SQL?

SQL, which stands for *Structured Query Language,* is a language designed to extract, organize, and update information in relational databases. Originally, SQL was envisioned as an English-like query language that untrained end users could use to access and update relational database data. But in reality, SQL is nothing like English, and it's far too complicated and esoteric for untrained users. But it has become the overwhelming favorite among programmers who develop applications that access relational databases.

How do you pronounce SQL?

Here's something you've probably wondered ever since you first saw the letters SQL: How do you pronounce it? Two schools of thought exist on the subject:

✦ Spell out the letters: *S-Q-L.*

✦ Pronounce it like the word *sequel.*

Either way is acceptable, but *sequel* is hipper.

You can always tell how a writer pronounces SQL by checking to see if the author writes "a SQL query" or "an SQL query."

You can impress even the staunchest SQL expert by pointing out that originally, the language was spelled *SEQUEL* by the IBM engineers who created the first version way back in the 1970s. SEQUEL stood for *Structured English Query Language.* Someone must have correctly pointed out that aside from borrowing a few words from English such as `select` and `CREATE`, SEQUEL actually bore no resemblance whatsoever to English. So *English* was dropped from the name and the acronym was shortened from SEQUEL to just SQL.

SQL dialects

Like most computer languages, SQL has several different dialects. In fact, each major brand of SQL database server has its own dialect of SQL. These dialects are 95 percent the same, so a basic SQL statement is likely to work the same regardless of the database server you use it with. But there are many variations in how the more advanced features of SQL work.

The version of SQL used by Microsoft's SQL Server is known as *T-SQL*.

SQL statements

Like other programming languages, SQL uses statements to get its work done. Table 3-1 lists the most commonly used statements:

Table 3-1	Common SQL Statements
SQL Statement	*What It Does*
use	Identifies the name of the database that subsequent SQL statements apply to.
select	Retrieves data from one or more tables. This is the SQL statement that's used the most.
insert	Inserts one or more rows into a table.
delete	Deletes one or more rows from a table.
update	Updates existing rows in a table.
create	Creates tables and other database objects.
alter	Alters the definition of a table or other database object.
drop	Deletes a table or other database object.

Using the select statement

As the name *Structured Query Language* suggests, queries are what SQL is all about. Thus, the select statement is the most important of the SQL statements. A select statement extracts data from one or more tables in a database and creates a *result set* containing the selected rows and columns.

In a select statement, you list the table or tables from which you want to retrieve the data, the specific table columns you want retrieved (you might not be interested in everything that's in the table), and other clauses that indicate which specific rows should be retrieved, what order the rows should be presented in, and so on.

Here's a simple `select` statement that retrieves data from a table named `movies`, which contains information about your favorite movies:

```
select title, year
    from movie
    order by year
```

Let's take this statement apart piece by piece:

✦ `select title, year` names the columns you want included in the query result (title and year).

✦ `from movie` names the table you want the rows retrieved from (movie).

✦ `order by year` indicates that the result should be sorted into sequence by the `year` column so the oldest movie appears first.

In other words, this `select` statement retrieves the title and date for all the rows in the `movie` table and sorts them into `year` sequence.

If you want the query to retrieve all of the columns in each row, you can use an asterisk instead of naming the individual columns:

```
select * from movie order by year;
```

Both examples so far include an `order by` clause. In a SQL database, the rows stored in a table are not assumed to be in any particular sequence. As a result, if you want to display the results of a query in sequence, you must include an `order by` in the select statement.

Suppose you want to find information about one particular video title. To select certain rows from a table, use the `where` clause in a `select` statement. For example:

```
select title, year from movie
    where year <= 1980
    order by year
```

Here, the `select` statement selects all rows in which the `year` column is less than or equal to 1980. The results are ordered by the `year` column.

Perhaps you want to retrieve all rows except those that match certain criteria. For example, here's a query that ignores movies made in the 1970s (which is probably a good idea, with a few exceptions like *The Godfather* and *Young Frankenstein*):

```
select title, year from movie
    where year < 1970 or year > 1979
    order by year;
```

There is, of course, much more you can do with `select` statements. But this chapter isn't about SQL itself; it's about installing and using SQL Server. So let's get on to the good stuff.

Installing SQL Server 2008

Like Exchange Server, SQL Server is licensed separately from Microsoft; it isn't included with any version of SQL Server 2008. As a result, you'll have to install it on a Windows Server computer before you can use it to create and access SQL databases.

You will probably want to run this installation procedure at least twice. First, you'll want to run it on a server computer to install the SQL Server 2008 server components, thus creating a *SQL Server instance.* Then, you'll want to run the setup procedure on a client workstation computer to install the management components that you run from a local workstation to manage the server. Depending on the needs of your organization, you may also need to run the setup program additional times to install other components.

The following steps summarize the procedure for installing SQL Server 2008:

1. **Insert the SQL Server 2008 distribution disk in the server computer's CD/DVD drive.**

   The installation program should auto-start. If it doesn't, browse to the disk, open the Servers folder, and double-click the `Splash.hta` file. The screen shown in Figure 3-1 appears.

2. **Under the Install heading, click the Server Components, Tools, Books Online, and Samples link.**

   This starts the SQL Server 2008 Setup program, which begins by displaying a license agreement page.

3. **Select the "I accept. . . ." check box, and then click Next.**

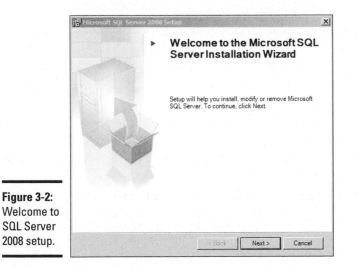

Figure 3-1:
Installing
SQL Server
2008.

4. **Be patient while the Setup program installs any prerequisites that are missing.**

Typically, this takes just a minute while the Setup program installs support files that are necessary for the installation to proceed.

5. **When the prerequisites have been installed, click Next.**

The Setup program next displays the SQL Server 2008 Setup Program welcome screen, as shown in Figure 3-2.

Figure 3-2:
Welcome to
SQL Server
2008 setup.

**Book VIII
Chapter 3**

**Using SQL
Server 2008**

6. **Click Next.**

The Setup program checks to make sure all of the requirements are in place for a successful installation of SQL Server 2008. This may take a few minutes. When all of the tests are complete, you'll see a screen such as the one shown in Figure 3-3. If any errors or warnings are detected, be sure to correct them before continuing.

Figure 3-3:
Checking the system requirements.

7. **Click Next.**

The Setup program prompts you to enter your name and your company name to personalize the installation.

8. **Enter your name (required) and company name (optional), and then click Next.**

The next screen, shown in Figure 3-4, lets you select which components of SQL Server 2008 you want to install.

9. **Select the components you want to install.**

At the minimum, you should select the first component, SQL Server Database Services.

You can select specific elements of any of the SQL Server components by clicking the Advanced button.

You should also install the Workstation components. However, you won't typically want to install them on the same computer that you install the SQL Database Services components. Instead, you'll want to repeat this entire procedure, installing the Workstation components on a client computer. You can then use these components to manage the SQL Server from a client computer, without having to log on to the server.

The remainder of this procedure assumes you have selected the SQL Server Database Services components to install a new SQL Server instance. If you are installing the Workstation components, the prompts and steps will vary slightly.

Figure 3-4:
Determining which components of SQL Server 2008 to install.

10. **Click Next.**

The Setup program next asks for the name of the Instance you want to create, as shown in Figure 3-5. You can leave this option set to Default Instance, which uses the name of the server as the instance name, or you can specify your own instance name if you prefer.

Figure 3-5:
Specifying an instance name.

11. **Choose the instance name, and then click Next.**

The Service Account screen appears, as shown in Figure 3-6. This screen lets you specify the Windows account that will be used to run the SQL Server services on the server computer. You can leave this set to the built-in system account, or if you prefer, you can choose a domain account to run the services. Note that if you choose to use a domain account, you must first use Active Directory Users and Computers to create the account, and you must make sure the account has adequate privileges.

Figure 3-6:
Specifying a service account.

12. **Select the service account, and then click Next.**

The Authentication Mode screen appears, as shown in Figure 3-7. This screen lets you choose one of two methods for authenticating users: Windows Authentication Mode, which relies entirely on Windows domain accounts, and Mixed Mode, which uses Windows domain accounts and accounts that are created within SQL Server. Unless you have a specific reason to use Mixed Mode (for example, you have older applications that depend on SQL Server accounts), I recommend that you select Windows Authentication Mode.

13. **Select the authentication mode, and then click Next.**

A screen called *Collation Settings* appears. This screen lets you change the way SQL Server sorts data. In most cases, you should leave this option set at its default.

14. **Click Next.**

A screen titled *Error and Usage Reporting Settings* appears. This screen lets you choose whether the server should send diagnostic information to Microsoft when errors occur and whether the server should send usage data to let Microsoft know which features of SQL Server you use the most. You can enable these features if you don't care about the privacy of this information or the small performance penalty the communication incurs. If you want to keep this information private or are obsessively concerned about performance, you can disable these features.

Figure 3-7:
Specifying
the
authentica-
tion mode.

15. **Enable or disable the reporting settings, and then click Next.**

The next screen displays a summary of what components of SQL Server will be installed, as shown in Figure 3-8.

Figure 3-8:
Summarizing
the
installation.

16. **Click Next to begin the installation.**

The Setup program proceeds with the installation, which can take a few minutes. A progress screen appears to indicate the installation's progress. When all components have been installed, the screen shown in Figure 3-9 appears.

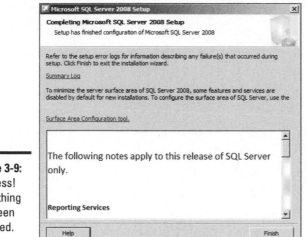

Figure 3-9:
Success!
Everything
has been
installed.

17. **Click Next to continue.**

One final completion screen appears to congratulate you on a job well done.

18. **Click Finish.**

You're done!

Using the SQL Server 2008 Management Studio

The SQL Server Management Studio is a component of SQL Server 2008 that runs on workstation computers and lets you manage any or all of the SQL Server instances on your network. You run it by choosing SQL Server Management Studio from the Start menu on a workstation computer. The Management Studio begins by displaying a Connect to Server dialog box, as shown in Figure 3-10. You can use this dialog box to connect to any SQL Server instance on your network.

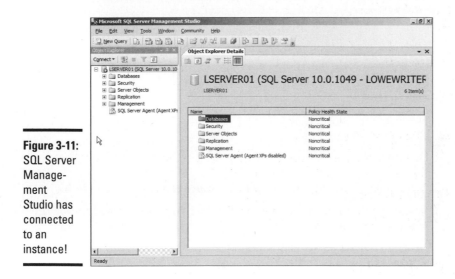

Figure 3-10:
Connecting
to a SQL
Server
instance.

To connect to a SQL Server instance, specify the instance name and your
login credentials, and then click Connect. After you have connected, the
Management Studio displays the screen shown in Figure 3-11.

Figure 3-11:
SQL Server
Manage-
ment
Studio has
connected
to an
instance!

The following sections explain how to perform some of the most common
SQL Server chores, such as creating databases and tables, viewing database
data, and so on.

Creating a New Database

To create a new database, follow these steps:

1. **Right-click the Databases node in the navigation pane (on the left side of the Management Studio window) and choose New Database from the menu that appears.**

This brings up the New Database dialog box, shown in Figure 3-12.

Figure 3-12:
Creating a
new
database.

2. **Type a name for the new database in the Database Name field.**

3. **Enter the domain username for the user who is responsible for the database in the Owner name field.**

You can leave this set to the default if you want yourself to be listed as the owner.

4. **If you want, change the settings for the database and log files.**

You can change the following settings:

• *Initial Size:* This refers to the amount of disk space initially allocated to the files. The defaults are a ridiculously small 2MB for the database and 1MB for the log files. Unless your databases are going to be extremely small, you should probably increase these defaults.

• *Autogrowth:* This setting sets the incremental amount by which the database grows when it exceeds the allocated capacity. Again, you'll probably want to change these amounts for any but the smallest databases.

- *Path:* This points the way to the folder where the files are stored. By default, the files are created under the Program Files folder on the server's C: drive. You may want to change this setting to a more appropriate location.

- *File Name:* You can change this setting if you want to use a filename that's different from the database name.

Note that you can change additional options by clicking Options or Filegroups near the left side of the New Database window. This links to additional pages of options you can set to tweak the behavior of the database.

5. **Click OK.**

SQL Server grinds and whirs for a few moments while it creates the new database. When it's finished, the database appears under the Databases node, as shown in Figure 3-13.

That's all!

The new database is ready to use. Of course, the database won't be very useful until you define some tables. So read on.

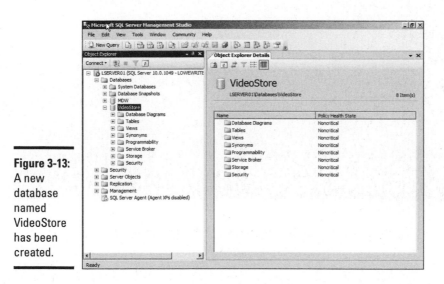

Figure 3-13: A new database named VideoStore has been created.

Book VIII
Chapter 3

Using SQL
Server 2008

Creating Tables

A database is nothing more than a container for various types of database objects. The most important of these objects are *tables*, which hold the actual data that makes up the database. A database isn't very useful without at least one table. Most real-world databases have more than one table — in fact, many databases have dozens of tables.

To create a table, follow these steps:

1. **Right-click the Tables node for the database and choose New Table.**

The window shown in Figure 3-14 appears.

Figure 3-14: Creating a new table.

2. **Type the name of the first column of the table, and then press the Tab key.**

3. **Choose the data type for the column, and then press the Tab key.**

SQL Server has several data types to choose from for each column. Use the drop-down list to choose the appropriate type.

4. **Use the Allow Nulls check box to indicate whether the column should allow null values, and then press the Tab key.**

Nulls are one of the more confusing aspects of database design and programming. In a SQL database, *null* means that the item does not have a value. It is different than zero (for numbers) or an empty string (for text). Allowing a column to have null values introduces programming complexities because when you retrieve the value of a column, the program has to anticipate that the value might be missing. But prohibiting nulls (by deselecting the check box) also introduces complexities because you have to make sure you always provide an explicit value for every column.

The phrase *null value* is actually an oxymoron. Because *null* means the absence of a value, it doesn't make sense to say a column can have a null value, or that the value of a column is null.

5. Repeat Steps 2 through 4 to create additional columns.

Figure 3-15 shows how the table looks after several columns have been defined.

Figure 3-15:
A table with several columns.

6. When all of the columns have been created, select the column you want to use as a key field for the table, and then right-click the column and choose Set Primary Key.

A little key icon will appear next to the column or columns to indicate the primary key.

(The *primary key* provides a unique value that can be used to identify each row in the table. Most tables use a single column, such as a Customer Number or an Invoice Number, as the primary key. But some tables create the primary key by combining two or more columns. This type of key is called a *composite key.*)

Book VIII
Chapter 3

**Using SQL
Server 2008**

7. **Right-click the table name tab that appears above the list of columns and choose Save.**

   A Save dialog box appears, prompting you to enter a name for the table.

8. **Type a name for the table, and then click OK.**

   The table is created.

Note that each column has a properties page that appears when you select the column. You can set a variety of properties for each column, including the following:

✦ **Default Value:** A value that is supplied for the column if no value is provided when a row is created. This property is especially useful for columns that do not allow null values.

✦ **Description:** A text description that you can use to explain the purpose of the column.

✦ **Identity Specification:** Used to create an *identity field,* which is a field whose value is automatically generated when rows are created. Identity fields are often used as the primary key field for a table when it is desirable for the table to have a primary key, but no other column in the table provides a unique value for each row.

   When you create an identity field, you can specify two settings that affect how the values are generated. The *seed* is the value used for the first row in the table. The *increment* is a value that's added to the seed for each subsequent row. For example, if you specify 1000 for the seed and 1 for the increment, the rows in the table will be numbered 1001, 1002, 1003, and so on.

Editing Tables

SQL Management Studio includes a spreadsheet-like feature that lets you directly edit the contents of database tables. To use it, right-click the table you want to edit and choose Open Table. The table is opened in a spreadsheet-like window. You can then add data to the table by entering table values for each row. Figure 3-16 shows a table after some data has been added via the Open Table command.

Note that in addition to inserting new rows, you can edit existing rows. You can also delete one or more rows by selecting the rows you want to delete and pressing the Delete key.

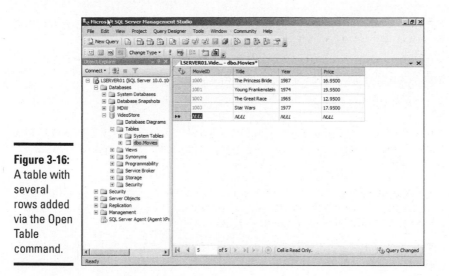

Figure 3-16:
A table with several rows added via the Open Table command.

Working with Queries

SQL Management Studio includes a query tool that lets you type SQL commands and execute them. You can type any SQL statement you want in a query Window, and then press the Execute button to execute the query.

There are two important rules to follow when you work with queries:

✦ First, each SQL statement in the query should end with a semicolon.

✦ Second, you should begin the query with a USE statement that provides the name of the database.

Here's an example of a query that follows these two rules:

```
use VideoStore;
select * from movies;
```

The USE statement indicates that the query applies to the VideoStore database, and the select statement retrieves all of the data from the Movies table.

To use the query tool, click the New Query button on the toolbar. Then, enter the statements for your query in the window and click the Execute button on the toolbar. The results of the query will be displayed in the window, as shown in Figure 3-17.

Figure 3-17:
A query that retrieves data from the Movies table.

Working with Scripts

One final feature of SQL Management Studio I want to cover in this chapter is the use of scripts. Although you can create databases by using the graphical features presented earlier in this chapter (in the sections "Creating a New Database" and "Creating Tables"), it's actually a much better practice to write SQL scripts that contain the CREATE commands necessary to create the database as well as its tables and other objects. That's because during the development and operation of any database application, there is often a need to delete the database and re-create it from scratch. By scripting these actions, you can delete the database and re-create it simply by running a script.

Fortunately, SQL Management Studio can generate scripts from existing databases and tables. Thus, you can use the visual design features of SQL Management Studio to initially create your databases. Then, you can generate scripts that will let you easily delete and re-re-create the database.

To create a script for a database or table, just right-click the database or table, and then choose one of the Script As commands. For example, Figure 3-18 shows the script that results when I right-click the Movies table and choose Script Table As⇨CREATE To⇨New Query Window. As you can see, this command generated a CREATE TABLE statement along with other advanced SQL statements to create the Movies table automatically.

Figure 3-18:
A script that creates the Movies table.

After you've created the script, you can save it to a text file by clicking the Save button. Then, you can run the script at any time by following these steps:

1. **Choose File➪Open➪File.**

2. **Select the file you saved the script to.**

3. **Click Open.**

4. **Click the Execute button to run the script.**

The only limitation of this technique is that although you can generate scripts to define your databases and tables, you can't automatically generate scripts to insert data into your tables. If you want scripts that insert data, you have to manually create the INSERT statements to insert the data.

Book VIII
Chapter 3

Using SQL
Server 2008

Chapter 4: Using SharePoint

*S*harePoint is a Web-based tool used mostly to create intranet sites that are designed to help people work together. The basic edition of SharePoint is free, included with Windows Server 2003 and 2008. A more advanced version, called *SharePoint Portal Server,* is available for an additional charge.

This chapter covers the basics of working with Windows SharePoint Services in Windows Server 2008. For more detailed information about SharePoint Portal Server, please refer to *SharePoint 2007 For Dummies,* by Vanessa L. Williams and published by Wiley, of course.

What Is SharePoint?

SharePoint is an extension to IIS that lets you create team Web sites that are designed to let your network users work together on projects. Among other things, these team Web sites can include the following features:

✦ Announcements and news

✦ Document libraries that can store and track documents

✦ Discussion forums where team members can discuss issues

✦ Task lists that help keep track of things that need to be done

✦ Contact lists

✦ Wikis, where users can work together to build a repository of interlinked articles

The basic version of SharePoint, called *Windows SharePoint Services,* is ideal for creating a company-wide intranet site with the above features. If your users end up loving the features provided by Windows SharePoint Services, you should consider upgrading to the SharePoint Portal Server. It provides additional features, such as the ability to create sites that individual users can customize themselves.

Installing Windows SharePoint Services

Before you can use SharePoint, you must configure your Web server computer to run Windows SharePoint Services. Here are the steps:

1. **Choose Start⇨Administrative Tools⇨Server Manager.**

2. **Click Roles in the console tree.**

3. **Click Add Roles.**

   The Add Roles Wizard screen appears, as shown in Figure 4-1.

4. **Select Windows SharePoint Services, and then click Next.**

   A dialog box appears informing you that certain services must be installed before SharePoint Services can run.

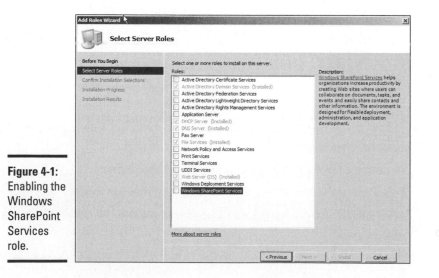

Figure 4-1:
Enabling the
Windows
SharePoint
Services
role.

5. Click Add Required Role Services.

The services are added. Then, an Introduction screen is displayed. This screen describes what Windows SharePoint Services is and provides some information you should read before you install it.

6. Click Next.

The wizard gives you the choice of two installation types:

- *Install Only on This Server,* which is the recommended option for small networks.

- *Install As Part of a Server Farm,* which you should use only if you are installing SharePoint on more than one Web server.

7. Choose Install Only on This Server, and then click Next.

Next, the Wizard asks what language to use for the setup and configuration pages.

8. Choose your language, and then click Next.

A final confirmation screen appears.

Note: If IIS has not already been installed on this server, you may see additional screens with IIS configuration information. Follow the wizard's steps to complete the configuration of IIS before proceeding to the next step.

9. Click Install.

The SharePoint Services components are installed. After the installation has finished, a final confirmation screen appears.

10. Click Close.

You're done!

After you've completed this procedure, two additional commands appear in the Start⇨Administrative Tools menu:

✦ **SharePoint 3.0 Central Configuration:** Click this link to display the Central Administration Web page, as shown in Figure 4-2. This page, which is a SharePoint site, provides useful links to basic configuration tasks, such as configuring incoming and outgoing e-mail settings or creating new SharePoint sites.

✦ **SharePoint Products and Technologies Configuration Wizard:** Click this link to run a tool that automatically restores the correct configuration for SharePoint's basic services. This is primarily a troubleshooting tool — if you are having problems with SharePoint, running this tool may solve them.

Figure 4-2:
The
SharePoint
Central
Administra-
tion page.

Connecting to a SharePoint Site

After you have installed Windows SharePoint Services, users can access the SharePoint site by opening a Web browser and entering the server name in the Address field. For example, Figure 4-3 shows the default home page of the SharePoint site on a server named LSERVER01.

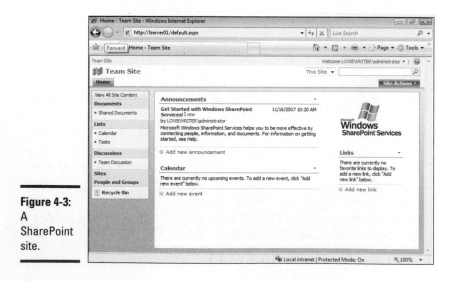

Figure 4-3:
A
SharePoint
site.

The default SharePoint site consists of the following pages:

+ A home page with announcements, a reminder of upcoming events on the site's calendar, and an area where you can add favorite links

+ A document library named Shared Documents, where you can store files that can be accessed by other SharePoint users

+ A calendar

+ A task list

+ A discussion area named *Team Discussion*

All of the pages on a SharePoint site have several elements in common, including the following:

+ At the top left, you'll find a title area that displays the name of the SharePoint site.

+ At the top right is a Help button that displays useful information about how to use SharePoint.

+ Just to the left of the Help button is a log on control that displays the name of the current user and includes a drop-down menu that lets you sign out, change users, or update your user settings.

+ Just below the log on control is a search box that lets you search the entire site for specific text. Just enter the text you want to search for, and then click the magnifying glass icon.

+ Below the search box is a button labeled Site Actions near the upper-right corner of the page. When you click this button, a menu appears with commands that let you create additional pages, edit the current page, or manage site settings.

+ Below the title area is a series of one or more tabs called the Top Link Bar. Initially, the Top Link Bar contains a single tab named Home, which takes you to the home page for the site. But you can add links. For more information, see the section "Creating a New Site" later in this chapter.

+ A navigation menu called *Quick Launch* runs down the left side of the window. It provides quick access to the individual pages on the site.

+ The main display area, in the center of each SharePoint page, contains one or more gadgets called *Web parts*. SharePoint comes with a collection of 14 different Web parts that can be added to this area, and additional Web parts are available from various sources. If you're handy with ASP.NET Web programming, you can even create your own Web parts.

Adding Users

One of the first things you'll want to do after you create a SharePoint site is add one or more users for the site. SharePoint recognizes three different *types,* also called *groups,* of users:

✦ **Team Site Owners,** who have full control over the site. Owners can add or remove pages, change the look and feel of pages, manage site settings, and perform any other administrative tasks necessary to keep the site running well. You should create a limited number of owners.

✦ **Team Site Members,** who can add content to the site but can't change the site's overall structure or modify its settings. Most of your users should be Team Site Members.

✦ **Team Site Visitors** have read-only access to the site: They can view the site's pages but cannot add content of their own.

Here is the procedure for adding a new member:

1. **Log on to the site as an Owner.**

Only an Owner can manage users. If you created the site yourself, you are already designated as an owner.

2. **Click the Site Actions button, and then choose Site Settings.**

This brings up the Site Settings page, shown in Figure 4-4. As you can see, this page contains links that lead to various site administration pages.

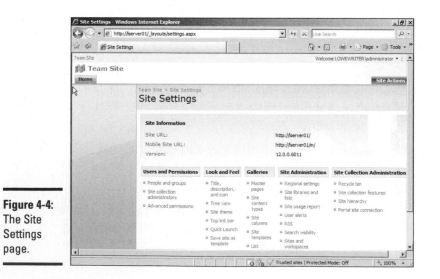

Figure 4-4:
The Site
Settings
page.

3. **Choose People and Groups.**

This brings up the People and Groups page, as shown in Figure 4-5.

Figure 4-5:
The People
and Groups
page.

4. **Choose the group you want to add the new user to.**

The site groups are listed in the Quick Launch area at the left of the page. In Figure 4-5, the Team Site Members group is selected.

5. **Click New, and then choose Add Users.**

The Add Users page appears, as shown in Figure 4-6.

6. **Type the name of the user you want to add in the Users/Groups text box.**

You must type the actual domain account name. To add more than one user, separate the names with semicolons. If you want, you can click the Browse button (represented by an address book icon) to browse for names.

7. **Select the permissions you want to provide for the user.**

You can specify the permissions by assigning the user to a group from the drop-down list, or you can bypass the group permissions and assign permission directly. In most cases, you should stick to group assignment.

Book VIII
Chapter 4

Using SharePoint

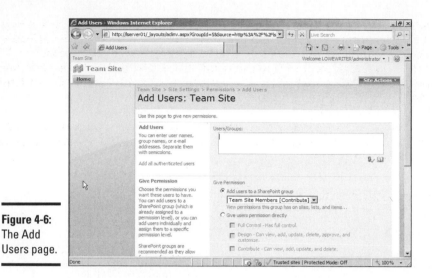

Figure 4-6:
The Add
Users page.

8. **Select the Send Welcome Message to New Users check box, and then enter a subject line and message text for the welcome e-mail.**

   These controls aren't shown in Figure 4-6; you'll have to scroll down to the bottom of the page to see them.

9. **Click OK.**

   The user is created. You're returned to the Users and Groups page, where the new user account is now listed. See Figure 4-7.

Figure 4-7:
A user
account has
been
created.

After you've created a new user, you can edit the user's settings by clicking the user's name. This brings up the User Information page, shown in Figure 4-8. Initially, there isn't much user information — just the user's name and Active Directory account. You can rectify that situation by clicking Edit Item, which brings up a form that lets you enter the user's e-mail address, descriptive "About Me" information, a picture, and so on.

Any SharePoint user can access his or her own User Information page by choosing My Settings from the logon control that appears at the top right of each SharePoint page.

Figure 4-8:
The User Information page for a new user doesn't contain any interesting information.

Adding and Removing Announcements

The home page includes an area for announcements. As the site owner, you'll want to periodically add new announcements to this page and remove old ones. Here are the steps for adding a new announcement:

1. **Click the Add New Announcement link.**

If you don't see an Add New Announcement link, you don't have adequate permissions to add new announcements. You can skip the rest of this procedure.

Assuming you have adequate permissions, the page shown in Figure 4-9 appears.

2. **Type a subject and body for the announcement.**

**Book VIII
Chapter 4**

Using SharePoint

Figure 4-9:
The
Announce-
ments page.

3. **Set an expiration date if you want.**

The Expiration date field isn't shown in Figure 4-9; you have to scroll down the page a bit to see it. When you set an expiration date, the message is automatically removed when it has expired.

4. **Click OK.**

The new announcement is added to the top of the list of announcements on the home page, as shown in Figure 4-10.

You're done! You and the site's users can now view and enjoy your latest announcement.

Figure 4-10:
Adding an
announce-
ment.

To edit or remove the announcement, click the announcement's title. This displays a page that lets you modify or delete the announcement.

Creating New Pages

The default SharePoint site consists of several standard pages, including a document library, calendar, and a discussion forum. You can add pages to your SharePoint site to customize it as needed. For instance, many SharePoint sites have more than one document library to store different types of documents.

To create a new SharePoint page, click Site Actions, and then click Create. The Create page is displayed, as shown in Figure 4-11.

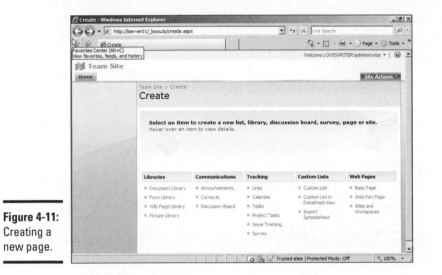

Figure 4-11: Creating a new page.

SharePoint lets you add the following standard page types to your site:

✦ **Document Library:** This is a repository of document files in a system of folders and subfolders. Document libraries can track multiple versions of documents, and they give users the ability to check documents in and out of the library. For more information about document libraries, see the section "Working with Document Libraries" later in this chapter.

✦ **Forms Library:** A *forms library* is a repository of XML-based business forms. Forms libraries are designed to work with a forms editor such as Microsoft's InfoPath.

✦ **Wiki Page Library:** A Wiki library is a collection of interconnected articles.

✦ **Picture Library:** This is a collection of pictures. Picture libraries can offer users the ability to view thumbnails, download picture files, and easily create slideshows.

✦ **Announcements:** This page is a place to record short items of interest to the entire team.

✦ **Contacts:** Here you'll find a list of names and addresses that can be integrated with other contact managers, including Microsoft Outlook and Exchange.

✦ **Discussion Board:** This is a message forum where users can post messages and post replies to other user's messages.

✦ **Links List:** This is a list of links to other Web pages.

✦ **Calendar:** SharePoint calendar pages track events related to the SharePoint site, but they can be integrated with users' personal calendar managers such as Outlook.

✦ **Project Task List:** This page contains a list of project-management tasks that can be viewed as a Gantt chart.

✦ **Issue Tracking List:** This list is designed to help you track issues or problems, from the initial problem or issue reporting through resolution.

✦ **Survey List:** Creates a list of questions that can be answered by users.

✦ **Custom List:** Creates a list in which you can specify the data to be recorded for each item in the list.

✦ **Basic Page:** This is a static Web page that you can edit any way you want.

✦ **Web Parts Page:** This is a Web page that you can add standard or customized Web parts to.

✦ **Sites and Workspaces:** This option lets you create not just a single page, but an entirely new SharePoint site based on one of several predefined templates. For more information, see the section "Creating a New Site" later in this chapter.

When you click one of the page types on the Create page, SharePoint displays a page that asks for the information necessary to create the type of page you selected. For example, the New page for a Document Library (shown in Figure 4-12) asks you to enter the name and description for the document library and lets you choose whether to include the library in the Quick Launch menu, whether to track version history for documents in the library, and the default file type for new documents added to the library. After you enter the requested information, you click Create to create the page.

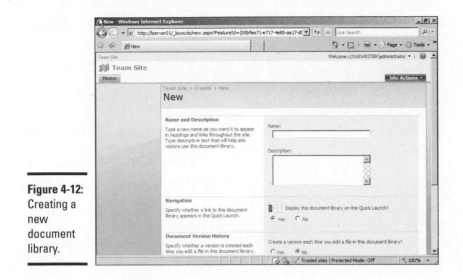

Figure 4-12:
Creating a new document library.

Editing the Quick Launch Menu

The Quick Launch menu is the menu that appears on the left side of Share Point pages. It provides one-click access to the most important pages in the site.

In most cases, you'll want to include any new pages you add to a SharePoint site to the Quick Launch menu. Otherwise, the site's users will have difficulty locating the pages. You can specify that a new page is added to the Quick Launch menu when you create the page, or you can add the page later if you forget.

To modify the Quick Launch menu, click Site Actions, choose Site Settings, and then click the Quick Launch link. This displays the page shown in Figure 4-13, which lets you modify the way items appear in the Quick Launch menu. You can use this page to add or remove items, change the order in which items appear, or to add or change existing headings.

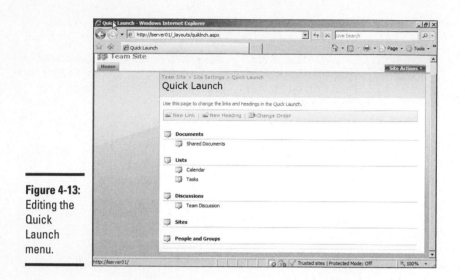

Figure 4-13:
Editing the Quick Launch menu.

Working with Document Libraries

In many ways, document libraries are the heart of SharePoint. They are often the most important and most frequently used pages in a SharePoint site. In fact, the purpose of many SharePoint sites is to enable a team of people to collaborate on the creation of the documents stored in a document library.

Figure 4-14 shows a document library named *Networking All-in-One Desk Reference For Dummies,* which I might use if I wanted to use SharePoint to help with the development of a book such as this. As you can see, I've added four Word documents to the library so far.

As a network administrator, the single most important thing to know about SharePoint document libraries (and maybe about SharePoint in general) is this: Documents stored in a SharePoint library are not stored as separate files on the server computer's file system. Instead, they are stored in a SQL database. The bottom-line result of this fact is this: After you (or a user) have created a document in a SharePoint library, that document can be accessed and managed only from SharePoint. You can't open Windows Explorer and navigate to the file via the Windows folder structure.

The following paragraphs describe some things you can do with documents in SharePoint document libraries:

✦ To add an existing file to a document library, click the Upload button, and then choose the Upload Document. This brings up the page shown in Figure 4-15, from which you can upload an existing file. Just type in the complete path and filename for the file, or click the Browse button to browse for the file. Then, click OK to upload the file.

✦ To open a file, just click the filename in the Document Library. This launches the application associated with the file and opens the document.

✦ You can display a shortcut menu with useful commands by hovering the mouse over a document name. In a moment, a border will appear around the filename, with a drop-down arrow at the right. Click this arrow to reveal the shortcut menu.

Figure 4-14:
A
SharePoint
document
library.

Figure 4-15:
Uploading
an existing
file to a
SharePoint
document
library.

✦ You can check out a document by choosing Check Out from the document's shortcut menu. This prevents other users from changing the file until you check the file back in by choosing Check In from the shortcut menu.

✦ You can organize documents in document libraries by creating folders. To create a folder, click the New button, and then choose the New Folder command.

Creating a New Site

When you install Windows SharePoint Services on a server computer, a default SharePoint site is created using the default IIS Web site. This site can be accessed by entering the server name in the address bar in a browser window.

You can create additional sites by clicking Site Actions, choosing the Create command, and then clicking the Sites and Workspaces link. This brings up the page shown in Figure 4-16.

The New SharePoint Site page asks you to enter the following information for the new site:

✦ **Title and Description:** Enter the title and description for the Web site.

✦ **Web Site Address:** The address that will be used to access the Web site begins with the name of the server but can end with any name you choose. For example, suppose I want to create a site devoted our company's Fantasy Football league. If the server name is LSERVER01, I could create a site with the address http://lserver01.Football.

Figure 4-16: Creating a new SharePoint site.

✦ **Template Selection:** SharePoint offers several templates to choose from when creating a new site. Pick the one that most closely matches your intended use for the site.

✦ **Permissions:** You can elect to use the same permissions as the main SharePoint site, or you can create separate permissions. Use the same permissions unless you want to restrict access to the new site.

✦ **Navigation:** These options let you choose whether to include the new site on the Quick Launch bar or on the top link bar.

✦ **Navigation Inheritance:** This option lets you select whether the top link bar for this site should be the same as for the main SharePoint site.

When you have entered the information for the new site, click OK to create the new site. After a few moments, the new site will appear, as shown in Figure 4-17.

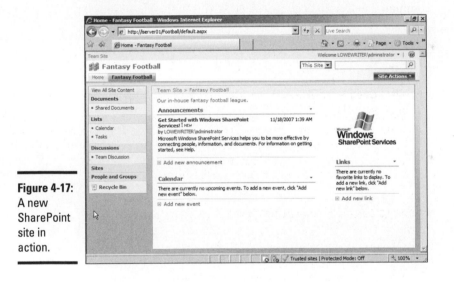

Figure 4-17: A new SharePoint site in action.

Book IX
Linux Networking Reference

The 5th Wave   By Rich Tennant

"It's called Linux Poker. Everyone gets to see everyone else's cards, everything's wild, you can play off your opponents' hands, and everyone wins except Bill Gates, whose face appears on the jokers."

Contents at a Glance

Chapter 1: Installing a Linux Server

In This Chapter

✓ Getting ready to install Linux

✓ Installing Linux

✓ Adding additional packages after installation

This chapter presents the procedures that you need to follow to install Linux on a server computer. The specific details provided are specifically for Fedora 7, a free Linux distribution from Red Hat. However, installing other distributions of Linux is similar, so you won't have any trouble adapting these procedures if you're using a different distribution.

Planning a Linux Server Installation

Before you begin the installation program, you need to make a number of preliminary decisions. The following sections describe the decisions that you need to make before you install Linux.

Checking system requirements

Before you install Linux, you should make sure that the computer meets the minimum requirements. Although the minimum requirements for Linux are considerably less than for the latest Windows or NetWare server operating systems, you can't run Linux on an abacus. The following paragraphs summarize the minimum capabilities you need.

+ **A Pentium-based computer.** Even a slow 100 MHz system will run some builds of Linux, although performance will be slow. The minimum recommended for Fedora Core is a 200 MHz Pentium.

+ **64MB of RAM or more.** Actually, 128MB or more is better, but Linux can make do with less.

+ **A hard drive with enough free space to hold the packages that you need to install.** The kernel itself needs about 850MB. If you choose not to install a graphical user interface, you can install a full-featured server in about 1.5GB. If you install everything, you need about 5GB.

✦ **A CD-ROM drive is almost a must, and it's helpful if the computer can boot from the CD.** If the computer doesn't have a CD, you can install over a network. If your computer can't boot from the CD, you can create a boot diskette from which to boot the computer.

✦ **Just about any video card and monitor combination.** You don't need anything fancy for a server. In fact, fancy video cards often lead to hardware compatibility issues. Stick to a basic video card.

✦ **A mouse is very helpful.** If you're converting an old junker computer to a Linux server and you've lost the mouse (that seems to happen a lot), pick one up at your local office supply store. A cheap one costs only about $15.

✦ **A network card.**

Choosing a distribution

Because the *kernel* (that is, the core operating functions) of the Linux operating system is free, several companies have created their own *distributions* of Linux, which include the Linux operating system along with a bundle of packages, such as administration tools, Web servers, and other useful utilities, as well as printed documentation. These distributions are inexpensive — ranging from $25 to $150 — and are well worth the small cost.

The following are some of the more popular Linux distributions:

✦ **Fedora** is one of the popular Linux distributions. At one time, Fedora was an inexpensive distribution offered by Red Hat. But Red Hat recently changed its distribution strategy by announcing that its inexpensive distribution would become a community project known as *Fedora,* so that it could focus on its more expensive Enterprise editions. As a result, you can't purchase Fedora, but you can download it free from `http://fedoraproject.com`. You can also obtain it by purchasing any of several books on Fedora that include the Fedora distribution on DVD or CD-ROM.

All the examples in this book are based on Fedora 8.

✦ **Mandriva Linux** is another popular Linux distribution, one that is often recommended as the easiest for first-time Linux users to install. This distribution was formerly known as *Mandrake Linux.* Go to `www.mandriva.com` for more information.

✦ **Ubuntu** is a Linux distribution that has gained popularity in recent years. It focuses on ease of use. For more information, go to `www.ubuntu.com`.

✦ **SUSE** (pronounced *SOO-zuh,* like the name of the famous composer of marches) is a popular Linux distribution sponsored by Novell. You can find more information at `www.suse.com`.

✦ **Slackware**, one of the oldest Linux distributions, is still popular — especially among Linux old-timers. A full installation of Slackware gives you all the tools that you need to set up a network or Internet server. See www.slackware.com for more information.

There are, of course, many other distributions of Linux available, including Knoppix (www.knoppix.net), Debian (www.debian.org), and Xandros Desktop (www.xandros.com). If you want, you can search a comprehensive database of Linux distributions at www.linux.org/dist.

All distributions of Linux include the same core components — the Linux kernel, an X Server, popular windows managers such as GNOME and KDE, compilers, Internet programs such as Apache, Sendmail, and so on. However, not all Linux distributions are created equal. In particular, the manufacturer of each distribution creates its own installation and configuration programs to install and configure Linux.

The installation program is what makes or breaks a Linux distribution. All the distributions I list in this section have easy-to-use installation programs that automatically detect the hardware that is present on your computer and configure Linux to work with that hardware, thus eliminating most — if not all — manual configuration chores. The installation programs also let you select the Linux packages that you want to install and let you set up one or more user accounts besides the root account.

Figuring out how you'll boot during installation

Before you can install Linux, you must have a working operating system in place so that you can boot the Linux installation program. There are two common ways to boot your computer to install Linux:

✦ If the computer has a bootable CD-ROM drive, you can boot the computer from the Linux distribution CD. To find out whether this technique will work, just put the Linux distribution CD-ROM in the drive and restart the computer. If the computer doesn't boot from the CD-ROM, don't despair. The problem may be that the computer's BIOS configuration isn't set to allow the computer to boot from the CD-ROM drive. Check the computer's BIOS configuration to see whether this is the problem.

✦ If the computer can't boot from the CD-ROM drive, you can create a bootable floppy disk. To do that, insert the CD-ROM into the CD drive on a Windows computer and then run the program that creates a bootable Linux disk. For Fedora, this program is called rawrite.exe. If you have access to a working Linux system, you can also use it to create a boot disk.

I can't see my C: drive!

Linux and Windows have a completely different method of referring to your computer's hard drives and partitions. The differences can take some getting used to for experienced Windows users.

Windows uses a separate letter for each drive and partition on your system. For example, if you have a single drive formatted into three partitions, Windows identifies the partitions as drives C:, D:, and E:. Each of these drives has its own root directory, which can, in turn, contain additional directories used to organize your files. As far as Windows is concerned, drives C:, D:, and E: are completely separate drives, even though the drives are actually just partitions on a single drive.

Linux doesn't use drive letters. Instead, Linux combines all the drives and partitions into a single directory hierarchy. In Linux, one of the partitions is designated as the *root* partition. The root partition is roughly analogous to the root directory of the C: drive on a Windows system. Then, the other partitions can be *mounted* on the root partition and treated as if they were directories on the root partition. For example, you may designate the first partition as the root partition and then mount the second partition as /user and the third partition as /var. Then, any files

stored in the /user directory would actually be stored in the second partition, and files stored in the /var directory would be stored in the third partition.

The directory to which a drive mounts is called the drive's *mount point.*

Notice that Linux uses regular forward slash characters (/) to separate directory names rather than the backward slash characters (\) used by Windows. Typing backslashes instead of regular slashes is one of the most common mistakes made by new Linux users.

While I'm on the subject, Linux uses a different convention for naming files, too. In Windows, filenames end in a three-letter extension that is separated from the rest of the filename by a period. The extension is used to indicate the file type. For example, files that end in .exe are program files, but files that end in .doc are word-processing documents.

Linux doesn't use file extensions, but periods are often used in Linux filenames to separate different parts of the name — and the last part often indicates the file type. For example, ldap.conf and pine.conf are both configuration files.

Thinking about multiboot

Linux comes with a boot loader program called *GRUB* that lets you choose from several installed operating systems when you start your computer. GRUB makes it possible to keep your existing Windows system on a computer and install Linux into a separate partition. Then, each time you start the computer, you can decide whether to start Windows or Linux.

I'm not a big fan of having multiple operating systems on one computer. If the computer is going to be a production server, you're not going to need to reboot the computer into Windows anyway. However, installing Linux into a separate partition while keeping your Windows system intact may be a viable alternative if you want to experiment with Linux before you commit to it.

Planning your partitions

Linux handles partitions a little differently than Windows. The Windows operating system installs itself into a single partition. However, Linux installations typically require three or more hard drive partitions:

✦ **A boot partition:** This should be small — 16MB is recommended. The boot partition contains the operating system kernel and is required to start Linux properly on some computers.

✦ **A swap partition:** This should be about twice the size of your computer's RAM. For example, if the computer has 256MB of RAM, allocate a 512MB swap partition. Linux uses this partition as an extension of your computer's RAM.

✦ **A root partition:** In most cases, this uses up the remaining free space on the drive. The root partition contains all the files and data used by your Linux system.

You can also create additional partitions if you want. The installation program includes a disk-partitioning feature that lets you set up your drive partitions and indicate the mount point for each partition. The installation program can make a recommendation for partitioning your drives that will be appropriate in most situations. (For more information about drive partitions, see the sidebar, "I can't see my C: drive!" earlier in this chapter.)

Deciding your TCP/IP configuration

Before you install the operating system, you should have a plan for how you will implement TCP/IP on the network. Here are some of the things you need to decide or find out:

✦ What is the public IP subnet address and mask for your network?

✦ What is the domain name for the network?

✦ What is the host name for the server?

✦ Will the server obtain its address from DHCP?

✦ Will the server have a static IP address? If so, what?

✦ Will the server be a DHCP server?

✦ What is the Default Gateway for the server? (That is, what is the IP address of the network's Internet router?)

✦ Will the server be a DNS server?

If the server will host TCP/IP servers (such as DHCP or DNS), you'll probably want to assign the server a static IP address.

For more information about planning your TCP/IP configuration, see Book IV.

Installing Fedora 7

Now that you've planned your installation and prepared the computer, you're ready to actually install Linux. The following procedure describes the steps you must follow to install Fedora 7 on a computer that has a bootable DVD-ROM drive.

1. **Insert the Fedora 7 CD in the DVD drive and restart the computer.**

The computer boots from the DVD drive and displays a Linux boot prompt, which looks like this:

        Boot:

If you don't have the installation DVD, download the DVD images from http://www.fedoraproject.com. Then, use DVD burning software to create a DVD from the image.

2. **Press Enter.**

The computer starts Linux from the installation disk. The screen shown in Figure 1-1 soon appears.

This screen gives you several options for starting the installation. The most common is to simply press Enter.

3. **Press Enter.**

Now a bunch of text messages fly by your screen as Linux starts up. Eventually, the screen shown in Figure 1-2 appears, offering to test the CD media you're installing from to make sure you have downloaded and burned the CD images correctly.

Figure 1-1: Selecting an installation option.

Figure 1-2:
Testing the
CD media.

4. **Press tab, and then press Enter to skip the test.**

Still more text messages fly by, but soon Fedora switches into graphics
mode and displays the Welcome to Fedora Core screen, as shown in
Figure 1-3.

Figure 1-3:
Welcome to
Fedora.

5. **Click Next.**

The Language Selection screen appears, offering quite a few language
choices, as shown in Figure 1-4.

6. **Choose your language, and then click Next.**

The Keyboard Configuration screen appears. It lets you choose from
about 55 different keyboard styles.

7. Choose your keyboard type and then click Next.

Next, Fedora warns you that it is about to wipe out any existing data on your hard disk.

8. Click Yes.

The screen shown in Figure 1-5 is displayed.

Figure 1-4:
Choosing a language.

Figure 1-5:
Partitioning the disk.

Virtual consoles and the installation program

Linux is inherently a command line oriented operating system. Graphical user interfaces — including the installation program's GUI — are provided by an optional component called *X Window System.* However, while you're working with the graphical user interface of the installation program, Linux keeps several additional command line consoles open. Normally, you don't need to use every one of these consoles during installation. However, if something goes wrong during installation, these consoles may be useful.

The following list describes the consoles:

✓ **Console 1: The Installation dialog box.** This is the main installation console. You see it when Setup first starts. After the graphical user interface takes over, it's hidden in the background. You can call it up by pressing Ctrl+Alt+F1.

✓ **Console 2: Shell prompt.** This console provides you with a shell prompt, from which you can enter Linux commands. If you need to do something manually during installation, you can do it from this console. The keyboard shortcut is Ctrl+Alt+F2.

✓ **Console 3: Install log.** This console lists messages generated by the installation program. You can get to it by pressing Ctrl+Alt+F3.

✓ **Console 4: System log.** This console displays system-related messages. You can get to it by pressing Ctrl+Alt+F4.

✓ **Console 5: Other messages.** Still more messages may appear in this console, which you can open by pressing Ctrl+Alt+F5.

✓ **Console 6: X graphical display.** This is the console where the graphical user interface of the installation program is displayed. If you use a Ctrl+Alt keyboard combination to view any of the other logs, press Ctrl+Alt+F7 to return to the installation GUI.

9. **Click Next. Then, when asked if you are sure, click Yes.**

Now the Network Configuration screen appears, as shown in Figure 1-6. This screen lists each network adapter detected in the server along with the adapter's configuration information. By default, the installation program assumes that this server will use DHCP to obtain its configuration information. If that's the case, skip ahead to Step 15.

10. **Click the Edit button and manually configure the network information, and then click OK.**

When you click the Edit button, the dialog box shown in Figure 1-7 appears. To use this dialog box to configure the server's network information, first check Manual Configuration. Then, enter the IP address and netmask that you want to use for the server and click OK. When you're returned to the Network Configuration screen, you need to enter the following information:

- **Host name:** Enter the host name to use for the computer.

- **Gateway:** Type the IP address of the router that you connect to for your Internet connection.

- **DNS servers:** Enter up to three IP addresses for your DNS servers.

Figure 1-6:
Network
options.

Figure 1-7:
The Edit
Interface
dialog box.

11. **Click Next.**

The Time Zone Selection screen appears, as shown in Figure 1-8. On this screen is a map of the world with dots representing about 500 different locations throughout the world.

12. **Click the location that's closest to you and then click Next.**

Next, the Set Root Password screen appears, as shown in Figure 1-9. This screen lets you enter the all-important root account password. It's vital that this account be protected by a strong password, so choose a good one. Write down the password somewhere and store it in a secure location away from the computer.

Figure 1-8:
Choose a
time zone.

Figure 1-9:
Setting the
root
password.

Don't lose the root password! If you do, you'll be in a world of hurt.

13. Type the root account password twice, and then click Next.

Next, the installation program displays the screen shown in Figure 1-10, which lets you choose the optional features you want to install.

14. Select the Web Server and Customize Now options, then click Next.

The screen shown in Figure 1-11 appears. This screen allows you to further customize the packages to be installed.

Figure 1-10: Choosing optional features.

Figure 1-11: Selecting additional packages.

15. Click Servers.

The list of optional server packages appears, as shown in Figure 1-12.

16. Select the server packages you want to install, and then click Next.

When you click Next, the installation program does some double-checking to make sure that none of the packages you have chosen depend on other packages you have not chosen. If it finds such a dependency, it adds the dependent package so that your system will function properly.

Next, the screen shown in Figure 1-13 appears. You have now reached the moment of truth.

Figure 1-12:
Selecting
optional
server
packages.

17. Take a deep breath and click Next.

The installation program installs Linux on your system. This will take awhile — maybe a long while — so now would be a good time to grab a book or take a nap.

When the installation finishes, the screen shown in Figure 1-14 is shown. Pat yourself on the back for your ingenuity and perseverance.

18. Remove the installation disk from the drive and then click Reboot.

The system is rebooted. Installation is done!

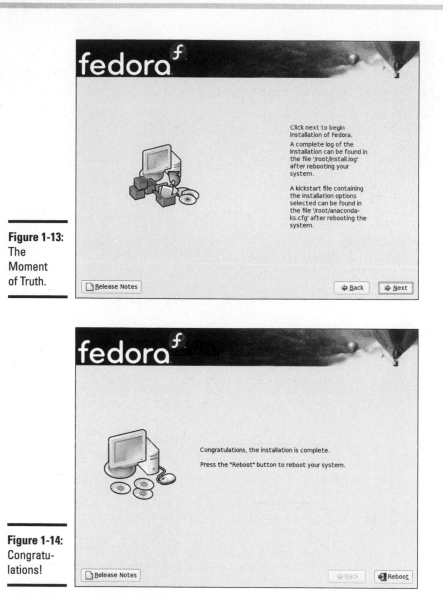

Figure 1-13:
The
Moment
of Truth.

Figure 1-14:
Congratu-
lations!

Using the Setup Agent

When Fedora restarts the first time after completing the installation program, it launches a handy feature called the *Setup Agent,* as shown in Figure 1-15. (The Setup Agent runs only if you installed a GUI.) The Setup Agent resembles the installation program, but it asks a few questions that the installation program forgot to ask.

Figure 1-15:
The Setup
Agent.

When the Setup Agent starts, follow these steps to see it through to completion:

1. **On the Welcome screen, click Forward to get started.**

The Setup Agent displays the License Agreement, as if after going through the previous 18 steps to install Fedora, you're now going to decide you don't agree to their terms. It is useless to resist.

2. **Select the Yes, I Agree Blah Blah Blah option, and then click Forward.**

The Setup Agent next displays the Firewall options, which let you specify how you want the built-in firewall to be configured. The firewall can be configured to allow or block access to various services, such as FTP or e-mail. See Figure 1-16.

3. **Select the services you want to enable, and then click Forward.**

The default services are adequate for most users. However, you should peruse this list and enable any additional services you might need.

4. **Click Forward.**

The Setup Agent now asks you to set the date and time.

5. **Select the correct date and time, and then click Forward.**

Now the Setup Agent asks if you want to submit details about your hardware configuration as part of an effort to improve Linux's support for various hardware devices.

6. **Click Send Profile or Do Not Send Profile, and then click Forward.**

The Setup Agent asks you to create a user account so that you don't have to access the system by using the root account.

7. **Type a name and password for the user account and then click Finish.**

You have to type the password twice to verify that you typed it correctly.

That's all there is. Your Linux system is now set up and ready to go.

Welcome
License Information
› Firewall
SELinux
Date and Time
Hardware Profile
Create User

Firewall

You can use a firewall to allow access to specific services on your computer from other computers and prevent unauthorized access from the outside world. Which services, if any, do you wish to allow access to?

Firewall: Enabled

Trusted services:
- [ ] FTP
- [ ] Mail (SMTP)
- [ ] NFS4
- [x] SSH
- [ ] Samba
- [ ] Secure WWW (HTTPS)

▷ Other ports

fedora

◀ Back   ▶ Forward

Figure 1-16: Configuring the firewall.

Installing Additional Packages

No matter how carefully you think things through when you install Linux, you're bound to discover that you wish you had installed some package that you didn't think you'd need. So you're faced with the prospect of figuring out how to install additional packages after you already have Linux up and running.

Fortunately, Fedora includes a package manager called *Pirut* that makes it easy to install additional packages. Just follow these steps:

1. **Choose Applications⇨Add/Remove Software.**

You'll be prompted for the Root account's password.

2. **Enter the Root account's password, then click OK.**

The Package Manager program comes to life and displays the window shown in Figure 1-17.

Figure 1-17:
The
Package
Manager.

3. **Select the package or packages you want to add.**

You can add an entire group of packages, or you can click the Optional
Packages button to display a dialog box that lets you add selected packages from a group. Note that most of the groups include some packages
that aren't selected by default when you select the group. As a result,
you should click Optional Packages to make sure that the specific
package in which you're interested is selected.

4. **Click Apply.**

Be patient while the Package Manager determines which packages need
to be upgraded. When it's done, the Package Manager displays a window
listing the packages that will be installed.

5. **Click Continue.**

The packages are installed. If asked, you may need to insert one of the
distribution discs.

When the packages have been installed, the Package Installation
Complete page appears, announcing that the packages have been
installed successfully.

6. **Click Finish.**

The Package Manager closes.

Chapter 2: Getting Used to Linux

In This Chapter

✓ Getting used to the Linux way of thinking

✓ Logging on and off Linux

✓ Using a GUI

✓ Working with commands

✓ Setting up user accounts

*B*efore you can set up Linux to do serious networking, you need to discover the basics of getting around Linux. In this chapter, you find out those basics. You see how to log on and off Linux, how the Linux file system works, and how to use commands. I also introduce you to GNOME, the graphical user interface that's used most with Fedora and many other Linux distributions. Finally, I show you the basics of setting up a Linux user account.

In this chapter, I assume that you have plenty of experience with Windows, so I focus mostly on the differences between Linux and Windows — which, unfortunately, are many.

Linux: It Isn't Windows

Before I get into the details of actually using a Linux system, you need to understand some basic differences between Linux and Windows that will puzzle you at first. Linux looks a lot like Windows, but underneath, it's very different. You won't have any trouble finding out how to point and click your way through the GNOME user interface, but before long, you'll run into Linux file-naming conventions, terminal windows, configuration files, and a host of other significant differences.

The following sections describe some of the more important differences between Linux and Windows.

X Window

Linux doesn't have a built-in graphical user interface (GUI) as Windows does. Instead, the GUI in Linux is provided by an optional component called *X Window System.* You can run Linux without X Window, in which case you interact with Linux by typing commands. If you prefer to use a GUI, you must install and run X Window.

X Window is split into two parts: a server component, called an *X server,* which handles the basic chores of managing multiple windows and providing graphics services for application programs, and a user interface component, called a *window manager,* which provides user interface features such as menus, buttons, toolbars, a taskbar, and so on. Several different window managers are available, each with a different look and feel. The most popular is GNOME. I describe it in more detail later in this chapter, in the section, "Using GNOME."

Virtual consoles

Linux is a true multiuser operating system. This means that you can log on to Linux by using one user account and then log on by using a different account, so that you are logged on twice at the same time. You switch back and forth between the different user sessions, and actions that you take in one session don't affect any of your other sessions.

In addition to an X Window client such as GNOME, Linux provides a traditional text-based environment called a *console,* through which you can enter Linux commands to perform any function available in Linux. The more you work with Linux, the more you'll discover the limitations of even a sophisticated GUI such as GNOME. When that happens, you'll turn to a console where you can enter brute-force commands.

Because Linux is a multiuser system, it lets you work with more than one console. In fact, you actually have six virtual consoles at your disposal. You can switch to a particular virtual console by pressing Ctrl+Alt+F1 through F6. For example, to switch to virtual console 3, press Ctrl+Alt+F3.

When a GUI such as GNOME is running, you can switch to it by pressing Ctrl+Alt+F7.

Understanding the file system

The Linux file system is a bit different from the Windows file system. Two of the most obvious differences are actually superficial:

✦ Linux uses forward slashes rather than backward slashes to separate directories. Thus, /home/doug is a valid path in Linux; \Windows\ System32 is a valid path in Windows.

✦ Linux filenames don't use extensions. You can use periods within a file-name, but unlike Windows, the final period doesn't identify a file extension.

The fundamental difference between the Linux and Windows file system is that Linux treats everything in the entire system as a file, and it organizes everything into one gigantic tree that begins at a single root. When I say, "Everything is treated as a file," I mean that hardware devices such as floppy drives, serial ports, and Ethernet adapters are treated as files.

The root of the Linux file system is the root partition from which the operating system boots. Additional partitions, including other devices that support file systems such as CD-ROM drives, floppy drives, or drives accessed over the network, can be grafted into the tree as directories called *mount points*. Thus, a directory in the Linux file system may actually be a separate hard drive.

Another important aspect of the Linux file system is that the directories that compose a Linux system are governed by a standard called the *Filesystem Hierarchy Standard* (FHS). This standard spells out which directories a Linux file system should have. Because most Linux systems conform to this standard, you can trust that key files will always be found in the same place.

Table 2-1 lists the top-level directories that are described in the FHS.

Table 2-1	**Top-Level Directories in a Linux File System**
Directory	*Description*
/bin	Essential command binaries
/boot	Static files of the boot loader
/dev	Devices
/etc	Configuration files for the local computer
/home	Home directories for users
/lib	Shared libraries and kernel modules
/mnt	Mount point for file systems mounted temporarily
/opt	Add-on applications and packages
/root	Home directory for the root user
/sbin	Essential system binaries
/tmp	Temporary files
/usr	Read-only, shared files such as binaries for user commands and libraries
/var	Variable data files

On Again, Off Again

Any user who accesses a Linux system, whether locally or over a network, must be authenticated by a valid user account on the system. In the following sections, you find out how to log on and off of a Linux system and how to shut down the system.

Logging on

When Linux boots up, it displays a series of startup messages as it starts the various services that compose a working Linux system. Assuming that you selected X Window when you installed Linux, you're eventually greeted by the screen shown in Figure 2-1. To log on to Linux, type your user ID on this screen, press Enter, and then type your password and press Enter again. (Note that this logon screen is for Fedora. Other distributions have similar logon screens.)

Figure 2-1: Logging on.

As a part of the installation process, the Setup Agent created a user account for you. You should use this user account rather than the root user account whenever possible. Use the root account only when you are making major changes to the system's configuration. When you're doing routine work, log on as an ordinary user in order to avoid accidentally corrupting your system.

When you log on, Linux grinds its gears for a moment and then displays the GNOME desktop, which I describe later in this chapter.

If you didn't install X server, you see a text-mode Login prompt that resembles this:

```
Fedora release 7 (Moonshine)
Kernel 2.6.21-1.3194.fc7 on an i686
localhost login:
```

The Login prompt displays the Linux version (Fedora release 7), the kernel version on which it's based (2.6.21), the CPU architecture (i686), and the server's hostname (localhost). To log in, type your user ID, press Enter, and then type the password and press Enter again.

After you've successfully logged on, you are greeted by a semi-friendly prompt similar to this:

```
Last login: Sun Sep 23 20:00:56 on :0
[dlowe@localhost doug]$
```

The prompt character in the standard Linux shell is a dollar sign ($) rather than a greater-than sign (>) as it is in MS-DOS or Windows. Also, notice that prompt indicates your username and server (dlowe@localhost), as well as the name of the current directory (dlowe).

Even if you've installed X server, you can still log on to a command shell by pressing Ctrl+Alt+F1. This switches you to a *virtual console,* which I describe in more detail in the section "Virtual consoles," earlier in this chapter.

Logging off

After you've logged on, you'll probably want to know how to log off. If you logged on to GNOME, you can log off by clicking the main menu and choosing the Log Out command. A dialog box asks whether you're sure that you want to log out. Click OK.

In a command shell, you can log out in three ways:

✦ Enter the logout command.

✦ Enter the exit command.

✦ Press Ctrl+D.

Shutting down

As with any operating system, you should never turn off the power to a Linux server without first properly shutting down the system. You can shut down a Linux system by using one of these three techniques:

✦ Press Ctrl+Alt+Delete.

✦ From GNOME, click the main menu and choose Log Out. Then, when the confirmation dialog box appears, select Shut Down or Restart and click OK.

✦ From a command shell, enter the `halt` command.

Using GNOME

Although you can do all your Linux configuration chores from the command line, Fedora includes a number of GNOME-based configuration tools for many configuration tasks. Although you can do most of your Linux configuration from GNOME, you will need to use a command shell once in awhile.

Figure 2-2 shows a typical GNOME desktop with the Text Editor application open. As you can see, the GNOME desktop looks a lot like Microsoft Windows. In fact, many of the basic skills for working with Windows — such as moving or resizing windows, minimizing or maximizing windows, and using drag-and-drop to move items between windows — work almost exactly the same in GNOME. So you should feel right at home.

Figure 2-2:
The
desktop.

The following paragraphs describe some of the key features of the GNOME desktop:

✦ On the desktop, you'll find several icons that let you access common features. The Home icon lets you access your home directory. The Computer icon is similar to the Windows My Computer icon. And the Trash icon is similar to the Recycle Bin in Windows.

✦ The panel at the top of the desktop area includes several menus and icons. The Applications menu lists applications you can run, and the Actions menu lists actions you can perform.

✦ Although Figure 2-2 doesn't show any open windows, you'll discover when you open a Window that each window provides a down arrow at the top-left corner of the window that reveals a menu of things that you can do with the window. Try the Roll Up command; it reduces a window to its title bar but leaves the window on the desktop. To restore the window, click the down arrow and choose Unroll. This menu also lets you move the window to a different workspace.

✦ Workspaces, you ask? A *workspace* is like a separate desktop where you can keep windows open in order to reduce the clutter on your screen. The panel beneath the desktop area contains a tool called the *Workspace Switcher,* which lets you switch active workspaces by clicking one of the rectangles in the grid.

Getting to a Command Shell

You can get to a command shell in one of two basic ways when you need to run Linux commands directly. The first is to press Ctrl+Alt+F*x* to switch to one of the virtual consoles. (If you aren't sure which function key to use to open a virtual console, take a look back at the "Virtual consoles" section in this chapter.) Then, you can log on and run commands to your heart's content. When you're done, press Ctrl+Alt+F7 to return to GNOME.

Alternatively, you can open a command shell directly in GNOME by choosing Applications⇨System Tools⇨Terminal. This opens a command shell in a window right on the GNOME desktop, as shown in Figure 2-3. Because this shell runs within the user account that GNOME is logged on as, you don't have to log on. You can just start typing commands. When you're done, type **Exit** to close the window.

Figure 2-3:
A terminal
window.

Managing User Accounts

One of the most common network administration tasks is adding a user account. The Setup Agent prompts you to create a user account the first time you start Linux after installing it. However, you'll probably need to create additional accounts.

Each Linux user account has the following information associated with it:

✦ **Username:** The name the user types to log on to the Linux system.

✦ **Full name:** The user's full name.

✦ **Home directory:** The directory that the user is placed in when he or she logs on. In Fedora, the default home directory is /home/username. For example, if the username is blowe, the home directory will be /home/blowe.

✦ **Shell:** The program used to process Linux commands. Several shell programs are available. In most distributions, the default shell is /bin/bash.

✦ **Group:** You can create group accounts, which make it easy to apply identical access rights to groups of users.

✦ **User ID:** The internal identifier for the user.

You can add a new user by using the useradd command. For example, to create a user account named slowe and using default values for the other account information, open a Terminal window or switch to a virtual console and type this command:

```
# useradd slowe
```

The `useradd` command has many optional parameters that you can use to set account information, such as the user's home directory and shell.

Fortunately, most Linux distributions come with special programs that simplify routine system management tasks. Fedora is no exception. It comes with a program called *User Manager,* shown in Figure 2-4. To start this program, choose System⇨Administration⇨User and Groups.

Figure 2-4:
Managing
users and
groups.

To create a user by using User Manager, click the Add User button. This brings up a dialog box that asks for the user's name, password, and other information. Fill out this dialog box and then click OK.

The User Manager also lets you create groups. You can simplify the task of administering users by applying access rights to groups rather than individual users. Then, when a user needs access to a resource, you can add the user to the group that has the needed access.

To create a group, click the Add Group button. A dialog box appears, asking for the name of the new group. Type the name you want and then click OK.

To add a user to a group, click the Groups tab in the User Manager. Then, double-click the group to which you want to add users. This brings up the Group Properties dialog box. Click the Group Users tab and then select the users that you want to belong to the group.

Chapter 3: Basic Linux Network Configuration

In This Chapter

✔ Configuring network interfaces

✔ Looking directly at network configuration files

✔ Using the `ifconfig` command to display network status

*I*n many cases, configuring a Linux server for networking is a snap. When you install Linux, the installation program automatically detects your network adapters and installs the appropriate drivers. Then, you're prompted for basic network configuration information, such as the computer's IP address, host name, and so on.

However, you may need to manually change your network settings after installation. You may also need to configure advanced networking features that aren't configured during installation. In this chapter, you discover the basic procedures for configuring Linux networking services.

Using the Network Configuration Program

Before you can use a network interface to access a network, you have to configure the interface's basic TCP/IP options, such as its IP address, host name, Domain Name System (DNS) servers, and so on. In this section, I show you how to do that by using Fedora's Network Configuration program. You can access this program by choosing Main Menu⇨System Settings⇨Network.

If you prefer a more masochistic approach to configuring your network, see the section "Working with Network Configuration Files," later in this chapter.

The Network Configuration program lets you configure the basic TCP/IP settings for a network interface by pointing and clicking your way through tabbed windows. Here are the steps:

1. Choose System⇨Administration⇨Network.

The Network Configuration window appears, as shown in Figure 3-1.

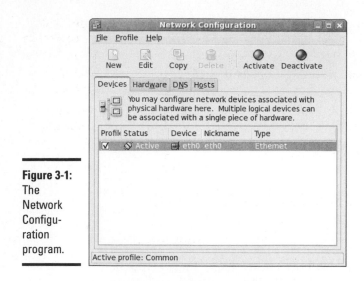

Figure 3-1:
The
Network
Configu-
ration
program.

2. Select the adapter that you want to configure, and then click Edit.

The main window of the Network Configuration lists all the network interfaces installed in your computer. If your computer has more than one interface, make sure that you select the correct one before proceeding.

When you click Edit, the Ethernet Device window appears, as shown in Figure 3-2.

3. To configure the device to use DHCP, select the Automatically Obtain IP Address Settings with DHCP radio button, type the computer's name in the Hostname text box, and select the Automatically Obtain DNS Information from Provider option.

If you plan on setting up this computer to be your network's DHCP or DNS server, you shouldn't select this check box. Instead, you should assign a static IP address as described in Step 4.

Some DHCP servers can't provide DNS information. In that case, you shouldn't select the Automatically Obtain DNS Information from Provider option. Instead, you should manually configure your DNS information, as described in Steps 6 and 7.

4. To configure the device with a static IP address, select the Statically Set IP Addresses option and then enter the IP address, subnet mask, and Default Gateway that you want the adapter to use.

The IP address is most likely located on one of the standard private subnets. You should almost always use a private address in the form 192.168.*x*.*x*.

If you are setting up this computer to be the gateway router that will manage traffic between your local network and the Internet, use a static address that is easy to remember, such as 192.168.1.1.

The subnet mask should be the mask that's appropriate for the IP address you choose. For a 192.168.*x.x* address, use 255.255.255.0.

The default gateway address should be the address of the gateway router that links your network to the Internet. If this computer *is* the gateway router, specify the gateway address provided to you by your Internet Service Provider (ISP).

Figure 3-2:
Configure
basic
TCP/IP
settings in
the Ethernet
Device
window.

```
┌─────────────────── Ethernet Device ──────────────────── x ┐
│ General  Route  Hardware Device                            │
│ Nickname: eth0                                             │
│ ☑ Activate device when computer starts                    │
│ ☐ Allow all users to enable and disable the device        │
│ ☐ Enable IPv6 configuration for this interface            │
│ ⦿ Automatically obtain IP address settings with: [dhcp ◆] │
│  ┌DHCP Settings────────────────────────────────────────┐  │
│  │ Hostname (optional): [                            ]  │  │
│  │ ☑ Automatically obtain DNS information from provider │  │
│  └──────────────────────────────────────────────────────┘ │
│ ○ Statically set IP addresses:                            │
│  ┌Manual IP Address Settings──────────────────────────┐   │
│  │ Address:          [                             ]   │   │
│  │ Subnet mask:      [                             ]   │   │
│  │ Default gateway address: [                      ]   │   │
│  └─────────────────────────────────────────────────────┘  │
│ ☐ Set MTU to: [1    ⬍]                                    │
│                                 [ ✗ Cancel ] [ ◆ OK ]     │
└────────────────────────────────────────────────────────────┘
```

5. Click OK.

You're returned to the Network Configuration window.

6. Click the DNS tab.

The DNS configuration settings appear, as shown in Figure 3-3.

7. Enter the IP addresses for the DNS servers that you want to use.

If your network runs its own DNS server, you can specify its address here. Otherwise, you have to get the DNS server addresses from your ISP.

Figure 3-3:
Configuring
the DNS.

8. Choose File➪Save.

Any changes that you've made to the network configuration are saved.
Then, an informative dialog box appears with the following message:

```
Redhat-config-network:
Changes are saved.
You may want to restart
the network and network services
or restart the computer.
```

9. Click OK.

You can now close the Network Configuration window.

10. Restart the network services.

To find out how to restart, see the next section, "Restarting Your
Network."

Restarting Your Network

Whenever you make a configuration change to your network, you must
restart Linux networking services in order for the change to take effect. If
you find that annoying, just be thankful that you don't have to restart the
entire computer. Simply restarting the network services is sufficient.

You can restart the network services from a GNOME desktop by following
these steps:

1. **Choose System⇨Administration⇨Server Settings⇨Services.**

The Service Configuration window appears, as shown in Figure 3-4.

Figure 3-4:
The Service
Configu-
ration
window.

2. **Select the Network service.**

You have to scroll down the list of services to find it.

3. **Click the Restart button.**

The service is stopped and then started again. When finished, a small dialog box appears, displaying the message, "Network restart successful."

4. **Click OK.**

You return to the Service Configuration window.

5. **Close the Service Configuration window.**

That's all!

If you prefer working in a command shell, you can restart the network by entering the command `service network restart`. This results in a display similar to the following:

```
Shutting down interface eth0:              [  OK  ]
Shutting down loopback interface:          [  OK  ]
Setting network parameters:                [  OK  ]
Bringing up loopback interface:            [  OK  ]
Bringing up interface eth0:                [  OK  ]
```

Working with Network Configuration Files

Like other operating system services, the Linux network is configured by settings that are specified in configuration files that you can find in the /etc directory or in one of its subdirectories. Graphical configuration programs such as Red Hat Network Configuration are actually little more than glorified text editors that enable you to select network configuration options from user-friendly screens and then save your configuration changes to the standard configuration files. If you prefer to do the grunt work yourself, you can open the configuration files in a text editor and make changes to them directly.

Any time you open a configuration file in a text editor, you run the risk of messing up your system's configuration. So be careful!

Table 3-1 lists the main Linux network configuration files and describes what each file does. The details of these files are described in the sections that follow.

Table 3-1	Linux Network Configuration Files	
File	**Location**	**Description**
network	/etc/sysconfig	Basic network configuration.
hostname	/etc	Specifies the host name (obsolete, but should still be present).
ifcfg-eth0	~/etc/sysconfig/	IP settings for the first Ethernet adapter network-scripts.
ifcfg-eth1	~/etc/sysconfig/	IP settings for the second Ethernet adapter network-scripts.
hosts	/etc	Lists host address mappings.
resolv.conf	/etc	Lists DNS nameservers.
nsswitch.conf	/etc	Specifies the name search order.
xinetd.conf	/etc	Specifies which network services are started automatically.

The Network file

The Network file, which lives in /etc/sysconfig, specifies basic configuration settings for your network. Here's a typical Network file:

```
NETWORKING=yes
HOSTNAME=LSERVER
GATEWAY=192.168.1.1
```

This file specifies that networking is enabled, the computer's host name is LSERVER, and the default gateway address is 192.168.1.1.

The following paragraphs describe all the settings that are valid for this file:

✦ **NETWORKING:** Specifies YES or NO to enable or disable networking for the computer.

✦ **HOSTNAME:** Specifies the host name for this computer. You should also specify this name in /etc/hostname, although that file is considered obsolete and is used only by some old programs. Note that this can be a simple host name (like LSERVER) or a fully qualified domain name (like Lserver.LoweWriter.com).

✦ **FORWARD_IPV4:** Specifies YES or NO to enable or disable IP forwarding. Specify FORWARD_IPV4=YES to set up a router.

✦ **GATEWAY:** Specifies the IP address of the computer's Default Gateway. If the network has a gateway router, specify its address here. If this computer is the network's gateway router, specify the gateway IP address provided by your ISP.

✦ **GATEWAYDEV:** Specifies the interface (such as eth0) that should be used to reach the gateway.

The ifcfg files

Each network interface has an ifcfg configuration file located in /etc/sysconfig/network-scripts. The device name is added to the end of the filename. So, for example, the configuration file for the first Ethernet interface is called ifcfg-eth0.

This file is created and updated by the Network Configuration program, so you don't have to edit it directly (if you don't want to).

Here's a typical ifcfg file for an interface that has a static IP address:

```
DEVICE=eth0
BOOTPROTO=none
ONBOOT=yes
USERCTL=no
IPADDR=192.168.1.200
NETMASK=255.255.255.0
BROADCAST=192.168.1.255
NETWORK=192.168.1.0
```

Here's an example for an interface that uses DHCP:

```
DEVICE=eth0
BOOTPROTO=dhcp
ONBOOT=yes
USERCTL=no
```

Here, the `ifcfg` file doesn't have to specify the IP address information because the interface gets that information from a DHCP server.

The following paragraphs describe the settings that you're most likely to see in this file:

✦ **DEVICE:** The name of the device, such as `eth0` or `eth1`.

✦ **USERCTL:** Specifies YES or NO to indicate whether local users are allowed to start or stop the network.

✦ **ONBOOT:** Specifies YES or NO to indicate whether the device should be enabled when Linux boots up.

✦ **BOOTPROTO:** Specifies how the device gets its IP address. Possible values are NONE for static assignment, DHCP, or BOOTP.

✦ **BROADCAST:** The broadcast address used to send packets to everyone on the subnet. For example: 192.168.1.255.

✦ **NETWORK:** The network address. For example: 192.168.1.0.

✦ **NETMASK:** The subnet mask. For example: 255.255.255.0.

✦ **IPADDR:** The IP address for the adapter.

The Hosts file

The Hosts file is a simple list of IP addresses and the host names associated with each address. You can think of the Hosts file as a local DNS database of sorts. Whenever Linux needs to resolve a DNS name, it first looks for the name in the Hosts file. If Linux finds the name there, it doesn't have to do a DNS lookup; it simply uses the IP address found in the Hosts file.

For small networks, common practice is to list the host name for each computer on the network in the Hosts file on each computer. Then, whenever you add a new computer to the network, you just update each computer's Hosts file to include the new computer. That's not so bad if the network has just a few computers, but you wouldn't want to do it that way for a network with 1,000 hosts. That's why other name resolution systems are more popular for larger networks.

The default Linux Hosts file looks something like this:

```
# Do not remove the following line, or various programs
# that require network functionality will fail.
127.0.0.1  localhost.localdomain  localhost
```

Here, the names `localhost.localdomain` and `localhost` both resolve to 127.0.0.1, which is the standard local loopback address.

Here's an example of a Hosts file that has some additional entries:

```
# Do not remove the following line, or various programs
# that require network functionality will fail.
127.0.0.1  LServer localhost.localdomain  localhost
192.168.1.1     linksys
192.168.1.100   ward.cleaver.com ward
192.168.1.101   june.cleaver.com june
192.168.1.102   wally.cleaver.com wally
192.168.1.103   theodore.cleaver.com theodore beaver
```

Here, I've defined host names for each of the Cleaver family's four computers and their Linksys router. Each computer can be accessed by using two names (for example, `ward.cleaver.com` or just `ward`), except the last one, which has three names.

The resolv.conf file

The `resolv.conf` file lists the DNS nameservers that can be consulted to perform DNS lookups. A typical `resolv.conf` file looks like this:

```
nameserver 192.168.1.110
nameserver 204.127.198.19
nameserver 63.249.76.19
```

If you have set up a nameserver on your own network, its IP address should be the first one listed.

The nsswitch.conf file

This configuration file controls how name resolution works when looking up various types of objects, such as host addresses and passwords. Listing 3-1 shows the sample `nsswitch.conf` file that comes with Fedora Linux. As you can see, this file is loaded with comments that explain what the various settings do.

You can use the `files`, `db`, and `dns` keywords to specify how objects should be retrieved. `files` specifies that the local file should be used, `db` specifies a database lookup, and `dns` specifies that a DNS server should be consulted.

The order in which you list these keywords determines the order in which the data sources are searched. Thus, if you want host names to be resolved first by the local Hosts file and then by DNS, you should include the following line in `nsswitch`:

```
hosts:   files dns
```

Listing 3-1:   A Sample /etc/nsswitch.conf File

```
#
# /etc/nsswitch.conf
#
# An example Name Service Switch config file. This file should be
# sorted with the most-used services at the beginning.
#
# The entry '[NOTFOUND=return]' means that the search for an
# entry should stop if the search in the previous entry turned
# up nothing. Note that if the search failed due to some other reason
# (like no NIS server responding) then the search continues with the
# next entry.
#
# Legal entries are:
#
#      nisplus or nis+    Use NIS+ (NIS version 3)
#      nis or yp          Use NIS (NIS version 2), also called YP
#      dns                Use DNS (Domain Name Service)
#      files              Use the local files
#      db                 Use the local database (.db) files
#      compat             Use NIS on compat mode
#      hesiod             Use Hesiod for user lookups
#      [NOTFOUND=return]  Stop searching if not found so far
#
# To use db, put the "db" in front of "files" for entries you want to be
# looked up first in the databases
#
# Example:
#passwd:    db files nisplus nis
#shadow:    db files nisplus nis
#group:     db files nisplus nis
passwd:     files
shadow:     files
group:      files
#hosts:     db files nisplus nis dns
hosts:      files dns
# Example - obey only what nisplus tells us...
#services:   nisplus [NOTFOUND=return] files
#networks:   nisplus [NOTFOUND=return] files
#protocols:  nisplus [NOTFOUND=return] files
#rpc:        nisplus [NOTFOUND=return] files
#ethers:     nisplus [NOTFOUND=return] files
#netmasks:   nisplus [NOTFOUND=return] files
bootparams: nisplus [NOTFOUND=return] files
ethers:     files
netmasks:   files
networks:   files
protocols:  files
rpc:        files
services:   files
netgroup:   files
publickey:  nisplus
automount:  files
aliases:    files nisplus
```

The xinetd.conf file

Xinetd is a service that oversees a variety of networking services, such as Telnet or Finger. Xinetd listens for requests on the ports on which these services talk and automatically starts the service when a connection is made. Xinetd is controlled by the configuration file xinetd.conf, which is found in the /etc directory, and each of the services controlled by xinetd is in turn controlled by a configuration file found in the /etc/xinet.d directory.

You should leave most of the settings in these configuration files alone unless you've studied up on xinetd. (You can find out more about it at www.xinetd.org.) However, you may want to modify the configuration files in order to enable or disable specific services.

Each of the services controlled by xinetd has a configuration file in the /etc/xinet.d directory. Each of these configuration files ends with a line that enables or disables the service. For example, here's the configuration file for Telnet, /etc/xinet.d/telnet:

```
# default: on
# description: The telnet server serves telnet sessions; it uses \
#      unencrypted username/password pairs for authentication.
service telnet
{
    Flags           = REUSE
    socket_type     = stream
    wait            = no
    user            = root
    server          = /usr/sbin/in.telnetd
    log_on_failure  += USERID
    disable         = yes
}
```

Here, the last line disables Telnet. You can enable the Telnet service by changing the last line to disable = no.

Displaying Your Network Configuration with the ifconfig Command

Linux doesn't have an ipconfig command like Windows. Instead, the command that you use to display information about your network configuration is ifconfig. You can also use this command to set network configuration options, but in most cases, using the Network Configuration program or directly editing the network configuration files is easier.

If you enter `ifconfig` without any parameters, you get output similar to the following:

```
Eth0      Link encap:Ethernet  HWaddr 00:40:05:80:51:F3
          inet addr:192.168.1.200  Bcast:192.168.1.255  Mask:255.255.255.0
          UP BROADCAST RUNNING MULTICAST  MTU:1500  Metric:1
          RX packets:17293 errors:0 dropped:0 overruns:0 frame:0
          TX packets:334 errors:0 dropped:0 overruns:0 carrier:0
          collisions:0 txqueuelen:100
          RX bytes:1124153 (1.0 Mb)  TX bytes:45726 (44.6 Kb)
          Interrupt:3 Base address:0xc000
lo        Link encap:Local Loopback
          inet addr:127.0.0.1  Mask:255.0.0.0
          UP LOOPBACK RUNNING  MTU:16436  Metric:1
          RX packets:202939 errors:0 dropped:0 overruns:0 frame:0
          TX packets:202939 errors:0 dropped:0 overruns:0 carrier:0
          collisions:0 txqueuelen:0
          RX bytes:13856758 (13.2 Mb)  TX bytes:13856758 (13.2 Mb)
```

From this output, you can tell that the IP address of the Ethernet adapter (eth0) is 192.168.1.200, the broadcast address is 192.168.1.255, and the netmask is 255.255.255.0. You can also see transmit and receive statistics as well as information about the hardware configuration, such as the MAC address and the adapter's interrupt and memory base address assignments.

Linux offers many other commands that can help you configure and troubleshoot a network. Many of these commands are described in detail in Chapter 9 of this minibook.

Chapter 4: Running DHCP and DNS

In This Chapter

✔ Dealing with DHCP

✔ Running a DNS server

✔ Understanding BIND configuration files

*O*ne of the main reasons that many network administrators add Linux servers to their networks is to run Internet services such as DHCP and DNS. These services were originally developed for the Unix environment, so they tend to run better under Linux than they do under Windows.

Well, that's the theory, at least. The most recent versions of Windows are probably just as good at running these services as Linux. Still, if you prefer to set up these services on a Linux server, this chapter is for you.

Running a DHCP Server

DHCP is the TCP/IP protocol that automatically assigns IP addresses to hosts as they come on the network. For a very small network (say, fewer than ten hosts), you don't really need DHCP: You can just configure each computer to have a static IP address. For larger networks, however, DHCP is almost a must. Without DHCP, you have to manually plan your entire IP address scheme and manually configure every computer with its IP information. Then, if a critical address such as your Internet gateway router or your DNS server address changes, you have to manually update each computer on the network. As you can imagine, DHCP can save you a lot of time.

 Even for small networks, however, DHCP can be a timesaver. For example, suppose that you have a notebook computer that you take back and forth between home and office. If you don't set up a DHCP server at home, you have to change the computer's static IP address each time you move the computer. With DHCP, the computer can change IP addresses automatically.

For the complete lowdown on DHCP, please refer to Book IV, Chapter 3. In the following sections, I show you how to install and configure a DHCP server on the Fedora Core 3 Linux distribution.

Installing DHCP

You can quickly find out whether DHCP is installed on your system by entering the following command from a shell prompt:

```
rpm -q dhcp
```

If DHCP has been installed, the package version is displayed. If not, the message `package dhcp is not installed` is displayed.

If DHCP isn't installed on your Linux server, you can install it by following these steps:

1. **Insert the Fedora distribution disk in the drive.**

2. **When prompted to run the Autorun file, click Yes.**

The Package Manager window opens.

3. **Click Forward.**

The Package Manager tallies up the packages that you've already installed on your computer. This may take a few moments. After it's done, the Package Manager displays a list of all the package groups that it can install.

4. **Scroll down the list, select Network Servers, and then click the Details link.**

This step brings up a list of specific packages in the Network Servers group.

5. **Select the DHCP package and then click Close.**

6. **Click Forward.**

Package Manager decides which packages it needs to install based on your selection. (This decision isn't as simple as it seems because many packages are dependent on other packages.)

7. **When Package Manager displays the list of packages that it proposes to install, click Forward.**

Package Manager updates your system. This step may also take awhile.

8. **When Package Manager program is done, click Finish.**

You're done! DHCP is now installed.

If you prefer to install DHCP manually, you can insert the Fedora distribution disk in the drive and then enter this command:

```
rpm -ivh /media/cdrom/RedHat/RPMS/dhcp*
```

This command installs the DHCP package with a single command.

Configuring DHCP

You configure DHCP settings through a file called `dhcpd.config` that lives
in the `/etc` directory. Red Hat provides you with a sample configuration
file located in the directory `/usr/share/doc/dhcp-version/dhcpd.`
`conf.sample`. Open this file in the text editor and then save it to the `/etc`
directory, changing its name from `dhcpd.conf.sample` to just `dhcpd.`
`conf`. Then, edit the file to reflect the settings that you want to use.

Listing 4-1 shows the sample configuration file that comes with Fedora.

Listing 4-1:   A Sample dhcpd.conf File

```
ddns-update-style interim;
ignore client-updates;
subnet 192.168.0.0 netmask 255.255.255.0 {
# --- default gateway
        option routers                  192.168.0.1;
        option subnet-mask              255.255.255.0;
        option nis-domain               "domain.org";
        option domain-name              "domain.org";
        option domain-name-servers      192.168.1.1;
        option time-offset              -18000;   # Eastern Standard Time
#       option ntp-servers              192.168.1.1;
#       option netbios-name-servers     192.168.1.1;
# --- Selects point-to-point node (default is hybrid). Don't change this
# -- unless you understand Netbios very well
#       option netbios-node-type 2;
        range dynamic-bootp 192.168.0.128 192.168.0.255;
        default-lease-time 21600;
        max-lease-time 43200;
        # we want the nameserver to appear at a fixed address
        host ns {
                next-server marvin.redhat.com;
                hardware ethernet 12:34:56:78:AB:CD;
                fixed-address 207.175.42.254;
                }
}
```

The following paragraphs describe some of the key points of this file:

✦ **ddns-update-style:** The DHCP standards group is in the midst of
   deciding exactly how DHCP will handle changes to DNS data. This
   option specifies that the interim method should be used. This line is
   required — so don't mess with it.

- ✦ **subnet:** This line specifies a subnet that's managed by this DHCP server. Following the subnet ID and netmask is an opening bracket; all the options that appear between this bracket and the closing bracket in the last line of the file belong to this subnet. In some cases, your DHCP server may dole out IP configuration information for two or more subnet groups. In that case, you'll need additional subnet groups in the configuration file.

- ✦ **option routers:** This line provides the IP address of the Default Gateway.

- ✦ **option subnet mask:** This line provides the subnet mask for the subnet.

- ✦ **option nis-domain:** This line provides the NIS domain name. This line is important only if you've set up one or more NIS servers.

- ✦ **option domain-name:** This line provides the domain name for the network.

- ✦ **option domain-name-servers:** This line provides the IP addresses of your DNS servers.

- ✦ **range:** This line specifies the range of addresses that the DHCP server will assign for this subnet.

- ✦ **default-lease-time:** This line determines the default lease time in seconds.

- ✦ **max-lease-time:** This line determines the maximum life of a lease.

- ✦ **host:** This line specifies a reservation. The host group specifies the MAC address for the host and the fixed IP address to be assigned.

Starting DHCP

After you've set up the configuration file, you can start DHCP by opening a terminal window or virtual console and entering the following command:

```
dhcpd start
```

If an error exists in the configuration file, a message to that effect is displayed. You have to edit the file in order to correct the error and then start the DHCP service again.

You should also restart the service whenever you make a change to the configuration file. To restart DHCP, enter this command:

```
dhcpd restart
```

To automatically start DHCP whenever you start the computer, run this command:

```
chkconfig -level 35 dhcpd on
```

Running a DNS Server

Linux comes with BIND, the best DNS server that money can buy. BIND is an extremely powerful program. Some people make entire careers of setting up and configuring BIND. In these few short pages, I just touch on the very basics of setting up a DNS server on your network.

You can find plenty of details about DNS in Book IV, Chapter 4. Please review that chapter before playing with BIND on your Linux system.

Installing BIND

You can quickly find out whether BIND is installed on your system by entering the following command from a shell prompt:

```
rpm -q bind
```

If BIND has been installed, the package version is displayed. If not, the message package bind is not installed is displayed.

BIND is usually installed by default when you install Linux as a network server. If it isn't, you can easily install it by following these steps:

1. Insert the Fedora distribution disk in the drive.

2. When prompted to run the Autorun file, click Yes.

The Package Manager window opens.

3. Click Forward.

The Package Manager displays a list of all the package groups that it can install.

4. Scroll down the list and select the DNS Name Server group.

5. Click Forward.

The Package Management spends a few moments deciding which packages it needs to install based on your selection.

6. When the Package Management program displays the list of packages it proposes to install, click Forward.

The Package Management program updates your system. This step can take awhile, so be patient.

7. When the Package Management program is done, click Finish.

That's all there is. BIND is now installed and ready to configure.

If you prefer to install BIND manually, you can insert the distribution disk in the drive and then enter this command:

```
rpm -ivh /media/cdrom/RedHat/RPMS/bind*
```

This command installs the BIND package with a single command.

Looking at BIND configuration files

Although Red Hat Linux includes a handy BIND configuration tool, you still need to know the location and purpose of each of BIND's basic configuration files. These files are described in the following sections.

named.conf

This file, found in the `/etc` directory, is the basic BIND configuration file. This file contains global properties and links to the other configuration files.

Because the Fedora BIND configuration tool edits this file, you shouldn't edit this file directly. If you need to set your own configuration options, use `named.custom` instead.

Here's a typical `named.conf` file:

```
## named.conf - configuration for bind
#
# Generated automatically by redhat-config-bind, alchemist et al.
# Any changes not supported by redhat-config-bind should be put
# in /etc/named.custom
#
controls {
        inet 127.0.0.1 allow { localhost; } keys { rndckey; };
};

include "/etc/named.custom";
include "/etc/rndc.key";
zone   "0.0.127.in-addr.arpa" {
                type master;
                file   "0.0.127.in-addr.arpa.zone";
};
zone   "localhost" {
                type master;
                file   "localhost.zone";
};
zone   "lowewriter.com" {
                type master;
                file   "lowewriter.com.zone";
};
```

The line `include "/etc/named.custom";` is what causes the
`named.custom` file to be read in. The `zone` lines name the zone files for
each domain for which the server is responsible.

By default, this file always includes two zones: `0.0.127.in-addr.arpa`,
which is the reverse-lookup zone for `localhost`, and `localhost`, the zone
file for the local computer. Any other zones that you've added through the
Red Hat BIND configuration tool appear in this file as well.

named.custom

This file, also found in `/etc`, lets you add information to the `named.conf`
file. Here's a typical `named.custom` file:

```
## named.custom - custom configuration for bind
#
# Any changes not currently supported by redhat-config-bind should be put
# in this file.
#
zone   "." {
     type hint;
     file  "named.ca";
};
options {
        directory "/var/named/";
};
```

One reason to use this file is if you want to include zone files that you create
yourself without the aid of the Red Hat BIND configuration program. If you
want to include your own zone file, just add a zone statement that names the
zone file. For example, suppose that you want to add a zone named
`cleaver.com`, and you've manually created the cleaver.com.zone. To
include this zone, add these lines to the named.custom file:

```
zone   "cleaver.com" {
     type master;
     file  "cleaver.com.zone";
};
```

named.ca

This file, located in the `/var/named` directory, lists the names and
addresses of the Internet's root servers. It's a fascinating file to look at
because it helps to unveil the mystery of how the Internet really works. You
shouldn't change it, however, unless, of course, you happen to be the administrator of one of the Internet's root servers — in which case, I hope you're
not reading this book to learn how BIND works.

Here's the `named.ca` file that ships with Fedora Core 3:

```
;       This file holds the information on root name servers needed to
;       initialize cache of Internet domain name servers
;       (e.g. reference this file in the "cache  .  <file>"
;       configuration file of BIND domain name servers).
;
;       This file is made available by InterNIC
;       under anonymous FTP as
;           file                /domain/named.cache
;           on server           FTP.INTERNIC.NET
;       -OR-                    RS.INTERNIC.NET
;
;       last update:    Jan 29, 2004
;       related version of root zone:   2004012900
;
;
; formerly NS.INTERNIC.NET
;
.                          3600000  IN  NS   A.ROOT-SERVERS.NET.
A.ROOT-SERVERS.NET.        3600000      A    198.41.0.4
;
; formerly NS1.ISI.EDU
;
.                          3600000      NS   B.ROOT-SERVERS.NET.
B.ROOT-SERVERS.NET.        3600000      A    192.228.79.201
;
; formerly C.PSI.NET
;
.                          3600000      NS   C.ROOT-SERVERS.NET.
C.ROOT-SERVERS.NET.        3600000      A    192.33.4.12
;
; formerly TERP.UMD.EDU
;
.                          3600000      NS   D.ROOT-SERVERS.NET.
D.ROOT-SERVERS.NET.        3600000      A    128.8.10.90
;
; formerly NS.NASA.GOV
;
.                          3600000      NS   E.ROOT-SERVERS.NET.
E.ROOT-SERVERS.NET.        3600000      A    192.203.230.10
;
; formerly NS.ISC.ORG
;
.                          3600000      NS   F.ROOT-SERVERS.NET.
F.ROOT-SERVERS.NET.        3600000      A    192.5.5.241
;
; formerly NS.NIC.DDN.MIL
;
.                          3600000      NS   G.ROOT-SERVERS.NET.
G.ROOT-SERVERS.NET.        3600000      A    192.112.36.4
;
; formerly AOS.ARL.ARMY.MIL
;
.                          3600000      NS   H.ROOT-SERVERS.NET.
H.ROOT-SERVERS.NET.        3600000      A    128.63.2.53
;
; formerly NIC.NORDU.NET
;
.                          3600000      NS   I.ROOT-SERVERS.NET.
I.ROOT-SERVERS.NET.        3600000      A    192.36.148.17
```

```
;
; operated by VeriSign, Inc.
;
.                       3600000    NS    J.ROOT-SERVERS.NET.
J.ROOT-SERVERS.NET.     3600000    A     192.58.128.30
;
; operated by RIPE NCC
;
.                       3600000    NS    K.ROOT-SERVERS.NET.
K.ROOT-SERVERS.NET.     3600000    A     193.0.14.129
;
; operated by ICANN
;
.                       3600000    NS    L.ROOT-SERVERS.NET.
L.ROOT-SERVERS.NET.     3600000    A     198.32.64.12
;
; operated by WIDE
;
.                       3600000    NS    M.ROOT-SERVERS.NET.
M.ROOT-SERVERS.NET.     3600000    A     202.12.27.33
; End of File
```

An organization named *InterNIC* keeps the `named.ca` file up to date. You can download the most current version of `named.ca` from InterNIC's FTP site at `ftp.internic.net`. Every once in awhile, InterNIC publishes a new version of this file, so you should check now and then to make sure that your file is current.

named.local

This file, located in `/var/named`, is a zone file for your local computer — that is, for the `localhost` domain. Rarely (if ever) do you need to modify it. It typically looks like this:

```
$TTL 86400
@       IN   SOA    localhost. root.localhost.   (
                    1997022700 ; Serial
                    28800      ; Refresh
                    14400      ; Retry
                    3600000    ; Expire
                    86400 )    ; Minimum
        IN   NS     localhost.
1       IN   PTR    localhost.
```

Zone files

Each zone for which your DNS server is authoritative should have a zone file, named *domain*.`zone` and located in the `/var/named` directory. If you like to edit DNS records directly, you can create this file yourself. Or you can use the point-and-click interface of the Red Hat BIND configuration tool to automatically create the file.

Here's a typical zone file, named `lowewriter.com.zone`:

```
$TTL 86400
@       IN      SOA     ns207.pair.com.  root.localhost (
                        2 ; serial
                        28800 ; refresh
                        7200 ; retry
                        604800 ; expire
                        86400 ; ttl
                        )
        IN      NS      ns000.ns0.com.
        IN      NS      ns207.pair.com.
@       IN      MX      1     sasi.pair.com.
www     IN      A       209.68.34.15
```

Table 4-1 lists the most common types of records that appear in zone files. For a complete description of each of these record types, refer to Book IV, Chapter 4.

Table 4-1	Common Resource Record Types	
Type	*Name*	*Description*
SOA	Start Of Authority	Identifies a zone.
NS	Name Server	Identifies a name server that is authoritative for the zone.
A	Address	Maps a fully qualified domain name to an IP address.
CNAME	Canonical Name	Creates an alias for a fully qualified domain name.
MX	Mail Exchange	Identifies the mail server for a domain.
PTR	Pointer	Maps an IP address to a fully qualified domain name for reverse lookups.

Restarting BIND

BIND runs as a service called `named`. As a result, when you make changes to your DNS configuration, you have to restart the `named` service to apply the changes. To do that, use this command:

```
service named restart
```

You can also restart the `named` service from the Service Configuration tool. Choose Main Menu⇨System Settings⇨Server Settings⇨Services. Then, scroll down the list to find `named` and click the Restart button.

Chapter 5: Doing the Samba Dance

*U*ntil now, you probably thought of Samba as a Brazilian dance with intricate steps and fun rhythms. In the Linux world, however, *Samba* refers to a file and printer-sharing program that allows Linux to mimic a Windows file and print server so that Windows computers can use shared Linux directories and printers. If you want to use Linux as a file or print server in a Windows network, you'll need to know how to dance the Samba.

Understanding Samba

Because Linux and Windows have such different file systems, you can't create a Linux file server simply by granting Windows users access to Linux directories. Windows client computers wouldn't be able to access files in the Linux directories. Too many differences exist between the file systems. For example:

✦ Linux filenames are case sensitive, whereas Windows filenames are not. For example, in Windows, `File1.txt` and `file1.txt` are the same file. In Linux, they are different files.

✦ In Linux, periods are not used to denote file extensions. Linux filenames don't use extensions.

✦ Windows has file attributes like *read-only* and *archive*. Linux doesn't have these.

More fundamentally, Windows networking uses a protocol called *SMB,* which stands for *server message block,* to manage the exchange of file data among file servers and clients. Linux doesn't have SMB support built in.

That's why Samba is required. Samba is a program that mimics the behavior of a Windows-based file server by implementing the SMB protocol. So when you run Samba on a Linux server, the Windows computers on your network see the Linux server as if it were a Windows server.

Like a Windows server, Samba works by designating certain directories as shares. A *share* is simply a directory that is made available to other users via the network. Each share has the following elements:

✦ **Share name:** The name by which the share is known over the network. Share names should be eight characters whenever possible.

✦ **Path:** The path to the directory on the Linux computer that's being shared, such as `\Users\Doug`.

✦ **Description:** A one-line description of the share.

✦ **Access:** A list of users or groups who have been granted access to the share.

Samba also includes a client program that lets a Linux computer access Windows file servers.

Why did Samba's developers choose to call their program *Samba?* Simply because the protocol that Windows file and print servers use to communicate with each other is called *SMB,* which stands for *server message block.* Add a couple of vowels to *SMB,* and you get *Samba.*

Installing Samba

If you didn't install Samba when you installed Linux, you'll have to install it now. You can do so in one of two basic ways. You can use Fedora's GNOME-based package management tool to install Samba. Just insert the Fedora distribution CD (disc 1) in the CD drive and click Yes when you're asked whether you want to run the `autorun` program. Then, when the Package Management window appears, select the Windows File Server group, which installs the Samba packages for you.

If you prefer to work from the command line, you can use the RPM command to install the Samba packages manually. Open a terminal window or log on to a virtual console. Insert the Linux distribution disk in the drive and then use this command:

```
rpm -ivh /media/cdrom/Fedora/RPMS/samba*
```

This will install all the Samba packages from the distribution CD.

One sure way to render a Samba installation useless is to enable the default Linux firewall settings on the computer that runs Samba. The Linux firewall is designed to prevent users from accessing network services such as Samba. It's designed to be used between the Internet and your local network — not between Samba and your local network. Although it's possible to configure the firewall to allow access to Samba only to your internal network, a much better option is to run the firewall on a separate computer. That way, the firewall computer can concentrate on being a firewall, and the file server computer can concentrate on being a file server.

Starting and Stopping Samba

Before you can use Samba, you must start its two daemons, smbd and nmbd. Both can be started at once by starting the SMB service. From a command shell, use this command:

```
service smb start
```

Whenever you make a configuration change, such as adding a new share or creating a new Samba user, you should stop and restart the service with these commands:

```
service smb restart
```

If you prefer, you can stop and start the service with separate commands:

```
service smb stop
service smb start
```

If you're not sure if Samba is running, enter this command:

```
service smb status
```

You get a message indicating whether the smbd and nmbd daemons are running.

To configure Samba to start automatically when you start Linux, use this command:

```
chkconfig -level 35 smb on
```

To make sure that the chkconfig command worked right, enter this command:

```
chkconfig -list smb
```

You should see output similar to the following:

```
Smb      0:off  1:off  2:off  3:on   4:off  5:on   6:off
```

You can independently configure services to start automatically for each of the six *boot levels* of Linux. Boot level 3 is normal operation without an X server; level 5 is normal operation with an X server. So setting SMB to start for levels 3 and 5 makes SMB available — regardless of whether you're using a graphical user interface.

You can also start and stop Samba by using the Service Configuration tool, shown in Figure 5-1. Scroll down the list of services until you find the SMB service. You can use the three buttons on the toolbar at the top of the window to start, stop, or restart a service.

Figure 5-1:
Using the
Service
Configu-
ration tool.

You can also use the Service Configuration tool to start Samba automatically, although frankly, the chkconfig command is easier to use. To configure Samba to start automatically for levels 3 and 5, follow these steps:

1. **Choose Edit Runlevel⇨RunLevel 3.**

2. **Select the check box next to SMB in the list of services.**

3. **Choose File➪Save Changes.**

4. **Choose Edit Runlevel➪RunLevel 5.**

5. **Select the check box next to SMB in the list of services.**

6. **Choose File➪Save Changes.**

Using the Samba Server Configuration Tool

Fedora includes a handy GNOME-based configuration tool that simplifies the task of configuring Samba. To start it, choose Applications➪System Settings➪Server Settings➪Samba Server. When you do so, the Samba Server Configuration window appears, as shown in Figure 5-2. This tool lets you configure basic server settings and manage shares.

Figure 5-2:
Using the Samba Configuration tool.

Not all of Samba's configuration options are available from the Samba Server Configuration tool. For advanced Samba server configuration, you need to edit the `smb.conf` file directly, as described in the section, "Editing the smb.conf File," later in this chapter.

Also, if you don't like the GNOME-based configuration tool, you can use a new Web-based configuration tool called *SWAT.* For more information, use Google or another Web search service to search for the package `samba-swat`.

Configuring server settings

To make your Samba server visible on the network, you need to configure its server settings. Follow these steps:

1. Choose Preferences⇨Server Settings.

The Server Settings dialog box springs to life, as shown in Figure 5-3.

Figure 5-3:
Configuring
the server
preferences.

2. Enter the workgroup name and a description for your server.

The workgroup name must match the workgroup or domain name used by the computers that will be accessing the server.

3. Click the Security tab.

The security settings appear, as shown in Figure 5-4.

Figure 5-4:
Configuring
security
options.

4. Set the authentication mode the way you want.

The Authentication Mode drop-down list offers four basic types of security:

- *Domain:* This mode configures the Samba server to use a Windows domain controller to verify the user. If you specify this option, you must provide the name of the domain controller in the Authentication Server text box. Also, you must set the Encrypted Passwords drop-down list to Yes if you use Domain mode.

- *Server:* This mode configures Samba to use another Samba server to authenticate users. If you have more than one Samba server, this feature lets you set up user accounts on just one of the servers. Specify the name of the Samba server in which you want to perform the authentication in the Authentication Server text box.

- *Share:* This mode authorizes users separately for each share that they attempt to access.

- *User:* This is the default mode. It requires that users provide a valid username and password when they first connect to a Samba server. That authentication then grants them access to all shares on the server, subject to the restrictions of the account under which they are authorized.

5. **Set the Encrypt Passwords drop-down list to Yes.**

   This option is required to allow users of Windows 98 or later versions to connect.

6. **Set the Guest Account drop-down list to the account that you want anonymous users to access.**

   Normally, this account is set to Nobody, which is a user account that doesn't have access to anything. This essentially prevents anonymous users from access shares.

7. **Click OK.**

   The Server Settings dialog box is dismissed.

Configuring server users

You must create a separate Samba user account for each network user who needs to access the Samba server. In addition, you must first create a Linux user account for each user. The Samba user account maps to an existing Linux user account, so you must create the Linux user account first.

To create a Samba user account, follow these steps:

1. **From the Samba Server Configuration window, choose Preferences⇨Samba Users.**

   The Samba Users dialog box appears, as shown in Figure 5-5.

Figure 5-5:
The Samba
Users dialog
box lists
your Samba
users.

2. **Click Add User.**

The dialog box in Figure 5-6 appears.

Figure 5-6:
Adding a
Samba user.

3. **From the Unix Username drop-down list, select the Linux user that you want this user to log on as.**

If you forgot to create the Linux user account for this user, choose System➪Administration➪Users and Groups and create the account now.

4. **Enter the Windows username for the user.**

This is the name of the user's Windows user account.

5. **Type the user's password into the password fields.**

6. **Click OK.**

You're returned to the Samba Users dialog box, which should now list the user that you just created.

7. **Repeat Steps 2 through 6 for any other users you want to create.**

8. **After you're done, click OK.**

The Samba Users dialog box is dismissed.

Creating a share

To be useful, a file server should offer one or more *shares* — directories that have been designated as publicly accessible via the network. You can see a list of the current shares available from a file server by firing up the Samba Server Configuration program.

To create a new share, follow these steps:

1. **Click the Add button.**

The dialog box shown in Figure 5-7 appears.

Figure 5-7:
Creating a
share.

2. **Type the path for the directory that you want to share in the Directory text box.**

If you aren't sure of the path, you can click the Browse button. This action calls up a dialog box that lets you search the server's file system for a directory folder to share. You can also create a new directory from this dialog box if the directory that you want to share doesn't yet exist. After you've selected or created the directory to share, click OK to return to the Create Samba Share dialog box.

3. **Type a description of the share in the Description text box.**

The description is strictly optional but can sometimes help users to determine the intended contents of the folder.

You may be wondering why there's no text box labeled Share Name in the Create Samba Share dialog box. Unfortunately, the Samba Configuration program doesn't let you specify the share name for the share. Instead, it just uses the name of the directory being shared. If a share already exists by that name, the configuration program adds a number to the end of the directory name in order to make the share name unique.

Don't despair, however. You can change the share name by editing the smb.conf file, as described later in this chapter.

4. Specify whether you want the share to be read-only or read/write.

The default is read-only. If you want to let users save their files on your Samba server, you need to change this setting to read/write.

5. Click the Access tab.

The Access Tab of the Create Samba Share dialog box appears, as shown in Figure 5-8.

Figure 5-8: Allowing access to a Samba share.

6. If you want to limit access to the share, select the Only Allow Access to Specific Users check box and then select the users to whom you want to grant access.

The Nobody user here is a little confusing. At first glance, you may think that selecting Nobody would deny access to everyone, thus making the share completely inaccessible. However, that isn't how it works. Instead, Nobody is a special user account that is used by default when a network user anonymously accesses a Samba server. As a result, enabling access for Nobody allows guest users to access the share.

7. Click OK.

You're returned to the Samba Configuration window, where the share that you just added appears in the list of shares.

When you create a new share by using the Samba Configuration program, the share should be immediately visible to other network users. If it isn't, try restarting the Samba server as described in the section, "Starting and Stopping Samba," earlier in this chapter.

Editing the smb.conf File

If you like the feeling of raw power that comes from editing configuration files, fire up your favorite text editor and play with the Samba configuration file. It's called `smb.conf` and is usually located in the `/etc/samba` directory, although some distributions may place this file in another location. Figure 5-9 shows you the `smb.conf` file being edited in the standard Text Editor program, which you can access by choosing Applications⇨Accessories⇨Text Editor.

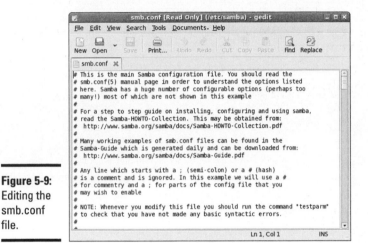

Figure 5-9:
Editing the
smb.conf
file.

Any line in the `smb.conf` file that begins with a hash mark (#) or semicolon (;) is a comment. The default `smb.conf` file is loaded with comments that describe what each configuration line does. Plus, you can find many sample configuration entries that are commented out. The sample configuration lines are marked with a semicolon to distinguish them from explanatory text lines, which begin with a hash mark.

The overall structure of the `smb.conf` file is something like this:

```
[global]
    workgroup = workgroup
    server string = samba server
    security = USER
    encrypt passwords = yes
    smb passwd file = /etc/samba/smbpasswd
    guest ok = yes
    other global settings...
[sharename]
    comment = comment
    path = path
    writeable = yes
```

The first section of the file, marked by the [global] line, contains options that apply to the entire server. These are the options that are set by the Preferences⇨Server Settings command in the GNOME Samba Server Configuration program. Table 5-1 lists a few of the more common settings that you can use in the global section.

Table 5-1	Common Global Settings for the smb.conf File
Setting	*Description*
workgroup	The name of the workgroup or domain.
server string	The comment that describes the server.
hosts allow	Lets you limit access to the Samba server to the IP addresses listed. If a partial IP address is listed (for example, 192.168.1), it is treated as a subnet.
guest ok	Specify Yes to allow guest access.
guest account	Specifies the Linux account to be used.
security	Specifies the security mode: Domain, Server, Share, or User.

Located after the global section is a section for each share that begins with the [sharename] line. The settings in these groups specify the details of a share, such as the comment and path. Table 5-2 lists the settings that you can specify for a share.

Table 5-2	Share Settings for the smb.conf File
Setting	*Description*
[sharename]	The name used by the share.
path=path	The path to the directory to be shared.
comment=comment	A description of the shared resource.
guest ok	Specify Yes to allow guest access.
writeonly	Specify Yes for read/write, No for read-only.
browseable	Specify Yes to make the share visible in My Network Places.
valid users	A list of users who can access the share.
hosts allow	Lets you limit access to the Samba server to the IP addresses listed. If a partial IP address is listed (for example, 192.168.1), it is treated as a subnet.

After you modify the smb.conf file and save your changes, you need to restart the SMB service in order for the changes to take effect. See the section, "Starting and Stopping Samba," earlier in this chapter, for more information.

Using the Samba Client

Earlier in this chapter, I show you how to set up Samba's server program so that you can enable a Linux computer to operate as a file server in a Windows network, thus allowing Windows clients to access files in shared directories on the Linux computer. That's the most common reason for using Samba.

But Samba can also work the other way around: It includes a program called *smbclient* that lets you access Windows file servers from a Linux computer. The smbclient program works much like an FTP client, so if you've used FTP before, you'll have no trouble understanding how it works.

Smbclient is a command line tool, so you need to log on to a virtual console or open a terminal window. Then, enter the smbclient command, followed by the server and share name, like this:

```
smbclient //server01/share01
```

When the client successfully accesses the share, you are greeted by the friendly SMB prompt:

```
smb:\>
```

Then, you can enter smbclient commands to access the data in the shared directory. Table 5-3 summarizes the more common commands that are available at the smb:\> prompt.

Table 5-3	Commonly Used smbclient Commands
Command	*Description*
cd *directory*	Changes to the specified directory on the remote system.
del *filename*	Deletes the specified file or files on the remote system.
dir	Lists files in the current directory on the remote system.
exit	Terminates the session.
get *remote-file local-file*	Copies the specified remote file to the specified local file.
lcd *directory*	Changes the local current directory to the specified directory.
md *directory*	Creates a directory on the remote system.
mget *wildcard-mask*	Copies all files that match the wildcard mask from the remote system to the local system.

(continued)

Table 5-3 *(continued)*

Command	Description
mput *wildcard-mask*	Copies all files that match the wildcard mask from the local system to the remote system.
put *local-file remote-file*	Copies the specified file from the local system to the remote system.
rd *directory*	Deletes the specified directory on the remote system.

Chapter 6: Running Apache

In This Chapter

- ✔ Getting Apache up and running
- ✔ Using the HTTP configuration tool
- ✔ Restricting access
- ✔ Creating virtual hosts
- ✔ Creating Web pages

*A*ll the popular Linux distributions come with Apache, the most popular Web server on the Internet today. In most cases, Apache is installed and configured automatically when you install Linux. Then, setting up a Web server for the Internet or an intranet is simply a matter of tweaking a few Apache configuration settings and copying your HTML document files to Apache's home directory.

Installing Apache

You can quickly find out whether Apache is installed on your system by entering the following command from a shell prompt:

```
rpm -q httpd
```

If Apache has been installed, the package version is displayed. If not, the message `package httpd is not installed` is displayed.

If Apache is not installed on your Linux server, you can install it by following these steps:

1. Insert the Fedora distribution disk in the drive.

2. When prompted to run the Autorun file, click Yes.

The Package Manager window opens.

3. Click the Forward button.

The Package Manager tallies up the packages that you've already installed on your computer. This may take a few moments. When it's done, it displays a list of all the package groups it can install.

4. **Scroll down the list, select Web Servers, and then click the Forward button.**

   The Package Manager decides which packages it needs to install based on your selection.

5. **When the Package Manager program displays the list of packages it proposes to install, click the Forward button.**

   The Package Manager program updates your system. This step may also take awhile.

6. **When the Package Manager program is done, click Finish.**

   Apache is now installed.

If you prefer to install Apache manually, you can insert the distribution CD in the CD-ROM drive and then enter this command:

```
rpm -ivh /media/cdrom/Fedora/RPMS/httpd*
```

This command installs Apache without muddling through the Package Manager screens.

Starting and Stopping Apache

Before you can use Apache, you must start the httpd daemon. From a command shell, use this command:

```
service httpd start
```

Whenever you make a configuration change, you should stop and restart the service with this command:

```
service httpd restart
```

If you prefer, you can stop and start the service with separate commands:

```
service httpd stop
service httpd start
```

If you're not sure if Apache is running, enter this command:

```
service httpd status
```

You get a message indicating whether the smbd and nmbd daemons are running.

To configure Apache to start automatically when you start Linux, use this command:

```
chkconfig --level 35 httpd on
```

To make sure that the `chkconfig` command worked right, enter this command:

```
chkconfig --list httpd
```

You should see output similar to the following:

```
httpd    0:off  1:off  2:off  3:on   4:off  5:on   6:off
```

Confirming that Apache Is Running

You can test to see whether Apache is up and running by trying to display the default home page shipped with Apache from another computer on your network. You can do that by firing up a Web browser such as Internet Explorer and typing the IP address of your Linux server in the Address bar. If Apache is running on the server, a page such as the one shown in Figure 6-1 appears.

Figure 6-1: Apache is running!

If this doesn't work, first make sure that you can ping your Linux server from the remote system. To do that, type **ping** followed by the IP address of the Linux server. If the ping command times out, you have a connectivity problem you need to correct.

If you can ping the Linux server but still can't reach the Apache server home page, here are a few things to check:

✦ Make sure that the httpd service is running as described in the "Starting and Stopping Apache" section, earlier in this chapter.

✦ Make sure that the Linux firewall is turned off or configured to allow HTTP traffic. In Fedora, you can manage the firewall settings from the GNOME-based Security Level Configuration tool. To run it, choose System➪Security Level. Then, either disable the firewall altogether or enable it but select WWW (HTTP) in the list of trusted services. Figure 6-2 shows the System Settings Configuration tool with the firewall enabled and the HTTP service trusted.

Do not disable the firewall altogether unless you have another firewall, such as a firewall router, between your Linux server and your Internet connection.

Figure 6-2:
Trusting the
HTTP
service.

Using the HTTP Configuration Tool

Apache should run fine using the default configuration settings made when you install it. However, you can change various configuration settings either by editing the Apache configuration files or by using the HTTP configuration tool, as shown in Figure 6-3. To start this tool, choose System⇨Server Settings⇨Http.

HTTP

| Main | Virtual Hosts | Server | Performance Tuning |

Basic Setup

Server Name: `www.lowewriter.com`

Webmaster email address: `webmaster@lowewriter.com`

Available Addresses

All available addresses on port 80

✦ Add...

✦ Edit...

✦ Delete

Set addresses for Apache to listen for requests on.

Help   ✖ Cancel   ✔ OK

Figure 6-3:
Configuring Apache's HTTP settings.

The Main tab of the HTTP configuration tool provides the basic configuration settings for Apache. Here, you can set the following options:

✦ **Server Name:** This option sets the name that the Apache server will return. If you leave this name blank, Apache will figure out the actual name of the Linux server and return it. So you need to set this option only if you want to use a different name for your Apache server.

✦ **Webmaster E-Mail Address:** This is the e-mail address of the Webmaster for this Web server.

✦ **Available Addresses:** This list box shows the addresses that Apache will service HTTP requests for. By default, Apache will reply to HTTP requests for any computer that makes the request on port 80, the standard HTTP port. However, you can change the port or restrict access, as described in the following section.

Whenever you use the HTTP configuration tool to change Apache's configuration, you need to restart Apache. You can do so by entering this command from a console prompt:

```
service httpd restart
```

Restricting Access to an Apache Server

To restrict access to your Apache server, you can alter the Available Addresses list in the Main tab of the HTTP Configuration tool by using the Add, Edit, or Delete buttons. If all you want to do is change the port that the Apache server uses, select All Available Addresses on Port 80 in the Available Addresses list and click Edit. This brings up the dialog box shown in Figure 6-4. Then, specify the port you want to use and click OK.

Figure 6-4:
The Edit an
Address
dialog box.

If you want to restrict access to certain IP addresses, select the All Available Addresses line, click the Edit button, select the Address radio button, and then enter the address you want to allow access to. You can enter a single IP address, but you're more likely to enter a partial IP address or an IP/netmask combination. For example, to allow access to all addresses from 212.66.5.0 to 212.66.5.255, you could enter either of the following:

```
212.66.5
212.66.5.0/255.255.255.0
```

If you want to allow access to a list of specific IP addresses, you can add lines to the Available Addresses list box. First, though, you should remove the All Available Addresses line or edit it to allow just a single address. Then, click the Add button to add addresses you want to allow.

Configuring Virtual Hosts

A *virtual host* is simply a Web site with its own domain name hosted by an Apache server. By default, Apache is set up to serve just one virtual host. However, you can add additional virtual hosts. As a result, a single Apache server is able to host more than one Web site.

For example, if I were so inclined, I might set up an Apache server to host my own personal Web site (www.lowewriter.com) that has information about my books and a second Web site (www.hauntedlowes.com) that has information about my favorite hobby, decorating my house for Halloween. Both of these Web sites could be implemented as virtual hosts on a single Apache server.

To configure a virtual host (including the default virtual host if you have only one), you use the Virtual Hosts tab of the HTTP configuration tool, as shown in Figure 6-5.

Figure 6-5:
The Virtual
Hosts tab.

Configuring the default host

Even if you don't plan on creating additional virtual hosts, you can still use the Virtual Hosts tab to configure the default virtual host for your Web site. To do so, select the virtual host in the Virtual Hosts list and click the Edit button. This brings up the Virtual Host Properties dialog box, as shown in Figure 6-6.

From this dialog box, you can configure a variety of important settings for the virtual host:

+ **Virtual Host Name:** The name you use to refer to the virtual host. For the default virtual host, the default name is — drum roll, please — Default Virtual Host. (Don't blame me, it isn't my fault.)

+ **Document Root Directory:** This is the filesystem location that contains the HTML documents for the Web site. The default is /var/www/html, but you can specify a different location if you want to store your HTML files somewhere else.

✦ **Webmaster E-mail Address:** Each virtual host can have its own Webmaster e-mail address. If you leave this option blank, the address specified for the main HTTP configuration (refer to Figure 6-3) is used.

✦ **Host Information:** This section of the dialog box lets you specify what HTTP requests should be serviced by this virtual host. In most cases, you should leave this set to the default setting, Handle All Remaining Unhandled Requests.

Figure 6-6:
The Virtual
Host
Properties
dialog box.

You can use the other tabs of the Virtual Host Properties dialog box to configure additional options. For example, Figure 6-7 shows the Page Options tab. Here, you can set the following options:

✦ **Directory Page Search List:** This list specifies the default page for the Web site. The default page is displayed if the user doesn't indicate a specific page to retrieve. Then, Apache looks for each of the pages listed in the Directory Page Search list and displays the first one it finds. You can use the Add, Edit, or Delete buttons to modify this list.

✦ **Error Pages:** This list lets you change the default error pages that are displayed when an HTTP error occurs. The most common HTTP error, Not Found, happens when the user requests a page that doesn't exist. If you want to create a custom error page to let the user know that the page doesn't exist or that some other error has occurred, this is the place to do it.

Figure 6-7:
The Page
Options tab
lets you
set the
directory
search list
and custom
error pages.

Creating a virtual host

If you want to host more than one Web site on an Apache server, you can
create additional virtual hosts. Just follow these steps:

1. **Click the Add button on the Virtual Hosts tab of the HTTP configuration tool.**

   This brings up the Virtual Host dialog box, which you've already seen in
   Figure 6-6.

2. **In the Host Information section, choose Name Based Virtual Host in
   the drop-down list.**

   The Virtual Host Properties dialog box morphs into the dialog box
   shown in Figure 6-8.

3. **Enter the IP address and the host name for the virtual host.**

   The IP address is usually the IP address assigned to the Apache server,
   and the host name is the DNS name used to access the virtual host.

4. **If you want to provide an alias for the virtual host, click the Add
   button, enter the alias name, and click OK.**

An alias is often used for Web sites that are used on an intranet rather than on public Web sites. For example, if you're setting up an intranet Web site for your company suggestion box, the full DNS name for the virtual host might be `suggestionbox.mycompany.com`. But if you provide just `suggestionbox` as an alias, users can access the suggestion box Web site by using `suggestionbox` rather than `suggestionbox.mycompany.com` as the Web site address.

5. **Use the other tabs of the Virtual Host Properties dialog box to configure additional options.**

   For example, you might want to use the Page Options tab to change the directory page search list or designate custom error pages.

6. **Click OK.**

   The virtual host is created. You're returned to the HTTP configuration tool, and the new virtual host will appear in the Virtual Hosts list.

Figure 6-8:
Creating a new virtual host.

Setting the Apache User Account

The Server tab of the HTTP configuration tool lets you set several configuration options, the most important of which is the user account that Apache will run under. By default, this account is named `apache`, and it belongs to a group named `apache`. This account is created automatically when you install Apache, so you don't have to do anything special to configure it.

Although it may be tempting, resist the urge to change this user setting to a user account with more rights. If you do so, you run the risk of a major security breach. An intelligent hacker can use a Web browser to break into your system. But the hacker will be constrained by the rights granted to the user account that Apache runs under. One of the worst mistakes you could make would be to change this user account from `apache` to `root`. Then, a hacker who manages to exploit a security hole in your Web site will have virtually free reign over your Linux server.

Manually Editing Apache's Configuration Files

If you're allergic to GUI configuration tools, you can configure your Apache server by directly editing the configuration files. Apache's configuration settings are found in three separate configuration files, named `httpd.conf`, `srm.conf`, and `access.conf`. These files are located in `/etc/httpd/conf` in Fedora Core Linux, but they may be in a different location in other Linux distributions. Be sure to study the Apache documentation before you start messing with these files!

Whenever you make a configuration change to Apache, you should restart Apache by using the `service httpd restart` command.

Creating Web Pages

This section is about how to create and edit HTML content for your Web site. Plenty of good books are available on how to do that, including my own *Creating Web Pages For Dummies Quick Reference* (Wiley Publishing). Rather, I just want to point out a few key things that you need to know in order to set up a Web site using Apache:

✦ The default location for Web documents is `/var/www/html`. When you create Web pages for your site, save them in that directory.

✦ When a user visits your Web site by typing just the domain name without out a filename (for example, `www.mydomain.com` instead of `www.mydomain.com/file1.html`), Apache displays the file named `index.html` or `index.htm`. You should give the home page for your Web site one of these two names.

✦ If you're a programmer, you can build complicated Web-based applications using PHP, which is installed along with Apache.

Chapter 7: Running Sendmail

In This Chapter

✔ **Looking at how e-mail works**

✔ **Installing and starting Sendmail**

✔ **Basic Sendmail configuration**

✔ **Blocking spam with SpamAssassin**

✔ **Reading e-mail with mail and Evolution**

Sendmail, which is a standard part of most Linux distributions, is one of the most popular mail server programs on the Internet. You can use Sendmail as an alternative to expensive mail server programs, such as Microsoft Exchange Server, to provide e-mail services for your LAN. This chapter shows you how to set up and use Sendmail on a Linux server.

Spam artists — unscrupulous marketers who clutter the Internet with millions of unsolicited e-mails — are constantly on the prowl for unprotected Sendmail servers, which they can use to launch their spam campaigns. If you don't protect your server, sooner or later a spammer will coax your computer into spending almost all its time sending out the spammer's e-mail. To protect your server from becoming an indentured spam servant, you can configure it to refuse any mail that merely wants to use your computer to relay messages to other computers. See the sidebar, "Don't be an open relay!" later in this chapter.

Understanding E-Mail

Before I get into the details of installing and configuring Sendmail, I want to review some basics of how Internet e-mail works. First, you need to understand that e-mail consists of messages that are delivered according to an Internet protocol commonly referred to as *SMTP*. SMTP, which stands for *Simple Mail Transfer Protocol,* was first codified in 1983, long before Al Gore invented the Internet. Several enhancements have been made along the way, but most e-mail on the Internet today is delivered using this nearly ancient protocol.

Interestingly, the software that delivers 70 percent of all the e-mail on the Internet — Sendmail — also originated in the same year. In 1983, Eric Allman developed the first version of the Sendmail program as part of the Berkeley Software Distribution (BSD) of Unix, one of the earliest versions of Unix made publicly available.

The following paragraphs describe some of the key features of e-mail that you should know about if you plan on setting up a Linux server running Sendmail:

✦ **Mailbox:** A *mailbox* is a simple text file that holds incoming e-mail messages until they are processed by a mail user agent. In Fedora Linux, each user has a mailbox file in /var/mail.

✦ **Mail User Agent (MUA):** A program that end users can use to send and receive mail. The most widely used MUA is Microsoft Outlook. Linux comes with several MUAs. The most basic is Mail, a text-based MUA that lets you read and compose e-mail messages from a console prompt. Fedora also includes a sophisticated graphical MUA called *Evolution,* which is similar in many ways to Microsoft Outlook. Both are described later in this chapter.

✦ **Mail Transfer Agent (MTA):** A program that transfers e-mail messages between computers. Sendmail, which most of this chapter is devoted to, is an MTA. When a user uses an MUA to send an e-mail message, the MUA delivers the message to an MTA, which then transfers the message to the intended recipient.

✦ **Mail Delivery Agent (MDA):** A program that accepts incoming mail from an MTA and places it in the intended recipient's mailbox. A basic MDA simply copies each message to the mailbox, but more advanced MDAs can be used to filter the incoming mail to eliminate spam or check for viruses. The default MDA for Fedora Linux is Procmail. Fedora also includes SpamAssassin, which you can use to filter spam from your incoming mail.

Installing Sendmail

You can quickly find out whether Sendmail is installed on your system by entering the following command from a shell prompt:

```
rpm -q sendmail
```

If Sendmail has been installed, the package version is displayed. If not, the message package sendmail is not installed is displayed.

While you're at it, you should check to make sure that m4 is installed by running the command `rpm -q m4`. Then check to make sure that `sendmail-c4` is installed by running the command `rpm -q sendmail-c4`. M4 and `sendmail-c4` are required if you want to make changes to your Sendmail configuration. They're installed by default when you install Sendmail, so they should be there if Sendmail is installed. It never hurts to check.

If Sendmail isn't installed, you can install it by following these steps:

1. **Insert the Fedora distribution disk in your CD/DVD drive.**

2. **When prompted to run the Autorun file, click Yes.**

   The Package Manager window opens.

3. **Click the Forward button.**

   The Package Manager ushers forth a list of all the package groups that it can install.

4. **Scroll down the list and select Mail Server.**

5. **Click the Forward button.**

   Be patient while the Package Manager decides which packages it needs to install based on your selection.

6. **When the Package Manager program displays the list of packages it proposes to install, click the Forward button.**

   The Package Manager program updates your system. Be patient some more.

7. **When the Package Manager program is done, click Finish.**

   You are now the proud owner of a computer with Sendmail.

If you prefer to install Sendmail manually, you can insert the distribution disk in the CD/DVD drive and then enter this command:

```
rpm -ivh /mnt/cdrom/RedHat/RPMS/sendmail*
```

The Sendmail package installs with a single command.

Modifying sendmail.mc

Sendmail is probably one of the most difficult programs to configure that you'll ever encounter. In fact, the basic configuration file, `sendmail.cf`, is well over a thousand lines long. You don't want to mess with this file if you can possibly avoid it.

Fortunately, you don't have to. The `sendmail.cf` configuration file is generated automatically from a much shorter file called `sendmail.mc`. This file contains special macros that are processed by a program called m4. The m4 program reads the macros in the `sendmail.mc` file and expands them to create the actual `sendmail.cf` file.

Even so, the `sendmail.mc` file is a few hundred lines long. Configuring Sendmail isn't for the faint of heart.

You can find the `sendmail.mc` and `sendmail.cf` files in the `/etc/mail` directory. Before you edit these files, you should make backup copies of the current files. That way, if you mess up your mail configuration, you can quickly return to a working configuration by reinstating your backup copies.

After you've made backup copies, you can safely edit `sendmail.mc`. When you're finished, you can regenerate the `sendmail.cf` file by entering these commands:

```
cd /etc/mail
m4 sendmail.mc > sendmail.cf
service sendmail restart
```

The first command changes the current working directory to `/etc/mail`. Then, the second command compiles the `sendmail.mc` command into the `sendmail.cf` command. Finally, the third command restarts the Sendmail service so that the changes will take effect.

You need to be aware of two strange conventions used in the `sendmail.mc` file:

✦ Unlike most configuration files, comments don't begin with a hash mark (#). Instead, they begin with the letters dnl.

✦ Strings are quoted in an unusual way. Instead of regular quotation marks or apostrophes, strings must begin with a backquote (`` ` ``), which is located to the left of the numeral 1 on the keyboard and ends with an apostrophe ('), located to the right of the semicolon. So a properly quoted string looks like this:

```
MASQUERADE_AS(`mydomain.com')
```

Pretty strange, eh?

The following sections describe the common configuration changes that you may need to make to `sendmail.mc`.

Don't be an open relay!

An *open relay* is a mail server that is configured to allow anyone to use it as a relay for sending mail. In short, an open relay sends mail when neither the sender nor the recipient is a local user. Spammers love open relays because they can use them to obscure the true origin of their junk e-mail. As a result, open relays are a major contributor to the Internet spam problem.

Fortunately, the default configuration for the current version of Sendmail (8.14) is to not allow open relaying. As a result, you have to go out of your way to become an open relay with Sendmail. In fact, you'll have to look up the lines you'd need to add to `sendmail.mc` to enable open relaying. I'm certainly not going to list them here.

If you do need to allow relaying for specific hosts, create a file named `relay-domains` in `/etc/mail`. Then, add a line for each domain you want to allow relaying for. This line should contain nothing but the domain name. Then restart Sendmail.

Enabling connections

The default configuration allows connections only from localhost. If you want Sendmail to work as a server for other computers on your network, look for the following line in the `sendmail.mc` file:

```
DAEMON_OPTIONS(`Port-smtp,Addr=127.0.0.1, Name=MTA')dnl
```

Add `dnl  #` to the beginning of this line to make it a comment.

Enabling masquerading

Masquerading allows all the mail being sent from your domain to appear as if it came from the domain (for example, `wally@cleaver.net`) rather than from the individual hosts (like `wally@wally.cleaver.net`). To enable masquerading, add lines similar to these:

```
MASQUERADE_AS(`cleaver.net')dnl
FEATURE(masquerade_envelope)dnl
FEATURE(masquerade_entire_domain)dnl
MASQUERADE_DOMAIN(`cleaver.net')dnl
```

Setting up aliases

An *alias* — also known as a *virtual user* — is an incoming e-mail address that is automatically routed to local users. For example, you may want to create a generic account such as `sales@mydomain.com` and have all mail sent to that account delivered to a user named *willie*. To do that, you edit the file `/etc/mail/virtusers`. This file starts out empty. To create a virtual user, just list the incoming e-mail address followed by the actual recipient.

For example, here's a `virtusers` file that defines several aliases:

```
sales@mydomain.com       willie
bob@mydomain.com         robert
marketing@mydomain.com   robert
```

After you make your changes, you should restart the Sendmail service.

Using SpamAssassin

SpamAssassin is a spam-blocking tool that uses a variety of techniques to weed the spam out of your users' mailboxes. SpamAssassin uses a combination of rule filters that scan for suspicious message content and other telltale signs of spam, as well as blacklists from known spammers. The following sections explain how to install and use it.

Installing SpamAssassin

To configure SpamAssassin for basic spam filtering, follow these steps:

1. Ensure that Procmail is installed as your MDA.

In Fedora, Procmail is installed by default. To make sure it is enabled, open the file `/etc/mail/sendmail.mc` and make sure it includes the following line:

```
FEATURE(local_procmail,`',`procmail -t -Y -a $h -d
    $u')dnl
```

If this line is missing, add it, and then restart Sendmail.

2. Ensure that the `spamassassin` daemon is running.

You can do that by choosing Applications⇨System Settings⇨Server Settings⇨Services and looking for `spamassassin` in the services list. Or, at a console prompt, enter this command:

```
service spamassassin status
```

If SpamAssassin isn't running, enter this command:

```
chkconfig --level 35 spamassassin on
```

Whenever you make a configuration change, you should stop and restart the service with this command:

```
service spamassassin restart
```

3. Create a file named `procmailrc` in the `/etc` directory.

Use gedit or your favorite text editor. The file should contain these two lines:

```
:0fw
| /usr/bin/spamc
```

These lines cause Procmail to run all incoming mail through the SpamAssassin client program.

4. **Restart Sendmail and SpamAssassin.**

You can do this from Applications⇨System Settings⇨Server Settings⇨ Services, or you can enter these commands at a console prompt:

```
service sendmail restart
service spamassassin restart
```

SpamAssassin should now be checking for spam. To make sure it's working, send some e-mail to one of the mailboxes on your system, then open the mailbox file for that user in \var\mail and examine the message that was sent. If the message headers include several lines that begin with *X-Spam,* SpamAssassin is doing its job.

Customizing SpamAssassin

You can configure SpamAssassin by editing the configuration file /etc/mail/spamassassin/local.cf. This file contains SpamAssassin rules that are applied system wide, though you can override these rules for individual users by creating a user_prefs file in each user's $HOME/. spamassassin directory.

In Fedora, the default local.cf file contains the following lines:

```
required_hits 5
report_safe 0
rewrite_header Subject [SPAM]
```

These lines cause SpamAssassin to add the word [SPAM] to the start of the subject line for any message that scores 5 or higher on SpamAssassin's spam scoring algorithm.

Although you can configure SpamAssassin to automatically delete messages that score above a specified value, most anti-spam experts recommend against it. Instead, adding a word such as [SPAM] to the header lets each user decide how he or she wants to handle spam by using a message filter on his or her e-mail client that either deletes the marked messages or moves them to a Spam folder.

No matter how you configure SpamAssassin, you will inevitably get some false positives. For example, a long-lost friend who moved to Nigeria will e-mail you a joke about Viagra using a Hotmail account. Odds are that SpamAssassin will mark this message as spam. That's why arbitrarily deleting messages marked as spam isn't such a great idea, especially on a system-wide basis. Better to simply mark the messages and then let your users decide how to deal with the spam.

Blacklisting and whitelisting e-mail addresses

SpamAssassin lets you blacklist or whitelist a specific e-mail address or an entire domain. When you *blacklist* an address, any mail from the address will automatically be blocked, regardless of the message contents. Conversely, when you *whitelist* an address, all mail from the address will be allowed through, even if the message would otherwise be blocked as spam.

Whitelisting is a powerful tool for making sure that the people you correspond with on a regular basis don't get their e-mail accidentally blocked by SpamAssassin. As a result, it's a good idea to add your friends, relatives, and especially your customers to a whitelist.

Likewise, blacklisting lets you mark spammers who have managed to get their spam into your system in spite of SpamAssassin's best efforts to detect their true intent.

To whitelist an address, add a line such as the following to `/etc/mail/spamassassin/local.rc`:

```
whitelist_from wally@cleaver.com
```

This allows all mail from `wally@cleaver.com` to be delivered, even if the mail might otherwise look like spam.

To blacklist an address, add a line like this:

```
blacklist_from auntida@myrelatives.com
```

This will block all mail from your Aunt Ida.

Using the Mail Console Client

The most basic client for creating and reading e-mail is the `mail` command. Although it doesn't have many advanced features, it is fast. So some Linux users like to use it for sending simple messages. (It is also sometimes used in scripts.)

To read mail, open a command console, log on using the account whose mail you want to read, and enter the command `mail`. A list of all messages in your mailbox will be displayed. You can then use any of the commands listed in Table 7-1 to work with the messages in the mailbox or compose new mail messages.

Table 7-1	Mail Commands
Command	*Explanation*
?	Display a list of available commands.
q	Quit.
h	List the headers for all messages in the mailbox.
n	Type the next message.
t *list*	Type the specified messages. For example, t 3 types message 3 and t 4 5 types messages 4 and 5.
d *list*	Deletes one or more messages. For example, d 4 deletes message 4.
R *list*	Reply to message sender.
r *list*	Reply to message sender and all recipients.
m *user*	Compose a new message addressed to the specified user.

To compose a new message from a command prompt, follow these steps:

1. **Type** mail **followed by the e-mail address of the recipient.**

For example:

```
mail wally@cleaver.com
```

Mail responds by prompting you for the subject.

2. **Type the subject line and press Enter.**

Mail then waits for you to enter the text of the message.

3. **Type the message text. Use the Enter key to start new lines.**

You can enter as many lines as you wish for the message.

4. **Press Ctrl+D to finish the message.**

The following prompt will appear:

```
Cc:
```

5. **Enter one or more carbon copy addresses if you want others to receive a copy. Otherwise, press Enter.**

You're done! The message is on its way.

Using Evolution

Evolution is a graphical e-mail client that's similar in many ways to Microsoft Outlook, as Figure 7-1 shows. It includes not only e-mail features, but also a contact list, a calendar, a task manager, and other Outlook-like features.

To start Evolution, click the E-Mail icon that's located in the panel at the top of the GNOME screen. The first time you run Evolution, a configuration wizard will guide you through the necessary configuration. You need to supply basic information about your e-mail account, such as your e-mail address and the name of your mail server.

Figure 7-1:
Evolution
looks a lot
like Outlook.

Chapter 8: Running FTP

In This Chapter

✓ Installing and starting the **vsftpd** server

✓ Configuring **vsftpd**

*F*TP is one of the oldest and still most common methods for sending files over the Internet. This chapter shows you how to install and configure the basic FTP server that comes with most Linux distributions, Very Secure FTP Daemon (vsftpd). For complete information about this server, visit the official Web site at www.vsftpd.beasts.org.

If you need to access files from someone's FTP site or instructions on setting up an FTP server on a Windows machine, please refer to Book IV, Chapter 5.

Installing vsftpd

You can quickly find out whether vsftpd is installed on your system by entering the following command from a shell prompt:

```
rpm -q vsftpd
```

If vsftpd has been installed, the package version is displayed. If not, the message package vsftpd is not installed is displayed.

If vsftpd isn't installed, you can install it by following these steps:

1. **Insert the Fedora distribution disk in your CD/DVD drive.**

2. **When prompted to run the Autorun file, click Yes.**

The Package Manager window opens.

3. **Click the Forward button.**

The Package Manager ushers forth a list of all the package groups that it can install.

4. **Scroll down the list and select FTP Server.**

5. **Click the Forward button.**

   Be patient while the Package Manager decides which packages it needs to install based on your selection.

6. **When the Package Manager program displays the list of packages it proposes to install, click the Forward button.**

   The Package Manager program updates your system. Be patient some more.

7. **When the Package Manager program is done, click Finish.**

   The vsftpd package is now installed on your computer.

Starting the vsftpd Service

After you have installed the vsftpd package, you can start the FTP service by following these steps:

1. **Choose System⇨Administration⇨Server Settings⇨Services.**

   This brings up the Service Configuration tool.

2. **Select the vsftpd service.**

   You'll have to scroll through the list of services to find it.

3. **Click the Start button.**

4. **Wait for the service to start.**

   It should only take a few seconds to start up. A dialog box confirming that the service has started will appear.

Whenever you make a change to any of the vsftpd configuration files, you should use the Service Configuration tool to restart the vsftpd service.

You can also start the vsftpd service from a terminal window by typing this command:

```
/etc/init.d/vsftpd start
```

To restart the service, use this command:

```
/etc/init.d/vsftpd restart
```

Configuring FTP

You configure `vsftpd` though a configuration file named `vsftpd.conf`, located in `/etc`. The default `vsftpd.conf` file is shown in Listing 8-1. You can learn a lot about how `vsftpd` works simply by reading through this configuration file.

Listing 8-1: The vsftpd.conf File

```
# Example config file /etc/vsftpd.conf
#
# The default compiled in settings are fairly paranoid. This sample file
# loosens things up a bit, to make the ftp daemon more usable.
# Please see vsftpd.conf.5 for all compiled in defaults.
#
# READ THIS: This example file is NOT an exhaustive list of vsftpd options.
# Please read the vsftpd.conf.5 manual page to get a full idea of vsftpd's
# capabilities.
#
# Allow anonymous FTP? (Beware - allowed by default if you comment this out).
anonymous_enable=YES
#
# Uncomment this to allow local users to log in.
#local_enable=YES
#
# Uncomment this to enable any form of FTP write command.
#write_enable=YES
#
# Default umask for local users is 077. You may wish to change this to 022,
# if your users expect that (022 is used by most other ftpd's)
#local_umask=022
#
# Uncomment this to allow the anonymous FTP user to upload files. This only
# has an effect if the above global write enable is activated. Also, you will
# obviously need to create a directory writable by the FTP user.
#anon_upload_enable=YES
#
# Uncomment this if you want the anonymous FTP user to be able to create
# new directories.
#anon_mkdir_write_enable=YES
#
# Activate directory messages - messages given to remote users when they
# go into a certain directory.
dirmessage_enable=YES
#
# Activate logging of uploads/downloads.
xferlog_enable=YES
#
# Make sure PORT transfer connections originate from port 20 (ftp-data).
connect_from_port_20=YES
#
# If you want, you can arrange for uploaded anonymous files to be owned by
# a different user. Note! Using "root" for uploaded files is not
# recommended!
```

(continued)

Listing 8-1: *(continued)*

```
#chown_uploads=YES
#chown_username=whoever
#
# You may override where the log file goes if you like. The default is shown
# below.
#xferlog_file=/var/log/vsftpd.log
#
# If you want, you can have your log file in standard ftpd xferlog format
#xferlog_std_format=YES
#
# You may change the default value for timing out an idle session.
#idle_session_timeout=600
#
# You may change the default value for timing out a data connection.
#data_connection_timeout=120
#
# It is recommended that you define on your system a unique user which the
# ftp server can use as a totally isolated and unprivileged user.
#nopriv_user=ftpsecure
#
# Enable this and the server will recognise asynchronous ABOR requests. Not
# recommended for security (the code is non-trivial). Not enabling it,
# however, may confuse older FTP clients.
#async_abor_enable=YES
#
# By default the server will pretend to allow ASCII mode but in fact ignore
# the request. Turn on the below options to have the server actually do ASCII
# mangling on files when in ASCII mode.
# Beware that on some FTP servers, ASCII support allows a denial of service
# attack (DoS) via the command "SIZE /big/file" in ASCII mode. vsftpd
# predicted this attack and has always been safe, reporting the size of the
# raw file.
# ASCII mangling is a horrible feature of the protocol.
#ascii_upload_enable=YES
#ascii_download_enable=YES
#
# You may fully customise the login banner string:
#ftpd_banner=Welcome to blah FTP service.
#
# You may specify a file of disallowed anonymous e-mail addresses. Apparently
# useful for combatting certain DoS attacks.
#deny_email_enable=YES
# (default follows)
#banned_email_file=/etc/vsftpd.banned_emails
#
# You may specify an explicit list of local users to chroot() to their home
# directory. If chroot_local_user is YES, then this list becomes a list of
# users to NOT chroot().
#chroot_list_enable=YES
# (default follows)
#chroot_list_file=/etc/vsftpd.chroot_list
#
# You may activate the "-R" option to the builtin ls. This is disabled by
# default to avoid remote users being able to cause excessive I/O on large
# sites. However, some broken FTP clients such as "ncftp" and "mirror" assume
# the presence of the "-R" option, so there is a strong case for enabling it.
#ls_recurse_enable=YES
```

You can edit this file via the text editor. (Choose Applications⇨Accessories⇨ Text Editor.) After you save your changes, you'll need to restart the `vsftpd` service for the changes to take effect, as described in the previous section.

The following paragraphs describe some of the more common modifications to the `vsftpd.conf` file:

✦ **Anonymous access:** By default, anonymous access is allowed. To prevent users from accessing the FTP site anonymously, change the `anonymous_enable` line to:

```
anonymous_enable=NO
```

If you disable anonymous access, your users will have to have a Linux account on the server to access the FTP site. By default, each user will be directed to his or her home directory.

✦ **Allowing local users:** By default, local users are allowed to access the FTP site. To prevent local users from accessing the FTP site, change the `local_enable` line to:

```
local_enable=NO
```

Note that you may want to disable anonymous users or local users, but you shouldn't disable both!

✦ **Creating a read-only FTP site:** If you want to make your FTP site read-only, so that users can download files but not upload, change the `write_enable` line to:

```
write_enable=NO
```

✦ **Customizing the welcome banner:** You can customize the welcome banner by uncommenting the `ftpd_banner` line and adding your banner. For example:

```
Ftpd_banner=Welcome to my FTP site!
```

Chapter 9: Linux Commands

In This Chapter

✔ Discovering the basics of command shells

✔ Identifying file and directory commands

✔ Discovering commands that help with packages and services

✔ Figuring out commands for managing users and groups

✔ Becoming familiar with networking commands

*L*inux has several nice graphical user interfaces to choose from, and many of the more common Linux networking functions have graphical configuration utilities. Still, many Linux configuration tasks can only be done from a command shell. In many cases, the configuration utility provides access only to the most basic configuration parameters. So if you want to configure advanced features, you have to use commands. In fact, some network features don't have a graphical configuration utility, so you have no choice but to use commands.

Even when GNOME-based alternatives are available, you'll often resort to using commands because, frankly, that's what Linux was built to do. Unlike Windows, Linux relies on commands as its primary means of getting things done. So if you're going to work with Linux, knowing the basic commands presented in this chapter is a must.

Command Shell Basics

A *shell* is a program that accepts commands from a command prompt and executes them. The shell displays a prompt to let you know it's waiting for a command. When you type the command and press the Enter key, the system reads your command, interprets it, executes it, displays the results, and then displays the prompt again so that you can enter another command.

Getting to a shell

You can work with Linux commands directly from one of the six virtual consoles. If you like the responsiveness of text mode, virtual consoles are for you. To switch to a virtual console, press Ctrl+Alt+F*x*. For example, press Ctrl+Alt+F1 to switch to virtual console 1. After you're in a virtual console, you have to answer the logon prompt with a valid username and password. To return to GNOME, press Ctrl+Alt+F7.

The alternative is to work in a terminal window within the GNOME environment. If you have an older computer, you may find that the terminal window is a little unresponsive. If your computer is relatively new, however, the terminal window will be just as responsive as the text-mode virtual console. Plus, you'll have the benefit of a scroll bar that lets you scroll to see text that otherwise would have flown off the screen.

To open a terminal window, choose Applications⇨System Tools⇨Terminal. This opens a command shell in a window right on the GNOME desktop, as shown in Figure 9-1. Because this shell runs within the user account GNOME is logged on as, you don't have to log on. You can just start typing commands. When you're done, type **Exit** to close the window.

```
dlowe@localhost:~
File  Edit  View  Terminal  Tabs  Help
[dlowe@localhost ~]$
```

Figure 9-1:
A terminal
window.

For normal Linux users, the command shell prompt character is a dollar sign ($). If you see a hash mark (#) as the prompt character, it means you're logged on as `root`. Whenever you see a hash prompt, you should be extra careful about what you do because you can easily get yourself into trouble by deleting important files or otherwise corrupting the system.

Editing commands

Most of the time, you just type commands using the keyboard. If you make a mistake, you just type the command again, being careful not to repeat the mistake. However, Linux shells have several built-in editing features that can simplify the task of correcting a mistaken command or entering a sequence of similar commands:

✦ If you want to repeat a command that you've used recently, press the up-arrow key. This recalls your most recently executed commands. You can press Enter to execute a command as is, or you can edit the command before you execute it.

✦ The shell has a handy auto-complete feature that can finish partially spelled directory, file, or command names. Just type part of the name and then press the Tab key. If you've typed enough for the shell to figure out what you mean, the shell finishes the name for you. Otherwise, it just beeps, in which case you can type a few more letters and try again. In some cases, the shell displays a list of items that match what you've typed so far to help you know what to type next.

Wildcards

Wildcards are one of the most powerful features of command shells. With wildcards, you can process all the files that match a particular naming pattern with a single command. For example, suppose that you have a folder with 500 files in it, and you want to delete all the files that contain the letters Y2K and end with `.doc`, which happens to be 50 files. If you try to do this in GNOME, you'll spend ten minutes picking these files out from the list. From a shell, you can delete them all with the single command `rm *Y2K*.doc`.

You can use two basic wildcard characters. An asterisk (*) stands for any number of characters, including zero, while an exclamation mark (!) stands for just one character. Thus, `!Text.doc` matches files with names like `aText.doc`, `xText.doc`, and `4Text.doc`, but not `abcText.doc` or just `Text.doc`. However, `*Text.doc` would match any of the names I mentioned.

You can also use brackets to indicate a range of characters to choose from. For example, `report[123]` matches the files `report1`, `report2`, or `report3`. You can also specify `report[1-5]` to match `report1`, `report2`, `report3`, `report4`, or `report5`. The wildcard `r[aeiou]port` matches files named `raport`, `report`, `riport`, `roport`, or `ruport`. As you can see, the possibilities are almost endless.

Redirection and piping

Redirection and piping are related techniques. *Redirection* lets you specify an alternate destination for output that will be displayed by a command or an alternate source for input that should be fed into a command. For example, you can save the results of an `ifconfig` command to `/home/doug/myconfig` like this:

```
$ ifconfig > /home/doug/myconfig
```

Here, the greater-than sign (>) is used to redirect the command's console output.

If a command accepts input from the keyboard, you can use input redirection to specify a file that contains the input that you want to feed to the command. For example, you can create a text file named `lookup.commands` with subcommands for a command such as `nslookup`. Then, you can feed those scripted subcommands to the `nslookup` command, like this:

```
$ nslookup < /home/doug/lookup.commands
```

Piping is a similar technique. It takes the console output from one command and feeds it into the next command as input. One of the most common uses of piping is to send the output of a command that displays a lot of information to the more program, which displays the output one page at a time. For example:

```
$ ifconfig | more
```

The vertical bar (|) is often called the *pipe character* because it's the symbol used to indicate piping.

Environment variables

The shell makes several *environment variables* available to commands. You can use an environment variable anywhere in a command by typing **$** (dollar sign) followed by the environment variable name. For example, this command

```
$ echo This is $HOSTNAME running on an $HOSTTYPE
```

displays a line such as

```
This is LSERVER running on an i386
```

Table 9-1 lists some of the more useful environment variables that are available to you and your commands.

Table 9-1	Environment Variables
Variable	*Description*
HOME	The current user's home directory.
HOSTNAME	The computer's host name.
HOSTTYPE	The host computer type.
OSTYPE	The operating system.
PATH	The search order for executable programs.
PROMPT_COMMAND	The command used to generate the prompt.

Variable	Description
PWD	The present working directory.
SHELL	The shell being used.
USERNAME	The current username.

Shell scripts

A *shell script* is simply a text file that contains one or more commands. Shell scripts are similar to MS-DOS/Windows batch files, but shell scripts can be much more complex. The simplest shell scripts are just lists of commands, but advanced shell scripts can include complicated scripting statements that border on a full-featured programming language.

You can create shell scripts by using any text editor. The easiest text editor to use is *gedit,* which you can access from the GNOME desktop by choosing Main Menu⇨Accessories⇨Text Editor. If you want your friends to think you're a Linux guru, however, take a few moments to learn how to use *vi,* a powerful text mode editor. To create or edit a file in vi, type the command **vi** followed by a filename. Then, type away. To use a vi command, press the Escape key and then type one of the commands listed in Table 9-2.

Table 9-2	Common vi Commands
Command	*Explanation*
i	Enters insert mode so that you can enter text at the cursor location. Move the cursor to the point where you want to enter the text first. When you're finished inserting text, press Esc to return to command mode.
:w	Saves the file (*w* stands for *write*).
:q	Quit.
:wq	Write and then quit.
:q!	Quit without saving.
/string	Search forward for *string*.
?string	Search backward for *string*.
n	Repeat the last search.
u	Undo the previous command.

After you've created a shell script, you have to grant yourself execute permission to run the script. To do that, use a command similar to this:

```
$ chmod 755 myscript
```

To run a shell script, you use the sh command and provide the name of the script file, like this:

```
$ sh myscript
```

Directory and File Handling Commands

Because much of Linux administration involves working with configuration files, you frequently need to use the basic directory and file handling commands presented in this section.

The pwd command

This command displays the current directory, which is called the *present working directory* — hence the command name pwd. Here's the syntax:

```
pwd
```

Enter this command, and you get output similar to the following:

```
$ pwd
/home/doug
```

The cd command

The cd command changes the current working directory. The syntax is as follows:

```
cd directory
```

You may want to follow the cd command up with a pwd command to make sure that you changed to the right directory. For example:

```
$ cd /etc/mail
$ pwd
/etc/mail
```

To change to a subdirectory of the current directory, omit the leading slash from the directory name. For example:

```
$ pwd
/home
$ cd doug
$ pwd
/home/doug
```

You can also use the double-dot (..) to represent the parent of the current directory. Thus, to move up one level, use the command cd .. as follows:

```
$ pwd
/home/doug
$ cd ..
$ pwd
/home
```

The mkdir command

To create a new directory, you use the mkdir command. It has the following syntax:

```
mkdir directory
```

Here's an example that creates a subdirectory named images in the current directory:

```
$ mkdir images
```

This example creates a directory named /home/doug/images:

```
$ mkdir /home/doug/images
```

The rmdir command

The rmdir command removes a directory. It has the following syntax:

```
rmdir directory
```

Here's an example:

```
$ rmdir /home/doug/images
```

Here, the /home/doug/images directory is deleted. Note that the directory must be empty to be removed, so you have to first delete any files in the directory.

The ls command

The ls command lists the contents of the current directory. Here's the syntax:

```
ls [options] directory
```

The following paragraphs describe the more important options for the `ls` command:

✦ **-a:** Lists all the files in the directory, including files that start with a period.

✦ **-c:** Sorts entries by the time the files were last modified.

✦ **-d:** Lists only directory names.

✦ **-l:** Displays in long format.

✦ **-r:** Displays files in reverse order.

✦ **-R:** Lists the contents of all subdirectories, and subdirectories of subdirectories, and subdirectories of subdirectories of subdirectories . . . in other words, lists subdirectories recursively.

✦ **-s:** Displays file sizes.

✦ **-S:** Sorts files by size.

✦ **-t:** Sorts files by timestamp.

✦ **-u:** Sorts files by the time the files were last accessed.

✦ **-x:** Sorts files by their extensions.

Without arguments, the `ls` command lists all the files in the current directory, like this:

```
$ pwd
/etc/mail
$ ls
access          helpfile          Makefile       submit.cf        virtusertable
access.db       local-host-names  sendmail.cf    submit.cf.bak    virtusertable.db
domaintable     mailertable       sendmail.mc    submit.mc
domaintable.db  mailertable.db    statistics     trusted-users
```

You can limit the display to certain files by typing a filename, which can include wildcards. For example:

```
$ ls a*
access          access.db
```

You can also specify the directory that you want to display, like this:

```
$ ls /etc/httpd
conf  conf.d  logs  modules  run
```

To display detailed information about the files in the directory, use the `-l` switch, as in this example:

```
$ ls /etc/mail/s* -l
-rw-r--r--    1 root      root        57427 Jul 19 16:35 sendmail.cf
-rw-r--r--    1 root      root         5798 Feb 24 16:15 sendmail.mc
-rw-------    1 root      root          628 Jul 24 17:21 statistics
-rw-r--r--    1 root      root        39028 Jul 19 17:28 submit.cf
-r--r--r--    1 root      root        39077 Feb 24 16:15 submit.cf.bak
-rw-r--r--    1 root      root          953 Feb 24 16:15 submit.mc
```

The cp command

The cp command copies files. Here's the basic syntax:

```
cp [options] source-file destination-file
```

The following list describes the more important options for the ls command:

- ✦ **-a:** The same as -dpR.
- ✦ **-b:** Makes backup copies of existing files before they are overwritten. Sounds like a good plan to me.
- ✦ **-d:** Copies links rather than the files the links point to.
- ✦ **-f:** Removes files that will be overwritten.
- ✦ **-i:** Interactively prompts for each file to be overwritten.
- ✦ **-l:** Creates links to files rather than actually copying file contents.
- ✦ **-p:** Preserves ownership and permissions.
- ✦ **-R:** Copies the contents of subdirectories recursively.
- ✦ **-s:** Creates symbolic links to files rather than actually copying file contents.
- ✦ **-u:** Replaces destination files only if the source file is newer.

To make a copy of a file within the same directory, use cp like this:

```
$ cp sendmail.cf sendmail.cf.backup
```

If you want to copy a file to another directory without changing the filename, use cp like this:

```
$ cp sendmail.cf /home/doug
```

You can use wildcards to copy multiple files:

```
$ cp send* /home/doug
```

To include files in subdirectories of the source file, use the -R switch, like this:

```
$ cp -R /etc/*.cf /home/doug
```

In this example, all files in the /etc directory or any of its subdirectories that end with .cf are copied to /home/doug.

The rm command

The rm command deletes files. The syntax is as follows:

```
rm [options] file
```

The options are described in the following paragraphs:

- ✦ **-f:** Removes files that will be overwritten.
- ✦ **-i:** Interactively prompts for each file to be overwritten.
- ✦ **-R:** Copies the contents of subdirectories recursively.

To delete a single file, use it like this:

```
$ rm any.old.file
```

To delete multiple files, use a wildcard:

```
$ rm any.*
```

To delete an entire directory, use the -r switch:

```
$ rm -r /doug/old.files
```

The mv command

The mv command moves files or renames them. In Linux, moving and renaming a file is essentially the same thing. Moving a file changes the file's directory location but leaves its name the same. Renaming a file leaves the file in the same directory but changes the file's name.

The syntax of the mv command is

```
mvp [options] source-file destination
```

The following paragraphs describe the options:

✦ **-b:** Makes backup copies of existing files before they are overwritten. Sounds like a good plan to me.

✦ **-f:** Removes files that will be overwritten.

✦ **-i:** Interactively prompts for each file to be overwritten.

✦ **-u:** Replaces destination files only if the source file is newer.

To move a file to another directory, provide a filename for the first argument and a directory for the second, like this:

```
$ mv monthly.report /home/Debbie/
```

To rename a file, provide filenames for both arguments:

```
$ mv monthly.report august.monthly.report
```

The touch command

The `touch` command is one of the more interesting Linux file management commands. Here's the syntax:

```
touch [options] file
```

Here are some of the options that you can use:

✦ **-a:** Changes the access time only.

✦ **-c:** Doesn't create files that don't exist.

✦ **-m:** Changes the modification time only.

The basic form of the `touch` command looks like this:

```
$ touch monthly.report
```

If you use `touch` on an existing file, the `touch` command changes the modification date of the file. If you use it on a command that doesn't exist, the `touch` command creates a new, empty file.

The cat command

The `cat` command displays the contents of a file. It has the following syntax:

```
cat [options] [filename...]
```

Notice that the filename is optional. If you omit the filename, the cat command obtains its input from the console, which you can redirect if you want.

Also notice that you can specify more than one filename. If you do, the files are combined to create a single output stream.

Here are some of the options you can use:

✦ **-A:** Displays new line characters as $, tab characters as ^I, and control characters with a caret (^).

✦ **-b:** Numbers all nonblank lines as they are displayed.

✦ **-e:** Displays new line characters as $ and control characters with a caret (^).

✦ **-E:** Displays new line characters as $.

✦ **-n:** Numbers lines as they are displayed.

✦ **-s:** Squeezes multiple spaces down to a single space.

✦ **-t:** Displays tab characters as ^I and control characters with a caret (^).

✦ **-T:** Displays tab characters as ^I.

✦ **-v:** Shows nonprinting control characters with a caret (^).

Here's a basic example:

```
$ cat /etc/hosts
# Do not remove the following line, or various programs
# that require network functionality will fail.
127.0.0.1       LSERVER localhost.localdomain   localhost
$
```

If you don't provide any filename arguments, the cat command copies text from the keyboard and displays it on the console. You can use the cat command along with output redirection to quickly create a short text file, like this:

```
$ cat >mytext
This is line one.
This is line two.
This is line three.
<ctrl+D>
```

For the last line, press Ctrl+D. This signals the end of the input to the `cat` command.

Commands for Working with Packages and Services

As a Linux administrator, you frequently need to start and stop services and check the status of installed packages or install new packages. The following sections describe the Linux commands that help you to perform these tasks.

The service command

You use the `service` command to check the status of services and to start, stop, or restart services. You need to restart a service whenever you make a configuration change in order for your changes to take effect. Here's the basic syntax:

```
service [service] [ start | stop | restart ]
```

The following paragraphs describe some typical uses of the service command:

+ To check the status of the `httpd` service (Apache), use this command:

    ```
    $ service httpd status
    ```

+ To stop the `httpd` service:

    ```
    $ service httpd stop
    ```

+ To start the `httpd` service:

    ```
    $ service httpd start
    ```

+ To restart the `httpd` service:

    ```
    $ service httpd restart
    ```

The only trick to using the `service` command is that you have to know the name of the service. If you're not sure of the name, you can run the `service` command to display the status of all services, like this:

```
$ service --status-all
```

It will take a few moments to list all the services, but after the command is done, you can scroll through the list to find the service that you're looking for.

Table 9-3 lists some of the more common services.

Table 9-3	Common Linux Services
Service	*Description*
atd	Runs commands scheduled by the at command.
autof	Automatically mounts file systems.
crond	Runs programs at specified times.
dhcpd	The DHCP server.
finger	The Internet finger service.
httpd	The Apache Web server.
imap	The IMAP mail protocol.
imaps	Secure IMAP service (SSL).
ipop3	The POP3 mail protocol.
iptables	Automatic packet filtering for firewalls.
isdn	ISDN services.
named	The Bind DNS server.
netf	The network file system.
network	Activates and deactivates all network interfaces.
nfs	Native Unix/Linux network file sharing.
pop3s	Secure POP3 service (SSL).
sendmail	The Sendmail service.
smb	The Samba file and printer sharing service.
snmpd	Simple Network Management Protocol.
telnet	The Telnet server.

The rpm command

Rpm is the Red Hat Package Manager, a tool that simplifies the task of managing packages on your Linux system. Although rpm was originally developed for Red Hat Linux, it is now found on many Linux distributions, including Fedora (which is, of course, based on the Red Hat distribution).

Here's the basic syntax for querying the status of a package:

```
rpm -q [options] package
```

To install, upgrade, or remove a package, the basic syntax is more like this:

```
rpm [ -i | -u | -e ] [options] package-file
```

You can use quite a few options with the rpm command, but the most common are

✦ **-v:** Displays verbose output. You may as well know what rpm is doing while it chugs along.

✦ **-h:** Displays hash marks (#) periodically to reassure you that the program hasn't died.

You can use rpm to determine the status of installed packages on your system by using the -q switch. For example, to find out what version of Sendmail is installed, use this command:

```
$ rpm -q send*
Sendmail-8.12.8-4
```

Notice that you can use a wildcard with the package name. If you don't have a package whose name matches the package name you supply, you get the message package not installed.

To install a package, you use the -i switch and specify a wildcard filename that indicates the location of the package file. It's also a good idea to use the -v and -h switches. For example, to install Sendmail from a mounted CD-ROM drive, you use this command:

```
$ rpm -ivh /mnt/cdrom/RedHat/RPMS/sendmail*
```

If you want to update to a newer version of a package, you can use the -u switch instead of the -i switch:

```
$ rpm -uvh /mnt/cdrom/RedHat/RPMS/sendmail*
```

Finally, you can remove a package by using the -e switch:

```
$ rpm -e send*
```

Note that to use the rpm command, you should log on as root.

Commands for Administering Users

The following sections describe the Linux commands that you can use to create and manage user accounts from a command shell.

You should log on as root to perform these tasks.

The useradd command

The `useradd` command creates a user account. Here's the basic syntax for adding a new user:

```
useradd [options] user-name
```

You can also use this command to change the default options for new users. In that case, the syntax is more like this:

```
useradd -D [options]
```

The options are as follows:

- ✦ **-c** *comment:* Typically, the comment is the user's full name.
- ✦ **-d** *home-dir:* The home directory of the new user.
- ✦ **-e** *date:* The expiration date for the user.
- ✦ **-f** *time:* The number of days between logons before the user is considered expired.
- ✦ **-g** *group:* The initial logon group for the user.
- ✦ **-G** *groups:* Additional groups the user should belong to.
- ✦ **-m:** Creates the new user's home directory if it doesn't exist already.
- ✦ **-s** *shell-path:* Specifies the user's logon shell.

The following option is valid only with -D:

- ✦ **-b** *base-dir:* Provides the default base directory if a home directory is not specified.

Its most basic form, the `useradd` command creates a user with default option settings:

```
$ useradd theodore
```

This command creates a user named *theodore*.

Here's a command that specifies the user's full name in the comment option:

```
$ useradd -c 'Theodore Cleaver' theodore
```

The following command creates a temporary account named *ghost* that expires on Halloween 2008:

```
$ useradd -e 2008-10-31 ghost
```

If you want to see what the default values are for account options, use the -D option without any other parameters:

```
$ useradd -D
GROUP=100
HOME=/home
INACTIVE=-1
EXPIRE=
SHELL=/bin/bash
SKEL=/etc/skel
```

The usermod command

The usermod command modifies an existing user. It has the following syntax:

```
usermod [options] user-name
```

The options are as follows:

- ✦ **c** *comment:* Typically, the comment is the user's full name.
- ✦ **-d** *home-dir:* The home directory of the new user.
- ✦ **-e** *date:* The expiration date for a logon.
- ✦ **-f** *time:* The number of days between logons before the user is considered expired.
- ✦ **-g** *group:* The initial logon group for the user.
- ✦ **-G** *groups:* Additional groups the user should belong to.
- ✦ **-m:** Creates the new user's home directory if it doesn't exist already.
- ✦ **-s** *shell-path:* Specifies the user's logon shell.
- ✦ **-1:** Locks an account.
- ✦ **-u:** Unlocks an account.

Here's an example that changes a user's full name:

```
$ usermod -c 'The Beave' theodore
```

The userdel command

The userdel command deletes a user. It has a simple syntax:

```
userdel [-r] user-name
```

If you specify -r, the user's home directory is deleted along with the account.

The chage command

The chage command modifies date policies for a user's passwords. It has the following syntax:

```
chage [options] user-name
```

The following paragraphs describe the options you can use:

+ **-m** *days:* Specifies the minimum number of days allowed between password changes.

+ **-M** *days:* Specifies the maximum number of days allowed between password changes.

+ **-d** *date:* The date of the last password change.

+ **-E** *date:* The date on which the account will expire.

+ **-W** *days:* The number of days prior to the password expiring that the user will be warned the password is about to expire.

+ **-I** *days:* The number of days of inactivity after the password has expired that the account is locked out. Specify 0 to disable this feature.

Here's an example that sets an account to expire on Halloween 2006:

```
$ chage -E 2006-10-31 ghost
```

If you specify a username but no other options, you are prompted to enter each option. This is a lot easier than trying to remember all the switches!

The passwd command

This command changes the password for a user account. Its syntax is

```
passwd [user]
```

If you don't supply a user, the password for the current user is changed.

The passwd prompts you to enter the new password twice in order to prevent the possibility of mistyping the password.

The newusers command

The newusers command provides an easy way to create a group of new user accounts. It reads a text file that contains one line for each new user, listing the user's name and password.

Here's the syntax of the `newusers` command:

```
newusers [filename]
```

If you omit the filename, `newusers` accepts input from the console.

Suppose that you have a file named `/root/island.users` that contains these lines:

```
gilligan    ml9jiedr
skipper     1hiecr8u
professor   dr0uxiaf
maryann     choe7rlu
ginger      jiuqled5
mrhowell    j1emoaf1
lovie       zo2priak
```

You can then create these seven stranded user accounts by issuing this command:

```
$ newusers /root/island.users
```

Because the `newusers` file contains unencrypted passwords, you shouldn't leave it lying around. Require these new users to change their passwords immediately and delete the file you used to create the users.

The groupadd command

The `groupadd` command creates a new group. It has the following syntax:

```
groupadd [options] group
```

Although you have several possible options to use, the only one you're likely to need is `-r`, which creates a system group that has special privileges.

Here's an example that creates a group named *castaways:*

```
$ groupadd castaways
```

That's all you have to do to create a new group. To administer the group, you use the `gpasswd` command.

The groupdel command

The `groupdel` command deletes a group. It has the following syntax:

```
groupdel group
```

Here's an example that deletes a group named *castaways:*

```
$ groupdel castaways
```

Poof! The group is gone.

The gpasswd command

You use the gpasswd command to administer a group. This command has several different syntax options.

To change the group password:

```
gpasswd [ -r | -R ]  group
```

To add a user:

```
gpasswd -a user group
```

To remove a user:

```
gpasswd -d user group
```

To create group administrators and/or members:

```
gpasswd [-A administrators...]  [-M members... ]  group
```

The options are as follows:

- ✦ **-r:** Removes the password from the group.
- ✦ **-R:** Disables access to the group via the newgrp command.
- ✦ **-a:** Adds the specified user to the group.
- ✦ **-d:** Deletes the specified user from the group.
- ✦ **-A:** Specifies one or more group administrators. Use commas with no intervening spaces to separate the administrators from each other. Each administrator must be an existing user.
- ✦ **-M:** Specifies one or more group members. Use commas with no intervening spaces to separate the members from each other. Each member must be an existing user.

The following example adds seven group members and one administrator to a group called *castaways.*

```
$ gpasswd -A skipper -M skipper,gilligan,professor,maryann,
ginger,mrhowell,lovie castaways
```

If the rest of the group finally decided to throw Gilligan off the island, they can remove him from the group with this command:

```
$ gpasswd -d gilligan castaways
```

Commands for Managing Ownership and Permissions

This section presents the details of the chown and chmod commands, which are the essential tools for assigning file system rights in the Linux environment.

You can view the ownership and permissions for a file using the ls command with the -l option.

The chown command

The chown command changes the owner of a file. Normally, the user who creates a file is the owner of the file. However, the owner can transfer the file to someone else via this command. The basic syntax of this command is

```
chown user file
```

For example, to change the owner of a file named rescue.plans to user professor, use this command:

```
$ chown professor rescue.plans
```

To change ownership of all the files in the directory named /home/island to professor, use this command:

```
$ chown professor /home/island
```

Issuing the following command would be a really bad idea:

```
$ chown gilligan rescue.plans
```

The chgrp command

Every file not only has an individual owner but also a group owner. You can change the group ownership using the chgrp command, which has the following basic syntax:

```
chgrp group file
```

For example, to grant the castaways group ownership of the file `rescue.plans`, use this command:

```
$ chgrp castaways rescue.plans
```

To change group ownership of all the files in the directory named `/home/island` to `castaways`, use this command:

```
$ chgrp castaways /home/island
```

The chmod command

The `chmod` command lets you change the permissions for a Linux file. Before explaining the syntax of the `chmod` command, you need to look at the cryptic way Linux reports file permissions. Linux grants three different types of permissions — *read, write, and execute* — for three different scopes: *owner, group, and everyone.* That's a total of nine permissions.

When you use the `ls` command with the `-l` option, the permissions are shown as a ten-character string that begins with a hyphen if the entry is for a file or a *d* if the entry is for a directory. Then, the next nine letters are the nine permissions, in this order:

+ Read, write, execute for the owner

+ Read, write, execute for the group

+ Read, write, execute for everyone

The letters *r, w,* or *x* appear if the permission has been granted. If the permission is denied, a hyphen appears.

For example, suppose the `ls -l` command lists these permissions:

```
-rw-r--r--
```

You interpret this permission string like this:

+ The first hyphen indicates that this is a file, not a directory.

+ The next three positions are `rw-`. Therefore, the owner has read and write permission on this file, but not execute permission.

+ The next three positions are `r--`. That means the group owner has read permissions but not write or execute permission.

✦ The last three positions are also `r--`. That means that everyone else has read permission but not write or execute permission.

The full syntax of the `chmod` command is pretty complex. However, you can do most of what you need to do with this form:

```
chmod specification file
```

Here, *specification* is in the form `u=rwx`, `g=rwx`, or `o=rwx` to set the permissions for the user (owner), group, and others (everyone). You don't have to specify *r, w,* and *x;* you just list the permissions that you want to grant. For example, to grant read and write permission for the user to a file named *rescue.plans,* use this command:

```
$ chmod u=rw rescue.plans
```

You can also combine specifications, like this:

```
$ chmod u=rw,g=rw,o=r rescue.plans
```

To revoke all rights for the user, group, or others, don't type anything after the equal sign. For example, this command revokes all rights for others:

```
$ chmod o= rescue.plans
```

Networking Commands

The following sections present Linux commands that are used to display information about the network or configure its settings.

You can find more detail about some of these commands in Book IV, Chapter 6.

The hostname command

The `hostname` command simply displays the computer's host name. It has the following syntax:

```
hostname [name]
```

If you use this command without any parameters, the computer's host name is displayed. If you specify a name, the computer's host name is changed to the name you specify.

The ifconfig command

`ifconfig` displays and sets configuration options for network interfaces. Although you can configure an Ethernet adapter using this command, you'll rarely have to. Linux does a pretty good job of automatically configuring network adapters, and the GNOME-based Network Configuration tool supplied with the Red Hat distribution should be able to handle most network configuration chores. So you'll use `ifconfig` mostly to display network configuration settings.

The basic syntax for `ifconfig` is

```
ifconfig interface [address] [netmask mask]
        [broadcast broadcast]
```

The following paragraphs describe the options that you can use on the `ifconfig` command:

✦ ***Interface:*** The symbolic name for your network adapter. It's typically `eth0` for the first Ethernet adapter or `eth1` for the second adapter.

✦ ***Address:*** The IP address you want to assign to the interface, such as 192.168.1.100.

✦ **netmask:** The subnet mask to use, such as 255.255.255.0.

✦ **broadcast:** The broadcast, which should be the highest address on the subnet. For example: 192.168.1.255.

If you enter `ifconfig` without any parameters, the `ifconfig` command displays the current status of your network adapters, like this:

```
eth0      Link encap:Ethernet  HWaddr 00:20:78:16:E0:6A
          UP BROADCAST RUNNING MULTICAST  MTU:1500  Metric:1
          RX packets:0 errors:0 dropped:0 overruns:0 frame:0
          TX packets:11 errors:0 dropped:0 overruns:0 carrier:0
          collisions:0 txqueuelen:100
          RX bytes:0 (0.0 b)  TX bytes:2916 (2.8 Kb)
          Interrupt:11 Base address:0xd000
eth1      Link encap:Ethernet  HWaddr 00:40:05:80:51:F3
          inet addr:192.168.3.100  Bcast:192.168.3.255  Mask:255.255.255.0
          UP BROADCAST RUNNING MULTICAST  MTU:1500  Metric:1
          RX packets:2358 errors:0 dropped:0 overruns:0 frame:0
          TX packets:1921 errors:0 dropped:0 overruns:0 carrier:0
          collisions:0 txqueuelen:100
          RX bytes:265194 (258.9 Kb)  TX bytes:424467 (414.5 Kb)
          Interrupt:3 Base address:0xc000
lo        Link encap:Local Loopback
          inet addr:127.0.0.1  Mask:255.0.0.0
          UP LOOPBACK RUNNING  MTU:16436  Metric:1
          RX packets:93707 errors:0 dropped:0 overruns:0 frame:0
          TX packets:93707 errors:0 dropped:0 overruns:0 carrier:0
          collisions:0 txqueuelen:0
          RX bytes:6393713 (6.0 Mb)  TX bytes:6393713 (6.0 Mb)
```

To change the IP address of an adapter, use `ifconfig` like this:

```
$ ifconfig eth0 192.168.1.200
```

The netstat command

The `netstat` command lets you monitor just about every aspect of a Linux server's network functions. This command can generate page after page of interesting information — if you know what it all means.

The two most common reasons to use `netstat` are to display the routing table and to display open TCP/IP connections. The syntax for displaying the routing table is

```
netstat -r
```

This results in a display similar to this:

```
Kernel IP routing table
Destination     Gateway         Genmask         Flags   MSS Window  irtt Iface
192.168.1.0     *               255.255.255.0   U         0 0        0 eth1
192.168.1.0     *               255.255.255.0   U         0 0        0 eth0
127.0.0.0       *               255.0.0.0       U         0 0        0 lo
```

To display TCP/IP connections, use this syntax:

```
netstat -l
```

This results in a display similar to the following:

```
Active Internet connections (only servers)
Proto Recv-Q Send-Q Local Address           Foreign Address         State
tcp        0      0 *:1024                  *:*                     LISTEN
tcp        0      0 LSERVER:1025            *:*                     LISTEN
tcp        0      0 *:netbios-ssn           *:*                     LISTEN
tcp        0      0 *:sunrpc                *:*                     LISTEN
tcp        0      0 *:http                  *:*                     LISTEN
tcp        0      0 *:x11                   *:*                     LISTEN
tcp        0      0 *:ssh                   *:*                     LISTEN
tcp        0      0 LSERVER:ipp             *:*                     LISTEN
tcp        0      0 LSERVER:smtp            *:*                     LISTEN
tcp        0      0 *:https                 *:*                     LISTEN
udp        0      0 *:1024                  *:*
udp        0      0 LSERVER:1026            *:*
udp        0      0 192.168.1.20:netbios-ns *:*
udp        0      0 192.168.1.20:netbios-ns *:*
udp        0      0 *:netbios-ns            *:*
udp        0      0 192.168.1.2:netbios-dgm *:*
udp        0      0 192.168.1.2:netbios-dgm *:*
udp        0      0 *:netbios-dgm           *:*
udp        0      0 *:940                   *:*
udp        0      0 *:sunrpc                *:*
udp        0      0 *:631                   *:*
```

```
Active UNIX domain sockets (only servers)
Proto RefCnt Flags      Type      State       I-Node Path
unix  2      [ ACC ]    STREAM    LISTENING   2663   /dev/gpmctl
unix  2      [ ACC ]    STREAM    LISTENING   2770   /tmp/.font-unix/fs7100
unix  2      [ ACC ]    STREAM    LISTENING   3144   /tmp/.ICE-unix/1953
.
.
.
```

From this display, you can tell which Linux services are actively listening on TCP/IP ports.

The ping command

The `ping` command is the basic troubleshooting tool for TCP/IP. You use it to determine whether basic TCP/IP connectivity has been established between two computers. If you're having any kind of network trouble between two computers, the first troubleshooting step is almost always to see whether the computers can ping each other.

The basic syntax of `ping` is straightforward:

```
ping [options] address
```

The options can be

➤ **-c:** The number of packets to send. If you omit this, `ping` continues to send packets until you interrupt it.

➤ **-d:** Floods the network with packets, as many as 100 per second. Use with care!

➤ **-i:** Specifies how many seconds to wait between sending packets. The default is one second. If you're having intermittent connection problems, you may try letting `ping` run for a while with this option set to a higher value, such as 60, to send a packet every minute.

➤ **-R:** Displays the route the packets take to get to the destination computer.

Ping will continue to ping the destination computer until you interrupt it by pressing Ctrl+Z.

You can specify the host to ping using an IP address, as in this example:

```
$ ping 192.168.1.100
PING 192.168.1.100 (192.168.1.100) 56(84) bytes of data.
64 bytes from 192.168.1.100: icmp_seq=1 ttl=128 time=0.382 ms
64 bytes from 192.168.1.100: icmp_seq=2 ttl=128 time=0.345 ms
64 bytes from 192.168.1.100: icmp_seq=3 ttl=128 time=0.320 ms
64 bytes from 192.168.1.100: icmp_seq=4 ttl=128 time=0.328 ms
```

You can also ping using a DNS name, as in this example:

```
$ ping www.lowewriter.com
PING www.lowewriter.com (209.68.34.15) 56(84) bytes of data.
64 bytes from www.lowewriter.com (209.68.34.15): icmp_seq=1 ttl=47 time=88.9 ms
64 bytes from www.lowewriter.com (209.68.34.15): icmp_seq=2 ttl=47 time=87.9 ms
64 bytes from www.lowewriter.com (209.68.34.15): icmp_seq=3 ttl=47 time=88.3 ms
64 bytes from www.lowewriter.com (209.68.34.15): icmp_seq=4 ttl=47 time=87.2 ms
```

The route command

The `route` command displays or modifies the computer's routing table. To display the routing table, use `route` without any parameters. To add an entry to the routing table, use this syntax:

```
route add [ -net | -host ] address [options]
```

To delete an entry, use this syntax:

```
route del [ -net | -host ] address [options]
```

The available options are as follows:

+ **netmask *mask*:** Specifies the subnet mask for this entry.

+ **gw *address*:** Specifies the Gateway Address for this entry.

+ **dev *if*:** Specifies an interface (such as `eth0` or `eth1`) for this entry.

If you enter `route` by itself, with no parameters, you'll see the routing table, as in this example:

```
$ route
Kernel IP routing table
Destination     Gateway         Genmask         Flags Metric Ref    Use Iface
192.168.1.0     *               255.255.255.0   U     0      0        0 eth1
192.168.1.0     *               255.255.255.0   U     0      0        0 eth1
169.254.0.0     *               255.255.0.0     U     0      0        0 eth1
127.0.0.0       *               255.0.0.0       U     0      0        0 lo
default         192.168.1.1     0.0.0.0         UG    0      0        0 eth1
```

Suppose that your network has a second router that serves as a link to another private subnet, 192.168.2.0 (subnet mask 255.255.255.0). The interface on the local side of this router is at 192.168.1.200. To add a static route entry that sends packets intended for the 192.168.2.0 subnet to this router, use a command like this:

```
$ route add 192.168.2.0 netmask 255.255.255.0 gw
    192.168.1.200
```

The traceroute command

The `traceroute` command displays a list of all the routers that a packet must go through in order to get from the local computer to a destination on the Internet. Each one of these routers is called a *hop*. If you're unable to connect to another computer, you can use `Tracert` to find out exactly where the problem is occurring.

Here's the syntax:

```
traceroute [-i interface] host
```

Although several options are available for the `traceroute` command, the one you're most likely to use is `-i`, which lets you specify an interface. This is useful if your computer has more than one network adapter.

Book X
Appendixes

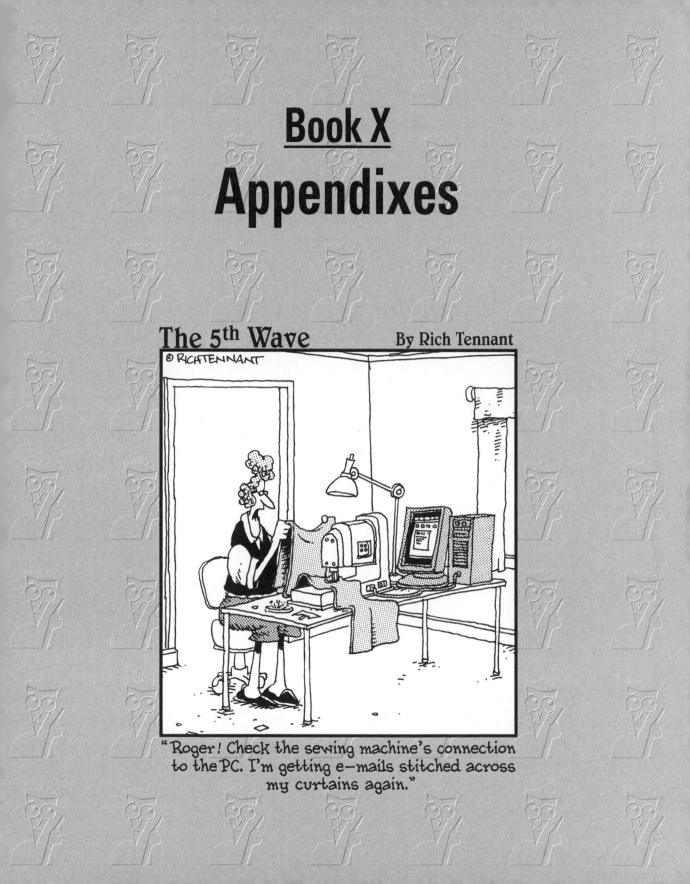

The 5th Wave   By Rich Tennant

"Roger! Check the sewing machine's connection
to the PC. I'm getting e-mails stitched across
my curtains again."

Contents at a Glance

Appendix A: Directory of Useful Web Sites

Throughout this book, I mention many Web sites that you can visit to glean more information about various networking topics. This appendix gathers those sites into one convenient location and adds a bunch more that are also worth visiting from time to time. Happy surfing!

Certification

Here are the sites to check out for official certification information:

✦ www.microsoft.com/learning/mcp: Microsoft's certification headquarters

✦ www.comptia.org: Independent certification including A+, Network+, and Security+

✦ www.novell.com/training/certinfo: The home page for Novell certification

✦ www.ibm.com/certify: IBM's certification home page

✦ www.cisco.com/certification: Cisco's certification home page

✦ www.redhat.com/training/certification: Red Hat's Linux certification home page

Hardware

The following Web sites are general resources for researching computer hardware:

✦ http://reviews.cnet.com: CNET's reviews section offers reviews on all types of computer hardware, with a special section devoted to networking.

✦ www.hardwarecentral.com: HardwareCentral is another good source for general computer hardware information, reviews, and advice.

✦ www.tomshardware.com: Tom's Hardware Guide is the place to go if you want detailed information about the latest in computer components.

The following manufacturers offer high-end networking products, including servers, routers, switches, and so on:

✦ `www.networking.ibm.com`: IBM's networking portal is a must-see site.

✦ `http://welcome.hp.com/country/us/en/prodserv/servers.html`: This site is the home page for Hewlett-Packard's server products.

✦ `www.dell.com`: This is the home page for Dell computers, which includes links that take you to the pages that describe Dell's server products.

✦ `www.sun.com/servers`: This page is the home page for Sun servers.

Home and Small Business Networking

The following Web sites have general information about home and small business networking:

✦ `www.homenethelp.com`: This excellent Web site is devoted to helping people get their home networks up and running, loaded with step-by-step procedures and flowcharts.

✦ `www.practicallynetworked.com`: This site is a great source of information for home networking, with general networking information, technology backgrounders, product reviews, troubleshooting advice, and more.

✦ `www.hometoys.com`: This site provides information on all sorts of gadgets for the home, including networks.

✦ `www.ehpub.com`: This is the home page of EH Publishing, which publishes several magazines for home technology.

✦ `www.homepna.org`: This is the home page of the Home Phone Networking Alliance.

✦ `www.homeplug.org`: This is the home page of the HomePlug PowerLine Alliance, which promotes PowerLine networking.

✦ `www.linksys.com`: This is the home page for Linksys, one of the most popular manufacturers of networking devices for homes and small offices, including 10/100BaseT, wireless, and even phone and PowerLine devices.

✦ `www.netgear.com`: This is home page for NETGEAR, which makes home and small office networking devices, including 10/100BaseT adapters and switches, wireless devices, and phone-line systems.

Linux

The following Web sites have general information about Linux:

✦ www.linux.org: One of the best overall Web sites for everything Linux. It's a central source of Linux information and news and many links to Linux distributions and downloadable applications.

✦ www.justlinux.com: This site includes a popular discussion forum where you can ask questions and, with luck, get answers.

Here are the home pages for some of the most popular distributions:

✦ www.redhat.com: The Web site of the most popular Linux distribution

✦ www.redhat.com/fedora: The home page for the Fedora project

✦ www.suse.com: The SUSE distribution

✦ www.caldera.com: The Caldera distribution from SCO

✦ www.mandrivalinux.com: The Mandriva Linux distribution (formerly called *Mandrake Linux)*

✦ www.slackware.com: Slackware, one of the oldest Linux distributions

Here are the home pages for some popular Linux networking software:

✦ www.isc.org/products/BIND: The official page for BIND, the most popular DNS nameserver on the Internet

✦ www.sendmail.org: Official site for Sendmail, the SMTP mail exchange server

✦ www.apache.org: Official site for the Apache HTTP server

✦ www.samba.org: Official site for the Samba file and print server

Magazines

Here are some links to various magazines on networking topics:

✦ www.informationweek.com: *InformationWeek*

✦ www.infoworld.com: *InfoWorld*

✦ www.networkcomputing.com: *Network Computing*

✦ www.networkmagazine.com: *Network Magazine*

- ✦ www.winitpro.com: *Windows IT Pro Magazine*
- ✦ www.2600.com: *2600 Magazine*
- ✦ www.linuxjournal.com: *Linux Journal*
- ✦ www.linux-magazine.com: *Linux Magazine*

Microsoft

Microsoft's Web site is vast. Here are some links to a few useful areas within this huge Web site:

- ✦ www.microsoft.com/windows: The home page for the Windows family of products
- ✦ www.microsoft.com/windowsserver2003: The home page for Windows Server 2003
- ✦ www.microsoft.com/windowsserver2008: The home page for Windows Server 2008
- ✦ www.microsoft.com/windowsxp: The home page for Windows XP
- ✦ www.microsoft.com/windowsvista: The home page for Windows Vista
- ✦ www.microsoft.com/windowsserversystem: The home page for Microsoft server products
- ✦ http://technet.microsoft.com: TechNet, a great source for technical information on Microsoft technologies
- ✦ http://support.microsoft.com: Microsoft's general support site

Network Standards Organizations

The following Web sites are useful when you're researching network standards:

- ✦ www.ansi.org: The American National Standards Institute (ANSI), the official standards organization in the United States.
- ✦ www.ieee.org: The Institute of Electrical and Electronic Engineers (IEEE), an international organization that publishes several key networking standards, including the official Ethernet standards (known as *IEEE 802.3*).
- ✦ www.iso.org: The International Organization for Standardization (ISO), a federation of more than 100 standards organizations from throughout the world.

+ www.isoc.org: The Internet Society, an international organization for global coordination and cooperation on the Internet.

+ www.ietf.org: The Internet Engineering Task Force (IETF), responsible for the protocols that drive the Internet.

+ www.iana.org: The Internet Assigned Numbers Authority, which has responsibility for the IP address space.

+ www.w3c.org: The World Wide Web Consortium (W3C), an international organization that handles the development of standards for the World Wide Web.

+ www.rfc-editor.org: This is the official repository of RFCs. It includes a search facility that lets you look up RFCs by name or keyword.

Reference

A number of general-purpose and computer-specific reference sites provide encyclopedia-style articles or simple definitions of computer and networking terms. If you aren't sure what some new technology is, start at one of these sites:

+ www.webopedia.com: The Webopedia is a great online dictionary of computer and Internet terms. Not sure what *direct sequence spread spectrum* means? Look it up at the Webopedia!

+ www.wikipedia.org: Wikipedia is a huge user-written online encyclopedia.

+ www.whatis.com: Whatis.com is another great dictionary of computer and networking terms.

+ www.howstuffworks.com: This site has general information about many different types of technology: computers, automobiles, electronics, science, and more. The computer section provides good low-level introductions to various computer topics, including computer hardware, the Internet, and security.

Search

Search engines are often the first place you turn to when you're trying to solve a network problem and you need information fast:

+ www.google.com: Google is the most popular search site on the Internet today, with a huge database of Web sites and newsgroup articles that's constantly updated. Google has a powerful keyword search features that lets you refine your search as you go.

✦ www.yahoo.com: Yahoo!, one of the original Web site catalogs, is still the best place to go if you want to browse categories rather than search for keywords.

✦ www.msnsearch.com: The search page of Microsoft's MSN.com portal.

✦ www.webfetch.com: Webfetch is a meta-search tool that searches multiple search engines at the same time.

TCP/IP and the Internet

The following sites have interesting information about the Internet:

✦ www.internic.net: The InterNIC Web site is a central point of information for domain registration. Check here for a list of accredited domain registrars.

✦ www.networksolutions.com: The home of Network Solutions, the most popular site for registering domain names.

✦ www.register.com: Register.com is another domain registration site.

✦ www.isc.org: Members of the Internet Systems Consortium are the folks who do the twice-a-year domain survey to try to estimate how big the Internet really is.

✦ www.broadbandreports.com: This site asks for your zip code to help you determine what broadband network options are available in your area. It also includes loads of other information about broadband connections.

For DNS information, try www.dnsreport.com, which lets you perform a variety of DNS lookups to make sure that your DNS zones are set up correctly.

Check these sites to find information about Web browsers:

✦ www.microsoft.com/ie: The official home page for Internet Explorer.

✦ www.netscape.com: Netscape, the makers of Navigator.

✦ www.mozilla.org: The home of Firefox, a popular alternative Web browser. Many users consider Firefox to be the best Web browser around.

✦ www.opera.com: The home of Opera, another alternative to Internet Explorer.

Wireless Networking

Here are some Web sites with general information about wireless networking:

✦ `www.wi-fiplanet.com`: Wi-Fi Planet is a large site devoted to news, information, and product reviews for wireless networking

✦ `http://wifinetnews.com`: Wi-Fi Networking News is a source for daily news on wireless networking

Here are the Web sites for the most popular manufacturers of wireless networking products:

✦ `www.linksys.com`: Linksys is a manufacturer of wireless network cards and access points.

✦ `www.netgear.com`: NETGEAR is another manufacturer of wireless components.

✦ `www.dlink.com`: D-Link is yet another manufacturer of inexpensive wireless products.

✦ `www.smc.com`: The home page for SMC, another manufacturer of wireless network products.

✦ `www.cisco.com`: Cisco is the place to go for high-end wireless networking.

✦ `www.3com.com`: 3Com is another good place to go for wireless networking components.

The following Web sites have interesting information about wireless network security:

✦ `www.netstumbler.com`: The makers of NetStumbler, software that detects wireless network access and security problems.

✦ `www.airwave.com`: The makers of AirWave, a software-based tool that snoops for unauthorized access points.

✦ `www.wardriving.com`: An extensive site devoted to the practice of wardriving.

Appendix B: Glossary

10Base2: A type of coax cable that was once the most often used cable for Ethernet networks. Also known as *thinnet* or *cheapernet*. The maximum length of a single segment is 185 meters (600 feet).

10Base5: The original Ethernet coax cable, now pretty much obsolete. Also known as *yellow cable* or *thick cable*. The maximum length of a single segment is 500 meters (1,640 feet).

10BaseT: Twisted-pair cable, commonly used for Ethernet networks. Also known as *UTP, twisted pair,* or *twisted sister* (just kidding!). The maximum length of a single segment is 100 meters (330 feet). Of the three Ethernet cable types, this one is the easiest to work with.

100BaseFX: The Ethernet standard for high-speed fiber-optic connections.

100BaseT4: An alternative standard for 100 Mbps Ethernet using four-pair Category-3 cable.

100BaseTX: The leading standard for 100 Mbps Ethernet, which uses two-pair, Category-5 twisted-pair cable.

100VG AnyLAN: A standard for 100 Mbps Ethernet that isn't as popular as 100BaseT. Like 100BaseT, 100VG AnyLAN uses twisted-pair cable.

1000BaseT: A new standard for 1,000 Mbps Ethernet using four-pair, Category-5, unshielded twisted-pair cable. 1000BaseT is also known as *Gigabit Ethernet*.

1000000000BaseT: Well, not really. But if current trends continue, we'll get there soon.

802.2: The forgotten IEEE standard. The more glamorous 802.3 standard relies upon 802.2 for moral support.

802.3: The IEEE standard known in the vernacular as *Ethernet*.

802.11: The IEEE standard for wireless networking. Three popular variants are 802.11a, 802.11b, and 802.11g.

8088 processor: The microprocessor chip around which IBM designed its original PC, marking the transition from the Bronze Age to the Iron Age.

80286 processor: *Computo-habilis,* an ancient ancestor of today's modern computers.

80386 processor: The first 32-bit microprocessor chip used in personal computers, long since replaced by newer, better designs.

80486 processor: The last of Intel's CPU chips to have a number instead of a name. Replaced years ago by the Pentium processor.

AAUI: Apple Attachment Unit Interface, a type of connector used in some Apple Ethernet networks.

access rights: A list of rights that tells you what you can and can't do with network files or directories.

account: You can't get into the network without one of these. The network knows who you are and what rights you have on the network by virtue of your account.

acronym: An abbreviation made up of the first letters of a series of words.

Active Directory: The directory service in Windows networks.

Active Server Pages: An Internet feature from Microsoft that enables you to create Web pages with scripts that run on the server rather than on the client. Also known as *ASP.* The newest version is called *ASP.NET.*

ActiveSync: A windows component used to synchronize data between computers.

adapter card: An electronic card that you can plug in to one of your computer's adapter slots to give it some new and fabulous capability, such as displaying 16 million colors, talking to other computers over the phone, or accessing a network.

address book: In an e-mail system, a list of users with whom you regularly correspond.

administrator: The big network cheese who is responsible for setting things up and keeping them running. Pray that it's not you. Also known as the *network manager.*

AFP: Apple Filing Protocol, a protocol for filing used by Apple. (That helps a lot, doesn't it?)

AGP: Advanced Graphics Port, a high-speed graphics interface used on most new computer motherboards.

allocation unit: Windows allocates space to files one allocation unit at a time; the allocation unit is typically 2,048 or 4,096 bytes, depending on the size of the disk. Also known as *cluster*. Windows Server uses allocation schemes that are more efficient than standard Windows.

antivirus program: A program that sniffs out viruses on your network and sends them into exile.

Apache: The most popular Web server on the Internet. It comes free with most versions of Linux.

AppleTalk: Apple's networking system for Macintoshes.

application layer: The highest layer of the OSI reference model, which governs how software communicates with the network.

archive bit: A flag that's kept for each file to indicate whether the file has been modified since it was last backed up.

ARCnet: An ancient network topology developed originally by Datapoint, now found only in history books.

Athlon: A competitor to Intel's Pentium CPU chip manufactured by AMD.

attributes: Characteristics that are assigned to files. DOS alone provides four attributes: system, hidden, read-only, and archive. Network operating systems generally expand the list of file attributes.

AUI: Attachment Unit Interface, the big connector found on older network cards and hubs that's used to attach yellow cable via a transceiver.

auto attendant: A feature of PBX systems that eliminates or reduces the need for human operators.

AUTOEXEC.BAT: A batch file that DOS executes automatically every time you start your computer.

backbone: A trunk cable used to tie sections of a network together.

BackOffice: A suite of Microsoft programs designed to run on a Windows server.

backup: A copy of your important files made for safekeeping in case something happens to the original files; something you should make every day.

banner: A fancy page that's printed between print jobs so that you can easily separate jobs from one another.

batch file: A file that contains one or more commands that are executed together as a set. You create the batch file by using a text editor and run the file by typing its name at the command prompt.

BDC: In Windows NT, a *backup domain controller* that provides backup management for a domain. Active Directory doesn't use BDCs.

benchmark: A repeatable test you use to judge the performance of your network. The best benchmarks are the ones that closely duplicate the type of work you routinely do on your network.

Bluetooth: (1) A Viking king who united Denmark and Norway in the 10th century. (2) A wireless networking protocol for short-range networks, used mostly for devices such as wireless keyboards, mice, and cell phones.

BNC connector: The connector that's used with 10Base2 cable.

bottleneck: The slowest link in your network, which causes work to get jammed up. The first step in improving network performance is identifying the bottlenecks.

bridge: Not the popular card game, but a device that enables you to link two networks together. Bridges are smart enough to know which computers are on which side of the bridge, so they allow only those messages that need to get to the other side to cross the bridge. This device improves performance on both sides of the bridge.

broadband: A high-speed connection used for wide-area networking.

buffer: An area of memory that holds data en route to somewhere else. For example, a hard drive buffer holds data as it travels between your computer and the hard drive.

bus: A type of network topology in which network nodes are strung out along a single run of cable called a *segment.* 10Base2 and LocalTalk networks use a bus topology. *Bus* also refers to the row of expansion slots within your computer.

cable tie: Little strips of plastic that are especially handy for securing cables or bundling them together.

cache: A sophisticated form of buffering in which a large amount of memory is set aside to hold data so that it can be accessed quickly.

call forwarding: A feature of PBX systems that automatically forwards unanswered calls to another destination, such as another extension or a voice mailbox.

call parking: A feature of PBX systems that lets you place a call on hold such that the call can be retrieved from any other extension on the system.

call transfer: A feature of PBX systems that lets you redirect a call from one extension to another.

Category 3: An inexpensive form of unshielded twisted pair (UTP) cable that is suitable only for 10 Mbps networks (10BaseT). Avoid using Category 3 cable for new networks.

Category 5: The higher grade of UTP cable that is suitable for 100 Mbps networks (100BaseTX) and Gigabit Ethernet (1000BaseT).

Category 6: An even higher grade of UTP cable that's more reliable than Category 5 cable for Gigabit Ethernet.

CD-R drive: A CD drive that can read and write CDs.

CD-ROM: A high-capacity disc that uses optical technology to store data in a form that can be read but not written over.

CD-RW drive: A CD drive that can read, write, and then rewrite CDs.

Centrex: A type of phone system similar to a PBX, but where the system is not located on a customer's premises rather on the phone company's premises.

Certified NetWare Engineer: Someone who has studied hard and passed the official exam offered by Novell. Also known as *CNE*.

Certified Network Dummy: Someone who knows nothing about networks but nevertheless gets the honor of installing one. Also known as *CND*.

chat: What you do on the network when you talk *live* with another network user.

Chaucer: A dead English dude.

cheapernet: See *10Base2.*

CHKDSK: A DOS command that checks the record-keeping structures of a DOS hard drive for errors.

circuit: An end-to-end connection between transmitters and receivers, typically in phone systems.

click: What you do in Windows to get things done.

client/server: A vague term meaning roughly that the workload is split between a client and server computer.

client: A computer that has access to the network but doesn't share any of its own resources with the network. See *server.*

Clouseau: The most dangerous man in all of France. Some people say he only plays the fool.

cluster: See *allocation unit.*

coaxial cable: A type of cable that contains two conductors. The center conductor is surrounded by a layer of insulation, which is then wrapped by a braided-metal conductor and an outer layer of insulation.

Com1, Com2: The first two serial ports on a computer.

computer name: A unique name assigned to each computer on a network.

cone of silence: A running gag on the old TV series *Get Smart* in which a security device would be lowered over two people who needed to have a secure conversation. Unfortunately, the cone of silence worked so well that the people in it couldn't hear each other. (However, anyone outside of the cone of silence could easily hear what the people in the cone were saying.)

conference call: A feature of PBX systems that lets three or more users join together in a single call.

CONFIG.SYS: A file on old-style Windows computers that contains configuration information. CONFIG.SYS is processed every time you start your computer.

console: In Linux, a text-mode command prompt.

Control Panel: In Windows, an application that enables you to configure various aspects of the Windows operating system.

CPU: The *central processing unit,* or brains, of the computer.

crimp tool: A special tool used to attach connectors to cables. No network manager should be without one. Try not to get your fingers caught in it.

cross-over cable: A cable used to daisy-chain two hubs or switches together.

CSMA/CD: Carrier Sense Multiple Access with Collision Detection, the traffic-management technique used by Ethernet.

daisy-chain: A way of connecting computer components in which the first component is connected to the second, which is connected to the third, and so on. In Ethernet, you can daisy-chain hubs together.

DAT: Digital audiotape, a type of tape often used for network backups.

Data Link layer: The second layer of the OSI model, responsible for transmitting bits of data over the network cable.

dedicated server: A computer used exclusively as a network server.

delayed write: A hard drive-caching technique in which data written to the hard drive is placed in cache memory and actually written to the hard drive later.

dial tone: The distinctive tone produced on a phone system to indicate the system is ready to accept a call.

DID: *Direct Inward Dialing,* a feature of PBX systems that lets you associate an external phone number with an extension on the PBX system.

differential backup: A type of backup in which only the files that have changed since the last full backup are backed up.

DIP switch: A bank of switches used to configure an old-fashioned adapter card. Modern cards configure themselves automatically, so DIP switches aren't required. See *jumper block.*

direct inward dialing: See *DID.*

directory hash: A popular breakfast food enjoyed by Linux administrators.

disk: Also known as a *hard drive.* A device that stores information magnetically on a hard drive. A hard drive is permanently sealed in an enclosure and has a capacity usually measured in thousands of megabytes, also known as *gigabytes.*

distribution: A publicly available version of the Linux operating system. There are many different distributions. One of the most popular is Fedora.

DMA channel: A direct pipeline for I/O that's faster than normal I/O. Network cards use DMA for fast network access.

DNS: See *Domain Name System.*

domain: (1) In a Windows network, one or more network servers that are managed by a single network directory. (2) In the Internet, a name assigned to a network.

Domain Name System (DNS): The naming system used on the Internet, in which a network is given a domain name and individual computers are given host names.

DOS: Disk Operating System, the original operating system for IBM and IBM-compatible computers.

dot-matrix printer: A prehistoric type of printer that works by applying various-colored pigments to the walls of caves. Once the mainstay printer for PCs, dot-matrix printers have given way to laser printers and inkjet printers. High-speed matrix printers still have their place on the network, though, and matrix printers have the advantage of being able to print multipart forms.

DTMF: *Dual Tone Multiple Frequency,* the tones used when dialing a phone number on a touch-tone phone system.

Dual Tone Multiple Frequency: See *DTMF.*

dumb terminal: Back in the heyday of mainframe computers, a monitor and keyboard attached to the central mainframe. All the computing work occurred at the mainframe; the terminal only displayed the results and sent input typed at the keyboard back to the mainframe.

DVD drive: A type of optical drive similar to a CD-ROM drive but with much higher storage capacity.

Eddie Haskell: The kid who's always sneaking around, poking his nose into other people's business and generally causing trouble. Every network has one.

editor: A program for creating and changing text files.

e-mail: Messages that are exchanged with other network users.

emoticon: A shorthand way of expressing emotions in e-mail and chats by combining symbols to create smiles, frowns, and so on.

encryption: A security technique in which data is stored in an encoded (encrypted) form that can be decoded (or decrypted) only if the key used to encrypt the data is known.

enterprise computing: A trendy term that refers to a view of an organization's complete computing needs, rather than just a single department's or group's needs.

Ethernet: The World's Most Popular Network Standard.

EtherTalk: What you call Ethernet when you use it on a Macintosh.

ETLA: Extended Three-Letter Acronym, an acronym with four letters. See *TLA*.

Exchange Server: The software that handles e-mail services on a Windows server.

Extension: In a PBX system, a telephone that can be used for internal or external calls. Also known as a *station*.

Fast Ethernet: 100 Mbps Ethernet. Also known as *100BaseT* or *100BaseTX*.

FAT: File allocation table, a record-keeping structure once used on DOS and Windows computers to keep track of the location of every file on a hard drive.

FAT32: An improved way of keeping track of hard drive files that can be used with Windows 98 and later.

FDDI: Fiber Distributed Data Interface, a 100 Mbps network standard used with fiber-optic backbone. When FDDI is used, FDDI FDDI/Ethernet bridges connect Ethernet segments to the backbone.

Fedora: A popular distribution of Linux.

ferrule: The outer metal tube that you crimp on to attach a BNC connector to the cable.

fiber-optic cable: A blazingly fast network cable that transmits data using light rather than electricity. Fiber-optic cable is often used as the backbone in large networks, especially where great distances are involved.

file rights: The ability of a particular network user to access specific files on a network server.

file server: A network computer containing hard drives that are available to network users.

firewall: A special type of router that connects a LAN to the Internet while preventing unauthorized Internet users from accessing the LAN.

fish tape: A gadget that helps you pull cable through walls.

forest: A group of Active Directory domains.

FTP: File Transfer Protocol, a method for retrieving files from the Internet.

full backup: A backup of all the files on a hard drive, whether the files have been modified since the last backup. See *differential backup.*

gateway: A device that connects dissimilar networks. Gateways often connect Ethernet networks to mainframe computers or to the Internet.

GB: Gigabyte, roughly a billion bytes of hard drive storage (1,024MB to be precise). See *K, MB,* and *TB.*

generation backup: A backup strategy in which several sets of backup disks or tapes are retained; sometimes called *grandfather-father-son.*

generation gap: What happens when you skip one of your backups.

glass house: The room where the mainframe computer is kept. It's symbolic of the mainframe mentality, which stresses bureaucracy, inflexibility, and heavy iron.

GNOME: A graphical user interface that's popular on Linux systems.

group account: A type of security account that lets you group user accounts that have similar access rights.

groupware: An application that enables collaborative work.

guest: A user account that has no privileges. The guest account is designed to provide minimal network access to users who don't have a regular network account.

guru: Anyone who knows more about computers than you do.

hotspot: An area that has access to a public wireless network. Hotspots are commonly found in airports, hotels, and trendy coffee shops.

HTML: Hypertext Markup Language, the language used to compose pages that can be displayed via the World Wide Web.

HTTP: Hypertext Transfer Protocol, the protocol used by the World Wide Web for sending HTML pages from a server computer to a client computer.

HTTPS: A secure form of HTTP that is used to transmit sensitive data such as credit card numbers.

hub: In Ethernet, a device that is used with 10BaseT and 100BaseT cabling to connect computers to the network. Most hubs have from 5 to 24 ports. See also *switch.*

hunt group: A group of extensions that a PBX system transfers incoming calls to.

I/O port address: Every I/O device in a computer — including network inter-face cards — must be assigned a unique address. In the old days, you had to configure the port address using DIP switches or jumpers. Newer network cards automatically configure their own port addresses so that you don't have to mess with switches or jumper blocks.

IACI: *International Association of the Computer Impaired.*

IDE: Integrated Drive Electronics, the most common type of hard drive interface in use today, popular because of its low cost and flexibility. For server computers, SCSI is the preferred drive interface. See *SCSI.*

IEEE: Institute of Electrical and Electronic Engineers, where they send computer geeks who've had a few too many parity errors.

incremental backup: A type of backup in which only the files that have changed since the last backup are backed up. Unlike a differential backup, an incremental backup resets each file's archive bit as it backs it up. See *archive bit, differential backup,* and *full backup.*

inkjet printer: A type of printer that creates full-color pages by spraying tiny jets of ink onto paper.

Internet: A humongous network of networks that spans the globe and gives you access to just about anything you could ever hope for, provided that you can figure out how to work it.

Internet Explorer: Microsoft's popular Web browser.

interoperability: Providing a level playing field for incompatible networks to work together, kind of like NAFTA.

intranet: A network that resembles the Internet but is accessible only within a company or organization. Most intranets use the familiar World Wide Web interface to distribute information to company employees.

IP address: A string of numbers used to address computers on the Internet. If you enable TCP/IP on your network, you must provide an IP address for each computer on the network.

IPX: A transport protocol used by NetWare.

IRQ: Interrupt ReQuest, network interface cards must be configured for the proper IRQ in order to work. In olden times, you had to use DIP switches or jumper blocks to set the IRQ. Nowadays, network cards configure themselves.

ISA bus: Industry Standard Architecture, a once-popular type of expansion bus for accommodating adapter cards. Now replaced by PCI.

ISDN: A digital telephone connection that lets you connect to the Internet at about twice the speed of a regular phone connection. It was once popular, but there are now more cost-effective forms of high-speed Internet connections.

ISO: International Standards Organization, whom we can thank for OSI.

ISP: Internet service provider, a company that provides access to the Internet for a fee.

Java: A programming language popular on the Internet.

JavaScript: A popular scripting language that can be used on Web pages.

JetDirect: A device made by Hewlett-Packard that enables printers to connect directly to the network without the need for a separate print server computer.

jumper block: A device used to configure an old-fashioned adapter card. To change the setting of a jumper block, you remove the jumper from one set of pins and place it on another.

K: Kilobytes, roughly one thousand bytes (1,024 to be precise). See *GB, MB,* and *TB.*

Kerberos: (1) The mythical three-headed dog that guards the gates of Hades. (2) A network security protocol that authenticates users when they log on and grants the user a ticket that allows the user to access resources throughout the network.

LAN: Local area network, what this book is all about.

LANcache: The disk caching program that comes with LANtastic.

LAN Manager: An obsolete network operating system that Microsoft used to sell. Microsoft long ago put all its networking eggs in the Windows basket, so LAN Manager exists only on isolated islands along with soldiers who are still fighting World War II.

LAN Server: IBM's version of LAN Manager.

LANtastic: A peer-to-peer network operating system that was once the most popular choice for small networks. When the good folks at Microsoft saw how popular LANtastic was, they decided to add free networking features to Windows. As a result, not too many people use LANtastic anymore.

laser printer: A high-quality printer that uses lasers and photon torpedoes to produce beautiful output.

LATA: *Local Access Transport Area,* an area within which a local carrier provides service. Calls between phones in different LATAs require the use of a long distance carrier.

LEC: See *local carrier.*

lemon-pudding layer: A layer near the middle of the OSI reference model that provides flavor and moistness.

Linux: An open source version of the Unix operating system that is becoming popular as a network server.

LLC sublayer: The *logical link sublayer* of layer 2 of the OSI model. The LLC is addressed by the IEEE 802.2 standard.

local area network: See *LAN.*

local carrier: A company that provides telephone service within a limited area of service. Also known as a *Local Exchange Carrier* or *LEC.*

local resources: Disk drives, printers, and other devices that are attached directly to a workstation rather than accessed via the network.

LocalTalk: Apple's scheme for cabling Macintosh networks by using the Mac's printer ports. *PhoneNET* is a cabling scheme that's compatible with LocalTalk but less expensive.

log in: Same as *log on.*

log on: The process of identifying oneself to the network (or a specific network server) and gaining access to network resources.

logon name: In a Windows network, the name that identifies a user uniquely to the network. Same as *user name* or *user ID.*

logon script: A batch file that is executed when a user logs on to a Windows domain.

log out: The process of leaving the network. When you log out, any network drives or printers you were connected to become unavailable to you.

long distance carrier: A telephone carrier that provides service between distinct local areas. See also *LATA.*

LPT1: The first printer port on a PC. If a computer has a local printer, it more than likely is attached to this port. That's why you should set up printer redirections using LPT2 and LPT3.

Macintosh: A cute little computer that draws great pictures and comes with built-in networking.

Mac OS X: The latest and greatest operating system for Macintoshes.

Mac OS X Server: Apple's most powerful server operating system for Macintosh computers.

MAC sublayer: The *media access control* sublayer of layer 2 of the OSI model. The MAC is addressed by the IEEE 802.3 standard.

mail server: The server computer on which e-mail messages are stored. This same computer also may be used as a file and print server, or it may be dedicated as a mail server.

mainframe: A huge computer kept in a glass house on raised floors and cooled with liquid nitrogen. The cable that connects the hard drives to the CPU weighs more than most PCs.

mapping: Assigning unused drive letters to network drives or unused printer ports to network printers. See *redirection.*

MB: Megabytes, roughly one million bytes (1,024K to be precise). See *K*, *GB*, and *TB*.

memory: The electronic storage where your computer stores data that's being manipulated and programs that are running. See *RAM.*

metaphor: A literary construction suitable for Shakespeare and Steinbeck but a bit overused by writers of computer books.

MMC: Microsoft Management Console, the primary management tool used to configure Windows features.

modem: A device that converts signals the computer understands into signals that can be accurately transmitted over the phone to another modem, which converts the signals back into their original form. Computers use modems to talk to each other. *Modem* is an abbreviation of *modulator-demodulator.*

mouse: The obligatory way to use Windows. When you grab it and move it around, the cursor moves on the screen. After you get the hand-eye coordination down, using it is a snap. *Hint:* Don't pick it up and talk into it like Scotty did in *Star Trek IV.* That's very embarrassing, especially if you've traveled millions of miles to get here.

Mr. McFeeley: The nerdy-looking mailman on *Mr. Rogers' Neighborhood.* He'd make a great computer geek. Speedy delivery!

multiboot: A technique that lets you install two or more operating systems on a single computer. When you power up a computer that uses multiboot, you must select which of the installed operating systems you want to boot.

My Network Places: An icon on the Windows XP desktop that enables you to access network servers and resources. (In older versions of Windows, this icon is known as *Network Neighborhood*. In Windows Vista, it is called *Network Places.*)

.NET: A Windows application environment that promises to simplify the task of creating and using applications for Windows and for the Web.

NETBIOS: Network basic input output system, a high-level networking standard developed by IBM and used by most peer-to-peer networks. It can be used with NetWare as well.

Netscape: The company that makes Navigator, a popular program for browsing the World Wide Web.

NetWare: A popular network operating system, the proud child of Novell, Inc.

NetWare Directory Services: A feature of NetWare first introduced with version 4, in which the resources of the servers are pooled together to form a single entity.

network: What this book is about. For more information, see Books I through IX.

network drive: A drive that resides somewhere out in the network rather than on your own computer.

network interface card: An adapter card that lets the computer attach to a network cable. Also known as *NIC*.

network layer: One of the layers somewhere near the middle of the OSI reference model. It addresses the interconnection of networks.

network manager: Hope that it's someone other than you.

Network Neighborhood: An icon used on older versions of Windows that enables you to access network servers and resources. In newer Windows versions, this icon is known as *My Network Places* or *Network Places*.

network operating system: An operating system for networks, such as Linux or Windows Server 2003. Also known as *NOS.*

Network Places: An icon on the Windows Vista desktop that enables you to access network servers and resources. (In older versions of Windows, this icon is known as *Network Neighborhood* or *My Network Places.)*

network resource: A disk drive, printer, or other device that's located in a server computer and shared with other users, in contrast with a *local resource,* which is located in a user's computer.

newsgroup: Internet discussion groups in which people leave messages that can be read and responded to by other Internet users.

NIC: See *network interface card.*

node: A device on the network, typically a computer or printer. A router is also a node.

NOS: See *network operating system.*

Novell: The folks you can thank or blame for NetWare, depending on your mood.

NTFS: A special type of disk format that you can use on Windows Server and Windows XP hard drives for improved performance and security.

obfuscation: A security technique that relies on using obscure names for security objects or particular user accounts. Avoiding obvious user account names can slow would-be intruders.

octet: A group of eight bits. In an IP address, each octet of the address is represented by a decimal number from 0 to 255.

off-hook: A condition in a phone system that occurs when a telephone handset is removed from its cradle. Dial tone is produced when a circuit goes off-hook.

offline: Not available on the network.

online: Available on the network.

operator: A user who has control over operational aspects of the network but doesn't necessarily have the power to grant or revoke access rights, create user accounts, and so on.

organizational unit: A grouping of objects in an Active Directory domain.

OSI: The agency Lee Majors worked for in *The Six Million Dollar Man.* Also the *Open System Interconnection* reference model, a seven-layer fruitcake framework upon which networking standards are hung.

Outlook: A mail client from Microsoft, part of the Microsoft Office suite.

package: In Linux, a software component that can be separately installed and configured.

packet filter: A security technique used by firewalls. The firewall examines each packet that passes through it and blocks certain types of packets while allowing others to pass.

packet sniffer: See *protocol analyzer.*

packets: Data is sent over the network in manageable chunks called *packets,* or *frames.* The size and makeup of a packet is determined by the protocol being used.

parallel port: A port normally used to connect printers, sometimes called a *printer port.* Parallel ports send data over eight "parallel" wires, one byte at a time. See *serial port.*

partition: A division of a single hard drive into several smaller units that are treated by the operating system as if they were separate drives.

password: The only thing protecting your files from an impostor masquerading as you. Keep your password secret, and you'll have a long and happy life.

patch cable: A short cable used to connect a computer to a wall outlet, or one running from a patch panel to a hub.

PBX: *Private Branch Exchange,* a phone system that manages shared access to one or more phones (called *extensions* or *stations*) to a limited number of external phone lines.

PCI: Peripheral Component Interconnect, the high-speed bus design found in modern Pentium computers.

PDC: *Primary Domain Controller,* a server computer that has the main responsibility for managing a domain. See *BDC.*

peer-to-peer network: A network in which any computer can be a server if it wants to be. Kind of like the network version of the Great American Dream. You can easily construct peer-to-peer networks by using Windows.

permissions: Rights that have been granted to a particular user or group of users enabling them to access specific files.

physical layer: The lowest layer of the OSI reference model (whatever that is). It refers to the parts of the network you can touch: cables, connectors, and so on.

ping: A program that determines whether another computer is reachable. Ping sends a message to the other computer and waits for a reply. If the reply is received, the other computer is reachable.

plenum cable: Fire-retardant cable that has a special Teflon coating.

pocket protector: A status symbol among computer geeks.

port: A connector on the back of your computer that you can use to connect a device such as a printer, modem, mouse, and so on.

PPP: Point to Point Protocol, the most common way of connecting to the Internet for World Wide Web access.

presentation layer: The sixth layer of the OSI reference model, which handles data conversions, compression, decompression, and other menial tasks.

print job: A report, letter, memo, or other document that has been sent to a network printer but hasn't printed yet. Print jobs wait patiently in the queue until a printer agrees to print them.

Print Manager: In old-style Windows (Windows 3.1 and Windows for Workgroups), the program that handles print spooling.

print queue: The line that print jobs wait in until a printer becomes available.

print server: A computer that handles network printing or a device such as a JetDirect, which enables the printer to attach directly to the network.

PRN: The DOS code name for the first parallel port. Also known as *LPT1*.

protocol: (1) The droid C-3PO's specialty. (2) The rules of the network game. Protocols define standardized formats for data packets, techniques for detecting and correcting errors, and so on.

protocol analyzer: A program that monitors packets on a network. Also called a *packet sniffer*.

punch-down block: A gadget for quickly connecting a bunch of wires, used in telephone and network wiring closets.

QIC: Quarter-inch cartridge, the most popular and least expensive form of tape backup. Now known as *Travan drives*. See *DAT* and *Travan*.

queue: A list of items waiting to be processed. The term usually refers to the list of print jobs waiting to be printed, but networks have lots of other types of queues as well.

RAID: Redundant Array of Inexpensive Disks, a bunch of hard drives strung together and treated as if they were one drive. The data is spread out over several drives, and one of the drives keeps checking information so that if any one of the other drives fails, the data can be reconstructed.

RAM: Random access memory, your computer's memory chips.

redirection: One of the basic concepts of networking, in which a device, such as a disk drive or printer, appears to be a local device but actually resides on the network. The networking software on your computer intercepts I/O requests for the device and redirects them to the network.

registry: The file where Windows keeps its configuration information.

Remote Desktop Connection: A Windows feature that lets you log on to a Windows server from a remote computer so that you can manage it without physically going to the server.

Remote Installation Service: See *RIS*.

repeater: A device that strengthens a signal so that it can travel on. Repeaters are used to lengthen the cable distance between two nodes. A *multiport repeater* is the same as a *hub*.

resource: A hard drive, hard drive directory, printer, modem, CD-ROM, or other device that can be shared on the network.

ring: (1) A type of network topology in which computers are connected to one another in a way that forms a complete circle. Imagine the Waltons standing around the Thanksgiving table holding hands, and you have the idea of a ring topology. (2) In phone system wiring, the wire that carries voltage (typically, -48 volts). It is called *ring* because in the days of manual switchboard operators, the negative voltage wire was connected to the ring around the shaft of the plugs used to connect incoming calls to their destinations. See also *tip*.

RIS: Remote Installation Service, a feature of Windows Server operating systems that lets you install from a remote location without actually being present at the server.

RJ-11: The kind of plug used by phone system cabling.

RJ-45: The kind of plug used by 10BaseT and 100BaseT networks. It looks kind of like a modular phone plug, but it's bigger.

root: (1) The highest-level directory in a file system. (2) The administrator account in Linux.

root server: One of 13 powerful DNS servers located throughout the world that provide the core of the Internet's DNS service.

router: A device that interfaces two networks and controls how packets are exchanged between them. Routers are typically used to link a local Ethernet network to a broadband Internet connection.

Samba: A program that runs on a Linux server, allowing the Linux computer to work as a file and print server in a Windows network.

ScanDisk: A Windows command that examines your hard drive for physical defects.

scheduling software: Software that schedules meetings of network users, which works only if all network users keep their calendars up to date.

scope: In DHCP, a range of IP addresses that a DCHP server manages.

SCSI: Small computer systems interface, a connection used mostly for hard drives but also suitable for CD-ROM drives, tape drives, and just about anything else. Also winner of the Acronym Computer Geeks Love to Pronounce Most award.

segment: A single-run cable, which may connect more than two computers, with a terminator on each end.

Sendmail: A Mail Transfer Agent used on Unix and Linux systems. By some estimates, 70 percent or more of all mail on the Internet is handled by a version of Sendmail.

serial port: A port normally used to connect a modem or mouse to a DOS-based computer, sometimes called a *communications port.* See **parallel port.**

server: A computer that's on the network and shares resources with other network users. The server may be *dedicated,* which means that its sole purpose in life is to provide service for network users, or it may be used as a client as well. See **client.**

service pack: A collection of patches that are bundled together to bring an operating system up to a particular service level.

session layer: A layer somewhere near the middle of the beloved OSI reference model that deals with sessions between network nodes.

SFT: System Fault Tolerance, a set of networking features designed to protect the network from faults, such as stepping on the line (known as a *foot fault).*

share name: A name that you assign to a network resource when you share it. Other network users use the share name to access the shared resource.

shared folder: A network server hard drive or a folder on a server hard drive that has been shared so that other computers on the network can access it.

shared resource: A resource, such as a hard drive or printer, that is made available to other network users.

shielded twisted pair: Twisted-pair cable with shielding, used mostly for Token Ring networks. Also known as *STP.* See **twisted pair.**

SMB: *Server Message Block,* the protocol that enables file sharing on Windows networks.

smiley: A face made from various keyboard characters; often used in e-mail messages to convey emotion. : -)

SNA: Systems Network Architecture, a networking standard developed by IBM that dates from the mid-Mainframerasic Period, approximately 65 million years ago. Used by fine IBM mainframe and AS/400 minicomputers everywhere.

sneakernet: The cheapest form of network, in which users exchange files by copying them to disks and walking them between computers.

SNMP: Simple Network Management Protocol, a standard for exchanging network management information between network devices that is anything but simple.

spooling: A printing trick in which data that is intended for a printer is actually written to a temporary hard drive file and later sent to the printer.

SSID: A name that identifies a wireless network.

star: A type of network topology in which each node is connected to a central wiring hub. This gives the network a star-like appearance.

Stateful Packet Inspection: An intelligent type of packet filtering that examines packets in groups rather than individually.

station: In a PBX system, a telephone that can be used for internal or external calls. Also known as an *extension*.

subnet mask: A bit pattern that is used to determine which bits of an IP address represent the subnet.

subnetting: An IP addressing technique that designates the first *n* bits of an IP address as the subnet address and the remaining bits as the host address.

switch: An efficient type of hub that sends packets only to the port that is connected to the packet's recipient rather than sending packets to all of the ports, as a simple hub does.

system fault tolerance: See *SFT*.

tape drive: The best way to back up a network server. Tape drives have become so inexpensive that even small networks should have one.

task: For a technically accurate description, enroll in a computer science graduate course. For a layperson's understanding of what a task is, picture the guy who used to spin plates on *The Ed Sullivan Show*. Each plate is a task. The poor guy had to frantically move from plate to plate to keep them all spinning. Computers work the same way. Each program task is like one of those spinning plates; the computer must service each one periodically to keep it going.

TB: Terrazzo bytes, imported from Italy. Approximately one trillion bytes (1,024GB to be precise). (Just kidding about terrazzo bytes. Actually, TB stands for terabytes. It won't be long before you can buy hard drives that can hold a terabyte or more.)

TCP/IP: Transmission Control Protocol/Internet Protocol, the protocol used by the Internet.

terminator: (1) The little plug you have to use at each end of a segment of thin coax cable (10BaseT). (2) The governor of Caleefornia.

tip: In phone system wiring, the wire that's connected to ground. It is called *tip* because in the days of manual switchboards, the ground wire was connected to the tip of the plugs used to manually connect calls to their correct destinations. See also *ring.*

thinnet: See *10Base2.*

three-letter acronym: See *TLA.*

time sharing: A technique used on mainframe computers to enable several users to access the computer at the same time.

time-out: How long the print server waits while receiving print output before deciding that the print job has finished.

TLA: Three-letter acronym, such as FAT (File Allocation Table), DUM (Dirty Upper Memory), and HPY (Heuristic Private Yodel).

token: The thing that gets passed around the network in a Token Ring topology. See *Token Ring.*

Token Ring: A network that's cabled in a ring topology in which a special packet called a *token* is passed from computer to computer. A computer must wait until it receives the token before sending data over the network.

top-level domain: In DNS, a domain that appears immediately beneath the root domain. The common top-level domains include com, net, org, edu, gov, mil, and int.

topology: The shape of the network; how its computers and cables are arranged. See *bus, star,* and *ring.*

touch-tone dialing: A form of phone dialing that uses a sequence of DTMF tones to indicate the number being dialed.

transceiver: A doohickey that connects a network interface card (NIC) to a network cable. A transceiver is always required to connect a computer to the network, but 10Base2 and 10BaseT NICs have built-in transceivers. Transceivers were originally used with yellow cable. You can also get transceivers that convert an AUI port to 10BaseT.

transport layer: One of those layers somewhere near the middle of the OSI reference model that addresses the way data is escorted around the network.

Travan: A technology for tape backup that can record up to 800MB on a single tape cartridge. See *QIC* and *DAT.*

Trojan horse: A program that looks interesting but turns out to be something nasty, like a hard-drive reformatter.

trust: A relationship between domains in which one domain (the *trusting domain*) honors the information in the other domain (the *trusted domain*).

trustee rights: In NetWare, rights that have been granted to a particular user or group of users enabling them to access specific files.

twisted pair: A type of cable that consists of one or more pairs of wires that are twisted in a certain way to improve the cable's electrical characteristics. See *unshielded twisted pair* and *shielded twisted pair.*

uninterruptible power supply: See *UPS.*

unshielded twisted pair: Twisted-pair cable that doesn't have a heavy metal shield around it. Used for 10BaseT networks. Also known as *UTP.* See *twisted pair.*

UPS: Uninterruptible power supply, a gizmo that switches to battery power whenever the power cuts out. The Enterprise didn't have one of these, which is why the lights always went out until Spock could switch to auxiliary power.

URL: Uniform Resource Locator, a fancy term for an Internet address. URLs are those familiar "dot" addresses, such as "www-dot-microsoft-dot-com" or "www-dot-dummies-dot-com."

USB: A high-speed serial interface that is found on most new computers. USB can be used to connect printers, scanners, mice, keyboards, network adapters, and other devices.

user ID: The name by which you're known to the network.

User Manager for Domains: The program you use on Windows NT to manage user accounts.

user profile: The way Windows keeps track of each user's desktop settings, such as window colors, wallpaper, screen savers, Start menu options, favorites, and so on.

user rights: Network actions that a particular network user is allowed to perform after he or she has logged on to the network. See *file rights.*

users' group: A local association of computer users, sometimes with a particular interest, such as networking.

UTP: Unshielded twisted pair. See *10BaseT.*

VBScript: A scripting language that can be used to add fancy features to Web pages or create macros for Microsoft Office programs.

VGA: Video Graphics Array, the current standard in video monitors. Most VGA adapters these days are actually Super VGA adapters, which are compatible with VGA adapters but have extra bells and whistles.

Vines: A network operating system made by Banyan, comparable to NetWare or Windows Server.

virtual memory: An operating system technique in which the system simulates more memory than is physically present in the computer by swapping portions of memory out to disk.

virus: An evil computer program that slips into your computer undetected, tries to spread itself to other computers, and may eventually do something bad like trash your hard drive.

Visio: A program from Microsoft that draws diagrams. It's especially good at drawing network diagrams.

voice mail: A feature of PBX and other types of phone systems in which a caller can record a message for the intended recipient of his or her call.

VoIP: *Voice over IP,* a technique for routing telephone calls over the Internet instead of over traditional phone carriers.

warchalking: The practice of using chalk to write special symbols on the sidewalk near open wireless networks.

wardriving: Cruising the streets with special equipment designed to detect open wireless networks and then publicizing their locations.

Web browser: A program that enables you to display information retrieved from the Internet's World Wide Web.

WEP: Wired Equivalent Privacy, a security standard for wireless networks that makes wireless networking almost (but not quite) as secure as cabled networks.

Wi-Fi: The common name for wireless networking using the 802.11 protocols.

Windows: The world's most popular operating system.

Windows 95: A version of Windows that became available in — you guessed it — 1995. Windows 95 was the first version of Windows that did not require DOS.

Windows 98: The successor to Windows 95, introduced in 1998. Windows 98 includes a new user interface that makes the Windows desktop resemble the World Wide Web.

Windows 2000 Server: The most popular Windows server operating system. Available in three editions: Windows 2000 Server, Windows 2000 Advanced Server, and Windows 2000 Datacenter Server for server computers.

Windows CE: A version of Windows for very small computers such as those found in phones and other hand-held devices. Windows Mobile is based on Windows CE.

Windows for Workgroups: Microsoft's first network-aware version of Windows, now pretty much defunct.

Windows Millennium Edition: The successor to Windows 98, designed especially for home users and featuring a Home Networking Wizard that simplifies the task of setting up a home network.

Windows Mobile: A version of the Windows operating system based on Windows CE and designed for handheld mobile devices, pocket computers, and smart phones.

Windows NT: The predecessor to Windows 2000. Windows NT is available in two versions: Windows NT Client for desktop computers and Windows NT Server for server computers.

Windows Server 2003: The Windows Server operating system version that replaced Windows 2000 Server.

Windows Server 2008: The newest version of Windows Server, which replaced Windows Server 2003 in early 2008.

Windows Vista: The most recent version of the Windows operating system for client computers, which replaced Windows XP in early 2007.

Windows XP: The most popular version of Windows, designed for home or professional users.

wireless: A method of networking that uses radio signals instead of cables to transmit data.

wireless access point: A device that connects wireless devices to a cabled network.

wiring closet: Large networks need a place where cables can congregate. A closet is ideal.

workstation: See *client.*

World Wide Web: A graphical method of accessing information on the Internet.

WPA: Wi-Fi Protected Access, a new and improved security standard for wireless networks.

WWW: See *World Wide Web.*

X10: A low-bandwidth protocol for home automation that runs over your home's power lines.

yellow cable: See *10Base5.*

zone: A portion of the DNS namespace which a particular DNS server is responsible for.

Index

B

E

F

H

V

BUSINESS, CAREERS & PERSONAL FINANCE

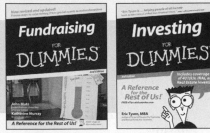

0-7645-9847-3   0-7645-2431-3

Also available:
- Business Plans Kit For Dummies
  0-7645-9794-9
- Economics For Dummies
  0-7645-5726-2
- Grant Writing For Dummies
  0-7645-8416-2
- Home Buying For Dummies
  0-7645-5331-3
- Managing For Dummies
  0-7645-1771-6
- Marketing For Dummies
  0-7645-5600-2

- Personal Finance For Dummies
  0-7645-2590-5*
- Resumes For Dummies
  0-7645-5471-9
- Selling For Dummies
  0-7645-5363-1
- Six Sigma For Dummies
  0-7645-6798-5
- Small Business Kit For Dummies
  0-7645-5984-2
- Starting an eBay Business For Dummies
  0-7645-6924-4
- Your Dream Career For Dummies
  0-7645-9795-7

HOME & BUSINESS COMPUTER BASICS

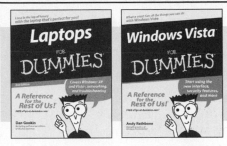

0-470-05432-8   0-471-75421-8

Also available:
- Cleaning Windows Vista For Dummies
  0-471-78293-9
- Excel 2007 For Dummies
  0-470-03737-7
- Mac OS X Tiger For Dummies
  0-7645-7675-5
- MacBook For Dummies
  0-470-04859-X
- Macs For Dummies
  0-470-04849-2
- Office 2007 For Dummies
  0-470-00923-3

- Outlook 2007 For Dummies
  0-470-03830-6
- PCs For Dummies
  0-7645-8958-X
- Salesforce.com For Dummies
  0-470-04893-X
- Upgrading & Fixing Laptops For Dummies
  0-7645-8959-8
- Word 2007 For Dummies
  0-470-03658-3
- Quicken 2007 For Dummies
  0-470-04600-7

FOOD, HOME, GARDEN, HOBBIES, MUSIC & PETS

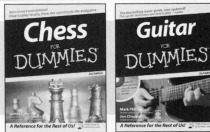

0-7645-8404-9   0-7645-9904-6

Also available:
- Candy Making For Dummies
  0-7645-9734-5
- Card Games For Dummies
  0-7645-9910-0
- Crocheting For Dummies
  0-7645-4151-X
- Dog Training For Dummies
  0-7645-8418-9
- Healthy Carb Cookbook For Dummies
  0-7645-8476-6
- Home Maintenance For Dummies
  0-7645-5215-5

- Horses For Dummies
  0-7645-9797-3
- Jewelry Making & Beading For Dummies
  0-7645-2571-9
- Orchids For Dummies
  0-7645-6759-4
- Puppies For Dummies
  0-7645-5255-4
- Rock Guitar For Dummies
  0-7645-5356-9
- Sewing For Dummies
  0-7645-6847-7
- Singing For Dummies
  0-7645-2475-5

INTERNET & DIGITAL MEDIA

0-470-04529-9   0-470-04894-8

Also available:
- Blogging For Dummies
  0-471-77084-1
- Digital Photography For Dummies
  0-7645-9802-3
- Digital Photography All-in-One Desk Reference For Dummies
  0-470-03743-1
- Digital SLR Cameras and Photography For Dummies
  0-7645-9803-1
- eBay Business All-in-One Desk Reference For Dummies
  0-7645-8438-3
- HDTV For Dummies
  0-470-09673-X

- Home Entertainment PCs For Dummies
  0-470-05523-5
- MySpace For Dummies
  0-470-09529-6
- Search Engine Optimization For Dummies
  0-471-97998-8
- Skype For Dummies
  0-470-04891-3
- The Internet For Dummies
  0-7645-8996-2
- Wiring Your Digital Home For Dummies
  0-471-91830-X

* Separate Canadian edition also available
† Separate U.K. edition also available

Available wherever books are sold. For more information or to order direct: U.S. customers visit www.dummies.com or call 1-877-762-2974.
U.K. customers visit www.wileyeurope.com or call 0800 243407. Canadian customers visit www.wiley.ca or call 1-800-567-4797.

SPORTS, FITNESS, PARENTING, RELIGION & SPIRITUALITY

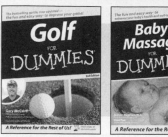

0-471-76871-5

0-7645-7841-3

Also available:

- Catholicism For Dummies
0-7645-5391-7
- Exercise Balls For Dummies
0-7645-5623-1
- Fitness For Dummies
0-7645-7851-0
- Football For Dummies
0-7645-3936-1
- Judaism For Dummies
0-7645-5299-6
- Potty Training For Dummies
0-7645-5417-4
- Buddhism For Dummies
0-7645-5359-3

- Pregnancy For Dummies
0-7645-4483-7 †
- Ten Minute Tone-Ups For Dummies
0-7645-7207-5
- NASCAR For Dummies
0-7645-7681-X
- Religion For Dummies
0-7645-5264-3
- Soccer For Dummies
0-7645-5229-5
- Women in the Bible For Dummies
0-7645-8475-8

TRAVEL

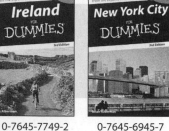

0-7645-7749-2

0-7645-6945-7

Also available:

- Alaska For Dummies
0-7645-7746-8
- Cruise Vacations For Dummies
0-7645-6941-4
- England For Dummies
0-7645-4276-1
- Europe For Dummies
0-7645-7529-5
- Germany For Dummies
0-7645-7823-5
- Hawaii For Dummies
0-7645-7402-7

- Italy For Dummies
0-7645-7386-1
- Las Vegas For Dummies
0-7645-7382-9
- London For Dummies
0-7645-4277-X
- Paris For Dummies
0-7645-7630-5
- RV Vacations For Dummies
0-7645-4442-X
- Walt Disney World & Orlando
For Dummies
0-7645-9660-8

GRAPHICS, DESIGN & WEB DEVELOPMENT

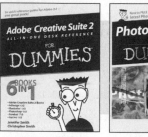

0-7645-8815-X

0-7645-9571-7

Also available:

- 3D Game Animation For Dummies
0-7645-8789-7
- AutoCAD 2006 For Dummies
0-7645-8925-3
- Building a Web Site For Dummies
0-7645-7144-3
- Creating Web Pages For Dummies
0-470-08030-2
- Creating Web Pages All-in-One Desk
Reference For Dummies
0-7645-4345-8
- Dreamweaver 8 For Dummies
0-7645-9649-7

- InDesign CS2 For Dummies
0-7645-9572-5
- Macromedia Flash 8 For Dummies
0-7645-9691-8
- Photoshop CS2 and Digital
Photography For Dummies
0-7645-9580-6
- Photoshop Elements 4 For Dummies
0-471-77483-9
- Syndicating Web Sites with RSS Feeds
For Dummies
0-7645-8848-6
- Yahoo! SiteBuilder For Dummies
0-7645-9800-7

NETWORKING, SECURITY, PROGRAMMING & DATABASES

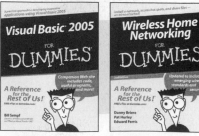

0-7645-7728-X

0-471-74940-0

Also available:

- Access 2007 For Dummies
0-470-04612-0
- ASP.NET 2 For Dummies
0-7645-7907-X
- C# 2005 For Dummies
0-7645-9704-3
- Hacking For Dummies
0-470-05235-X
- Hacking Wireless Networks
For Dummies
0-7645-9730-2
- Java For Dummies
0-470-08716-1

- Microsoft SQL Server 2005 For Dummies
0-7645-7755-7
- Networking All-in-One Desk Reference
For Dummies
0-7645-9939-9
- Preventing Identity Theft For Dummies
0-7645-7336-5
- Telecom For Dummies
0-471-77085-X
- Visual Studio 2005 All-in-One Desk
Reference For Dummies
0-7645-9775-2
- XML For Dummies
0-7645-8845-1

HEALTH & SELF-HELP

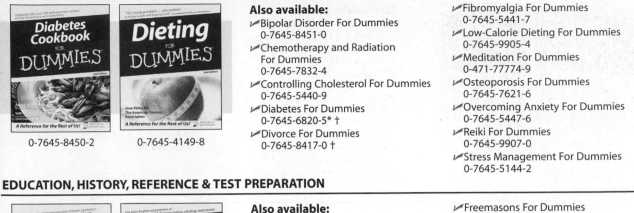

0-7645-8450-2   0-7645-4149-8

Also available:
- Bipolar Disorder For Dummies
  0-7645-8451-0
- Chemotherapy and Radiation
  For Dummies
  0-7645-7832-4
- Controlling Cholesterol For Dummies
  0-7645-5440-9
- Diabetes For Dummies
  0-7645-6820-5* †
- Divorce For Dummies
  0-7645-8417-0 †

- Fibromyalgia For Dummies
  0-7645-5441-7
- Low-Calorie Dieting For Dummies
  0-7645-9905-4
- Meditation For Dummies
  0-471-77774-9
- Osteoporosis For Dummies
  0-7645-7621-6
- Overcoming Anxiety For Dummies
  0-7645-5447-6
- Reiki For Dummies
  0-7645-9907-0
- Stress Management For Dummies
  0-7645-5144-2

EDUCATION, HISTORY, REFERENCE & TEST PREPARATION

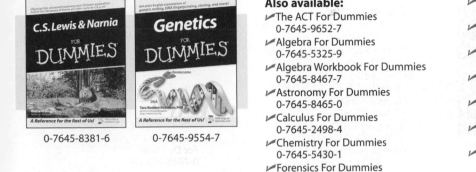

0-7645-8381-6   0-7645-9554-7

Also available:
- The ACT For Dummies
  0-7645-9652-7
- Algebra For Dummies
  0-7645-5325-9
- Algebra Workbook For Dummies
  0-7645-8467-7
- Astronomy For Dummies
  0-7645-8465-0
- Calculus For Dummies
  0-7645-2498-4
- Chemistry For Dummies
  0-7645-5430-1
- Forensics For Dummies
  0-7645-5580-4

- Freemasons For Dummies
  0-7645-9796-5
- French For Dummies
  0-7645-5193-0
- Geometry For Dummies
  0-7645-5324-0
- Organic Chemistry I For Dummies
  0-7645-6902-3
- The SAT I For Dummies
  0-7645-7193-1
- Spanish For Dummies
  0-7645-5194-9
- Statistics For Dummies
  0-7645-5423-9

Get smart @ dummies.com®

- **Find a full list of Dummies titles**
- **Look into loads of FREE on-site articles**
- **Sign up for FREE eTips e-mailed to you weekly**
- **See what other products carry the Dummies name**
- **Shop directly from the Dummies bookstore**
- **Enter to win new prizes every month!**